Japanese/Korean Linguistics

Volume 14

Japanese/Korean Linguistics

Volume 14

Edited by
Timothy J. Vance and
Kimberly Jones

Published for the
Stanford Linguistics Association by
CSLI Publications
Center for the Study of Language and Information
Stanford, California

Copyright © 2006
CSLI Publications
Center for the Study of Language and Information
Leland Stanford Junior University
Printed in the United States
10 09 08 07 06   1 2 3 4 5

Library of Congress Cataloging-in-Publication Data

Conference on Japanese/Korean Linguistics (1st : 1989 : University of Southern California)
Japanese/Korean Linguistics / edited by Hajime Hoji.

Volume 14 / edited by Timothy J. Vance and Kimberly Jones.
p.   cm.

Includes bibliographical references and index.
ISBN-13 978-1-57586-519-5
ISBN-10   1-57586-519-X
ISBN-13 978-1-57586-520-1 (pbk.)
ISBN-10   1-57586-520-3 (pbk.)
1. Japanese language—Congresses. 2. Korean language—Congresses.
3. Japanese language—Grammar, Comparative—Korean—Congresses.
4. Korean language—Grammar, Comparative—Japanese—Congresses.
5. Linguistics—Congresses. I. Hoji, Hajime. II. Stanford Linguistics Association.
III. Center for the Study of Language and Information (U.S.) IV. Title.
PL503.C6 1989
495.6–dc20   90-2550
                                                                    CIP

∞ The acid-free paper used in this book meets the minimum requirements of the American National Standard for Information Sciences—Permanence of Paper for Printed Library Materials, ANSI Z39.48-1984.

For a list of volumes in this series, along with a cumulative table of contents, please visit
http://cslipublications.stanford.edu/site/JAKO.html

CSLI was founded in 1983 by researchers from Stanford University, SRI International, and Xerox PARC to further the research and development of integrated theories of language, information, and computation. CSLI headquarters and CSLI Publications are located on the campus of Stanford University.

CSLI Publications reports new developments in the study of language, information, and computation. Please visit our web site at
http://cslipublications.stanford.edu/
for comments on this and other titles, as well as for changes and corrections by the authors, editors, and publisher.

Contents

Acknowledgments

The 14th Japanese/Korean Linguistics Conference was held in Tucson at the Marriott University Park near the campus of the University of Arizona on November 5–7, 2004. There were 42 presentations over the course of the three days, including six by invited speakers. The two keynote lectures were delivered by Shigeru Miyagawa (MIT) and Ho-min Sohn (University of Hawai'i at Mānoa), and the other invited speakers were Shoko Hamano (George Washington University), Shoichi Iwasaki (UCLA), Sun-Ah Jun (UCLA), and Hyo Sang Lee (Indiana University). The remaining 36 presentations were chosen by blind review from the 131 abstracts submitted in response to the call for papers. A few of the presenters opted not to rework their presentations for publication, but 37 of the papers appear in this volume. Our thanks go to all of the presenters and also to the many people who served as session chairs at the meeting.

The success of each J/K conference is due in large measure to the generosity of the busy scholars who agree to referee the abstracts. We are extremely grateful to the 40 people whose input allowed us to put together the J/K14 program. We are also indebted to the Standing Organizing Committee (Noriko Akatsuka, Pat Clancy, Hajime Hoji, Sung-Ock Sohn, and Shoichi Iwasaki) and to the organizers of J/K12 (Bill McClure) and J/K13 (Mutsuko Endo Hudson) for their advice and encouragement.

J/K14 was supported entirely by funds from the University of Arizona, principally by contributions from the Office of the Vice President for Research and from the Department of East Asian Studies. The Department of Linguistics also contributed.

Brenda Fraker in the East Asian Studies department office kept track of finances and led us through the maze of state and university regulations. Registration and on-site support were in the capable hands of student volunteers from the Department of East Asian Studies, the Department of Linguistics, and the Second Language Acquisition and Teaching Program. The staff at the Marriott did a thoroughly professional job of handling the meeting space and the catering, especially the memorable banquet in the exhibit hall of the Arizona Historical Society.

Thanks are due also to Dikran Karagueuzian at CSLI for endless patience in helping us get the manuscript into publishable shape.

Finally, we are grateful beyond words to Paul Lyddon, who maintained the conference website, worked with the Marriott to arrange accommodations, meeting space, and catering, and recruited and organized the volunteers. Without his logistical genius, J/K14 never would have happened.

Timothy J. Vance and Kimberly Jones
Department of East Asian Studies
University of Arizona

Part I

Phonology

Accent and Sound Symbolism in Japanese

SHOKO HAMANO

George Washington University

1. Introduction

Recent studies have shown that sound-symbolic words in Japanese are governed by phonological, morphological, and syntactic principles much the same way as the rest of the language (Hamano 1998, Tamori and Schourup 1999, Nasu 1995, Asano 2003, Kageyama 2004).

For instance, the distribution of palatalized consonants in the mimetic system is extremely regular and predictable because of stringent phonological constraints, not unlike those operating in the Yamato stratum. The concept of template is useful in both strata, and compound mimetic adverbs must conform to one of the two templates, $C_1aC_2a\text{-}C_1oC_2o$ or $C_1V_1C_2V_2\text{-}C_3V_3C_2V_2$. The mimetic and the Yamato stratum also share many phonological and morphological features. For instance, /r/ can only appear medially in both strata. The minimum word constraint is in operation in both strata. The minimum size of a mimetic adverb is two moras. There are morphological processes shared by the mimetic and the Yamato stratum, such as insertion of mora consonants and vowel lengthening for intensification or emphasis, appending of mora obstruents for indication of finality, and reduplication with the sense of repetition and distribution. Verbs and adjectives

3

that are productively derived from mimetic words exhibit standard semantic and syntactic properties of Yamato lexical items.

A cursory survey of some non-Tokyo dialects suggests that such characteristics are widely shared by various dialects of Japanese. The mimetic stratum seems to be an area worthy of serious linguistic research in any dialect. Unfortunately, however, previous studies of the mimetic stratum have concentrated on the Tokyo dialect. Information on the mimetic stratum in other dialects is almost non-existent or at best haphazard. I believe that the study of mimetic vocabulary across dialects provides insight into the phonology of Japanese to the extent that the mimetic stratum has close ties with the rest of the language. The northern dialects, particularly those in Aomori, are the most logical starting point in this direction because of the richness of their mimetic vocabulary and their unique phonological characteristics. In this paper, by exploring accentual phenomena in the sound-symbolic stratum of the Tsugaru dialect, I will try to demonstrate that the study of sound symbolic vocabulary across dialects can provide a new insight into our understanding of Japanese phonology.

2. The Optimatility-Theoretic Account of Accent in the Mimetic Stratum

In Hamano 1998, I pointed out the three types of accent in (1) for the mimetic adverbs in the Tokyo dialect.[1]

(1) Accent Types in the Tokyo Dialect
   a. The accent falls on the syllable before -*ri*: koro̱ri
   b. The accent falls on a heavy syllable: sa̱t-to, kata̱t-to, kata-kata̱t-to
   c. The accent falls on the initial syllable: ka̱ta-kata-to

Asano (2003), within the framework of Optimality Theory, proposes that these Tokyo data can be accounted for by the constraints in (2), which are ranked as in (3).

---

[1] In this paper, I mark the accent by underlining an accented syllable, although what constitutes accent is not uniform across dialects. According to Uwano (1986), the accent in a Tsugaru word is realized as the first high-pitched syllable. This contrasts with the situation in the Tokyo dialect, in which accent is identified as the initial pitch fall. Further, in the Tsugaru dialect, a non-distinctive fall in pitch may occur anywhere after the accented syllable. This is not the case in the Tokyo dialect, of course. Consequently, four syllables carrying the pitch patterns of LHLL, LHHL, and LHHH, for instance, are phonologically equivalent in the Tsugaru dialect, whereas they are distinct in the Tokyo dialect. Still, the two dialects behave in remarkably similar ways with regard to where in a mimetic word an accent is placed. This justifies the uniform marking of the accent for both dialects in this paper.

(2) Accentual Constraints in the Tokyo Dialect
    a. Culmin: Every accentual domain has one and only one accent.
    b. Pre-RI: The accent falls on the syllable preceding -*ri*.
    c. WSP: Heavy syllables are prominent.
    d. Lmost: The head syllable is leftmost in a prosodic word.

(3) Culmin >> Pre-RI >> WSP >> Lmost

    The Tsugaru dialect exhibits more accentual varieties. Nevertheless, similar constraints seem to be in operation, supporting the optimality-theoretic claim that these constraints are universal.

    The pre-accenting of -*ri* found in the Tokyo dialect has a close counterpart in the Tsugaru dialect in the form of accenting of -*ra*, as shown in (4). The difference is that in the Tsugaru dialect, -*ra* itself is accented, as in *katara-do*, while in the Tokyo dialect, instead of -*ri* being accented, the preceding syllable is accented, as in *sappari-to*. This constraint almost totally dominates the other constraints among speakers of the Tsugaru dialect, although not to the extent of its counterpart in the Tokyo dialect. Some Tsugaru speakers seem to be influenced occasionally by the presence of a heavy syllable, producing forms such as *gaŋŋara-do*, *sokkora-do*, and *jakkura-do*. Nevertheless, among most speakers, young and old alike, the pattern found in (4) is the normative one.

(4) a. kata<u>rat</u>-to
    b. maho<u>ra</u>-do
    c. sokko<u>ra</u>-do, jakku<u>ra</u>-do, gaŋŋa<u>ra</u>-do, gappa<u>ra</u>-do, katta<u>ra</u>-do, dokki<u>ra</u>-do

Note that the accent is placed on -*ra* whether it is part of a heavy syllable, as in (4a), or it forms a light syllable, as in (4b), or there is a heavy syllable elsewhere, as in (4c).

    The other constraints observed for the Tokyo dialect are relevant for Tsugaru adverbial forms as well. Particularly significant is the constraint involving heavy syllables. A large number of mimetic adverbs that contain a heavy syllable have the accent placed on the heavy syllable, as shown in (5) from the recordings accompanying Kokuritsu Kokugo Kenkyūjo 1980 and the story-telling tapes recorded by Ryūji Sasaki in the 1980s.

(5) a. <u>Ut</u>-te busukaede-naa.
             was scolded
      'I was scolded severely.'

    b. maa <u>don</u>do-do hupparu-dogodee
      horse   pull   because
      'because the horse pulls hard'

   c. zyo<u>rot</u>-to odosute
               drop
        'dropping it sloppily'

   d. <u>mok</u>ku-do tatsuagatte
                  rise
        'rising suddenly'

   e. Ketake<u>tat</u>-te waratta-zu.
               laughed-I hear
        'I hear that he cackled.'

Other examples can be cited from Ogasawara (1998, 1999a, 1999b), Narumi (1957–1961), and Miura (2001). Some examples are given in (6).

(6) a. <u>ban</u>-to, <u>sat</u>-to
     b. <u>guu</u>gu-do, <u>sas</u>sa-do, <u>bit</u>ta-do, <u>gap</u>pa-do
     c. ka<u>sat</u>-to, ka<u>tan</u>-to, ka<u>tak</u>kata-do

The pattern of accenting initial syllables, observed for the Tokyo dialect, is also observed primarily for phonomimes (imitations of sounds) in the Tsugaru dialect, as in (7).

(7) <u>bon</u>bon, <u>en</u>en-te, <u>kat</u>akata-do, gorogoro-te

Thus, the constraints in (2), ranked in the way Asano proposes for the Tokyo dialect, also seem to account for the Tsugaru mimetic forms so far.

3. Problems with the Above Account

The constraints and their ranking posited so far, however, fail to account for some types of mimetic adverbs in the Tsugaru dialect. For one thing, we observe a strong preference for accenting the second syllable. This preference accounts for the location of the accent in the examples in (8). These forms consist of light syllables, and the light, second syllable is accented.

(8) yu<u>ta</u>-do, zu<u>pa</u>-do, wa<u>ya</u>waya-do, yu<u>ki</u>yuki-do [2]

Apparently the constraint that places an accent on the second syllable dominates the leftmost constraint for these mimetic forms in the Tsugaru dialect.

    In addition, some speakers prefer to place a secondary accent on the fourth syllable, as in (9).

---

[2] Since pitch fall is non-distinctive in the Tsugaru dialect, the pitch of all but the first syllable may be raised. Some attested examples are: *su<u>ra</u>sura-do* (LHHHH or LHHHL), *su<u>po</u>supo-do* (LHHHH), and *yu<u>ra</u>yura-te* (LHHHL).

(9) piṇapiṇa-do, nepakapa-te

And only the fourth syllable may be raised, as in (10).

(10) a. nugunugu-do, zunazuna-do
     b. wasuwasu-te

Interestingly, speakers avoid accenting the third syllable alone. Among numerous forms reported in published sources, I found only one form with the accent exclusively on the third syllable, and none in my corpus.

The pattern of accenting light, even-numbered syllables of mimetic forms is unique to the northern dialects. In the Tokyo dialect, the accent is never placed on a non-initial light syllable. These forms would all be accented on the initial syllable in the Tokyo dialect due to the dominance of the leftmost constraint.

The second-syllable constraint can even dominate the weight constraint in the Tsugaru dialect as in (11) and (12), which are from the aforementioned recorded and published sources, respectively.

(11) a. Zuppa-do osaneba.
             if.don't.push
         'If you don't push sufficiently, (it won't do).'

     b. Mizu kurebanaa sokku-do haa umi-do   hutodu.
        water if.it.comes   ocean-with identical
        'When water comes, it looks exactly like the ocean.'

 (12) bekka-do, dotta-do, sokku-do, gittya-do, katta-do, kattakata-do

Note that the accent is placed on the second syllables in these forms, although their initial syllables are heavy. Except for the location of the accent, their structural descriptions are exactly the same as (6b), in which the heavy syllable in initial position is accented. In fact, an identical string can exhibit two different accent patterns, as shown in (13).

(13) sokku-do ~ sokku-do

Thus, it is clear that the second-syllable constraint is in close competition with the weight constraint.

When we take into consideration the significance of the second syllable, we can also understand why forms containing two heavy syllables have the accent on the second syllable. A couple of examples of this pattern are given in (14).

(14) kattan-to, gakkun-to

Further, we observe that, when a form contains only one heavy syllable and it is in the second syllable, the accent is invariably placed on that second syllable. In the story-telling tapes recorded by Ryūji Sasaki, I identified 39 forms like (15), all having the accent on the second syllable, and none having the accent on the initial, light syllable. This is easy to account for as the joint effect of the two constraints.

(15) be<u>rot</u>-to/*<u>be</u>rot-to, de<u>rat</u>-to/*<u>de</u>rat-to, ka<u>sat</u>-to/*<u>ka</u>sat-to,
      zu<u>bat</u>-to/*<u>zu</u>bat-to

Of the weight and the second-syllable constraints, can we decide which is stronger? There is a set of data that suggests that the second-syllable constraint is stronger. If both constraints were equally strong, we should expect about the same number for each of the accentual types in (16).

(16) a. The heavy syllable wins: <u>CVX</u>CV-to (e.g. <u>wa</u>tta-do)
      b. The second syllable wins: CVX<u>CV</u>-to (e.g. zup<u>pa</u>-do)

Actually, of the 29 forms conforming to this pattern in the corpus of recorded and published data I mentioned before, 8 exhibited the first pattern; 21 exhibited the second pattern, thus suggesting that the second-syllable constraint is stronger.

The ranking posited in (3) fails to account for two additional types of accentual patterns, which are semantically motivated. First, some mimetic expressions are accentless. Even in the Tokyo dialect, there are a few unaccented mimetic adverbs such as *sat-to* 'lightly' and *kat-to* 'angrily'. Their accented counterparts *<u>sat</u>-to* 'wiping motion' and *<u>kat</u>-to* 'flaring up or hitting hard' are phonomimes (imitations of sounds) or phenomimes (descriptions of physical conditions). The accentless ones are degree adverbs or psychomimes (mimetic words describing psychological conditions).

In the Tsugaru dialect, also, there are a large number of unaccented mimetic forms. The examples of unaccented monosyllabic mimetic adverbs in (17) are from Kokuritsu Kokugo Kenkyūjo 1980.

(17) a. Ut-te   ninju   atte.
          in.a.large.number   number.of.people exist
          'There are a lot more people.'

      b. adama-sa   zut-to   kaputede
          head-to   for.a.long.time be.wearing
          'wearing it on the head for a long time'

The accented and unaccented counterparts are slightly different in their meanings, as shown in (18).

(18)   accented (phono-/phenomime)   unaccented (degree adverbial)

    a. <u>ut</u>-te (uttering a forceful sound)   ut-te 'a lot'

    b. <u>zut</u>-to (dragging over a distance)   zut-to 'for a long time'

    c. <u>sat</u>-to (light touch)   sat-to 'lightly'

    d. <u>pat</u>-to (explosive movement)   pat-to 'quickly'

As in the Tokyo dialect, most of the unaccented counterparts are used as degree adverbs. This tendency of a mimetic form to lose accent when its meaning is less iconic is also realized in derived verbs such as *zawa-dugu* 'to be agitated' and *dao-megu* 'to slacken' and derived nominal adjectives such as *hura-hura-no* 'worn-out'.

The role of semantics is also clear in the fact that the semantic distinction between phono-/phenomimes and psychomimes, which is suppressed for their counterparts in the Tokyo dialect, is accentually significant for reduplicative mimetic forms in the Tsugaru dialect. Tsugaru psychomimes such as *ma<u>ho</u>-maho-do* 'absent-mindedly' never exhibit the leftmost accentual pattern prevalent in the Tokyo dialect.

4. The Implication of the New Observation: Nativization and Accent

What is the relevance of this to the study of the Japanese language? As Nasu (2001) points out, the accentual phenomena in the mimetic system are not isolated phenomena. In this section, I will compare the accentual patterns of Tsugaru mimetic words with the accentual patterns of loan words in the Tokyo dialect analyzed by Kubozono (in Kubozono and Ōta 1998). This will reveal significant similarities between the two in the way they are nativized into the Yamato stratum.

The forms in (19) are instances of the so-called "−3 rule" for compounds and loan words (see McCawley 1968), which is formulated as in (20).

(19) sa<u>ban</u>na 'Savanna', a<u>ren</u>zi 'arrange', gu<u>roo</u>bu 'globe', <u>gu</u>rasu 'glass'

(20) The syllable containing the antipenultimate mora is accented (Kubozono and Ōta 1998).

Kubozono's discussion clarifies that there are two types of exceptions that do not conform to this rule. In one, the words are deaccented, as in (21).

(21) burando 'brand', saraebo 'Sarajevo'

Unlike previous researchers, who reduced the problem solely to the degree of familiarity in terms of exposure or usage, Kubozono identifies phonological conditions for this deaccenting process. The conditions are either (22a) or (22b).

(22) a. The word is four mora long, and the last two syllables are light: e.g. *saraebo* 'Sarajevo'.[3]

    b. The word is four mora long, the penultimate syllable is heavy, and the vowel of the ultimate syllable is an epenthetic /o/: e.g. *burando* 'brand'.

When the last vowel is a reflex of the final vowel in the source word or when it is an epenthetic /u/ or /i/, deaccenting does not occur: e.g. *sabanna* 'savanna', *arenzi* 'arrange', *guroobu* 'globe'.

The other exceptional types of loan words are accented but do not observe the −3 rule. The accent is placed on the heavy syllable. They can also be phonologically characterized. One type has the characteristics summarized in (23).

(23) The last syllable is heavy, and the word-initial syllable contains an epenthetic vowel: e.g. *buruu* 'blue', *dorai* 'dry', and *surii* 'three'.

In the other type, the words have the segmental make-up to which the −3 rule should apply, but the actual rule that applies is the second half of the Latin accent rule in (24).

(24) If the penultimate syllable is light, the antepenultimate syllable is accented.

The application of this rule produces: *amazon* 'Amazon', *intabyuu* 'interview', and *enerugii* 'energy'. The Japanese accent rule would have produced: *amazon, *intabyuu, and *enerugii respectively. Younger people are applying this Latin-type rule to more forms: hence, *kuudetaa* instead of the older *kuudetaa*. Kubozono demonstrates that the outcomes of the Japanese rule and the Latin rule are not very different to begin with, the difference being limited to cases where the penult is light. He argues that the alternative forms are the results of applying the syllable-weight sensitive Latin rule across the board.

For our purpose, we can reinterpret Kubozono's analysis to mean that loan words line up on a scale of nativization as in the following.

---

[3] The sequence /ae/ is parsed as two syllables.

(25) (less nativized)   (more nativized)
    buruu   dorinku   saraebo
      enerugii   gurasu   pureeto
                kuudetaa   burando

The middle category in (25) invokes the language-specific weight-insensitive accent rule. The accent is placed on the head of a syllable containing an antepenultimate mora. When this rule is at its strongest stage, it should apply to all the forms in (25). However, the rule is constantly in negotiation with various other factors.

The right-most category in (25) contains the most nativized forms. They are four mora long, and their last two syllables are light, or their last syllable consists of a dental stop and epenthetic /o/. These phonological characteristics signal either that a word of foreign origin already conforms to the native template or that a word of foreign origin has undergone a significant degree of nativization. Such forms tend to be deaccented.

The left-most category in (25) apparently contains the outcomes of more universal constraints which center on the weight factor. Increasingly, the Japanese accent rule is also giving way to more general constraints.

Thus, in the Tokyo dialect, loan words are being tugged from two opposite ends by contradictory forces: the more universal, weight-sensitive, syllable-based constraints and the more Japanese-specific deaccenting pattern. The weight-insensitive accent rule is losing ground. We will observe a similar pattern among Tokyo mimetic forms when we compare them with Tsugaru mimetic forms.

Not unlike loan words, Tsugaru mimetic forms can be divided into three major accentual types along the scale of nativization, as shown in (26).

(26) (less nativized)   (more nativized)
     sat-to   katta-do   sat-to
    katta-do   mahomaho-do   zawa-dugu
     katat-to   hurahura-to
  katakata-do

The middle category contains bisyllabic forms containing a heavy syllable and reduplicative forms consisting of four light syllables. Old speakers of the Tsugaru dialect are likely to report that they place an accent on the second syllable for these forms. Written sources also predominantly report this pattern. In other words, this is the normative type.

Most forms containing heavy syllables and reduplicative light syllable phonomimes and phenomimes belong to the less nativized category. Those having a heavy syllable get the heavy syllable accented and those consisting of light syllables get the initial syllable accented. This latter is probably due to the universal function of the highest pitch in initial position—of introducing an independent intonational phrase. The most nativized category contains degree adverbs and derived verbs and adjectives. They are deaccented.

Thus, in the Tsugaru dialect, the normative accentuation is constantly in negotiation with opposite forces, the more universally motivated accentuation and the more Japanese-specific deaccentuation.

The three-way distinction is not clear in the case of Tokyo mimetic forms. In the Tokyo dialect, the type corresponding to *katta-do* is absent. Further, mimetic forms consisting of four light syllables are either accented on the initial syllable or unaccented. The intermediate type of accent—second-syllable or antipenultimate accent—is reserved for non-mimetic reduplicative forms such as those given in (27).

(27) nobinobi-to 'freely', yamayama 'mountains', kawarugawaru 'taking turns', kaesugaesu 'most regrettably'

When we turn to younger speakers and neighboring areas, we observe generational and regional gradations along the same parameter. A 21-year old speaker of a Nambu dialect from Nagawa, Aomori, exhibits a strong tendency to place the accent on the initial syllable. In addition, she uses unaccented forms as well as forms accented on the second syllable. Based on introspection, she says that she prefers accenting the initial syllable of mimetic forms consisting of four light syllables. In her perception, younger people use, for instance, *katakata-do* (realized as HHHHL), and older people *katakata-do* (LHLLL).

A 35-year old woman from Maesawa, Iwate, accents a heavy syllable if there is one. She uses the initial accent pattern for phonomimes consisting of four light syllables and the accentless pattern for other mimetic forms. Her parents also uniformly accent heavy syllables, but they prefer the antipenultimate accent pattern for forms containing four light syllables.

These differences means that the accent rule that places the accent on the second syllable is losing ground among young people in the tug of war between the more universal constraints and the more Japanese-specific deaccenting pattern. Thus, the parallelism between loan words and mimetic words is clear. Taking the regional and generational gradations into account, it would be reasonable to hypothesize that the Tokyo dialect once had the antipenultimate or second-syllable accent rule for mimetic forms.

5. Need for Further Studies

This study has not looked at how loan words are accented in the Tsugaru and other northern dialects. It remains to be seen if the prediction of a parallelism between loan word accentuation and mimetic accentuation will be borne out. The issue is worth pursuing in many more dialects. For instance, Kibe 2000 contains brief descriptions of loan word and mimetic accentuation patterns in the Kagoshima dialect. Predictably, there are three accent types among the Kagoshima loan words and mimetic forms: heavy syllable or initial accentuation, penultimate accentuation, and final accentuation. In my view, they correspond to the three accent types among Tsugaru mimetic forms. Systematic research in many more dialects across Japan will surely shed light on the motivations behind the changes in accentuation patterns.

References

Asano, M. 2003. The Optionality of the Quotative Particle -to in Japanese Mimetics. *Japanese/Korean Linguistics 12*, ed. W. McClure, 91–102. Stanford: CSLI.

Hamano, S. 1998. *The Sound-Symbolic System of Japanese*. Stanford: CSLI.

Kageyama, T. 2004. The Semantics and Syntax of Mimetic Light Verb Constructions. Paper presented at the Second Oxford-Kobe Linguistics Seminar, Kobe, Japan.

Kibe, N. 2000. *Seinanbu Kyūshū nikei akusento-no kenkyū* [A study of accent in the southeastern Kyūshū dialects]. Tokyo: Bensei Shuppan.

Kokuritsu Kokugo Kenkyūjo, ed. 1980. *Hōgen danwa shiryō* [Dialectal conversation data]. Tokyo: Kokutitsu Kokugo Kenkyūjo.

Kubozono, H., and S. Ōta 1998. *On'in-kōzō to akusento* [Phonological structure and accent]. Tokyo: Kenkyūsha.

McCawley, J. 1968. *The Phonological Component of a Grammar of Japanese*, Mouton, The Hague.

Miura, Y. 2001. *Aomori-shi kyū-Yasuda no hōgen-goi* [Dialectal vocabulary of the former Yasuda area in Aomori City]. Aomori: Kitanomachisha.

Narumi, S. 1957–1961. *Tsugaru no kotoba* [The vocabulary of the Tsugaru dialect]. Vols. 1–10. Hirosaki: Tsugaru no Kotoba Kankō Iinkai.

Nasu, A. 1995. Onomatope no keitai ni yōkyū-sareru inritsu jōken [Prosodic restrictions on Japanese onomatopoeia]. *Onseigakkai Kaihō* 209: 9–20.

Nasu, A. 2001. Onomatope no gokeisei to akusento [Word formation and accent in Japanese mimetics]. *Studies in Japanese Language and Culture* 11: 9–24.

Ogasawara, I. 1998. *Chimei Tsugaru Aomori-kō: Tsugaru-ben no sekai III* [Place names in Tsugaru and Aomori: The world of the Tsugaru dialect III]. Hirosaki: Hoppō Shinsha.

Ogasawara, I. 1999a. *Tsugaru-ben no sekai: Sono on'in gogen o saguru* [The world of the Tsugaru dialect: Phonology and etymology]. Hirosaki: Hoppō Shinsha.

Ogasawara, I. 1999b. *Tsugaru-ben no sekai II* [The world of the Tsugaru dialect II]. Hirosaki: Hoppō Shinsha.

Tamori, I., and L. Schourup. 1999. *Onomatope: keitai to imi* [Onomatopoetic expressions: Their morphology and semantics]. Tokyo: Kuroshio.

Uwano, Z. 1986. Aomori-shi hōgen no dōshi no akusento [Accentuation of verbs in the dialect of Aomori City]. *Nihonkai Bunka* 13:1–49.

Intonational Phonology of Seoul Korean Revisited

SUN-AH JUN

University of California, Los Angeles

1. Introduction

An autosegmental-metrical model of intonational phonology, developed by Pierrehumbert and her colleagues (Pierrehumbert 1980, Beckman and Pierrehumbert 1986, Pierrehumbert and Beckman 1988; see Ladd 1996 for a review) analyzes a pitch contour in terms of two distinct tonal targets (High and Low) and their combinations (e.g. LH for a rising contour and HL for a falling contour). Furthermore, each tone is associated with either a metrically prominent syllable or the edge of a prosodic unit. Thus, an intonation structure captures the prominence relation among words and the hierarchical structure of prosodic units. Though languages vary in the number of prosodic units above the **Word**, ranging from one to three, prosodic units higher than a Word are often marked by tone, pitch range, and/or final lengthening. Observations of cross-linguistic data (Jun 2005b) suggest that the highest prosodic unit marked by intonation is an **Intonation Phrase** (IP). Below this unit is an **Intermediate Phrase** (ip), which in turn is higher than an **Accentual Phrase** (AP), a unit slightly larger than a Word.

An intonational phonology of Seoul Korean adopting the same framework was proposed in Jun 1993, 1998, 2000, 2005a. This model proposed two tonally defined prosodic units above the Word: Intonation Phrase and

Accentual Phrase. Both levels have been shown to be psychologically real in studies of sentence processing and word segmentation. Korean listeners are sensitive to AP boundary cues in parsing the Adjective + Noun1 + Noun2 structure (e.g., *wise baby's daddy*; from Schafer and Jun 2002) as well as IP boundary cues in parsing a complex sentence (e.g. Kang and Speer 2003, Kim 2004). Sensitivity to IP boundary cues by children has also been shown in processing data (Choi and Mazka 2003).

However, prosodic analysis of attachment data (Jun and Kim 2004) suggests that Korean has a prosodic unit lower than an IP and higher than an AP, which I call an Intermediate Phrase (ip). The prosodic criteria defining the ip are not localized as in the IP. The boundary of an ip is perceived either by pitch reset at ip-initial or by a higher boundary (Ha) at ip-final. Unlike an IP, it does not show substantial phrase-final lengthening. It either has no lengthening or only a slight degree of final lengthening. In this paper, I will propose a revision of the intonational phonology of Seoul Korean by discussing the motivations for adding this prosodic unit.

The organization of the paper is as follows. In §2, the IP and the AP in Korean are briefly described. In §3, three motivations for adding the new prosodic unit, ip, are given. §4 proposes a revised model, and §5 discusses difficulties in defining the ip and proposes further research.

2. Intonation Phrase and Accentual Phrase in Seoul Korean

An Intonation Phrase (IP) can have one or more Accentual Phrases and is marked by a boundary tone (%) which is realized on the phrase-final syllable. Nine boundary tones have been identified so far: L%, H%, LH%, HL%, LHL%, HLH%, LHLH%, HLHL%, LHLHL%. In addition, an IP is marked by phrase-final lengthening. The phrase-final syllable is about twice as long as the same syllable in the middle of an IP. Finally, an IP is optionally followed by a pause. An Accentual Phrase (AP) can have one or more Words and is marked by a tonal pattern, phrase-initial rise and phrase-final rise, i.e. LH-LH or HH-LH. The phrase-initial tone is High or Low depending on the phrase-initial segment: High (H) in the case of a tense consonant, an aspirated consonant, /s/, or /h/, but Low otherwise. Typically, an AP does not show any phrase-final lengthening and is not followed by a pause.

The four tones marking an AP are associated with certain locations within an AP. The first two tones (HH or LH) are associated with the first two syllables of an AP and the last two tones (LH) are associated with the last two syllables of an AP. When an AP has four or more syllables, all four tones are realized, but when an AP has fewer than four syllables, the second or third tone (H and L), or both, is often not realized, i.e. undershot. It is not clear yet what determines which tone to undershoot. Schematic contours of common AP tonal patterns when an AP has fewer than four syllables are shown in Figure 1. The tones undershot are in parentheses. The first three contours are when an AP begins with a Low tone, and the other two are when it begins with a High tone. The AP-final tone is, however, sometimes realized as a Low tone (i.e. La) due to the tonal context or its location within an IP. The La tone occurs most commonly when a short AP beginning with a High tone is followed by a High-tone initial AP. Kim (2004:48) shows that H-initial APs have a higher percentage of La tones than L-initial APs (28.9% vs. 11.1%).

| L(HL)H | LH(L)H | L(H)LH | H(H(L))H | H(H)LH |

Figure 1. Common AP Tonal Patterns When AP Has Fewer than 4 Syllables

Example pitch tracks of Seoul intonation are shown below. Figure 2 and Figure 3 show one IP forming three APs, one AP per word: Topic-Object-Verb. The sentences are: Figure 2, *yEQmaninenIN yEQarIR miwEhAyo* 'Youngman's family hates YoungAh'; Figure 3, *hyEQmininenIN yEQarIR miwEhAyo* 'Hyungmin's family hates YoungAh'. The words in the words tier are written in the Korean romanization used in Korean ToBI (Jun 2000).

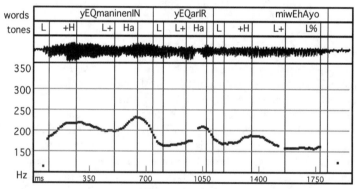

Figure 2. Pitch Track Example of the Sentence *yEQmaninenIN yEQarIR miwEhAyo* 'Youngman's family hates YoungAh' (The first AP (*yEQmaninenIN*) shows an LHLH pattern.)

A major difference between Figure 2 and Figure 3 is in the tonal contour of the first AP and their pitch ranges. The AP beginning with [h] (Figure 3) has an HHLH pattern and the f0 value of the initial High tone is much higher than that of the LHLH pattern AP in Figure 2. However, this pitch range difference due to an AP-initial segment disappears at the end of the AP, as shown in these figures (see Lee 1999 for a detailed description of

AP tone realizations). The second AP both in Figure 2 and in Figure 3, being three syllables long, shows an LH or LLH pattern. The third, IP-final, AP shows an LHL pattern (L, +H, (L+), L%) because it is four syllables long (+H on the second syllable of the AP). The final tone is not H because the AP-final syllable is also IP-final; hence, the H tone (Ha) is overridden by the IP-final Low boundary tone (L%), which marks a declarative meaning.

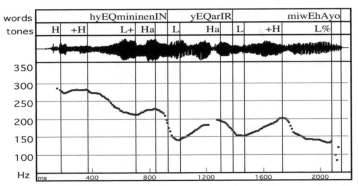

Figure 3. Pitch Track Example of the Sentence *hyEQmininenIN yEQarIR miwEhAyo* 'Hyungmin's family hates YoungAh' (The first AP shows an HHLH pattern.)

3. Proposal: Intermediate Phrase

In this paper, I am proposing a third prosodic unit above the Word in Seoul Korean. Since this unit is smaller than an IP and larger than an AP, it will be called an Intermediate Phrase (ip). This prosodic unit serves as the domain of "phonetic" downstep. This is different from the Intermediate Phrase proposed for English and Japanese in Beckman and Pierrehumbert (1986), where the Intermediate Phrase is the domain of downstep triggered by a phonological tone (i.e. bitonal pitch accent). In Korean, a sequence of APs (when all APs begin with the same type of initial tone; see §5 for more discussion on AP-initial tone types) shows a downstep-like f0 lowering within a domain which forms a coherent unit of meaning and/or syntactic structure. Pitch range is reset across this domain, an ip, and the reset in pitch can be cued in more than one way. Three motivations for adding this new prosodic unit are given below.

3.1. First Motivation for Revision

The first motivation comes from the difference between a focused AP and a default AP. A focused word in Korean is realized with expanded pitch range and the lengthening/strengthening of a word-initial segment (Jun and Lee 1998), providing a larger disjuncture from the previous AP than the juncture of a default AP boundary. In K-ToBI (Korean ToBI), the break index before a focused word would be lower than '3' (corresponding to the IP juncture) and higher than '2' (corresponding to the AP juncture).

The size of an AP also differs between a focused AP and a default AP. Typically one AP contains one word (Schafer and Jun 2002, Kim 2004, Jun 2005b), but a focused phrase can include multiple words, with post-focus words being dephrased or phrased in a very reduced pitch range. The figures below show pitch tracks of a sentence produced without focusing any word (Figure 4) and and focusing the object noun *minari* 'dropwort' (Figure 5). (The other words in the sentence are *EmEni* 'mother' and *mEGnINdeyo* 'eat-ending'.)

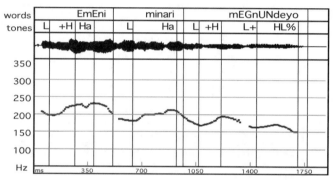

Figure 4. Pitch Track of the Sentence *EmEni minari mEGnINdeyo* 'Mother eats dropwort' without Focusing Any Word (f0 peaks show a downstep-like lowering over the sentence.)

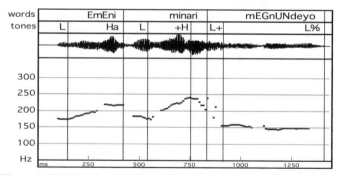

Figure 5. Pitch Track of the Same Sentence as in Figure 4, but Focusing the Object *minari* 'dropwort' (The focused AP shows a higher f0 peak than the preceding AP and includes the focused word and the following word, Verb.)

Figure 4 shows a downstep-like lowering of f0 peaks over the sentence. The focused AP in Figure 5, however, breaks this downstep-like chain and shows a higher pitch range than that of the preceding AP, thus higher than the corresponding second AP in Figure 4. The focused AP is also larger than the neutral AP, including two words ('eat dropwort'). Therefore, categorizing a focused AP as the same unit as the default AP would not reflect their acoustic and perceptual correlates.

3.2. Motivation 2 for Revision

A boundary of a syntactic clause or a complex syntactic phrase is often marked by a larger boundary than an AP. For example, in the Relative clause (RC) + NP1 + NP2 structure, the end of the RC is often marked by an IP-final boundary tone (%) and phrase-final lengthening. Figure 6 shows an example pitch track showing an HL% boundary tone after an RC and pitch reset at NP1: RC (*byEQwEne ibwENhan* 'who is hospitalized') + NP1 (*do-QryoU* 'colleague's') + NP2 (*buinIN* 'wife-TOP'). The phrase shown in Figure 6 is taken from the sentence *byEQwEne ibwENhan doQryoU buinIN ne doQseQU dehaG doQchaQiEDda* '(My) colleague's wife who is hospitalized was my younger sibling's college classmate'.

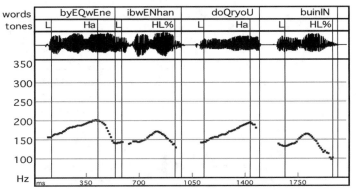

Figure 6. Pitch Track Showing an IP Boundary (HL%) after the Relative Clause *byEQwEne ibwENhan* 'who is hospitalized' (Pitch is reset at NP1 (doQryoU).

But, sometimes, we observe no IP boundary tone or lengthening at the end of the RC, even though we perceive a larger juncture than the default AP boundary. In this case, we observe a higher AP-final Ha boundary at the end of the RC or pitch reset at NP1. A pitch track example of an RC boundary marked by a higher AP-final boundary tone but no lengthening is shown in Figure 7. Compare Figure 7 with the pitch track of the same phrase shown in Figure 8, where the RC boundary is marked by an AP. In Figure 8, each word forms one AP, and the first AP-final H tone is higher than the second AP-final H tone (marking the end of the RC), which in turn is higher than the third AP-final H tone (marking the end of NP1). The last AP, an IP-final AP, shows an HL% tone, another type of declarative marking IP-boundary tone in Korean.

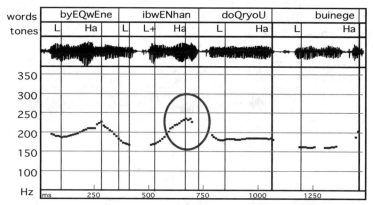

Figure 7. Pitch Track of the Same Phrase as in Figure 6 (The RC-final syllable is not lengthened, but the juncture after the RC is perceived to be bigger than the default AP because the AP-final tone (circled), marking the end of the RC, is higher than the preceding AP.)

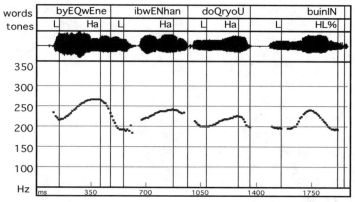

Figure 8. Pitch Track of the Same Phrase as in Figure 7 (Except for NP2's Postposition, *-ege* LOCATIVE vs. *-IN* TOPIC) (Each word is produced in one AP, thus the juncture after the RC is not perceived to be bigger than the default AP. The f0 peak of each AP is lowered throughout the phrase (except for the HL% boundary tone).)

A pitch track example of a larger-than-AP juncture after an RC, marked by pitch reset at NP1 and no lengthening, is shown in Figure 9. The phrase shown in the figure is RC (*sENgEe* 'in the election' *chuRmahhaN* 'who runs'), NP1 (*sENbeU* 'senior's'), NP2 (*chiNgunIN* 'friend'). Since all AP-initial segments are [s] or aspirated affricates, each AP begins with a High tone. Here, the end of the RC is not marked by a higher Ha boundary tone as in Figure 7. Instead, the beginning of the third AP, which contains NP1, is higher than that of the second AP (marking the end of the RC), thus cueing a bigger juncture than AP after the RC.

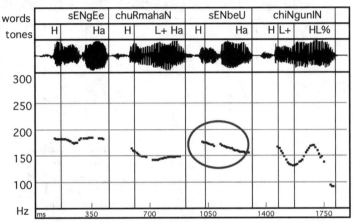

Figure 9. Pitch Track of the RC + NP + NP2 Structure *sENgEe chuRmahaN sENbeU chiNgunIN* 'My senior's friend who runs in the election' (The RC-final syllable is not lengthened, but the juncture after the RC is perceived to be bigger than the default AP because the pitch is reset at NP1 (*sENbeU*). The AP-initial High tone (circled) is higher than that of the preceding AP.)

The same phenomenon is found in Chonnam dialect, whose prosodic structure is the same as that of Seoul but has a different AP tonal pattern from Seoul's (Jun 1993, 1998). A pitch track example of the same phrase as in Figure 7 is shown in Figure 10. As seen in the figure, the tonal pattern of the AP is LHL (it would be HHL if the AP-initial segment were an H-tone trigger as in Seoul). Here, the boundary after the RC is perceived to be bigger than the default AP. That is, a bigger juncture after the RC is cued by pitch reset at NP1.

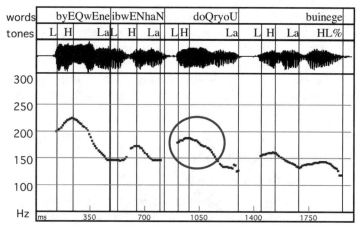

Figure 10. Pitch Track of the Same Phrase as in Figure 7 in Chonnam Dialect
(The RC-final syllable is not lengthened but the juncture after the
RC is perceived to be bigger than the default AP because the AP-
initial tone of NP1 (circled) is higher than that of the preceding
AP.)

3.3. Motivation 3 for Revision

The next motivation is from sentence processing data, which suggest that
the presence of an intermediate prosodic unit between an IP and an AP is
psychologically real.

In the RC NP1's NP2 structure, Korean speakers tend to prefer high attachment of the RC, i.e. RC modifying NP2 (Jun and Kim 2004). Production data show that the most common prosodic phrasing of this structure is
{RC}{NP1 NP2}, i.e. a bigger boundary after the RC than after NP1. In this
case, the RC was marked by an IP or an ip, and the NP1 was marked by an
AP. When the RC was longer, more IP or ip breaks were found after the
RC, and listeners interpreted them as high attachment more often (see Jun
2004 for details). A similar phenomenon was found in Japanese (Jun and
Koike 2003).

4. Intonation of Seoul Korean – Revised

In sum, the prosodic structure of Seoul Korean proposed in Jun 1993, 1998,
2000, forthcoming, does not distinguish the difference in juncture between
the default AP and the focused AP, and it does not capture the prosodic cues
used to disambiguate syntactically ambiguous structures. These problems
would be solved if we assume an intermediate prosodic unit between an IP
and an AP. That is, an Intermediate Phrase (ip) in Seoul Korean is the domain of focus and the domain of phonetic downstep. It often marks the edge
of a syntactic clause or a complex phrase structure. Phonetically, either the

beginning or the end of an ip boundary is marked. The end of an ip is marked by a higher AP-final tone (which could be interpreted as a boundary tone of an ip) than the preceding AP-final tone. The beginning of an ip is marked by "higher initial pitch" than the preceding AP. The higher initial pitch can come from either the beginning or the end of the ip-initial AP. Therefore, the revised prosodic units above the Word in Seoul Korean, from the highest to the lowest, are shown in Figure 11.

Intonation Phrase (IP) > Intermediate Phrase (ip) >Accentual Phrase (AP)

Figure 11. Three Tonally Defined Prosodic Units above the Word in Seoul Korean

5. Problems and Future Research

Pitch-range related phenomena such as downstep and pitch reset have been used as a criterion to define a prosodic unit in other languages (e.g. Intermediate Phrase in English and Japanese). Then, why was pitch range ignored before in defining a prosodic unit in Korean? One of the main reasons is that, as mentioned earlier, pitch range can change in Korean depending on the properties of the segment at the beginning of a phrase. APs beginning with a tense consonant, an aspirated consonant, /s/, or /h/ have a higher pitch range than those beginning with other segments. An example pitch track showing a higher pitch range due to an H-initial AP, but not marking the beginning of a larger prosodic unit, is shown in Figure 12 (*maIR sara-MdIri* 'the village people', *sirhEhanIN* 'hate-RC marker', *mudaQU* 'the exorcist's', *goyaQinIN* 'the cat-TOP', meaning 'The cat of the exorcist that the village people hate . . .').

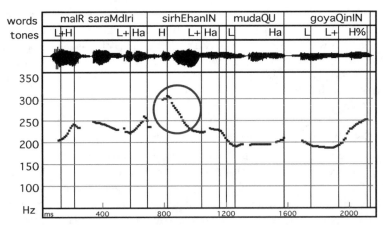

Figure 12. Pitch Track of a Phrase, RC (*maIR saraMdIri sirEhanIN*) + NP1 (*mudaQU*) + NP2 (*goyaQinIN*) (The predicate of the RC (*sirhEhanIN*) forms one AP, but its beginning pitch (circled) is higher than the preceding AP due to the AP-initial segment [s].)

Here, due to the [s] sound, the AP containing the predicate of the RC (*sir-hEhanIN*) begins with a higher pitch than the preceding AP, which is the subject of the RC. However, as the tonal transcription suggests, the juncture between the subject and the predicate is not bigger than an AP.

It is difficult, therefore, to define an ip based on only pitch range when a sentence has words whose initial segment is a different tone trigger, especially when a Low-beginning AP is followed by a High-beginning AP.[1] In this case, the initial High tone of a High-beginning AP either keeps the same f0 height as the preceding Ha of the Low-beginning AP or starts higher than the preceding Ha value (as in Figure 12). Informal observation suggests that we need to consider the speaker's pitch range to decide an ip boundary. If an AP-initial H tone value belongs to the top of the speaker's pitch range, the AP begins a new ip. We need more data to define an ip when an utterance has APs with mixed initial tone triggers.

The next question concerns whether an IP is exhaustively parsed in ips and an ip is exhaustively parsed in APs. This would be true if we assume Selkirk's (1986) Strict Layer Hypothesis (SLH). But, it is not easy to answer this question straightforwardly. It seems that there exist some constraints on the realization of an ip. Data (used in Jun 1993, 2000, and in Jun and Kim 2004) suggest that some ips (e.g. ips containing only a short, monosyllabic, pronoun or a short adverb) are not fully realized but degenerated before a main/full ip, similar to a pro-clitic or an extrametrical segment in segmental phonology. A similar phenomenon seems to be found in the last ip of an IP. It is not clear if this small phrase should be analyzed as an ip. If not, the SLH would be violated. Another interesting tendency observed in the data is that, when the syntactic structure is the same, a sequence of L-initial APs showed a chain of downstep more often than a sequence of H-initial APs. This implies that there is an interaction between the tone type and the phrasing: H-initial APs tend to begin an ip more often than L-initial APs.

Finally, the degree of phrase-final lengthening is another issue that needs to be examined. As mentioned earlier, most ip-final syllables are not lengthened, similar to AP-final syllables. But there are some cases where the ip-final syllable is slightly longer than the AP-level duration (though clearly shorter than the IP-level duration). It is possible that an ip has a small degree of final lengthening. A perception experiment should be performed to confirm a qualitative difference between the prosodic units.

---

[1] For this reason, all RC + NP1 + NP2 structures examined in this paper were chosen because they contain words whose initial segments are either all H-tone triggers or all L-tone triggers.

References

Beckman, M. E., and J. Pierrehumbert. 1986. Intonational Structure in Japanese and English. *Phonology Yearbook* 3:255–309.

Choi, Y., and R. Mazuka. 2003. Young Children's Use of Prosody in Sentence Parsing. *Journal of Psycholinguistic Research* 32(2):197–217.

Jun, S.-A. 1993. The Phonetics and Phonology of Korean Prosody. Doctoral dissertation, Ohio State University. [Published in 1996. New York: Garland.]

Jun, S.-A. 1998. The Accentual Phrase in the Korean Prosodic Hierarchy. *Phonology* 15(2):189–226.

Jun, S.-A. 2000. K-ToBI (Korean ToBI) Labelling Conventions: Version 3. *Speech Sciences* 7:143–69. [Version 3.1, *UCLA WPP* 99:149–73]

Jun, S.-A. 2005a. Korean Intonational Phonology and Prosodic Transcription. *Prosodic Typology: The Phonology of Intonation and Phrasing*, ed. S.-A. Jun, 201–29. Oxford: Oxford University Press.

Jun, S.-A. 2005b. Prosodic Typology. *Prosodic Typology: The Phonology of Intonation and Phrasing*, ed. S.-A. Jun, 430–58. Oxford: Oxford University Press.

Jun, S.-A. Forthcoming. The Intermediate Phrase in Korean Intonation: Its Role in Sentence Processing. *Tones and Tunes: Studies in Word and Sentence Prosody*, eds. C. Gussenhoven and T. Riad. Berlin: Mouton de Gruyter.

Jun, S.-A., and S. Kim. 2004. Default Phrasing and Attachment Preference in Korean. Paper presented at INTERSPEECH 2004 – ICSLP, Jeju, Korea.

Jun, S.-A., and C. Koike. 2003. Default Prosody and RC Attachment in Japanese. Paper presented at the 13th Japanese/Korean Linguistics Conference, East Lansing, Michigan. [To appear in *Japanese/Korean Linguistics 13*. Stanford: CSLI.]

Jun, S.-A., and H.-J. Lee. 1998. Phonetic and Phonological Markers of Contrastive Focus in Korean. *Proceedings of the 5th ICSLP* 4:1295–8.

Kang, S., and S. Speer. 2003. Prosodic Disambiguation of Syntactic Clause Boundaries in Korean. Paper presented at WCCFL XXII, San Diego, California.

Kim, S. 2004. The Role of Prosodic Phrasing in Korean Word Segmentation. Doctoral dissertation, UCLA.

Ladd, R. 1996. *Intonational Phonology*. Cambridge: Cambridge University Press.

Lee, H.-J. 1999. Tonal Realization and Implementation of the Accentual Phrase in Seoul Korean. Master's thesis, UCLA.

Pierrehumbert, J. 1980. The Phonology and Phonetics of English Prosody. Doctoral dissertation, MIT.

Pierrehumbert, J., and M. E. Beckman. 1988. *Japanese Tone Structure*. Cambridge: MIT Press.

Schafer, A., and S.-A. Jun. 2002. Effects of Accentual Phrasing on Adjective Interpretation in Korean. *East Asian Language Processing*, ed. M. Nakayama, 223–55. Stanford: CSLI.

Selkirk, E. 1986. On Derived Domains in Sentence Phonology. *Phonology Yearbook* 3:371–405.

Consonant Cooccurrence Restrictions in Yamato Japanese

SHIGETO KAWAHARA*
University of Massachusetts, Amherst

HAJIME ONO
University of Maryland, College Park

KIYOSHI SUDO
New York University

1. Introduction

This paper points out previously unnoticed dissimilatory restrictions in Japanese. Often, similar consonants, especially those that have the same place of articulation, are prohibited from cooccurring within a particular domain such as a stem or a word. Such restrictions have been found in many languages, sometimes under the rubric of the **Obligatory Contour Principle (OCP)**. Languages that have been shown to have such effects include Arabic (McCarthy 1986), English (Berkley 1994), Javanese (Mester 1986), Muna (Coetzee and Pater 2005), Rotuman (McCarthy 2003), Russian (Padgett 1992), and others. The primary aim of this paper is to argue that similar consonant cooccurrence restrictions are found in the native vocabulary of Japanese (Yamato Japanese). We show that homorganic consonants

---

* We wish to thank Bjarke Frellesvig, Shōsuke Haraguchi, Markus Hiller, Kazu Kurisu, John McCarthy, Joe Pater, Adam Ussishkin, Tim Vance, Cheryl Zoll, the audience at University of Maryland, the members of the UMass Summer Phonology/Phonetics Group, the audience at the Tokyo Circle of Phonologists, and the audience at the 14th Japanese/Korean Conference for very useful comments on this project. Any shortcomings of interpretation and exposition of the data rest solely with us.

are less likely to cooccur than expected within a root, although this tendency is not an absolute prohibition.

The remainder of this paper is structured as follows. §2 presents the method of our survey. §3 discusses several aspects of the consonant cooccurrence restrictions we have found. In §4 we discuss crosslinguistic implications of this study. Throughout, we focus on descriptive aspects of our findings, although theoretical implications are touched upon where appropriate. One final remark before closing this introductory section. Due to space limitations, it is impossible to provide detailed data for all aspects of findings presented in this paper, but more complete data are found in the following website, which can be consulted for further information: http:// www.people.umass.edu/kawahara/yamato.htm.

2. Method

The first step of our investigation was to extract all monomorphemic Yamato roots from a large dictionary of Japanese, *Kōjien* (Shinmura 1998). Loanwords, mimetics, affixes, and interjections were excluded.[1] Obsolete words, noted as such in the dictionary, were also excluded for two reasons: this study focused on the synchronic grammar, and the morphological composition of such words was often not clear. In the case of a morphologically related paradigm (e.g. *sadamari* 'law', *sadameru* 'to define', *sadamaru* 'to fix') the root was counted only once. The database contained 4,011 roots at the end of this procedure.

From the collected set of monomorphemic roots, adjacent pairs of consonantal sequence were extracted. For instance, a root that contains {s d m r} yielded three pairs: {s d}, {d m}, and {m r}. This resulted in 4,737 adjacent consonantal pairs. Two notes are in order regarding this procedure. First, coda consonants, which place-assimilate to the following consonant, were systematically ignored. For example, given a word like *tombo* 'dragonfly', only {t b} was counted, but not {m b}; we focused on onset-adjacency. Second, our study was based on surface forms. For example, [ʃi], which is arguably derived from /si/, was counted as [ʃ] (see §4.3 for discussion on this choice).

Then, for all adjacent consonant pairs, the frequency of cooccurrence was counted and summarized, as illustrated in Table 1. Table 1 is a simplified table listing only three consonants, for the sake of illustration. It lists the number of pairs with a particular consonant configuration. For example, there are three pairs in which C_1 is [m] and C_2 is [b]; call these **observed** numbers.

---

[1] Dissimilatory restrictions on mimetics have been pointed out by Hamano (1998:41–2).

C_1 \ C_2	m	b	t	Total
m	9	3	6	18
b	2	2	9	13
t	8	7	8	23
Total	19	12	23	54

C_1 \ C_2	m	b	t	Total
m	6.3	4.0	7.7	18
b	4.6	2.9	5.5	13
t	8.1	5.1	9.8	23
Total	19	12	23	54

Table 1. Observed Numbers   **Table 2.** Expected Numbers

From Table 1 we can calculate the **expected** number of consonant pairs. For example, the probability of [m] occurring as C_1 in Table 1 is $18/54 = .33$. Similarly, the probability of [b] occurring in C_2 is $12/54 = .22$. Therefore, if these two events are independent (i.e. their probabilities do not influence one another), then the probability of both events occurring is $.33 \times .22 = .074$. Since there are 54 pairs in total, we should expect $.074 \times 54 = 4$ pairs that have [m] followed by [b]. This is the **expected** number for the {m b} pair, if the two consonants are combined at random. In general, an expected number for pairs of {x y} can be calculated as $E(C_1 = x, C_2 = y) = P(C_1 = x) \times P(C_2 = y) \times N$ (where N is a total number of pairs).

Expected numbers were calculated for each consonantal pair, as shown in Table 2. Next, so-called O/E values were calculated by dividing each observed number by the corresponding expected number. O/E values smaller than 1 indicate that consonantal pairs are underrepresented (i.e. occur less often than expected); O/E values larger than 1 indicate overrepresentation.

A χ^2 test was used to check the statistical significance of the deviations of O/E values from 1. The χ^2 value for each {x y} pair is the sum of $(O - E)^2/E$ over the four cells, {x, y}, {x, non-y}, {non-x, y}, and {non-x, non-y}. {non-x} and {non-y} are defined as all the sounds (or classes of sounds) other than {x} and {y}, respectively. For example, for χ^2 of two adjacent labials, the relevant cells are {lab, lab}, {lab, non-lab}, {non-lab, lab}, and {non-lab, non-lab}. The degree of freedom is thus $(2-1) \times (2-1) = 1$.

To investigate the existence of general cooccurrence restrictions based on place homorganicity, consonants were classified according to their major place of articulations (labial, coronal, palatal, dorsal). Further, the coronal class was divided into two classes (coronal sonorants and coronal obstruents), because previous studies (see works cited above) found that such a division is observed. We refer to these classes as "identity classes", following Yip's (1989) terminology.

Given the findings of the previous studies, the a priori prediction was that any pair of two consonants from the same identity class should be underrepresented. We set our α-level at .05; if $\chi^2 > 3.84$, then p < .05. Since the the multiple applications of the same test were preplanned, no familywise error α-level adjustment was used.

3. Results

3.1. General Patterns

The procedure described above revealed that there are indeed consonant cooccurrence restrictions in Yamato Japanese, as summarized in Table 3, where pairs that are underrepresented to a statistically significant degree are indicated by shading. Note that the linear order is abstracted away; see the website for the table with a preserved linear order.

	Labial p, b, m, ɸ, w	Cor-Obs t, d, ts, s, z, ʃ, ʒ, tʃ, dʒ	Cor-Son n, r	Palatal ç, j	Dorsal k, g
Labial	O = 43 O/E = 0.22 χ^2 = 180.11	O = 404 O/E = 1.35 χ^2 = 67.78	O = 222 O/E = 1.20 χ^2 = 11.43	O = 41.5 O/E = 1.08 χ^2 = 0.31	O = 225 O/E = 1.07 χ^2 = 1.72
Cor-Obs		O = 247 O/E = 0.53 χ^2 = 218.75	O = 295.5 O/E = 1.02 χ^2 = 0.27	O = 62 O/E = 1.03 χ^2 = 0.09	O = 417 O/E = 1.27 χ^2 = 45.36
Cor-Son			O = 69 O/E = 0.39 χ^2 = 104.25	O = 37.5 O/E = 1.01 χ^2 = 0.00	O = 266.5 O/E = 1.31 χ^2 = 31.43
Palatal				O = 3 O/E = 0.39 χ^2 = 3.15	O = 42 O/E = 0.99 χ^2 = 0.00
Dorsal					O = 66 O/E = 0.29 χ^2 = 193.31

Table 3. O/E Values by Identity Classes – Adjacent Pairs (Significant underrepresentation is indicated by shading. If $\chi^2 > 3.84$, p < .05. N = 4,737.)

Table 3 clearly shows OCP effects. All pairs of consonants from the same identity class show underrepresentation to a statistically significant degree, with the exception of palatals.[2] For instance, a labial occurs with another labial only about 20 percent as often as expected. Even palatal pairs are underrepresented, but only barely significantly (p = .075), due to the small number of data points. Note also that none of the nonhomorganic pairs are

---

[2] "Palatal" allophones of coronal obstruents (ʃ, ʒ, tʃ, dʒ) pattern with coronal consonants: they are underrepresented with coronal obstruents (O/E = .57, χ^2 = 21.89, p < .001). They are prepalatals, and thus are treated as coronals with [−ant] specification in Japanese (see Zoll 1997 for phonological evidence that they are coronals).

underrepresented. These results suggest that, in Yamato Japanese, a pair of adjacent consonants from the same identity class occurs much less likely than expected, quite similar to the effect observed in other languages cited in the introduction. The χ^2 tests show that the probability of these effects occurring by chance is quite small; even for the smallest χ^2 (104.3 for coronal sonorants) the associated probability is smaller than .001.

In Table 3 we only computed values for pairs of adjacent consonants, since it is known that the OCP applies most stringently to adjacent consonants. We also checked whether nonadjacent consonants exhibit any restrictions. The results are given in Table 4, where only weaker (if any) OCP effects hold. Only the shaded cells (coronal sonorants and obstruents) are statistically significant, and the effects are even weaker than those found in Table 3.

	Labial p, b, m, φ, w	Cor-Obs t, d, ts, s, z, ʃ, ʒ, tʃ, dʒ	Cor-Son n, r	Palatal ç, j	Dorsal k, g
Labial	O = 45 O/E = 0.87 χ^2 = 1.39	O = 88.5 O/E = 1.01 χ^2 = 0.03	O = 65 O/E = 0.98 χ^2 = 0.06	O = 11 O/E = 0.95 χ^2 = 0.03	O = 74.5 O/E = 1.15 χ^2 = 2.15
Cor-Obs		O = 121 O/E = 0.83 χ^2 = 8.76	O = 140 O/E = 1.25 χ^2 = 13.13	O = 17.5 O/E = 0.91 χ^2 = 0.26	O = 110 O/E = 1.01 χ^2 = 0.02
Cor-Son			O = 49 O/E = 0.57 χ^2 = 25.78	O = 19 O/E = 1.29 χ^2 = 1.63	O = 81 O/E = 0.10 χ^2 = 0.10
Palatal				O = 1 O/E = 0.39 χ^2 = 1.03	O = 16 O/E = 1.11 χ^2 = 0.23
Dorsal					O = 70 O/E = 0.86 χ^2 = 2.59

Table 4. O/E Values by Identity Classes – Nonadjacent Pairs (N = 1679)

One point that merits discussion is the fact that coronal sonorants and coronal obstruents constitute a separate identity class, that is, coronal sonorants and coronal obstruents happily cooccur even in adjacent positions (O/E = 1.02, χ^2 = .27, p = .60). No evidence for such a distinction is found for labials or dorsals. Such a tendency (i.e. a sonority split for coronals) is observed in many languages, including all the languages listed in the introduction. Further evidence is found in an identity-driven cluster reduction in Wintu (McGarrity 1999). The fact that this generalization holds also in Yamato Japanese suggests the robustness of this crosslinguistic tendency, and this generalization might arguably be universal. Here, we have nothing new to say about why there is such a division only for coronals and not for other classes (see Frisch et al. 2004 for a hypothesis; see Coetzee and Pater 2005 and McCarthy 2003 for a counterexample to their claim).

Next, we checked the O/E values of pairs of identical consonants. It is known that totally identical consonants avoid violating the OCP (see the works cited in the introduction). In Yamato Japanese, two voiced obstruents are disallowed within a stem (Lyman's Law; see e.g. Itô and Mester 1986), and even when they are identical, two voiced obstruents cannot cooccur. Besides these cases, however, total identity does seem to provide an escape hatch from the OCP. Each of [p], [ɸ], [w], [t], [ts], [s], [n], [ʃ], [tʃ], [ç], [j], [h] seems to freely occur with itself ([n] and [ʃ] show slight underrepresentation). Cases that are underrepresented to a statistically significant degree are [m], [r], and [k].[3]

Finally, as mentioned above, Yamato Japanese prohibits two voiced obstruents within the same stem, and this restriction holds regardless of the place of articulation. We tested whether two other manner features, [±cont] and [±nasal], are subject to similar restrictions. The results demonstrate that continuancy results in very slight underrepresentation ([+cont] O/E = .80; [−cont] O/E = .90), but [m] and [n] are not underrepresented with one another). Voicing seems to have a special status in Japanese.

3.2. Similarity Correlates with Underrepresentation?

Frisch et al. (2004) argue that the degree of similarity correlates with the degree of underrepresentation: the more similar two consonants are, the less likely they cooccur (see Frisch et al. 2004 on how to measure similarity). Coronal consonants provide a nice testing ground concerning whether this generalization applies in the case of Yamato Japanese or not. We will see that it is (at least partially) supported. Here we present only a subset of the segment-by-segment cooccurrence data (see the aforementioned website for more information).

Starting with [±voice], consider the following observations (the numbers in parentheses represent O/E values).

(1) [±voice]
   [t] is more underrepresented with [s] (.35) than with [z] (.58).
   [ts] is more underrepresented with [s] (.21) than with [z] (.52).
   [ʃ] is more underrepresented with [s] (.29) than with [z] (1.11).

All these suggest that two voiceless consonants are less likely to cooccur

---

[3] With 20 applications of the same χ^2 test, α is adjusted by the Bonferroni method, α = .05/20 = .0025. If $\chi^2 > 9.14$, p < .0025. See the website for O/E and χ^2 values.

than pairs with different voicing specifications. In other words, within the coronal class, having two voiceless consonants is disfavored. This suggests that agreeing in [±voice] contributes to more similarity, which leads to more underrepresentation. It is important to notice, however, that this assumes place homorganicity; [t] and [k], for example, happily cooccur (O/E = .99 χ^2 = .00).

The only other relevant feature is [±cont], as a difference in [±nas] entails a difference in [±son]. Here, an unexpected pattern is observed:

(2) [±cont]
[d] is more underrepresented with [s] (.66) than with [t] (1.91).
[z] is more underrepresented with [t] (.58) than with [s] (1.04).

The generalization appears to be that it is better to agree in continuancy. We do not, however, simply submit to the view that this constitutes a counterexample to the generalization that similarity correlates with the degree of underrepresentation. The reason is that pairs like [d]-[t] and [z]-[s] are not only less underrepresented, but not underrepresented at all.

We suggest that pairs like [d]-[t] and [z]-[s], which differ only in terms of [voice], can be treated as identical for OCP computations. Recall that total identity usually provides an escape hatch from OCP violations. Perhaps [d] and [t], for example, are not different enough to be treated as different, and hence there is no underrepresentation.

This hypothesis points to special properties of voicing in Japanese. On the one hand, although it can affect cooccurrence rates, it can also be ignored in the computation of identity. On the other hand, it is subject to a cooccurrence restriction independent of place homorganicity (see above).[4] Here we suggest two tentative explanations for these peculiar properties of voicing in Japanese. First, it has a special status in Japanese phonology in that it is a diacritic (autosegmental) feature, as Unger (1977) argues. Thus, just as tones can be ignored in the computation of identity, voicing can potentially be ignored, total identity being defined in terms of features other than [±voice]. Further, since it constitutes its own autosegmental tier, it is specifically subject to OCP(voi).

Another plausible explanation is to assume that voicing is perceptually nonsalient. If it is nonsalient, it is easily lost (Steriade 2001), and it can also be ignored in the identity computation. These special properties of voicing in Japanese merit further discussion in future research.

---

[4] These properties are also found in Muna's prenasalization, as identified by Coetzee and Pater (2005). It might be noteworthy that, historically, Japanese voicing used to be prenasalization (Unger 1977).

3.3. Further Support: Evidence from Rendaku

We have identified a general restriction in Japanese that two adjacent consonants with the same place of articulation are disfavored. We show in this section that such a restriction manifests itself in a morphophonemic alternation as well, namely, Rendaku. Rendaku voices the first consonant of a second member in compound. By this process, [h] alternates with [b], as in *nui* 'sew' + *hari* 'needle' → *nui-bari* 'sewing needle'.

However, stems that begin with [h] followed by [m] do not usually undergo Rendaku, as shown by the examples in (3).[5]

(3) Creation of [b...m] blocked.

suna 'sand' + hama 'shore'	→	suna-hama	*suna-bama
oo 'big' + hamo 'fish name'	→	oo-hamo	*oo-bamo
tema 'trouble' + hima 'boredom'	→	tema-hima	*tema-bima
mai 'dance' + hime 'princess'	→	mai-hime	*mai-bime
kutsu 'shoe' + himo 'lace'	→	kutsu-himo	*kutsu-bimo
oo 'big' + hema 'mistake'	→	oo-hema	*oo-bema

This blockage of Rendaku should be compared to a minimally different case in which [h] is followed by [n]; in such a case, Rendaku is not blocked:

(4) Creation of [b...n] not blocked.

ai 'purple' + hana 'flower'	→	ai-bana	*ai-hana
te 'hand' + hane 'wing'	→	te-bane	*te-hane
nagasi 'float' + hina 'doll'	→	nagasi-bina	*nagasi-hina
oo 'big' + huna 'gibel'	→	oo-buna	*oo-huna
oo 'big' + hune 'ship'	→	oo-bune	*oo-hune

The blockage of Rendaku in (3) can be explained in terms of the cooccurrence restriction effects we identified above. Given an underlying /h...m.../ sequence, changing /h/ into [b] would result in two adjacent labials within the same stem, which is avoided. This explanation receives further support from the fact that when /h/ and /m/ are nonadjacent, Rendaku is not blocked (e.g. *ryoori-basami* 'cooking scissors', *naga-bakama* 'long hakama'). This is predicted because only weaker (if any) OCP restrictions hold on nonadjacent consonantal pairs.

3.4. Restrictions on Verbal Stems

Finally, we present yet another novel finding about the Japanese lexicon. It is well known that in Semitic languages, verbal roots in which the first and

---

[5] Verbs and deverbal nouns undergo Rendaku even in this configuration; e.g. *musi-bamu* 'to corrupt' and *asi-bumi* 'stepping'. We do not have a good explanation for this fact besides noting that the applying force of Rendaku might be stronger for verbs than for nouns.

second consonants are identical are banned, while roots where the second and third consonants are identical are permitted (McCarthy 1979). For example, there is a root like *smm* but not a root like *ssm*.

We tested whether a similar restriction holds on Japanese verbal stems. The results revealed a mirror-image restriction: roots with identical consonants in the first and second syllables are common, while verbs with identical consonants in the second and third syllables are highly underrepresented. In other words, roots like those in (5) are rare; out of 1,266 roots, we found only 8 instances (O/E = .1, $\chi^2 = 63.38$, p < .001). On the other hand, roots like those in (6) are rather common (60 instances; O/E = .9, $\chi^2 = .68$, p = .41).

(5) exceptional $(C_i)C_jC_j$ roots (exhaustive)

atatamaru 'to warm up', ononoku 'to be frightened', omomuku 'to visit', kuwawaru 'to add', sitatameru 'to write down', sitataru 'to drip', tumamu 'to pick', wananaku 'to be scared'

(6) $C_iC_iC_j$ roots (examples)

kakeru 'to pour', kakumau 'to hide', sasuru 'to rub', sosogu 'to pour', tataku 'to hit', tatoeru 'to analogize', nonoshiru 'to curse', mamireru 'to immerse', ninau 'to take on', . . .

This is the mirror image of the Semitic pattern, and a similar pattern is found in Javanese (Mester 1986; though see Yip 1989:355 for an argument that this actually involves prefixing reduplication, since the first two vowels also agree).

These examples show that total identity is not always an escape hatch from OCP restrictions. Another implication is that the Japanese case identified here provides a counterexample to Frisch's (2004) claim that OCP effects are due to processing difficulty in segment linearization, and that the problem of repetition for processing is ameliorated as the loci of repetition get closer to the end of a word. This evidence is stronger than the Javanese case; (6) cannot be treated as reduplication because there are a number of forms that have different vowels in the first and second syllable.

4. Discussion

4.1. Tendencies, Not Prohibitions

One implication of this study is that consonant cooccurrence restrictions are not **categorical prohibitions** but **tendencies**. The cooccurrence restrictions found in Yamato Japanese are much weaker than what is found in Arabic (see Frisch et al. 2004:168; their O/E values for pairs from the same identity class are usually less than 0.1). The O/E values in Japanese are between 0.2 and 0.6 (Table 3). Further, nonadjacent pairs barely show any underrepresentation (Table 4). Thus, it is not that homorganic pairs of consonants are absolutely prohibited; they just occur much less often than expected.

Our study thus shows that such cooccurrence restrictions are general tendencies rather than categorical prohibitions (see, e.g. Berkley 1994, Frisch et al. 2004; see also Moreton et al. 1998 for other aspects of phonological tendencies in the Japanese lexicon). How to capture such tendencies in the current framework of Optimality Theory (Prince and Smolensky 1993) remains an interesting theoretical question. See Coetzee and Pater 2005 for recent discussion.

4.2. The OCP and CV Segregation

It has been thought that OCP effects are tied to CV segregation: in languages that show the OCP, consonants and vowels are organized into different autosegmental tiers, the most famous example being Semitic languages, as proposed by McCarthy (1979). Thus, Yip (1989:352) notes that "[when OCP effects are observed], at some level adjacency is always involved and that apparent nonadjacent instances *always* involve separation of consonant and vowel melodies underlyingly" (emphasis in the original). Frisch (2004) also claims a connection between the OCP and CV segregation.

However, it is unlikely that Japanese has CV segregation (relative order of consonants and vowels is highly predictable, but not completely: *nata* 'hatchet', *anta* 'you').[6] Thus, OCP restrictions may have nothing to do with CV segregation. See Berkley 1994 for similar arguments.

4.3. Underlying Form or Surface Form?

Our study was based on surface forms, but as Adam Ussishkin reminded us (p.c.), such OCP restrictions used to be captured as Morpheme Structure Conditions, imposed on the lexicon. For example, McCarthy (1979) prohibits two adjacent identical consonants underlyingly by positing that the OCP operates on underlying forms, and roots like *smm* are derived by long distance consonantal spreading of the second consonant.

Since underlying and surface forms are usually similar, it is hard to distinguish at which level consonant cooccurrence restrictions are operative. Yet we maintain that such restrictions are computed on surface forms, as predicted from a surface-oriented theory of phonology such as Optimality Theory. To recap, in building our database of consonantal sequences, surface forms were used. For instance, surface [ɸu], which arguably derives

---

[6] See McCarthy (1989) for discussion on the relation between predictability of CV order and segregation. One piece of indirect evidence for CV segregation in Japanese is the fact that hiphop rhymes are computed on the basis of identity of vowels from the end of lines, ignoring consonants (Kawahara 2002). This evidence, however, is weak at best.

from /hu/, was treated as a labial, not as a pharyngeal [h]. This is first of all due to a current claim of Optimality Theory that there is no reason for [ɸu] to have to be underlyingly /hu/. Rather, from the perspective of language learners, it might be more natural to regard [ɸu] as stemming from /ɸu/ (Lexicon Optimization; Prince and Smolensky 1993).

Further, we found empirical evidence that what is at issue might be surface forms rather than underlying forms. Recall that words that have initial [h] followed by [m] generally do not undergo Rendaku to avoid creating [b...m] (§3.3). However, there is one exception: [ɸumi] 'letter' does become [bumi] when compounded, as in *koi-bumi* 'love letter'. This exception makes sense if we assume that [ɸumi] already violates OCP(lab) so that it freely undergoes Rendaku; not undergoing Rendaku does not ameliorate the OCP violation. This explanation assumes that the OCP is enforced on surface forms rather than underlying /humi/, since it distinguishes cases of surface [h...m] (Rendaku blocked) from cases of surface [ɸ...m] (Rendaku not blocked).

Also, [t] and [ts], allophones of /t/, differ slightly in their cooccurrence behavior. And [ç], a surface form of /h/ before [i], is underrepresented with palatal [j], although the effect was only marginally significant (p = .075). Finally, [ɸ], the allophone of /h/ before [u], is underrepresented with all other labial consonants [p, b, m, w], even though this pattern does not reach statistical significance because there are not enough words containing this sound. On the other hand, [h], which appears before nonhigh vowels, is underrepresented only with [m, w] (this underrepresentation makes sense because [h] was historically [p]). Therefore, at the very least, we can conclude that, even though /h/ in general can be underrepresented with other labial sounds, the restriction is stronger when /h/ becomes [ɸ] at the surface.

5. Concluding Remarks

This paper has pointed out several previously unnoticed restrictions on consonant cooccurrence in Yamato Japanese. We have shown that a pair of adjacent consonants from the same identity class is strongly disfavored, and Rendaku can be blocked by a prohibition against two adjacent labials. We also pointed out that verbs with identical consonants in the second and third syllables are highly underrepresented. These are rather surprising results in that Yamato Japanese is not historically related to any languages that have been shown to have similar OCP effects. This study thus contributes to the generality of consonant cooccurrence restrictions in natural language.

References

Berkley, D. 1994. The OCP and Gradient Data. *Studies in the Linguistic Sciences* 24:59–72.

Coetzee, A., and J. Pater. 2005. Lexically Gradient Phonotactics in Muna and Optimality Theory. Manuscript, University of Massachusetts, Amherst.

Frisch, S. 2004. Language Processing and Segmental OCP Effects. *Phonetically-Based Phonology*, eds. B. Hayes, R. Kirchner, and D. Steriade, 346–71. Cambridge: Cambridge University Press.

Frisch, S., J. Pierrehumbert, and M. Broe. 2004. Similarity Avoidance and the OCP. *Natural Language and Linguistic Theory* 22:179–228.

Hamano, S. 1998. *The Sound-Symbolic System of Japanese*. Stanford: CSLI.

Itô, J., and A. Mester. 1986. The Phonology of Voicing in Japanese. *Linguistic Inquiry* 17:49–73.

Kawahara, S. 2002. Aspects of Hip-Hop Rhymes in Japanese. Paper presented at the Language Study Workshop at International Christian University, Tokyo.

McCarthy, J. 1979. Formal Problems in Semitic Morphology and Phonology. Doctoral dissertation, MIT.

McCarthy, J. 1989. Linear Order in Phonological Representation. *Linguistic Inquiry* 20:71–99.

McCarthy, J. 2003. Rotuman Consonant Cooccurrence Restrictions. Manuscript, University of Massachusetts, Amherst.

McGarrity, L. 1999. A Sympathy Account of Multiple Opacity in Wintu. *Indiana University Working Papers in Linguistics* 1:93–107.

Mester, A. 1986. Studies in Tier Structure. Doctoral dissertation, University of Massachusetts, Amherst.

Moreton, E, S. Amano, and T. Kondo. 1998. Statistical Phonotactics in Japanese. *Transactions of Technical Committee on Psychological Acoustics*, H-98-120.

Padgett, J. 1992. OCP Subsidiary Features. *Proceedings of North East Linguistic Society* 22:335–46.

Prince, A., and P. Smolensky. 1993. Optimality Theory: Constraint Interaction in Generative Grammar. Manuscript, University of Colorado, Boulder, and Rutgers University.

Shinmura, I., ed. 1998. *Kōjien*. Tokyo: Iwanami Shoten.

Steriade, D. 2001. The Phonology of Perceptibility Effect: The P-map and Its Consequences for Constraint Organization. Manuscript, UCLA.

Unger, J. 1977. *Studies in Early Japanese Morphophonemics*. Bloomington: Indiana University Linguistics Club.

Yip, M. 1989. Feature Geometry and Co-occurrence Restrictions. *Phonology* 6: 349–74.

Zoll, C. 1997. Conflicting Directionality. *Phonology* 14:263–86.

Phonological Structure and Unaccented Nouns in Tokyo and Osaka Japanese

HARUO KUBOZONO*
Kobe University

MISA FUKUI
Kobe University

1. Introduction

One of the most distinctive features characterizing Japanese phonology is the existence of so-called "unaccented" words, or words that are pronounced without an abrupt pitch fall in the phonetic output. The distinction between "accented" and "unaccented" words has been a mystery in Japanese phonology and, in fact, is believed to be basically arbitrary, with every morpheme specified in the lexicon with respect to its accentedness. Kubozono (1996, 1999) argued against this traditional view by demonstrating that emergence of the unaccented pattern is largely predictable in loanwords in Tokyo Japanese on the basis of phonological information. Specifically, he showed that the unaccented pattern tends to emerge if the following conditions are met: (a) four-mora length, (b) word-final sequence of light (i.e.

---

* We would like to thank Donna Erickson for checking this manuscript. All errors that remain are of course ours. This work has been supported by the following grants to the first author: Grant-in-Aid for Scientific Research (B) (Japan Society for the Promotion of Science, Grant no. 14310222) and Grant-in-Aid for Exploratory Research (Ministry of Education, Culture, Sports, Science and Technology, Grant no. 15652027).

monomoraic) syllables, and (c) non-epenthetic (i.e. underlying) vowel in word-final position.

The primary goal of this paper is to reinforce and extend Kubozono's phonological generalization from a more statistical viewpoint by looking at a novel source of data from Tokyo Japanese as well as new data from Osaka Japanese. We will first report on our dictionary-based statistical survey of loanwords in Tokyo Japanese (§3.1). Building upon Kubozono's earlier generalization, we will show that the word-initial syllable structure is also a relevant factor. Namely, four-mora loanwords beginning with a sequence of light syllables show a stronger tendency towards the unaccented pattern than those beginning with a heavy syllable. Secondly, we will demonstrate that the phonological generalization thus obtained can be extended to Osaka Japanese, which is supposed to have a considerably different accent system from Tokyo Japanese (§3.2).

In the second half of this paper, we will analyze the accentuation of the so-called "alphabetic acronyms" such as *NHK* 'Nihon Hoso Kyokai' and *JR* 'Japan Railways' in Tokyo and Osaka Japanese (§4). On the basis of original fieldwork on 80 acronyms, we will demonstrate that the emergence of the unaccented pattern is indeed phonologically predictable in both dialects: It emerges only in four-mora acronyms that end in a sequence of light syllables, particularly in those that consist of four light syllables.

The data presented and analyzed in §3 are based on the NHK pronunciation and accent dictionary (NHK 1985/1998) and Sugitō's (1995) CD-ROM. The latter provides original data about Osaka Japanese as well as digital data compiled in the 1985 version of the former accent dictionary. We principally used the CD-ROM version of the NHK dictionary (1998) for Tokyo Japanese and Sugitō 1995 for Osaka Japanese, unless otherwise stated.

2. Unaccented Words

By way of introduction to 'unaccented words', let us look at the following famous song by the Beatles ("Get Back").

(1) Jo-Jo was a man
     Who thought he was a loner
     But he knew it couldn't last
     Jo-Jo left his home
     In Tucson, Arizona
     For some California grass
     Get back, get back
     Get back to where you once belonged
     Get back, get back
     Get back to where you once belonged

This passage contains three place names: *Tucson, Arizona,* and *California.* Of these, the first word is borrowed as an accented word, whereas the second and third are borrowed as 'unaccented' words in Japanese. In (2) and the rest of this paper, lexically accented words are marked by accent marks (´) on relevant vowels; unaccented words are unspecified. Dots (.) indicate syllable boundaries.

(2) a. túu.son
     b. a.ri.zo.na, ka.ri.fo.ru.ni.a

The accented/unaccented distinction is found in native and Sino-Japanese (SJ) words as well, as exemplified in (3).

(3) a. ha.ná 'flower', a.ói 'blue', kú.ru 'to come', pá.sa.pa.sa (mimetic expression), kyóo.to 'Kyoto', ná.go.ya 'Nagoya', kóo.be 'Kobe', na.gá.sa.ki 'Nagasaki'
     b. ha.na 'nose', a.kai 'red', i.ku 'to go', pa.sa.pa.sa (mimetic expression), too.kyoo 'Tokyo', oo.sa.ka 'Osaka', yo.ko.ha.ma 'Yokohama', hi.ro.si.ma 'Hiroshima'

However, the unaccented pattern occurs to considerably different degrees in the three types of words in Tokyo Japanese. As shown in Table 1, this accent pattern is very popular in native words but hardly so in loanwords. Due to this as well as other facts, loanword accentuation has been treated in quite different ways from the accentuation of native and SJ words in the literature (Akinaga 1985).

Word Type:	Native	SJ	Loan
Percentage:	71%	53%	7%

Table 1. Percentage of the Unaccented Pattern in Three-mora
Words in Tokyo Japanese (Total = 7,937 Words)

The accented vs. unaccented distinction is predictable to a certain extent in compound nouns and relatively long words. For example, so-called "deaccenting morphemes" yield unaccented compound nouns (McCawley 1968, Kubozono 1997). Similarly, certain endings such as /i.a/ and /in.gu/ tend to produce unaccented loanwords, which explains why /ka.ri.fo.ru.ni.a/ in (2b) is unaccented. These two cases are illustrated in (4) and (5), respectively, where "deaccenting" morphemes and endings are underlined.

(4) a. native morphemes
        orenzi-iro 'orange color', takara-zima (< sima) 'Treasure Island'
     b. SJ morphemes
        minsyu-too 'Democratic Party', sinzoo-byoo 'heart disease'

(5) kariforun<u>ia</u> 'California', karedon<u>ia</u> 'Caledonia', makedon<u>ia</u>
    'Macedonia', sukuur<u>ingu</u> 'schooling', tyuun<u>ingu</u> 'tuning'

Apart from these relatively long words and compound nouns, it was largely unclear how the same accent pattern emerges. In fact, it was long believed that the accented/unaccented distinction is basically unpredictable and specified in the lexicon for morphologically simplex words. Kubozono (1996) challenged this traditional analysis and claimed, on the basis of an analysis of some 700 foreign place names, that the distinction is largely pre-dictable from phonological information as far as loanwords are concerned.[1] He specifically argued that the unaccented pattern tends to emerge if the three phonological conditions in (6) are met.

(6) a. 4 mora length
    b. sequence of light syllables in word-final position
    c. non-epenthetic vowel in word-final position

According to Kubozono (1996), syllable structure exerts the most pro-found effect among the three phonological factors. This is shown in Table 2, which illustrates the correlation between syllable structure and accent pat-tern in four-mora foreign place names in Tokyo Japanese. In this table as well as in the rest of this paper, "H" and "L" stand for heavy (bimoraic) and light (monomoraic) syllables, respectively, whereas "UR" means 'unaccent-edness ratio', that is, the percentage of words that are unaccented.

Syllable Structure:	#LL<u>LL</u># #H<u>LL</u>#	#LHL#	#LLH#	#HH#	Average
UR:	60%	5%	3%	0%	34%

Table 2. Correlation between Syllable Structure and Accent Pattern in Four-mora Foreign Place Names in Tokyo Japanese

3. Loanwords in Accent Dictionaries

3.1. Tokyo Japanese

We conducted a dictionary-based survey to see if Kubozono's (1996) ob-servation in (6) can be supported by an analysis of a larger corpus of data. Table 3 shows the relationship between accent pattern and word length, or the number of moras, in the total of 1,863 loanwords. The unaccented pat-tern is a few times more popular in four-mora loanwords than in words of other phonological lengths, thus supporting the claim in (6a). The UR for four-mora loanwords goes up to 29 percent in the 1998 version of the NHK Dictionary.

---

[1] See Kubozono et al. 1997 and Ogawa 2004 for some other phonological factors responsible for unaccented SJ and other compound nouns in Tokyo Japanese.

Word Length:	3-mora	4-mora	5-mora	Average
UR:	5%	19%	8%	13%

Table 3. Word Length and UR in Loanwords (NHK 1985)

Table 4 depicts effects of syllable structure on accent patterns in the corpus of 963 four-mora loanwords (NHK 1998). The data in this table resemble those in Table 2, with about a half of the words that end in a sequence of light syllables, i.e. #LLLL# and #HLL#, taking the unaccented pattern. In contrast, the UR goes down remarkably in words ending in a heavy syllable, i.e. #LLH# and #HH#. This supports Kubozono's (1996) claim stated in (6b) above.

Syllable Structure:	#LL<u>LL</u>#	#H<u>LL</u>#	#LHL#	#LLH#	#HH#	Average
UR:	54%	45%	24%	19%	7%	29%

Table 4. Syllable Structure and UR in Four-mora Loanwords

In addition to this, the data in Table 4 further show that #LLLL# and #LLH# exhibit higher URs than #HLL# and #HH#, respectively. This suggests that syllable structure of word-initial position exerts a certain effect on accent patterns, although this effect is not as large as the effect exerted by syllable structure in word-final position.

Finally, let us look at Table 5, which shows the effect of word-final vowels on accent in 355 four-mora loanwords ending in a sequence of light syllables, i.e. #LLLL# and #HLL#. #..L<L># means that the final vowel is epenthetic, i.e. inserted in the process of borrowing (e.g. /rái.ba.r<u>/ 'rival', /pá.ra.so.r<u> 'parasol'), whereas #..LL# means that the same vowel is underlying, i.e. non-epenthetic (e.g. /mo.na.ri.za/ 'Mona Lisa', /su.te.re.o/ 'stereo', /ho.no.ru.ru/ 'Honolulu'). The data in this table clearly show that the UR greatly varies depending on the nature of the word-final vowel; specifically, the UR goes up remarkably if the final vowel is non-epenthetic. This is in full accord with Kubozono's claim in (6c).

Epenthetic/Non-epenthetic:	..LL#	..L<L>#	Average
UR:	90%	32%	50%

Table 5. Epenthetic Vowel and UR in Four-mora #..LL# Loanwords

Indeed, nine out of ten loanwords become unaccented if they satisfy all three conditions in (6). This is an extremely high ratio—even higher than the UR of four-mora native words, which is sixty-six percent according to Sibata (1994). This explains why the word /a.ri.zo.na/ 'Arizona' in (2b) is unaccented: It has good phonological reason to take the unaccented pattern.

In sum, the unaccented pattern predominantly occurs if the following phonological conditions are met.

(7) a. four-mora length
 b. a sequence of light syllables in word-final position
 c. a sequence of light syllables in word-initial position
 d. non-epenthetic vowel in word-final position

3.2. Osaka Japanese

The discussion in the preceding section has provided statistical support for Kubozono's (1996) claim that loanwords tend to become unaccented if they satisfy the three phonological conditions in (6). It has also shown that syllable structure in word-initial position exerts a certain additional effect on accent patterns. Let us now discuss the accentuation of loanwords in Osaka Japanese, which is supposed to have a rather different prosodic (accent) system from Tokyo Japanese (Hirayama 1960, Haraguchi 1977).

The data in Tables 6–8 exhibit basically the same tendencies that were observed in Tables 3–5 for Tokyo Japanese. First, the data in Table 6 show a clear effect of word length on accent patterns in Osaka Japanese. The only difference between Table 3 and Table 6, in fact, is that the average UR as well as the UR for each word length is lower in Osaka than in Tokyo. The data in Tables 7 and 8 also resemble those in Tables 4 and 5, respectively, indicating that the phonological factors in (6b) (= 7b) and (6c) (= 7d) are at work in Osaka as well as in Tokyo. In Table 7, moreover, #LLLL# and #LLH# exhibit higher URs than #HLL# and #HH#, respectively. This suggests that syllable structure in word-initial position also plays a certain role in the choice between accented and unaccented patterns in Osaka, just as it does in Tokyo.

Word Length:	3-mora	4-mora	5-mora	Average
UR:	3%	16%	5%	9%

Table 6. Word Length and UR in Loanwords

Syllable Structure:	#LLLL#	#HLL#	#LHL#	#LLH#	#HH#	Average
UR:	39%	20%	12%	8%	5%	16%

Table 7. Syllable Structure and UR in Four-mora Loanwords

Epenthetic/Non-epenthetic:	..LL#	..L<L>#	Average
UR:	71%	13%	31%

Table 8. Epenthetic Vowel and UR in Four-mora #..LL# Loanwords

In sum, Osaka Japanese follows basically the same rule as Tokyo Japanese with respect to the emergence of the unaccented pattern in loanwords. Given this, one may naturally wonder why the unaccented pattern tends to emerge when the phonological conditions in (7) are met in Tokyo and Osaka Japanese alike. This question can be answered, at least in part, by looking at the structure and accentuation of native nouns. One basic fact about native accentuation is that four-mora nouns exhibit a considerably higher UR than their three-mora and five-mora counterparts (Sibata 1994). Given this, it is not difficult to understand why four-mora loanwords exhibit a higher UR than loanwords of other phonological lengths: Loanwords simply follow the native pattern regarding the interaction between word length and accent pattern.

Likewise, (7b–d) represent phonological structures characteristic of native words. Unlike many loanwords, native words do not generally contain a heavy syllable, especially in word-final position, and they do not end in an epenthetic vowel. Hence, a typical native word consists of a sequence of light syllables and of underlying vowels. Loanwords satisfying the phonological conditions in (7b–d) indeed look like native words in phonological shape, and they do exhibit a native-like accent pattern by favoring the unaccented pattern over the accented one (see Kubozono, forthcoming, for a more detailed discussion).

4. Alphabetic Acronyms

4.1. Experimental Design

In the preceding section we have seen the reality of the four phonological conditions in (7) through a statistical analysis of loanwords listed in accent dictionaries in both Tokyo and Osaka Japanese. In this section we will look at a novel source of data to reinforce the generalization in the two dialects. The data we are going to examine here are "alphabetic acronyms" (AAs) such as those in (8).

(8) a. /ii.tíi/ 'ET', /bii.zii.é.mu/ 'BGM', /wai.e.mu.sii.ée/ 'YMCA'
     b. /zyee.áa.ru/ 'JR', /oo.e.ru/ 'OL', /e.nu.ei.ti.kée/ 'NHK'

These acronyms consist of an initial alphabetic letter of each component. Some of them are loans from English (e.g. /ii.tíi/ 'ET', /wai.e.mu.sii.ée/ 'YMCA'), while others were coined in Japanese (e.g. /oo.é.ru/ 'office lady, female office worker', /e.nu.ei.ti.kée/ 'NHK, i.e. Nihon Hōsō Kyōkai').

In order to examine the accentuation of these words in Tokyo and Osaka Japanese, we had thirty-eight native speakers of these dialects pronounce a total of eighty AAs (see Appendix for a full list). These test words fall into the four major classes in Table 9 according to their length: the number of letters, syllables, and moras, respectively. Forty-two of them consist of two letters (Classes A–C), whereas the remaining thirty-eight words consist of three letters (Class D). The former further falls into two groups depending on whether they are four moras long (Classes A and B) or longer (Class C). Class A and Class B differ from each other in whether the second element (letter) is monosyllabic or bisyllabic. As we will see below, Class B can be divided into two subgroups according to the syllable structure, i.e. monosyllabic vs. bisyllabic, of the first element/letter.

In the experiment, each informant pronounced each test word twice. The accent pattern of each utterance was identified by the experimenters on an auditory basis.

Class	Examples	No. of Letters	No. of Moras	Final Element	No. of Test Words	
A	JA, PC, MD	2	4	1 syllable, 2 moras	19	42
B	OL, SF, BS			2 syllables, 2 moras	17	
C	HB, JR, PR		5–6	—	6	
D	NHK, JCB	3	6–	—	38	

Table 9. Test Words

4.2. Tokyo Japanese

As for Tokyo Japanese, we asked twenty-five informants, eleven male and fourteen female speakers, to pronounce the eighty test words. This yielded a total of 2,000 tokens (= 80 words × 25 informants). Table 10 shows the percentage of the unaccented pattern, or unaccentedness ratio (UR), for each phonological type of test word (μ = mora).

Syllable Structure:	#LLLL#	#HLL#	#LLH#	#HH#	5μ–
Examples:	SL, FM	OL. AM	FA, ST	ET, PK	JR, NHK
UR:	97%	70%	0%	0%	0%

Table 10. Phonological Structure and UR in AAs in Tokyo Japanese

The data in this table show that the unaccented pattern is observed in a highly restricted environment, i.e. only in words of Class B in Table 9. This accent pattern actually accounts for nearly all words that consist of four light syllables and seventy percent of words that have #HLL# structure. In contrast, it does not appear at all either in five-mora or longer words (Classes C and D) or in four-mora words that end in a heavy syllable (Class A).

This indicates that the word length condition in (7a) and syllable structure condition in (7b) are necessary conditions for the emergence of unaccented AAs in this dialect. On top of this, the syllable structure condition in

(7c) exerts a secondary effect, raising the UR from seventy percent to nearly one hundred percent in Class B words. This means that the three factors combined serve as necessary and sufficient conditions for the emergence of the unaccented pattern in AAs. Seen conversely, this means that none of the three factors serves as a sufficient condition: AAs do not become unaccented if they satisfy only one of the three phonological conditions. For example, /bii.zii.é.mu/ 'BGM' does not become unaccented even though it satisfies the condition in (7b), since it does not meet the condition in (7a).

On the other hand, the vowel condition in (7d) does not seem to play a role in AAs. In fact, all AAs that fulfill the syllable structure condition in (7b) end in an epenthetic vowel: e.g. /e.su.e.hu̲/ 'SF', /oo.e.ru̲/ 'OL'. However, they almost invariably become unaccented if they meet the other phonological conditions in (7a–c). In the absence of an LL sequence ending in a non-epenthetic vowel, it is impossible to evaluate the role of (7d) in AAs, but it is a noteworthy fact that AAs show an extremely high UR even if they do not satisfy the vowel condition in (7d).[2]

In sum, AAs are subject to basically the same phonological conditions as ordinary loanwords with respect to the emergence of the unaccented pattern. This further reinforces the reality of the phonological conditions given in (7).

4.3. Osaka Japanese

We tested the validity of the phonological conditions in (7) in AAs in Osaka Japanese, too. We looked at thirteen native speakers of this dialect—four male and nine female speakers—who pronounced the same set of eighty test words illustrated in Table 9. The results of this survey are summarized in Table 11.

Syllable Structure:	#LLLL#	#HLL#	#LLH#	#HH#	5μ–
Examples:	SL, FM	OL. AM	FA, ST	ET, PK	JR, NHK
UR:	78%	33%	6%	2%	0%

Table 11. Phonological Structure and UR in AAs in Osaka Japanese

The distribution of the unaccented pattern in this table looks very similar to the one we saw in Table 10. Namely, the unaccented pattern is popular in

---

[2] Another difference between ordinary loanwords and AAs is that they take an accent in different positions when they are accented. Ordinary loanwords obey the famous antepenultimate rule whereby an accent docks onto the syllable containing the antepenultimate mora: e.g. /o.rén.zi/ 'orange', /ku.ri.sú.ma.su/ 'Christmas'. In contrast, accented AAs generally take an accent on the initial syllable of their final member: /ii.tíí/ 'ET', /pii.tii.ée/ 'PTA'. The latter can be attributed either to the stress pattern of English acronyms or to the compound accent rule of Japanese which tends to preserve the lexical accent of the final member of compounds.

two phonological structures, #LLLL# and #HLL#, while it accounts for a very low percentage of words that have other phonological structures. Admittedly, Osaka Japanese shows a lower UR for #LLLL# and #HLL# than Tokyo Japanese, which is in line with the dialectal difference that we saw in Section 3. Moreover, Osaka Japanese admits the unaccented pattern in some words that have other phonological structures. However, these facts should not distract our attention from the fact that the unaccented pattern is virtually restricted to those AAs that fulfill the phonological conditions in (7a, b). In this respect, the data in Table 11 resemble the data of AAs in Tokyo Japanese (i.e. Table 10) as well as the data of ordinary loanwords in Osaka Japanese summarized in Tables 6–7.

5. Conclusion

In summary, we have shown that the unaccented pattern is a marked accent pattern in loanwords in both Tokyo and Osaka Japanese and that its emergence is largely predictable on the basis of certain phonological information. Particularly important is information on word length as measured in terms of the number of moras and on syllable structure in word-final position.

We presented statistical evidence from two sources of data: (a) hundreds of ordinary loanwords listed in accent dictionaries and (b) alphabetic acronyms frequently used in Japanese. It is worth emphasizing that these two sources of data display basically the same type of correlation between phonological structure and accent patterns. It is also important to emphasize that Tokyo and Osaka Japanese are subject to the same set of phonological conditions despite the fact that their prosodic/accent systems are considerably different from each other.

This study has several important implications for Japanese phonology. First of all, syllable structure plays a very important role in the accentuation of Tokyo and Osaka Japanese. This lends support to the idea that the syllable serves as an indispensable prosodic unit in so-called mora languages like Tokyo and Osaka Japanese (Kubozono 1999).

Secondly, the present study has shown that loanwords tend to become unaccented if they are given the phonological shape of native words. This suggests that loanwords are not as different from native words as they first appear to be. Quite the contrary, they follow basically the same accent patterns/rules as native words. This clearly speaks against the traditional view that loanwords constitute a separate prosodic group from native words because of the scarcity of the unaccented pattern. Loanwords do certainly exhibit different accentual tendencies from native words, but they do so because they have different phonological structures from the latter. In particular, if we control syllable structure and nature of the final vowel, the two types of words display much the same accent patterns and preferences.

Finally, the fact that the emergence of the unaccented pattern is phonologically predictable to a considerable extent in loanwords has an implication for the accentuation of native words, too. It has been assumed in the literature that the accented vs. unaccented distinction is basically unpredictable in native morphemes. Given the phonological conditions for the unaccented pattern in loanwords, however, it is expected that the same phonological account can be extended to native words in both Tokyo and Osaka Japanese. Native words do not exhibit such a rich variation in syllable structure as loanwords, but a statistical survey will be called for to examine the phonological basis of the accented/unaccented distinction in native words. This is certainly an important issue for future research.

Appendix

The list below contains the alphabetic acronyms used in the experiments described in §4, classified according to the phonological structure as in Table 9 and rearranged in an alphabetic order. (A)–(D) below correspond to Classes A–D in the same table.

(A) AO, AP, CT, DJ, ET, EU, FA, IQ, IT, JA, JT, LP, MD, NG, PC, PK, QP, SP, TC

(B) AM, BS, CM, FM, GM, LL (language laboratory), LL (size of clothes), OL, ON, OS, PL, PM, SF, SL, SM, UN, YS

(C) DH, JR, PR; HB, WC, XP

(D) AFS, AGF, ASL, ATM, BGM, BMW, CIA, CPU, DDI, DNA, ESP, FBI, GHQ, IBM, IHI, IPA, IRA, JCB, KGB, MRI, NGO, NHK, NKK, NTT, OCP, OHP, PPM, PTA, QQR, SOS, TDK, TDL, USA, USJ, VHS, VTR, WHO, YKK

References

Akinaga, K. 1985. Kyōtsūgo no akusento [Accent of standard Japanese]. In the appendix to *Nihongo hatsuon akusento jiten*, ed. NHK. Tokyo: Nihon Hōsō Kyōkai.

Haraguchi, S. 1977. *The Tone Pattern of Japanese: An Autosegmental Theory of Tonology*. Tokyo: Kaitakusha.

Hirayama, T. 1960. *Zenkoku akusento jiten* [All-Japan accent dictionary]. Tokyo: Tōkyōdō.

Kubozono, H. 1996. Syllable and Accent in Japanese: Evidence from Loanword Accentuation. *The Bulletin* (Phonetic Society of Japan) 211:71–82.

Kubozono, H. 1997. Lexical Markedness and Accent: A Nonderivational Account of Japanese Compound Accent. *WCCFL* 15:273–87.

Kubozono, H. 1999. Mora and Syllable. *The Handbook of Japanese Linguistics*, ed. N. Tsujimura, 31–61. Oxford: Blackwell.

Kubozono, H. Forthcoming. Loanword Accentuation in Japanese. To appear in *Lingua*, a special issue on loanword phonology.

Kubozono, H., J. Itô, and A. Mester 1997. On'in kōzō kara mita go to ku no kyōkai [The phonological boundary between the word and the phrase]. *Bunpō to Onsei* [Speech and grammar], ed. Spoken Language Research Group, 147–166. Tokyo: Kurosio Publishers.

McCawley, J. D. 1968. *The Phonological Component of a Grammar of Japanese*. The Hague: Mouton.

NHK, ed. 1985/98. *Nihongo hatsuon akusento jiten*. Tokyo: Nihon Hōsō Kyōkai.

Ogawa, S. 2004. Sino-Japanese Word Accent and Syllable Structure. *Phonological Studies* (The Phonological Society of Japan) 7:41–48.

Sibata, T. 1994. Gairaigo ni okeru akusento kaku no ichi. (On the location of accent in loanwords). *Gendaigo hōgen no kenkyū* [Studies on modern dialects], ed. K. Satō, 338–418. Tokyo: Meiji Shoin.

Sugitō, M. 1995. *Ōsaka-Tōkyō akusento onsei jiten* (CD-ROM). Tokyo: Maruzen.

Theoretical Implications of Mimetic Voicing in Japanese

KAZUTAKA KURISU*
Kobe College

1. Introduction

This paper explores mimetic voicing in Japanese. This voicing process adds rather unfavorable semantic connotations such as heaviness, dullness, and coarseness. On the phonological side, when a CVCV mimetic root is given, usually only the initial consonant undergoes voicing. The interesting fact is that both consonants are voiced if the medial consonant is /p/. Nasu (1999) develops a theoretical analysis of the voicing process within the framework of constraint-based Optimality Theory (OT; Prince and Smolensky 1993). He essentially views voicing of medial /p/ as emergence of the unmarked, building on earlier observations that [p] is a marked segment in Japanese.

Nasu's account is attractive, but it encounters several serious problems, so it cannot be upheld as it stands. I provide an alternative analysis, crucially capitalizing on the notion of transderivational correspondence proposed by Benua (1995, 1997). I demonstrate that my analysis successfully

* This is part of the paper presented at the Phonological Association in Kansai (July 17, 2004) and at the 14th Japanese/Korean Linguistics Conference (November 5–7, 2004). I express my gratitude to Junko Itô, Shigeto Kawahara, Armin Mester, Philip Spaelti, and Adam Ussishkin for useful comments and discussion. Any remaining errors and infelicities are mine.

51

circumvents the problems with Nasu 1999. But this is not the ultimate goal of this study. I argue that my analysis based on output-output correspondence has a significant implication in light of the core-periphery model of Japanese phonological lexicon (Itô and Mester 1995a, 1995b, 1999). The mimetic vocabulary has been excluded from consideration due to its peculiar behavior. I argue that Faith-IO and Faith-OO constraints together allow mimetic items to be successfully included in the core-periphery system.

The rest of this paper is organized as follows. In §2, I present a set of relevant data and critically review Nasu 1999. §3 presents an analysis which overcomes the problems with Nasu 1999. In §4, I discuss how the mimetic vocabulary can be incorporated into the overall core-periphery model articulated by Itô and Mester (1995a, 1995b, 1999). In conclusion, the gist of the paper is summarized in §5.

2. Mimetic Voicing (Nasu 1999)

This section provides a set of examples discussed below, and I give a quick overview of the analysis by Nasu (1999). Mimetic roots are either monosyllabic or disyllabic. The mimetic voicing of relevance here occurs with disyllabic roots. As exemplified in (1), the initial consonant is the target of voicing.

(1)

MIMETIC FORM	GLOSS	VOICED FORM	GLOSS
toku-toku	'pouring little'	doku-doku	'pouring much'
saku-saku	'crispy'	zaku-zaku	'jingling'
kata-kata	'clattering'	gata-gata	'rattling'
koto-koto	'pattering silently'	goto-goto	'pattering loudly'

If the medial consonant is /p/, however, not only the initial consonant but also medial /p/ undergoes the voicing process, as shown in (2).

(2)

MIMETIC FORM	GLOSS	VOICED FORM	GLOSS
tapu-tapu	'tumbling (of water)'	dabu-dabu	'full (of water)'
kapo-kapo	'lightly sounded'	gabo-gabo	'squelchy'
supo-supo	'push in/out softly'	zubo-zubo	'push in/out hard'
supa-supa	'unsparingly'	zuba-zuba	'forcefully'

This is at first glance surprising because many mimetic forms contain [p], as illustrated in (3). This means that [p] is eschewed in the environment of mimetic voicing, but it is admitted when voicing does not occur.

(3) pika-pika 'shining'   tapu-tapu 'tumbling (of water)'
    piri-piri 'tingling'   supa-supa 'unsparingly'

Nasu (1999) argues that avoidance of [p] in the voicing context is to be attributed to the *[p] constraint, which militates against non-geminated [p].

This constraint is actually active in Yamato and Sino-Japanese, so [p] does not appear unless it is (partially) geminated. Nasu further claims that avoidance of [p] in the voicing context is an instance of emergence of the unmarked (McCarthy and Prince 1994). This is confirmed by the examples in (4). /p/ occupies the root-initial position, so normal initial voicing suffices to avoid marked [p]. The position of /p/ is therefore crucial.

(4) | MIMETIC FORM | GLOSS | VOICED FORM | | GLOSS |
|---|---|---|---|---|
| puka-puka | 'buoyant' | buka-buka | *buga-buga | 'baggy' |
| pata-pata | 'pattering' | bata-bata | *bada-bada | 'rattling' |
| peta-peta | 'sticking' | beta-beta | *beda-beda | 'pasty' |
| paku-paku | 'munching' | baku-baku | *bagu-bagu | 'devouring' |
| poso-poso | 'silently' | boso-boso | *bozo-bozo | 'secretly' |

The gist of analysis developed by Nasu (1999) is sketched in (5). As in (5a), the floating voicing feature is linked to the initial consonant. When the root-internal consonant is /p/, the [voi] feature is doubly linked, as in (5b), so that the normally uninhibited appearance of [p] is suppressed.

(5) a. /pika,[voi]/ → [bika]   b. /tapu,[voi]/ → [dabu]

          [voi]   [voi]

Nasu assumes the three constraints in (6).

(6) a. Align-L([voi],Stem): A [voi] feature is left-aligned to a stem.
    b. *[p]:   Single [p] is prohibited.
    c. Ident-IO-[voi]:   No voicing change between input and output.

(1) is analyzed in (7), where double linking of a single [voi] feature is indicated by italicizing the relevant consonants. To respect Align-L([voi], Stem), the input [voi] feature must be linked to the initial consonant. In (7c), double linking of the [voi] feature incurs a gratuitous violation of Ident-IO-[voi].

(7) | /toku,[voi]/ | | Align | *[p] | Ident |
|---|---|---|---|---|
| a. | togu | *! | | * |
| b. ☞ | doku | | | * |
| c. | *do*gu | | | **! |

If a mimetic root contains /p/ in medial position, the floating [voi] feature is doubly linked, as can be seen from (8c). As a consequence, neither Align-L([voi],Stem) nor *[p] is violated by the optimal candidate.

(8)

	/tapu,[voi]/	Align	*[p]	Ident
a.	tabu	*!		*
b.	dapu		*!	*
c. ☞	*da*b*u*			**

[p] is admitted without voicing, however, since Dep-IO-[voi] is ranked over *[p], as depicted in (9). Furthermore, underparsing the floating feature is not a viable possibility due to high ranked Max-IO-[voi].

(9)

	/pika/	Dep	*[p]	Ident
a. ☞	pika		*	
b.	bika	*!		*

In a nutshell, Nasu (1999:62) provides the constraint ranking in (10).

(10) Dep/Max-IO-[voi]

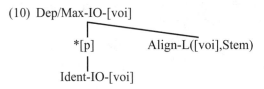

    *[p]   Align-L([voi],Stem)

    |
Ident-IO-[voi]

This analysis has several nontrivial deficits. I discuss two of them here. First, Nasu posits multiple feature associations. This means that long distance geminates could be generated. Gafos (1996, 1998) develops a cogent argument against long distance spreading in general, noting that it gives rise to non-existing place assimilation (e.g. /nap/→[map]) or voicing assimilation (e.g. /pad/→[bad]). No such assimilation is attested, but long distance geminates allow for such assimilatory patterns, contrary to fact.

Second, emergence of the unmarked obtains through Faith-IO >> Markedness >> Faith-IO. Mimetic voicing involves morphological derivation in the sense that it adds semantic effects like heaviness, dullness, and coarseness, as stated above. But input-output correspondence alone is not enough to represent morphological derivedness. Rather, emergence of the unmarked normally comes out of the ranking of Faith-IO >> Markedness >> Faith-OO.

In the next section, I develop an alternative account with essential reference to the transderivational model articulated by Benua (1995, 1997). My analysis overcomes the problem of long distance geminates too.

3. Transderivational Voicing

In order to elucidate the mimetic voicing effect presented in the last section, I propose the transderivational model in (11). This model is akin to the transderivational correspondence model articulated by Benua (1995, 1997) in the context of truncation effects. IO-faithfulness constraints regulate input-output disparities while OO-faithfulness constraints evaluate identity between a base and its voiced counterpart. This OO-correspondence reflects the fact that mimetic voicing produces morphologically derived forms.

(11) **Input:** /saku-RED/

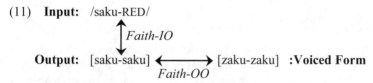

Output: [saku-saku] ⟷ [zaku-zaku] :**Voiced Form**
                                Faith-OO

The fact that [p] is normally permitted suggests that Ident-IO-[voi] outranks *[p]. As a result, [p] is not suppressed in the IO-dimension, as in (12).

(12)

/pika-RED/	Ident-IO	*[p]
a. ☞ pika-pika		**
b. bika-bika	*!	

Before presenting my analysis of mimetic voicing, I must note that I adopt an alignment constraint different from that in Nasu 1999. In his analysis, the alignment constraint in (6a) requires every [voi] feature to be aligned to the left edge of a stem. My alignment constraint, on the other hand, as defined in (13), specifically refers to the floating [voi] feature that triggers mimetic voicing. This morpheme is denoted by π. This specificity is required for an empirical reason that I will discuss shortly. Another minor difference is that (6a) refers to a stem while (13) refers to a prosodic word. This difference is simply due to the fact that Nasu does not consider reduplicated forms. But this difference does not have any crucial repercussion on the subsequent discussion.

(13) Align-L([voi]π,PrWd): Floating [voi] is left-aligned to a prosodic word.

My analysis of voiced forms is given below. (14) represents an analysis of (1), where consonants in boldface are the ones voiced by the influence of [voi]π. One violation mark is assigned to each non-initial consonant that undergoes voicing to realize [voi]π. Because Align-L([voi]π,PrWd) is highly ranked, applying voicing to PrWd-initial /t/ is more harmonic than voicing medial /k/. Although Ident-OO-[voi] is ranked the lowest, it plays an important role in minimizing the number of consonants undergoing voicing. Unless the medial consonant is /p/, additional voicing meaninglessly increases violations of Ident-OO-[voi].

(14)

/toku-toku,[voi]π/		Alignπ	*[p]	Ident-OO
a.	togu-togu	**!		**
b. ☞	doku-doku	*		**
c.	dogu-dogu	*		***!*
d.	dogu-dogu	**!*		****

One question arising here is why [doku-toku] is not chosen as the winning candidate, given that this incorrect output incurs no violation of Align-L([voi]π,PrWd). In terms of morpheme realization, minimal deviance from the input form suffices to fulfill the requirement of Max-IO-[voi] (Kurisu 2001). The answer is that Ident-BR-[voi] is undominated. As shown in (15), this faithfulness constraint outranks Align-L([voi]π,PrWd).

(15)

/toku-toku,[voi]π/		Ident-BR	Alignπ	Ident-OO
a. ☞	doku-doku		*	**
b.	doku-toku	*!		*

When the input contains /p/ root-internally, both consonants are subject to voicing. As illustrated in (16), this is because *[p] is ranked above Ident-OO-[voi]. Although (16c) and (16d) are identical segmentally, they do not fare equally well. Again, boldface indicates voiced consonants under the influence of input [voi]π. This means that the voicing change of /p/→[b] in (16d) incurs violations of Align-L([voi]π,PrWd), whereas that in (16c) does not. Importantly, note that I do not adopt multiple linking of a single [voi] feature, unlike Nasu (1999). Each consonant undergoing voicing due to the input floating feature violates the alignment constraint unless it is in the PrWd-initial position. This suggests that there are two independent sources of voicing: floating [voi]π and *[p] >> Ident-OO-[voi]. More concretely, initial /t/ undergoes voicing to manifest [voi]π, and medial /p/ is independently voiced to better satisfy the ranking of *[p] >> Ident-OO-[voi]. In my analysis, therefore, voicing of root-medial /p/ has nothing to do with the existence of the [voi]π feature, although the result is still emergence of the unmarked, as argued by Nasu.

(16)

/tapu-tapu,[voi]π/		Alignπ	*[p]	Ident-OO
a.	tabu-tabu	**!		**
b.	dapu-dapu	*	*!*	**
c. ☞	dabu-dabu	*		****
d.	dabu-dabu	**!*		****

We are now in a position to explain why the alignment constraint needs to be morpheme-particular. Suppose that the alignment constraint is general, meaning that the two kinds of voiced consonants separated above are treated in a unified fashion. As tabulated in (17), when /p/ is in the root-internal position, applying voicing only to medial /p/ is wrongly expected to be better than the actual output. This problem arises precisely because each voiced obstruent has its own [voi] feature. This observation strongly justifies the morpheme-particular nature of the alignment constraint.

(17)

/tapu-tapu,[voi]π/	Align	Ident-OO
a. ☞ tabu-tabu	**	**
b. ☹ dabu-dabu	***!	****

Summarizing my analysis, the overall constraint ranking is encapsulated in (18). *[p] is sandwiched between Faith-IO and Faith-OO, so this constraint ranking reflects the schema of emergence of the unmarked. The marked segment [p] is therefore avoided only in the voicing context.

(18)   Ident-IO-[voi]   Ident-BR-[voi]

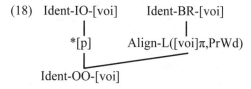

   *[p]   Align-L([voi]π,PrWd)

   Ident-OO-[voi]

As emphasized above, my analysis does not postulate long distance geminates at all. This aspect of my analysis has a favorable theoretical consequence. As pointed out by Hamano (1998:40), the two consonants are never identical in C_1VC_2V mimetic roots (i.e. $C_1 \neq C_2$). Were long distance partial geminates permitted, total geminates across a vowel should also appear legitimately. Rose (2000) develops a rigorous argument that $[C_\alpha V C_\alpha]$ without multiple linking of feature [α] (i.e. the configuration in (19)) violates the OCP (Leben 1973, McCarthy 1986). Complete absence of C_1-C_2 identity in the mimetic vocabulary is ascribed to the OCP, so abolishment of multiple feature linking successfully accounts for the robust phonotactic restriction that two consonants are never identical within a mimetic root.

(19)   C   V   C
       | |
      [αF]   [αF]

4. Implication for Lexical Stratification

In addition to the desirable consequence discussed immediately above, the transderivational analysis developed in the previous section has a larger theoretical implication in light of the core–periphery model of the Japanese lexicon.

Roughly speaking, the Japanese vocabulary is classified into the Yamato, Sino, Mimetic, and Foreign classes. The foreign class is further divided into assimilated and unassimilated loanwords. Itô and Mester (1995a, 1995b, 1999) show that these five classes exhibit different phonological behavior with respect to the markedness constraints in (20). SyllStruc is a combination of *Complex and the relevant coda condition (Itô 1986).

(20) a. SyllStruc: A set of relevant syllable markedness constraints.
     b. *VoiGem: Voiced geminates of obstruents are banned.
     c. *[p]:   Single [p] is prohibited.
     d. *NC̥:   No sequence of a nasal and a voiceless obstruent.

The different behavior of the five lexical classes with respect to these constraints is summarized in (21). Here and below, the unassimilated foreign class is labeled Foreign$_U$, and the assimilated foreign class is labeled Foreign$_A$. A horizontal line indicates that no such item is found, meaning that the pertinent markedness constraint is respected. SyllStruc is not violated anywhere (i.e. is undominated) in Japanese, so it is omitted in (21) and the subsequent discussion.

(21)

	*VoiGem	*[p]	*NC̥
Yamato	—	—	—
Sino	—	—	sam-po
Mimetic	—	pika-pika	—
Foreign$_A$	—	paN	sento
Foreign$_U$	baggu	petto	tento

The general tendency is that native (i.e. Yamato) items are most stringently regulated by the four markedness constraints, and these phonological restrictions are increasingly loosened as a given lexical item becomes more alien. But this general pattern is not completely clear given mimetics. Excluding mimetics, the remaining four lexical strata exhibit an implicational relationship: Foreign$_U$ ⊃ Foreign$_A$ ⊃ Sino ⊃ Yamato. This means that satisfaction of *NC̥ implies that of *[p], and satisfaction of *[p] in turn implies that of *VoiGem. Alternatively, exclusion of Sino-Japanese succeeds in incorporating mimetics, obtaining the following implicational relationship:

Foreign$_U$ ⊃ Foreign$_A$ ⊃ Mimetic ⊃ Yamato. This relationship indicates that satisfaction of *[p] implies that of *NÇ, and satisfaction of *NÇ implies that of *VoiGem. Either way, mimetics or Sino-Japanese must be kept outside the overall lexicon of Japanese to establish a coherent implicational relationship. For this reason, earlier literature has not taken mimetics into serious consideration. The obvious question is how the mimetic vocabulary is to be successfully embedded in the core-periphery structure.

As a first step toward a solution, I propose that the *NÇ constraint is decomposed into a domain-restricted one and a domain-free one. More specifically, *NÇ is divided into a morpheme-internal constraint and a general constraint, as defined in (22).

(22) a. *NÇ$_{MI}$: Nasals must not be immediately followed by a voiceless obstruent morpheme-internally.

 b. *NÇ: Nasals must not be immediately followed by a voiceless obstruent anywhere (both tautomorphemically and heteromorphemically).

Now, look at the distribution of NÇ clusters summarized in (23). Most notably, a sequence of a nasal followed by a voiceless obstruent is disallowed within a morpheme but permitted heteromorphemically in the mimetic vocabulary. NÇ clusters are to be prohibited according to the generalization by Itô and Mester, as shown in (21). In reality, a morpheme boundary plays an essential role in determining whether NÇ clusters are sanctioned or not in the mimetic vocabulary (see Kawahara et al. 2003 for similar discussion).

(23)

	Tautomorphemic *NÇ	Heteromorphemic *NÇ
Yamato	—	—
Sino	—	sam-po
Mimetic	—	pan-to (underived) ban-to (derived)
Foreign	tempo	pan-suto (trunc.)

Next, consider the distribution of [p]. It is summarized in (24). Focusing on mimetics, [p] appears on the surface in an underived context but not in a derived environment involving the voicing process discussed in the previous section.

(24)

Yamato	—
Sino	—
Mimetic	pika-pika (underived) — (derived)
Foreign	piano

Equipped with the argument thus far, the generalization regarding the phonological characteristics of the mimetic vocabulary is restated below. First, mimetics and Sino-Japanese are similar in that they permit NÇ clusters only across morphemes. Second, derived mimetic forms are like Sino-Japanese in the sense that [p] is prohibited. Third, underived mimetic forms respect *NÇ morpheme-internally like derived mimetic forms and Sino-Japanese items, but differ from them in that *[p] is copiously violated.

Segregation of *NÇ into a morpheme-internal constraint and a general constraint makes it possible to capture all lexical strata in terms of an implicational relationship. Positioning *[p] between *NÇ$_{MI}$ and *NÇ, mimetic items can be embedded in the implicational hierarchy, as recapitulated in (25). Derived mimetic items are labeled Mimetic$_D$, and underived mimetic items are labeled Mimetic$_U$, respectively.

(25)

	*VoiGem	*NÇ$_{MI}$	*[p]	*NÇ
Yamato	✓	✓	✓	✓
Sino	✓	✓	✓	*
Mimetic$_D$	✓	✓	✓	*
Mimetic$_U$	✓	✓	*	*
Foreign$_A$	✓	*	*	*
Foreign$_U$	*	*	*	*

To convert this observation into a concrete OT account, suppose that a markedness hierarchy is given as indicated in (26). Unlike in Itô and Mester 1995a, 1995b, 1999, context-specific (morpheme-internal) *NÇ is added, and *[p] outranks context-free *NÇ. I assume that this markedness hierarchy is fixed.

(26) SyllStruc >> *VoiGem >> *NÇ$_{MI}$ >> *[p] >> *NÇ

Building on my analysis of mimetic voicing in the last section, Faith-Mimetics is now separated into two sub-constraints: Faith-IO and Faith-OO. Faith-IO-Mimetic is in charge of underived mimetic items, while Faith-OO-Mimetics is responsible for derived mimetic forms. As demonstrated in (27), ranking class-particular faithfulness constraints differently in various loci of the markedness hierarchy generates the implicational relationship in (25).

(27) SyllStruc
    | ← Faith-Foreign$_U$
  *VoiGem
    | ← Faith-Foreign$_A$
  *NÇ$_{MI}$
    | ← Faith-IO-Mimetic
  *[p]
    | ← Faith-OO-Mimetic/Faith-Sino
  *NÇ
          ← Faith-Yamato

Notice that the Faith-OO constraint in (27) is specific to the mimetic vocabulary. Given that different lexical classes could display different behavior in the OO-dimension, faithfulness constraints sensitive to other lexical classes could be ranked independently of Faith-OO-Mimetic. The ranking in (27) therefore does not a priori exclude the possibility that [p] is faithfully parsed in the surface representation in other lexical strata. Due to space limitations, I will not discuss this issue in more detail here.

5. Conclusion

I examined mimetic voicing in Japanese. As Nasu (1999) points out, avoidance of medial [p] in the voicing context is considered as emergence of the unmarked. Critically reviewing his analysis, I argued that transderivational correspondence desirably accounts for this descriptive observation. My analysis militating against [p] in the OO-dimension has the significant implication that the mimetic class is successfully incorporated in the core-periphery model of the Japanese phonological lexicon. To achieve this goal, I proposed to separate the *NÇ constraint into a morpheme-specific constraint and a general constraint.

References

Benua, L. 1995. Identity Effects in Morphological Truncation. *University of Massachusetts Occasional Papers in Linguistics 18: Papers in Optimality Theory*, eds. J. Beckman, L. Walsh, and S. Urbanczyk, 77–136.

Benua, L. 1997. Transderivational Identity: Phonological Relations between Words. Doctoral dissertation, University of Massachusetts, Amherst.

Gafos, A. 1996. The Articulatory Basis of Locality in Phonology. Doctoral dissertation, John Hopkins University.

Gafos, A. 1998. Eliminating Long-distance Consonantal Spreading. *Natural Language and Linguistic Theory* 16:223–78.

Hamano, S. 1998. *The Sound-Symbolic System of Japanese*. Stanford: CSLI.

Itô, J. 1986. Syllable Theory in Prosodic Phonology. Doctoral dissertation, University of Massachusetts, Amherst.

Itô, J., and A. Mester. 1995a. Japanese Phonology. *The Handbook of Phonological Theory*, ed. J. Goldsmith, 817–38, Oxford: Blackwell.

Itô, J., and A. Mester. 1995b. The Core-Periphery Structure of the Lexicon and Constraints on Reranking. *University of Massachusetts Occasional Papers in Linguistics 18: Papers in Optimality Theory*, eds. J. Beckman, L. Walsh, and S. Urbanczyk, 181–209.

Itô, J., and A. Mester. 1999. The Phonological Lexicon. *The Handbook of Japanese Linguistics*, ed. N. Tsujimura, 62–100. Oxford: Blackwell.

Kawahara, S., K. Nishimura, and H. Ono. 2003. Unveiling the Unmarkedness of Sino-Japanese. *Japanese/Korean Linguistics 12*, ed. W. McClure, 140–51. Stanford: CSLI.

Kurisu, K. 2001. The Phonology of Morpheme Realization. Doctoral dissertation, University of California, Santa Cruz.

Leben, W. 1973. Suprasegmental Phonology. Doctoral dissertation, MIT.

McCarthy, J. 1986. OCP Effects: Gemination and Antigemination. *Linguistic Inquiry* 17:207–63.

McCarthy, J., and A. Prince. 1994. The Emergence of the Unmarked: Optimality in Prosodic Morphology. *Proceedings of the North East Linguistic Society* 24:333–79.

Nasu, A. 1999. Onomatope ni okeru yūseika to [p] no yūhyōsei [Voicing in onomatopoeia and the markedness of [p]]. *Onsei Kenkyū [Journal of the Phonetic Society of Japan]* 3:52–66.

Prince, A., and P. Smolensky 1993. Optimality Theory: Constraint Interaction in Generative Grammar. Manuscript, Rutgers University and University of Colorado, Boulder.

Rose, S. 2000. Rethinking Geminates, Long-Distance Geminates, and the OCP. *Linguistic Inquiry* 31:85–122.

Loan Phonology Is Not All Perception: Evidence from Japanese Loan Doublets

JENNIFER L. SMITH*
University of North Carolina, Chapel Hill

1. Introduction

When loanwords from a source language (L_S) enter a borrowing language (L_b), they may be altered to conform to L_b phonology. This phenomenon, known as **loanword adaptation**, has long been considered a source of evidence about the phonological grammar of L_b. However, Peperkamp and Dupoux (2003) (see also Peperkamp forthcoming) have developed an alternative proposal, in which loanword adaptation takes place **not** in the UR→SR mapping of the phonological grammar but at the level of speech perception.

This paper presents evidence from English-to-Japanese **loan doublets**, L_S words with two L_b outcomes, showing that the perception-only model of loanword adaptation is too restrictive. While perceptual factors are important, the phonological grammar must play a role in loanword adaptation as

* Many thanks for comments and discussion to Misha Becker, Shigeto Kawahara, Craig Melchert, Jeff Mielke, David Mora-Marín, Elliott Moreton, Tim Vance, Natasha Warner, and Andy Wedel. Thanks also to the participants in Phonology II at UNC-CH in Fall 2004, and to audiences at Japanese/Korean Linguistics 14 and the UNC-CH, U. of Arizona, and Kyushu U. linguistics departments. Any remaining errors or oversights are the author's sole responsibility.

well. (For additional discussion supporting this claim, see Yip 2002, Kenstowicz 2004, and Smith forthcoming.) First, the traditional phonological approach to loanword adaptation and the alternative perception-only approach are summarized in §2 and §3, respectively. §4 then presents the loan-doublet evidence and discusses the problems that it raises for the perception-only model. Finally, §5 outlines a new phonological approach based on output-output faithfulness (Benua 1997).

2. The Phonological Approach to Loanword Adaptation

Much previous work holds that loanword adaptation is carried out by the **phonological grammar** of Lb (Hyman 1970, Lovins 1975, Yip 1993, Jacobs and Gussenhoven 2000, Shinohara 2004). The underlying representation (UR) of a loanword in Lb closely resembles the Ls form, at least for those speakers who first borrow a given word through contact with Ls (the situation may be different for subsequent generations of monolingual Lb speakers). The Lb phonological grammar then maps that UR to a surface representation (SR). As part of this mapping, the loanword may be altered (that is, adapted) to better satisfy Lb phonological requirements.

For example, English *cream* [kɹiːm] is borrowed as Japanese *kuriimu*. In the phonological approach to loanword adaptation, shown in (1), the Japanese UR is /kriːm/. Constraints (defined in (2)) against onset clusters and certain codas compel epenthesis, producing the SR [kɯ.riː.mɯ]. (In candidate (1c) and subsequent examples, deletion sites are indicated with a short underline.)

(1) Loanwords: {*COMPONS, CODACOND, MAX-IO} >> DEP-IO

/kriːm/ 'cream'	*COMP ONS	CODA COND	MAX-IO	DEP-IO
a. kriːm	*(!)	*(!)		
☞ b. kɯ.riː.mɯ				**
c. _riː_			*!*	

(2) Constraint Definitions (Prince and Smolensky 1993, Itô 1989, McCarthy and Prince 1995)

    a. *COMPLEXONSET   Onset clusters are prohibited.
    b. CODACONDITION   Codas with Place features are prohibited.
    c. MAX-IO ('no deletion')   Input segments have output correspondents.
    d. DEP-IO ('no epenthesis')   Output segments have input correspondents.

A crucial aspect of (1) is the ranking MAX-IO >> DEP-IO, which ensures that epenthesis, not deletion, is the preferred repair strategy.

However, this ranking leads to a problem for the view that loanword adaptation is entirely driven by the Lb phonological grammar. In the non-loan phonology of Japanese, the preferred repair is deletion (McCawley 1968), as shown by the verb-suffix alternations in (3) involving nonpast /-ɾɯ/ and causative /-sase/.

(3) Deletion Repairs in Japanese Nonloan Phonology

    a. Vowel-final Verbs: Suffixes surface unchanged.
       'see'   /mi-ɾɯ/ [mi.ɾɯ]   /mi-sase/ [mi.sa.se]
       'eat'   /tabe-ɾɯ/ [ta.be.ɾɯ]   /tabe-sase/ [ta.be.sa.se]

    b. Consonant-final Verbs: Suffix consonants delete.
       'read' /jom-ɾɯ/ [jo.m_ɯ]   /jom-sase/ [jo.m_a.se]
       'fly'   /tob-ɾɯ/ [to.b_ɯ]   /tob-sase/ [to.b_a.se]
       'wait' /mat-ɾɯ/ [ma.tˢ_ɯ] /mat-sase/ [ma.t_a.se]

Here, because deletion is chosen, the opposite ranking would have to hold between the faithfulness constraints: DEP-IO >> MAX-IO, as in (4).

(4) Nonloans: {*COMPONS, CODACOND, DEP-IO} >> MAX-IO

/jom-sase/ 'read-CAUS'	*COMP ONS	CODA COND	DEP-IO	MAX-IO
a. jom.sa.se		*!		
b. jo.mV.sa.se			*!	
☞ c. jo.m_a.se				*

The fact that Japanese uses epenthesis repairs only for loanwords, while preferring deletion repairs in the nonloan phonology, turns out to be part of a larger pattern. Paradis and LaCharité (1997), in their cross-linguistic survey of loanword adaptation repairs, have discovered a strong cross-linguistic tendency to avoid deletion repairs for loanwords (which they name the Preservation Principle). The ranking paradox illustrated in (2) and (4) above represents the most extreme manifestation of this tendency: a language that uses deletion as the default repair in nonloan phonology, but chooses epenthesis repairs **specifically** for loanword adaptation. Korean shows similar behavior, in that the native phonology uses feature change or deletion repairs, but loanword adaptation involves epenthesis (Kang 2003, Kenstowicz 2004; for additional discussion of languages with loan-specific repair strategies, see also Yip 2002, Smith 2004, Peperkamp forthcoming).

Languages like Japanese, with epenthesis only for loanwords, are significant because they clearly demonstrate that the nonloan phonology cannot be the only mechanism responsible for loanword adaptation. If it were, then the same repair strategy that is used for the nonloans would be chosen for loanwords as well. The question remains, however, just what factors beyond the native L*b* phonology are responsible for adaptation effects. Some researchers have proposed adding loanword-specific principles or constraints to the phonological system (Silverman 1992, Paradis and La Charité 1997, Yip 2002, Kang 2003). But Peperkamp and Dupoux (2003) and Peperkamp (forthcoming) take a different approach, which is summarized in the following section.

3. The Perception-Only Approach to Loanword Adaptation

Peperkamp and Dupoux (2003; see also Peperkamp forthcoming) develop a model of loanword adaptation in which all adaptation occurs **during perception**. On this view, there is no UR→SR mapping regulated by the L*b* phonology that turns L*s*-based source forms into L*b* outputs. The L*b* phonology is involved in loanword adaptation only in that it determines how L*s* words are (mis-)perceived by a native speaker of L*b*, as shown in (5).

(5) Perception of a Nonnative Form (Peperkamp and Dupoux 2003)

    a. L*s* **acoustic signal** (Eng. *cream*, [kɹiːm])

    b. L*b* speaker's **phonetic decoding module** maps acoustic signal to closest native phonetic categories (Jpn. SR [kɯ.ɾiː.mɯ]).

    c. L*b* speaker's **phonological decoding module** maps surface phonetic representation to a corresponding UR (Jpn. UR /kɯriːmɯ/).

Step (5b), where the L*s* acoustic signal is mapped onto L*b* phonetic categories, models a psycholinguistic effect known as **perceptual assimilation**: the tendency for one's native phonology to distort the perception of nonnative forms. In particular, a form that is illicit in language L is hard for speakers of L to distinguish from a similar, legal form (Best 1994, Hallé et al. 1998, Dupoux et al. 1999, Moreton and Amano 1999, Kabak 2003, Mielke 2003). Peperkamp and Dupoux (2003:369) emphasize that perceptual assimilation can occur even with prosodic constituents such as syllables. For example, Dupoux et al. (1999) and Dehaene-Lambertz et al. (2000) find that Japanese listeners have difficulty distinguishing between auditory stimuli with illicit VCCV versus well-formed VC[ɯ]CV sequences. This suggests that the Japanese phonetic decoding module maps both VCCV and VC[ɯ]CV onto VC[ɯ]CV. That is, VCCV is perceived as VC[ɯ]CV—a type of perceptual assimilation that can be called **perceptual epenthesis**.

According to the perception-only model of loanword adaptation, the very same effect is responsible for the 'epenthetic' vowels that appear in loanwords in Japanese. The presence of these non-L*s* vowels is held to be an automatic consequence of the way that illicit codas or consonant clusters in the L_S form are perceived by an L_b speaker. On this view, Japanese listeners directly perceive English *cream* as *kuriimu*, so their UR is already /kɯuɾiːmɯu/ with the "epenthetic" vowels included, and no UR→SR process involving epenthesis need be postulated. It is important to note that the perception-only model does not require all loanword adaptation to occur by epenthesis; it is an empirical question what the "closest available native phonetic category" for an illicit syllable type would be in each language. However, since Japanese loanwords **are** productively repaired by epenthesis, the perception-only model views the presence of those non-L_S vowels as the consequence of perceptual assimilation.

As Peperkamp (forthcoming) argues, a major advantage of adopting the perception-only model for Japanese loanwords is that it can straightforwardly account for the mismatch between loanword epenthesis and nonloan deletion repairs. If loanword adaptation is not a UR→SR mapping, then all repairs that **are** driven by a UR→SR mapping (that is, nonloan repairs) consistently involve deletion. There would be no need to complicate the phonological grammar with loanword-specific mechanisms.

However, there is some reason to question the ultimate success of the perception-only approach. For one thing, as Kenstowicz (2003) observes, if Japanese loanwords gain vowels as a direct consequence of perception, then such vowels could not have a phonological status different from the non-"epenthetic" vowels in loanwords. But this prediction is contradicted by Shinohara (2000), who shows that Japanese loans from French have an accent assignment process that treats inserted and L_S-based vowels differently.

The following section presents a new set of data that pose a problem for the perception-only approach to loanword adaptation in Japanese: loanwords that have doublet forms, one with epenthesis and one with deletion.

4. Evidence from Loan Doublets

Epenthesis is by far the most productive repair strategy in Japanese loanword adaptation for L_S forms containing L_b-illicit codas or consonant clusters. However, there are also cases of adaptation involving deletion. Typically, loanwords with deletion repairs have doublet forms with epenthesis. This section argues that in such doublets, it is the deletion form that more closely reflects perceptual factors, so perceptual assimilation cannot be responsible for all epenthesis repairs in loanwords.

Examples of deletion/epenthesis loan doublets are given in (6). The deletion forms are from Arakawa 1977, Ichikawa 1929, and Miura 1993. The epenthesis forms are either from the same source as the corresponding deletion form, or from Arakawa 1977.

(6) Deletion/Epenthesis Loanword Doublets (19th–20th century loans)[1]

   a. Onset Cluster Simplification by Deletion   Epenthesis Form

[ɾi.sɯ.ɾiɴ]	< *glycerine*	I25	[gɯ.ɾi.se.ɾiɴ]
[wai.ʃa.tˢɯ]	< *white shirt*	'white/dress shirt' I8	[ho.wai.to]

   b. Final Coda Deletion   Epenthesis Form

[dʒi.ɾɯ.ba]	< *jitterbug*	A577	[dʒit.ta:.bag.gɯ]
[pok.ke]	< *pocket*	I7	[po.ket.to]
[ɾa.mɯ.ne]	< *lemonade*	'l.-flavor drink' I3,M171	[ɾe.mo.ne:.do]
[haɴ.ke.tʲi]	< *handkerchief* I7, M136		[haɴ.ka.tʲi:.fɯ]
♦[o:.ɾai]	< *all right*	I32	[o:.ɾɯ.rai.to]

   c. Final Coda-Cluster Simplification by Deletion   Epenthesis Form

[ka.ɾaɴ]	< *crank*	I26	[kɯ.ɾaɴ.kɯ]
[ne.ba:.ma.iɴ]	< *never mind*	(cheer a team) M28	[ne.ba:.ma.iɴ.do]
[se.meɴ]	< *cement*	I26	[se.meɴ.to]
♦[bo:.ɾɯ]	< *board*	'pasteboard' I30	[bo:.do]/[bo:.ɾɯ.do]
♦[ɾo:.sɯ]	< *roast*	'meat for roast' I3,M135	[ɾo:.sɯ.to]

   d. Coda [ŋ] as [ɴ], not [ɴgɯ]   Epenthesis Form

[pɯ.ɾiɴ]	< *pudding*	I3	[pɯ.diɴ.gɯ]
[taɴ]	< *tongue*	(food) I4, M177	[o.kɯ.sɯ.taɴ.gɯ]
[sa:.fiɴ]	< *surfing*	M139	[sa:.fiɴ.gɯ]

   e. Medial Coda Deletion   Epenthesis Form

[he.boɴ]	< *Hepburn*	'(J. C.) Hepburn' M58	[hep.pɯ.ba:ɴ] (Katharine, Audrey)
[wai.ʃa.tˢɯ]	< *white shirt*	'white/dress shirt' I8	[ho.wai.to]
♦[bi.sɯ.te.ki]	< *beefsteak*	I2	[bi:.fɯ.sɯ.te:.ki]
♦[doɴ.mai]	< *don't mind*	(cheer a team) M28	[doɴ.to.mai.ɴ.do]
♦[o:.ɾai]	< *all right*	I32	[o:.ɾɯ.rai.to]

Since most loanwords show epenthesis, why are there cases like (6)
with deletion doublets? Additional examples of deletion loans, shown in (7)
and (8) below, help answer this question. It is well known that loanwords
usually enter Japanese through written materials rather than spoken English
(Lovins 1975, Miura 1993). But the forms in (7) and (8) involve borrowing

---

[1] The symbol ♦ in (6) indicates a deletion form that only differs from its epenthesis doublet
form in having the prosodic shape [(μμ)(μμ)] or [(μμ)μ], and moreover matches the epenthesis
form at the left edge(s) of the L_s morpheme(s). A case like this may have an alternative analysis as a metrically motivated truncation of the epenthesis form (see Itô 1990 on the phonology
of loan truncation). But if a deletion form that meets these prosodic criteria has different counterparts to the L_s vowels than the epenthesis form has (especially L_s reduced vowels), this is
taken as evidence of auditory borrowing rather than metrically motivated truncation; such
cases are not marked with ♦. Finally, the form [sa:.fiɴ] 'surfing' in (6d) does have the prosodic
shape of a possible truncation form, but Miura (1993:139) explicitly labels this as a likely
auditory loan, noting that other sport-name loans consistently have [...iɴ.gɯ].

situations that are probably auditory, and thus less likely to have been determined by English orthography. ("Standard" Japanese epenthesis forms from Arakawa (1977) are also listed in (7) and (8) where applicable.)

The examples in (7) are English loanwords into Hawai'ian Japanese, the language of a population that would have interacted with English speakers directly rather than primarily through English-language written materials.[2]

(7) English Loanwords in Hawai'ian Japanese (Higa 1970)

a. Deletion of Final Voiced Stop, V_# (H137)

[iɴ.sai̯] 'inside' cf. [iɴ.sai.do̲]
[au̯.sai̯] 'outside' cf. [au̯.to.sai.do̲]

b. Deletion of Final Voiced Stop, N_# (H131)

[ha.zu.beɴ̲] 'husband' cf. [ha.zu.baɴ.do̲]

c. Deletion of Final Voiceless Stop, S_# (H136)

[ne.ki.su̲ (i.ja)] 'next (year)' cf. [ne.ki.su.to̲] + *generation*
[ɾa.su̲ (i.ja)] 'last (year)' cf. [ɾa.su.to̲]

d. Deletion of Medial-Coda Voiceless Stop (H137)

[au̯̲.sai] 'outside' cf. [au̯.to̲.sai.do]

The examples in (8) are from English phrasebooks written for 19th-century merchants interacting with English speakers in the ports newly open to foreign trade. As Kamei et. al (1965) note, the users of these books were not involved in the academic study of English-language materials; they were simply interested in communicating with English-speaking customers.

(8) Items from 19th-century English Phrasebooks (Kamei et al. 1965)

a. Final Coda Deletion

[wa.ɾi.waɴ̲] K147
gloss: *nan de gozaru* 'what is it?' probable source: *what (do) you want*
[nai̲] K148, from *Nihon gaikoku shoonin dokutsuushi*
gloss: *yoru* 'evening, night' probable source: *night*; cf. [nai.to̲]

b. Medial Coda (Geminate) Simplification by Deletion

[goː̲.deː.mu̲] K148, from *Nihon gaikoku shoonin dokutsuushi*
gloss: *okoru* 'become angry' probable source: *goddamn*; cf. [go̲d.de.mu̲]

---

[2] It is possible that the Hawai'ian Japanese examples in (7) were borrowed from English indirectly, by way of Hawai'ian Creole English (Hawai'ian Pidgin), which also has deletion repairs. Therefore, we cannot be absolutely certain that these forms are true examples of deletion repairs **in Japanese**. But this point actually brings up another problem for the perception-only model of loanword adaptation: If the cross-linguistic preference for epenthesis repairs in loanword adaptation is an automatic consequence of perceptual epenthesis, then why are deletion repairs quite commonly found in situations of pidgin and creole formation? See Smith (forthcoming) for additional discussion of the phonological implications of deletion repairs in pidgins and creoles.

Thus, the items in (7), and especially in (8), provide examples of how loanwords from English were represented by Japanese speakers who presumably encountered those English forms in spoken-language contexts. These examples indicate that when the influence of English orthography is lessened or removed, deletion repairs can be found. An auditory-borrowing explanation is also likely for many of the deletion loans in (6) (see also Ichikawa 1929 and Miura 1993 for discussion of some of these examples). In support of this claim, we may note that other differences between the deletion loans in (6) and their epenthesis doublet forms are also consistent with an auditory source for the deletion form and an orthographic source for the epenthesis form. For example, the penultimate vowel in the deletion loan [ɾi.sɯ.ɾiɴ]<*glycerine* is similar to the English reduced vowel in that syllable, while the corresponding vowel in the epenthesis doublet [gɯ.ɾi.se.ɾiɴ] is more consistent with English orthography than with English pronunciation. Other examples from (6) in which deletion loans represent English reduced vowels more accurately include [dʒi.ɾɯ.ba] vs. [dʒit.taː.bag.gɯ]<*jitterbug* and [ɾa.mɯ.ne] vs. [ɾe.mo.neː.do]<*lemonade*. Deletion loans are also more likely to represent an English intervocalic flap as [ɾ] instead of [t] or [d]; compare [pɯ.ɾiɴ] vs. [pɯ.diɴ.gɯ]<*pudding* and, again, [dʒi.ɾɯ.ba] vs. [dʒit.taː.bag.gɯ]<*jitterbug*.[3]

Summing up the results of this section, we find that although epenthesis is by far the most common repair strategy for loanwords in Japanese, there are examples of deletion repairs as well—particularly when the medium of borrowing is auditory rather than orthographic. This indicates that the outcome of actual auditory perception of English L_s forms by Japanese L_b speakers, at least in certain contexts, often involves **perceptual deletion** rather than perceptual epenthesis. Another, nonperception explanation is needed for the prevalence of epenthesis repairs, especially for cases with known deletion doublet forms.

5. An OO-Faith Account of Japanese Loanword Adaptation

The preceding section has shown that the prevalence of epenthesis repairs for Japanese loanwords, far from being an automatic consequence of the perception of a nonnative form by a Japanese speaker, is actually related to the availability of L_s orthographic forms. In particular, L_s consonants that might not have been perceived in auditory input become accessible when the input is orthographic. The difference between perceptually based deletion and orthographically influenced preservation of a word-final coda is il-

---

[3] S. Kawahara (p.c.) notes that English loans in Japanese rap songs may also involve deletion repairs; this is plausibly another context in which auditory similarity to English is valued.

lustrated with the loan doublet *jiruba/jittaabaggu* from English *jitterbug* in (9).

(9) Deriving the doublet from L_S *jitterbug*

a. **Auditory** Borrowing (following perception model from (5))

i. L_S phonetic form	[dʒɪ.ɾɚ.bʌg̚]	
ii. L_b phonetic decoder	[dʒi.ɾɯ.ba_]	([g]→Ø: **perception**)
iii. L_b underlying form	/ziɾɯba/	
iv. L_b surface form	[dʒi.ɾɯ.ba]	

b. **Orthographic** Borrowing

i. L_S spelling	<*jitterbug*>	
ii. assumed target → UR	/dʒit.taː.bag(g)/	(via orthography)
iii. L_b surface form	[dʒit.taː.bag.gɯ]	(Ø→[ɯ]: **phonology**)

Crucially, the form in (9b) provides evidence for **phonological** epenthesis. The final [g] in the L_S form is "perceived" on the basis of orthographic decoding; therefore, it can be represented in the L_b UR. However, the final [ɯ] that appears in the L_b surface form is not provided by the English orthography. On the contrary, the orthography provides evidence that the L_S form does **not** end in a vowel. The best explanation for the presence of this non-L_S vowel is the Japanese phonotactic constraint that makes [g] an illicit final coda. That is, the epenthetic vowel is the result of a UR→SR mapping; it is supplied **by the phonological grammar**. This means that the perception-only view of loanword adaptation, according to which "loanword adaptations are not due to the phonological grammar" (Peperkamp and Dupoux 2003:367), is too strong.[4]

Having concluded that at least some instances of epenthesis repairs in Japanese loanwords are the effect of the phonological grammar, however, we must now address the problem outlined at the end of §2: How can there be phonological epenthesis in loanword adaptation if deletion is the default repair in the nonloan phonology? A number of researchers have proposed that the phonological UR→SR mapping involved in loanword adaptation is regulated not only by the constraints relevant for the native phonology of L_b but also by constraints that enforce similarity to L_S forms (Yip 2002, Kang 2003, Kenstowicz 2003). Such constraints account for loan-specific repair strategies as seen in Japanese. Smith (forthcoming) shows that these L_S-L_b

[4] Peperkamp and Dupoux (2003:369) acknowledge orthography as a possible **confound** in the investigation of loanword adaptation, noting that "orthography can be expected to play a role in all adaptations that are either based on written input or done by speakers who know the spelling of the loanwords in the source language." However, they do not consider cases comparable to orthographically borrowed loans in Japanese, where orthographic information sets the stage for **subsequent phonological adaptation** that is not itself motivated by the orthography.

similarity constraints can be systematically formalized as **output-output (OO) faithfulness constraints** (Benua 1997), requiring only a minimal extension to the phonological framework.

Invoking the independently motivated OO-FAITH system allows us to define a correspondence relation (call it the **SB relation**) between L_S output forms as perceived by L_b speakers (pL_S forms), which may include information gleaned from orthography as well as from auditory perception, and L_b outputs. One faithfulness constraint on the SB relation is the anti-deletion constraint MAX-SB, which penalizes L_b output forms when they lack segments found in their corresponding pL_S forms. MAX-SB is vacuously satisfied for nonloans, which, by definition, have no pL_S correspondents. So the ranking MAX-SB >> {DEP-SB,{DEP-IO >> MAX-IO}} produces a grammar where loans have epenthesis repairs, because MAX-SB dominates both DEP constraints (10a), but nonloans have deletion repairs, because DEP-IO dominates MAX-IO (10b).

(10) SB-FAITH Constraints and Loanword-Specific Epenthesis in Japanese

a.

/best/ 'best' pL_S form: < Eng [bɛst]	CODA COND	MAX-SB	DEP-SB	DEP-IO	MAX-IO
i. best	*!				
☞ ii. be.sɯ.to			**		
iii. be_ _		**!			**

b.

/jom-sase/ 'read-CAUS' pL_S form: *none*	CODA COND	MAX-SB	DEP-SB	DEP-IO	MAX-IO
i. jom.sa.se	*!				
ii. jo.mV.sa.se				*!	
☞ iii. jo.m_a.se					*

The OO-FAITH approach to loanword adaptation captures the fact that adaptation often includes an attempt to match the perceived L_S form, but also that this process is driven by violable constraints, rather than being a mandatory outcome of speech perception as the perception-only approach to adaptation would require. (See Smith forthcoming for further discussion of this point; for more evidence that L_S similarity in loanword adaptation is violable and interacts with other aspects of the phonological grammar, see Davidson and Noyer 1997, Yip 2002, Kang 2003, Kenstowicz 2004.)

In conclusion, perception is certainly influenced by native-language phonology, but perceptual assimilation is not the only force in loanword adaptation. A phonological analysis that includes OO-FAITH between L_S

forms (as perceived by L*b* speakers) and L*b* forms is able to model the diverse forces that influence loanword phonology, including not only perceptual effects, but also orthographic information, and even interactions between loanword adaptation and other phonological constraints active in L*b*.

References

Arakawa, S. 1977. *Gairaigo jiten*, 2nd ed. Tokyo: Kadokawa.

Benua, L. 1997. *Transderivational Identity*. Doctoral dissertation, University of Massachusetts.

Best, C. 1994. The Emergence of Native-Language Phonological Influence in Infants: A Perceptual Assimilation Model. *The Development of Speech Perception*, ed. J. Goodman and H. Nusbaum, 167–224. Cambridge: MIT Press.

Davidson, L., and R. Noyer. 1997. Loan Phonology in Huave: Nativization and the Ranking of Faithfulness Constraints. *WCCFL* 15:65–79.

Dehaene-Lambertz, G., E. Dupoux, and A. Gout. 2000. Electrophysiological Correlates of Phonological Processing: A Cross-Linguistic Study. *Journal of Cognitive Neuroscience* 12:635–47.

Dupoux, E., K. Kakehi, Y. Hirose, C. Pallier, and J. Mehler. 1999. Epenthetic Vowels in Japanese: A Perceptual Illusion? *JEP:HPP* 25:1568–78.

Hallé, P., J. Segui, U. Frauenfelder, and C. Meunier. 1998. Processing of Illegal Consonant Clusters: A Case of Perceptual Assimilation? *JEP:HPP* 24:592–608.

Higa, M. 1970. The Sociolinguistic Significance of Borrowed Words in the Japanese Spoken in Hawaii. *University of Hawaii Working Papers in Linguistics* 2:125–40.

Hyman, L. 1970. The Role of Borrowing in the Justification of Phonological Grammars. *Studies in African Linguistics* 1:1–48.

Ichikawa, S. 1929. *Foreign Influences on the Japanese Language*. Tokyo: Japanese Council Institute of Pacific Relations.

Itô, J. 1989. A Prosodic Theory of Epenthesis. *NLLT* 7:217–59.

Itô, J. 1990. Prosodic Minimality in Japanese. *CLS* 26, vol. 2:213–39.

Jacobs, H., and C. Gussenhoven. 2000. Loan Phonology: Perception, Salience, the Lexicon, and OT. *Optimality Theory: Phonology, Syntax, and Acquisition*, ed. J. Dekkers, F. van der Leeuw, and J. van de Weijer, 193–209. Oxford: Oxford University Press.

Kabak, B. 2003. *The Perceptual Processing of Second Language Consonant Clusters*. Doctoral dissertation, University of Delaware.

Kamei, T., T. Ōtō, and T. Yamada. 1965. *Atarashii kokugo e no ayumi*. Tokyo: Heibonsha.

Kang, Y. 2003. Perceptual Similarity in Loanword Adaptation: English Postvocalic Word-final Stops in Korean. *Phonology* 20:219–73.

Kenstowicz, M. 2003. Salience and Similarity in Loanword Adaptation: A Case Study from Fijian. Manuscript, MIT.

Kenstowicz, M. 2004. Issues in Loanword Phonology. Paper presented at Phonetic Society of Japan workshop, Tokyo.

Lovins, J. 1975. *Loanwords and the Phonological Structure of Japanese*. Bloomington: IULC.

McCarthy, J., and A. Prince. 1995. Faithfulness and Reduplicative Identity. *Papers in Optimality Theory* (UMOP 18), ed. J. Beckman, L. Walsh Dickey, and S. Urbanczyk, 250–384. Amherst, Mass.: GLSA.

McCawley, J. 1968. *The Phonological Component of a Grammar of Japanese*. The Hague: Mouton.

Miura, A. 1993. *English in Japanese*. New York: Weatherhill.

Mielke, J. 2003. The interplay of Speech Perception and Phonology: Experimental Evidence from Turkish. *Phonetica* 60:208–29.

Moreton, E., and S. Amano. 1999. Phonotactics in the Perception of Japanese Vowel Length: Evidence for Long-Distance Dependencies. *Proceedings of EuroSpeech 6*.

Paradis, C., and D. LaCharité. 1997. Preservation and Minimality in Loanword Adaptation. *Journal of Linguistics* 33:379–430.

Peperkamp, S. Forthcoming. A Psycholinguistic Theory of Loanword Adaptations. *BLS* 30.

Peperkamp, S., and E. Dupoux. 2003. Reinterpreting Loanword Adaptations: The Role of Perception. *ICPhS* 15:367–70.

Prince, A., and P. Smolensky. 1993. *Optimality Theory: Constraint Interaction in Generative Grammar*. [Published by Blackwell, 2004.]

Shinohara, S. 2000. Default Accentuation and Foot Structure in Japanese: Evidence from Adaptations of French Words. *JEAL* 9:55–96.

Shinohara, S. 2004. Emergence of Universal Grammar in Foreign Word Adaptations. *Constraints in Phonological Acquisition*, ed. R. Kager, J. Pater, and W. Zonneveld, 292–320. Cambridge: Cambridge University Press.

Silverman, D. Multiple Scansions in Loanword Phonology: Evidence from Cantonese. *Phonology* 9:289–328.

Smith, J. 2004. On Loanword Adaptation as Evidence for Preferred Repair Strategies. Poster presented at International Conference on Linguistic Evidence, Tübingen.

Smith, J. Forthcoming. A Correspondence Theory Model of Loanword Adaptation. *Phonological Argumentation: Essays on Evidence and Motivation*, ed. Steve Parker. London: Equinox.

Yip, M. 1993. Cantonese Loanword Phonology and Optimality Theory. *JEAL* 2:261–91.

Yip, M. 2002. Perceptual Influences in Cantonese Loanword Phonology. *Journal of the Phonetic Society of Japan* 6:4–21.

Part II

Psycholinguistics

Effects of Intonational Phrase Boundaries on Ambiguous Syntactic Clause Boundaries in Japanese

SOYOUNG KANG
Ohio State University

SHARI R. SPEER
Ohio State University

MINEHARU NAKAYAMA
Ohio State University

1. Introduction

Recently, numerous spoken language studies have provided the evidence for the immediate use of prosodic information to resolve syntactic ambiguity. The results of these studies have been robust enough to be attested with different experimental paradigms ranging from auditory comprehension tasks (Lehiste 1973, Schafer et al. 2000, Schafer et al. 2005, Warren, et al. 2000. Price et al. 1991, Warren et al. 1995), cross-modal naming task (Marslen-Wilson et al. 1992, Kjelgaard and Speer 1999), ERP (Steinhaur et al. 1999) and eye-tracking (Snedeker and Trueswell 2004). However, most of these studies center around English, and only a few examined typologically distinct languages such as Japanese and Korean for prosodic effects on syntactic/semantic disambiguation (Venditti 1993, Jun and Oh 1996, Misono et al. 1998).

Kang and Speer (2003), using syntactic constructions unexamined previously, demonstrated that prosodic boundary information was crucially used by listeners in the resolution of syntactic clausal ambiguity in Korean. In contrast to English, Korean has neither lexical stress nor pitch accents (Jun 2005). In addition, Korean syntactic characteristics differ from those of English in that it includes *pro*-drop, verb-final word order, and the presence of complementizers at the end of but not the beginning of embedded clauses, the combination of which contributes to abundant syntactic clausal ambiguity. Despite this, Kang and Speer argued that prosodic boundaries could provide some pieces of the most salient and reliable information about the structure of spoken sentences, and prosodic boundaries play a fundamental role in spoken language processing in Korean.

Although it is well-known that Japanese shares many syntactic properties with Korean, its prosodic structure is distinctly different, including lexically assigned pitch accents (Venditti 2005, among others; see also the description in §3). Given syntactic similarity but intonational difference, we tested to see if Japanese sentence comprehension relies on prosodic boundary information like in Korean as listeners understand syntactic ambiguities. Japanese materials were temporarily and globally ambiguous sentences, with syntactic structures closely comparable to those used in Kang and Speer's (2003) Korean study. For example, the two-word sentence-initial fragment in (1) is ambiguous such that the initial nominative-marked NP may be the subject either of the immediately following verb or of the sentence-final main verb.[1]

(1) Ta'keshi-ga nyuuin-shiteiru . . . .
     -NOM was hospitalized . . . .

Depending on the types of head nouns (e.g. animate vs. inanimate) modified by relative clauses, this fragment can be continued as in (2) or as in (3).

(2) Ta'keshi-ga nyuuin-shiteiru   oba-o nagusa'meta
     -NOM was hospitalized aunt-ACC consoled
     'Takeshi consoled the aunt who was hospitalized.'

(3) Ta'keshi-ga nyuuin-shiteiru   byooin-o   sagashita
     -NOM was hospitalized hospital-ACC looked for
     a. '(Someone) looked for the hospital where Takeshi was hospitalized.'
     b. 'Takeshi looked for the hospital where (someone) was hospitalized.'

At the completion of the sentences, (2) is not ambiguous any more (temporary ambiguity) while (3) still shows ambiguity (global ambiguity). The critical difference for these two examples is that for (2), the initial noun *Takeshi* cannot be the subject of the following embedded verb *nyuuin-shiteiru*, whereas for (3), the initial noun may or may not be the subject of the embedded verb. In addition, for the type of sentence in (3), a null pro-

---

[1] "Word" here means *bunsetsu* in Japanese, which may include a case marker, and items in the same *bunsetsu* are joined by hyphens in the transcriptions. The two words in (1) can, of course, form a complete sentence if there are no words following them. The symbol ' means that the preceding syllable is accented.

noun *pro* needs to be posited for the subject of the main verb as in (3a) or of the embedded verb as in (3b), and the referent of this *pro* must be recovered from prior context. For the purposes of the discussion, the type of sentence in (2) will be called a **gap type** (since the embedded clause is analyzed as a kind of relative clause involving a gap in English) and the type in (3) will be called a ***pro* type** (since the ambiguity centers on the positing of an empty noun phrase).

In Kang and Speer's (2003) study on comparable Korean constructions, the presence of an Intonation Phrase (see Jun 1993) right after the initial NP caused processing difficulty for a gap type sentence such as (2) due to the mismatch between syntactic and prosodic structures, whereas the same prosodic boundary was critically used to retrieve two distinct meanings for a sentence such as (3). The fact that listeners were able to obtain the (3b)-type interpretation solely based on prosodic structures is remarkable, given the difficulty of this reading in the absence of a prior context. Note that in Korean (as in Japanese, but not in Italian or Spanish, for instance), the comprehension of syntactic forms that include a null pronoun for the subject of a verb cannot be attributed to the presence of any overt morpho-syntactic marker in the spoken signal. Given this, the results are particularly interesting, as they show that prosodic phrasing, an intrinsic part of the spoken language stream, can inform listeners of the presence of a syntactic interpretation for the sentence that posits a null pronoun.

Studies of Japanese language production have reported that naïve speakers mark syntactic boundaries prosodically for constructions such as those in (4). Specifically, nominative and dative markers were lengthened only when they were followed by a syntactic clause boundary. Syntactic boundaries were also marked by an inserted pause, and there was no downstep found on the words that began a new clause (Venditti 1993). Here, the subordinated clauses are enclosed in square brackets.

(4) a. [Ma'yuko-ga Nobu'yuki-ni me'ron-o na'geta]
          -NOM   -DAT melon-ACC threw

      e'ngi-wa   omoshiro'katta
      performance-TOP was-interesting

      'The performance in which Mayuko threw the melon to Nobuyuki was interesting.'

   b. Ma'yuko-ga [Nobu'yuki-ni me'ron-o na'geta]
           -NOM   -DAT melon-ACC threw

     e'nji-o   shikatta
     child-ACC scolded

     'Mayuko scolded the child who threw the melon at Nobuyuki.'

    c. Ma'yuko-ga   Nobu'yuki-ni [me'ron-o na'meta]
          -NOM   -DAT melon-ACC licked

    e'nji-o   azu'keta
    child-ACC left in care of

    'Mayuko left the child who licked the melon to Nobuyuki's care.'

Given this, it would be interesting to see if Japanese listeners are also sensitive to prosodically marked syntactic clause boundaries in a listening comprehension study. Such sensitivity would suggest that, despite distinct differences in prosodic structure, Japanese listeners, like Korean listeners, can critically utilize prosodic information in auditory sentence comprehension, and provide cross-linguistic evidence for prosodic effects.

For the two types of sentences given in (2) and (3), written and auditory sentence comprehension experiments were conducted. The written study assessed readers' preferred syntactic representation for these sentences in the absence of overt prosody, while the auditory study examined the effects of prosodic phrasing on the comprehension of these two types of sentences.

2. Written Experiment

A written comprehension study assessed the preferred interpretation of the two types of ambiguous sentences. For this test, two lists were created. Each list contained eighteen gap type sentences (like (2)) and eighteen *pro* type sentences (like (3)) along with thirty-six filler items with different syntactic structures. The gap, *pro*, and filler sentences were mixed and pseudo-randomized in a questionnaire so that no three sentences of the same type occurred consecutively. Sixteen native speakers of Japanese participated for the payment of $7.00 each. Each participant was given one of the two versions to read. On each trial, the participants read the sentences and answered comprehension questions. Since the critical information involved the subject of embedded predicates in both (2) and (3), the question took the form of "Who was hospitalized?". Along with the questions, three counterbalanced response choices were provided. For the gap type, these included NP1 (e.g. definitely *Takeshi*), NP2 (e.g. definitely *oba*), and either NP1 or NP2 (e.g. either *Takeshi* or *oba*). For the *pro* type, the response choices included NP1 (e.g. definitely *Takeshi*), NP2 (e.g. definitely someone other than *Takeshi*), and either NP1 or someone else (e.g. either *Takeshi* or someone other than *Takeshi*). Figure 1 shows the results from this written test.

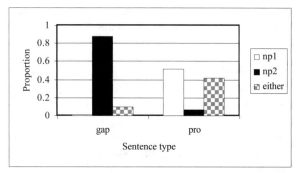

Figure 1. Mean Proportion of Three Response Types for Visually
Presented Gap and *pro* Type Sentences

Arcsine transformed proportions of responses in the three categories were analyzed in a two (sentence type) × three (response type) repeated measures analysis of variance (henceforth ANOVA). Throughout the text, statistical effects are significant at $p < .001$ unless otherwise noted. Analyses showed two main effects and an interaction (sentence type, $F_1(1,15) = 15.5$, $p < .005$; $F_2(1,35) = 37.91$; response type $F_1(2,30) = 9.15$; $F_2(2,70) = 51.12$; interaction $F_1(2,30) = 88.07$; $F_2(2,70) = 224.96$). Planned comparisons revealed that readers retrieved one clear meaning by sentence end for the temporarily ambiguous gap type sentences. The NP2 response was chosen as the answer to the comprehension question for these sentences on the vast majority of trials—significantly more often than both other response types combined $(F_1(1,2) = 27.64$; $F_2(1,2) = 67.0)$. On the other hand, responses for *pro* type sentences indicated a slight preference for the interpretation where the initial NP was the subject of the immediately following predicate, but a clear awareness of the presence of an ambiguous interpretation. Listeners chose NP1 more often than "either NP1 or someone else". However, planned comparisons showed that this difference was significant only by items $(F_1(1,1) = 1.55$, $p = 0.222$; $F_2(1,1) = 5.58$, $p < .05)$. Both of these responses combined were chosen significantly more often than "definitely someone else" $(F_1(1,2) = 27.64$; $F_2(1,2) = 67.0)$.

3. Japanese Intonation Model

We assume the intonation model of Tokyo Japanese described in Venditti 2005. According to this model, each utterance in Japanese consists of one or more than one Intonation Phrase (henceforth IP). Each IP, then, can have one or more than one Accentual Phrase (henceforth AP) and is marked by tonal patterns and perceived junctures and optional pauses. An AP, the lower-level phrase, is typically characterized by an initial rise around the second mora and by a following fall at the right edge of the phrase. Each word is lexically either accented or unaccented, and in each AP, one or more than one word can occur, although an unaccented word typically tends to be merged with an accented word to form a single AP.

4. Auditory Experiment

For all the test materials, which are like sentence (2) or sentence (3), two prosodic versions of each syntactic type were produced by a female, native Japanese phonetician—one with an IP boundary immediately following the initial NP (shown in Figure 2) and the other without an IP boundary at the same location (shown in Figure 3). Prosodic structures beyond this IP were held constant for each item.

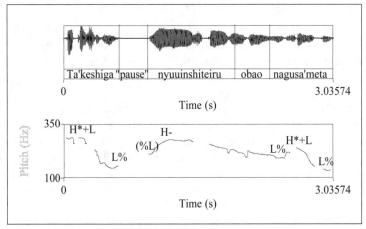

Figure 2. Waveform and Pitch Contour for a Gap IP Sentence

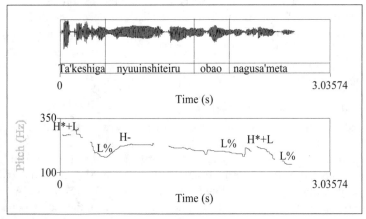

Figure 3. Waveform and Pitch Contour for a Gap No-IP Sentence

To make sure that two prosodic versions for each test item were produced as intended, duration measurements were also taken of critical words in each utterance. As can be seen in Figure 4, since the IP boundary was placed right after the initial NP-*ga*, *ga* (the last syllable of the word in IP boundary conditions) is longer than *ga* in no-IP conditions. In addition, while a considerable length of silence was found among all sentences in IP conditions, this was rarely so in no-IP conditions (ten out of seventy-two utterances).

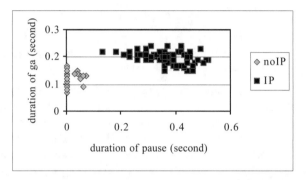

Figure 4. Durations of Pause Immediately Following Initial NP and of Nominative Marker *ga* in Two Prosodic Conditions

Four lists were created with a two × two factorial design (two syntactic types and two prosodic types). The same thirty-six test items used in the written experiment were pseudo-randomized with thirty-six filler items. Forty native speakers of Japanese from Daitō Bunka University in Tokyo participated in the experiment for the payment of ¥1,000. On each trial, each participant heard one prosodic version of either gap type or *pro* type and completed two tasks. First, they indicated as quickly as possible whether they understood each sentence or not. Then, they answered the same comprehension questions asked of readers in the written experiment, choosing one of the same three responses in each case.

For all sentence types, listeners indicated they understood the sentences more than 90% of the time (96% for the gap sentences with an IP, 94% for the gap sentences with no IP, 93% for the *pro* sentences with an IP, and 96% for the *pro* sentences with no IP). Figure 5 shows the mean end-of-sentence comprehension times for the understood sentences for four spoken sentence types, which are from the first task.

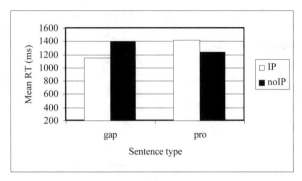

Figure 5. Mean End-of-Sentence Comprehension Times for Gap and *pro*
Type Sentences in Two Prosodic Conditions

Comprehension times were submitted to a two (syntactic forms) × two (prosodic structures) repeated measures ANOVA. Results indicated that listeners were slower to process gap type sentences without an IP boundary than they were to process those same sentences with an IP boundary after the first NP. Analyses showed a significant interaction of syntactic form and prosodic structure $(F_1(1,39) = 9.2,$ p < .005; $F_2(1,35) = 8.19,$ p < 0.01; all other Fs < 1). Planned comparisons showed that response times were shorter for gap sentences with IP boundaries (mean RT = 1144 ms) than for those without IP boundaries (mean RT = 1402 ms) $(F_1(1,1) = 6.34,$ p < .05; $F_2(1,1) = 5.84,$ p < .05). For these sentences, results were consistent with a model that predicts shorter processing time when prosodic and syntactic boundaries coincide than when they do not (Kjelgaard and Speer 1999).

In contrast, listeners were only numerically faster to process *pro* type sentences without an IP boundary (mean RT = 1234 ms) than they were to process those same sentences with an IP boundary after the first NP (mean RT = 1408 ms). Planned comparison showed that these response time differences did not reach significance $(F_1(1,1) = 3.14,$ p = .08; $F_2(1,1) = 2.65,$ p = .11).

The relative difficulty of processing *pro* type sentences that contained a prosodic boundary after the initial noun can be attributed to the effect of prosodic boundary information. Because the initial noun is an available and accessible candidate to be the subject of the embedded verb, this would seem the most obvious interpretation for listeners. However, the observed difficulty suggests the situation was otherwise; a prosodic boundary after the initial NP seems to lead them to build a structure where the initial NP was not the subject of the embedded verb. In such a case, listeners must also have posited a null pronoun (*pro*) for the subject of the embedded verb, which is possible in a *pro*-drop language like Japanese. Since it is pragmatically awkward to posit a null pronoun for the subject of an embedded predicate in the absence of any preceding context, sentences in the *pro* IP condition would have been more difficult to understand. Another possibility that can lead to increased difficulty for *pro* IP conditions is the fact that *pro* type sentences with an IP boundary can give rise to additional possible syntactic structure. Thus, the sentence in (3) could be analyzed syntactically as having the same structure as the one in (2), although this structure is semantically odd since the hospital cannot be hospitalized and there was no option involving *hospital* among the choices.

For ease of exposition, responses to the comprehension questions will be discussed separately for gap and *pro* type sentences. Comprehension question results for the temporarily ambiguous gap type sentences are shown in Figure 6.

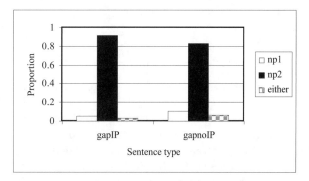

Figure 6. Mean Proportion of Each Response Choice for Gap Type
Sentences in Two Prosodic Conditions

Arcsine transformed data were submitted to a two (syntactic form) $\times$ two (prosodic structure) $\times$ three (response type) ANOVA. Results showed significant main effects for syntactic form ($F_1(1,39) = 72.47$; $F_2(1,35) = 79.14$) and response type ($F_1(2,78) = 170.39$; $F_2(2,70) = 189.25$), and significant interaction of prosodic structure with syntactic form ($F_1(1,39) = 14.61$; $F_2(1,35) = 5.54$, $p < .05$). All remaining interactions were significant (syntax $\times$ response type: $F_1(2,78) = 208.9$, $F_2(2,70) = 172.15$; prosody $\times$ response type: $F_1(2,78) = 44.06$, $F_2(2,70) = 23.43$; syntax $\times$ prosody $\times$ response type: $F_1(2,78) = 9.03$; $F_2(2,70) = 5.49$, $p < 0.05$). There were significantly more correct NP2 choices (the head noun in example (2)) for the gap IP condition, where syntactic and prosodic boundaries coincided (90.8%), than for the gap no-IP condition, where no IP boundary followed the initial NP (82.4%) ($F_1(1,1) = 15.96$; $F_2(1,1) = 8.87$). Therefore, when no IP boundary intervened between the initial NP and the following verb, prosodic grouping influenced syntactic grouping, inducing more erroneous responses even for these unambiguous sentences.

For *pro* type sentences, the presence or absence of an IP boundary was used to resolve standing syntactic ambiguity. The results are shown in Figure 7.

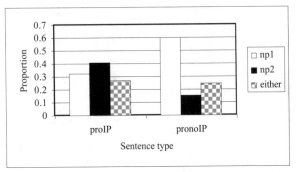

Figure 7. Mean Proportion of Each Response Choice for *pro* Type Sentences in Two Prosodic Conditions

There were significantly more choices of the initial NP (*Takeshi* in example (3)) when there was no IP boundary (60.2%) as compared to when there was an IP boundary at the same location (33.7%) ($F_1(1,1) = 49.38$, $F_2(1,1) = 30.07$). Hence, the absence of an IP boundary following the initial NP biased listeners toward the interpretation where the initial NP was the subject of the following embedded verb. The reverse pattern was found for NP2 choices (someone other than the initial NP). There were significantly more NP2 choices (40.4%) when there was an IP boundary after the initial NP than when there was no such boundary (15.4%) ($F_1(1,1) = 35.67$, $F_2(1,1) = 20.58$). These results suggest that listeners posited a *pro* subject for the embedded verb, which is remarkable, especially in the absence of any preceding context that could have identified its referent.

4. Discussion and Conclusion

These results demonstrate the fundamental importance of prosodic phrasal structure to the assignment of syntactic constituency during sentence comprehension, particularly in the case of head-final, *pro*-drop languages such as Japanese and Korean. Although the first reading experiment showed that our gap type sentences were only temporarily ambiguous, evidence was found that the absence of a prosodic boundary between the initial NP and the following verb induced longer reaction times and more erroneous answers to questions in the auditory sentence comprehension experiment. This suggests that the misalignment of prosodic and syntactic boundaries caused processing difficulty in this temporarily ambiguous structure. The *pro* type sentences, which were globally ambiguous, showed a clear effect of prosodic boundary information on resolving the location of syntactic clausal boundaries. Depending on the presence or absence of a prosodic boundary, listeners assigned a different syntactic clause boundary to the same word sequence even if this required them to posit a null pronoun for the embedded predicate, which is rare in the absence of any preceding context. The results of this study, along with those of Kang and Speer (2003), confirm the importance of prosodic structure during comprehension, and thus, further necessitate the inclusion of this component in models of spoken language processing for these two languages.

References

Jun, S. 1993. The Phonetics and Phonology of Korean Prosody. Doctoral dissertation, Ohio State University.

Jun, S. 2005. Prosodic Typology. *Prosodic Typology: The Phonology of Intonation and Phrasing*, ed. S. Jun, 761–806. Oxford: Oxford University Press.

Jun, S., and M. Oh. 1996. A Prosodic Analysis of Three Types of wh-phrases in Korean. *Language and Speech* 39(1):37–61.

Kang, S., and S. R. Speer. 2003. Prosodic Disambiguation of Ambiguous Clause Boundaries in Korean. *WCCFL 22 Proceedings*, eds. G. Garding and M. Tsujimura, 259–72. Somerville, Mass.: Cascadilla Press.

Kjelgaard, M., and S. R. Speer. 1999. Prosodic Facilitation and Interference in the Resolution of Temporary Syntactic Closure Ambiguity. *Journal of Memory and Language* 38:153–94.

Lehiste, I. 1973. Phonetic Disambiguation of Syntactic Ambiguity. *Glossa* 7(2): 107–22.

Marslen-Wilson, W. D., L. K. Tyler, P. Warren, P. Grenier, and C. S. Lee. 1992. Prosodic Effects in Minimal Attachment. *The Quarterly Journal of Experimental Psychology* 45A(1):73–87.

Misono, Y., R. Mazuka, T. Kondo, S. Kiritani. 1998. Effects and Limitations of Prosodic and Semantic Biases on Syntactic Disambiguation. *Journal of Psycholinguistic Research* 26(2):319–44.

Price, P.J., M. Ostendorf, S. Shattuck-Hufnagel, and C. Fong. 1991. The Use of Prosody in Syntactic Disambiguation. *Journal of the Acoustical Society of America* 90(6):2956–70.

Schafer, A., S. R. Speer, P. Warren, and D. White. 2000. Intonational Disambiguation in Sentence Production and Comprehension. *Journal of Psycholinguistic Research* 29(2):169–82.

Schafer, A., S. R. Speer, and P. Warren. 2005. Prosodic Influences on the Production and Comprehension of Syntactic Ambiguity in a Game-Based Conversation Task. *Approaches to Studying World-Situated Language Use: Bridging the Action and*

Product Traditions, eds. J. C. Trueswell and M. K. Tanenhaus, 209–25. Cambridge: MIT Press.

Snedeker, J., and J. C. Trueswell. 2003. Using Prosody to Avoid Ambiguity: Effects of Speaker Awareness and Referential Context. *Journal of Memory and Language* 48(1):103–30.

Steinhaur, K., K. Alter, and A. D. Friederici. 1999. Brain Potentials Indicate Immediate Use of Prosodic Cues in Natural Speech Processing. *Nature Neuroscience* 2(2):191–6.

Venditti, J. J. 1993. Disambiguation of Potential Garden Path Sentences in Japanese: A Baseline Study. Manuscript, Ohio State University.

Venditti, J. J. 2005. The J_ToBI Model of Japanese Intonation. *Prosodic Typology: The Phonology of Intonation and Phrasing*, ed. S. Jun, 172–200. Oxford: Oxford University Press.

Warren, P., E. Grabe, and F. Nolan. 1995. Prosody, Phonology and Parsing in Closure Ambiguities. *Language and Cognitive Processes* 10:457–86.

Warren, P., A. Schafer, S. R. Speer, and D. White. 2000. Prosodic Resolution of Prepositional Phrase Ambiguity in Ambiguous and Unambiguous Situations. *UCLA Working Papers in Phonetics* 99:5–33.

The Role of Prosody in Korean Sentence Processing

HEE-SUN KIM*
Stanford University

HYUCK-JOON LEE
University of California, Los Angeles

1. Introduction

The present study investigated the use of prosody in the resolution of syntactic ambiguity in Korean sentence processing. A number of studies have shown that prosodic grouping of an utterance can reflect its syntactic structure (Cooper and Paccia-Cooper 1980, Lehiste 1973), and prosody can provide helpful information for a listener to make parsing decisions in ambiguous sentence processing (Beach 1991, Kjelgaard and Speer 1999, Lehiste, Olive, and Streeter 1976, Price, Ostendorf, Shattuck-Hufnagel, and Fong 1991, Schafer, Carter, Clifton, and Frazier 1996). These studies indicate that there is a close relationship between prosody and syntactic structure. Language users have some knowledge about the relationship, and they are able to use that knowledge to segment speech input and to build the syntactic relationships of words.

However, there have been mixed results in demonstrating the capabilities of listeners to use prosody in sentence processing. Through cross-

* We would like to thank Sun-Ah Jun for her valuable comments on an earlier verson. We also thank all the people who participated in our experiments and Jeong-Woon Park at Hankuk University of Foreign Studies, who kindly helped us run the perception experiment.

linguistic studies, it is known that English and Japanese speakers rely on prosodic phrasing cues to resolve syntactic ambiguity more than Chinese and Dutch speakers do (Avesani, Hirschberg, and Prieto 1995, 't Hart, Collier, and Cohen 1990, Venditti and Yamashita 1994). Some ambiguous constructions were equally well disambiguated by prosody both in production and in perception, while other constructions were not. Lehiste (1973) showed that syntactic phrasal grouping ambiguity was successfully disambiguated by prosody, while grammatical category ambiguity was not. Also, production studies have shown that a syntactic structure can be realized more than one type of prosodic grouping, that is, a sentence can be produced with a variety of prosodic structures (Jun 1993). It is still questionable whether speakers spontaneously and reliably produce disambiguating prosodic cues (Allbritton, McKoon, and Ratcliff 1996, Schafer, Speer, Warren, and White 2000).

Apart from the effect of prosody in sentence processing, some researchers have argued that human sentence processing is guided by syntactic principles such as **minimal attachment** and **late closure** in the first stage of parsing without allowing any interference from other types of information (Frazier 1987). It is believed that these principles produce the preference for the simplest structure over others—the so-called "garden-path" effect. This claim has been regarded as controversial, and researchers have found mixed results (Kjelgaard and Speer 1999). Thus, it is interesting to examine how prosody influences the ultimate parsing decision relative to the syntactic preferences.

Several studies of Korean adults' and children's speech have found positive evidence of the use of prosodic phrasings in a small number of ambiguous constructions (Choi and Mazuka 2003, Schafer and Jun 1996), but the data were of limited use in terms of clarifying the issues outlined above. This study was designed to fill the gap by examining five types of syntactically ambiguous constructions in Korean. Specifically, this study addressed four questions. First, to what extent do native Korean speakers use prosodic phrasing cues to inform syntactic structure? Second, do speakers disambiguate various types of syntactic ambiguity equally well by prosody? Third, are there any processing differences depending on syntactic ambiguity types with the help of prosody? And fourth, is there any preference for choosing one type of syntactic structure over another in spite of disambiguating prosodic cues? To answer these questions, production and comprehension experiments were conducted. The production study examined the first two questions, and the comprehension study examined the other two.

2. Experimental Materials

The five types of syntactically ambiguous sentences used in this study were globally ambiguous in that each whole sentence could have more than one interpretation. The ambiguity in the first type arises from a double noun sequence, underlined in (1) below. In spoken forms, the two nouns can be separately parsed into two sentences if prosody signals a sentence boundary between the two, as in (1a). By contrast, the two nouns can form a single noun phrase if there is no clear prosodic boundary cue, as in (1b).

(1) Type 1 N1+N2: NP. NP vs. ModN+N

/jəgi-nɨn pusan   namdʒa-ga   mani   sa-nɨn   kosida/
here-TOP Pusan (./-POSS) man-SUBJ many.more live/be-REL place.be

   a. This is Pusan. (This is) a place, where the men outnumber (the women).

   b. This is the place where there are more men from Pusan than any other region.

Type 2 is a case of two predicate ambiguities. If a clause boundary intervenes beteween the two predicates, /andʒasə koŋbuha-nɨn/, as in (2a), SUBJ will be interpreted as the subject of Pred1, and Pred2 modifies the following noun N. On the other hand, the agent of both Pred1 and Pred2 is the N, as in (2b), if there is no clause boundary between the two.

(2) Type 2 NP+Pred1+Pred2+N: [SUBJ+Pred1]+[Pred2+N] vs.
                                 SUBJ+[Pred1+Pred2+N]

/əmma-ga   andʒasə   koŋbuha-nɨn   tʃinsu-rɨl pogois'ɨlk'əya/
mother-SUBJ being.seated.and to.study-REL Jinsu-OBJ see.(I) guess

   a. (I guess), the mother is seated, and sees Jinsu who is studying.

   b. (I guess), the mother sees Jinsu who is seated and studying.

Type 3 is an adverbial scope ambiguity construction. If the adverb, /kɨnalp'am/, modifies the main verb, /tʃʰadʒat'æ/, it leads to a wide scope interpretation, as in (3a). In this reading, a prosodic boundary is expected right after the adverb. If there is no clear prosodic boundary cue, the adverb modifies the next verb, /irəbəri-n/, which results in a narrow scope interpretation, as in (3b).

(3) Type 3 AdvP+VMod+N+V: AdvP+[VMod+N]+V vs.
                                   [AdvP+VMod+N]+V

/kɨnalp'am irəbəri-n   ton-ɨl   tʃʰadʒat'æ/
that.evening lost-REL money-OBJ discover.PAST

   a. He discovered [the money he had lost] that evening.

   b. He discovered [the money that he had lost that evening].

Type 4 is another double noun ambiguity construction. Ambiguity arises from omission of particles after the first noun. In (4a), the first noun is interpreted as the subject of the sentence if prosody marks a major syntactic boundary separating the subject NP and predicate VP. Otherwise, the first noun will be interpreted as the possessor of the second noun, as in (4b).

(4) Type 4 N1+N2: SUBJ+NP vs. PossN+N
/ɨna   tabaŋ-e kalk'ərago kɨrədəra/
Eunah(-SUBJ/POSS) café-to   go.will   say.PAST
   a. (Eunah) said (to me) that she would go to the café.
   b. (Someone) said (to me) that s/he would go to Eunah's café.

Type 5 is a plural vs. singular noun ambiguity. If there is a prosodic boundary after the first noun, the ambiguous string, N+Mod+N, can be interpreted as a conjunction of two noun phrases, as in (5a). If there is no such boundary signal, the N+Mod serves as a complex modifier of the following N, which results in a singular noun phrase interpretation, as shown in (5b).

(5) Type 5 N1+Mod+N2: N+[Mod+N] vs. [N+Mod]+N
/jəŋa-raŋ   katʃʰi   sa-nɨn   kjəŋmi-ga   pwadʒugiro   hæs'ə/
Youngah-and together live-REL Kyugmi-SUBJ take.care.of.FUT do.PAST
   a. Youngah and Kyungmi, who live together, would take care of (it).
   b. Kyungmi, who lives with Youngah, would take care of (it).

3. Experiment 1: Production

3.1. Method

For each type of ambiguous construction, four sentences were constructed and used in the production study, producing a total of twenty sentences. A pseudo-conversation task was employed to invoke natural prosody similar to that used in real conversation. For each target sentence, two different dialogues were made to elicit two readings, and the same target sentence was embedded in each. Four native Seoul Korean subjects (two males and two females) participated in this experiment. The experiments were conducted in two separate sessions with a two-week interval, and the dialogue pairs were not mixed in the same session. Each subject imitated real-life conversations with the experimenter based on the dialogues. Dialogues were produced three times and recorded in a sound-proof booth in the Stanford Phonetics Laboratory. The target sentences were prosodically transcribed in Korean ToBI (Jun 2000) by two annotators. The average transcription agreement on prosodic boundaries was 96 percent.[1]

---

[1] According to Jun (2000), Korean has two major prosodic phrasing boundaries, AP (accentual phrase) and IP (intonational phrase). An AP is smaller than an IP but larger than a phonological word, which is usually composed of a lexical item plus a case marker or postposition in Korean. The default AP tonal type is LHLH.

3.2. Results

The results of the production study are summarized in Table 1, which shows that speakers used distinct prosodic cues to mark syntactic boundaries very consistently. There was also some variability in the use of prosody. In general, however, speakers reliably used distinct prosody representing syntactic structures. The most frequently used prosodic phrasings of each reading and type are marked in bold in Table 1.

Ambiguity Types	Prosodic Phrasings	Reading (a)		Reading (b)	
		T1	T2	T1	T2
Type 1 N1+N2	**IP+IP**	**48**	**48**	0	0
	AP+AP	0	0	2	3
	AP (N1+N2)	0	0	**46**	**45**
Type 2 NP+Pred1+Pred2+N	**AP+IP+AP+AP**	**48**	**48**	0	0
	IP+AP+AP+AP	0	0	**41**	**43**
	IP+AP(Pred1+Pred2)+AP	0	0	7	5
Type 3 AdvP+Vmod+N+V	**IP+AP+AP+IP**	**41**	**43**	0	0
	IP+AP(Vmod+N)+IP	7	5	0	0
	AP+AP+AP+IP	0	0	**37**	**42**
	AP(AdvP+Vmod)+AP+IP	0	0	11	6
Type 4 N1+N2	**AP+AP**	**48**	**46**	5	6
	AP (N1+N2)	0	0	**43**	**42**
	IP+AP	0	2	0	0
Type 5 N1+Mod+N2	**IP+AP+AP**	**47**	**46**	0	0
	AP+AP+AP	1	1	**34**	**38**
	AP(N+Mod)+AP	0	1	14	10

Table 1. Summary of the Use of Prosody for Disambiguation in Types 1–5 (AP= Accentual Phrase, IP= Intonational Phrase (*see* footnote 1); T1= Transcriber 1, T2= Transcriber 2).

The following five figures show samples of prosodic realizations of each type of ambiguity. Figure 1 shows that the major prosodic difference in Type 1 was found after the first noun, N1, as we predicted. In the reading [NP. NP], significant final lengthening and a clear pause followed N1, indicating the existence of a large sentence boundary (a). On the other hand, the two nouns form one accentual phrase in the reading [Mod+N] (b).

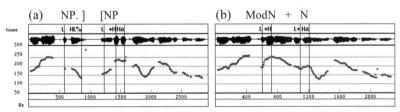

Figure 1. Utterances of Type 1: N1+N2

In Type 2, critical differences were found in the vicinity of Pred1. In the production of [SUBJ+Pred1]+[Pred2+N] (a), an IP boundary intervenes between Pred1 and Pred2. By contrast, a smaller prosodic boundary, AP, was found after Pred1, and an IP boundary was used after SUBJ in the production of SUBJ+[Pred1+Pred2+N] (b).

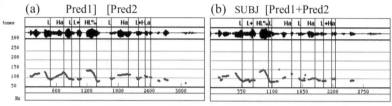

Figure 2. Utterances of Type 2: NP+Pred1+Pred2+N

Type 3 also showed prosodic phrasing differences reflecting the structural differences of the two readings. A large intonational boundary after AdvP marked the syntactic boundary, leading to the wide scope reading (a), while an accentual phrase boundary was used in the narrow scope reading (b).

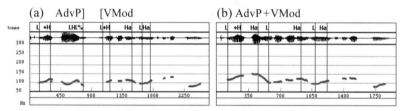

Figure 3. Utterances of Type 3: AdvP+VMod+N+V

In Type 4, subjects produced the noun sequence as one AP in the Poss+ N reading (b). Two separate phrases were used for the SUBJ+NP reading (a).

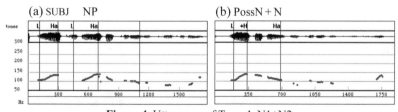

Figure 4. Utterances of Type 4: N1+N2

In Type 5, differences were found after the first noun, N1. [N1] and [Mod+N2] were separated by an IP in the (a) reading. In the (b) reading, however, an AP boundary was used to represent the syntactically closer relationship between the two.

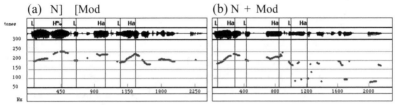

Figure 5. Utterances of Type 5: N1+Mod+N2

In sum, the production study showed that speakers were able to use prosodic cues to mark the structural differences between sentences. The use of prosody was fairly consistent across types and speakers.

3.3. Discussion

In the production study, we found a very close correspondence between prosody and syntactic structures in Korean. As shown in Table 1, however, it is not the case that all syntactic ambiguity types were uniformly well disambiguated by prosody. Speakers demonstrated larger prosodic variability in the production of the (b) readings in Types 3, 4, and 5. By contrast, Types 1 and 2 showed hardly any prosodic variability in either the (a) or the (b) readings. Note that in Type 4, the speakers used the (a) reading prosody (AP+AP) for the (b) reading syntax approximately 11 percent of the time. This suggests that some ambiguity types may not be prosodically disambiguated as proficiently by speakers as others.

Nonetheless, the results of Experiment 1 indicate a very systematic relationship between syntactic and prosodic boundaries. In a previous study, Jun (1993) proposed that the maximal projection boundaries (e.g. subject NP vs. predicate VP, topicalized or extracted XP, sentential AdvP, main vs. subordinate clause boundary, and coordinate clause boundary) are marked by either AP or IP. The results of this study support Jun's claim that the maximal projection boundaries match prosodic boundaries. However, speakers' use of an AP or IP does not seem to be entirely optional. Within sentences, speakers used AP more frequently than IP, but they tended to use IP if the next maximal projection contained a nested syntactic structure (i.e. a **phonologically heavy** structure). For example, in the (b) reading of Type 2, the subject was marked with IP when the following maximal projection included an embedded (relative) clause. On the other hand, the largest syntactic boundary within a sentence, between subject NP and predicate VP, was marked by a small boundary, AP, more often than IP in Type 4, where the next maximal projection only contained one word plus a particle. This suggests that the use of a prosodic boundary is sensitive not only to the syntactic structure but also to the phonological weight of the following constituent. The mapping relationship between syntax and prosody is summarized in (6).

(6) Mapping Relationship between Syntax and Prosody[2]

    a. Between sentences, an IP boundary with a pause is used.

    b. Within a sentence, a maximal projection boundary usually coincides with an AP boundary. However, speakers tend to use an IP boundary (with optional pause) instead of an AP if the next maximal projection contains a complex clause or is phonologically heavy.

In summary, a relatively systematic relationship held between prosody and syntax, but prosodic grouping did not mirror syntactic structure directly. We also found that there was more variation in the prosodic boundary marking of syntactic constituents within sentences (Types 3, 4, and 5) than of clause or sentence boundaries (Types 1 and 2).

4. Experiment 2: Comprehension

4.1. Method

The productions of the two subjects (one male and one female) who showed the fewest prosodic variations were used in the perception study. The sentences produced in the dominant types of disambiguating prosodic phrasings were selected as stimuli (see Table 1). In this experiment, only target (ambiguous) sentences were played to 97 subjects. After listening, the subjects then chose one of three responses for each: (i) reading (a), (ii) reading (b), and (iii) "I don't know." Subjects were native Korean speakers who used the Seoul dialect proficiently. The total number of test sentences was 80 (4 sentences × 2 readings × 2 speakers × 5 types). 64 filler sentences were also prepared. Filler sentences were segmentally or syntactically ambiguous sentences in different constructions. All 80 test sentences and 60 filler sentences were pseudo-randomized so that two versions of the same sentence spoken by two speakers did not appear one after the other. Four filler sentences were used as practice sentences before the experiment.

4.2. Results

As Table 2 illustrates, listeners were proficient at distinguishing different readings by prosody in every type. The correct response rates are far above chance level. The average correct response rates were 99 percent for Type

---

[2] From the production study, we found that if an IP was employed within sentences, speakers preferred to use a high boundary tone, (H%), whose tonal type is the same as the default final high tone in AP (Ha). Thus, critical difference was durational difference from the final lengthening marking IP.

1, 96 percent for Type 2, 94 percent for Type 3, 93 percent for Type 4, and 94 percent for Type 5.

Prosody		Correct Response Rate	Incorrect Response Rate	
			Wrong (a) or (b)	Don't Know (c)
Type 1	(a) NP. NP	99.4% (771)	0.4% (3)	0.2% (2)
	(b) ModN+N	99.1% (769)	0.5% (4)	0.4% (3)
Type 2	(a) ... Pred1]+[Pred2	95.1% (738)	2.3% (18)	2.5% (20)
	(b) ... [Pred1+Pred2...]	97.0% (752)	2.2% (17)	0.9% (7)
Type 3	(a)AdvP+[VMod+N]+V	90.5% (702)	7.5% (58)	2.1% (16)
	(b)[AdvP+VMod+N]+V	96.3% (747)	2.4% (19)	1.3% (10)
Type 4	(a) SUBJ+NP	86.2% (669)	11.2% (87)	2.5% (20)
	(b) PossN+N	99.3% (770)	0.5% (4)	0.2% (2)
Type 5	(a) N+[Mod+N]	89.9% (697)	7.8% (61)	2.3% (18)
	(b) [N+Mod]+N	98.9% (767)	0.6% (5)	0.5% (4)

Table 2. Summary of the Correct Comprehension Rates of Each Reading in Each Type (number of tokens in parentheses)

To make the responses measurable, those that correctly matched the interpretation based on prosody were scored as 1, while those that were incorrect were scored as 0. Subject-based means were used as the correct response rates. First, a two-way ANOVA (types × speakers) was performed to examine whether the degree of difficulty for subjects to disambiguate by prosody differed depending on ambiguity types. Results revealed that the ambiguity types were significantly different in difficulty [$F(4,384) = 15.4$, $p < .001$]. That is, listeners were not able to disambiguate all types of ambiguity equally proficiently; some types of ambiguity were much harder to disambiguate than others. In the analysis, we found neither a speaker effect on the correct response rates [$F(1,96) = .37$, $p = .55$] nor an interaction between type and speaker [$F(4,384) = .24, p = .9$].

To examine where the differences are from, a post-hoc test (Tukey HSD) was performed. We found four homogenous groups: Type1, Type2, Types 3 and 5, and Type 4. That is, Type 1 was the easiest for listeners to disambiguate, Type 2 was the next easiest, Types 3 and 5 were harder than Type 2, and Type 4 was the hardest.

Next, we further examined the data to determine whether subjects were equally proficient in identifying the two readings (reading (a) vs. reading (b)) in each type. Two-way ANOVA analyses (readings × speakers) were conducted in each type, and subject-based means were used as the dependent measure. The two readings in Types 1 and 2 were perceived similarly well (Type 1: [$F(1,96) = .88$, $p = .35$]; Type 2: [$F(1,96) = 1.98$, $p = .07$]). However, in Types 3, 4, and 5, we found a main effect of reading: listeners were better at identifying the (b) reading than the (a) reading (Type 3: [F(1, 96) = 13.9, $p < .001$]; Type 4: [F(1,96) = 68.3, $p < .001$]; Type 5: [F(1,96) = 41.3, $p < .001$]).This suggests that listeners had a preference for a particular reading (the garden-path effect) in Types 3, 4, and 5. The error response rates confirmed that these differences were from the subject's preference for the (b) readings (see Table 2). For example, in Type 4, the percentage of misjudgments of the (b) reading in the (a) prosody was nearly 11.2 percent, while the percentage of the (c) "I don't know" choice was only 2.5 percent. By contrast, misjudgments of the (a) reading in the (b) prosody did not show such bias (0.5 percent for (a) vs. 0.2 percent for (c)). This tendency also appeared in Types 3 and 5. In the ANOVA analyses, we found neither a speaker effect on the correct response rates nor an interaction effect between readings and speakers in any of the ambiguity types ($p > .05$ in all cases).

4.3. Discussion
Experiment 2 showed that listeners actively used prosodic phrasing information to resolve syntactic ambiguity. The average correct response rate was 95 percent. This indicates that prosodic boundary cues play a robust role in the sentence comprehension process. However, listeners were not equally adept at disambiguation across ambiguity types and readings. Some types of ambiguity were disambiguated easier than the others by prosody. In some types (3, 4, and 5), listeners favored a particular reading over the other even though disambiguating prosody was present.

Given the results of Experiments 1 and 2, the ambiguity types showing larger prosodic variations in Experiment 1 were harder to disambiguate by prosody in Experiment 2. Although all stimuli used in Experiment 2 were produced with disambiguating prosody, listeners could not successfully disambiguate the ambiguity types showing greater prosodic variation (Types 3, 4, and 5) as proficiently as the ambiguity types showing less prosodic variation in Experiment 1 (Types 1 and 2). This suggests that listeners may be aware of the unreliable relation between prosody and syntactic structure in ambiguity types such as Types 3, 4, and 5. They may also have had some difficulty choosing the meaning of a structurally ambiguous sentence when they linked prosodic cues to corresponding syntactic structure. Possibly, experience as speakers made them unsure of whether a particular prosodic phrasing truly corresponds to the syntactic structure in such cases.

As mentioned above, we also found that listeners showed some preference for a particular reading in Types 3, 4, and 5, which in turn seems to be the main reason behind the difficulty found in these types. As Table 2 shows, the correct response rates for reading (a) in Types 3, 4, and 5 (90.5 percent, 86.2 percent, and 89.9 percent, respectively) were relatively lower than those in Types 1 and 2 (99.4 percent and 95.1 percent, respectively). By contrast, the correct response rates for reading (b) in Types 3, 4, and 5 (96.3 percent, 99.3 percent, and 98.9 percent, respectively) were as high as those in Types 1 and 2 (99.1 percent and 97 percent, respectively).

Thus, we may ask where this preference comes from and why only some types of ambiguity showed such a preference. We suggest that the preference is due to the garden-path effect favoring one structure over the other.[3] That is, prosody and syntactic preference are interacting with each other in determining the ultimate parsing decision. As far as why only particular types of ambiguity showed such interactions, one possible explanation can be found in the relatively unreliable relations between prosody and syntactic structure in Types 3, 4, and 5 in Experiment 1. This would mean that listeners were not able to overcome the influence of the syntactic preference in parsing decisions. Another possibility is the phonetic features employed for disambiguation. In Types 1 and 2, the prosodic cues used for reading (a) were all IP boundaries with a large pause, which may eliminate the syntactic preference for reading (b). Our present study does not tell us which of the two possibilities is responsible for the results. Further study is needed to discover the sources of such differences.

5. Conclusion

In this study, production and comprehension experiments were carried out to see whether Korean speakers and listeners use prosodic cues for the resolution of syntactic ambiguity. In the production study, we found that speakers indeed use prosodic cues to mark syntactic structures consistently. We found some reliable mapping relationships between prosodic and syntactic structures. The comprehension study also showed that listeners were able to use prosodic cues in sentence processing. However, some ambiguity types proved to be more difficult than others in prosodic disambiguation.

References

Allbritton, D., G. McKoon, and R. Ratcliff. 1996. The Reliability of Prosodic Cues for Resolving Syntactic Ambiguity. *Journal of Experimental Psychology: Learning, Memory, and Cognition* 22:714–35.

Avesani, C., J. Hirschberg, and P. Prieto. 1995. The Intonational Disambiguation of Potentially Ambiguous Utterances in English, Italian, and Spanish. *Proceedings of the XIIIth International Congress of Phonetic Sciences*. Vol. 1:174–7.

---

[3] The garden-path effect refers here to a general preference for a certain syntactic structure over the other. We do not mean that the preferred structure must be consistent with the minimal attachment and late closure principles proposed by Frazier (1987). See Frazier and Rayner 1988 on the garden-path effect in head-final languages. For other explanations, see MacDonald, Permutter, and Seidenberg 1994.

Beach, C. 1991. The Interpretation of Prosodic Patterns at Points of Syntactic Structure Ambiguity: Evidence for Cue Trading Relations. *Journal of Memory and Language* 30:644–63.

Choi, Y., and R. Mazuka. 2003. Young Children's Use of Prosody in Sentence Parsing. *Journal of Psycholinguistic Research* 32:197–217.

Cooper, W., and J. Paccia-Cooper. 1980. *Syntax and Speech.* Cambridge: Harvard University Press.

Frazier, L. 1987. Sentence Processing: A Tutorial Review. *Attention and Performance,* ed. M. Coltheart, 559–86, Hillsdale, N.J.: Erlbaum.

Frazier, L., and K. Rayner. 1988. Parametrizing the Language Processing System: Left- vs. Right-Branching within and across Languages. *Explaining Language Universals*, ed. J. Hawkins, 247–79. Oxford: Blackwell.

Jun, S. 1993. The Phonetics and Phonology of Korean Prosody. Doctoral dissertation, Ohio State University.

Jun, S. 2000. K-ToBI Labeling Conventions (Version 3). *Speech Sciences* 7:143–69.

Kjelgaard, M., and A. Speer. 1999. Prosodic Facilitation and Interference in the Resolution of Temporary Syntactic Closure Ambiguity. *Journal of Memory and Language* 40:153–94.

Lehiste, I. 1973. Phonetic Disambiguation of Syntactic Ambiguity. *Glossa: An International Journal of Linguistics* 7:107–22.

MacDonald, M., N. Pearlmutter, and M. Seidenberg. 1994. Lexical Nature of Syntactic Ambiguity Resolution. *Psychological Review* 4:676–703.

Price, P., M. Ostendorf, S. Shattuck-Hufnagel, and C. Fong. 1991. The Use of Prosody in Syntactic Disambiguation. *Journal of Acoustical Society of America* 90:2956–70.

Schafer, A., and S. Jun. 2002. Effects of Accentual Phrasing on Adjective Interpretation in Korean. *East Asian Language Processing*, ed. M. Nakayama, 223–55. Stanford: CSLI.

Schafer, A., J. Carter, C. Clifton, and L. Frazier. 1996. Focus in Relative Clause Construal. *Language and Cognitive Processes* 11:135–63.

Schafer, A., S. Speer, P. Warren, and D. White. 2000. Intonational Disambiguation in Sentence Production and Comprehension. *Journal of Psycholinguistic Research* 29:169–82.

't Hart, J., R. Collier, and A. Cohen. 1990. *A Perceptual Study of Intonation: An Experimental-Phonetic Approach to Speech Melody.* Cambridge: Cambridge University Press.

Venditti, J., and H. Yamashita. 1994. Prosodic Information and Processing of Complex NPs in Japanese. *MIT Working Papers in Linguistics* 24:375–91.

Interaction between Case Marking and the Inalienable Possession Relation in Korean Double Nominative Constructions

KYUNG SOOK SHIN*
University of Hawai'i at Mānoa

1. Introduction

Head-final languages such as Korean and Japanese have syntactic properties that can generate multiple local ambiguities during sentence processing for several reasons (Inoue and Fodor 1995). First, crucial sources of syntactic information such as verbs and complementizers appear late in the sentence, as we can see in the basic word order of subject–object–verb and relative clause–head noun. Second, word order is relatively free; for example, we can use object–subject–verb order as well as subject–object–verb order. Finally, arguments can be omitted in a sentence; for example, we can use a subject–verb or an object–verb pattern rather than a subject–object–verb pattern. Due to these syntactic properties, the parser may face multiple local ambiguities during processing head-final languages, such as whether a noun phrase is a subject or an object, and whether a noun phrase belongs to a main clause or an embedded clause (Miyamoto 2002, Kim 1999).

* This is a revised version of the paper presented at the 14th Japanese/Korean Linguistics Conference, which was later presented at the 79th Annual Meeting of the Linguistic Society of America. I would like to thank William O'Grady, Amy Schafer, and Ho-Min Sohn for their valuable comments and suggestions.

In head-final languages, case marking is an important source of information concerning sentence structures (Carlson and Tanenhaus 1988, Kim 1999, Miyamoto 2002). For example, a nominative case marker generally indicates the beginning of a new clause, since a nominative-marked noun phrase is the subject of its clause. Moreover, in a sequence of two nominative-marked noun phrases, the second one is typically taken to be the subject of a new clause (Uehara 1997, Miyaoto 2002), as shown in (1).

(1) Yenghi-ka [s Chelswu-ka   naka-ss-ta-ko]   malhayssta[1]
        -NOM   -NOM go out-PAST-MOOD-COMP say-PAST-DEC
     'Yenghi said Chelswu went out.'

In sentence (1), the first nominative noun phrase, *Yenghi*, is the subject of the main clause and the second nominative noun phrase, *Chelswu*, is the subject of the embedded clause.

Even though case marking is crucial for recovering the structure and meaning of sentences, there are still many local ambiguities in processing head-final sentences. A typical case causing local ambiguities involves a sequence of two noun phrases with the same case marker. For example, contrary to the generalization outlined above, the second nominative-marked noun phrase is not always the subject of a center-embedded sentence. Korean has monoclausal constructions that include two nominative noun phrases, as shown in (2) and (3).[2]

(2) Psych-Verb Construction
     Yenghi-ka   Chelswu-ka   coh-ta
        -NOM   -NOM   like-DEC
     'Yenghi likes Chelswu.'

(3) Possession Ascension Construction
     a. Inalienable Possession Relation
        Yenghi-ka   son-i   khu-ta
           -NOM   hand-NOM   big-(be)DEC
        'Yenghi has a big hand.' (Literally, 'As for Yenghi, (her) hand is big')

---

[1] In transcribing Korean sentences, I use the Yale Romanization system. In addition, the following abbreviations are used: ACC = accusative, DEC = declarative, INST = instructive, MOOD = mood marker, NOM = nominative, PAST = past tense.

[2] Apparently, there are some other types of double nominative constructions such as existential verb constructions, and quantifier constructions. This study, however, dealt with only psych-verb constructions and possession ascension constructions.

b. Alienable Possession Relation

    Yenghi-ka   apeci-ka   uysa-ta
    -NOM   father-NOM   doctor-(be)DEC
    'Yenghi's father is a doctor.' (Literally, 'As for Yenghi, (her) father
    is a doctor')

A sequence of two nominative noun phrases can be constituents of a psych-verb construction (as in (2)) and a possession ascension construction (as in (3)).[3] The two nominative noun phrases in the double nominative constructions manifest different types of semantic relations. *Yenghi* and *Chelswu* in the psych-verb construction in (2) enter into no plausible semantic relation, *Yenghi* and *hand* in the inalienable possession ascension construction in (3a) enter into an inalienable possession relation, and *Yenghi* and *father* in the alienable possession ascension construction in (3b) enter into an alienable possession relation.[4]

Thus, a sequence of two nominative noun phrases is temporarily ambiguous; the noun phrases can be taken to be parts of a monoclausal double nominative construction, or arguments of a biclausal construction, where the second noun phrase is the argument of an embedded clause, as shown in (4)–(6).

(4) No Semantic Relation

    a. Yenghi-ka Chelswu-ka coh . . .
       -NOM   -NOM like

    b. Yenghi-ka Chelswu-ka   coh-ta
       -NOM   -NOM like-DEC
       'Yenghi likes Chelswu.'

    c. Yenghi-ka [s Chelswu-ka   coh-ta-nun] sonye-lul manna-ss-ta
       -NOM   -NOM like-MOOD-REL girl-ACC meet-PAST-DEC
       'Yenghi met the girl Chelswu likes.' or 'Yenghi met the girl who
       likes Chelswu.'

---

[3] There have been many debates in the literature on the syntactic nature of the DNC. Studies have previously looked into the DNC in terms of the subject-predicate (Park 1982, Yim 1985), or the topic/focus-comment relation (Yang 1997, Yoon 1989).

[4] Inalienable possession manifests a body-part relation (e.g. *Yenghi's hand*), a part-whole relation (e.g. *table's leg*), an attribute-holder relation (e.g. *Yenghi's character*), a time-event relation (e.g. *yesterday's weather*), or a locative relation (e.g. *the patch's strawberry*), while alienable possession indicates an interpersonal relationship (*Yenghi's father*) or a possessor-possessee relationship (e.g. *Yenghi's book*) (Chappell and McGregor 1996, Nichols 1988). Interestingly, kin-terms, which are inalienable in some languages, are regarded as alienable in Korean.

(5) Inalienable Possession Relation

    a. Yenghi-ka   meli-ka   khu . . .
       -NOM head -NOM big-(be)

    b. Yenghi-ka   meli-ka   khu-ta
       -NOM head-NOM big-(be)DEC
       'Yenghi's head is big.'

    c. Yenghi-ka [s meli-ka   khu-n] sonye-lul   manna-ss-ta
           -NOM head-NOM big-REC girl-ACC meet-PAST-DEC
       'Yenghi met the girl whose head is big.'

(6) Alienable Possession Relation

    a. Yenghi-ka   appa-ka   uysa . . .
       -NOM father-NOM doctor

    b. Yenghi-ka   appa-ka   uysa-ta
       -NOM father-NOM doctor-(be)DEC
       'Yenghi's father is a doctor.'

    c. Yenghi-ka [s appa-ka   uysa-i-n]   sonye-lul manna-ss-ta
           -NOM father-NOM doctor-be-REC girl-ACC meet-PAST-DEC
       'Yenghi met the girl whose father is a doctor.'

In the above sentences the second nominative noun phrase (*Chelswu, head,* and *father*) can be interpreted either as a constituent of a double nominative construction, as in (5b) and (6b), or as the argument of an embedded clause, as in (5c) and (6c).

The purpose of this study is to investigate how Korean native speakers resolve the local ambiguity in a sentence containing a sequence of two nominative noun phrases. I focus on two questions. First, do subjects initially give a biclausal interpretation with the help of only the grammatical information associated with case markers, or do they temporarily favor a monoclausal interpretation based on the information of the possible existence of a double nominative construction? And second, how do the different types of semantic relations manifested by a sequence of two nominative noun phrases affect the initial interpretation of such sentences?

2. Experiment

2.1. Subjects

Fifty-four Korean native speakers participated in the experiment. Forty subjects were undergraduates either at Sogang University or at Ehwa Women's University, and the others were undergraduates or graduates at the University of Hawai'i. Since they had not participated in a self-paced reading task before, they did not notice the purpose of the experiment.

2.2. Materials

The test sentences consisted of 24 sets of center-embedded clauses containing a sequence of two nominative-marked noun phrases. These sentences were constructed by using a Korean corpus program from the 21st Century Sejong Project. Two types of center-embedded clauses were designed: relative clause constructions and adverbial clause constructions, as shown in (7).

(7) a. Unrelated Condition

    Mina-ka   Jinhi-ka   sakolo   tachyess-ten elkwul-ul

    -NOM   -NOM by accident was injured-REL face-ACC

    salmyesi an-ass-ta[5]

    gently hug-PAST-DEC

    'Mina gently hugged Jinhi's face, which was injured by accident.'

  b. Inalienable Condition

    Mina-ka   elkwul-i   sakolo   tachyess-ten Jinhi-lul

    -NOM face- NOM by accident was injured-REL   -ACC

    salmyesi an-ass-ta

    gently hug-PAST-DEC

    'Mina gently hugged Jinhi, whose face was injured by accident.'

  c. Alienable Condition

    Mina-ka   enni-ka   sakolo   tachyess-ten Jinhi-lul

    -NOM sister-NOM by accident was injured-REL   -ACC

    salmyesi an-ass-ta

    gently hug-PAST-DEC

    'Mina gently hugged Jinhi, whose sister was injured by accident.'

  d. Adverbial Condition

    Mina-ka Jinhi-ka   sakolo   tachye-se   elkwul-ul

    -NOM   -NOM by accident was injured-because face-ACC

    salmyesi an-ass-ta

    gently hug-PAST-DEC

    'Mina gently hugged (her) face since Jinhi was injured by accident.'

The relative clause constructions manifested three different types of sequences of two nominative-marked noun phrases: those in which no relation between the two noun phrases was plausible (the Unrelated Condition in (7a)), those in which there was a potential relation of inalienable possession (the Inalienable Condition in (7b)), and those in which there was a potential

---

[5] In the literature it is taken for granted that the second nominative noun phrase cannot be relativized when it is a body-part term. The relative clause, however, becomes natural when the verb is unaccusative.

relation of alienable possession (the Alienable Condition in (7c)). The center-embedded adverbial clause constructions contain a sequence of two nominative-marked noun phrases which do not enter into any plausible semantic relation (the Adverbial Condition in (7d)).

The test sentences are potentially ambiguous at the second noun phrase; they can be interpreted as monoclausal double nominative constructions or as biclausal center-embedded relative clause constructions. This local ambiguity can be solved when the head noun is encountered, as it provides the information that the sentence is a biclausal relative clause construction. The center-embedded adverbial clauses were included as controls in order to examine whether a relative clause marker causes more processing burden than an adverbial clause marker.

A Latin square design, which was used to present each condition of any particular set of test sentences in each list, generated four test lists. Each of the four test lists contained 24 test sentences and 48 fillers, which were randomized by using Excel. The test sentences in each list consisted of 6 tokens of each of the 4 conditions with a sequence of two nominative-marked noun phrases. The fillers included sentences with a variety of structures and different lengths (16 five-word sentences, 16 six-word sentences, and 16 seven-word sentences). Subjects were evenly assigned to four lists: thirteen subjects each to Lists 1 and 2, and fourteen subjects each to Lists 3 and 4.

2.3. Procedures

This study used PsyScope for a self-paced reading task, with each sentence presented word-by-word on a Macintosh computer. Table 1 depicts how each word in each type of sentence was presented on the computer monitor.

Frame 1	Frame 2	Frame 3	Frame 4	Frame 5	Frame 6	Frame 7
NP1-NOM	NP2-NOM	Adverb	Relative Cl Adverb Cl	Head Noun	Adverb	Verb
Mina-ka	Jinhi-ka/ elkwul-i/ enni-ka/ Jinhi-ka	sako-lo	tachyess-ten tachye-se	elkwul-ul/ Jinhi-lul/ Jinhi-lul/ elkwul-ul	salmye-si	anassta
Mina-NOM	Jinhi-NOM/ face-NOM/ sister-NOM/ Jinhi-NOM	by accident	was injured -Rel Cl was injured -because	face-ACC/ Jinhi-ACC/ Jinhi-ACC/ face-ACC	gently	hugged

'Mina gently hugged (a) Jinhi's face, which was injured by accident'
(b) Jinhi, whose face was injured by accident'
(c) Jinhi, whose sister was injured by accident'
(d) (her) face since Jinhi was injured by accident'

Table 1. Regions for the Self-Paced Reading Presentation

The subject was asked to press any button when s/he finished reading the word on the screen. At the point of pressing the button, the word disappeared and the next word appeared to the right of the previous word position. At the end of each sentence, a yes/no question appeared on a new screen to prevent the subject from pressing buttons carelessly without catching the meaning of each word. The subject was instructed to answer by pressing the <YES> or <NO> button; no feedback was given. The computer recorded the time between the onset of each new word and the next button press in milliseconds. It took about 30 minutes for each subject to finish the whole experiment.

2.4. Data Analysis

Each subject's responses on comprehension questions were analyzed to calculate the response accuracy. Reading times falling beyond cutoffs established for each subject at mean plus three standard deviations were replaced with those cutoff values. The number of trimmed reading times was less than 2.4% of the total of 9,072 data points. Repeated measures ANOVAs and paired t-tests were performed separately at each word position to examine the three types of semantic relations as a main factor.

2.5. Results and Discussion

The results showed that each subject gave more than 95 percent correct answers to a total of 70 comprehension questions, which means the subjects read the test words carefully.[6] Figure 1 shows the reading times per region. A repeated measures ANOVA showed no significant differences across the four conditions at the first word position ($F(3,53) = 1.414, p = .2373$).

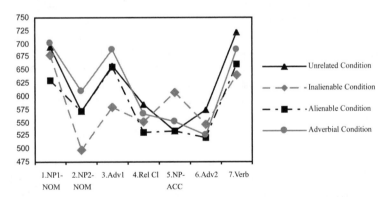

Figure 1. Reading Times for Each Region in the Embedded Clauses

---

[6] The percentages of correct answers for two subjects were low (75% and 79%), but the results of the experiment are not affected whether these subjects are excluded or not.

However, at the second word position, there was a significant difference among the four conditions ($F(3,53) = 6.927, p = .0001$). A paired t-test indicated that the Inalienable Condition showed the shortest reading times compared to the Unrelated Condition ($p = .0014$), the Alienable Condition ($p = .0018$), and the Adverbial Condition ($p < .0001$). This result suggests that the parser was sensitive to the type of possession relation and apparently needed less time to process the second nominative noun phrase in the inalienable possession pattern than in the other patterns. One possible interpretation of these results is that the second nominative noun phrase in the Inalienable Condition was initially interpreted as a constituent of a double nominative construction. On the other hand, the second nominative noun phrase in the other embedded clause constructions was interpreted as an argument of an embedded clause, and a clause boundary was inserted, which increased processing time.[7]

The reading pattern at the third word position was similar to that at the second word position. There was a significant difference among four conditions ($F(3,53) = 7.160, p < .0001$). Reading time for the third word in the Inalienable Condition was shorter than in the Unrelated Condition ($p = .0011$), the Alienable Condition ($p = .0099$), and the Adverbial Condition ($p < .0001$). This result may reflect the spillover effect of semantic relation, which appeared at the next word position. The reading pattern of each subject indicated that 26 percent of subjects showed shorter reading time in the Inalienable Condition than the other conditions at the second word position, 33 percent of subjects at the third word position, and 18.5 percent of subjects at both the second and third word positions. This indicates individual differences among subjects in relative timing between the button press and actual word comprehension.

At the fourth word position, a repeated measures ANOVA showed no significant difference among the three types of semantic relation ($F(3,53) = 1.526, p = .2062$). Interestingly, even though different types of complementizers such as the relative clause marker -$(n)un$ and the adverbial clause marker -se appeared at this region, no significant differences were found between relative clause constructions and adverbial clause constructions. This shows that the relative clause marker -$(n)un$ did not involve more processing cost than the adverb clause marker -se 'because'.

At the fifth word position, there was a significant difference in reading times among the four conditions ($F(3,53) = 3.507, p = .0144$). The Inalienable Condition showed the longest reading times compared to the Unrelated Condition ($p = .0062$), the Alienable Condition ($p = .0142$), and the Adver-

---

[7] Insertion of a clause boundary is known to increase processing load (Miyamoto 2002).

bial Condition ($p = .0394$). Evidently, the parser needed more time to shift its analysis of the inalienable possession relation pattern from a mono-clausal interpretation, in which the second nominative noun phrase is an argument of a double nominative construction, to a biclausal interpretation, in which it is an argument of an embedded relative clause.

At the sixth and seventh word positions, there was no significant difference in reading times among the four types of embedded clause constructions ($F(3,53) = .1657, p = .4.972; F(1,3) = 2.077, p = .1018$).

3. General Discussion

In this study two research questions were raised. First, are case markers the only source of information used in processing potentially ambiguous sentences which contain a sequence of two nominative-marked noun phrases, or does the possible existence of a double nominative construction also affect the initial interpretation of the sentences? Second, how are the different types of semantic relations manifested by the two nominative noun phrases relevant to the local ambiguity resolution?

The results of the experiment reveal two interesting facts about Korean sentence processing. First, Korean native speakers are sensitive to the type of semantic relations as well as the grammatical information associated with case markers in processing potentially ambiguous sentences containing a sequence of two nominative noun phrases. Different types of semantic relations resulted in different reading-time patterns.

Second, the reading time patterns of the test sentences indicated that an inalienable possession relation was utilized in a different way from the other semantic relations in processing sentences with a sequence of two nomina-tive-marked noun phrases. Compared to the other constructions, relative clauses with an inalienable possession relation showed the shortest reading time at the second nominative noun phrase and the longest reading time at the head noun of the relative clause, suggesting that the second nominative-marked noun phrase was initially interpreted as an argument of a double nominative construction and later reanalyzed as a part of an embedded clause. In other words, an inalienable possession relation induced parsers to take a sequence of two noun phrases with identical case markers as con-stituents of a double nominative construction.

Why does an inalienable possession relation have a different effect from the other types of relations in sentence processing? In an attempt to find an answer to this question, I examined the frequency of the three types of se-mantic relations (inalienable possession relation, alienable possession rela-tion, and irrelevant relation) in a Korean corpus consisting of 1,071,787 words from essays, novels, articles and editorials. There was a total of 329 double nominative constructions, and 55 were possession ascension constructions (51 inalienable possession and four alienable possession), while the rest were other types of double nominative constructions. In other words, the inalienable possession relation is used more frequently than the alienable possession relation in double nominative constructions, suggesting that frequency may be a factor in processing the ambiguous sentences.

Another possible factor is the prominence of the inalienable possession relation in Korean grammar. Even though possession is an important semantic concept in Korean grammar, the inalienable possession relation is relevant to more syntactic structures and processes than the alienable possession relation. Only the inalienable possession relation is allowed in double accusative constructions, and the second nominative noun phrase in double nominative constructions can be deleted, scrambled, clefted, etc., only when it enters into an inalienable possession relation with the first nominative noun phrase (Hong 1994, Shibatani 1976, Yim 1985). This highlights the fact that the two kinds of possessive relations behave differently in Korean grammar, suggesting that Korean native speakers are sensitive to the distinction between the two types.

These findings offer evidence that the parser processes sentences incrementally. It makes a parsing decision by rapidly integrating various sources of information—the grammatical information associated with case marking, the nature of the semantic relation between two nominative noun phrases, and the frequency of each type of semantic relation—and it revises its initial analysis when it turns out to be wrong, which results in an increase in processing cost.

Since double nominative constructions exist in a typologically varied set of languages, a study of their processing may shed light on how the parser employs language specific strategies in parsing. Whether other types of inalienable possession relations, such as body-part relations, part-whole relations, attribute-holder relations, time-event relations, and locative relations, are also relevant to the processing of a sequence of double nominative noun phrases is also an interesting question for future investigation.

References

Carlson, G. N., and M. K. Tanenhaus. 1988. Thematic Roles and Language Comprehension. *Syntax and Semantics 21*, ed. W. Wilkens, 263–300. New York: Academic Press.

Chappell, H., and W. McGregor. 1996. *The Grammar of Inalienability: A Typological Perspective on Body Part Terms and the Part-Whole Relation.* New York: Mouton de Gruyter.

Frazier, L. 1987. Sentence Processing: A Tutorial Review. *Attention and Performance*, ed. M. Coltheart. Hillsdale, N.J.: Erlbaum.

Frazier, L 1989. Against Lexical Generation of Syntax. *Lexical Representation and Process*, ed. W. D. Marslen-Wilson. Cambridge: MIT Press.

Frazier, L., and K. Rayner. 1982. Marking and Correcting Errors during Sentence Comprehension: Eye Movements in the Analysis of Structurally Ambiguous Sentences. *Cognitive Psychology* 14:178–210.

Gibson, E., and N. Pearlmutter. 2000. Distinguishing Serial and Parallel Parsing. *Journal of Psycholinguistic Research* 29:231–40.

Hirose, Y. 2002. Resolution of Reanalysis Ambiguity in Japanese Relative Clauses: Early Use of Thematic Compatibility Information and Incremental Processing. *Sentence Processing in East Asian Language*, ed. M. Nakayama. Stanford: CSLI.

Inoue, A., and J. D. Fodor. 1994. Information-Paced Parsing of Japanese. *Japanese Sentence Processing*, eds. R. Mazuka and N. Nagai. Hillsdale, N.J.: Erlbaum.

Keenan, E., and B. Comrie. 1977. Noun Phrase Accessibility and Universal Grammar. *Linguistic Inquiry* 8:63–99.

Kim, Y. 1999. The Effects of Case Marking Information on Korean Sentence Processing. *Language and Cognitive Processes* 14:687–714.

Miyamoto, E. T. 2002. Case Markers as Clause Boundary Inducers in Japanese. *Journal of Psycholinguistic Research* 31:307–47.

Nichols, J. 1988. On Alienable and Inalienable Possession. *In Honor of Mary Haas: From the Haas Festival Conference on Native American Linguistics*, ed. W. Shipley, 557–609. Berlin: Mouton de Gruyter.

O'Grady, W. 2005. *Syntactic Carpentry: An Emergentist Approach to Syntax*. Mahwah, N.J.: Erlbaum.

Park, B.-S. 1982. Double Subject Constructions Revisited. *Linguistics in the Morning Calm* 1:645–57.

Shibatani, M. 1976. Relational Grammar and Korean Syntax. *Language Research* 2: 241–51.

Trueswell, J. C., K. T. Michael, and M. G. Susan. 1994. Semantic Influences on Parsing: Use of Thematic Role Information in Syntactic Ambiguity Resolution. *Journal of Memory and Language* 33:285–318.

Uehara, K. 1997. Judgments of Processing Load: The Effect of NP-ga Sequences. *Journal of Psycholinguistics Research* 26:255–63.

Yim, Y.-J. 1985. Multiple Subject Constructions. *Harvard Studies in Korean Linguistics 1*, eds. S. Kuno et al., 101–12. Seoul: Hanshin.

Yoon, J. H-S. 1989. The Grammar of Inalienable Possession Constructions in Korean, Mandarin and French. *Harvard Studies in Korean Linguistics 3*, eds. S. Kuno et al., 357–68. Seoul: Hanshin.

Aspectual Asymmetries in Japanese: Insights from a Reaction Time Study

FOONG HA YAP*
Chinese University of Hong Kong

YUMI INOUE
Chinese University of Hong Kong

YASUHIRO SHIRAI
Chinese University of Hong Kong and Cornell University

STEPHEN MATTHEWS
University of Hong Kong

YING WAI WONG
Chinese University of Hong Kong

YI HENG CHAN
Chinese University of Hong Kong

1. Introduction

The concept of time is central to human thought and is often grammatically encoded in the languages of the world. Among the more common temporal devices, perfective and imperfective aspect markers have received considerable attention. Much is now known about the bounded vs. unbounded contrast between these two aspectual categories, and work within the psycholinguistic tradition has begun to focus on aspects of their processing. In a recent study involving English, Madden and Zwaan (2003) found that perfective constructions were processed faster than imperfective ones. For example, in a sentence-and-picture matching task, perfective constructions such as *He made a fire* yielded faster response speeds than imperfective constructions such as *He was making a fire*. According to Madden and Zwaan, one possible reason for this "perfective advantage" is that perfective sentences possess a telic endpoint, which arguably produces a more focused mental representation of the event. Imperfective sentences, on the other

* We thank Him Cheung, Karen Chong, Shoichi Iwasaki, Edson Miyamoto, Conrad Perry, Wai Ming Tsui, and Wei-ping Wu for their support and input. This research is funded by a Direct Grant for Research (#2010255) from the Chinese University of Hong Kong and a Competitive Earmarked Research Grant (#2110122) from the Research Grants Council of Hong Kong.

hand, are characterized by their durativity, relative homogeneity, and lack of a clear endpoint focus, and thus allow different readers to profile different phases of the imperfective situation or event. Thus, not only was the mean processing speed for imperfective sentences slower; their standard deviation was larger too.

Similar results have also been obtained for tenseless languages such as Cantonese and Mandarin Chinese (Chan et al. 2004, Yap et al. 2004). Thus, in Cantonese, perfective utterances such as *Popo zik zo gin laangsaam* ('Grandma **has** knitted a sweater') were processed faster than imperfective utterances such as *Popo zik gan gin laangsaam* ('Grandma **is/was** knitting a sweater'). The results for the two Chinese studies suggest that the perfective advantage is robust across tenseless languages as well.

The present study extends this investigation of aspectual asymmetries to Japanese. Our first objective is to determine whether the perfective advantage is also observed in verb-final languages such as Japanese. If aspectual asymmetry is confirmed, our second objective is to examine whether subtler aspectual distinctions also yield significant differences in processing speed. In other words, can we observe differences in processing speed not only **across** the perfective and imperfective domains, but also **within** each of these domains, namely, between perfective *V-ta* and *V-ta tokoro* constructions, and between imperfective *V-te iru* and *V-te iru tokoro* constructions?

2. Previous Studies on Aspectual Asymmetries

Our work builds on previous psycholinguistic studies such as Morrow 1990, Magliano and Schleich 2000, and Madden and Zwaan 2003. In this section, we briefly review findings from these studies that focus on **the reader's and hearer's mental representation of situations and events**.

A common assumption in psycholinguistics is that, when listening to a narrative, we construct situation models in the mind to represent the unfolding events. These situation models are multi-dimensional mental representations. Different types of linguistic elements contribute different types of information (e.g. time, space, causation, and agent intentionality) to these situation models. For example, Morrow (1990) reported that different prepositions identify different locations along a pathway, **not only spatially, but also temporally**. Magliano and Schleich (2000) found that different aspectual markers impose different interpretations on the temporal duration of activities. Crucially for the purpose of the present study, verbs with imperfective markers are more likely to be perceived as **ongoing** in subsequent context. On the other hand, verbs with perfective markers are more likely to be perceived as **completed** in subsequent context.

Magliano and Schleich (2000) further noted that in subsequent recall tasks, memory of verbs with imperfective marking decays at a slower rate.

This "lingering effect" is not surprising given that imperfective constructions lack a clear endpoint focus. One could say that verbs with perfective markings "disappear" (or rather dissipate) from working memory faster. What advantage might there be in such an arrangement? Apparently, more rapid "closure" in terms of memory activation allows perfective constructions to quickly give way to new sequences of events as narratives unfold in discourse time. The slower decay rate of imperfective constructions, on the other hand, makes them ideal for discourse backgrounding functions.

Madden and Zwaan (2003) showed that verbs with perfective marking are processed more accurately and significantly faster than verbs with imperfective marking. In their Experiment 1, participants were first shown either an imperfective sentence (e.g. *The man was drawing a picture*) or a perfective sentence (e.g. *The man drew a picture*). Participants were then shown a pair of contrastive pictures, one depicting an ongoing action and the other a completed action. For each sentence-and-picture sequence, participants were to choose the picture that matched the sentence they had just read. Results from this experiment reveal that readers were more accurate in matching perfective constructions with pictures depicting completed actions (76% accuracy rate). Performance for matched imperfective conditions was much poorer (56%)—only slightly above chance. Based on these results, Madden and Zwaan claimed that there is **perfective facilitation**, but not imperfective facilitation, in their forced choice comprehension task.

Madden and Zwaan's forced choice experiment (i.e. their Experiment 1) did not involve a reaction time component, but processing speed was measured in their Experiments 2 and 3. Results from these experiments reveal that perfective sentences yield **significantly faster reaction times** for **completed** pictures, while imperfective sentences did not yield faster reaction times for **ongoing** pictures. Based on these findings, Madden and Zwaan conclude that there is **perfective facilitation** in terms of processing speed, but imperfective facilitation is not significant, or even lacking.

Madden and Zwaan (2003) reported that their Experiment 1 scored highest in terms of power analysis for the perfective advantage phenomenon, suggesting that the forced choice design is likely to be the most robust for crosslinguistic replication. Given its greater sensitivity in distinguishing between the performance of perfective and imperfective constructions, we chose to retain the basic design of Experiment 1 to facilitate further crosslinguistic analyses. However, instead of visual stimuli (i.e. written sentences), we used **auditory stimuli** (i.e. spoken utterances) in our experiments. This is because auditory stimuli arguably provide more direct access to cognitive processing. We also added a **reaction time component** to our modified design. This yielded a single (and more economical) design that measures both accuracy and processing speed.

The results of our Cantonese and Mandarin Chinese studies also showed evidence of a perfective advantage, in that perfective utterances were processed significantly faster than imperfective utterances (Chan et al. 2004, Yap et al. 2004). However, unlike the English study, findings from our Chinese studies (based on accuracy scores) indicated both **perfective** facilitation and **imperfective** facilitation. Given that languages show variation in their tense-aspect systems, it remains to be seen whether there is a similar perfective advantage in verb-final languages such as Japanese, where tense-aspect information is typically provided much later toward the end of the clause.

3. The Present Study

In the present study, we first investigate whether a perfective advantage is also observed in Japanese. In addition, we investigate if more subtle aspectual asymmetries can be detected within the perfective domain and the imperfective domain. In the perfective domain, we compare the reaction times of -ta and -ta tokoro constructions, while in the imperfective domain, we compare the reaction times of -te iru and -te iru tokoro constructions.

3.1. Aspect Markers Tested in This Study

Of the two aspect markers that we here identify with the perfective domain, -ta can denote a wide range of perfective-related senses (see Bybee, Perkins and Pagliuca 1994), namely, anterior (or perfect) aspect, perfective aspect, and past tense, while -ta tokoro only denotes the perfect of recent past. The two aspect markers that we identify with the imperfective domain are no less complex: -te iru can denote imperfective readings such as progressive and habitual, but it can also yield resultative or perfect interpretations that imply or include a change-of-state or telic component; meanwhile -te iru tokoro is largely limited to an in-progress interpretation. In other words, -ta tokoro and -te iru tokoro have a narrower range of meaning than -ta and -te iru, respectively. In the present study, we will restrict tokens of -te iru to progresssive uses only. This allows us to focus our investigation on potential contrasts between canonical perfective and imperfective constructions.

Perfective uses of -ta and -ta tokoro are illustrated in (1) and (2), and imperfective uses of -te iru and -te iru tokoro in (3) and (4).

(1) Okaasan ga keeki o   yai-ta
    mother NOM cake ACC bake-PAST
    'Mother baked a cake.'

(2) Okaasan ga keeki o   yai-ta tokoro da
    mother NOM cake ACC bake-PERFECT
    'Mother has just baked a cake.'

(3) Okaasan ga keeki o yai-te iru
    mother NOM cake ACC bake-PROG
    'Mother is baking a cake.'

(4) Okaasan ga keeki o yai-te iru tokoro da
    mother NOM cake ACC   bake-PROG
    'Mother is (right in the middle of) baking a cake.'

Following Madden and Zwaan's (2003) experimental design, the present study focuses on the interaction of perfective and imperfective aspect markers with **accomplishment verbs** only. This decision was made because accomplishment verbs as a whole lend themselves more readily to either perfective or imperfective marking, the former yielding a reinforced endpoint reading, the latter yielding a stronger in-progress interpretation.

3.2. Methodology

The participants were 32 adult native-speakers of Japanese, most of them in their twenties. 25 of them were learning either Cantonese or Mandarin Chinese in Hong Kong, four were tourists visiting Hong Kong, and three were colleagues of the investigators. We used an utterance-and-picture matching task. As noted earlier, instead of visual stimuli (written sentences), **auditory stimuli** (spoken utterances) were used, and a reaction time component was added. The utterance-and-picture sequence is illustrated in Figure 1.

(1) The participant first hears   (2) The participant then sees a pair of
    a perfective or imperfective   pictures: one depicts an ongoing
    utterance.   event, the other a completed event.

Figure 1. Sequence of Utterance-and-Picture Matching Task
Used in Our Chinese and Japanese Studies

For the test items, 38 pairs of sentences were constructed, each describing an accomplishment according to the classification of situation types by Vendler (1957) and Smith (1991). We also tested the inherent semantics of each of the Japanese verbs using Shirai's (1998) classification tests. For each accomplishment event, one sentence was marked with a perfective aspect marker (*-ta* or *-ta tokoro*), and its counterpart marked with an imperfective aspect marker (*-te iru* or *-te iru tokoro*). The sentences were then recorded into sound wave files. The lengths of the recorded utterances were equalized pair by pair. These 38 pairs of perfective and imperfective utterances were matched by a corresponding 38 pairs of pictures drawn by a professional artist. For each picture pair, one picture depicted an in-progress stage of the action, while the other picture depicted its completed stage.

During the reaction time study, participants were first presented with an utterance describing an event, then immediately shown a pair of pictures— one depicting an ongoing action and the other a completed action. Each participant only heard either the perfective or the imperfective version of the utterance for each pair. The materials were counterbalanced, and each item was heard equally often as a perfective utterance and as an imperfective utterance. Each picture had an equal chance of appearing on the left or on the right. An additional seven pairs of utterances and pictures were prepared for a practice session, in which participants were told in Japanese that they would hear an utterance and then see two pictures, one on the left, and one on the right. They were asked to decide which picture best depicts the content of the utterance they heard and then press the corresponding key labeled on the keyboard. Throughout this practice phase and the experiment proper, the pictures appeared for 3 seconds after the utterance was played through. Stimuli were presented and reaction times were recorded using the Millisecond Software package INQUISIT. The mean reaction time for matched perfectives was compared to the mean reaction time for matched imperfectives, and the significance was tested by a series of ANOVAs.

3.3. Results and Discussion

3.3.1. Crosslinguistic Comparison

As shown in Table 1, the accuracy scores in the Japanese utterance-and-picture matching experiment were very high overall, with perfective *-ta* and *-ta tokoro* constructions showing only a slight advantage in percentage of correct matches than imperfective *-te iru* and *-te iru tokoro* constructions.

		Picture of Ongoing Action	Picture of Completed Action
Perfective Utterance	*V-ta*		96.48%
	V-ta tokoro		96.48%
Imperfective Utterance	*V-te iru*	91.41%	
	V-te iru tokoro	94.92%	

Table 1. Accuracy Percentages for Perfective and Imperfective Constructions in Japanese (Based on an Utterance-and-Picture Matching Task)

Both perfectives yielded a mean accuracy rate of 96.48%; the imperfectives fared only slightly lower, with *-te iru* at 91.41% and *-te iru tokoro* at 94.92%. These high accuracy scores imply strong and consistent facilitation from both perfective and imperfective morphology in the utterance-and-picture matching task. In this regard, Japanese shows a similar pattern to

Mandarin Chinese and Cantonese, but not to English as reported in Madden and Zwaan's (2003) study, where accuracy was only 56% for the imperfective aspect (see Table 2 for a crosslinguistic comparison).

	English	Cantonese	Mandarin	Japanese
Perfective Match	76%	87%	95%	96% *-ta* 96% *-ta tokoro*
Imperfective Match	56%	82%	91%	91% *-te iru* 95% *-te iru tokoro*
Type of Stimuli	*visual*	*auditory*	*auditory*	*auditory*

Table 2. Accuracy Percentages for Perfective and Imperfective Constructions in an Utterance-and-Picture Matching Task across Four Languages (English, Madden and Zwaan 2003; Cantonese, Chan et al. 2004; Mandarin Chinese, Yap et al. 2004; Japanese, Present Study)

Note that in the English study reported in Madden and Zwaan, after reading perfective sentences, participants were more likely to choose pictures showing completed events than pictures showing ongoing events. However, after reading imperfective sentences, **they chose either ongoing or completed pictures with about equal frequency** (Madden and Zwaan 2003). This is reflected in the 76% accuracy rate for perfectives vs. the 56% accuracy rate for imperfectives reported in their English study. In the case of our Chinese and Japanese studies, both perfective and imperfective facilitations were found. This means that after hearing perfective utterances, participants were inclined to choose completed pictures rather than ongoing ones, **and conversely, after hearing imperfective utterances, they tended to choose ongoing pictures instead of completed ones**. Note that the accuracy rates for Cantonese, Mandarin Chinese, and Japanese are high for both perfectives and imperfectives (above 80%).

The question arises why there should be this discrepancy between English and the other three languages we investigated. We argue this is because present progressive (*-te iru*) was used in our Japanese study, and "tenseless" (hence "pure") progressives (*gan2* and *zai*) were used in our Cantonese and Mandarin Chinese studies, while Madden and Zwaan used past progressive (*was/were V-ing*) in their English study. Thus, with the exception of Madden and Zwaan's study on English, all the other studies used the progressive imperfective, which is prototypically present progressive (Andersen and Shirai 1994) rather than past progressive. This would explain why imperfective facilitation was observed in our Chinese and Japanese studies, but not in Madden and Zwaan's English study. Table 3 highlights the nonprototypicality of the past progressive form used in the English study.

	English Madden and Zwaan 2003	**Cantonese** Chan et al. 2004	**Mandarin** Yap et al. 2004	**Japanese** the present study
Choice of Imperfective Construction	*was/were + V-ing*	*gan2*	*zai*	*-te iru -te iru tokoro*
Tense	past	—	—	nonpast/present
Aspect	progressive	progressive	progressive	progressive

Table 3. Choice of Imperfective Constructions Used in the Sentence/Utterance-
and-Picture Matching Tasks across Four Languages

Given that nonprototypical progressives were used in Madden and Zwaan's (2003) previous study on English, it would be useful in future work to test prototypical (i.e. present) progressives as well. To facilitate crosslinguistic comparison, the use of auditory stimuli in place of visual ones would be an important consideration. Such a replication study would, we suspect, show improved imperfective facilitation for English too.

3.3.2. Perfective Advantage in Reaction Time

While facilitation in terms of accuracy scores was robust for both perfective and imperfective Japanese utterances, it is worth noting that perfectives as a whole still retain a slight advantage over imperfectives, and this perfective advantage is much more visible in terms of processing speed (with statistical significance at $p < .001$ for English, Cantonese, and Mandarin; $p < .0001$ for Japanese *-ta* and *-te iru*).

		Picture of Ongoing Action	**Picture of Completed Action**
Perfective Utterance	*V-ta*		1512 ms (SD = 504)
	V-ta tokoro		1568 ms (SD = 519)
Imperfective Utterance	*V-te iru*	1809 ms (SD = 715)	
	V-te iru tokoro	1724 ms (SD = 734)	

Table 4. Mean Reaction Times for Perfective and Imperfective Constructions
in Japanese (Based on an Utterance-and-Picture Matching Task)

As shown in Table 4, the Japanese data show a clear perfective advantage in terms of processing speed. Perfective constructions with *-ta* and *-ta tokoro* yielded mean reaction times of 1512 ms and 1568 ms, respectively, while imperfective constructions with *-te iru* and *-te iru tokoro* yielded mean reaction times of 1809 ms and 1724 ms, respectively. All comparisons (except one; see §3.3.3) between perfective and imperfective yielded statistically significant differences ($p < .05$ between *-ta* (*tokoro*) and *-te iru* (*tokoro*); $p < .0001$ between *-ta* and *-te iru*; $p < .003$ between *-ta* and *-te iru* *tokoro*; and $p < .007$ between *-ta tokoro* and *-te iru*). Basically, imperfective constructions were slower overall, and their standard deviations much larger.

As highlighted in Table 5, Japanese is not alone in showing a perfective advantage in terms of processing speed. Other languages such as Cantonese and Mandarin likewise show evidence of this type of aspectual asymmetry. Also interesting is that languages differ in their range of processing speeds for equivalent constructions. For example, faster processing speeds were observed for Cantonese than for Mandarin Chinese (possible reasons for this observation are discussed in Yap et al. 2004). As seen from Table 5, equivalent constructions in Japanese yielded the slowest reaction times. This could in part be due to the delayed appearance of tense-aspect information, given that Japanese is a verb-final language. That is, temporal information related to telicity or boundedness could be processed much later in Japanese, and this could impose slightly longer processing times for this language. Future replication of this study with other verb-final languages such as Korean would be useful to help test this claim.

	English	Cantonese	Mandarin	Japanese
Perfective Match	NA	1118 ms (SD = 147)	1315 ms (SD = 320)	**1512 ms** *-ta* (SD = 504) **1568 ms** *-ta tokoro* (SD = 519)
Imperfective Match	NA	1253 ms (SD = 201)	1397 ms (SD = 339)	**1809 ms** *-te iru* (SD = 715) **1724 ms** *-te iru tokoro* (SD = 734)

Table 5. Mean Reaction Times for Perfective and Imperfective Constructions in an Utterance-and-Picture Matching Task across Four Languages (English, Madden and Zwaan 2003; Cantonese, Chan et al. 2004; Mandarin Chinese, Yap et al. 2004; Japanese, Present Study)

3.3.3. Asymmetries Among Related Aspect Markers

We now examine more closely the processing speeds of different aspectual markers in Japanese. Mean reaction times for the utterances were ranked according to aspectual markers as follows: *-ta* was fastest, followed by *-ta tokoro*, then *-te iru tokoro*, and finally *-te iru* (see Tables 4 and 5).

As mentioned earlier, there was a significant difference in reaction time between perfective *-ta* and imperfective *-te iru* constructions ($p < .0001$), as well as between perfective *-ta* and progressive *-te iru tokoro* constructions ($p < .003$). A significant difference was also found between perfect of recent past *-ta tokoro* and imperfective *-te iru* ($p < .007$). Overall, a significant difference ($p < .05$) was also found between the two perfective constructions combined (-*ta* and -*ta tokoro*) and the two imperfective constructions combined (-*te iru* and -*te iru tokoro*), confirming the perfective advantage.

However, no significant difference in reaction time was found between the two perfective constructions involving -*ta* and -*ta tokoro* ($p < .25$), or between the two imperfective constructions involving -*te iru* and -*te iru tokoro* ($p < .35$). There was also no significant difference between the perfective -*ta tokoro* and the imperfective -*teiru tokoro* constructions ($p < .1$).

If we map the observed processing times with what we know about grammaticalization pathways (Bybee et al. 1994), we would obtain the following interesting scenario (Figure 2).

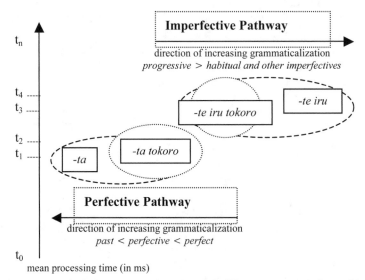

Figure 2. Mapping of Mean Reaction Times of Different Aspect Markers with Their Degree of Grammaticalization along Either the Perfective or Imperfective Pathway (t_1 is the mean reaction time for perfective -*ta*, t_2 for -*ta tokoro*, t_3 for -*te iru tokoro*, and t_4 for -*te iru*; see Table 4 for the means and standard deviations.)

Bybee et al. (1994) established that within the perfective domain, anterior or perfect aspect markers often grammaticalize further to become perfective aspect (and sometimes past tense) markers, while within the imperfective domain, progressive aspect markers often take on habitual, generic and other more general imperfective functions. Consistent with these cross-linguistic tendencies, Japanese perfective -*ta* is known to have evolved from perfect to perfective and past marking functions, with -*ta tokoro* being a recent development to mark perfect of recent past. Our findings are currently unable to distinguish significant differences in processing times between these two perfective markers when used with accomplishment verbs. Figure 2 above highlights their overlap both in range of processing speeds (measured via the vertical axis) and in range of grammatical functions (depicted via the horizontal perfective and imperfective trajectories). The lack of significant difference in processing speed suggests that perfective *-ta*, though more grammaticalized, still shares many features in common with perfect of recent past *-ta tokoro*, such as [+completion] and [+telicity].

The grammaticalization account for *-te iru* is more complicated, and still incomplete. Although on the basis of crosslinguistic tendencies we could posit a development from progressive to habitual for imperfective *-te iru*, and from resultative to anterior (perfect) for 'perfective uses' of *-te iru*, their exact relationship to each other still awaits further investigation, particularly from a diachronic perspective. However, the results from our Japanese study highlight a number of interesting possibilities. Recall that there was no significant difference in processing speed between *-te iru* and *-te iru tokoro* ($p < .35$). This is not surprising, given that the newer *-te iru tokoro* progressive marker forms a subset relationship with the older and more grammaticalized *-te iru* progressive imperfective. Clearly, the overlap between them is considerable, hence the lack of significant difference in processing speed.

Also of interest is the lack of significant difference between the young progressive marker *-te iru tokoro* and perfect of recent past marker *-ta tokoro*, since they are considered to belong to different aspectual domains, namely, the imperfective and the perfective categories, respectively. This does not mean that progressive *-te iru tokoro* and perfect of recent past *-ta tokoro* fail to show a perfective-imperfective contrast. It does suggest, however, that these two categories have features in common. One shared feature derives from the presence of the morpheme *tokoro* '(lit.) place', which in both aspectual constructions adds a temporal focus that can be called "contingency". Thus, with the addition of *tokoro*, the very general *-te iru* imperfective becomes progressive, past tense *-ta* becomes perfect of recent past, and nonpast *-ru* becomes proximative *-ru tokoro* 'be about to' (not examined in this study), all referring to the temporal contingency of the action.

4. Conclusion

The Japanese data confirm that there is both perfective and imperfective facilitation in utterance-and-picture matching tasks. This result differs from Madden and Zwaan's findings for English, but is consistent with our findings for Cantonese and Mandarin. We suggested that this may be due to the use of past progressive in the English study as opposed to the use of (default) present progressive for the other languages we studied. This needs to be tested by using present progressive for English speakers.

At the same time, we found that there is aspectual asymmetry in language processing favoring perfectives over imperfectives in Japanese. This asymmetry is observed with respect to both accuracy and speed, and is consistent with the "perfective advantage" observed in all the languages studied so far. We also observed that overall processing times were slower in Japanese than in the other languages studied. The SOV word order of Japanese could be a contributing factor here, in that aspectual cues related to telicity and boundedness get integrated later in the hearer's mental representation.

In this study we found no statistically significant aspectual asymmetries between the individual aspect markers -ta and -ta tokoro within the perfective domain, or between -te iru and -te iru tokoro within the imperfective domain. We interpret this to mean that aspect markers within the same domain typically share considerable overlapping features, and therefore fail to show significant contrast in processing speed. It is also possible, however, that we have not yet investigated aspectual functions within the same or related morphemes that are sufficiently distinct from each other. For example, in this study only progressive uses of -te iru were used. Whether aspectual asymmetry can be found between progressive and resultative uses of -te iru still awaits investigation.

References

Andersen, R. W., and Y. Shirai. 1994. Discourse Motivations for Some Cognitive Acquisition Principles. *Studies in Second Language Acquisition* 16:133–56.

Bybee, J., R. Perkins, and W. Pagliuca. 1994. *The Evolution of Grammar.* Chicago: University of Chicago Press.

Chan, Y. H., F. H. Yap, Y. Shirai, and S. Matthews. 2004. A Perfective Imperfective Asymmetry in Language Processing: Evidence from Cantonese. *Proceedings of the 9th International Symposium on Chinese Languages and Linguistics*, 383–91.

Madden, C. J., and R. A. Zwaan. 2003. How Does Verb Aspect Constrain Event Representation? *Memory and Cognition* 31:663–72.

Magliano, J. P., and M. C. Schleich. 2000. Verb Aspect and Situation Models. *Discourse Processes* 29:83–112.

Morrow, D. G. 1990. Spatial Models, Prepositions, and Verb-Aspect Markers. *Discourse Processes* 13:441–69.

Shirai, Y. 1998. The Emergence of Tense-Aspect Morphology in Japanese: Universal Predisposition? *First Language* 18:281–309.

Smith, C. 1991. *The Parameter of Aspect.* Dordrecht: Kluwer.

Vendler, Z. 1957. Verbs and Times. *Philosophical Review* 66:143–60.

Yap, F. H., Y. H. Chan, Y. Shirai, L. H. Tan, S. Matthews, and P. Li. 2004. The Perfective-Imperfective Asymmetry in the Human Mind: Evidence from Cantonese and Mandarin. Paper presented at the 28th International Congress of Psychology, Beijing.

Part III

Historical Linguistics

The Emergence of the Complementizer *no* in Japanese Revisited

YUMIKO NISHI*
Cornell University

1. Introduction

The particle *no* in Japanese has three grammatical functions: genitive, pronominal, and complementizer, which arguably developed in the order presented. In particular, it has been claimed that the complementizer *no* derived from the post-predicate pronominal *no* (e.g. Horie 1998, Nakayama 1950, Yanagida 1993b, Yoshimura and Nishina 2004). However, historical facts and cross-linguistic data seem to leave open the possibility that the complementizer *no* did not directly derive from the pronominal *no*. In this paper, I suggest that the complementizer *no* followed a distinct path from the development of other functions of *no*, which can be accounted for by the structural discontinuity observed between the properties of pronominal *no* and those of complementizer *no*. As an alternative account to the single, linear developmental path approach to the development of different func-

* I am grateful to Yoshihito Dobashi, Cristina Dye, Kaoru Horie, Carol Rosen, Kyoko Selden, John Whitman, and Foong Ha Yap for their invaluable comments and discussions on the earlier versions of the paper. I also thank the participants at the 14th Japanese/Korean Linguistics Conference, especially to Shigeru Miyagawa and Kunio Nishiyama. All remaining errors are mine.

tions of *no*, I propose two distinct paths: the **determiner path** and the **complementizer path**.

2. Grammatical Functions of *no*

The particle *no* has three grammatical functions: genitive, pronominal, and complementizer. Modern Japanese examples of genitive *no* are shown in (1).[1]

(1) a. Hanako **no** hon   b. sakura **no** ki
       GEN book   cherry GEN tree
    'Hanako's book'   'cherry tree'

(2) shows Modern Japanese examples of pronominal *no*, where each *no* refers to a specific entity. There are four types of pronominal *no*. The pronominal *no* follows a nominal in (2a), an adjectival in (2b), a postpositional phrase in (2c), and a verbal predicate in (2d).

(2) a. Hanako **no**   c. uti   kara **no**
           one   home from one
       'Hanako's one'   'one from home'
    b. akai **no**   d. kinoo   kai-ta   **no**
       red one   yesterday write-PAST one
       'red one'   'the one that (I) wrote yesterday'

Finally, (3) shows a Modern Japanese example of complementizer *no*.

(3) yuki ga huru **no**   o   mi-tei-ta
    snow NOM fall COMP ACC watch-ASP-PAST
    '(I) was watching the snow fall.'

3. A Linear Developmental Path of *no*

Although the development of these different functions of *no* has caught the attention of researchers in traditional Japanese linguistics for several decades, the developmental path of *no* has not been explicitly presented in a systematic way. In one attempt, Horie (1998:172) proposes a developmental path that is illustrated in (4), and provides an integrative account by introducing the perspectives of cognitive linguistics and grammaticalization theory.[2]

---

[1] For a list of abbreviations used in the examples in this paper, see the Appendix.

[2] Horie's (1998) analysis relies on data from Nakayama (1950) and *Nihon kokugo daijiten* [Japanese language dictionary].

(4) [Taroo **no** hon]   [Taroo **no**]   [Ø katta] **no**   [ame-ga hutta] **no**
   'Taro's book'   'Taro's' 'the one that (I) bought'   'that it rained'
    genitive   >   pronoun   >   pronoun   >   sentential nominalizer

The developmental path Horie proposes goes from genitive to pronoun following a nominal, to pronoun following a predicate, and then finally to complementizer, which he refers to as a sentential nominalizer.

As regards the rise of the complementizer, Yoshimura and Nishina (2004:59) make a more specific claim that the complementizer *no* derived from a categorical reanalysis of what they claim was a demonstrative pronominal *no*, as shown in (5), just like the emergence of complementizer *that* in Germanic languages.

(5) $[_{IP} i...]$ pro$i$ > $[[_{IP} ...]Ø]$ > $[_{DP} [_{IP} ...pro...][_D no]]$ > $[_{CP} [_{IP} ...][_C no]]$

They argue that the change from pronoun *no* to complementizer *no* involved semantic bleaching, with *no* losing its referentiality, that is, the feature [+ deictic].

4. Problems with the Linear Account

4.1. Timing of Emergence

The proposed paths of the diachronic changes discussed above rely heavily on work in traditional Japanese linguistics and are not without problems.

First, the path from post-predicate pronominal *no* to complementizer *no* is not actually attested by the actual historical data. For example, Nakayama (1950) states that the post-predicate pronominal *no* "probably" appeared late in the 16th century, admitting that this has not yet been attested by historical data. Yanagida (1993b) also argues for the "pronominal to complementizer" path. He speculates that the emergence of pronominal *no* took place earlier than that of complementizer *no*, simply because post-predicate pronominal *no* is similar in function to post-nominal pronominal *no*.

However, according to data in Yoshikawa (1950), the earliest credible examples of *no* as post-predicate pronominal and complementizer both appear in the same literary text, the 1642 *Toraakirabon kyōgen*. Yoshikawa cites the examples shown in (6) and (7) from this text.

(6) sendo   soti e   watai-ta **no** wa nan to si-ta   zo
    the other day you DAT pass-PAST PRON TOP what QT do- PAST EMPH
    'What did you do with the thing that I passed on to you the other day?'

(7) hudan   ogamiyaru **no** ni   sei takaku-ba . . .
    constantly pray-HON COMP DAT height tall- COND
    'In praying, if it is tall, it would probably be . . .'

In fact, Yoshikawa (1950) claims that the complementizer *no* seems to have existed already when post-predicate pronoun *no* was first attested. Given that both post-predicate pronominal *no* and complementizer *no* appeared at around the same time in the early 17th century, it seems difficult to claim that post-predicate pronominal *no* pre-dated complementizer *no*. We lack the evidence to confirm that one derived from the other.

Another relevant point is the timing of the rise of the post-predicate pronominal *no* and the complementizer *no*. The genitive *no* and the post-nominal pronominal *no* are attested as early as the 8th century. However, as we have seen earlier, the development of post-predicate pronominal *no* and complementizer *no* took place early in the 17th century. According to the historical facts discussed above, we can reconstruct the developmental path of *no* as in (8).

(8) GEN and post-nominal PRON > post-predicate PRON and COMP
    8th century   17th century

Here, we notice that there is a significant time gap between the attestation of the first two *no*s and the latter two *no*s. In other words, there is a time gap between the rise of the post-predicate pronominal *no* and other types of pronominal *no*s. Given that pronominal functions already existing in 8th century, it seems puzzling that the post-predicate pronoun *no* developed all of a sudden around the early 17th century when complementizer *no* also developed, after an interval of nine centuries in which *no* was restricted to post-nominal uses. Given these problems, it does not seem to be the case that the complementizer *no* is derived directly from post-predicate pronominal *no* as has been proposed in the research cited above.

4.2. Nondemonstrative Pronoun *no*

Yoshimura and Nishina (2004) refer to pronominal *no* as a demonstrative pronominal, and they analyze the development of *no* in the same vein as the development of the demonstrative pronoun *that* in English. However, we cannot automatically treat the case of Japanese *no* as parallel to the development of *that* in English. In English, complementizer *that*, which is a demonstrative pronoun, seems to have derived from pronoun *that* (see, e.g., Kiparsky 1995), but pronominal *no* in Japanese is not a demonstrative pronoun.

Pronominal *no* is a bound morpheme with a function close to that of *'s* in English. In Japanese, *kore*, *sore*, and *are* are the demonstrative pronouns. Examples of the demonstrative pronoun *are*, which is an equivalent of *that* in English, are given in (9).

(9) a. **Are** o mite.   b. **Ano**   hon   o mite.
       that ACC look   that:ADNM book ACC look
       'Look at that!'   'Look at that book.'

In contrast, *no* is clearly not a demonstrative pronoun, as shown in (10).

(10) a. ***No***   o mite.   b. ***No*** hon   o mite.
        PRON ACC look   PRON book ACC look

This suggests that the derivation of complementizer *no* from pronominal *no* cannot be straightforwardly justified by extending the arguments for the development of complementizer *that* in English. The distinction between demonstrative and nondemonstrative pronoun becomes important as we look into cross-linguistic data in §5.

4.3. Claims

To resolve the issues discussed above, I make the following two claims: (1) post-predicate pronominal *no* and complementizer *no* developed concurrently, and (2) it is unlikely that the complementizer *no* is derived directly from a nondemonstrative or non-*wh* pronoun simply by categorical reanalysis. I first provide evidence from cross-linguistic data, and then from semantic and syntactic analysis of the different types of *no*.

5. Cross-Linguistic Data

In their study of grammaticalization, Heine and Kuteva (2002) list the cases of complementizers that derived from demonstrative pronouns and w-questions (*wh*-pronouns), along with others, as shown in (11). However, there seem to be no known cases where a complementizer has derived from a non-demonstrative or non-*wh* pronoun.

(11)   allative
       demonstrative
       matter
       w-question   > complementizer
       relative
       resemble
       say
       thing

Simpson and Wu (2001) also argue that pronouns (determiners) can become Infl-elements, but not complementizers. What is more interesting is that, as different stages of grammaticalization process, Mandarin *de*, Cantonese *ge*, Hokkien *e*, Malay *punya*, and Singlish *one* share strikingly similar properties to Japanese *no*, yet none of them developed a function as a complementizer (Yap et al. 2002), as shown in Table 1.

Language	GEN	PRONOMINAL PHRASAL	CLAUSAL	REL	CLEFT	COMP	STANCE
Japanese (no)	✓	✓	✓	*	✓	✓	✓
Mandarin (de)	✓	✓	✓	✓	✓		✓
Cantonese (ge)	✓	✓	✓	✓	✓		✓
Hokkien (e)	✓	✓	✓	✓	✓		✓
Malay (punya)	✓	✓	✓		✓		✓
Singlish (one)	✓	✓	✓		?		✓

Table 1. Functions of Japanese *no* and Comparable Items in Other Languages (*Early Modern Japanese)

Yap et al. (2002) also refer to the case of Korean, in which the genitive marker *uy* has never been used as a complementizer nor even as a pronoun. Given these historical and cross-linguistic facts, it is difficult to establish that Japanese *no* extended its function from post-predicate pronoun to complementizer. Rather, cross-linguistic data seem to suggest structural discontinuity between pronominal *no* and complementizer *no*.

6. Two Types of Post-Predicate *no*

Although post-predicate pronominal *no* and complementizer *no* appear to be similar in that they both follow a predicate, they have distinct semantic and syntactic properties.

6.1. Difference in Meaning

In the case of the post-predicate pronoun, *no* has a specific entity as a referent, which is heavily context-dependent. In (12), *no* refers to a specific set of clothes that can be identified from the context.

(12)   kinoo   kat-ta   **no**   o   ki-ta
        yesterday buy-PAST PRON ACC wear- PAST
        '(I) wore the one that I bought yesterday.'

In contrast, complementizer *no* does not have a specific entity as a referent; it represents a proposition that is denoted within the clause that *no* follows as in (13), where *no* represents the proposition 'it rains'.

(13)   ame ga huru **no**   o   mi-tei-ta
        rain NOM fall COMP ACC see-ASP-PAST
        '(I) was watching the rain's falling' (i.e. '(I) was watching the rain fall).'

6.2. Difference in Structure

The two *no*s discussed above are different in terms of their syntactic properties as well. The sentence with pronominal *no* has a structure shown in (14).[3]

(14) kinoo kat-ta **no** o ki-ta

  [$_{DP}$ [$_{CP}$ OP$_i$ [$_{IP}$ kinoo t$_i$ kat-ta]] [$_{DP}$ **no**]] o ki-ta

The CP *kinoo katta* 'yesterday bought' adjoins to DP and constitutes a DP. However, in the case of complementizer *no*, *no* selects the preceding IP and together with it forms a CP, as shown in (15). Here, IP is a complement of the C that is realized as *no*. This is distinct from the case of pronominal *no* shown in (14), in which they each form a DP.

(15) ame ga furu **no** o mi-tei-ta

  [$_{CP}$ [$_{IP}$ ame ga furu] [$_C$ **no**]] o mi-tei-ta

Thus, the DP in (14) refers to an object, as DPs in general do, while the CP in (15) represents propositional content or an event, as CPs in general do. That is, the structural difference proposed here directly reflects the semantic difference between the two post-predicate *no*s that we examined earlier.

It is important to note here that the post-predicate pronominal *no* is both semantically and syntactically different from complementizer *no*, but it is very similar to other types of pronominal *no*s and also to genitive *no*. All pronominal *no*s share with genitive *no* the property of a modifying relationship within DP, while the construction in which complementizer *no* appears does not. Thus, I suggest that the complementizer *no* is purely grammatical (i.e. C, a head of CP) and is distinct from the pronominal *no*, which is more lexical and thus close to other nominalizers such as *koto* 'matter', *mono* 'thing', *toki* 'time', *tokoro* 'place', etc.

Given these semantic and syntactic differences between complementizer *no* and other functions of *no*, in addition to the historical and cross-linguistic data we have observed earlier, it is difficult to locate the rise of complementizer *no* along the same developmental path as the other functions. It seems more probable that post-predicate *no* and complementizer *no* developed concurrently, and that complementizer *no* developed as an analogy (or "extension"; see Harris and Campbell 1995) from pronominal *no*, rather than as a reanalysis. The loss of distinct adnominal inflection that took place in the 16th century was probably the major trigger for the rise of complementizer *no* and pronominal *no* (see, e.g. Shinta 1976).

---

[3] Kayne (1994) proposes that the N-final relative clause structure is derived by moving the relative clause to adjoin to DP so that the relative clause precedes the head noun. The present analysis shown in (14) is similar to Kayne's in that the relative clause is adjoined to DP, preceding the head DP.

7. An Alternative Account: The Dual Path Approach

Thus, I propose two distinct paths for the development of different grammatical functions of *no* as shown in Figure 1.

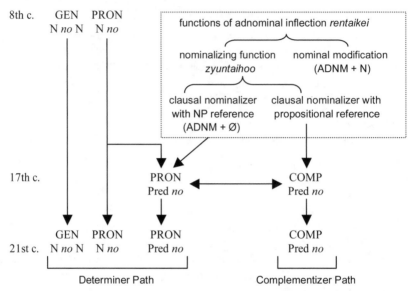

Figure 1. Dual Path Development of *no*

The above dual path approach well explains the distinct properties and the timing of the rise of complementizer *no* that cannot be explained by the single linear path approach. It also accords with cross-linguistic data.

I suggest that this dual path approach is motivated by the fact that there are two types of *no*: one constitutes a DP, and the other a CP, as discussed earlier. One is the path from the two post-nominal functions: genitive and post-nominal pronoun, to post-predicate pronoun, which I call the determiner path. Independent of this determiner path, the use of *no* as a complementizer emerged due to the loss of distinct adnominal inflection, which is a major shift in the morphology of predicates in Japanese that took place in the 16th century.[4] It seems that the function of *no* was extended to two contexts that were previously marked by adnominal inflection: clausal nominalization with NP reference, as in (16a), and clausal nominalization with pro-

---

[4] The relationship between the loss of distinct adnominal inflection and the emergence of post-predicate *no* is still a controversial issue in the field. See, for example, Horie 1995, Shinta 1976, 1987, Yanagida 1993, and Yoshimura and Nishina 2004.

positional reference, as in (16b), which are referred to as *zyuntaihoo* in traditional Japanese linguistics.[5]

(16) a. Clausal Nominalization with NP Reference
      [sakimori ni   iku]   wa   tagase   to tou hito   o . . .
      guarding to go.ADNM TOP whose.husband QT ask person ACC
      '. . . (person) asking whose husband it is that is going to coast guard
      service'
      (*Man'yōshū*, vol. 20, 4425; cited in Kondō 1981)

      b. Clausal Nominalization with Propositional Reference
      [sakura no hana   no   tiru]   o   yomeru
      cherry GEN flower NOM fall.ADNM ACC make.poem.ASP
      '(a poem) that composed on cherry blossoms scattering'
      (*Kokinwakashū*, 85, kotobagaki; cited in Kondō 1981)

This extension was simultaneous, and there may have been interaction between the two. Specifically, we might hypothesize that there was some kind of analogy at work between the derivations of post-predicate pronominal *no* and post-nominal pronominal *no*. This process may be explained by Horie's (1998) analysis of the structural and conceptual continuity observed among the properties of different functions of *no*.[6] But a complete understanding of the process will require more intensive study of material from around the 17th century when the two post-predicate patterns emerged.

8. Conclusion

I have proposed that the complementizer *no* is not directly derived from the pronoun *no*. My argument rests on a demonstration of a structural discontinuity between the two as well as on evidence from historical and crosslinguistic data.

    As mentioned earlier, both genitive and post-nominal pronominal *no* ex-

---

[5] There are two functions of adnominal inflection (*rentaikei*): a nominalizing function (*zyuntaihoo*) and nominal modification. An example of the nominalizing function is shown in (16), and the following is an example of nominal modification:
Nominal modification (Adnominal + N):
[siroku   sakeru]   hana
whitely bloom.ADNM flower
'a flower that blooms in white'

[6] Horie (1998) claims that the structural relatedness presented by *no* mirrors conceptual continuity, by introducing an ontological continuum based on Lyons (1977). He argues that three levels of ontological status can be semantically linked to the different functions of *no*, since genitive *no* characterizes a relationship between two first-order entities, pronoun *no* normally encodes first-order entities, and the sentential nominalizer (i.e. complementizer) *no* encodes both second and third-order entities. For details, see Horie (1998:170–5).

isted as early as the 8th century, and it is not the case that we have historical evidence that confirms that one is older than the other. However, it seems highly plausible to assume that genitive *no* and post-nominal pronominal *no* are closely related in terms of historical development, considering the lack of unidirectionality between the genitive and the post-nominal pronoun path claimed by Yap et al. (2002, 2004), which is apparent in the case of Malay and Chinese. What should be stressed here is not the possible developmental order between the two, but that it is this functional similarity that allows one to derive from the other, disregarding the direction. And in contrast, it is the functional discontinuity between determiners and complementizers that prohibits languages from deriving a complementizer from non-demonstrative or non-*wh* pronominals of genitive origin in the process of grammaticalization. The remaining questions of how the rise of the complementizer interacts with the loss of the distinct adnominal inflection, and why *no* came to be used as a complementizer, are discussed in Nishi 2005.

Appendix: Abbreviations

ACC	Accusative	DAT	Dative	PRON	Pronominal
ADNM	Adnominal	EMPH	Emphatic	REL	Relativizer
ASP	Aspect	GEN	Genitive	QT	Quotation
COMP	Complementizer	HON	Honorific	TOP	Topic
COND	Conditional	NOM	Nominative		

References

Harris, A. C., and L. Campbell. 1995. *Historical Syntax in Cross-Linguistic Perspective*. Cambridge: Cambridge University Press.

Heine, B., and T. Kuteva. 2002. *World Lexicon of Grammaticalization*. Cambridge: Cambridge University Press.

Horie, K. 1995. What the Choice of Overt Nominalizer *No* Did to Modern Japanese Syntax and Semantics. *Historical Linguistics 1993*, ed. H. Andersen, 191–203. Amsterdam: John Benjamins.

Horie, K. 1998. On the Polyfunctionality of the Japanese Particle *No*: From the Perspectives of Ontology and Grammaticalization. *Studies in Japanese Grammaticalization*, ed. T. Ohori, 169–92. Tokyo: Kurosio Publishers.

Kayne, R. S. 1994. *The Antisymmetry of Syntax*. Cambridge: MIT Press.

Kiparsky, P. 1995. Indo-European Origins of Germanic Syntax. *Clause Structure and Language Change*, eds. A. Battye and I. Roberts, 179–95. Oxford: Oxford University Press.

Kondō, Y. 1981. Chūkogo no juntaikōzō ni tsuite. *Kokugo to Kokubungaku* 58(5): 18–31.

Lyons, J. 1977. *Semantics*, vol. 2. Cambridge: Cambridge University Press.

Nakayama, T. 1950. Juntaijoshi *no* no tsūjiteki kenkyū: Toku ni katsuyōgo ni tsuku baai ni tsuite. *Nihonbungaku Kyōshitsu* 2:19–23.

Nishi, Y. 2005. The Decline of Adnominal Function and the Rise of Post-Predicate Pronoun and Complementizer *No* in Japanese. Paper presented at the Workshop on the Development of Nominalizers in Asian Languages at the 3rd New Reflections on Grammaticalization Conference. Santiago de Compostela, Spain.

Shinta, T. 1976. Juntaijoshi *no* no katsuyōgo shōsetsu ni tsuite. *Risshō Joshidai Kokubun* 5:16–25.

Shinta, T. 1987. *Amakusabon Heike monogatari* ni okeru rentaikei juntaihō ni tsuite: *Kakuitsubon* to no hikaku o chūshin ni shōmetsu katei no kentō nado. *Kindaigo Kenkyū* 7:121–39.

Simpson, A., and Z. Wu. 2001. The Grammaticalization of Formal Nouns and Nominalizers in Chinese, Japanese, and Korean. *Language Change in East Asia*, ed. T. E. McAuley, 250–83. Richmond, Surrey: Curzon.

Yanagida, S. 1993a. Mumeishi taigenku kara juntaijoshi taigenku (*Shiroku sakeru o* kara *shiroku saite iru no o*) e no henka. *Ehime Daigaku Kyōikugakubu Kiyō Dainibu Jinbun Shakai Kagaku* 25(2):11–36.

Yanagida, S. 1993b. *No* no tenkai – kodaigo kara kindaigo e no. *Nihongogaku* 12 (11):15–22.

Yap, F. H., S. Matthews, and K. Horie. 2002. On the Grammaticalization of Nominalizers into Pragmatic Markers: An East and Southeast Asian Perspective. Paper presented at the Conference on New Reflections on Grammaticalization 2, Amsterdam.

Yap, F. H., S. Matthews, and K. Horie. 2004. From Pronominalizer to Pragmatic Marker: Implications for Unidirectionality from a Crosslinguistic Perspective. *Up and Down the Cline – The Nature of Grammaticalization*, eds. O. Fischer, M. Norde, and H. Perridon, 137–68. Amsterdam: John Benjamins.

Yoshikawa, Y. 1950. Keishiki meishi *no* no seiritsu. *Nihonbungaku Kyōshitu* 3:29–38.

Yoshimura, N., and A. Nishina. 2004. The Emergence of the Japanese Complementizer *No*. Paper presented at the 6th Annual International Conference of the Japanese Society for Language Sciences, Hoshigaya, Aichi, Japan.

Grammaticalization of Postpositional Particles from Spatial Terms in Korean

SEONGHA RHEE*

Hankuk University of Foreign Studies

1. Introduction

Adpositions often grammaticalize from spatial terms, as has been widely attested in numerous studies across languages (see the lexicons in Heine et al. 1993 and in Heine and Kuteva 2002). Korean is not an exception in this respect. Certain members of the Korean postpositional system show on-going grammaticalization, which this paper intends to explicate.

The objectives of this paper are to examine eleven primary postpositional particles developed from spatial terms in Korean and to analyze six secondary postpositional particles in present-day Korean developed from spatial terms that are undergoing grammaticalization processes. Those in the second set exhibit various characteristics of the incipient grammaticalizing stage.

2. Data

Korean has a rich inventory of postpositional grammatical markers, many of which have developed from spatial terms. Korean makes use of ortho-graphic spacing to set apart words, which comprise a stem and its satellite

* This work was supported by the Hankuk University of Foreign Studies Research Fund.

particles. The spacing convention is very useful in that it reflects writers' perception of the degree of bondedness between linguistic forms. Drawing upon this orthographic convention, we differentiate two groups of postpositional particles: the primary postpositions, which must be directly affixed to their host noun without any spaces, and the secondary postpositions, which may be affixed to a noun with a space or may have internal morphosyntactic complexity and contain a space in them.

The primary postpositional particles with spatial origins are listed in Table 1. These are largely old grams, and many of them do not have semantically transparent lexical sources. For example, the source meaning of *-ey*, one of the highest ranking particles in Korean, has not been firmly established, but Kim (2004) claims that it was derived from the Old Korean (OK) noun *auy* 'middle/center'.

POSTPOSITION	MEANING	LEXICAL SOURCE MEANING
-taylo	as/like	place
-pakkey	only	outside
-kkaci	to/until/up.to	edge
-ey	to/at	middle
-hanthey	to	one place
-eykey	to	middle place
-kkey	to [+honorific]	that place
-kkeyse	NOM [+honorific]	that place + exist
-eyse	from/at	middle + exist
-hantheyse	from	one place + exist
-eykeyse	from	middle place + exist

Table 1. Primary Postpositions from Spatial Sources

There is also another group of secondary postpositions, as listed in Table 2, all of which have in common a genitive *-uy* 'of' and a locative *-ey* 'at'.

POSTPOSITION	MEANING	LEXICAL SOURCE MEANING
-uy aphey	before	at front of
-uy twiey	behind	at back of
-uy wiey	over/above/on	at top of
-uy alay(ey)	under	at lower region of
-uy mithey	under/beneath	at bottom of
-uy kawuntey(ey)	among/between	at center of

Table 2. Secondary Postpositions from Spatial Sources

2.1. Grammaticalization of Primary Postpositions

The primary postpositions listed in Table 1 have developed from various sources, but one noteworthy characteristic is that a large number of them are from nominal sources denoting 'place', i.e. *kuy* and *tA* of OK and MidK (Middle Korean) in seven out of the eleven cases, mostly affixed with a locative marker. The use of 'place' is not at all unusual crosslinguistically (see Blake 1994 for Finnish and Everbroeck 1958 for Lingala, among others), but the preference for this general term over more specific spatial terms (i.e. those having relational/directional meanings) is worth noting.

Another important aspect is that there is a high degree of nonisomorphism, i.e., there are multiple terms to encode the grammatical concepts of allative/dative 'to' and ablative 'from'. There exists a division of labor among them, based on fine-grained semantic and pragmatic distinctions of the goals, such as spatiality, animacy, colloquiality, humanness, and honorification. For example, the allative/dative function is carried by multiple terms with a division of labor as a result of different "specialization" (Hopper 1991), as shown in (1).

(1) *-kkaci* 'to/until/up.to'   [+terminative]
    -ey 'to/at'   [−animate], normally [+spatial]
    -eykey 'to'   [+animate]
    -hanthey 'to'   [+human], largely [+colloquial]
    -kkey 'to'   [+human] [+honorific]

The functional differentiation indicated in (1) is a schematic generalization glossing over an enormous number of subtleties. This generalization, however, suggests that linguistic forms that come into acute competition for survival and try to acquire primacy in carrying a grammatical function may divide up the function in a number of subcategories with various semantic properties and settle the conflict with a seemingly peaceful arrangement by distributing the subcategorized functions among them. An analogous specialization phenomenon is also attested with the ablatives.

The next issue involves the relationship between honorific forms and distal demonstratives. In Table 1 we have two forms that are inherently marked with honorification, and these recruit the distal demonstrative form, as shown in (2).

(2) a. *-kkey* 'to' [+honorific]
         (< that place) [*-s* GEN + *kungekuy* 'that place']
     b. *-kkeyse* NOM [+honorific]
         (< that place) [*-s* GEN + *kungekuy* 'that place' + *se* 'from']

There are two sources that have been generally acknowledged for *–kkeyse.* One is the one presented above, and the other involves an existence verb *kyesita* 'to exist', which does not concern us here. According to the current analysis, lexical expressions of distal deixis are used to refer to an honorable person. This is an example of metonymization, i.e. referring to honorable persons by their associated location. This is a strategy to avoid pinpointing honorable persons by direct mention or direct pointing, and the referent is still obvious, since people never say the names of their parents or other honorable persons in direct full forms. On the other hand, this same use of distal demonstrative for honorification is an instance of metaphorization, i.e., respect maintained by distancing (cf. "negative face") is encoded by a linguistic expression of distance. Encoding a discourse participant's face relates to intersubjectification (Traugott 1982, Traugott and König 1991, Traugott and Dasher 2002, Traugott 2003). In the cases of -*kkey* and -*kkeyse*, intersubjectification is realized by way of metaphorization.

2.2. Grammaticalization of Secondary Postpositions

Grammaticalization of secondary postpositions, as is evident from the label *secondary*, shows a lesser degree of grammaticalization in certain aspects. These morphologically complex constructions exhibit on-going grammaticalizing phenomena in reductions at the morpho-syntactic and phonological levels, orthographic changes, functional and semantic specialization, etc.

The first issue to be addressed is their formal reduction. Reduction in their phonological and/or morpho-syntactic shapes is common. This reductive process can be diagrammatically represented as in (3), where RN stands for a relational noun.

(3) [-*uy* GEN + RN + -*ey* 'at'] >> [RN]

As is evident in the example in (4), the particles -*uy* and -*ey* are often deleted from the source construction.

(4) X-uy   aph-ey   >> X-aph
    X-GEN front-at   X-front
    'at the front of X'   'in front of X'

The derivational pattern illustrated in (4) is uniformly, yet optionally, applied to all cases. One aspect relevant to this process is that the formation of the final product resembles compounding, and in fact, there is no theoretically sound way of separating these two processes, because the resultant form from the above process is composed of two nouns in juxtaposition, and they can be used as full-fledged nouns instead of prepositional phrases. It is possible that compounding and grammaticalization converge in these instances.

As has been often pointed out, discourse is the locus of grammaticalization (Hopper and Traugott 2003[1993]), and signs of grammaticalization of linguistic forms first surface in colloquial data. Thus, we can reasonably expect that the reduced forms should be common in spoken data. This is definitely true, but the reductive process is so prominent across genres and registers, though it is relatively less so in written data, that the use of reduced forms is very common even in balanced corpora. This is well illustrated in Table 3, where the more conservative forms (i.e. the nonreduced forms) and the more innovative forms (i.e. the reduced forms) are contrasted in terms of their token frequency.

	RN	RN-*ey*	RN-Ø
aph	'front'	14,211	2,531
twi	'back'	9,824	11,066
wi	'top'	15,837	24,400
alay	'below'	1,114	5,216
mith	'bottom'	2,936	452
kawuntey	'middle'	476	17,123
	TOTAL	44,398	60,788

Table 3. *-ey* Deletion (Based on the *KAIST KORTERM Corpus*)

The statistics in Table 3 suggest a number of interesting points. One of them is that there is a subtle pattern with the deletion of the particle *-ey*. In the case of relational nouns ending in an open syllable, such as *twi* 'back', *wi* 'top', *alay* 'below' and *kawuntey* 'middle', the final locative particle *-ey* is more commonly omitted. This seems to be attributable to the common tendency for language users to delete a segment from a string of successive vowels to economize the articulatory gestures.

Another relevant point is that the morphological/phonological reduction is applicable not only to the particles but also to their stems. The reductive process operated on some of the relational nouns, including *aph* 'front', *twi* 'back', and *wi* 'top'. In historical data the modern *aph* had the predecessors *alp* and *alph*, from which the lateral liquid or aspiration feature was deleted. A similar process affected *twi*, whose historical form is *twih*. A slightly different picture emerges in the case of *wi* 'top'. The MidK counterpart of *wi* /wi/ [wi] was *wuh* /uh/ [ut] by itself or /uh/ [uh] when followed by a vowel. Therefore, the reductive process occurred in such a direction that the final consonant was dropped and the remaining vowel compensated by way of diphthongization. Despite the fact that this process is not grammaticalization-specific but a more general process in Korean historical phonology, it is true that the stem forms under current consideration have undergone phonological reduction.

Still another point concerns Korean orthography, according to which, as mentioned earlier, spacing is used to separate words. Deletion of spaces between word groups reflects the perception of language that the two or more adjacent items form a single unit. When this orthographic space deletion is coupled with particle deletion, the outcome can be strikingly different from the source structure, as illustrated in (5).

(5) san-uy < space > alay-ey >> san-alay
    mountain-GEN   bottom-at   mountain-bottom
    'at the bottom of a mountain'   'below the mountain'

This type of space deletion is characterizable as an example of "univerbation" (Lehmann 1995[1982]), a process whereby multiple linguistic forms begin to behave as a single unit.

Functional specialization merits discussion as well. A very interesting aspect surfaces because these secondary postpositions come into competition with their Sino-Korean counterparts, i.e. those of Chinese origin. Therefore, this comparison relates to inter-systemic specialization, i.e. functional competition between two different systems over a set of identical grammatical functions. These competitors are listed in Table 4.

CONCEPT	NATIVE KOREAN	SINO-KOREAN
BEFORE	-uy aphey	-(uy) ceney
AFTER	-uy twiey	-(uy) hwuey
ON	-uy wiey	-(uy) sangey
UNDER	-uy alayey/mithey	-(uy) haey
AMONG	-uy kawunteyey	-(uy) cwungey

Table 4. Native Korean and Sino-Korean Postpositions

One peculiarity of the Sino-Korean system, as compared with the native Korean system, is that unlike the latter, where the formal variations occur between the full forms and those without the possessive -uy, the forms in the Sino-Korean system have a very strong tendency for use without the possessive -uy, thus resembling compounding. That cognitive mechanisms involved in compounding may be operative in this process is supported by the fact that these Sino-Korean forms prefer cooccurrence with Sino-Korean nominals and the fact that these forms tend to be written without a space in between. Considering that the core elements of the Sino-Korean postpositions are categorically nouns, that Korean compounding exhibits a strong preference for native-native or borrowed-borrowed combinations except for a handful of rare exceptional cases, and that borrowed-borrowed combinations (typically Sino-Korean combinations) are normally written without spaces, the use of Sino-Korean postpositions seems to be strongly influenced by nominal compounding.

Since the given relational concepts are encoded by two different sets of postpositions, their respective frequency of use should reveal their relative supremacy in carrying the grammatical functions concerned. Relative token frequencies of these forms can be retrieved from the *KAIST KORTERM Corpus*. Since this corpus is flawed by inconsistent tagging, the frequency figures are given in rounded form.

CONCEPT	NATIVE KOREAN	SINO-KOREAN
BEFORE	17,000	25,000
AFTER	21,000	11,000
ON	40,000	600
UNDER	10,000	400
AMONG	18,000	8,000
TOTAL	106,000	45,000

Table 5. Approximate Token Frequency of Postpositions

As is evident in the statistics, with the exception of the BEFORE words, the native Korean forms are more frequently used than their Sino-Korean counterparts, thus exhibiting primacy in use.

A similar specialization phenomenon relates to semantic specialization, i.e. division of labor between the native and Sino-Korean systems depending on their semantics. The general semantics of the two systems can be described as in Table 6. The primary meanings of these forms have been determined on the basis of the use frequency in the *KAIST KORTERM Corpus*.

CONCEPT	NATIVE KOREAN	SINO-KOREAN
BEFORE	spatial anteriority	temporal anteriority
AFTER	spatial/temporal posteriority	temporal posteriority
ON	spatial superiority	abstract relation
UNDER	spatial inferiority	abstract relation
AMONG	spatial/abstract inclusion	abstract inclusion

Table 6. Semantic Specialization

A semantic comparison of the two systems reveals an intriguing phenomenon. Sino-Korean words referred primarily to spatial location in Chinese, and speakers of Chinese typically associate these forms with spatial meanings as their primary semantic designation (Y. J. Kim, p.c.). This association is very robust, athough it is weaker with *cwungey* 'among', which is almost equally associated with the abstract meaning. It is therefore reasonable to suggest that the Sino-Korean forms denoted primarily spatial concepts in the source language. When they were brought into Korean, they became specialized and predominantly encode temporal and/or abstract (i.e. nonspatial) relations. This is interesting because, according to a widely accepted idea about semantic change, space terms are metaphorically used for spatial or quality terms, usually accompanying grammaticalization, not vice versa. In other words, the grams encoding temporal relations can be said to be more grammaticalized than the grams encoding spatial relations. However, in Table 6 we see that the borrowed terms encode more grammaticalized notions. We shall return to this issue in the following discussion.

3. Discussion

3.1. Source Lexemes and Grammaticalization

We have looked at the grammaticalization of the postpositions with reference to their semantic characteristics. These postpositions develop into grammatical markers that designate relationships between the referenced entity (normally encoded as the host NP; the "ground") and the entity in question (normally encoded as the external argument; the "figure"). Of particular interest with reference to the semantics of the postpositions is the fact that their relationships are largely static, as in the case of LIKE, AT, TO, FROM, BEFORE, AFTER, BEHIND, ON, UNDER, BELOW, AMONG, etc. Except for TO and FROM, they lack dynamicity in their semantics. Even TO and FROM may be said to be relatively weak in their dynamism in that they simply encode directionality instead of making direct reference to motions. On the other hand, postpositions developed from verbal sources encode highly dynamic concepts beyond designating simple topographic or relational contour, and they often encode the speaker's attitude (Rhee 2002). What this phenomenon suggests is that the semantics of the source lexemes determines the dynamicity of the grammaticalized marker. This is in consonance with such principles as "persistence" (Hopper 1991) and "source determination" (Bybee et al. 1994), which essentially say that the meaning of the source lexemes has a bearing on the grammaticalization paths and resultant semantics.

3.2. Source Construction and Grammaticalization

In the preceding discussion we have seen that the postpositions of spatial origins make use of relational nouns. These relational nouns often recruit the possessive marker -uy as a connecter between the host nominal and the relational noun. This possessive connecter has a strong tendency to resist assimilating into the host noun (with the rare exception of na-uy 'I-GEN', which changed into nay 'my'). When the possessive marker is eroded or deleted, it rarely causes any change in the adjacent forms. Consequently, the nominal-derived postpositions tend to maintain formal transparency. This is in contrast with the postpositions developed from verbal sources. Grammaticalization from verbal sources inevitably involves nonfinite markers, which often obscure formal transparency and promote conceptual relatedness, a process which consequently paves the way for a greater range of semantic change. In contrast, nominal source lexemes tend to maintain formal transparency and keep their semantics relatively stable, because the nominal parency and keep their semantics relatively stable, because the nominal source lexeme remains intact in form. This may relate to the preceding discussion about the relative static nature of the semantics of the postpositions developed from spatial nominals.

3.3. Semantics and Formal Transparency

The relation between the semantics of a grammatical form and its formal transparency has often been pointed out in literature. It is widely accepted that semantic generalization and formal reduction occur in parallel (the parallel reduction hypothesis; Bybee et al. 1994). It has also been pointed out that formal transparency/opacity has an effect on grammaticalization. With reference to the spatial postpositions discussed in the present study, we see that most nonrelational nominal sources have a high level of opacity (-*taylo*, -*kkaci*, -*ey*, -*eykey*, -*kkey*, -*kkeyse*, -*eyse*, -*eykeyse*) and that all relational nominal sources have a high level of transparency (-*uy aphey*, -*uy twiey*, -*uy wiey*, -*uy alayey*, -*uy mithey*, -*uy kawuntey*). The postpositions from the nonrelational nominal source group with the highest level of opacity are those that have the highest use frequency in general; those with a lower level of opacity are those that belong to the next group in terms of use frequency. The postpositions from the relational nominals are used with the lowest frequency. This supports the hypothesis that semantic generality, formal transparency, and use frequency are closely related in grammaticalization. In other words, formal transparency contributes to semantic persistence because formal transparency makes visible the semantics associated with the source lexeme.

3.4. Specialization and Grammaticalization

It has been pointed out that there is a large amount of nonisomorphism between form and meaning among the postpositions discussed here. For example, there are multiple forms for allative/dative and ablative. Each of the forms carries specialized subcategorical functions, and this division of labor, as previously indicated, depends on various semantic distinctions and other pragmatic and textual notions.

Our interest lies in the specialization of the two competing systems within the same grammatical domain of marking the spatio-temporal notions, i.e. the division of labor between the native and Sino-Korean postpositional systems. We have noted that in general the native Korean postpositions are more frequently used than the Sino-Korean postpositions. The primacy of the native Korean postpositions over their Sino-Korean counterparts is expected because, except for a small number of exceptions across languages, native forms are more commonly used when native forms and forms of foreign origin come into competition. However, the BEFORE words in the two systems show the opposite trend, i.e., the notion of BEFORE is expressed more frequently by Sino-Korean -(*uy*) *ceney* than by native Korean -*uy aphey*. This is peculiar for the reason stated above. One thing we may suspect is that the physical vs. nonphysical dichotomy between the native Korean *aphey* and the Sino-Korean *ceney* is more strict than in other pairs (cf. *twiey* and *hwuey*, both of which can express a nonphysical relationship), and in real-life language use, reference to a nonphysical relationship (i.e. 'before') is more common than reference to a physical relationship (i.e. 'in front of'). This claim, however, needs to be empirically tested for validation.

Another issue with respect to the specialization of native Korean vs. Sino-Korean systems involves the universal pattern of semantic change attested in grammaticalization. In their seminal work, Heine et al. (1991:55) proposed a direction of metaphorization along the ontological continuum as in (6).

(6) PERSON > OBJECT > PROCESS > SPACE > TIME > QUALITY

The above continuum shows the direction of metaphorical transfer, i.e. unidirectionally from left to right. This directionality seems to have crosslinguistic validity. The directionality can be interpreted such that if one grammatical form carries a spatial meaning while another carries a temporal meaning, the latter can be reasonably assumed to have undergone more grammaticalization. This general directionality is well illustrated with English *before* and *in front of*. Historically *before* had a source construction of something like *by the fore of*, where *fore* meant 'front'. When this construction underwent a univerbation process with grammaticalization, its meaning became more abstract. As a result, a new periphrastic form *in front of* came into existence to designate physical spatial location. The coexistence of these two forms shows that the older gram has the function of marking the more abstract concept, whereas the newer gram has the function of marking the less abstract concept.

It is interesting, however, that the general semantic distinction between the native Korean and Sino-Korean postpositional systems is such that the native Korean system is predominantly specialized for spatial concepts whereas the Sino-Korean system is largely specialized for temporal concepts. This is an anomaly, because we can reasonably suppose that the native Korean terms should have a longer history of grammaticalization as compared to the borrowed terms from Chinese. In other words, the situation is that the grams having a longer grammaticalization history are carrying the less developed semantic notions, while the grams having a shorter grammaticalization history are carrying the more developed semantic notions.

There does not seem to be an easy explanation for this anomaly. Such situations have not been addressed in the grammaticalization literature, and thus there are no empirically reliable sources of explanation or of analogy. However, what this situation suggests is that when a new competing system is imported for a certain grammatical paradigm, the extant system may not have to be pushed up to encode more abstract grammatical notions ("push-chain" change). Instead, the extant system may specialize in its robust function, giving a new domain to the new system, regardless of the relative degree of the abstraction that the semantics of the new domain may have. In other words, there may be no strict rule of division of labor in terms of the level of abstraction when linguistic forms come into competition and the competitors choose their functions for their specialization.

4. Conclusion

This paper has explored a special group of postpositions in Korean, i.e. those that developed from spatial sources. It has been noted that the primary postpositions have semantic generality and relative formal opacity, whereas the secondary postpositions were derived from relational nouns. Various aspects of the secondary postpositions and the competing Sino-Korean system have been compared, and certain issues that may have theoretical implications have been presented. A comparison of the grammaticalization processes of those that involve nominal sources with those that involve verbal sources led to the conclusion that there exists a close relationship among semantic generality, formal opacity, and use frequency. Further, it has been shown that the Sino-Korean postpositional system exhibits an anomaly as to the direction of metaphorization, which suggests that the notion of push-chain in grammaticalization is not supported.

References

Blake, B. J. 1994. *Case.* Cambridge: Cambridge University Press.

Bybee, J. L., W. Pagliuca, and R. Perkins. 1994. *The Evolution of Grammar: Tense, Aspect, and Modality in the Languages of the World.* Chicago: University of Chicago Press.

Everbroeck, R. v. 1958. *Grammarire et Exercises Lingala.* Anvers-Leopoldville: Standaard-Boekhandel S. A.

Heine, B., U. Claudi, and F. Hünnemeyer 1991. *Grammaticalization: A Conceptual Framework.* Chicago: University of Chicago Press.

Heine, B., T. Güldermann, C. Kilian-Hatz, D. A. Lessau, H. Roberg, M. Schladt, and T. Stolz 1993. *Conceptual Shift: A Lexicon of Grammaticalization Processes in African Languages.* AAP 34/35. Universität zu Köln.

Heine, B., and T. Kuteva 2002. *World Lexicon of Grammaticalization.* Cambridge: Cambridge University Press.

Hopper, P. J. 1991. On Some Principles of Grammaticalization. *Approaches to Grammaticalization*, vol. 1, eds. E. C. Traugott and B. Heine, 17–35. Amsterdam: John Benjamins.

Hopper, P. J., and E. C. Traugott 2003. *Grammaticalization*, 2nd ed. Cambridge: Cambridge University Press.

KAIST KORTERM Corpus. n.d. http://morph.kaist.ac.kr/kcp/.

Kim, S. G. 2004. *Kwuke thossi ewenkwa yongpep* [Etymology and usage of Korean particles]. Seoul: Yuklak Publishing.

Lehmann, C. 1995 [1982]. *Thoughts on Grammaticalization*. München: Lincom Europa.

Rhee, S. 2002. Grammaticalization of Postposition from Movement Verbs in Korean. Paper presented at the International Conference on Adpositions of Movement, Leuven, Belgium.

Traugott, E. C. 1982. From Propositional to Textual and Expressive Meanings: Some Semantic-Pragmatic Aspects of Grammaticalization. *Perspectives in Historical Linguistics*, eds. W. P. Lehmann and Y. Malkiel, 245–71. Amsterdam: John Benjamins.

Traugott, E. C. 2003. From Subjectification to Intersubjectification. *Motives for Language Change*, ed. R. Hickey, 124–42. Cambridge: Cambridge University Press.

Traugott, E. C., and R. Dasher 2002. *Regularity in Semantic Change*. Cambridge: Cambridge University Press.

Semantic Shift from Politeness to Expressive: A Case Study of the Japanese Inferential Auxiliary *soo*

HIDEMI S. RIGGS
University of California, Los Angeles

1. Introduction

The Japanese inferential auxiliary *soo* 'seemingly' is used in various con-texts in present day Japanese and has both an inferential and a figurative use. The typical grammatical account for these uses is, in the case of the inferen-tial *soo*, to indicate the speaker's uncertainty about the realization of the proposition (see, e.g. Nakahata 1991:1). On one hand, the hyperbolic use of *soo* is widely described as an extension of its inferential sense where-by the speaker/writer expresses an exaggerated description based on his inference (see Teramura 1984:241). In this view, the inferential use is canonical and the hyperbolic use is derived from it. Despite the development of other types of rhetorical uses, such as personification and its opposite, materiali-zation, researchers' attention seems to converge upon grammatical change from the inferential use *ame ga furi-soo* 'it looks like it is going to rain' to the hyperbole *ki ga kurui-soo* 'I feel as if I will go mad.'[1]

As the Japanese term for the auxiliary *yoodai no jodooshi* 'auxiliary of appearance' indicates, *soo* is widely acknowledged to denote an objective

---

[1] I use the term "materialization" to refer to a metaphor in which the speaker likens a person to a nonhuman entity.

inference based on what the speaker sees. Consequently, the development of the inferential use is typically explained in terms of the semantic change from objective to subjective. For instance, Sakurai (1972:213) notes that the historical development of the inferential auxiliaries exposes a directional pattern, i.e. the shift from a logical and analytical expression to an emotional and symbolical expression. The account for the semantic shift mechanism from an objective inference to an exaggeration is thus referred to as the course of subjectification.[2] The conventional hypothesis of the development of the auxiliary can be summarized as: **inference** (objective) > **hyperbole** (subjective).

However, the present diachronic study uncovered a prominent trait of the auxiliary, i.e. speaker's politeness, which hitherto has rarely been discussed. That is, numerous instances found in the data suggest that the auxiliary is used in contexts where the speaker apparently demonstrates civility as a way of presenting an inferential judgment. This peculiarity is observed in the literary works produced in the early Edo period (1600s and 1700s). Another finding is the fact that these instances are overwhelmingly found in conversations rather than narratives. Another significant finding of this research is an instance in which *soo* conveys no inferential sense what-soever (see (1) in §4.3 below). This invalidates the traditional construal of the auxiliary as inferential

After scrutinizing the data collected from novels and playbooks published in the 17th and 18th centuries, I came to the conclusion that the auxiliary is used in order to demonstrate the speaker's civility rather than present an inference based on the appearance of somebody or something. Hence, it is reasonable to analyze the meaning of the auxiliary in terms of linguistic interaction, focusing on the contexts in which participants are communicating. Thus, the discussion of this paper will employ terms such as "interpersonal domain" and "expressiveness domain" (Halliday and Hasan 1976), and "intersubjectification" (Traugott 1999).

Based on the findings aforementioned I postulate the semantic path of the auxiliary as follows:

1600s: politeness auxiliary > polite inferential auxiliary
1700s: fantasy marker (e.g. hyperbole, personification)

The aim of the paper is to show the increase of subjectivity denoted in the word as the language evolved.

---

[2] On the subject of subjectivity in inference, Palmer (1986:16) says modality in language is essentially subjective, and the human behavior of making an inference per se is very subjective conduct.

2. Theoretical Framework and Method of Analysis

The theoretical framework of this paper is **intersubjectification**, which is advocated by Traugott (1999). According to Traugott, in historical linguistics attention has been paid to the process called "subjectification", which is the semasiological process whereby meanings come over time to encode or externalize the speaker/writer's perspectives and attitudes as constrained by the communicative world of the speech event, rather than by the so-called "real world" characteristics of the event or situation referred to.

3. Etymology

There are two different opinions about the origin of the auxiliary *soo* in modern Japanese. Hypothesis 1, which is due to Matsushita (1930:193; as cited in Yoshida 1971:404), considers either the noun *sama* 'appearance' or the noun *soo* 'look' as the origin of *soo*. Similarly, Yuzawa (1970:290) notes that *soo* (*da*) derived from the noun *sama* 'appearance'. In the past several decades this noun-etymology opinion prevailed and was typically cited in dictionaries. Nonetheless, no textual evidence supports the theory. Hypothesis 2, proposed by researchers in recent decades, identifies the auxiliary *soo na* 'almost, looks like' that emerged in Middle Japanese (Kobayashi 1987:25) as the origin of *soo* (*da*). In this view, *soo na* is construed as "a new inferential auxiliary" that appeared in literary works such as Buddhist commentaries, collections of anecdotes on historical events, and the scripts of *kyoogen* plays. Senba (1976:522) notes that the established date of the inferential auxiliary *soo na* is based on Yuzawa's study of *soo na/ni/de/ nare* in data from the Muromachi period (1333–1603). Yet, the trajectory of how *soo na* started to be used as an inferential auxiliary in Muromachi period is considered unclear. Although the interpretation of the auxiliary (i.e. the inferential sense) is based on the actual uses of *soo na* documented by Rodrigues, who came to Japan in 1577 as a Portuguese missionary, the emergence of the auxiliary as such is unknown (Konoshima (1973:418–9).

This paper maintains the latter view, adducing the direct relationship between *soo na* and *soo* (*da*).

4. Current Research

4.1. Data

The source materials for this study are novels and playbooks produced by Ihara, Chikamatsu, Shikitei, Jippensha, and Tamenaga during the Edo period (1603–1867). The investigation focuses on the sense imbued in the auxiliary in the particular context in which it is used. Consequently, the investigation is characterized as qualitative rather than quantitative research.

Table 1 shows the emergence of the variety of usages of *soo na* along with the historical period in which each occurred.

Domain	Meaning	1600s	1700s	1800s
intersubjective	politeness	✓	✓	✓
expressive	exaggeration		✓	✓
expressive	materialization			✓
expressive	personification			✓

Table 1. Uses of *soo na*

The meaning of politeness includes polite inference. That is, while the sense of inference is not apparent in the contexts, the sense of politeness is clear from the presence of honorific morphemes. We will discuss this matter while examining specific examples below.

Table 2 indicates that the use of the auxiliary together with honorific words (e.g. honorific affixes and deferential verbs) has been consistent since the 1600s.

Late 1600s	Early 1700s	Late 1700s	Early 1800s	Late 1800s
✓	✓	✓	✓	✓

Table 2. Cooccurrence with Honorific Words

4.2. Findings

The main findings of this investigation can be summarized in three points:

(i) *Soo na* overwhelmingly appears in conversations recorded in literary works. This bias plausibly suggests that the auxiliary is used as a communicative device that conveys the speaker's courteousness, particularly to his addressee.

(ii) Although *soo na* is commonly characterized as an inferential auxiliary, in the data there are quite a few instances that do not convey the inferential sense.

(iii) An instance of *soo na* being used to exaggerate a proposition appears in dialogue in a playbook produced in 1703. It apparently suggests the advancement of subjectification, marking the speaker's unrealistic proposition.

4.3. *Soo na* as a Polite Marker

As noted earlier, the instances of noninferential uses of *soo na* are found in the data despite the prevailing explanation that the word inidicated a speaker's conjectural judgment. (1) is a counterexample to the traditional account. In this and all other examples in this paper, the italicized portions in the Japanese and in the English translation correspond.[3]

(1) *Yuugiri Awa Naruto* (1712)

Yoko ni naru Naruto no Awa daijin, Yuugiri ga uchikake ni ryooashi
   lie down   in   plutocrat   GEN gown LOC legs

gutto   irekereba satemo nametari   nametari, *kono Yuugiri*
forcefully thrust because very made light of me REP   this

ni ashi motasu wa korya chitto **ryogai-soo na**. Sore hodo ashi ga
DAT legs hold.CST TOP this   a bit impolite AUX   that much legs NOM

kuninaraba uchiotte   suteta ga yoi, to iisutete tsutto   tachi
 bother if break and discard is good QT flung suddenly stood up

tsugi no   ma   ni izure ba . . .
adjoining room LOC went out

'Plutocrat Awa thrust his legs into the long outer garment in which Yūgiri is robed. She was very upset with his rude manner and said, "*It is impolite to have me* [a prominent *dayu*] *hold your legs in my robe.* If your legs bother you that much, you should break them and throw them away." She suddenly stood up and walked away to the adjoining room. Then . . .'

The instance of *soo na* in this excerpt was found in a conversation in a playbook. The auxiliary demonstrates that the speaker does not use it to encode her inference but instead to express her anger, saying that she cannot bear such an insult. In the scene, the speaker (Yūgiri) shows her pride as a prominent *dayu*, so she refuses to be treated badly by Awa.[4] Nonetheless, the referent is the speaker's patron. The appearance of the auxiliary indicates that *ryogai-soo na* expresses the speaker's politeness toward the addressee. This instance guides us to judge that *soo na* was used in order to encode the speaker's civility to the addressee, that is, as a referent honorific auxiliary. If a person belonging to a higher social class is insulted by someone of a lower social class, then he or she would say *ryogai **nari*** 'it **is** rude' without the auxiliary *soo na*.

Iwasaki (1993) introduces types of speaker perspective based on the

---

[3] The abbreviations used in this example and throughout this paper are: AUX auxiliary, COP copula, CNJ conjunction, COM complementizer, CST causative, DAT dative, DSR desiderative, EP emphatic particle, FIL filler, FP final particle, GEN genitive, HBL humble, HON honorific, ITJ interjection, LOC locative, NOM nominative, POL polite, PSV passive, QT quotative, REP repetition, TOP topic.

[4] *Dayu* is the highest rank of geisha society. There were only limited numbers of *dayu* during the Edo period.

speaker's semantic role in the described event. According to Iwasaki, if the speaker composes a sentence in which he or she plays the dual role of "reporter" and "participant", then it involves **speaker-perspective**. The auxiliary in (1) unquestionably denotes this speaker's participant perspective. Consequently, this instance allows us to judge that the subjectivity encoded in the auxiliary had reached a considerably advanced phase in its subjectification course.

If *soo na* was an auxiliary conveying a speaker's surmise, as documented by a Portuguese missionary circa 1600, then the significance of the example in (1) is that it indicates the word had lost its original meaning or at the very least was subject to "bleaching" by 1700. That is to say, the word acquired an exaggerating sense (i.e. an expressive sense) a hundred years after it was first noted. The fact that *soo na* appears in a variety of morpho-syntactic contexts allows us to infer that the auxiliary was very frequently used in the Edo period. The productivity observed apparently is an indication of the further development of the auxiliary.[5]

Besides *soo* (*na*) in Late Middle Japanese, there is another polite auxiliary *soo* that is the shortened form of the classical polite auxiliary *sooroo* 'be (POLITE)'. According to researchers (e.g. Yuzawa 1958:168, Konoshima 1973:456), the clipping of the form is well documented in *Heike Monogatari*. Konoshima notes that the abbreviated form first appeared in this book and became common in the Muromachi period. As regards politeness relevant to the social status of speaker and addressee, Nishida (1968: 89) notes that *sooroo* in *Heike Monogatari* is used when the speaker is of lower status than the addressee.

If that is the case, it may be that speakers of Late Middle Japanese used the polite auxiliary in order to mark an inference about someone else's affairs. Making an inference about the addressee is doubtless obtrusive to the referent. The advantage of postulating Late Middle Japanese *soo* 'be (POLITE)' as the source of the inferential auxiliary *soo na* emerging in the same historical period (Kobayashi 1987:25) is that it allows us to comprehend the appearance of the word in a context in which the speaker politely introduces his inference about the addressee(s). In the following section, we will examine the instances found in the data.

4.4. Presenting a Polite Inference

The excerpt in (2) is found in a conversation in a playbook.

---

[5] The modern form *soo* (*da*) emerged in conjunction with the development of the copulative verb *da*. The modern form appears repeatedly in the *kokkeibon Ukiyodoko* (1812). This fact is evidence that there is a word boundary between *soo* and the copula forms (i.e. the old form *na* and its modern form *da*, respectively).

(2) *Daimyoo nagusami Soga* (1684)

Wakashu: Satewa *go-kyoodai-soo na.*
    then   HON-brother-INF
    'I *suppose you are brothers.*'

Onioo: Naruhodo kyoodai ni gozaimasuru.
    indeed brothers COP HBL-be
    'It is true. We are brothers.'

The first speaker in (2) uses *soo na* as he presents his inference about the relationship between the referents who are present. He uses the honorific prefix *go-* in referring to this relationship. It is reasonable to interpret the auxiliary as conveying the speaker's civility, i.e., he is guessing at the strangers' relationship.

Instances comprised of auxiliary and honorific constituents are found copiously in the data. The typical type involves adding the honorific prefix onto a noun, adjective, or verb. Examples (3) and (4) show typical combinations of an honorific prefix with another word.

    'Then I suppose that you *have not known* about it yet,'

(4) *o-ureshi* soo na kao
    'His face appears to *be happy,*'

The italicized expression in the excerpt in (5) is explicit flattery of the referents by the speaker.

(5) *Yotsugi Soga* (1683)

Mottomokashi. *Mina-sama wa o-daimyoo soo nari.* Tono wa yoshi.
    correct   everyone-HON TOP HON-lord INF COP lord TOP good
    'Absolutely right. *You all look like lords.* You are all nice looking.'

The audience members at this play are well aware that the referents are not actually lords. This example clearly reveals the speaker's angle in an interpersonal situation.

In the sentence in (6) two honorific expressions appear.

(6) *Mizuki Tatsunosuke tachi burumai* (1690)

Satemo migoto. Sadamete are   wa   *oku-sama   no otooto*
indeed wonderful surely that one TOP madam-HON GEN brother

Fusanojoo-sama no mari soo na
    HON GEN kick INF

'It's indeed a wonderful kick. I'm sure that *madam's younger brother Mr. Fusanojō kicked it.*'

The deferential term *oku-sama* 'madam' contains the deferential suffix *sama*. At the time of this play, the suffix was exclusively used to address or refer to a samurai's wife. In (6), it specifically refers to the speaker's employer. The speaker uses the honorific suffix referring to the woman and her younger brother. Backhouse (1993:91) explains that referent honorifics encode respect on the part of the speaker toward the person talked about (the madam's younger brother in the excerpt) and contrast with non-honorific terms, which encodes no such respect. Thus, it is reasonable to suppose that the use of *soo na* was required in the context because of the different social standing of the speaker and referent. Accordingly, it is natural to infer that *soo na* in this instance conveys respect.

The excerpt in (7) demonstrates a teaming use of honorifics.

(7) *Kichijooten koyasu no tama* (1704)

    Saizen   kara mimasure ba   *tabi   no   o-hito-sama-soo na*
    a while ago from watch.HBL since travel GEN HON-person-HON-AUX

    ga   dochira kara gozanshita.
    CNJ where   from   came.PLT

    'I *suppose that you are a visitor to this vicinity.* Where are you from?'

The prefix *o* and suffix *sama* both attach to *hito* 'person' (*o-hito-sama*), and this is an indication of the speaker's civility and distal "angle" toward a total stranger. Since the social element is "interpersonal", the auxiliary expresses the speaker's socially polite attitude toward his inferential judgment *tabi no o-hito-sama* 'you are a visitor to this vicinity'. It is apparent that the auxiliary is imbued with a clear sense of politeness in the context.

The excerpt in (8) is similar and contains three honorific expressions.

(8) *Yushi hogen* (1770)

    Kyoo no   wa *kyuu na   go-yoo   no o-fumi-soo de* gozaimashita.
    today's one TOP pressing HON-matter GEN HON-letter-INF   HON.was

    'The one delivered today *looked like a pressing letter.*'

The polite prefixes *go* and *o*, respectively, precede *yoo* 'matter' and *fumi* 'letter'. The predicate *gozaimashita* contains the most polite form of the copulative verb. In this scene the speaker, who is the madam of a brothel, is speaking to a patron, who is a samurai. The polite language of course reflects the relationships between the speaker and the addressee in terms of lower/higher. The interesting point here is, however, that the auxiliary fits into the series of honorific. That the new copula *da* replaces *na* in the construction demonstrates that the speakers in the 18th century were cognizant of the word boundary between the auxiliary *soo* and the copula. That is, this instance is a manifestation of the loose linkage between the clitic *soo* and the copula *da*. Consequently, it indicates that *soo* is the only morphemic constituent in which the speaker's "interpersonal angle" is encoded.

As the examples in this section demonstrate, the auxiliary denotes the speaker's courteousness toward the addressees and referents in the conversation. The data suggest, however, that speakers' sense of courtesy was demoted with the passing of time. This downgrade phenomenon is vividly revealed in instances of the auxiliary found in the genre commonly called *kokkeibon* 'ludicrous books'.[6] These comical books were widely produced in the 1800s, during which the decline of the samurai class finally ended with its abolition. The use of the auxiliary perhaps could not evade these social needs. Example (9) shows the speaker attempting to entertain the addressee with her lighthearted talk.

(9) *Zeni no waraji* (1813)

Kono hito san no *hana wa   moo   dokoka   de torarete*
this person PLT GEN nose TOP already somewhere LOC take.PSV

kinasareta soo de. Hana no hikui   o-kata   ja.
came.POL INF   nose NOM low HON.person COP

'This person seems to have had his nose taken by some one somewhere. He has such a short nose.'

In this excerpt an employee of an inn attempts to draw a traveler's attention to her inn. She mocks the addressee, who is a potential customer. This social relationship demands her to use polite expressions such as the polite suffix *san* and the polite prefix *o*. Despite the appearance of these polite elements, they tend to indicate a lesser degree of politeness than their honorific counterparts. For instance, the suffix *san* indicates less politeness than *sama*, and the verb *kinasareta* 'came' is less polite than the exalting phrasal verb *oide ni naru* 'to come'. Nevertheless, it can plausibly be argued that the use of polite words along with the previously polite auxiliary is suitable in a context in which the speaker is communicating with a total stranger.

5. Hyperbolic Uses in Early Modern Japanese

In this section we will examine uses of *soo* that indicate exaggeration rather than polite inference.

In the excerpt in (10), the speaker politely stops the interlocutor from going any further.

---

[6] The same downgrade phenomenon is observed in the history of the second person singular pronoun *omae* 'you.' It was an exalting term in Classical Japanese and is relegated to a vulgar term in Contemporary Japanese.

(10) *Sonezaki shinjuu* (1703)

Aa iya moo ifute kudasun-na.   Kikeba kiku hodo mune itami,
ITJ   more talk HON.give-HON.don't   more hear more   heart aches
warawa kara sakihe shini-soo na. Isso   shinde   noke-tai.
I   from first   die-INF   would rather die accomplish-DSR
'Oh please don't say that. The more I hear the more my heartaches, so *I feel as if I will die first.* I would rather commit suicide.'

The excerpt in (11) is found in a dinner table conversation in a novel, and the speaker mischievously gives an excuse for his drinking habit to the rest of the participants in the conversation.

(11) *Ukiyodoko* (1812)

Sake mo nomite ga   nakucha *sabishi-soo da*   kara   ne. Miru mo
saké EP drinker SBJ absent.TOP lonely-INF COP because FP seeing EP

kinodoku de   tsui   nonde ageru ki ni naru   no sa.
sorry because involuntarily drink give feel like to COM FP

'The sake *looks like it is feeling lonely*, having no one to drink it. I felt so sorry that I involuntarily feel I must drink it on its behalf.'

The speaker in (11) personifies *sake* 'Japanese rice wine' saying that it feels lonely since nobody is drinking it. This use of *soo* is a clear example that exhibits the speaker's epistemic shift from the realis/irrealis domain (i.e. inferential use) to clear irrealis (i.e. figurative use). This instance shows that the speakers of Early Modern Japanese shifted the basis of observation from physical to conceptual. There is no doubt that this usage had penetrated into everyday conversation by the time the novel was published in 1812.

In the excerpt in (12), the speaker uses the emotive adverb *ikasama* 'certainly' to indicate that he relishes the high quality of the article that belongs to the addressee.

(12) *Ukiyodoko* (1812)

(Hinekurite shibaraku mi) Naruhodo ii   kawa da. Ikasama anpera
turn over for a while look   indeed nice leather COP certainly

to iu no   wa, ano nandano, anosore, *kobitojima no   negoza*
such thing TOP FIL   FIL   FIL   midget.island GEN sleeping.mat

to mo ii-soo na mono dakkeno.
QT also say-INF thing is.FP

'(Looking at the tobacco case for a while) This leather is as amazing as I heard. Indeed, this one called *anpera* is certainly, well, umm, we would call it, *a sleeping mat for a midget* on Midget Island, right?'

The speaker (i.e. the author of this comic story) may have used the unusual metaphor to elicit a humorous response from the interlocutor (i.e. reader).

Besides metaphors in which the speaker likens an object to another object (as in the previous example), there are instances in which a person is likened to an object. Such human and object metaphors, as well as object and object metaphors, allow us to infer that speakers are introducing entertainment elements (what Halliday and Hasan (1976:234) call "additives") into their discourse. Examples (13) and (14) illustrate this matter. Note the modern forms of the copula in parentheses attached to the auxiliary.

(13) *Zeni no waraji* (1813)

    Manju   yorika *kami sama ga uma-soo (ja).*
    sweet.bun than madam HON NOM tasty-INF COP
    '*The madam looks more delicious* than a bun with a bean jam filling.'

(14) *Zeni no waraji* (1813)

    Soba yorika *koko no   musume ga tonda   uma-soo   (da).*
    noodle than this.family's daughter NOM very good.tasting-INF COP
    'The daughter of this noodle shop looks more delicious than the buckwheat noodle served at this shop.'

As the examples in this section demonstrate, speakers could use nonsensical metaphors with *soo* to make conversation more interesting. This entertainment sense is not observed in earlier uses (cf. (1) above). Thus, the instances of metaphorical use lead us to judge that the semantic quality of the auxiliary advanced into an expressive phase in its course of its intersubjectification. Regarding the conative function of language Halliday and Hasan (1976:26–7) note that it expresses the speaker's "angle," showing his or her attitude, judgment, encoding of role relationships, and motive in saying anything at all. That the advent of the modern forms of the copula *ja* and *da* took place by the time the auxiliary developed the expressive uses is a significant indication of the advancement of the auxiliary.

6. Conclusion

After closely examining instances of the inferential auxiliary *soo* (*na*) and putting it under the light of intersubjectification, the present study came to the conclusion that the auxiliary is used on the interpersonal plane in the domain of language use, in which the speaker encodes his role relationship in the situation, and his motivation in saying anything at all (see Halliday and Hasan 1976:27). For this reason, the speaker can use the auxiliary when presenting a fantasy as well as a polite inference. Particularly in the texts produced in the 1600s and 1700s, the auxiliary tends to be used to show the speaker's civility toward a referent. The speakers in the data are apt to use the auxiliary when they make inferences about the referent. Since doing so is considered intrusive, it is reasonable to expect a polite auxiliary in such a context.

By contrast, in the 1800s the auxiliary is used to present a speaker's fantasy in contexts in which the participants in the conversation are enjoying the interaction. The auxiliary increased its degree of subjectivity and became a much more "expressive" auxiliary, whereby speakers could evoke a lighthearted response from their interlocutors. In sum, the path of the auxiliary is analyzed as: polite marker > polite inferential > entertaining surmise. The direction of these semantic changes can be understood as from politeness to expressiveness, and these concepts should be comprehended under the scope of the intersubjectification process.

The question why politeness is inherent in *soo na* (see Table 2) is postponed to a future study.

References

Backhouse, A. E. 1993. *The Japanese Language*. Oxford: Oxford University Press.

Halliday, M. A. K., and R. Hasan. 1976. *Cohesion in English*. London: Longman.

Iwasaki, S. 1993. *Subjectivity in Grammar and Discourse: Theoretical Considerations and a Case Study of Japanese Spoken Discourse*. Amsterdam: John Benjamins.

Kobayashi, C. 1987. Kindai-go no bunpō. *Kokubunpō kōza 5: Jidai to bunpō*, ed. A. Yamguchi, 1–31. Tokyo: Meiji Shoin.

Konoshima, M. 1973. *Kokugo jodōshi no kenkyū: Taikei to rekishi*. Tokyo: Ōfūsha.

Nakahata, T. 1991. Futashika na yōsō—yō da to sō da. *Mie Daigaku Nihongo Bungaku* 2:26–33.

Traugott, E. C. 1999. From Subjectification to Intersubjectification. http://www.stanford.edu/~traugott/papers/subject2intersubject.pdf.

Yuzawa, K. 1970. *Tokugawa jidai gengo no kenkyū*. Tokyo: Kazama Shobō.

Part IV

Syntax and Semantics

Toward a Unified Approach to Negative Polarity Triggered by Inherently Negative Predicates

DAEHO CHUNG
Hanyang University

1. Introduction

As exemplified below, some inherently negative predicates (INPs) can license negative polarity items (NPIs) embedded under their complement clauses but not NPIs appearing as their direct complements.[1] (See Klima 1964, Linebarger 1987, Progovac 1988, 1993, Laka 1990 for English, and Sohn 1995, 2004, Lee 1996, Choi 1999, Lee, Chung, and Nam 2000 for Korean.)

(1) a. The witness denied that anybody left the room before dinner.
    b. The professor doubts that the students understood any explanation.

(2) a. *The witness denied anything.
    b. *The professor doubts any explanation.

(3) John-un [e amwuto manna-ki] silheha-n-ta. (= Sohn 1995:42, (57a))
    -TOP   anyone   meet-C dislike-PRES-DE
    'John dislikes seeing anyone.'

---

[1] See Hoeksema and Klein (1995) for some counterexamples and their semantic type approach.

165

(4) *John-un amwuto silheha-n-ta. (= Sohn 1995:42, (56a))
　　　-TOP anyone dislike-PRES-DE
　　'John dislikes anyone.'

The anti-locality displayed in NPI licensing in the INP context led some linguists (Progovac 1988, 1993, Laka 1990, among others) to claim that NPIs are not directly licensed by INPs but by an intervening negative operator (NO) in the complementizer position of the embedded clause, as schematically illustrated in (5).

(5) ... INP [$_{CP}$ Op$_{[+neg]}$ [$_{IP}$ ... NPI ...]]

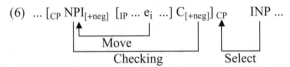

　　Select　　　C-command/License

Under this negative operator analysis (NOA), the NPIs in (1), for example, will be licensed by the NO in C, while no NO in C is available for the NPIs in (2), since the complement is a nominal projection.

　　To explain the similar anti-locality restriction observed in the Korean data in (3) and (4), Sohn (1995, 2004) essentially maintains the NOA except for the use of a checking device. As shown in (6), NPIs first move to the CP-SPEC and the [+neg] feature contained in the NPIs gets checked against the matching [+neg] feature in C.[2]

(6) ... [$_{CP}$ NPI$_{[+neg]}$ [$_{IP}$ ... e$_i$ ...] C$_{[+neg]}$] CP　　INP ...

　　　　　Move
　　　　Checking　　　Select

The NPI in (3) will be appropriately checked, while no checking takes place for the NPI in (4) since there is no negative complementizer available.

　　In this paper, however, I observe a puzzling case in Korean where the anti-locality generalization collapses. As will be made concrete in §2, INPs may license NPIs in the subject position (as well as those embedded under the complement clause) when they select a certain clausal complement. The puzzling case cannot be taken care of by the NOA as it stands, because the subject NPI is not embedded under a CP.

　　Logically there seem to be two possible ways to resolve the puzzle. One possibility is to push the NPI in the matrix subject position down to some position in the embedded clause, while keeping the NOA intact, so that the NPI may be c-commanded/licensed by the NO in C at least at some point of

---

[2] According to Sohn (1995, 2004), NPIs move or stay in situ in overt syntax, depending on the strength of their [+neg] feature. Korean NPIs happen to contain a strong [+neg] feature and move to the appropriate SPEC position: NegP-SPEC or CP-SPEC.

derivation. The other is to abandon the NOA altogether and propose an alternative analysis. The second will be opted for in this paper.

2. A Puzzling Case in Korean

There is an empirical problem with the NOA, which assumes a NO in C. Consider the sentences in (7).

(7) a. amwuto$_i$ [e$_i$ kulen telewun il-ul   ha-ki] silheha-ess-ta.
     anyone   that   dirty work-ACC do-KI dislike-PST-DE
     'No one likes to do that sort of dirty job.'

   b. amwuto$_i$ [e$_i$ na-wa   ccakha-ki]   silheha-ess-ta.
     anyone   I-with become.partner-KI dislike-PST-DE
     'No one liked to be my partner.'

Notice NPI *amwuto* resides in the matrix subject position. This indicates that the NPI licensing domain in the INP context is not necessarily confined to the complement clause. Thus, the NOA or any theory that crucially resorts to a NO in C will erroneously predict sentences like (7) to be ill-formed since the NPIs are not embedded under a CP.

One cannot plainly say, however, that the verb *silheha* can license its NPI argument. Recall from §1 that NPIs in the direct object position are not licensed by an INP, as exemplified in (4). NPIs are not licensed in the subject position, either, when INPs take a nominal complement:

(8) *amwuto John-ul   silheha-n-ta.
    anyone   -ACC dislike-PRES-DE
    'Anyone dislikes John.'

The correct generalization that emerges as to the NPI distribution in the Korean INP context is that NPIs may be embedded under the complement clause or appear in the subject position when the INP introduces a clausal complement.[3]

3. Approach I: Generate NPIs in the Embedded Clause

How can the puzzle then be resolved? Logically, there are two routes to pursue, depending on whether we keep or abandon the NOA. The first route is to abandon the NOA altogether and propose a new analysis, as will be advocated in §§4–6 of this paper. In this section, however, I consider (but ultimately discard) a second possibility, in which the NOA is kept intact with a novel interpretation of the puzzling data.

If, by some syntactic manipulation, subject NPIs in sentences like (7) can be "pushed down" to a position in the embedded clause at the appropri-

---

[3] It is hard to find a clause mate non-subject NPI that goes with an INP.

ate level, they may be licensed by the NO in C. This line of reasoning does not sound completely untenable because the puzzling case happens to be a control structure in which a null element coindexed with an (overt) element in the matrix clause resides in the embedded clause. The null element used to be interpreted as a pronominal anaphor, PRO, in the LGB stage of generative grammar. It is reinterpreted, however, as a copy (trace) of its antecedent in the matrix clause in Hornstein 2001.[4] Under Hornstein's theory of control, (7a), for example, will be derived as follows.

(9) a. Phase I: [$_{CP}$ amwuto kulen telewun il-ul ha]
     b. Phase II: amwuto [$_{CP}$ (amwuto) kulen telewun il-ul ha]-ki silheha-n-ta

Now that the NPI originates from the embedded clause, it can be checked at the embedded CP-SPEC, as described in (6), resolving the puzzle in question under the NOA.

There are non-trivial problems with this approach, however. First, notice that NPIs must pass through the embedded CP-SPEC for the [+neg] feature checking to take place, giving rise to an instance of so-called improper movement as in (10), which is banned in grammar.[5]

(10) NPI ...   [$_{CP}$ (NPI) C$_{[+neg]}$ [$_{IP}$ ... (NPI) ...]] INP ...
      A-position   A'-position   A-position

Another serious problem with the raising approach is that it incorrectly predicts sentences like (11b) below to be grammatical.

(11) a. amwuto an-cwuk-ess-ta.
          anyone Neg-die-PST-DE
          'No one died.'

      b. *amwuto an-cwuk-ki   pala-n-ta.
          anyone Neg-die-KI hope-PRES-DE
          'No one wants to die.'

---

[4] In this system, (controlled) PRO is dispensed with but the theta-theory is modified such that theta-roles are not assigned but theta-features are checked. In the control structure, a multiple theta-feature checking takes place.

[5] According to Tanaka (2002), the Japanese ECM (subject-to-object raising) construction involves an A-position at the edge of CP through which the accusative case marked NP moves to AgroP. See also Bruening 2001. (I thank Sung-Eun Cho for informing me of the references.) If an A-position is available at the edge of CP also in the control structure, there will be no improper movement problem with the theta-feature checking theory. However, there is no definite evidence pointing in this direction. Furthermore, the A-position hypothesis (combined with the NOA) cannot be carried over to the construction at issue because the NPIs are generally assumed to be licensed at an A'-position.

If the NPI in (11b) originated from the embedded clause, then it should be licensed, just as in (11a).[6]

4. Approach II: Two Types of INPs

As an alternative solution this section suggests a predicate type approach. As was seen at the outset and is schematically represented in (12), INPs select an NP or a clausal complement (a *ki*-clause, in particular) as an internal argument.

(12) a. INP I: [NP __]
　　　b. INP II: [CP __]

Assume that only the latter type of INP bears a negative force "strong enough" to license NPIs.

Once a negative predicate is strong enough, it can license NPIs, as long as a certain locality requirement is satisfied, regardless of whether the NPIs reside in the complement clause or in the subject position. Notice that there is no subject-object asymmetry in NPI licensing in Korean, as exemplified in (13).

(13) a. John-i amwuto ani-manna-ess-ta.
　　　　　 -NOM anything Neg-meet-PST-DE
　　　　　 'John did not meet anyone.'

　　　b. amwuto John-ul ani-manna-ess-ta.
　　　　　 anyone　　 -ACC Neg-meet-PST-DE
　　　　　 'No one met John.'

The NPI licensing in the subject position of (7) is not peculiar at all, since the INP is strong enough to license NPIs and the locality requirement is met.

The INP type in (12a) is not strong enough to license NPIs. Thus, it never licenses NPIs, whether the NPIs reside in the object position, as in (4), or in the subject position, as in (14) below.

(14) *amwuto John-ul　 silheha-n-ta.
　　　 anyone　　 -ACC dislike-PRES-DE
　　　 'Anyone dislikes John.'

To sum up, INPs that select a -*ki* complement clause are strong enough in their negative force and license NPIs that appear in the complement clause or in the subject position. In contrast, INPs that select a nominal

---

[6] Another way to push the NPIs in (7) down to a position in the embedded clause is to exploit the counter-equi NP deletion rule entertained in Kuroda 1965 and Harada 1973. See also Harley 1995 and Miyagawa 2002 for an LF movement analysis of this mechanism. Because of space limitations, I do not discuss the potential problems with these approaches.

complement are not strong enough in their negative force and never license NPIs, irrespective of the syntactic position of the NPIs.

5. V-*ki*-INP Reanalysis

In this section, it will be observed that NPI licensing in the INP context is possible only when V-*ki* and INP are adjacent. Based on this observation, I claim that V-*ki* and INP are reanalyzed as a complex predicate.

V-*ki* and INP must be adjacent to license NPIs. Consider the contrast in (15) and (16).

(15) a. amwuto$_i$ [e$_i$ ilen nalssi-ey kongpwuha-ki] silheha-n-ta.
        anyone   such weather-at   study-KI   hate-PRES-DE
        'No one likes to study in such weather.'

   b. *[e$_i$ ilen nalssi-ey kongpwuha-ki]$_j$ amwuto e$_j$ silheha-n-ta.
        such weather-at   study-KI   anyone   hate-PRES-DE

(16) a. John-i$_i$ [e$_i$ amwuto manna-ki] silheha-n-ta. (= (3))
        -NOM   anyone   meet-KI dislike-PRES-DE
        'John dislikes seeing anyone.'

   b. *[e$_i$ amwuto manna-ki]$_j$ John-i$_i$ e$_j$ silheha-n-ta.
        anyone meet-KI   -NOM dislike-PRES-DE

V-*ki* and an INP are adjacent in a string in (15a) and (16a), while the adjacency is destroyed due to the scrambling of the complement clause in (15b) and (16b). The NPIs are licensed only in the (a) sentences. If only the predicate type mattered, then the grammaticality difference displayed would be mysterious, since there is no difference in the predicate types: both select a clausal complement. Notice also that scrambling itself does not alter the licensing domain in simple overt negation cases.

(17) a. John-i amwuto manna-ci ani-ha-ess-ta.
        -NOM anyone   meet-CI Neg-do-PST-DE
        'John did not meet anyone.'

   b. amwuto$_i$ John-i e$_i$ manna-ci ani-ha-ess-ta.
        anyone   -NOM meet-CI Neg-do-PST-DE
        'John did not meet anyone.'

(18) a. amwuto John-ul manna-ci ani-ha-ess-ta.
        anyone   -ACC meet-CI Neg-do-PST-DE
        'No one met John.'

   b. John-ul$_i$ amwuto$_i$ e$_i$ manna-ci ani-ha-ess-ta.
        -ACC anyone   meet-CI Neg-do-PST-DE
        'No one met John.'

Thus, it seems to be the case that the string V-*ki* plus INP is strong enough to license NPIs only when they form a complex predicate.

6. A Unified NPI Licensing Mechanism

It will be argued in this section that, given the process of the complex predicate formation, it is possible to achieve a unified NPI licensing mechanism: NPI licensing takes place uniquely at the NegP-SPEC, dispensing with the possibility of NPI licensing at the CP-SPEC. I will first examine some further facts (other than the contrast between (3) and (4)) that Sohn (2004) takes to support his checking mechanism at the embedded CP-SPEC and then show that all this can be accommodated under the analysis proposed in this paper.

Sohn (2004) takes the following two facts to support his checking mechanism at the embedded CP-SPEC. First, negation-quantifier (QP) scope interaction shows up in the INP context, just as in the context of overt negation. Consider the sentences in (19) and (20), cited from Sohn (2004):

(19) na-nun mahn-un haksayng-tul-eykey i   wenli-lul   kaluchi-ki
     I-TOP   many   student-PL-DAT this principle-ACC teach-KI
    silh-ta.
    hateful-DE

    R1: 'There are a lot of students I hate to teach this principle to.'
       (QP > Neg)

    R2: 'I hate to teach this principle to a lot of students.'
       (QP < Neg)

(20) a. na-nun mahn-un haksayng-tul-eykey amwu wenli-to   kaluchi-ki
       I-TOP   many   student-PL-DAT   any principle-TO teach-KI
      silh-ta.
      hateful-DE

      R1: 'There are a lot of students I hate to teach any principle to.'
         (QP > Neg)

      #R2: 'I hate to teach any principle to a lot of students.'
         (QP < Neg)

    b. na-nun amwu wenli-to mahn-un haksayng-tul-eykey kaluchi-ki
       I-TOP   any principle-TO many   student-PL-DAT   teach-KI
      silh-ta.
      hateful-DE

      #R1: 'There are a lot of students I hate to teach any principle to.'
         (QP > Neg)

      R2: 'I hate to teach any principle to a lot of students.'
         (QP < Neg)

If there is no NPI present in the sentence, as in (19), the QP may have scope over or under the (implicit) negation. This may be explained in Sohn's (2004) checking mechanism as follows. When the QP scrambles over the negative complementizer, then the first reading ensues. When the QP remains in situ, then it has scope under negation. Now consider the case where there is an NPI present, as in (20). In this case, a scope freezing effect shows up such that a QP to the left of the NPI has scope over negation, as in (20a), while a QP to its right has scope under negation, as in (20b). All this is captured by Sohn's NPI licensing mechanism, in which the NPI moves to the embedded CP-SPEC and its strong [+neg] feature gets checked against the negative complementizer with a [+neg] feature.

Another piece of evidence Sohn (2004) uses for his checking approach is the fact that NPIs in the INP context are subject to a one-notch loosened clause mate condition: NPIs can be in the complement clause of an INP but not further embedded, as is schematically represented in (21) and exemplified in (22), cited from Sohn 2004.

(21) *... $[_{CP1}$ $C_{[+neg]}$ ... $[_{CP2}$ ... NPI ...] ...] INP

(22) a. *ku-nun amwukesto mek-un salam-ul manna-ki silheha-n-ta.
      he-TOP anything eat-RE man-ACC meet-KI hate-PRES-DE
      'He hates to meet a man who ate anything.'

    b. *ku-nun amwuto Mary-uy cip-ey iss-ta-ko sayngkakakha-ki
      he-TOP anyone -GEN house-at stay-DE-C think-KI
      silheha-n-ta.
      hate-PRES-DE
      'He hates to think that anyone stays at Mary's place.'

Sohn's checking approach predicts the sentences in (22) to be ill-formed: The NPIs cannot move to the appropriate licensing position (i.e. CP1-SPEC in (21)), because another CP (i.e. CP2) intervenes.

All the facts discussed thus far can be explained under the predicate type approach without resort to checking or licensing at the CP-SPEC if some adjustment is made in the implementation of the licensing process. Recall from §5 that the string of V-*ki* and INP becomes strong enough to license NPIs only when they form a complex predicate. Given the process of complex predicate formation, it suffices to assume Sohn's (1995) original NPI licensing mechanism (i.e. licensing at NegP-SPEC), which was assumed for the overt negation context. Notice that the complex predicate formation eliminates the clausal boundary between V-*ki* and INP (or at least makes it invisible). Now that no barrier intervenes, NPIs can directly move to the NegP-SPEC, where they are checked against Neg with an appropriate licensing/checking feature, as illustrated in (23).[7]

(23)

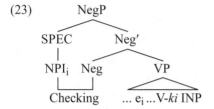

With this simplified version of the NPI licensing mechanism, all the relevant data considered so far can be accounted for. Let us first consider the sentences in (3), (4), (7), (14), and (22). (Put aside the scope related facts in (19) and (20) for the moment.) NPIs are licensed when they satisfy the following two conditions. First, there has to be a negative predicate strong enough to license NPIs. Second, NPIs and their licensing predicates must be in the same clause. Let us call the first requirement the **Negative Force Condition** (NFC) and the latter the **Clause Mate Condition** (CMC). Then the grammaticality can be accounted for, as summarized in the Table 1.

	NFC	CMC
(3)	✓	✓
(4)	*	✓
(7)	✓	✓
(14)	*	✓
(22)	✓	*

Table 1. Grammaticality by NFC and CMC

With complex predicate formation, all the data above except for (22) satisfy the locality condition, i.e. the CMC. The sentences in (4) and (14) are ruled out since there is no predicate strong enough to license NPIs. The sentences in (3) and (7) are acceptable since they satisfy both of the conditions. The sentences in (7), our original puzzling sentences, are well-formed because Korean shows no subject-object asymmetry in NPI licensing (see the discussion of (13)).

Now turn to the scope facts observed in (19) and (20). The scope interactions in the INP context are no different from those in the context of overt negation. As observed in Sohn 1995, QPs may have wide scope over or

---

[7] In Chung (1995), I assumed three types of negation: Neg is licensed by incorporating a negative predicate in a language like Korean, by attracting a negative operator to its SPEC in a language like English, and by both operations in a language like French. With the structure at hand, the complex predicate V-*ki* INP is assumed to be incorporated into Neg for the negation licensing.

narrow scope under negation when there is no NPI present in the sentence, as in (24) below. If, however, there is an NPI present, a scope freezing effect emerges: QPs to the left of the NPI have wide scope over negation, as in (25), while QPs to the right have narrow scope under negation, as in (26).

(24) John-un Tom-eykey manhun chayk-ul cwu-ci ani-ha-ess-ta.
　　　 -TOP 　　　-DAT 　many book-ACC give-CI Neg-do-PST-DE
　　　 R1: 'There are many books that John didn't give to Tom.'
　　　 R2: 'There aren't many books that John gave to Tom.'

(25) John-un manhun salam-eykey amwu chayk-ul cwu-ci ani-ha-ess-ta.
　　　 -TOP many 　　man-DAT 　　any book-ACC give-CI Neg-do-PST-DE
　　　 R1: 'There are many people who John didn't give any book to.'
　　　 #R2: 'There aren't many people who John gave any book to.'

(26) John-un amwu-eykey-to manhun chayk-ul cwu-ci ani-ha-ess-ta.
　　　 -TOP anyone-DAT 　　many book-ACC give-CI Neg-do-PST-DE
　　　 #R1: 'There are many books that John didn't give to Tom.'
　　　 R2: 'There aren't many books that John gave to Tom.'

Sohn (1995) explains these scope facts in terms of his checking mechanism in NegP, according to which NPIs move to the NegP-SPEC in order for their [+neg] feature to be checked against the matching feature in the Neg head. NPIs take the left edge position of NegP, and QPs to the left lie outside of NegP, having wide scope over negation. In contrast, QPs to the right stay inside NegP, therefore remaining within the negation scope. When there is no NPI present, then QPs may lie outside or inside NegP, displaying scope ambiguity.

　　　 Exactly the same story can be repeated for the scope facts in INP contexts, given complex predicate formation. When there is no NPI present, QPs may stay outside or inside NegP, leading to scope ambiguity as in (19). When there is an NPI present, it is located at the SPEC of NegP, due to complex predicate formation. QPs to the left of the NPI lie outside of NegP, having wide scope over negation, as in (20a). In contrast, QPs to the right stay inside of NegP, having narrow scope under negation, as in (20b).

References

Bruening, B. 2001. Syntax at the Edge: Cross-clausal Phenomena and the Syntax of Passamaquoddy. Doctoral dissertation, MIT.

Choi, J. 1999. The Distribution and Meaning of the NPI *te isang*: With Focus on Implied Negative Predicate. Master's thesis, Seoul National University. [in Korean]

Chung, D. 1995. A Negation Typology and Distribution of NQs and NPIs. Paper presented at the annual meeting of the Linguistic Society of America, New Orleans, Lousiana.

Harada, S.-I. 1973. Counter Equi NP Deletion. *Annual Bulletin of the Research Institute of Logopedics and Phoniatrics* 7:113–47.

Harley, H. 1995. Subject, Events, and Licensing. Doctoral dissertation, MIT.

Hoeksema, J., and H. Klein. 1995. Negative Predicates and Their Arguments. *Linguistic Analysis* 25:146–80.

Hornstein, N. 2001. *Move! A Minimalist Theory of Construal.* Malden, Mass.: Blackwell.

Klima, E. 1964. Negation in English. *The Structure of Language*, eds. J. Fodor and J. Katz. Englewood Cliffs, N.J.: Prentice Hall.

Kuroda, S.-Y. 1965. Generative Grammatical Studies in the Japanese Language. Doctoral dissertation, MIT. [Published 1979. New York: Garland.]

Laka, M. I. M. 1990. Negation in Syntax as Inherent Scope Relation. Doctoral dissertation, University of Iowa.

Lee, C. 1996. Negative Polarity Items in English and Korean. *Language and Science* 18:505–23.

Lee, C, D. Chung, and S. Nam. 2000. The Semantics of *amu* N-*to*/-*ilata*/-*ina* in Korean: Arbitrary Choice and Concession. *Language and Information* 4(2):107–23.

Linebarger, M. 1987. Negative Polarity and Grammatical Representation. *Linguistics and Philosophy* 11:325–87.

Miyagawa, S. 2002. Causatives. *The Handbook of Japanese Linguistics*, ed. N. Tsujimrua, 269–96. Oxford: Blackwell.

Progovac, L. 1988. A Binding Approach to Polarity Sensitivity. Doctoral dissertation, University of Southern California.

Progovac, L. 1993. Negative Polarity: Entailment and Binding. *Linguistics and Philosophy* 16:140–80.

Sohn, K.-W. 1995. Negative Polarity Items, Scope, and Economy. Doctoral dissertation, University of Connecticut.

Sohn, K.-W. 2004. On the Types of Korean NPIs. *Eneyennkwu* 9(3):450–68.

Tanaka, H. 2002. Raising to Object out of CP. *Linguistic Inquiry* 33(4):637–52.

Control into Adverbial Predicate PPs

STANLEY DUBINSKY*
University of South Carolina

SHOKO HAMANO
George Washington University

1. Introduction

This paper examines the control properties of the adverbial clause in (1), consisting of an accusative NP and a locative *ni* phrase.

(1) Masao wa [kiseru o   kuti ni] aruita
        TOP pipe ACC mouth at walked
    'Masao walked with a pipe in [his] mouth.'

This adverbial is special in several ways: (i) neither *kiseru o* nor *kuti ni* are arguments of the main verb *aruita* 'walked'; (ii) *kuti ni* is a stative predicate depicting *kiseru o* and their order is fixed (i.e. **kuti ni kiseru o*); (iii) accusative Case on *kiseru* does not involve the verb *aruita*; and (iv) *kiseru o kuti ni* involves Obligatory Control (OC) from the matrix subject when *site* is not present. The key curiosities lie in the accusative Case marking on the "subject" of a PP, and OC into an adverbial PP. The former is

---

* For helpful questions, our thanks to Olena Aydarova, Anne Bezuidenhout, Barbara Broome, Anna Mikhaylova, Mila Tasseva-Kurktchieva, Henry Yum, and Lan Zhang, all of USC. For errors, we thank ourselves.

treated extensively in Dubinsky and Hamano 2003, and this paper will motivate an OC analysis of (1), showing that OC into Japanese PPs is subject to the same transparency/opacity effects as OC into VPs (that is, they are both sensitive to the blocking effects of the same inflectional morphemes/ functional projections).

The adverbial clause in (1) appears to alternate with a similar adverbial construction, shown in (2), that is extended from (1) by the addition of the 'light' verb *suru* (here *si*) and the gerundive marker *-te*.

(2) Masao wa [kiseru o   kuti ni site] aruita
      TOP   pipe ACC mouth at do.TE walked
    'Masao walked with a pipe in [his] mouth.'

Examples (1) and (2) are not exactly identical in meaning, in that the latter involves separate events of 'having a pipe in one's mouth' and of 'walking' (more on this later). Nevertheless, the meaning is close enough that some (e.g. Martin 1975) have claimed that (1) is derived from (2) via deletion of *site*.

In this paper, §2 will show that the adverbial clause in (1) does not freely alternate with (2). §3 will present arguments for subject Control of the possessor of *kuti* in the bare *ni* adverbial phrase in (1), and show that the *ni site* adverbial in (2) is not an OC structure. §4 will show that the *ni site* adverbial is a tense phrase (TP) while the bare *ni* adverbial is a bare PP or perhaps an aspect phrase (AspP). §5 will discuss the role of gerundive *-te* in particular and tense in general, in blocking Control in Japanese.

2. (1) Does Not Involve Ellipsis of the Verb in (2)

As (1) and (2) appear to alternate, we must show that (1) does not involve deletion of *site*, an analysis which would most readily explain the accusative postposition *o* on *kiseru*. Martin (1975:471) quite explicitly claims the opposite, namely that the alternation between (1) and (2) arises from the ellipsis of *site*. While some examples may involve ellipsis, the whole class of constructions cannot be so derived. Specifically, we can show (i) that some of these adverbials do not admit *site*, (ii) that some of the *site* adverbials do not allow it to be omitted, and (iii) that when *ni* and *ni site* appear to alternate, the apparent alternation correlates with differences in meaning.

2.1. *ni/*ni site*

Notice first that the sentences in (3) do not admit *site* (with the intended meaning).

(3) a. [hana   o   ryoote ni (*site)] yatte-kita
        flower ACC both.hands at do.TE   came
       'He came with flowers in both hands.' (e.g. to give them to s.o.)

b. [tue   o   katate   ni (*site)] yatte-kita
   cane ACC one.hand at do.TE   came
   'He came with a cane in his hand.' (i.e. depends on cane for support)

If the "NP *o* NP *ni*" construction involved deletion of *site*, then the data in (3) would have no source.

2.2. *ni site/*ni*

Correspondingly, (4) illustrates a case in which *site* itself cannot be deleted felicitously.

(4) [kagi o   te   ni *(site)] benkyoo-siteita
    key ACC hands at do.TE study-was.doing
    'She was studying with keys in [her] hands.'

If the alternation of *ni site* and *ni* were simply due to the optional deletion of *site*, then the obligatory appearance of *site* in (4) would have no explanation.

2.3. *ni ≠ ni site*

Even where *ni/ni site* alternation appears to occur, it is found to correlate with a clear difference in meaning. Observe (5).

(5) a. Mariko wa [tue   o   yoko ni] tatiagatta
            TOP cane ACC side at   stood.up
       'Mariko stood up, with the cane at [her] side.' ONLY
    b. Mariko wa [tue   o   yoko ni site] tatiagatta
            TOP cane ACC side at do.TE stood.up
       'Mariko stood up, with the cane at [her] side.' OR
       'Mariko stood up, having laid the cane flat [i.e. on its side].'

As the translations in (5) show, the insertion of *site* results in interpretations that are not possible when it is absent.

3. (1), but Not (2), Involves Obligatory Control

Further reinforcing the claim that simple phonological deletion of *site* is not in play is the fact that the bare *ni* construction involves OC, while the *ni site* construction does not. There are several arguments for this claim: (i) the NP preceding *ni* must be inalienably possessed by the sentential subject (its controller), (ii) the possessor of this NP cannot be replaced by any overt pronominal or anaphor, and (iii) the bare *ni* phrase cannot be a sentential subject or topic.

3.1. "NP *o* NP *ni*" Requires an Inalienably Possessed Noun

Notice first that *yoko ni* in (5a), without *site*, can only be interpreted as 'at her side' (a possessed body part), while in (5b) it can mean 'at her side' or 'on its [the cane's] side'. This is illustrated further by the data in (6) and (7). In (6), where the *ni* phrase contains the inalienably possessed noun *kokoro* 'heart', either *ni* or *ni site* is possible.

(6) a. Taroo wa [ziten   o **kokoro** no sasae   ni] benkyoo-siteita
           TOP dictionary ACC heart GEN support at study-was.doing
    b. Taroo wa [ziten   o **kokoro** no sasae   ni site]
           TOP dictionary ACC heart GEN support at do.TE
      benkyoo-siteita
      study-was.doing
      'Taroo was studying with a dictionary as psychological support (lit: support for [his] heart).'

(7) a. *Taroo wa [ziten   o **tukue** no   sasae ni] benkyoo-siteita
           TOP dictionary ACC desk GEN support at study-was.doing
    b. Taroo wa [ziten   o **tukue** no   sasae ni site]
           TOP dictionary ACC desk GEN support at do.TE
      benkyoo-siteita
      study-was.doing
      'Taroo was studying with a dictionary as support for the desk.'

In (7), though, *kokoro* is felicitously replaced by the noun *tukue* 'desk' only in (7b), which contains *ni site*, and not in (7a), which has a bare *ni* phrase.

3.2. Possessor of "NP *ni*" Is PRO Rather than pro

Second, we find that the bare *ni* construction in contrast with the *ni site* adverbial may not have the reflexive *zibun* appearing before the noun *aite* 'companion'(similar facts are reported in Miyamoto 1999, regarding the behavior of controlled verbal nouns (VNs)). This is seen in (8). Notice that *zibun* is not categorically ruled out of a bare *ni* adverbial. *Zibun* is possible before *neko* 'cat', and (9a) contrasts in this regard with (8a).

(8) a. Taroo$_1$ wa [neko o (***zibun**$_1$ no)   aite   ni] syokuzi o sita
            TOP cat ACC self   GEN companion as   meal ACC did
      'Taroo$_1$ ate a meal with a cat as [self's$_1$] companion.'
    b. Taroo$_1$ wa [neko o (**zibun**$_1$ no)   aite   ni site] syokuzi o sita
            TOP cat   ACC self   GEN companion as do.TE   meal ACC did
      'Taroo$_1$ ate a meal with a cat as [self's$_1$] companion.'

(9) a. Taroo$_1$ wa [(**zibun**$_1$ no) neko o   aite   ni] syokuzi o sita
            TOP   self   GEN cat ACC companion as   meal ACC did
      'Taroo$_1$ ate a meal with a [self's$_1$] cat as [his] companion.'

b. Taroo$_1$ wa [(**zibun$_1$** no) neko o   aite   ni site] syokuzi o sita
       TOP   self   GEN cat ACC companion as do.TE   meal ACC did
       'Taroo$_1$ ate a meal with a [self's$_1$] cat as [his] companion.'

The ungrammaticality of *zibun* in (8a) is understandable under the hypothesis that (8a), but not (8b), involves Obligatory Control of the *ni*-marked nominal in the bare *ni* adverbial.

3.3. "NP *o* NP *ni*" Cannot Be a Matrix Subject/Topic

Alongside the facts presented thus far is the contrasting distribution of the bare *ni* and *ni site* adverbials in subject/topic position. Observe (10).

(10) a. Zisyo   o   katate ni   site wa kangaekonda
       dictionary ACC one.hand at do.TE TOP   think-fell
       '(every time) I held a dictionary (in hand), I fell deep into thought.'
   b.*Zisyo   o   katate ni   wa kangaekonda
       dictionary ACC one.hand at TOP   think-fell

The ungrammaticality of (10b) is consistent with the assumption that the possessor of *katate* in the bare *ni* construction is a controlled PRO. The licit placement of the *ni site* phrase in (10a) accords with the hypothesis that this phrase involves little pro.

3.4. Conclusion: "NP *ni*" Has an OC PRO Possessor

These observations support the analysis of the adverbial phrases in (1) and (2), shown in (11a) and (11b).

(11) a. Masao$_1$ wa [kiseru o [PRO$_1^{poss}$ kuti] ni]   aruita   = (1)
   b. Masao$_1$ wa [kiseru o [pro$_1^{poss}$ kuti] ni site] aruita   = (2)

In (11a), the possessive pronominal in the projection of *kuti* is controlled PRO, and in (11b) it is little pro. In addition to explaining the facts already presented, this analysis can account for the interpretations observed in (5), repeated here with appropriate structural annotation.

(5) a. Mariko$_1$ wa [tue   o [PRO$_1^{poss}$ yoko] ni] tatiagatta
       TOP cane ACC   side   at stood.up
       'Mariko$_1$ stood up, with the cane at [her$_1$] side.'
   b. (i)   Mariko$_1$ wa [tue$_2$ o [pro$_1^{poss}$ yoko] ni site] tatiagatta
           TOP cane ACC   side   at do.TE stood.up
           'Mariko$_1$ stood up, with the cane at [her$_1$] side.'
     (ii)   Mariko$_1$ wa [tue$_2$ o [pro$_2^{poss}$ yoko] ni site] tatiagatta
           TOP cane ACC   side   at do.TE stood.up
           'Mariko stood up, having laid the cane$_2$ on [its$_2$] side.'

Example (5a) only has one interpretation on account of the fact that controlled PRO must be coindexed with the matrix subject *Mariko*. Example (5b) on the other hand contains little pro, which may be freely coindexed with either *Mariko* (giving an interpretation equivalent to (5a)) or with *tue* 'cane'.

4. "NP *o* NP *ni*" Clause Is PP, "NP *o* NP *ni site*" Clause Is TP

The bare *ni* adverbial and the *ni site* adverbial differ in meaning, and in a way that goes beyond the alternation between controlled PRO and little pro. The key difference lies in the event-splitting nature of the *te* projection, which, following Nakatani 2003 among others (see also Matsuo 1936, Yoshikawa 1973, Nishida 1977, and Ogihara 1998, along with Hasegawa 1996 for a different perspective), we will assume to be TP. Notice first the second interpretation given for (5b), in which the laying of the cane on its side is followed by Mariko's standing up. Sequentiality of this sort correlates with the *ni site* adverbial, while the state depicted by the bare *ni* adverbial is always part of the event/state denoted by the matrix clause.

4.1. Aspectual Dependency between Matrix VP and Bare *ni* Adverbial

The *ni site* adverbial clause expresses an event/state that is independent of the main clause. Compare (12) and (13). (12a) has the atelic main verb *miteita* 'was watching', and (12b) has the telic main verb *mita* 'saw/noticed'. In contrast, (13b) is infelicitous because the telic achievement of seeing [i.e. noticing or catching site of] is incompatible with the stative meaning expressed by the bare *ni* adverbial.

(12) a. John wa   kasa   o   katate ni site Mary o   **miteita**
           TOP umbrella ACC one.hand at do.TE   ACC was.watching
           'Holding an umbrella in his hand, John was watching Mary.'
     b. John wa   kasa   o   katate ni site Mary o   **mita**
           TOP umbrella ACC one.hand at do.TE   ACC saw
           'Holding an umbrella in his hand, John saw Mary.'

(13) a. John wa   kasa   o   katate ni Mary o   **miteita**
           TOP umbrella ACC one.hand at   ACC was.watching
           'John was watching Mary, holding an umbrella in his hand.'
     b.#John wa   kasa   o   katate ni Mary o   **mita**
           TOP umbrella ACC one.hand at   ACC saw
           'John saw Mary, holding an umbrella in his hand.'

While the stative bare *ni* adverbial is incompatible with the main predicate in (13b), the stative *ni site* adverbial does not conflict with it in (12b). Example (13a) is fine. This supports the hypothesis that the *ni site* clause denotes an event/state that is separate from the main clause. Note that it is VP-aspect, rather than any particular verbal inflection, that constrains the occurrence of the bare *ni* adverbial.

4.2. ATB Extraction and *ni site* Adverbials

Additionally, we find that the accusative nominal in a bare *ni* adverbial cannot be shared by a matrix (transitive) verb, while in a *ni site* adverbial it can. Consider the contrast in (14) and (15), observed in Kuwahira 1998.

(14) Denpoo   o   katate   ni site yonda
    telegram ACC one.hand at do.TE read
    'She held the telegram$_1$ in her hand and read it$_1$.'

(15) Denpoo   o   katate   ni yonda
    telegram ACC one.hand at read
    (i)   'She read it$_1$ with the telegram$_2$ in her hand.'
    (ii) #'She held the telegram$_1$ in her hand and read it$_1$.'

While *denpoo* 'telegram' in (14) can simultaneously function as the object of *katate ni site* and *yonda*, this is not possible in (15), where *denpoo* is only associated with *katate ni*. Note also that the null object of *yonda* in (15) can be replaced by an overt nominal as in (16).

(16) Denpoo   o   katate   ni zikokuhyoo o yonda
    telegram ACC one.hand at   timetable ACC read
    'She read the timetable with the telegram in her hand.'

The contrast between *ni* and *ni site* adverbials is more salient when object-scrambling facts are considered. Consider (17).

(17) a. Sono denpoo o,   Mariko wa katate   ni site   yonda
       that telegram ACC M   TOP one.hand at do.TE read
       'That telegram$_1$, Mariko held it$_1$ in her hand and read it$_1$.'
    b.*Sono denpoo o,   Mariko wa katate   ni yonda
       that telegram ACC M   TOP one.hand at read
       (That telegram$_1$, Mariko held it$_1$ in her hand and read it$_1$.)

We would suggest that (17a) involves ATB extraction, as illustrated in (18). Similar extraction is not possible for (17b), because the adverbial is not a separate clause, as depicted in (19).

(18) Denpoo-o$_1$ [$_{TP}$ [$_{TP}$ __$_1$ katate ni site] __$_1$ yonda]   = (17a)

(19)*Denpoo-o$_1$ [$_{TP}$ [$_{PP}$ __$_1$ katate ni]   __$_1$ yonda]   = (17b)

4.3. Conclusion

These observations support the further articulation of the analysis of the adverbials in (1) and (2), shown in (20a) and (20b), where the first is a bare PP or AspP and the second is a TP.[2]

(20) a. Masao$_1$ wa   [$_{\text{AspP/PP}}$ kiseru o [PRO$_1$^{poss} kuti] ni]   aruita

     b. Masao$_1$ wa [$_{\text{TP}}$ [$_{\text{AspP/PP}}$ kiseru o [pro$_1$^{poss} kuti] ni] site] aruita

We would suggest that it is the TP phrase headed by *-te*, which blocks Control in (20b)/(2).

5. Control Is Blocked by Tense

We have seen now that the bare *ni* adverbial is transparent for Control by the matrix subject, in contrast with the *ni site* adverbial. We assume, along with Nakatani (2003:380), that *-te* and *-ta* are morphological realizations of past tense, where the tense feature is "realized as *-ta* when governed by C, and as *-te* otherwise." Examining the contrast between (1) and (2) more closely, it is clear that it is the TP projection headed by *-te*, and not the associated VP headed by *si* 'do', that blocks Control in (2). This is confirmed by examining an analogous pair of constructions involving the verbal stem *tabe-* 'eat', shown in (21).

(21) a. Tabe-tai   b. Tabete-hosii
     eat-want   eat.te-want
     'I want to eat.'   'I want him to eat.'

The phrase *tabetai* (21a) is an OC construction which can only mean 'I want to eat', while *tabete hosii* (21b) can normally mean only that I want someone else to eat. Shown in (22a), the verb stem *tabe* forms a phrase that is subject to OC from the matrix subject of *-tai* 'want'. In (22b), however, the TP headed by *-te* blocks Control into the VP, just as it does with the PP in (2), and the matrix and embedded clauses each have their own null pronouns.

(22) a. pro$_1$ [$_{\text{VP}}$ PRO$_1$ tabe]   tai
     b. pro$_1$ [$_{\text{TP}}$ [$_{\text{VP}}$ pro$_2$ tabe] te] hosii   (pro$_1$ ≠ pro$_2$)

Obviation between the two pronouns in (22b), i.e. pro$_1$ ≠ pro$_2$, is forced by pragmatic implicature (that is, the availability of (21a) precludes using (21b) to express its meaning). The obviation in (21b)/(22b) can be overridden by context, showing that it truly is pragmatically induced rather than syntactic. Consider (23).

---

[2] In these representations and those that follow, we represent Control structures as containing 'PRO'. This is simply a notational convenience, as we do not take a position here as to whether Control involves PRO, movement, and/or Case.

(23) Mazu zibun ni ganbatte hosii   yo   nee?
     first self DAT persist.TE want to.be.sure isn't.it
     'Don't you agree that you want yourself to do your best before anyone
     else?'

Other constructions involving the non-past tense morpheme -*ru* show
similar effects. Consider (24), in which the semantically similar morphemes
soo 'seem/look' and *yoo* 'appear/look' are used.

(24) a. Tabe-soo da
        eat-seem is
        'She looks like she's about to eat.'
     b. Taberu   yoo da
        eat.nonpast appear is
        'It looks like she's going to eat (at some later time).'

In (24a), "evidential" *soo* (see Martin 1975:991–95) is attached to a bare
VP, and the two predicates share a semantic subject. In contrast, the *yoo*
construction in (24b) is impersonal and has a matrix expletive subject (see
Martin 1975:731–35). The representations for these two sentences are given
in (25).[3]

(25) a. pro$_1$ [$_{VP}$ PRO$_1$ tabe]   soo da
     b. Ø   [$_{TP}$ [$_{VP}$ pro$_1$ tabe] ru] yoo da

In light of these facts, let us reconsider classic examples of control
verbs in Japanese, as shown in (26).

---

[3] Like the past tense affix -*te*/-*ta*, the intrusion of -*ru*/-*u* in a complement denotes an event
independent of the main clause. Accordingly, in (i), the tensed embedded verb *nomu* 'drink'
can felicitously support the temporal adjunct *sanzin ni* 'at three o'clock'.

(i) [kusuri   o (sanzi ni) nomu]   no   o wasureta
    medicine ACC 3:00 at drink NOMINALIZER ACC forgot
    'I forgot that [I would take my medicine (at 3 o'clock)]'

In (ii), on the other hand, the embedded VP has no tense inflection, and there is no event of
medicine-taking that is separable from the event of forgetting. Here the appearance of a temporal adjunct between the embedded verb and its object is unacceptable.

(ii) [kusuri   o (*sanzi ni) nomi]-wasureta
     medicine ACC 3:00 at drink-forgot
     'I forgot [take my medicine (#at 3 o'clock)]'

Unlike the English infinitival '*to* [verb]', which is deemed to denote 'unrealized future tense'
(see Bresnan 1972 and Stowell 1982), it would appear that Japanese infinitival verb forms bear
no tense at all.

(26) Taroo ga Mary$_1$ ni [PRO$_1$ sono hon   o yomu   yoo-ni]   meizita
         NOM   DAT   that book ACC read manner-AS ordered
    'Taroo ordered Mary to read that book.'

In Monahan (2003), it is shown that Korean allows both forward and backward control, as shown here in (27) and (28) [=Monahan 2003:(3) and (4)].

(27) Chelswu$_1$ nun Yenghi$_1$ lul [PRO$_1$ kakey ey ka-tolok]
          TOP   ACC   store LOC go-COMP
      seltukha-ess-ta
      persuade-PAST-DECL
      'Chelswu persuaded Yenghi to go to the store.' (forward control)

(28) Chelswu$_1$ nun PRO$_1$ [Yenghi$_1$ ka kakey ey ka-tolok]
          TOP   NOM store LOC go-COMP
      seltukha-ess-ta
      persuade-PAST-DECL
      'Chelswu persuaded Yenghi to go to the store.' (backward control)

Monahan (2003) claims that *Yenghi* moves from the embedded clause, overtly in (27) and after spell-out in (28). In (28), "nominative case is licensed on the subject of [−tense] clauses in Korean because of a default nominative case (DNC) mechanism" (367).

As pointed out by Fujii (2004), Japanese contrasts with Korean in this regard, allowing forward Control (as in (26)) but not backward Control. The ungrammatical (29) here below is intended to parallel (28).

(29)*Taroo ga PRO$_1$ [Mary$_1$ ga sono hon   o yomu yoo-ni]   meizita
         NOM   NOM that book ACC read manner-AS ordered
    (Taroo ordered Mary to read that book.)

The key difference between the Japanese and Korean subordinate clauses in these examples is that the latter are not specified for tense. If tense serves to block backward Control (involving **covert** movement) in Japanese, in contrast with Korean, then it might also block forward Control (involving overt movement) as well. This leads to the possibility that (26) does not involve syntactic Control at all. Some tentative support comes from the fact that the null subject of (26) can sometimes be rendered overt, as in (30). Here, (30) is comparable to the *ni site* clause in (8b) rather than the controlled bare *ni* phrase in (8a). Further, the subject of the *yoo ni* clause may, exceptionally, be other than the object of *meizita*, as (31) shows. To the extent that (30) and (31) are possible, the analysis of (26) as Control is called into question.

(30) Mary$_1$ ni, Taroo zyanakute, kanozyo$_1$ ga sono kaisya   o
      DAT   is.not   she   NOM that company ACC
      tyoosa suru yoo-ni   meizita
      investigate do manner-AS ordered
      'I ordered Mary that she, not Taroo, should investigate that company.'

(31) Mary$_1$ ni,   kanozyo$_1$ zyanakute, Taroo ga sono   kaisya   o
      DAT   she   is.not   NOM that company ACC
      tyoosa suru yoo-ni   meizita
      investigate do manner-AS ordered
      'I ordered Mary that Taroo, not she, should investigate that company.'

At the same time, it cannot be denied that the null subject in (26) displays (many of) the properties normally attributed to obligatorily controlled PRO (such as requiring a local, c-commanding, non-split antecedent).

One possibility is that Control may very well subsume two differently derived constructions that share many of the same properties. The classic "Control" cases would be instances of "semantic" control, while the Control cases we have examined here would involve "syntactic" control and perhaps movement. A reexamination of Control constructions involving a tensed clause lies beyond the scope of this paper but is certainly wanted, given the facts presented here.

References

Aoshima, S. 2003. Control Structures and Scrambling. *University of Maryland Working Papers in Linguistics* 12:1–25.

Bresnan, J. 1972. Theory of Complementation in English Syntax. Doctoral dissertation, MIT.

Dubinsky, S., and S. Hamano. 2003. Case Checking by AspP: The Syntax and Semantics of Predicative Postpositions. *Japanese/Korean Linguistics 12*, ed. W. McClure, 231–42. Stanford: CSLI.

Fujii, T. 2004. Binding and Scope in Japanese Backward Control. Paper presented at the Workshop on Control Verbs in Cross-linguistic Perspective, Zentrum für Allgemeine Sprachwissenschaft, Typologie und Universalienforschung (ZAS), Berlin.

Hasegawa,Y. 1996. The (Non-vacuous) Semantics of TE-linkage in Japanese. *Journal of Pragmatics* 25:763–90.

Iida, M. 1987. Case-Assignment by Nominals in Japanese. *Working Papers in Grammatical Theory and Discourse Structure*, eds. M. Iida, S. Wechsler, and D. Zec, 93–138. Stanford: CSLI.

Kuno, S. 1973. *The Structure of the Japanese Language.* Cambridge: MIT Press.

Kuwahira, T. 1998. Bunshōtai ni arawareru shōchaku genshō no kōsatsu. Paper presented at the Sixth Princeton Japanese Pedagogy Workshop, Princeton.

Martin, S. 1975. *A Reference Grammar of Japanese.* New Haven: Yale University Press.

Matsuo, S. 1936 [1961]. *Kokugo hōronkō* [Considerations on Japanese grammar]. Tokyo: Hakuteisha.

Miyamoto, T. 1999. *The Light Verb Construction in Japanese: The Role of the Verbal Noun.* Amsterdam: John Benjamins.

Monahan, P. 2003. Backward Object Control in Korean. *Proceedings of the 22nd West Coast Conference on Formal Linguistics*: 356–69. Somerville, Mass.: Cascadilla Press.

Nakatani, K. 2003. Analyzing -*te*. *Japanese/Korean Linguistics 12*, ed. W. McClure, 277–87. Stanford: CSLI.

Nishida, N. 1977. Joshi (1) [Auxiliary particles (1)]. *Iwanami kōza Nihongo 7: Bunpō II* [Iwanami courses in Japanese 7: Grammar II], eds. S. Ōno and T. Shibata (eds.), 191–289. Tokyo: Iwanami.

Ogihara, T. 1998. The Ambiguity of the -*te iru* Form in Japanese. *Journal of East Asian Linguistics* 7:87–120.

Stowell, T. 1982. The Tense of Infinitives. *Linguistic Inquiry* 13:561–70.

Yoshikawa, T. 1976. Gendai Nihongo dōshi no asupekuto no kenkyū [A study of aspect in Japanese]. *Nihongo dōshi no asupekuto*, ed. H. Kindaichi, 155–327. Tokyo: Mugishobō.

It's Time to Say Goodbye to Syntactic Analyses of the SIKA–NAI Construction

YUKIO FURUKAWA*
McGill University

1. Introduction

The primary goal of this paper is to compositionally analyze the meaning of
the construction in Japanese exemplified in (1) below. It is called the SIKA–
NAI **construction**, since *nai* (negation) and a constituent followed by the
sika particle (henceforth a *sika*-phrase) must cooccur in a single clause, as
(1) and (2) show. This cooccurrence is often called the **clause-mate condition**.

(1) a. **John sika** *gakusei ga* ko*(-nakat)-ta (koto)
       SIKA student NOM come-NEG-PAST (fact)
       '(the fact that) for every student except John, he or she did not
       come.'

   b. John ga **LGB sika** *hon o* yom*(-anakat)-ta (koto)
      NOM   SIKA book ACC read-NEG-PAST (fact)
      '(the fact that) for every book except LGB, John did not read it.'

---

* I would like to thank Brendan Gillon, Nobuko Hasegawa, Kazuko Inoue, Yasuo Ishii, Kazuki
Kuwabara, Kyle Johnson, Jon Nissenbaum, and Akira Watanabe for helpful comments and
suggestions.

(2) Mary wa   [John ga (*LGB sika)   *hon o*   yom-da   to]
     TOP [John NOM   SIKA book ACC read-PAST COMP]
     omow-<u>anakat</u>-ta.
     think-NEG-PAST

Most previous analyses of the SIKA–NAI construction focus their attention on the clause-mate condition and try to reduce it to a syntactic dependency. In fact, none of them cares anything about the semantics of the construction, and, unfortunately, such a syntactic dependency fails to bear its meaning (see §2). Contrary to those syntactic analyses, this paper first makes a proposal about the semantics of *sika* (see §§3–4). Then, I claim that its semantic conditions control the distribution of a *sika*-phrase (see §5).

Before proceeding, I would like to note one important aspect of the *sika*-phrase: it is an associative element. While a *sika*-phrase rejects Nominative and Accusative Case particles, it can instead be associated with a Nominative or Accusative Case-marked NP, as is shown in (1). (1) further shows that *sika*-phrases and Case-marked NPs form semantic units which are close to 'no student but John' and 'no book except LGB'.

(3) a. **John sika**   ko-nakat-ta   (koto).
         SIKA come-NEG-PAST (fact)
         '(the fact that) for everyone except John, he or she did not come.'[1]

     b. *e* **John sika** ko-nakat-ta   (koto).

     c. **John sika** *e* ko-nakat-ta   (koto).   (*e* = a null object)

I suspect that this association is obligatory for the exceptive meaning of the construction (see §3). Moreover, since (3a) presupposes a set of people, it can be equivalent to (1a) by context. Thus, I assume that the underlying structure of (3a) is either (3b) or (3c), where the *sika*-phrase is associated with a covert host which is responsible for the presupposition.[2] In short, (3a) has the same structure as that of (1a).

2. Problems in Syntactic Analyses

By appealing to the clause-mate condition observed in (1) and (2), many syntactic analyses assume that the *sika*-phrase is a negative polarity item (NPI), and, therefore, put it in the scope of negation.[3] The biggest problem

---

[1] Some previous analyses assign '(the fact that) only John came' to (3a) as its translation, but this translation does not reflect its meaning (see Appendix).

[2] This assumption is not unreasonable. It is well-known that Japanese allows null objects (e.g. *pro*) rather freely. Also, (8c) in §3 provides strong evidence for the presence of its covert host.

[3] Tanaka (1997) reports that (2) is acceptable, and also, Yamashita (2003) reports that judgments are improved if the *sika*-phrase is scrambled to the clause initial position of the embed-

in NPI-analyses is that they fail to bear the meaning of the construction. Consider (4a). As is indicated by its translation, John is not a student that did not come but rather a student that came. Since NPI-analyses have to put *John* (*sika*) in the scope of negation, their LF-representation bears the opposite interpretation, as shown in (4b).

(4) a. **John sika** *gakusei ga* ko-<u>nakat</u>-ta (koto)
SIKA student NOM come-neg-past (fact)
'(the fact that) John came and no other student came'

    b. ¬[... John ...]

    c. λx. ¬come(x)

    d. λx. come(x)

This problem is not solved by raising *John sika* out of the scope of negation. *John* is still involved in the negative proposition, since the predicate (4c) is applied to *John* after its raising. Rather, (4d) should be applied to *John* for the meaning of (4a). As far as I can see, no syntactic analysis solves this interpretational problem. It also casts doubt on a direct dependency between the *sika*-phrase and negation, which those syntactic analyses usually assume. That is, semantically, such a dependency is not motivated. The only thing that might support syntactic analyses is the locality between the *sika*-phrase and negation, but §5 shows that it is only apparent.

3. A Semantic Analysis: A *sika*-Phrase as an Exception Phrase

The necessity of the predicate (4d) for the meaning of (4a) apparently suggests that the negation *nai* does not contribute to a negative meaning in this particular construction. Other than rhetorical questions, however, I have never seen such cases in Japanese. Moreover, *nai* really contributes to the negativity of the negative proposition in (4a). While the complement of *sika* (*John* in (4a)) does not participate in the negative proposition, every other member of the set of students is really involved in it, as is indicated by its translation.

This property seems identical to the property that the exception con-

---

ded clause (see (ia)). However, the clause-mate condition is real. As far as I can see, neither (2) nor (ia) is acceptable for many native speakers. Also, Aoyagi and Ishii (1994b) point out that, since the matrix predicate *omow* 'think' can be associated with a major object, this type of example needs verification as to whether or not the *sika*-phrase stays in the embedded clause. In short, those who accept (ia) may use not (ia) but (ib) as an underlying structure.

(i) a. Mary wa [(*LGB sika$_i$) John ga t$_i$ *hon o* yom-da to] omow-<u>anakat</u>-ta.
     -TOP [SIKA NOM book ACC read-PAST COMP] think-NEG-PAST

    b. Mary wa *e* **LGB sika** [John ga *hon o* yom-da to] omow-<u>anakat</u>-ta.
    'Mary thought of no book except LGB that John read it.'

struction (EC) has. Moltmann (1995) provides the following three generalizations about the EC.

(5) a. *The Condition of Inclusion*
The exceptions must belong to the restriction of the host QP.
#Every *boy* **except Mary** came.

    b. *The Quantifier Constraint* (approximation)
The NP that hosts an exception phrase must denote a universal or negative universal QP.
{#*A lot of boys*/#*Three boys*/#*At least three boys*}**except John** came.

    c. *The Negative Condition*
Applying the predicate to the exceptions yields the opposite truth value from applying the predicate to non-exceptions.
Every boy **except John** came.
≠ John came and every boy other than John came.

The SIKA–NAI construction obeys both the Condition of Inclusion and the Negative Condition. (6a) is not felicitous since *LI* (a journal) is not a member of the set of books. (6b) is not felicitous, either, since what is meant by the second conjunct is contradictory to the meaning of the first conjunct.

(6) a. John ga (#**LI sika**) *hon o*   yom-anakat-ta (koto)
         NOM   SIKA book ACC read-NEG-PAST (fact)
     '(the fact that) for every book (#except LI), John did not read it'

    b. John wa **LGB sika** *hon o*   yom-anakat-ta
         TOP   SIKA book ACC read-NEG-PAST
    (#ga <u>Barriers wa</u>   yom-da).
    but   FOC read-PAST
    'For every book except LGB, John did not read it
    (#but he read Barriers).'

The SIKA–NAI construction obeys the Quantifier Constraint, too. Although the host of the *sika*-phrase is realized as a bare NP, it really bears a universal reading. Modifiability by *almost*-type adverbs is used as a diagnostic for the universality of a modified element, and *hotondo* 'almost' can modify the bare NP host *hon* 'book', as is shown in (7a).[4] Furthermore, existential QPs cannot host a *sika*-phrase (see (7b)).

---

[4] As pointed out by Lee and Horn (1994) and Horn (2000), *almost* in English can modify existential QPs with higher values in scales (see (ia)). However, *hotondo* in Japanese does not do this, as shown in (ib). In this sense, *hotondo*-modification is more reliable as a diagnostic for universality than *almost*-modification. Note that *hotondo* is ambiguous between 'almost' and (floated) 'most', but prenominal *hotondo* unambiguously means 'almost'.

(7) a. John ga (<u>hotondo</u>) **LGB sika** *hon o* yom-anakat-ta (koto)
   NOM almost   SIKA book ACC read-neg-past (fact)
   '(the fact that) for (almost) every book except LGB, John did
   not read it'

   b. LGB sika {*takusan/*san-satu/*sukunakutomo san-satu} no hon o
      SIKA { many / three-CL / at least three-CL } GEN book ACC

Note that compatibility with *hotondo*-modification in (8c) shows (i) that a
cover subject really hosts the *sika*-phrase and (ii) that it is universally quantified. Since the matrix predicate is an individual-level predicate and neither
(8a) nor (8b) is compatible with *hotondo*-modification, its compatibility in
(8c) can be taken as strong evidence for the presence of a universally quantified covert host.

(8) a. (*<u>hotondo</u>) John ga   eigo ga   umai (koto)
      almost   NOM English NOM good (fact)
      '(the fact that) John is (?almost) good at English'

   b. (*<u>hotondo</u>) John ga   eigo ga   umak-nai (koto)
      almost   NOM English NOM good-NEG (fact)
      '(the fact that) John isn't (?almost) good at English'

   c. <u>hotondo</u> **John sika** *e* eigo ga   umak-nai (koto)
      almost   SIKA English NOM good-NEG (fact)
      '(the fact that) for almost everyone except John, he or she is good at
      English'

Since the SIKA–NAI construction obeys the three conditions in (5), I conclude that it is an instance of the EC.

4. A Compositional Analysis of *sika*

Let us assume that the exceptive meaning of (9a) (i.e. 'John came and no
other student came') is logically asserted. People might think that, for the
sake of the Quantifier Constraint, the conditional statement (9b) can be the
logical representation for (9a). However, it does not express the meaning,
correctly. Since its antecedent is false by the application of John to x, (9b)
itself returns true as the truth value in this case. As is observed in the Negative Condition, however, the truth value in this case must be false.

(i) a. I could solve <u>almost</u> {all / any / half / none / 50 / *many / *most / *few} of the
      problems. (Horn 2000)

   b. boku wa <u>hotondo</u> {*subete* / *gozyuu-mon*} no   mondai o   to-ita.
      I   TOP almost { all /   50-CL   } GEN problems ACC solve-PAST

(9) a. **John sika** *gakusei ga* ko-nakat-ta (koto)
        SIKA student NOM come-NEG-PAST (fact)
        '(the fact that) for every student except John, he or she did not come'

    b. $\forall x \, [[x \mid x \in [\text{student}] \land x \neq j] \rightarrow \neg\text{come}(x)]$

In fact, difficulties exist in expressing the meaning of the EC in terms of a universal quantifier. A (nonnegative) universal quantifier requires subsethood of its restriction with respect to its nuclear scope. In the case of (9a), however, the set of students is not a subset of the set denoted by the matrix predicate ([not come]) for exceptive {John}, as is shown in (10) (see also von Fintel 1993).

(10) a.

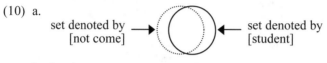

    set denoted by   set denoted by
     [not come]   [student]

    b. $[\text{student}] - [\text{not come}] = \{\text{John}\} \neq \varnothing$

To capture the meaning of (9a) in a compositional way, this paper adopts half of Moltmann's (1995) analysis, which holds that exceptions involve a subtraction operation on the set denoted by a QP.[5] The basic idea of (11) is the following. The universally quantified *gakusei* 'every student' (= [NP1]) in (9a) denotes the set of sets containing all students, in other words, the set consisting of every superset of [student]. The subtraction operation subtracts each member of the set of witness sets for {John} (= [NP2]) from every member of the set denoted by the QP.[6]

---

[5] The reason I adopt only half of Moltmann's analysis is that her definition of the negative EC (i.e. *no … except*) has a problem in the Condition of Inclusion. Also, since Japanese uses wide scope universal quantification (with respect to negation) as its strategy for the meaning of total negation that sentences like (i) express (see Furukawa 2005), I adopt her definition of the non-negative EC (i.e. *every … except*). However, see Lappin (1996), who raises a problem in her analysis.

(i) *gakusei ga* ko-nakat-ta (koto)
    student NOM come-NEG-PAST (fact)
    '(the fact that) for all students, they did not come'

[6] The witness set for {John} is {John}, and hence, trivial. The notion of a witness set is crucial in (i), since the cardinality of the exceptive students is either two, one, or zero. Note that $W([\text{NP2}]^M)$ in (11) denotes the set of witness sets for [NP2] in the model.

(i) **ookutemo huta-ri sika** *gakusei ga* ko-nakat-ta (koto)
    at most two-CL SIKA student NOM come-neg-past (fact)
    '(the fact that) for every student except at most two, he or she did not come'

(11) $([sika]^M([NP2]^M))([NP1]^M)$

$= \cup_{V' \in W([NP2]M)} \{V - V' : V \in [NP1]^M\}$ where NP1 is a universally quantified bare NP, if for every appropriate extension M' of M, for every $V \in [NP1]^{M'}$, and for every $V' \in [NP2]^{M'}$, $V' \subseteq V\}$,

= undefined otherwise. (cf. Moltmann 1995)

Then, one of the members of the set denoted by $([sika]([John]))([gakusei])$ can match up with the set denoted by the predicate ([not come]). Hence, the proposition obtained by the application of the latter to the former can be false with respect to John but true with respect to students other than John.

5. The Clause-Mate Condition

§1 observes that a *sika*-phrase is an associative element. Then, what kind of NP can host it?

(12) a. John ga *LGB sika* { **hon o** / ***sorera no hon o** /
         NOM   SIKA {book ACC/those GEN book ACC /

   subete no   hon o**[7] /go-satu no hon o** }yom-anakat-ta (koto)
   all GEN book ACC / 5-CL GEN book ACC} read-NEG-PAST (fact)

   '(the fact that) for {all books/all of those books/all of the books/all of the five books} except LGB, John didn't read them'

b. John ga (**LGB sika*) **[Aspects to LGB to Barriers] o**
      NOM   SIKA [and   and   ] ACC

   yom-anakat-ta (koto)
   read-NEG-PAST (fact)

   '#Except for LGB, John read none of the three books, i.e. Aspects, LGB, and Barriers.'

As observed in §3, a *sika*-phrase can be associated with a bare NP. Here, I assume that only bare NPs can host it. As far as I can see, it cannot be associated with any other kind of NP (e.g. definite NPs,[8] quantificational NPs, "listing" NPs, etc.). Further investigation is warranted.

---

[7] The Quantifier Constraint may not exclude this. At this stage, I leave the issue of why NPs with overt universal quantifiers cannot host a *sika*-phrase for future research.

[8] Some native speakers may point out that (ia) is acceptable, but (ia) does not show that a definite NP can host a *sika*-phrase. Since Japanese allows major subjects rather freely, it is plausible to think that the *John sika* in (ia) is associative to a covert subject (see (ib)). In fact, a *sika*-phrase is never associative to a definite object NP, as is shown in (12a).

(i) a. sorera no gakusei ga John sika ko-nakat-ta   (koto)
       those GEN student NOM John SIKA come-NEG-PAST (fact)
       '(the fact that) as for those students, no one except John came'

   b. sorera no gakusei ga John sika *e* ko-nakat-ta (koto)

Consider the meanings that a bare NP can bear. Since a bare NP has no overt determiner, it is ambiguous in several ways (e.g. definite, indefinite, kind, universal, etc.). Remarkably, if it is a clause-mate of negation, it can bear a universal reading, which is confirmed by *hotondo*-modification, as in (13). Furthermore, its universal reading is not free; it cannot bear a universal reading unless it is a clause-mate of negation. This is confirmed by its incompatibility with *hotondo*-modification, as in (14).

(13) John ga (<u>hotondo</u>) **hon o**   yom-anakat-ta (koto)
      NOM   almost book ACC read-NEG-PAST (fact)
      '(the fact that) for (almost) every book, John did not read it'

(14) a. John ga (*<u>hotondo</u>) **hon o**   yom-da (koto)
          NOM   almost book ACC read-PAST (fact)

     b. Mary wa [John ga (*<u>hotondo</u>) **hon o**   yom-da   to]
          TOP [NOM   almost book ACC read-PAST COMP]
          iw-anakat-ta.
          say-NEG-PAST
          (lit.) 'Mary did not say that John read (*almost) the books/books.'

At this stage, we have three observations: (i) the *sika*-phrase is associated with a bare NP, (ii) its bare NP host must be universally quantified for an exceptive meaning, and (iii) a bare NP cannot bear a universal reading unless it is a clause-mate of negation. These observations demonstrate that a universal reading of its host bare NP creates an apparent clause-mate condition between the *sika*-phrase and negation. Thus, I conclude that the clause-mate condition is a byproduct of its universal reading.

Then, why can a bare NP bear a universal reading only in this environment? Because of space limitations, I will not discuss this issue here, and I refer readers to Furukawa 2005.

6. Anti-Multiplicity of *sika*

Semantic analyses have one benefit. While English allows multiple exceptions (see (15)), Japanese does not allow multiple *sika* (see (16)). As far as I can see, no syntactic analysis provides a well-articulated explanation for absence of multiple *sika*.[9] Based on truth conditions, semantic analyses have an explanation for its absence. Compare (15) (see Moltmann 1995) and (16) (see Aoyagi and Ishii 1994a, 1994b).

---

[9] Among the syntactic analyses, only Aoyagi and Ishii (1994a, 1994b) address the unacceptability in (16a). However, I do not think that their analysis is problem free (see Furukawa 2003).

(15) a. *Every man* **except John** danced with *every woman* **except Mary**.

    b. *No man* **except John** danced with *any woman* **except Mary**.

(16) a. ***John sika ringo sika** tabe-nakat-ta.
          SIKA apple-SIKA eat-NEG-PAST

    b. ***John sika** *gakusei ga* **ringo sika** *kudamono o* tabe-nakat-ta.
         SIKA student NOM apple SIKA fruit ACC   eat-NEG-PAST
     'No student except John ate any fruit except apples.'

Let us first look at multiple exceptions in English. (15a) can be true in two situations, namely (17a) and (17b). The truth table in (17c) summarizes its truth conditions.[10]

(17) a. Every man other than John danced with every woman other than Mary, but not with Mary. John did not dance with any woman other than Mary but with Mary.

    b. Every man other than John danced with every woman other than Mary, but not with Mary. John danced neither with any woman other than Mary nor with Mary.

    c.

dance with $<$x,y$>$	application of c to y	application of d to y
application of a to x	TRUE	FALSE
application of b to x	FALSE	UNDFINED

    where $a \in \{x \mid x \in [\text{man}] \wedge x \neq j\}$, $b \in \{j\}$,
          $c \in \{y \mid y \in [\text{woman}] \wedge y \neq m\}$, $d \in \{m\}$

The difference between (17a) and (17b) is whether or not John danced with Mary. The fact that (15a) can be true in both situations indicates that it does not have any truth value with respect to the 'dance with' relation between John and Mary. Therefore, strictly speaking, the truth value of (15a) is indeterminate. However, it is a natural utterance, and used in a meaningful way. I suspect that since matters of non-exceptive members (i.e. those men other than John and those women other than Mary) are conversationally more significant than matters of exceptive members (i.e. John and Mary), speakers of the utterance and its hearers do not care anything about their 'dance with' relation.

If we assume that the truth table in (17c) is a logical consequence of multiple exceptions in general, (16) has no truth value with respect to the

---

[10] For some native speakers, *except* in (15a) is weak, and they have an intuition that (15a) is almost equivalent to (i) (see von Fintel 1993, Hoeksema 1987, 1995).

(i) Except for John, every man danced with every woman except Mary.

'(not) eat' relation between John and apples, either.[11] Then, why is (16) unacceptable? A difference between English and Japanese is that, in Japanese, matters of exceptive members have conversational significance. As is observed above, the host of the *sika*-phrase is often realized as a null object. In fact, some previous analyses claim that the *sika*-phrase is a focus (see Futagi 2003). In short, since the '(not) eat' relation between John and apples that (16) tries to convey has no truth value, the utterance (16) is meaningless, and hence, unacceptable.[12]

7. Conclusion

Previous analyses of the SIKA–NAI construction claim that the *sika*-phrase is dependent on negation, and, therefore, propose a direct dependency between them. As we have seen, however, these analyses cannot express the meaning of the construction correctly, and moreover, the semantics does not motivate such a dependency. To express its exceptive meaning in a compositional way, I propose that *sika* is a subtraction function from an exception and a QP. I further claim that the clause-mate condition between the *sika*-phrase and negation is only apparent—a byproduct derived from the availability of a universal reading of its bare NP host.

Note that to explain the basic idea of the subtraction operation, (11) is defined in a loose way. Also, I leave one issue for future research, that is, why only bare NPs can host a *sika*-phrase.

Appendix: *sika* ≠ 'only'

Some previous analyses assign '(the fact that) only John came' to (18) as its translation, but this is an incorrect translation. First, none of these analyses is explicit about why negation disappears from translations with *only*.

(18) **John sika** *e* ko-nakat-ta (koto)
      SIKA come-NEG-PAST (fact)
      '(the fact that) for everyone except John, he or she did not come'

Another problem is the following. Although the meaning of *only* is a debat-

---

[11] Context sometimes plays a role in truth-value indeterminacy. For example, the truth value of 'John is tall' can be determinate with appropriate context. However, context provides no help for the truth-value indeterminacy in multiple exceptions, since its indeterminacy is a logical consequence (see also note 12).

[12] Alternatively, it might be possible to say that multiple exceptions assert contradictory things; (15a) asserts both 'John danced with Mary' and 'John did not dance with Mary'. Then the unacceptability in (16) may be restated in the following way: since matters of exceptive members have conversational significance, (16) tries to convey contradictory things (i.e. 'John ate apples' and 'John did not eat apples'). If so, the definition in (11) should be modified to bear such contradictory meanings.

able issue, suppose that the logical representation (19b) and its presupposition (19c) express the meaning of (19a). As is shown in (19b), the presupposition introduced by (19c) does not correspond to the domain of quantification for the universal quantifier. In the SIKA–NAI construction, however, a (hidden) universal quantifier quantifies over a set of presupposed individuals, denoted by either an overt bare NP or a null object (see (8c)). Hence, the meaning of (19a) is completely different from the meaning of (18).

(19) a. Only John came.

　　b. assertion: $\exists x \ [x = j \wedge \text{come}(x)] \wedge \neg \exists y [\text{come}(y) \wedge y \neq x]$
　　　　 or, $\exists x \ [x = j \wedge \text{come}(x)] \wedge \forall y [\text{come}(y) \rightarrow y = x]$

　　c. presupposition: There exists at least one person that is distinct
　　　　 from John.

References

Aoyagi, H., and T. Ishii. 1994a. On Agreement-Inducing vs. Non-Agreement-Inducing NPIs. *NELS 24*, ed. M. González, 1–15. Amherst, Mass.: GLSA Publications.

Aoyagi, H., and T. Ishii. 1994b. On NPI Licensing in Japanese. *Japanese/Korean Linguistics 4*, ed. N. Akatsuka, 295–311. Stanford: CSLI.

von Fintel, K. 1993. Exceptive Constructions. *Natural Language Semantics* 1:123–48.

von Fintel, K. 1994. Restrictions on Quantifier Domains. Doctoral dissertation, University of Massachusetts, Amherst.

Furukawa, Y. 2003. Semantics of *Sika*. Manuscript, McGill University.

Furukawa, Y. 2005. Why Can Bare NPs in Japanese Bear Universal Readings in Certain Environments? *Proceedings of ConSOLE XIII*, eds. S. Blaho, L. Vicente, and E. Schoorlemmer, 91–105. Leiden: SOLE.

Futagi, Y. 2003. Japanese Focus Particle at the Syntax-Semantics Interface. Doctoral dissertation, Rutgers University.

Hasegawa, N. 1994. Economy of Derivation and A'-Movement. *Current Topics in English and Japanese*, ed. M. Nakamura. Tokyo: Hituzi.

Hoeksema, J. 1987. The Logic of Exception. *Proceedings of the Fourth Eastern States Conference on Linguistics*, eds. A. Miller and J. Powers, 100–13. Columbus: The Ohio State University.

Hoeksema, J. 1995. The Semantics of Exception Phrases. *Quantifiers, Logic, and Language*, eds. J. van der Does and J. van Eijck, 145–77. Stanford: CSLI.

Horn, L. R. 1996. Only and the Dynamics of Vertical Inference. *Journal of Semantics* 13:1–40.

Horn, L. R. 2000. Pick a Theory (Not Just Any Theory). *Negation and Polarity*, eds. L. R. Horn and Y. Kato, 147–92. Oxford: Oxford University Press.

Kawashima, R., and H. Kitahara. 1992. Licensing of Negative Polarity Items and Checking Theory. *Proceedings of the Formal Linguistic Society of MidAmerica* 3:139–54.

Keenan, E. L., and D. Westernståhl. 1997. Generalized Quantifiers. *Handbook of Logic and Language*, eds. J. van Benthem and A. ter Meulen, 837–93. Amsterdam: Elsevier.

Lappin, S. 1996. Generalized Quantifiers, Exception Phrases and Logicality. *Journal of Semantics* 13:197–220.

Lee, Y.-S., and L. R. Horn. 1994. Any as Indefinite plus Even. Manuscript, Yale University.

Moltmann, F. 1995. Exception Phrases and Polyadic Quantification. *Linguistics and Philosophy* 18:223–80.

Muraki, M. 1978. The Sika Nai Construction and Predicate Restructuring. *Problems in Japanese Syntax and Semantics*, eds. J. Hinds and I. Howard, 155–77. Tokyo: Kaitakusha.

Oyakawa, T. 1975. On the Japanese Sika-Nai Construction. *Gengo Kenkyū* 67:1–20.

Shimoyama, J. 2004. Wide Scope Universal NPIs in Japanese. Paper presented at Georgetown University Round Table, Washington, D.C.

Takahashi, D. 1990. Negative Polarity, Phrase Structure and the ECP. *English Linguistics* 7:129–46.

Tanaka, H. 1997. Invisible Movement in SIKA-NAI and the Linear Crossing Constraint. *Journal of East Asian Linguistics* 6:143–88.

Yamashita, H. 2003. On the Distribution and Licensing of Negative Polarity Items in Japanese and the Phase-Impenetrability Condition. *Proceedings of the Fourth Tokyo Conference on Psycholinguistics*, ed. Y. Otsu, 313–37. Tokyo: Hituzi.

Formal Grammar of Evidentiality and Implicatures: A Case Study of Japanese Contrastive *wa*

YURIE HARA*
University of Delaware

1. Introduction

The Japanese contrastive marker (CTopic) *wa* can appear within a *because*-clause, as in (1), while it cannot appear within a temporal clause with *toki* 'when', as in (2), or an *if*-clause, as in (3).[1]

(1) Itsumo uchi ni Mary **wa** kuru **node**, kodomo ga yorokob-u.
     always house DAT   CTOP come because, children NOM happy-PRES
     'Because Mary$_{CTop}$ always comes to our house, the children are happy.'

(2) *Itsumo uchi ni Mary **wa** kuru **toki**, keeki o motteku-ru.
     always house DAT   CTOP come when, cake ACC bring-PRES
     'When Mary$_{CTop}$ comes to our house, she always brings a cake.'

---

* I have greatly benefited from the valuable comments, suggestions and discussions with Satoshi Tomioka, Maribel Romero, Anna Papafragou, and Benjamin Bruening. I also thank the audience at the 14th Japanese/Korean Linguistics Conference for their comments and criticisms. Needless to say, all remaining errors are my own.
[1] The same asymmetry is also found in Sawada and Larson (forthcoming).

(3) *Moshi John ga hon o 3-satsu **wa** yom-eba, gookaku-suru.
    if   NOM book ACC 3-CLASS CTOP read-COMP   pass-do
    'If John reads 3_{CTop} books, he will pass.'

This paper has several goals. First, I will give an account for this contrast using two "pragmatic" concepts: implicatures and evidentiality. Second, the analysis gives evidence for syntax-pragmatics interfaces. These concepts (implicatures and evidentiality) are previously treated as purely pragmatic. However, some recent studies show that there are syntactic representations for implicatures (Chierchia 2001) and for evidentiality (Cinque 1999, Speas 2004, Tenny 2002). Lastly, the analysis suggests that there is a syntactic and pragmatic connection between implicatures and evidentiality.

2. Japanese Contrastive Topic

In previous work (Hara forthcoming a, forthcoming b) I argue that propositions that cannot induce implicatures are not compatible with contrastive topics. For example, in (4a) the proposition 'Some people came' is marked by contrastive *wa*, and the marking induces implicature. On the other hand, (4b) shows that the proposition 'Everyone came' cannot be marked by *wa*, since it can-not induce implicatures.

(4) a. Nanninka   **wa**   ki-ta.
      some.people CTOP come-PAST
      'Some people came.'
      (Implicature: It is possible that it is not the case that everyone came.)

    b. #Minna   **wa**   ki-ta.
      everyone CTOP come-PAST
      (No implicature is possible.)

Here is a brief sketch of the explanation. The asserted proposition 'Everyone came' is the strongest (most informative) among the alternatives ('Some people came', 'Most people came', etc.). Therefore, there is no room to implicate and hence, the proposition is not compatible with contrastive *wa*. In the following section, I will give a formal mechanism for computing implicatures.

2.1. Presuppositional Requirement

In Hara forthcoming a, I claimed that contrastive topics always induce scalar implicatures that express the uncertainty of the alternatives as defined in (5). I employed the mechanism developed by Sauerland (2004) to compute implicatures and proposed that if a sentence contains a CTopic, it presupposes a particular set of scalar alternatives. A scalar alternative becomes an implicature "only if the scalar alternative is stronger than the assertion." In our case, since CTopic-marked sentences always induce implicatures, they must have a scalar alternative stronger than the assertion in order to be interpreted properly. In other words, as in (5b), there must be a scalar alternative that entails but is not entailed by the original assertion. If the presupposition is satisfied, contrastive *wa* implicates that the negation of the stronger alternative is possible, as in (5c).

(5) CONTRASTIVE$(w)(x)(B)(T)$ (w: world variable, x: speaker or attitude-bearer, B: background, T: contrastive-marked element)

    a. asserts: $B(T)(w)$

    b. presupposes: $\forall w' \in min_w[w' \in Dox_x(w)] : \exists T'[T' \in ALT_C(T)$ & $B(T')(w')$ entails $B(T)(w')$ & $B(T)(w')$ doesn't entail $B(T')(w')]$

    c. implicates: $\exists w' \in min_w[w' \in Dox_x(w)] : \forall T'[T' \in ALT_C(T)$ & $B(T')(w')$ entails $B(T)(w')$ & $B(T)(w')$ doesn't entail $B(T')(w')]$ $[B(T')(w') = 0]$

To illustrate, let us see how (4a), repeated below, induces its implicature.

(4) a. Nanninka   **wa**   ki-ta.
     some.people CTOP come-PAST
     'Some people came.'
     (Implicature: It's possible that not everyone came.)

The asserted proposition $\exists x[[person(x)][come(x)]]$ has a stronger scalar alternative $\forall(x)[[person(x)][came(x)]]$. $\forall(x)[[person(x)][came(x)]]$ entails $\exists[[person(x)][come(x)]$ but not the other way around. Therefore, the asserted proposition is compatible with *wa* and induces the implicature 'It is possible that it is not the case that everyone came':

(6) a. $\exists x[[person(x)][come(x)]$ $(= B(T)(w'))$

    b. Stronger Scalar Alternative: $\forall(x)[[person(x)][came(x)]]$ $(= B(T')(w'))$

    c. $B(T')(w')$ entails $B(T)(w')^2$

    d. $B(T)(w')$ does not entail $B(T')(w')$

    e. Implicature: $Poss(\neg\forall(x)[[person(x)][came(x)]])$ $(= \neg B(T')(w'))$

On the other hand, (4b), repeated below, does not induce implicatures.

(4) b. #Minna   **wa**   ki-ta.
     everyone CTOP come-PAST
     (No implicature is possible.)

The asserted proposition $\forall(x)[[person(x)][came(x)]]$ does not have a

---

^{2} I ignore the case where there is no person in the domain. The entailment does not hold in this case, since $B(T')(w')$ is vacuously true, while $B(T)(w')$ is false.

stronger scalar alternative. None of its scalar alternatives $(\exists(x)[[\text{person}(x)]$ $[\text{came}(x)]]$, $\text{few}(x)[[\text{person}(x)][\text{came}(x)]]$, $\text{most}(x)[[\text{person}(x)][\text{came}(x)]]$, more-than-half$(x)[[\text{person}(x)][\text{came}(x)]]$, etc.) entails the original assertion. Since the asserted proposition causes a presupposition failure, therefore, it is not compatible with wa:[3]

(7) a. $\forall(x)[[\text{person}(x)][\text{came}(x)]]$ $(= B(T)(w'))$
    b. Scalar Alternative: $\exists x[[\text{person}(x)][\text{came}(x)]$ $(= B(T')(w'))$
    c. $B(T')(w')$ does not entail $B(T)(w')$
    d. $B(T)(w')$ entails $B(T')(w')$
    e. no implicatures

In summary, contrastive topics always induce scalar implicatures, and this property is pronounced as a presuppositional requirement on the proposition that wa takes. The point which is relevant to this paper is that the induced implicatures are always attributed to some attitude-holder. In other words, as depicted in the definition (5), an attitude-holder (the value of x) is required in order to compute the presupposition and the implicature of wa.

3. Implicatures and Attitudes

In the last section, we have seen that contrastive topics induce scalar implicatures that are associated with some attitude-holder. This fact leads us to another interesting set of data. First, if wa is embedded within an attitude predicate, another attitude-holder is introduced (the subject of the attitude predicate). As a result, the sentence becomes ambiguous. To illustrate, (8) is ambiguous depending on (i) which attitude-holder (the speaker or Mary) is responsible for the implicatures, and (ii) which propositions are contrasted (i.e. what propositions are in the alternative set).

(8) Nanninka   **wa**   kita   to Mary ga   shinjite-iru
    some.people CTOP came COMP   NOM believe-PROG
    'Mary believes [some people]$_{CTop}$ came'

    a. Local: The speaker asserts [Mary believes some people came and she doesn't believe everyone came].

    b. Global: The speaker asserts [Mary believes some people came] and the speaker doesn't assert [Mary believes everyone came].

In (8a), the embedded proposition 'Some people came' is contrasted, and the induced implicature 'It's possible that not everyone came' is attributed to Mary. In (8b), the matrix proposition 'Mary believes some people came'

---

[3] Some readers might notice that this analysis is very similar to Büring's (1997) analysis of German Topic-Focus contour. For a comparison with Büring, see Hara 2004.

is contrasted, and the induced implicature 'It's possible that Mary doesn't believe everyone came' is attributed to the speaker.

Secondly, remember that *wa* within a *when*-clause is ungrammatical as in (2), repeated below. However, *wa* under *toki* 'when' becomes acceptable if *wa* is further embedded in an attitude predicate, as in (9).

(2) *Itsumo uchi ni Mary **wa** kuru **toki**, keeki o motteku-ru.
     always house DAT   CTOP come when, cake ACC bring-PRES
     'When Mary$_{CTop}$ comes to our house, she always brings a cake.'

(9) John ga Mary **wa** kuru to   **omot**-ta   **toki**, kanojo ga heya ni
     NOM   **CTOP** come COMP **think**-PAST **when** 3SG   NOM room DAT
     haitte   ki-ta.
     enter come-PAST
     'When John thought that Mary$_{CTop}$ would come, she came into the room.'

To summarize the facts so far, *wa*-induced implicatures are always attributed to some attitude-holder. If *wa* is embedded within an attitude predicate, the induced implicature could be attributed to the subject of the predicate or to the speaker. Also, *wa* within 'when' is unacceptable. However, if *wa* is further embedded in an attitude predicate, *wa* within 'when' becomes acceptable. Based on these facts, I propose the following syntactic account.

I speculate that there exists a movement operation involved in the computation of *wa*-implicatures. Specifically, I propose that the use of *wa* introduces an implicature operator, which contains an attitude-holder variable. The motivation for this movement is that the implicature operator needs to saturate its attitude-holder variable. The attitude-holder could be either the speaker or the subject of the attitude predicate. Recall example (8), repeated below.

(8) Nanninka   **wa**   kita   to Mary ga shinjite-iru
     some.people CTOP came COMP   NOM believe-PROG
     'Mary believes [some people]$_{CTop}$ came'

If Op identifies *Mary* as its attitude-bearer (i.e. it moves below *Mary* as in (10)), sentence (8) is interpreted as Mary's implicature reading (8a). If Op moves below [the speaker], as in (11), sentence (8) is interpreted as the speaker's implicature reading (8b).

(10)

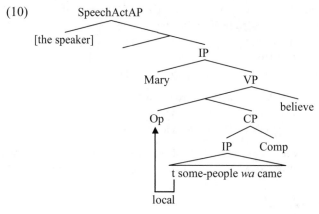

(11)

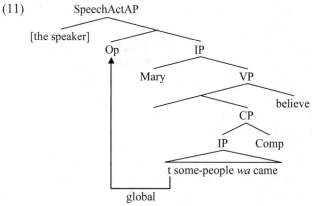

Then, we could say that (2), repeated below, is unacceptable since it causes an adjunct-island violation.

(2) *Itsumo uchi ni Mary **wa** kuru *toki*, keeki o motteku-ru.
    always house DAT   CTOP come when, cake ACC bring-PRES
    'When Mary$_{CTop}$ comes to our house, she always brings a cake.'

The operator cannot find a local attitude predicate. Therefore, it tries to target the global implicature (the speaker's uncertainty), and then it has to cross an adjunct island.

(12) *[[speaker] [$_{XP}$ toki Op [$_{XP}$ ... [$_{AdjunctP}$ [$_{IP}$ *t* Mary wa kuru] toki]]]] (2)
                               *

One might feel uncomfortable introducing a syntactic operation like movement in order to explain a semantic-pragmatic object like implicature. However, having a contrasted argument within a conditional *per se* should be allowed semantically, i.e. semantically interpretable. In (13), the *wa*-marked NP coindexed with an argument within the *when*-clause is allowed if it is overtly outside the *when*-clause. Therefore, it is reasonable to think that the ungrammaticality of (2) is due not to semantic constraints but to syntactic ones.

(13) Mary **wa**$_i$ itsumo uchi ni *pro*$_i$ kuru **toki**, keeki o motteku-ru.
       CTOP always house DAT   come when, cake ACC bring-PRES
       'As for Mary, when she comes to our house, she always brings a cake.'

This speculation raises two questions. First, where exactly does this operator move? And second, why does a *because*-clause not constitute an island? In the next section, I am going to answer these two questions using the notion of evidentiality.

4. Evidentiality

There are some languages (Japanese, Korean, Turkish, and Quechua, to name a few) that have means of encoding an information source of an uttered statement. This encoding is called **evidentiality**. On the assumption that there exist **speech act phrases** (Rivero 1994, Rizzi 1997) and **evidential phrases** (Cinque 1999, Speas 2004), Tenny (2002) argues for the existence of an evidential argument in syntax. The evidential argument refers to an individual who is "responsible for evaluating the truth of a proposition."

In Korean, for example, a sentence with an *e* ending indicates that the speaker of the sentence has direct evidence for the statement, while a sentence with a *tay* ending indicates that the truth value of the statement is based on reported evidence. The examples in (14) are from Papafragou et al. 2004.

(14) a. Toli-ka   mantwu-lul   mek-ess-**e**
            -NOM dumpling-ACC eat-PAST-DECL
         'Toli ate dumplings.'

     b. Toli-ka   mantwu-lul   mek-ess-**tay**
            -NOM dumpling-ACC eat-PAST-DECL
         '(I heard that) Toli ate dumplings.'

According to Tenny (2002), this is mapped in syntax in the following way: the evidential phrase projected by *e* contains [the speaker] as an invisible argument:

(15)

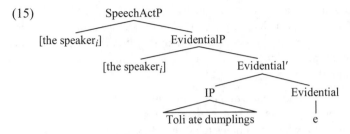

On the other hand, if the evidential phrase is projected by *tay*, someone other than the speaker, x_j, is occupying the position:

(16)

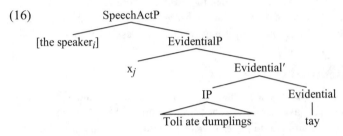

Tenny proposes that *node* 'because' is the head of an evidential projection, and that *node* introduces two arguments: a proposition and an evidential argument.

(17) node [p   x]
         Prop Evid

Tenny provides different interpretations of direct experience predicates within a *because*-clause and a *when*-clause (see Tenny 2002 for details).[4]

In summary, the pragmatic concept of evidentiality is mapped in syntax as an **evidential projection**. This evidential projection contains an evidential argument, which refers to an individual who is responsible for the truth value of the proposition. Japanese *node* 'because' is a head of an evidential projection.

5. Back to Contrastives

Implicatures induced by contrastive topic *wa* also give evidence for the existence of evidential arguments and projections. *Wa* contains a variable which corresponds to the attitude-holder of the induced implicature. I equate this attitude-holder of *wa* to the evidential argument in Tenny's framework.

To illustrate, let us consider the case when a speaker utters (18).

---

[4] See §6.

(18) Nannin-ka wa kita
'[Some people]$_{CTop}$ came.'

In (18), the individual who knows the truth value of the asserted proposition 'some people came' (the evidential argument) is identical to the individual who is not sure about the truth value of the stronger alternative, namely, the individual who implicates 'probably not everyone came' (the attitude-holder of the implicature)—**the speaker**.

Both an evidential argument and an attitude-holder are holders of a point of view towards a proposition. In addition, the implicature operator needs to find an entity for its attitude-holder. Therefore, the attitude-holder variable of *wa* should be saturated by the evidential argument. This saturation is implemented in syntax: the implicature operator adjoins to the evidential projection. This is the answer to the first question.

Now, let us move on to the second question. Why does a *because*-clause not constitute as an island? Why is there an asymmetry between (1) and (2), both repeated below?

(1) Itsumo uchi ni Mary **wa** kuru **node**, kodomo ga yorokob-u.
    always house DAT   CTOP come because, children NOM happy-PRES
    'Because Mary$_{CTop}$ always comes to our house, the children are happy.'

(2) *Itsumo uchi ni Mary **wa** kuru **toki**, keeki o motteku-ru
    always house DAT   CTOP come when, cake ACC bring-PRES
    'When Mary$_{CTop}$ comes to our house, she always brings a cake.'

In (1), the operator finds the local evidential projection which is headed by *node* 'because':

(19) [$_{SpeechActP}$ [speaker] [$_{EvidP}$ ...
     [$_{EvidP}$ Op [$_{EvidP}$ [evid-arg] [$_{Evid'}$ [$_{IP}$ *t* Mary wa kuru] node]]]]]   (1)

In (2), *toki* 'when' does not introduce an evidential projection. The operator cannot find a local landing site within an adjunct. Thus, having *wa* within *toki* causes an island violation:

(20) *[$_{SpeechActP}$ [speaker] [$_{EvidP}$ ...
     [$_{EvidP}$ Op [$_{EvidP}$ ... [$_{AdjunctP}$ [$_{IP}$ *t* Mary wa kuru] toki]]]]   (2)
                                                              *

Wa in a *because*-clause does not cause an island violation, since the *because*-clause itself is the evidential projection that can host the implicature operator.

6. Concluding Remarks and Future Research

By examining the distribution of *wa*, we can see the connection between implicature and evidentiality both pragmatically and syntactically. In terms of pragmatics, both concepts involve a holder of a point of view towards a proposition. With respect to syntax, an implicature operator adjoins to an evidential projection. The analysis accounts for the asymmetry between *because* and *when*. I would like to point out that this analysis crucially requires a framework of syntax-pragmatics interfaces: some pragmatic features are represented in syntax. Without the notion of interfaces, that is, if the interaction between pragmatics and syntax were minimal as traditionally viewed, it would be very difficult to give a unified account for the distribution of *wa*, especially the island-sensitivity of implicature computation.

A reader might notice that my account for the asymmetry between *because* and *when* heavily depends on Tenny's (2002) assumption that *because* introduces an evidential projection, whereas *when* does not. Tenny gives an analysis for different interpretations of direct experience predicates and logophors within a *because*-clause and a *when*-clause, arguing that, unlike *node* 'because', *toki* 'when' does not project an evidential phrase. Although Tenny gives a number of empirical data that are compatible with her claim, she does not provide a conceptual argument that explains why *because* projects an evidential phrase and *when* does not.

In my work in progress, therefore, I modify Tenny's (2002) analysis in a way that *because* takes an evidential phrase as its complement rather than itself projecting the phrase, following Johnston (1994) and Sawada and Larson (forthcoming). Now, in order for the syntactic island analysis to go through, I need to establish two points regarding the syntax of adjuncts. First, there is no evidential phrase under *when*. Second, there could be an evidential phrase under *because*.

According to Johnston (1994), *when* necessarily combines with an open event predicate $<ev, t>$. Since an evidential argument is defined as a sentient being "who holds for the evidence for the truth of a proposition" (Tenny 2002), it is plausible to say that an evidential projection takes a closed event sentence (type t). One cannot hold for the evidence for the truth of an open predicate, since the expression is not saturated to be a truth-condition. Given Johnston's analysis of *when*, therefore, there is no evidential projection under *when*. On the other hand, it is not clear whether *because* necessarily takes an evidential projection as its complement. According to Johnston (1994), *because* takes a closed event proposition t. Johnston's analysis of *because* is certainly compatible with the speculation in which *because* takes an evidential phrase as its complement. Since it is the speaker's or some attitude-bearer's reasoning that connects two conjuncts of *because*, it is plausible to introduce evidentiality (point of view) in the complement of *because*.

References

Büring, D. 1997. The Great Scope Inversion Conspiracy. *Linguistics and Philosophy* 20:175–94.

Chierchia, G. 2001. Scalar Implicatures, Polarity Phenomena, and Syntax/Pragmatics Interface. Manuscript, University of Milan.

Cinque, G. 1999. *Adverbs and Functional Heads: A Cross-Linguistic Perspective.* Oxford: Oxford University Press.

Hara, Y. Forthcoming a. Scope Inversion in Japanese: Contrastive Topics Require Implicatures. *Japanese/Korean Linguistics 13*. Stanford: CSLI.

Hara, Y. Forthcoming b. Implicature Unsuspendable: Japanese Contrastive *wa*. *Proceedings of Texas Linguistics Society* 8.

Johnston, M. 1994. *The Syntax and Semantics of Adverbial Adjuncts.* Doctoral dissertation, University of California Santa Cruz.

Papafragou, A., P. Li, Y. Choi, and C. Han. 2004. Evidentiality in Language and Cognition. Manuscript, University of Delaware, Harvard University, University of Pennsylvania, and Simon Fraser University.

Rivero, M.-L. 1994. Clause Structure and V-movement in the Languages of the Balkans. *Natural Language and Linguistic Theory* 12(1):63–120.

Rizzi, L. 1997. The Fine Structure of the Left-Periphery. *Elements of Grammar*, ed. L. Haegeman, 281–337. Dordrecht: Kluwer.

Sauerland, U. 2004. Scalar Implicatures in Complex Sentences. *Linguistics and Philosophy* 27:367–91.

Sawada, M., and R. Larson. Forthcoming. Presupposition & Root Transforms in Adjunct Clauses. *Proceedings of NELS 34*.

Speas, M. 2004. Evidentiality, Logophoricity and the Syntactic Representation of Pragmatic Features. *Lingua* 114:255–276.

Tenny, C. 2002. Evidentiality, Experiencers, and the Syntax of Point of View in Japanese. Manuscript, Carnegie-Mellon University.

(A)symmetric Nominalization of Measure Expressions in Japanese and Korean

YOUNGJUN JANG*
Chung-Ang University

CHUNG-KON SHI
KAIST

1. Introduction

This paper compares a group of adjectives in English, Japanese, and Korean and observes that so-called measuring expressions in these languages are best characterized when classified into two groups, namely Group I, with positive values, and Group II, with negative values. We show that the members of one group share their own morphological, syntactic, and/or semantic properties that those of the other do not. For example, only the members of Group I, and not of Group II, allow some morphological rule applications. They also allow more basic morphological suffixes. This kind of observation seems to follow from the fact that the members of Group I measure adjectives are more basic (unmarked) compared to those of Group II, and that they have positive values as opposed to the negative values of the members of Group II. We will provide evidence for this claim by analyzing measure expressions in English, Japanese, Korean, and other languages. In

* An earlier version of this paper was presented at the 14th Japanese/Korean Linguistics Conference at the University of Arizona on November 6, 2004. We appreciate the comments and questions from the audience. In particular, we thank many Japanese scholars for providing data and grammatical judgments.

particular, we show that the uniform pattern of nominalization of measure adjectives in Japanese is only superficial/misleading and that Japanese also recognizes the distinction between Group I and Group II measure adjectives, just like English and Korean.

2. Background

As is well known, a set of English adjectives can be grouped into pairs of opposites. Let us call this group of words **measure adjectives**, since they are used for measurement in a sense.

(1) English   Group I   Group II
         high   *low*
         wide   *narrow*
         deep   *shallow*
         broad   *narrow*

Interestingly, the nominalizer -*t*/-*th* in English can attach only to the members of Group I, while another nominalizer, -*ness*, can attach to the members of either group.[1] This is illustrated in the following examples.

(2) English   Group I   Group II
         high – height   *low – *lowth* (cf. *lowness*)
         wide – width   *narrow – *narrowth* (cf. *narrowness*)
         deep – depth   *shallow – *shallowth* (cf. *shallowness*)

It is sometimes claimed that which affix attaches to which root is always quite arbitrary and unpredictable: it is not a matter of rule but must be stated separately for each root as, for example, in a dictionary (Marchand 1969). That is, derivation is part of the lexicon, not part of the grammar of a language. However, we found that even though derivation is in general quite idiosyncratic and a matter of the lexicon of a given language, choosing a particular suffix form in measure expressions is typical cross-linguistically.

Our working hypothesis is that the morphological behavior observed in (2) above is by no means random. Rather it is a rule-based, systematic morphological phenomenon. We will show that this kind of systematic pattern is a universal linguistic property found in languages like Japanese, Korean, English, and other languages that are genealogically or typologically unrelated to each other. In particular, we observe that only the members of

---

[1] The suffix -*t*/-*th* seem to have been widely used for forming nouns from adjectives at an earlier period in English. For example, Marchand (1969) cites the first appearance of the following nominal forms: *growth* (1557), *spilth* (1607), *breadth* (1523), *width* (1627), *coolth* (1547), *warmth*, *illth* (1860, Ruskin), *lowth* (Bacon), *greenth* (Horace Walpole).

Group I measure adjectives allow so-called primary nominalizers and/or adverbializers, while those of Group II allow secondary ones.

3. Two Types of Measure Adjectives

In this section we show that two types of measure adjectives should be recognized and that they behave quite differently with regard to various morphological changes. We provide several tests for establishing two types of measure adjectives in this section.

3.1. Question Formation

Only measure adjectives that are unmarked (Group I in our terms) are felicitous in forming questions out of the blue. Consider the following examples.

(3) a. How high is the wall?
    b. #How low is the wall?

A sentences like (3a) is more natural/unmarked than one like (3b) in unmarked conversational situations. This is true of Japanese and Korean as well.

(4) a. Japanese: kabe wa dore kurai takai desu ka?
      Korean: pyek-un   elmana   nop-sumni ka?
              wall TOP   how   high is   Q
    b. Japanese: #kabe-wa dore kurai hikui-desu ka?
      Korean: #pyek-un   elmana   nac-sumni ka?
                                  low is

Of course, the sentences (3b) and (4b) might be natural in a limited/primed conversational situation. However, it is clear that those in (3a) and (4a) are more natural/basic in normal conversational situations. All the expressions in Group I behave the same way.

3.2. Nominalization

Japanese and Korean, despite so many shared grammatical features, seem to diverge in nominalizing measure adjectives. For example, the Japanese adjective nominalizer -sa can attach to either member of the following pairs, although the nominalizer -mi can attach only to those in Group I.

(5) Japanese

Group I	Group II
takai – takasa 'high'	hikui – hikusa 'low'
hiroi – hirosa 'wide'	semai – semasa 'narrow'
fukai – fukasa 'deep'	asai – asasa 'shallow'
takami	*hikumi
hiromi	*semami
fukami	*asami

In contrast to Japanese, however, Korean seems to behave just like English with regard to nominalizing measure adjectives. That is, only the members of Group I in the following examples allow the primary/lexical nominalizer *-i*, whereas the members of Group II do not.

(6) Korean   Group I   Group II

             nopta – nopi 'high'   *natta – *nati* 'low'

             nelpta – nelpi 'wide'   *copta – *copi* 'narrow'

             kipta – kipi 'deep'   *yatta – *yati* 'shallow'

Note that the secondary nominalizer *-ki* and gerundive marker *-um* can be attached to either Group I or Group II in Korean, as shown in (7).

(7) Korean   Group I   Group II

             nopta – nopki 'high'   *natta – natki* 'low'

             nelpta – nelpki 'wide'   *copta – copki* 'narrow'

             kipta – kipi 'deep'   *yatta – yatki* 'shallow'

                nopum   *natum*

                nelpum   *copum*

                kipum   *yatum*

Note that the Japanese nominalizer *-sa* seem to be equivalent to the secondary nominalizer *-ki* in Korean in the sense that it does not distinguish Group I from Group II.

3.3. Adjectival Conjugation: *-talan* Test

Group I and Group II measure adjectives behave differently in allowing a special adjectival conjugation in Korean. That is, *-talan* '-ish, -like' is a conjunctive that can be allowed only in Group I adjectives but not Group II adjectives. Consider the following examples.

(8)   Group I   Group II

     nopta – noptalan 'high'   *nacta – *nactalan* 'low'

     nelpta – nelptalan 'broad'   *copta – coptalan* 'narrow'

     kipta – ?kiptalan 'deep'   *yatta – *yattalan* 'shallow'

     khuta – khetalan 'big'   *cakta – *caktalan* 'small'

That is, the Korean adjectival suffix *-talan* is allowed only for the unmarked forms (namely Group I measure adjectives). Intriguingly, another type of adjectival morpheme, *-umakhan* '-ish', is allowed only for marked forms, as shown in (9).

(9) Group I   Group II
     *nopta – *nopumakhan* 'high'   *nacta – nacumakhan* 'low'
     *kipta – *kipumakhan* 'deep'   *yatta – yathumakhan* 'shallow'
     *kilta – *kilmakhan* 'long'   *ccalpta – ccalmakhan* 'short'
     *khuta – *khumakhan* 'large'   *cakta – cakumakhan* 'small'

In a nutshell, *-talan* is used only for unmarked forms, while *-umakhan* is used for marked ones.

3.4. Adverb Formation

Unmarked forms allow the primary/lexical adverbial suffix *-(l)i* in Korean, while marked ones do not. This is shown in (10).

(10) Group I   Group II
      nopta – nopi 'high (adv.)'   *natta – *nati* 'low (adv.)'
      kipta – kipi 'deep (adv.)'   *yata – *yati* 'shallowly'
      nelpta – nelli 'broadly'   *copta – *copi* 'narrowly'

Unlike the primary adverbial suffix *-li*, the secondary/complementizer-type suffix *-key* can be attached either members of either Group I or Group II, as in (11).

(11) Group I   Group II
      nopta – nopkey 'high (adv.)'   *natta – natkey* 'low (adv.)'
      kipta – kipkey 'deep (adv.)'   *yata – yatkey* (shallowly)'
      nelpta – nelkey 'broadly'   *copta – copkey* 'narrowly'

It seems that the Japanese adverbial suffix *-ku* behaves not like the Korean lexical adverbial suffix but like the secondary/complementizer-type suffix *-key*. Consider the following Japanese examples.[2]

(12) Group I   Group II
      takaku 'high (adv.)'   *hikuku* 'low (adv.)'
      fukaku 'deep (adv.)'   *asaku* 'shallow (adv.)'
      hiroku 'wide (adv.)'   *semaku* 'narrow (adv.)'

3.5. Causative Formation

Lexical causativization using the morpheme *-hi* seems to be possible only with unmarked forms and not with marked ones. Consider the following.

---

[2] The Japanese adverbial suffix *-ku* seems to behave very much like the Korean suffix *-key* for other functions, too. See Jang and Kim 2001 for discussion.

(13) Group I   Group II
      nopta – nophita 'heighten'   *natta – *nathita* 'make low'
      kipta – ?kiphita 'deepen'   *yatta – *yathita* 'make shallow'
      nelta – nelhita 'widen'   *copta – cophita* 'make narrow'

Interestingly, English also seems to behave like Korean in this sense. That is, the English verbal suffix *-en* seems to attach to the unmarked forms but not to the marked ones, as in (14).[3]

(14) Group I   Group II
      high – heighten   *low – *lowen*   cf. *make low*
      deep – deepen   *shallow – *shallowen* cf. *make shallow*
      wide – widen   *narrow – *narrowen*   cf. *make narrow*

Japanese also show the same pattern of nominalization for measure expressions. Consider the following examples.[4]

(15) Group I   Group II
      takameru 'heighten'   **hikumeru* 'make low'
      fukameru 'deepen'   **asameru* 'make shallow'
      hiromeru 'widen'   **semameru* 'make narrow'
      *shizumeru[5] 'make quiet' **urusameru* 'make loud'

On the other hand, Japanese also allows both unmarked and marked forms to use the periphrastic causative form *-ku suru*, as shown in (16).

(16) Group I   Group II
      takaku suru 'make high'   *hikuku suru* 'make low'
      fukaku suru 'make deep'   *asaku suru* 'make shallow'
      hiroku suru 'make wide'   *semaku suru* 'make narrow'

In this sense Japanese causativization of measure expressions is exactly the same as syntactic (but not lexical) causativization in Korean. Syntactic *-key hata* causativization in Korean can apply to both unmarked and marked forms, as shown in (17).

---

[3] For *long* and *short*, we see the opposite of the expected pattern. That is, *longen* is not acceptable, while *shorten* is OK. We do not have any comment on this phenomenon.

[4] This data was provided by Kunio Nishiyama.

[5] To the best of our knowledge, it is not clear why *shizumeru* is unacceptable. According to our hypothesis, it is expected to be well-formed, contrary to fact. At the moment, we speculate that this particular form might have undergone some idiosyncratic historical changes.

(17) Group I   Group II
    nopkey hata 'make high'   *nackey hata* 'make low'
    kipkey hata 'make deep'   *yatkey hata* 'make shallow'
    nelkey hata 'make wide'   *copkey hata* 'make narrow'

Therefore, it seems that there are two ways to causativize measure expressions in Japanese, just as in Korean, namely, lexical causativization as in (15) and syntactic causativization as in (16). This is why Japanese seems not to distinguish unmarked (Group I) measure expressions from marked ones if we consider only the data in (16).

4. Summary and Conclusion

In this paper we have analyzed so-called measure expressions in English, Japanese, and Korean. We have shown that the members of Group I are more basic or primitive than those of Group II and that only the former allows a set of morphological rule applications. In so doing, we made the following observations. First, Japanese has syntactic (and not lexical) nominalization of measure adjectives, which is similar to the secondary, nonlexical nominalization of measure adjectives in Korean. Korean allows lexical and syntactic nominalization of measure adjectives. Second, Japanese causativization of measure adjectives may in fact be a syntactic process, which does not distinguish unmarked from marked forms of measure adjectives. We conclude that the superficial differences between Japanese and Korean regarding the (a)symmetric behavior of measure expressions are due to the syntactic versus lexical properties of the relevant grammatical procedures. A further question to be pursued would be why then Japanese lacks a primary/lexical nominalizer similar to Korean *-i* and English *-t/-th* and lexical causativization for measure adjectives.

References

Aronoff, M. 1976. *Word Formation in Generative Grammar.* Cambridge: MIT Press.

Becker, W., R. Dixon, and L. Anderson-Inman. 1980. *Morphographic and Root Word Analysis of 26,000 High Frequency Words.* Technical Report 1980-I. Eugene: University of Oregon.

Im, J. 1988. A Study of Co-relation System of Meaning in Korean Opposition-Words. Doctoral dissertation, Kyungbuk University. [in Korean]

Jang, Y. 2002. Measure Expressions. Paper presented at the 2002 Spring Conference of the Modern Grammar Society, Daegu.

Jang, Y., and S.-Y. Kim. 2001. Small Clause Complementizers. *Harvard Studies in Korean Linguistics* 4:377–88.

Jang, Y, and C.-K. Shi. 2003. Measure Expressions in English and Korean. *Harvard Studies in Korean Linguistics* 10:746–52.

Kim, Y. 1995. *A Study of Opposition Words in Korean*. Seoul: Sejong Publisher. [in Korean]

Marchand, H. 1969. *The Categories and Types of Present-Day English Word-Formation: A Synchronic-Diachronic Approach*. München: C. H. Beck.

Shi, C.-K. 1993. The Principle of Word-Formation in Korean. Doctoral dissertation, Korea University. [in Korean]

Shin, J. 1992. The Principle of Markedness in Word-Formation. *Jwusikyenghakpo* 9: 107–11. [in Korean]

Song, C. 1990. A Study of Derivation in Korean. Doctoral dissertation, Seoul University, Seoul. [in Korean]

"Neg-sensitive" Elements, Neg-c-command, and Scrambling in Japanese

KIYOKO KATAOKA*
Nihon University

1. Goal

Most languages have some expressions which must occur with sentential negation. *XP sika* and *roku-na N* are instances of such elements in Japanese.

(1) a. Taroo wa manga **sika** yoma-**nai**. / *yomu (koto)
        TOP comics all:but read-NEG /   read (COMP)
        'Taro does not read any kind of book but comics.'

    b. Taroo **sika**   manga o yoma-**nai** / *yomu (koto)
        all:but comics ACC read-NEG /   read (COMP)
        'Nobody but Taro reads comics.'

---

* I am very grateful to Hajime Hoji, Yukinori Takubo, and Ayumi Ueyama for their careful comments and insightful suggestions. I also deeply appreciate the help and patient support by Teruhiko Fukaya, Maki Irie, Yasuhiko Miura, Emi Mukai, Yukiko Tsuboi, and other students at USC and Kyūshū University, though I cannot mention all of their names here because of space limitations. I have greatly benefited from discussions with them and their patient support. Lastly, I would like to thank to the participants at the 14th Japanese/Korean Linguistics Conference.

(2) a. Saikin **roku-na** sakka ga syoo o {tora-**nai** / *toru}.
   recently good writer nom   award ACC get-NEG / get
   'Recently, no good writers have gotten an award.'

   b. Taroo wa itumo **roku-na** koto o   {si-**nai** / *suru}.
   TOP always good thing ACC do-NEG / do
   'Taro always does damn things.'

In this paper, I will refer to such "Neg(ation)-sensitive" elements as NPIs for ease of exposition.[1] In general, the condition in (3) (Klima 1964) is assumed, and this assumption is widely accepted in the literature on Japanese syntax and semantics (Kato 1994, 2002, Kuno 1995, and others).

(3) An NPI must be c-commanded by Neg at LF.

The goal of this paper is to show, contrary to this general assumption, that not all NPIs in Japanese obey the condition in (3). More specifically, I will argue for (4) and (5) below.

(4) *Roku-na N* must be c-commanded by Neg at LF.

(5) *XP sika* must c-command Neg at LF.

I will first demonstrate that *roku-na N* is, but *XP sika* is **not**, subject to (3). For that purpose, we need to examine whether those items can occur in a position outside the c-command domain of Neg at LF. Though it appears that every NP in Japanese can be in the c-command domain of Neg at LF, as seen in (6) below, I will demonstrate that some elements in a certain configuration cannot be in the c-command domain of Neg at LF, and I will show how to identify such an element. Making use of the construction in question, I will first argue for (4), and then propose (5), on the basis of scope interactions between Neg and QP in the sentences containing *XP sika* and another QP. I will then discuss some consequences.

2. The Scrambling Construction, A-scrambled Object and Neg

It has been observed that the scope relation between Neg and QP is ambiguous in Japanese (Kuno 1980).[2] Given the general assumption that the

---

[1] The term *NPI* (Negative Polarity Item) has been widely used as a descriptive term to refer to such "Negation-sensitive" items, departing from the original notion of polarity in the terms of works such as Fauconnier 1975 and Ladusaw 1979. Chapter 1, §1.1 of Kataoka 2004 contains some relevant discussion.

[2] It has been observed that the wide scope reading for Neg over a QP is not easy to obtain compared with the one for the QP over Neg, especially for a subject QP. As pointed out in Imani 1993, however, the difference in acceptability can be attributed to pragmatic factors, and it is possible even for a subject QP to be in the scope of Neg. As also pointed out in Imani 1993, the interpretation in question can obtain more readily when the sentence is embedded in a con-

scope of α is its c-command domain at LF, this suggests that every NP α can be in the c-command domain of Neg where α and the Neg are clause-mates.

(6) a. [gonin-izyoo no seito]$_{QP}$ ga so-no hon o yoma-**na**-katta
five-or:more GEN student NOM that-GEN book ACC read-NEG-PAST
(koto)
(COMP)
'Five or more students did not read that book.' *QP > Neg, Neg > QP*

b. [gosatu-izyoo no hon]$_{QP}$ o so-no seito ga yoma-**na**-katta
five-or:more GEN book ACC that-GEN student NOM read-NEG-PAST
(koto)
(COMP)
'Five or more books, that student did not read.' *QP > Neg, Neg > QP*

A close examination of sentences with the *O(bject) S(ubject) V* order, however, reveals that this is not quite correct.

2.1. The Scrambling Construction and Its Structural Ambiguity

While it has been assumed since the mid 1980s that the subject asymmetrically c-commands the object in a non-scrambling sentence, the structural relation between the subject and the object is said to be ambiguous in the scrambling construction, and each case reveals its own properties, as illustrated below (Saito 1992, Ueyama 1998).[3]

(7) a. A-scrambling: A-properties (e.g. absence of WCO effects)
PF : NP-ACC/DAT NP-NOM V
LF : [NP-ACC/DAT [NP-NOM V]]

b. A'-scrambling: A'- properties (e.g. reconstruction effects)
PF : NP-ACC/DAT NP-NOM V
LF : [NP-NOM [NP-ACC/DAT V]]

2.2. A-scrambling or A'-scrambling?

I will show that the object in an A-scrambling case (henceforth **A-scrambled object**) is outside the c-command domain of Neg at LF. Since it is necessary, for that purpose, to know whether the relevant object is an A-

---

ditional clause, and it is for this reason that some of the examples here are embedded in a conditional clause.

[3] In this paper, I use the terms *scrambling* and *scrambled object* as purely descriptive terms. Though I do not discuss here how the two LF representations in (7) are derived, since the discussion here is not affected, Ueyama's base-generation analysis of A-scrambled objects is adopted in Kataoka 2004 on the basis of negation-related phenomena, including those which are not discussed in this paper.

scrambled object or not, I will first introduce two tests in order to identify an A-scrambled object.[4]

2.2.1. Test 1: Bound Variable Anaphora (BVA)

The availability of BVA has been regarded as a test to determine whether a given syntactic position is an A-position or an A'-position, and an NP is said to be in an A-position if the binding is possible from its position. The same test has been applied to the scrambled object in Japanese; if the scrambled NP can serve as a "binder", it is considered to be an A-scrambled NP (Ueyama 1998, Yoshimura 1992).[5] See (8), where the object QP is an A-scrambled object when the BVA obtains.[6]

(8) [Itutu-izyoo no ginkoo]$_i$ ni soko$_i$ no torihikisaki ga   Nissan o
    five-or:more GEN bank DAT   it GEN   client   NOM Nissan ACC
    suisensi-ta.
    recommend-PAST
    'To [each of five or more banks]$_i$, its$_i$ client recommended Nissan.'

2.2.2. Test 2: Resumption

Since it has been observed that "resumption" is allowed in A-scrambling but not in A'-scrambling (Hayashishita 1997, Hoji and Ueyama 1998, Hoji 2003), its use is another way to force the scrambled NP to be an A-scrambled NP. As in (9a), resumption (*soko*) is allowed when the object enters into BVA as a binder (i.e. when it is an A-scrambled object). However, it is not allowed in (9b), where the object enters into BVA as a bindee through reconstruction (i.e. when the object is an A'-scrambled object).[7]

---

[4] An A-scrambled object, according to Hayashishita 2004, can also be identified based on scope interpretation. See Kataoka 2004 (§3.3.2 and §3.4.2) for more details.

[5] Ueyama 1998 (§2.2.1 and Chapter 2, Appendix B, §B.1.3) contains a survey of much of the past literature and provide reasons why the tests that have often been used in the literature, such as the "anaphor-binding", are not reliable tests for our purposes.

[6] For what "binder-bindee" pairs should be used in the relevant paradigm and why, see Hoji 2003 and the references provided there.

[7] One might object that examples with resumption are less than perfect. However, I would like to report, according to a survey I have conducted, that 9 out of 14 people find (9a) acceptable, and, more crucially, all the speakers find (9b) unacceptable. The judgmental variation and fluctuation on resumption in the scrambled sentences is addressed in Hoji 2003. See Ueyama 1998 (Chapter 2, Appendix A.2) and Hoji 2003 (§3) for more details.

(9) a. [Itutu-izyoo   no ginkoo]$_i$ ni soko$_i$ no torihikisaki ga *soko* ni
        five-or:more GEN bank   DAT   it   GEN   client NOM it DAT
        Nissan o   suisensi-ta.
        Nissan ACC recommend-PAST
        '*To [each of five or more banks]$_i$*, its$_i$ client recommended Nissan
        to it.'

    b. *Soko$_i$ no torihikisaki ni [itutu-izyoo   no ginkoo]$_i$ ga *soko* ni
         it GEN   client   DAT five-or:more GEN bank   NOM it DAT
        Nissan o   suisensi-ta.
        Nissan ACC recommend-PAST
        '*To its$_i$ client*, [each of five or more banks]$_i$ recommended Nissan
        to it.'

2.3. A-scrambled Objects and Neg

I will now demonstrate, by making use of the two methods above, that the A-scrambled object is outside the c-command domain of Neg at LF.

First, observe that the QP in (10), which is an A-scrambled object, cannot be in the scope of Neg, while the QP in (11), which can be an A'-scrambled object, can be in the scope of Neg (see note 8 below).

(10) [Itutu-izyoo   no ginkoo]$_i$ ni soko$_i$ no torihikisaki ga   Nissan o
       five-or:more GEN bank   DAT   it   GEN   client NOM Nissan ACC
       suisensi-**na**-katta.
       recommend-NEG-PAST
       'To [each of five or more banks]$_i$, its$_i$ client did not recommend
       Nissan.'   *when BVA obtains:* ^{OK}*5-or-more > Neg*, **Neg > 5-or-more*

(11) [Itutu-izyoo   no ginkoo] ni Toyota ga Nissan o
       five:or:more GEN bank   DAT Toyota NOM Nissan ACC
       suisensi-**na**-katta.
       recommend- NEG-PAST
       'To five or more banks, Toyota did not recommend Nissan.'
       5-or-more > Neg, Neg > 5-or-more

Second, observe that the QP in (12), which is forced to be an A-scrambled object by the use of resumption, cannot be in the scope of Neg. Compare this again with (11) above, whose object can be in the scope of Neg.

(12) [Itutu-izyoo no ginkoo] ni   Toyota   ga *soko* ni   Nissan   o
     five-or:more GEN bank DAT Toyota NOM it DAT Nissan ACC
     suisensi-**na**-katta.
     recommend-NEG-PAST
     '*To five or more banks*, Toyota did not recommend Nissan *to it*.'
     *5-or-more > Neg, *Neg > 5-or-more*

Given the assumption that the scope of α is its c-command domain at LF, the observations above show that the A-scrambled object cannot be in the c-command domain of Neg at LF. Thus, it is reasonable to assume that the A-scrambled object is outside the c-command domain of Neg before QR. The structures before QR of the A/A'-scrambling cases should be as illustrated in (13). Notice that the general condition on movement in (14) should be assumed here.

(13) Structures before QR
      a. A-scrambling: [NP-ACC/DAT [$_{NegP}$ [$_{VP}$ NP-NOM V] [$_{Neg}$ -nai]]]
      b. A'-scrambling: [$_{NegP}$ [$_{VP}$ NP-NOM [NP-ACC/DAT V]] [$_{Neg}$ -nai]]

(14) Movement cannot be downward.

3. *XP sika, roku-na N* as A-scrambled Objects

Now I will turn to *XP sika* and *roku-na N*, and show that *XP sika* can, but *roku-na N* cannot, occur as an A-scrambled object.

3.1. The A-scrambling Case with BVA

As seen in §2.2.1, the scrambled object is forced to be an A-scrambled object with the BVA interpretation. *XP sika* can be a binder in the scrambled position for the dependent term in the subject NP, while *roku-na N* cannot, as illustrated in (15) and (16a).[8]

---

[8] Some speakers find the example (16a) acceptable, although the proposed analysis predicts it to be unacceptable. One possibility that comes to mind is as follows. For those speakers who find (16a) acceptable, BVA(*roku-na N*, soko) is not based on the c-command relation at LF, but it arises in a way that is sensitive to a PF-precedence relation ("co-I-indexation" in the terms of Ueyama 1998), and the condition on *roku-na N* in (4) is satisfied at LF "through re-construction". Although it was suppressed in the earlier discussion, some speakers also find the Neg > QP reading not impossible for (10). We might pursue essentially the same account for the availability of the Neg > QP reading in the examples like (10) for those speakers. The conclusions reached in this study in regard to *XP sika* and *roku-na N* (see (4) and (5)), however, are not affected by those observations, since the predictions to be discussed in §5 in regard to *XP sika* and *roku-na N* are borne out even for those speakers who do not agree with the reported judgment on (16a) and (10). Kataoka forthcoming contains further discussion.

(15) Mosi [Tookyoo-ginkoo ni   **sika**]$_i$ soko$_i$ no torihikisaki ga
     if   Bank of Tokyo DAT all:but   it GEN   client NOM
     syootaizyoo o okura-**na**-katta-ra, ...
     invitation ACC send-NEG-PAST-if
     'If, to [any company except Bank of Tokyo]$_i$, its$_i$ client did not send
     an invitation, ...' $^{OK}BVA(Tookyoo$-$ginkoo\ ni\ sika,\ soko)$

(16) a. *Mosi [**roku-na** ginkoo]$_i$ ni soko$_i$ no torihikisaki ga
         if   good   bank DAT it GEN   client NOM
         syootaizyoo o okura-**na**-katta-ra, ...
         invitation ACC send-NEG-PAST-if
         $*BVA(roku$-$na\ ginkoo,\ soko)$

     b. Mosi [**roku-na** ginkoo]$_i$ ga soko$_i$ no torihikisaki ni
         if   good   bank NOM it GEN   client DAT
         syootaizyoo o okura-**na**-katta-ra, ...
         invitation ACC send-NEG-PAST-if
         'If [no good banks]$_i$ send an invitation to its$_i$ client, ...'
         $^{OK}BVA(roku$-$na\ ginkoo,\ soko)$

3.2. The A-scrambling Case with Resumption

Resumption also forces the scrambled object to be an A-scrambled object.
As seen below, *XP sika* can, but *roku-na N* cannot, occur with resumption.

(17) Mosi Tookyoo-ginkoo ni   **sika**   Mitubisi   ga *soko* ni
     if   Bank of Tokyo DAT all:but Mitsubishi NOM it DAT
     syootaizyoo o okura-**na**-katta-ra, ...
     invitation ACC send-NEG-PAST-if
     'If, *to any company except Bank of Tokyo*, Mitsubishi did not send
     there an invitation, ...'

(18) *Mosi **roku-na** ginkoo ni   Mitubisi   ga *soko* ni syootaizyoo o
     if   good   bank DAT Mitsubishi NOM it DAT invitation ACC
     okura-**na**-katta-ra, ...
     send-NEG-PAST-if

The observations above show that *XP sika* can, but *roku-na N* cannot, occur
as an A-scrambled object. Given (13) and (14), I conclude that *roku-na N*
must be c-commanded by Neg at LF, but that *XP sika* can be outside the c-
command domain of Neg at LF. What then is the necessary condition on *XP
sika*? I will propose that *XP sika* **must c-command** Neg at LF.

4. Proposal

I will argue that *XP sika* must c-command Neg at LF, as stated in (5) above.

4.1. Scope Interaction between *XP sika* and QP

The argument for the proposal comes from the scope interaction between *XP sika* and QP. As noted above with the example in (6), the scope relation between Neg and QP is generally observed to be ambiguous. This scope ambiguity can be accounted for by assuming, as in (19), that there are two distinct landing sites for QR, an instance of an adjunction to a maximal projection (Hasegawa 1991: §1).

(19) a. PF : ... QP_1 ... V-nai
     b. LF1 : $[QP_1 [[_{VP} ... t_1 ...] [_{Neg} \text{-nai}]]]$ $\rightarrow QP_1 > Neg$
     c. LF2 : $[[_{VP} QP_1 [_{VP} ... t_1 ...]] [_{Neg} \text{-nai}]]$ $\rightarrow Neg > QP_1$

However, when *XP sika* and a QP are in the same clause, the ambiguity disappears. As in (20), where the *XP sika* is the subject of the sentence, the QP, which is c-commanded by *XP sika* before QR, cannot take scope over Neg. On the other hand, as shown in (21), a QP which c-commands *XP sika* before QR cannot be in the scope of Neg.

(20) Yamada-sensei   **sika** [sannin-izyoo no gakusei]$_{QP1}$ o
       -professor all:but three-or:more GEN student   ACC

   Mitubisi ni syookaisi-**nai** (koto)
   Mitsubishi DAT introduce-NEG (COMP)

   'All professors but Prof. Yamada do not introduce three or more
   students to Mitsubishi.'   (i) *$QP1 > Neg$, (ii) $^{OK}Neg > QP1$

(21) [sannin-izyoo no   sensei]$_{QP2}$ ga Taroo o   Mitubisi ni **sika**
     three-or:more GEN professor   NOM   ACC Mitsubishi DAT all:but

   syookaisi-nai (koto)
   introduce-NEG (COMP)

   'Three or more professors do not introduce Taro to any company but
   Mitsubishi.'   (i) $^{OK}QP2 > Neg$, (ii) *$Neg > QP2$

4.2. Analysis

The unambiguity suggests that, if c-commanded by *XP sika* before QR, a QP cannot raise to a position outside the c-command domain of Neg at LF, while if it c-commands *XP sika* before QR, it cannot be in a position c-commanded by Neg at LF.

Assuming that *XP sika* undergoes QR, and that the **Scope Rigidity Principle** (Huang 1982, Hoji 1985) holds in Japanese, I propose that *XP sika* must be in NegP-Spec at LF.

(22) Scope Rigidity Principle (SRP): The c-command relation between maximal projections XP_1 and XP_2 cannot be altered through LF movement.

(23) *XP sika* must be in NegP-Spec at LF.[9]

Given that the SRP prohibits the c-command relation between QPs from being altered after QR, a QP, if c-commanded by *XP sika* before QR, cannot raise beyond the *XP sika*, and therefore must stay inside the c-command domain of Neg at LF, since *XP sika* must be in NegP-Spec at LF after QR. (In what follows, "OK" means that the condition/principle is satisfied.)

(24) *XP sika$_1$ QP$_2$ V-nai*, where *XP sika$_1$* c-commands QP$_2$ before QR

a. LF1: $[[_{NegP}$ XP sika$_1$ $[_{Neg'}$ $[_{VP}$ QP$_2$ $[_{VP}$ t$_1$ $[_{V'}$ t$_2$ V$]]]$ $[_{Neg}$ -nai$]]]]$
   ^{OK}(23) **for *XP sika*,** ^{OK}(22) **SRP**

b. *LF2: $[_{IP}$ $[_{IP}$ QP$_2$ $[_{NegP}$ XP sika$_1$ $[_{Neg'}$ $[_{VP}$ t$_1$ $[_{V'}$ t$_2$ V$]]$ $[_{Neg}$ -nai$]]]]]$
   ^{OK}(23) **for *XP sika*,** *(22) **SRP**

c. *LF3: $[_{IP}$ XP sika$_1$ $[_{IP}$ QP$_2$ $[_{IP}$ $[_{NegP}$ $[_{Neg'}$ $[_{VP}$ t$_1$ $[_{V'}$ t$_2$ V$]]$ $[_{Neg}$ -nai$]]]]]]$
   *(23) **for *XP sika*,** ^{OK}(22) **SRP**

If the QP$_2$ raised to the position outside the NegP, it would violate the SRP, as in (24b), or the condition on *XP sika* would be unsatisfied, as in (24c). Consequently, the QP which is c-commanded by *XP sika* cannot be outside the c-command domain of Neg at LF, making its wide scope over Neg impossible (see (20)).

On the other hand, if it c-commands *XP sika* before QR, a QP must

---

[9] *XP sika* does not fall into the same category as the Negative Concord items found in Italian or Spanish (Zanuttini 1991), since *XP sika* cannot induce negation by itself, even in an ellipsis context with negation in the first "conjunct", as is observed below.

(i) Hoka-ni dare-ka   ko-na-katta   no?
    else   anybody come-NEG-PAST Q
    'Didn't anybody else come?'

    Taroo sika   ko-na-katta. / *Taroo sika kita. / *Taroo sika.
    all:but come-NEG-PAST /   all:but came /   all:but
    'Nobody but Taro came.'

The original idea for the hypothesis in (23) was suggested to me by Y. Takubo in 1998. Aoyagi and Ishii (1994) also propose a condition along the same lines based on the one-to-one relation between *XP sika* and Neg, claiming that *XP sika* must be licensed by Spec-head agreement with Neg at LF. The important point of my proposal, however, is not whether there is some kind of agreement or not, but that, at LF, *XP sika* must c-command and be close enough to Neg, just like the structural relation between Spec and head. Further discussion can be found in Kataoka 2004 (§5.2) and Kataoka forthcoming, including the differences between the two analyses.

raise beyond the *XP sika*, due to the SRP, and therefore must be outside the c-command domain of Neg, since *XP sika* must be in NegP-Spec at LF.

(25) QP_2 *XP* $sika_1$ *V-nai*, where QP_2 c-commands *XP* $sika_1$ before QR

    a. LF1: $[[_{IP} QP_2 [_{IP} [_{NegP}$ XP-$sika_1 [_{Neg'} [_{VP} t_2 [_{V'} t_1 V]] [_{Neg}$ -nai$]]]]]]$
        ^{OK}(23) **for *XP sika*,** ^{OK}(22) **SRP**

    b. LF2: $[[_{NegP}$ XP-$sika_1 [_{Neg'} [_{VP} QP_2 [_{VP} t_2 [_{V'} t_1 V]]] [_{Neg}$ -nai$]]]]$
        ^{OK}(23) **for *XP sika*,** *(22) **SRP**

    c. LF3: $[_{IP} [_{NegP} [_{Neg'} [_{VP} QP_2 [_{VP}$ XP-$sika_1 [_{VP} t_2 [_{V'} t_1 V]]]] [_{Neg}$ -nai$]]]]$
        *(23) **for *XP sika*,** ^{OK}(22) **SRP**

In order for the QP to be in the c-command domain of Neg at LF, the QP must either be in the c-command domain of the *XP sika*, violating the SRP as in (25b), or be in the c-command domain of Neg, leaving the condition on *XP sika* unsatisfied as in (25c). Therefore, the QP which c-commands *XP sika* before QR cannot be in the c-command domain of Neg at LF.

    Thus the condition in (23), together with (22), accounts for the observation in (20) and (21). A QP which is c-commanded by *XP sika* before QR cannot take scope over Neg because it cannot be outside the c-command domain of Neg at LF, while a QP which c-commands *XP sika* before QR cannot be interpreted in the scope of Neg because it cannot be in the c-command domain of Neg at LF.

5. Some Consequences and Predictions

I argued in §3 that *roku-na N* must be c-commanded by Neg at LF (see (4)). I then argued in §4 that, given (22) and (23), a QP which c-commands *XP sika* before QR cannot be in the c-command domain of Neg at LF, while a QP c-commanded by *XP sika* before QR must be in the c-command domain of Neg at LF. Assuming that *roku-na N* undergoes QR at LF (see (16b) above), it follows that *roku-na N*, if it c-commands *XP sika* before QR, must c-command the *XP sika* at LF due to the SRP, and hence be outside the c-command domain of Neg, violating (4). We thus deduce that *roku-na N* cannot occur in the position c-commanding *XP sika* before QR.

5.1. *XP sika* and *roku-na N* in the Non-scrambling Construction

Given the assumption that the subject asymmetrically c-commands the object in a non-scrambling sentence, the first prediction we make is (26).

(26) **Prediction 1**: *Roku-na N* cannot occur as the subject of a non-scrambling sentence where *XP sika* occurs as the object in the same sentence, with both being related to the same Neg.

(27) a. LF1: *$[_{IP}$ roku-na N$_2$ $[_{IP}$ $[_{NegP}$ XP sika$_1$ $[_{Neg'}$ $[_{VP}$ t$_2$ $[_{V'}$ t$_1$ V]]
       $[_{Neg}$ - nai]]]]]
       *(4) for *roku-na N*, ^{OK}(23) for *XP-sika*, ^{OK}(22) **SRP**

      b. LF2: *$[_{IP}$ $[_{NegP}$ XP sika$_1$ $[_{Neg'}$ $[_{VP}$ roku-na N$_2$ $[_{VP}$ t$_2$ $[_{V'}$ t$_1$ V]]]
       $[_{Neg}$ -nai]]]
       ^{OK}(4) for *roku-na N*, ^{OK}(23) for *XP sika*, *(22) **SRP**

This first prediction is borne out, as illustrated in (28), which should be compared with acceptable (29a), where the subject *XP sika* c-commands the object *roku-na N*.

(28) *[**roku-na** sensei   ga] [Taroo **sika**]   Mitubisi   ni   syookaisi-**nai**
        good professor NOM   all:but Mitsubishi DAT introduce-NEG
      (koto)
      (COMP)

(29) a. [Mori-sensei **sika**] [**roku-na** kaisya   o] Taroo ni   syookaisi-**nai**
          -professor all:but   good   company ACC   DAT introduce-NEG
        (koto)
        (COMP)
        (roughly) 'All professors but Prof. Mori do not introduce any decent company to Taro.'

      b. LF: $^{OK}[_{IP}$ $[_{NegP}$ XP sika$_1$ $[_{Neg'}$ $[_{VP}$ rokuna-N$_2$ $[_{VP}$ t$_1$ $[_{V'}$ t$_2$ V]]]
         $[_{Neg}$ -nai]]]
         ^{OK}(4) for *roku-na N*, ^{OK}(23) for *XP sika*, ^{OK}(22) **SRP**

The status of (29) is as expected. A QP which is c-commanded by *XP sika* before QR can be in the c-command domain of Neg at LF, and hence there can be a legitimate LF representation, given in (29b), with all the conditions in question satisfied.

5.2. *XP sika* and *roku-na N* in the Scrambling Construction

The second prediction concerns the scrambling construction. Given the structural ambiguity of a scrambled sentence, two distinct c-command relations between *roku-na N* and *XP sika* are possible at LF for a phonetic string of the form *roku-na N* ACC *XP sika*$_{(subj)}$ *V*.

(30) a. A'-scrambling: *XP sika*$_{(subj)}$ >> *roku-na N* ACC
      b. A-scrambling: *roku-na N* ACC >> *XP sika*$_{(subj)}$
         (where α >> β means that α c-commands β)

It is thus expected that (31), which is the scrambled counterpart of (29a), can be acceptable, since it can be analyzed as an A'-scrambling case, where *roku-na N* is c-commanded by *XP sika* before QR.

(31) [**roku-na** kaisya   o] [Mori-sensei **sika**] Taroo ni syookaisi-**nai**
     good company ACC   -professor all:but   DAT introduce-NEG
     (koto)
     (COMP)
     (roughly) 'All professors but Prof. Mori do not introduce any decent
     company to Taro.'

Now, if we 'force' (31) to be an instance of A-scrambling, *roku-na N* should be in a position c-commanding *XP sika* before QR, and hence could not be in the c-command domain of Neg at LF, given (14). Thus we predict (32), since resumption forces (31) to be an instance of A-scrambling, as seen in §2.2.2.

(32) **Prediction 2**: Resumption makes (31) unacceptable.

This prediction is also borne out, as indicated in (33a), whose LF representation should be (33b).

(33) a. *[**roku-na** kaisya o] [Mori-sensei **sika**] Taroo ni *soko* o
        good company ACC   -professor all:but   DAT there ACC
        syookaisi-**nai** (koto)
        introduce-NEG (COMP)

    b. LF: $[_{IP}$ roku-na N_2 ACC $[_{IP}$ t_1 $[_{NegP}$ XP sika$_2$ $[_{Neg'}$ $[_{VP}$ t_2 $[_{V'}$ *soko* ACC
       V]] $[_{Neg}$ -nai]]]]
      *(4) **for** *roku-na N*

6. Concluding Remarks

I first demonstrated that the A-scrambled object is outside the c-command domain of Neg at LF. I then argued for (4) and (23) (which entails (5) by definition).

(4)   *Roku-na N* must be c-commanded by Neg at LF.

(5)   *XP sika* must c-command Neg at LF.

(23) *XP sika* must be in NegP-Spec at LF.

References

Aoyagi, H., and T. Ishii. 1994. On NPI Licensing in Japanese. *Japanese/Korean Linguistics 4*, ed. N. Akatsuka, 295–311. Stanford: CSLI.

Fauconnier, G. 1975. Pragmatic Scales and Logical Structure. *Linguistic Inquiry* 6: 353–75.

Hasegawa, N. 1991. On Non-Argument Quantifiers: Floating Quantifiers and the Narrow Scope Reading. *Metropolitan Linguistics* 11: 52–78.

Hayashishita, J.-R. 1997. On the Scope Ambiguity in the Scrambling Construction in Japanese. Manuscript, University of Southern California.

Hayashishita, J.-R. 2004. Syntactic Scope and Non-Syntactic Scope. Doctoral dissertation, University of Southern California.

Hoji, H. 1985. Logical Form Constraints and Configurational Structures in Japanese. Doctoral dissertation, University of Washington.

Hoji, H. 2003. Falsifiability and Repeatability in Generative Grammar: A Case Study of Anaphora and Scope Dependency in Japanese. *Lingua* 113:377–446.

Hoji, H., and A. Ueyama. 1998. Resumption in Japanese. Manuscript, University of Southern California. (http://www.gges.org/work/hoji/WECOL-handout-3.pdf)

Huang, C.-T. J. 1982. Logical Relations in Chinese and the Theory of Grammar. Doctoral dissertation, MIT.

Imani, I. 1993. Hitei-ryōkabun o zenken ni motsu jōkenbun ni tuite (On conditional clauses including quantifiers and negative element). *Nihongo no jōken-hyōgen*, ed. T. Masuoka, 203–22. Tokyo: Kurosio.

Kataoka, K. 2004. Nihongo hiteibun no kōzō: Kakimaze-bun to hiteikō-hyōgen (Syntactic structure of Japanese negative sentences: Scrambling construction and negation-sensitive elements). Doctoral dissertation, Kyūshū University. (A slightly revised version will be published by Kurosio, Tokyo.)

Kataoka, K. Forthcoming. Two Types of Neg-sensitive Elements.

Kato, Y. 1994. Negative Polarity and Movement. *MIT Working Papers in Linguistics* 24:101–20.

Kato, Y. 2002. Negation in English and Japanese: Some (A)symmetries and Their Theoretical Implications. *Proceedings of the Sophia Symposium on Negation*, 1–21. Tokyo: Sophia University.

Klima, E. S. 1964. Negation in English. *The Structure of Language*, eds. J. Fodor and J. Katz, 246–323. Englewood Cliffs, N.J.: Prentice-Hall.

Kuno, S. 1980. The Scope of the Question and Negation in Some Verb-Final Languages. *CLS* 16:155–69.

Kuno, S. 1995. Negative Polarity Items in Japanese and English. *Harvard Working Papers in Linguistics* 5:165–97.

Ladusaw, W. A. 1979. *Polarity Sensitivity as Inherent Scope Relations.* New York: Garland.

Saito, M. 1992. Long Distance Scrambling in Japanese. *Journal of East Asian Linguistics* 1:69–118.

Ueyama, A. 1998. Two Types of Dependency. Doctoral dissertation, University of Southern California.

Yoshimura, N. 1992. Scrambling and Anaphora in Japanese. Doctoral dissertation. University of Southern California.

Zanuttini, R. 1991. Syntactic Properties of Sentential Negation: A Comparative Study of Romance Languages. Doctoral dissertation, University of Pennsylvania.

A Theory of Number Marking: Syntax-Semantics Interface Approach

CHONGHYUCK KIM*
University of Delaware

1. Introduction

In languages such as English, number is transparently reflected in the morphological shape of a nominal expression. In general, the presence or absence of the plural marker *s* determines the plurality/singularity of the nominal expression:

(1) a. John met my student.
 b. John met my students.

My student in (1a) can only refer to a singular individual. In order to refer to a plural individual, the plural marker *s* must be added to *student*, as shown in (1b). Many languages, however, do not have this straightforward one-to-one relationship between number and morphology. Consider the following Chinese example.

(2) Zuotian wo mai le shu.
 Yesterday I buy ASP book
 'Yesterday, I bought one or more books.' (Rullmann and You 2003:1)

* I would like to thank Satoshi Tomioka, Benjamin Bruening, Peter Cole, and Christine Brisson for their insightful comments and encouragement.

As indicated in the translation of (2), the nonplural nominal *shu* 'book' can be construed as singular or plural depending on context. The morphology of the word *shu* does not provide any clue to what the number interpretation of the word would be. A striking contrast exists between English-type languages and Chinese-type languages in terms of number marking.

The contrast between (1) and (2) is just one of several striking differences that exist between English-type languages and Chinese-type languages, but it serves well to illustrate the purpose of this paper: How is number marking achieved in a language without a transparent number-morphology correspondence?[1] In an effort to answer this question, this paper examines the number marking patterns of Korean, another language that does not have a transparent relationship between number and morphology. The main proposal of this paper is that a number interpretation of a nominal expression is regulated by an intricate interaction of NumP with a semantic principle.

The organization of this paper is as follows. §2 introduces three Korean facts that will be at the heart of our discussion. A theory of number marking is developed in §3 that accounts for the Korean facts. §4 concludes the paper.

2. Number Marking in Korean

Just like Chinese nonplural nominals, Korean nonplural nominals are in general interpreted as singular or plural depending on context:

(3) Chelswu-nun   ecey chinkwu-lul manna-ss-ta.
      -TOP yesterday friend-ACC meet-PST-DC
      'Chelswu met friend yesterday.' (literal)[2]

The argument *chinkwu*, whose literal meaning is 'friend', does not have to be plural-marked even if *Chelswu* met more than one friend. In this plural context, (3) has the same truth condition as its plural-marked counterpart in (4).

---

[1] The contrast between English-type languages and Chinese-type languages raises many other important questions than the one in the text. That is, where do the differences between the two types of languages come from? Do the languages employ the same number marking mechanism or not? Unfortunately, I cannot discuss these important issues here for space reasons. See Kim 2005 for a detailed discussion of these issues.

[2] A Korean bare noun is underspecified in many respects. The number and definiteness information of a bare noun is retrieved by the context in which the bare noun is uttered. So, it can in principle be definite/indefinite or singular/plural depending on context. Rather than listing all the possible interpretations (e.g. 'Chelswu met a/the student/students' for (3)) for a bare noun in the translation line, I put the literal meaning of it when its actual meaning is not of our concern.

(4) Chelswu-nun   ecey   chinkwu-tul-lul manna-ss-ta.
        -TOP yesterday friend-PL-ACC meet-PST-DC
    'Chelswu met friends (*a friend) yesterday.'

In other words, the plural marking is not necessary.
    It is not the case, however, that a Korean nonplural is always interpreted as singular or plural. As noted by Kang (1994), they are unambiguously interpreted as singular in a demonstrative context:

(5) Chelswu-nun   ecey   ku/i   chinkwu-lul manna-ss-ta.
        -TOP yesterday that/this friend-ACC meet-PST-DC
    'Chelswu met that/this friend (*those/these friends) yesterday.'

The nonplural phrase *ku chinkwu* 'that student' can only refer to a singular student, as the translation indicates. As a result, the plural marker *tul* is obligatory in order to refer to a plural individual in this context:

(6) Chelswu-nun   ku/i chinkwu-tul-ul manna-ss-ta.
        -TOP that/this friend-PL-ACC meet-PST-DC
    'Chelswu met those/these friends (*that/this friend).'

Notice that the demonstratives *ku/i* are not inherently singular, as they can combine with plural nouns.
    Even in demonstrative contexts, however, number marking is not always obligatory. When there is some other plural expression (e.g. a numeral), *tul* becomes optional:

(7) Chelswu-nun   ecey   ku/i chinkwu-(tul) twu myeng-ul manna-ss-ta.
        -TOP yesterday that/this friend-(PL) two CL-ACC meet-PST-DC
    'Chelswu met those/these two friends yesterday.'

To summarize, there are three Korean facts we need to account for:

(8) Fact I: A Korean nonplural can be singular or plural. Hence, *tul* is
              optional.

    Fact II: A Korean nonplural is interpreted as singular in a demonstra-
              tive context. Hence, *tul* is obligatory.

    Fact III: *Tul* becomes optional even in a demonstrative context, when
              there is some other plural element.

In the next section, I consider these facts one by one and provide an analysis.

3. Analysis

3.1. Apparent Ambiguity of a Korean Nonplural Noun

Let us consider the first fact, that is, the apparent ambiguous interpretation of a Korean nonplural noun. Standard analyses of plurality, which have been developed mainly based on English, do not have much to say on this matter. Most analyses of plurality (Link 1983, Landman 1996, Kamp and Reyle 1993, Schwarzchild 1996, Chierchia 1998a, 1998b, and others) agree that a bare (count) noun in English denotes a set of singularities, whereas the extension of its plural counterpart includes sums of these individuals, although there is a debate on whether to include singularities in the denotation of a plural noun.[3] This is illustrated in (9).

(9) a. $[student]] = \{a, b, c\}$

   b. $[students]] = \{a{\oplus}b, a{\oplus}c, b{\oplus}c, a{\oplus}b{\oplus}c\}$

To give an example, a *student* will have *a*, *b*, or *c* as its value, while its plural counterpart *students* picks out one plurality out of the four plural individuals. Although these analyses correctly predict English nonplural nouns to be interpreted as singular, they **wrongly** predict their Korean counterparts to be interpreted as singular, as shown in (10).

(10) $[haksayng \text{ 'student'}]] = \{a, b, c\}$

An indefinite reading of *haksayng* 'student' picks one entity out of *a*, *b*, *c*, which will lead to a singular reading, contrary to fact.

One common solution for this problem is that a Korean nonplural noun is **morphologically ambiguous** between singular and plural. This hypothesis is what Chung (2000) explores in discussing Indonesian nonplurals. Consider the following excerpt (Chung 2000:165–6).

> Whereas a reduplicated noun is always construed as plural, the corresponding unreduplicated noun can be construed as singular or plural depending on context. This amounts to saying that semantically plural nouns can be realized morphologically in two ways.

According to Chung, a Korean nonplural is interpreted as singular or plural because the plural morpheme *tul* can be realized as a zero morpheme. I will call this hypothesis the **ambiguity hypothesis**. Under the ambiguity hypothesis, the Korean *haksayng* 'student' is ambiguous between *haksayng* [a set of singularities] and *haksayng*-∅ [a set of pluralities] in which ∅ is a zero plural morpheme (a zero realization of the Korean plural marker *tul*). This amounts to saying that the Korean nonplural noun *haksayng* 'student'

---

[3] While Link (1983), Landman (1996, 2000), and Schwarzchild (1996) include singular entities in the extension of an English plural noun, Chierchia (1998a, 1998b), Kamp and Reyle (1993), and Rullmann and You (2003) exclude them from the extension. Since the debate on the extension of a plural noun is not directly related to what I have to say in this work, I will simply assume, following Chierchia (1998), Kamp and Reyle (1993) and Rullmann and You (2003), that an English plural noun does not include singularities in its denotation.

is ambiguous between English *a student* and *students* when it is interpreted as an indefinite.

There are many reasons to doubt the ambiguity hypothesis. In a recent paper, Rullmann and You (2003) have established a crosslinguistic relationship between number and scope. Their generalization is that if a bare noun is singular, it takes scope, while if a bare noun is truly numberless, it is scopeless. For instance, a noun such as English *a student* takes scope because it is singular:

(11) a. John did not meet a student. [*a student* > *not* or *a student* > *not*]

    b. A student is here and a student is not here. [*a student* > *not*]

The ability of *a student* to take scope explains the ambiguous status of (11a). In (11b), only the wide scope reading of *a student* is available, because the narrow scope reading leads to a contradictory situation where the same student is claimed to be present and absent at the same time, which is pragmatically excluded. If the Korean *haksayng* 'student' were ambiguous between *a student* and *students*, a wide scope reading is predicted to be available in line with English (11). Contrary to this prediction, Korean nonplurals are generally scopally inert. A comparable example to (11) is given in (12).

(12) a. Chelswu-nun   ecey   **haksayng**-ul *an* manna-ss-ta.

           -TOP yesterday student-ACC not meet-PST-DC

          'Chelswu did not meet students.' [*not* > *haksayng*, *haksayng > *not*]

    b. #**Haksayng**-i yeky iss-ko   *haksayng*-i yeky **epsta**.

      student-NOM here exist-and student-NOM here not.exist

      '#Students are here and students are not here.'

The nonplural *haksayng* 'student' can only have narrow scope in (12a), as evidenced by (12b). If Rullmann and You's claim is correct that scope is related to number, Korean nonplurals must be numberless, not ambiguous.

Let me add three more arguments: what I call **how-many**, **demonstrative**, and **disjunction** tests. Consider the sentences in (13).

(13) a. Joe has written *a book*,

      and #I can tell you exactly how many. (Just one.)

    b. Joe has written *books*,

      and I can tell you exactly how many. *Just one.*

(13a) is very odd. Although (13b) is felicitous, it comes as a surprise or a joke to the hearer, since *just one* is unexpected. If a Korean nonplural were ambiguous between singular and plural, we would expect it to be either odd as in (13a) or a surprise as in (13b). But this is not the case, as shown in (14), which is the Korean counterpart of (13).

(14) Chelsuw-ka   chayk-ul ssessnun-tey, chenghwakhi myec-kwen-ul
       -NOM book-ACC wrote-CONJ   exactly   how.many-CL-ACC
    ssessnun-ci malhaycwul-swu-iss-ta. Han-kwen pakkey an ssessta.
    wrote-COMP   tell-can-exist-DC   one-CL   except NEG wrote
    'Chelswu has written book, and I can tell you exactly how many. Just
    one.' (literal)

(14) is neither odd nor sudden. Another argument comes from one of the facts we have already seen in §2, which can be used as a test for the ambiguity hypothesis. Recall that a Korean nonplural noun is always interpreted as singular in a demonstrative context. This poses a difficulty for the ambiguity hypothesis, according to which the nonplural is predicted to be either singular or plural. Finally, consider the English disjunctive sentence in (15).

(15) Did you meet a (one) student or students?

If the Korean *haksayng* were ambiguous between singular and plural, the Korean equivalent of (15) would be expected to be fine, since (16) is always available according to the ambiguity theory.

(16) [haksayng han myeng 'student one CL'] or [PL haksayng-∅ 'student']

This prediction does not hold, as shown in (17).

(17) #Ne-nun [haksayng han-myeng]-ul manna-ss-ny? Ani-myen
     you-TOP   student one-CL$_{human}$-ACC meet-PST-Q   NEG-if
    [haksayng]-ul manna-ss-ny?
    student-ACC   meet-PST-Q
    'Did you meet one student or students?' (intended meaning)

In order to make (17) felicitous, we need to add *tul* to *haksayng*.

Based on these arguments, I conclude that a Korean nonplural is truly numberless, and claim, along with Rullmann and You's (2003) claim for Chinese nonplurals, that a Korean nonplural includes both singular and plural entities in its extension. This is depicted in (18).

(18) a. [*haksayng* 'student'] = {a, b, c, $a{\oplus}b$, $a{\oplus}c$, $b{\oplus}c$, $a{\oplus}b{\oplus}c$}
    b. [*haksayng-tul* 'students'] = {$a{\oplus}b$, $a{\oplus}c$, $b{\oplus}c$, $a{\oplus}b{\oplus}c$}

Under the analysis given in (18), it is straightforward to explain why a Korean nonplural is interpreted as either singular or plural. If we pick out a singular entity from the denotation of a bare noun, it has a singular interpretation. If we pick out a plural entity instead, we get a plural interpretation.

Turning to the narrow scope fact of a Korean nonplural noun, there are two possible explanations available in the literature: the kind approach (Chierchia 1998b) and what I call the property approach (Dobrovie-Sorin 1997 and others). Although the two theories differ in what the basic denotation of a nonplural noun is (a kind for the former, and a property for the latter), their idea for deriving the narrow scope is basically the same. An argument which denotes a kind or a property does not have a suitable type (or sort) to serve as an argument of a predicate. This creates a sort/type mismatch, which is resolved by a type shifting operation that introduces an existential quantifier locally. For our purposes, both approaches will do. Since I assume here that a nonplural is a property, I use Dobrovie-Sorin's (1997) existential predication to derive the narrow scope reading. A sample derivation of (12a) is provided in (19).

(19) $[\![$I did not meet student$]\!]$
   $= \lambda x \lambda y\ [\text{meet}(x)(y)]\ (\lambda v\ \text{student}(v))$
   $= \lambda P \lambda y \exists x [\text{meet}(x)(y) \wedge P(x)]\ (\lambda v\ \text{student}(v))$ (Existential predication)
   $= \lambda y \exists x\ [\text{meet}(x)(y) \wedge \text{student}\ (x)]$
   $= \neg \exists x\ [\text{meet}(I)(x) \wedge \text{student}\ (x)]$

We can also account for the **how-many** and **disjunction** facts without any difficulty. Reconsider the **how-many** sentence in (13). (13a) is odd. When the speaker utters *a book*, he commits himself to a singular book. This commitment contradicts the continuation *I can tell you exactly how many*. Hence the oddity arises. (13b) is okay, but comes as a joke or a surprise to the hearer. When the speaker utters *books*, as in (13b), he does not commit himself to a specific number of books. But the hearer implicitly expects the number of books to be more than one. Hence, *just one* comes as a surprise. Unlike the English *a book* or *books*, the Korean *chayk* 'book' ranges over both singularities and pluralities, and thus the continuation 'just one' is expected by the denotation of the bare noun. Hence, no oddity/suddenness obtains in (14). Finally, consider the disjunction facts in (20).

(20) a. ✓[a/one student]   or [students]
    b. # [two students]   or [students]

In the grammatical disjunction of (20a), the denotations of disjunctive nominals are mutually exclusive, since the singular nominal ranges over singular entities while the plural one ranges over pluralities. In contrast, the denotations of the infelicitous disjunctive nominals are not exclusive because the extension of *students* includes that of *two students*. This contrast shows that the denotations of disjunctive nominals must be mutually exclusive. Joining the nondisjunctive two Korean NPs by a disjunctor in (17) is correctly predicted to be odd under our analysis, since the denotation of the one includes that of the other. One remaining fact to explain is the demonstrative one: a Korean nonplural is interpreted as singular in a demonstrative context. This is actually the second fact we observed in (8). I will consider it in the next section.

In this subsection, I discussed the issue of how to capture the apparent ambiguous interpretation of a Korean nonplural. Standard semantic theories of plurality and the ambiguity hypothesis were shown to have some difficulties in this regard. I claimed that the apparent ambiguous interpretation of a nonplural is best captured by the hypothesis that Korean nonplurals are numberless.

3. 2. Obligatory Number Marking in Demonstrative Contexts

The singular interpretation of a nonplural demonstrative nominal poses a problem for the proposal made in §3.1 that a Korean nonplural ranges over both singularities and pluralities. The nonplural form *ku haksayng* 'that student' is predicted to be either singular or plural, contrary to fact. This is shown in (21), where I assume for the sake of simplicity that *ku* 'that' is interpreted in a fashion similar to English *the* (iota ι).

(21) a. Situation 1: there are three students a, b, c.
      $[\![$ku haksayng 'that student'$]\!]$ $= \iota\{a, b, c, a\oplus b, b\oplus c, a\oplus c, a\oplus b\oplus c\}$
      ι picks out the largest entity from the denotation of *student*
      $= a\oplus b\oplus c$ (plural)

   b. Situation 2: there is only one student a.
      $[\![$ku haksayng 'that student'$]\!]$ $= \iota\{a\}$
      $= a$ (singular)

In order to solve this problem, I propose that overt D material forces the projection of NumP. We can formalize this idea by adopting Chomsky's (1998) *Agree* in the following way. A D comes with an uninterpretable number feature, which needs to be checked off by agreeing with an interpretable number feature in NumP which hosts a [+pl] or [−pl] feature. A schematic structure of DP and the meanings of the features are in (22).

(22)

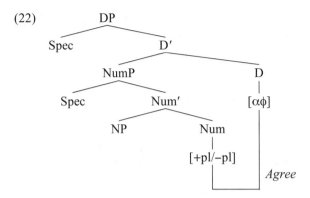

$[\![+pl]\!] = \lambda P.\ \lambda x.\ [P(x) \wedge \neg Atom(x)]$, $[+pl]$ is realized as *tul*.
$[\![-pl]\!] = \lambda P.\ P$ (identity function), $[-pl]$ is **not** realized since it is vacuous.

The uninterpretable number feature in D, $\alpha\phi$, must be valued by an interpretable number feature, $[+pl]$ or $[-pl]$ in Num. This forces the projection of NumP whenever there is an overt D. Let us now look at the meanings of the features. The $[+pl]$ feature, as a pluralizer, takes the denotation of an NP and subtracts the atomic entities from it. We can think of the $[+pl]$ feature as some kind of a filter. Given a set of entities, it examines each entity and filters out atomic entities, leaving entities that consist of more than one atom. Unlike the $[+pl]$ feature, which has its own semantic force, $[-pl]$ is characterized as the lack of the pluralization process. The $[-pl]$ feature does not change the denotation of its argument in any way. Notice that, in this proposal, $[-pl]$ does not mean 'singular'. It is in a sense number neutral in that it takes its argument's denotation (whatever that is) as the input and produces the same thing as the output.

The proposal in (22) alone does not solve our problem yet. We need another concept called Semantic Polarization, which is quoted from Ojeda 1998:225 in (23).

(23) Semantic Polarization (SP)

If a language L contains two forms α and β such that the denotation of α is a proper subset of the denotation of β, then L contains a third form β' which is homophonous with β but denotes the difference between the denotation of β and the denotation of α.

(23) means that given two forms A and B, if the meaning of A is a proper subset of the meaning of B, B denotes the difference between the two. Rather than applying SP across the board, I propose to apply semantic polarization at the level of NumP. That is, two NumPs are compared, and if the denotation of one NumP has the denotation of the other NumP as its subset, it denotes the difference between the two.

Given the proposal in (22) and SP, we can now turn to solve our original problem, the obligatory number marking in demonstrative contexts. Consider the structure in (24).

(24)

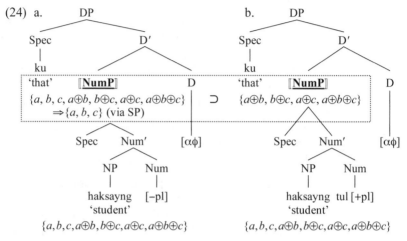

The overt demonstrative *ku* 'that' forces DP to be projected, which, in turn, forces the projection of NumP. Notice that the denotation of NumP in (24b) is a proper subset of the denotation of NumP in (24a). This satisfies the condition for semantic polarization to occur. SP removes the plural entities from the denotation of *haksayng* 'student' in (24a). Therefore, the NumP in (24a) ends up having only singular entities in its denotation. This is why a nonplural can only refer to a singular entity in a demonstrative context.

The proposed analysis has several important consequences. First, we can maintain a strong claim that number marking is obligatory in Korean, not just in a demonstrative context, with the assumption that functional structures are not projected in Korean unless they are forced to be. That is, number marking is obligatory in Korean whenever NumP is projected. The generalization that number marking is obligatory only in a demonstrative context is a result of the fact that functional projections are not projected unless they are forced to be. Second, there is no [sg] feature under the proposed analysis. The singular interpretation is not an inherent property of a noun but something that is derived by a semantic comparison with its plural counterpart in a certain syntactic context. Third, there is a straightforward one-to-one mapping between features and their morphological realization: the [+pl] feature is always realized as *tul*, while the [−pl] feature is never realized, since it is semantically vacuous.

Let me sum up. In this subsection, I provided an explanation for why number marking is required in a demonstrative context in Korean. An overt

D, which hosts an uninterpretable number feature, forces the projection of NumP, which has an interpretable number feature. A NumP hosts either [+pl] or [−pl]. While the [+pl] feature, as a pluralizer, pluralizes its argument by removing the atomic parts from the denotation of the argument, the [−pl] feature simply indicates the lack of the pluralization process. A NumP with the [−pl] feature, however, gains its semantic force via semantic polarization and thus has a singular interpretation when it is compared with its plural counterpart.

3.3. Fact IV: Optional Plural Marking

Let us now consider the final fact: number marking becomes optional when there is some other plural element in a DP. Compare the two structures in (25).

(25) a.

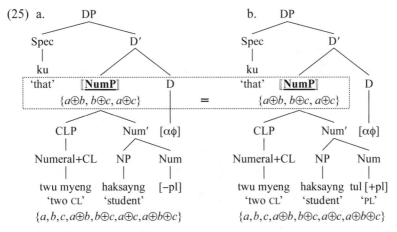

As usual, D forces NumP to be projected in (25). Notice, however, that the denotations of the two NumPs are exactly the same due to the presence of the numeral *twu* 'two'. The numeral *two* picks out the plural individuals that consist of two atoms. As a result, both NumPs have $\{a\oplus b, b\oplus c, a\oplus c\}$ as their denotations. None of them is a subset of the other, which fails to satisfy the condition for semantic polarization to occur. Hence, no singular interpretation obtains in this context.

Before closing this section, let me note a consequence of the proposed analysis regarding optional number marking. It is customary in the literature to attribute the optional marking to the optional projection of NumP. Under the proposed analysis here, the optional number marking does not necessarily correspond to the optional projection of NumP. In a non-DP context, the presence or absence of a plural marker is controlled by the projection of NumP. In a DP context, however, NumP is always there. The presence or absence of a plural marker is determined by what feature is generated under Num.

4. Conclusion

In this paper, I have developed a theory of number marking in Korean. In the course of doing so, I made several important claims regarding number. Two major proposals are: (1) nonplurals in Korean include both singular and plural individuals; and (2) the singular interpretation of a nonplural is derived by semantic comparison of a NumP with its plural counterpart.

References

Chierchia, G. 1998a. Plurality of Mass Nouns and the Notion of Semantic Parameter. *Events and Grammar*, ed. S. Rothstein, 53–103. Dordrecht: Kluwer.

Chierchia, G. 1998b. Reference to Kinds across Languages. *Natural Language Semantics* 6:339–405.

Chomsky, N. 1998. *Minimalist Inquiries: The Framework* (MIT Occasional Papers in Linguistics 15). Cambridge: MITWPL.

Chung, S. 2000. On Reference to Kinds in Indonesian. *Natural Language Semantics* 8:151–71.

Dobrovie-Sorin, C. 1997. Types of Predicates and the Representation of Existential Readings. *Proceedings of SALT VII*, ed. A. Lawson, 117–34. Ithaca: CLC Publications.

Kamp, H., and U. Reyle. 1993. *From Discourse to Logic*. Dordrecht: Kluwer.

Kang, B. 1994. Plurality and Other Semantic Aspect of Common Nouns in Korean. *Journal of East Asian Linguistics* 3(1):1–25.

Kim, C. 2005. The Korean Plural Marker *Tul* and Its Implications. Doctoral dissertation, University of Delaware.

Landman, F. 1996. Plurality. *Handbook of Contemporary Semantics,* ed. S. Lappin, 425–57. London: Blackwell.

Link, G. 1983. The Logical Analysis of Plurals and Mass Terms: A Lattice Theoretical Approach. *Meaning, Use, and the Interpretation of Language*, eds. R. Bäuerle, C. Schwarze, and A. von Stechow, 302–23. Berlin: de Gruyter.

Ojeda, E. A. 1998. The Semantics of Collectives and Distributives in Papago. *Natural Language Semantics* 6:245–70.

Rullmann, H., and A. You. 2003. General Number and the Semantics and Pragmatics of Indefinite Bare Nouns in Mandarin Chinese. Manuscript, University of Calgary (http://www.ucalgary.ca/~rullmann/).

Schwarzschild, R. 1996. *Pluralities*. Dordrecht: Kluwer.

The Classifier in Japanese Numeral Quantification

MANA KOBUCHI-PHILIP*
Utrecht University

1. Two Types of Japanese Numeral Quantifier

The Japanese numeral quantifier (NQ) has two basic types of surface syntactic distribution. It can occur in the nominal domain, as illustrated in (1), or it can occur in the verbal domain, as exemplified in (2).

(1) DP-internal NQ (DNQ)

    a. [**gakusei san-nin**] ga   pai o tabeta.
        student   3-CL NOM pie ACC ate

    b. [**gakusei** no **san-nin**] ga   pai o tabeta.
        student GEN 3-CL NOM pie ACC ate

    c. [**san-nin** no **gakusei**] ga   pai o tabeta.
        3-CL GEN student NOM pie ACC ate

    d. [**gakusei** ga **san-nin**] pai o tabeta.
        student NOM 3-CL pie ACC ate

'Three students ate a pie.'

---

* I would like to thank members of the audience of J/K14 for their helpful comments.

(2) Floating NQ (FNQ)

  a. **gakusei** ga [**san-nin** pai o tabeta].
     student NOM 3-CL pie ACC ate

  b. **san-nin**$_i$ **gakusei** ga t$_i$ pai o tabeta.
     3-CL   student NOM pie ACC ate

  'Three students ate a pie.'

In all cases in (1) the NQ appears in the nominal domain, forming a constituent with an NP which is construed with it (host NP). Let us call this type of NQ a DP-internal NQ, or simply **DNQ**.[1]

On the other hand, in (2a) the NQ appears in a verbal domain, occupying an adverbial position and forming a constituent with the following predicate. Since this type of NQ is generally regarded as a subcase of the floating quantifier (FQ), let us call it a floating NQ, or **FNQ**. We assume here a base-generated adverbial hypothesis for all FQs, rather than a transformational hypothesis.[2] Thus, assuming that the NQ in (2a) is an adverb, we further assume that (2b) is derived from (2a) by scrambling the FNQ from its base-generated pre-VP position to the sentence-initial position.

2. Two Previous Approaches to the Japanese FNQ

In the previous literature there are two basic approaches to the semantics of the Japanese FNQ. Consider (3).

(3) a. gakusei ga   kinoo **san**-nin odotta.
     student NOM yesterday 3-CL danced
     'Three students danced yesterday.'

  b. There are **3 students** who danced yesterday.

  c. There were **3 dancing events** (each by a student) yesterday.

Under one approach (Fukushima 1991; cf. Dowty and Brodie 1984, Link 1987), the numeral of the FNQ indicates the number of elements which have the properties denoted by the host NP and the predicate. Thus, the numeral *san* '3' in the FNQ sentence (3a) counts three members of the host NP denotation, namely students, yielding the interpretation in (3b). In con-

---

[1] Strictly speaking, the NQ in (1d) might not be DP-internal (see Terada 1990, Kitahara 1992, Koizumi 1995). However, because it must at least be internal to a syntactic constituent that contains the host NP and that functions as an argument for the predicate, I consider it a kind of DNQ. (See Kamio 1983 for the constituency argument of the NQ and the host NP.)

[2] A contemporary version of the transformational analysis of the FQ is Sportiche 1988, adopted for Japanese by Kitahara (1992). See, e.g., Inoue 1978, Fukushima 1991, and Nakanishi 2003 for empirical arguments for the adverbial hypothesis. Also see Bobaljik 1998 for an overview of general problems concerning transformational analyses of FQs in other languages.

trast, under the other approach (Gunji and Hasida 1998, Nakanishi 2003; cf. Junker 1990), the VP (taken as a set of events) functions as the domain of quantification. Here, the numeral *san* '3' in (3a) counts three dancing events, yielding the interpretation in (3c).

The principal problem with the first approach is that it fails to capture the truth conditions of the kind of FNQ sentence illustrated in (4). Here the FNQ contains *hatsu* 'shot', a kind of classifier which I will call an **event classifier**.

(4) **pisutoru** ga soko de **san-patsu** utareta.

    pistol NOM there at   3-CL were-shot

    'There were three pistol shots there.'

    (**NOT**) 'There were **three pistols** that were shot there.'

If *pisutoru* 'pistol' is taken as the domain of quantification or the nuclear scope, as the first approach would have us do, then *san* '3' of *san-patsu* '3-CL' would have to count pistols. However, for (4) to be true, the number of pistols is irrelevant. This sentence would also be perfectly true of a situation in which only one pistol was shot with, as long as it was shot three times.

The principal problem for the second basic approach is that it fails to capture the basic intuition that a sentence like (3a) is used to count objects, not events. Without an auxiliary assumption, it makes an incorrect prediction about canonical FNQ sentences. For example, consider the situation in (5), in which student s_1 dances at three different times.

(5) e_1: Student s_1 danced yesterday at time t_1.

    e_2: Student s_1 danced yesterday at time t_2.

    e_3: Student s_1 danced yesterday at time t_3.

According to the second approach, (5) should make sentence (3a) true. The numeral *san* in (3a) is supposed to be counting three dancing events, and indeed there are three dancing events in (5). However, since the same student s_1 dances in all three of the dancing events, the number of students in (5) is just one, not three. For this reason, (3a) is in fact false of a situation like (5).

It will be noted that a sentence structurally similar to (3a) could be true of situation similar to (5) if it could be assigned an "event related reading" of the type discussed by Krifka (1990), as shown by his example in (6).

(6) 4,000 ships passed through the lock last year.

    Object related reading: 'There were 4,000 ships.'

    Event related reading (*nobeyomi*): 'There were 4,000 passages.'

However, this event related reading requires special contextual licensing, and these licensing conditions clearly are not met in the case of (3a) because the number is too small.[3] Consequently, the only way to describe a situation like (5) is by means of a sentence like (7), which makes use of the event classifier *kai* 'time'.

(7) gakusei ga   kinoo san-**kai** odotta.
    student NOM yesterday 3-CL danced
    'A student danced three times yesterday.'

3. A New Approach

In view of the empirical and theoretical problems of the previous approaches, we propose a different approach, according to which it is not the host NP or the VP that functions as the domain of quantification, but rather the classifier that is morphologically composed with the numeral. This new approach entails rejection of the implicit (or sometimes explicit) general assumption in the literature that the numeral classifier is merely a syntactic agreement morpheme. Rather, the classifier is seen to have a denotation of its own, the objects that it refers to being the objects that the numeral counts. The principal motivation for this idea comes from the simple observation that sentences such as those in (8) constitute a minimal pair.

(8) a. gakusei ga, go-**nin** kita.   → 5: # of persons
        student NOM 5-CL came
        'Five (**individual**) students came.'

    b. gakusei ga, go-**kumi** kita.   → 5: # of sets
        student NOM   5-CL came
        'Five **sets** of students came.'

The sentence in (8a) uses the classifier *nin*, which is a unit for counting people, and thus means '5 individual students came'. In contrast, (8b) uses the classifier *kumi*, which is a unit for counting sets, and therefore means '5 groups of students came'. Minimal pairs like (8) clearly show that (i) the classifier directly affects the meaning of the sentence, i.e. each classifier is meaningful, and (ii) that the numeral counts objects of the type denoted by the classifier, rather than objects of the type denoted by the host NP. In other words, the classifier functions as the domain of quantification.

If the classifier functions as the domain of quantification, it must denote a set of atoms in the sense of Link (1983), rather than a set containing both atoms and sums. As Kratzer (1989) and Chierchia (1998) note, this is due to the logic of enumeration: Numeral quantification requires the numeral to

---

[3] It seems that a general pragmatic condition on the felicitous use of the event related reading of an NQ sentence is that the number in question be far too large for the object related reading to be verified by enumeration.

indicate the number of relevant objects and the number of quantified elements in the domain of quantification simultaneously. If sums were included in the domain of quantification, the number of elements and the number of quantified objects would no longer necessarily be identical. Thus, under the proposed analysis we represent the denotation of the classifier as shown in (9), in which the atomicity is expressed with Link's (1983) atomic individual-part operator $^\bullet\Pi$.

(9) a. nin_{CL}: $\lambda u_e \exists v_e[\text{nin}'(v) \wedge u^\bullet \Pi v]$ ($<e,t>$)
    b. hatsu_{CL}: $\lambda e_{1s} \exists e_{2s}[\text{hatsu}'(e_2) \wedge e_1{}^\bullet \Pi e_2]$ ($<s,t>$)

Note that there are two kinds of classifiers, one for objects (e.g. *nin* for counting people) and another for events (e.g. *hatsu* for counting shots). This distinction is encoded in (9) as a difference in semantic type.

Next, adhering closely to the surface syntax, we propose that the host NP and the predicate function as the nuclear scope in DNQ and FNQ quantification, respectively, as shown in (10).

(10) a. DNQ: NP-modifier   b. FNQ: Predicate-modifier

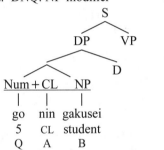

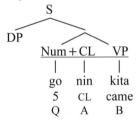

Finally, we propose that the denotation of the numeral is as shown in (11).

(11) The numeral denotation
    n: $\lambda C_{<e,t>} \lambda P_{<e,t>} \lambda x_e \exists K[K \subseteq (C \cap P) \wedge |K| \geq n \wedge \sqcup K = x]$
    (C: CL denotation, P: Predicate denotation)

Applying lambda calculations, we obtain the interpretations of DNQ and FNQ sentences in the manner illustrated in (12)–(14).

(12) a. DNQ sentence:
      san-nin no gakusei ga peepaa o   kaita.
       3-CL GEN student NOM paper ACC wrote
      'Three students wrote a paper.'

b. $\exists y[\exists K[K\subseteq(\lambda u\exists v[nin'(v)\wedge u^{\bullet}\Pi v]\cap gakusei')\wedge|K|\geq 3\wedge\sqcup K=y]$
  'nin'   'student'

  $\wedge peepaa\ o\ kaita'(y)]$
  'wrote a paper'

(13) a. FNQ sentence with an object classifier:
  gakusei ga, san-nin peepaa o kaita.
  student NOM 3-CL   paper ACC wrote
  'Three students wrote a paper.'

  b. $\exists y[gakusei'(y)\wedge\exists K[K\subseteq(\lambda u\exists v[nin'(v)\wedge u^{\bullet}\Pi v]\cap peepaa\ o\ kaita')$
  'student'   'nin'   'wrote a paper'

  $\wedge|K|\geq 3\wedge\sqcup K=y]]$

(14) a. FNQ sentence with an event classifier:
  pisutoru ga, san-patsu utareta
  pistol NOM   3- CL were shot
  'Three shots were shot from a pistol.'

  b. $\lambda e_3\exists K[K\subseteq(\lambda e_1\exists e_2[hatsu'(e_2)\wedge e_1^{\bullet}\Pi e_2]$
  'hatsu'

  $\cap\lambda e_4\exists y[pisutoru'(y)\wedge utareta'(y)(e_4)])\wedge|K|\geq 3\wedge\sqcup K=e_3]$
  'pistol'   'were shot'

In the DNQ quantification in (12), the classifier and the host NP denotations intersect, with three elements in the intersection. Thus, the sentence asserts that there are three people, each of whom is a student, and these people (each) wrote a paper. In the FNQ quantification with an object classifier in (13), the classifier and the predicate denotations intersect, again with three elements in the intersection. This sentence asserts that there are three people, each of whom is a paper-writer, and each of these paper-writers is a student. In (14), since the classifier is of the event type, the quantification is over events instead of objects. Here the secondary role of the so-called host NP is even more obvious. The subject NP *pisutoru* 'pistol' is not construed with the NQ in any way; rather, it merely denotes a participant in the type of event denoted by the predicate. Again, the classifier and the predicate denotations intersect, with three elements in the intersection. (14a) asserts that there are three shots, each of which is a shot from a pistol (rather than an arrow shot or a cannon shot).

4. Advantages of the New Approach

The proposed analysis has a number of advantages. First, it provides a unified analysis for the DNQ and the FNQ, as shown below.

(15)

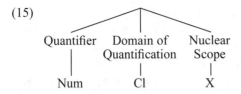

Quantifier	Domain of Quantification	Nuclear Scope
Num	Cl	X

The quantificational structure can be generalized as shown in (15), in which the numeral, the classifier, and what follows it function as the quantifier, its domain of quantification, and the nuclear scope, respectively. This applies to both DNQ and FNQ quantification.

Second, the analysis provides a straightforward mapping from syntax to semantics:

(16)

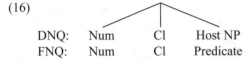

DNQ:	Num	Cl	Host NP
FNQ:	Num	Cl	Predicate

As shown in (16), the DNQ and the FNQ quantifications differ only as to the identity of the nuclear scope. However, this difference directly corresponds to a syntactic difference, such that the proposal observes the Principle of Compositionality in the simplest possible way.

Third, my proposal provides a unified analysis of FNQ sentences with object and event classifiers:

(17)

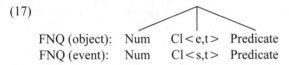

FNQ (object):	Num	Cl$<$e,t$>$	Predicate
FNQ (event):	Num	Cl$<$s,t$>$	Predicate

The difference between the two types of classifier is represented in the semantic type, as we mentioned above. This is specified directly in the lexical content of each classifier. Thus, we account for the correct quantification of each type of classifier (object or event) without any additional stipulation or any special mechanism.

Fourth and most significantly, the proposed analysis straightforwardly accounts for the observation in the literature that a Japanese FNQ sentence requires a distributive reading while a DNQ sentence does not (e.g. Terada 1990, Sasaki Alam 1997, Kato 1997, Nakanishi 2003). Observe the instance of this phenomenon in (18).

(18) a. **san-nin** no **butsurigakusha** ga sono genshoo ni tsuite
      3-CL GEN physicist NOM the phenomenon to pertaining
      atarashii riron o happyooshita.
      new theory ACC presented
      'Three physicists presented a new theory about the phenomenon.'

    b. **butsurigakusha** ga, sono genshoo ni tsuite **san-nin**
      physicist NOM the phenomenon to pertaining 3-cl
      atarashii riron o happyooshita.
      new theory ACC presented
      'Three physicists (**each**) presented a new theory about the
      phenomenon.'

The DNQ sentence in (18a) is ambiguous. It asserts either that three physicists presented a new theory together or else that they did so individually. In contrast, (18b), with an FNQ, can only be interpreted as an assertion that these physicists presented a new theory individually. The obligatorily distributive interpretation of the FNQ sentence can be accounted for quite trivially as a set-theoretical logical consequence of the analysis. Recall that under our analysis of FNQ quantification the classifier denotation is a set of atoms that intersects with the predicate denotation. Since one of the intersecting sets only contains atoms, all the elements in a successful intersection must also be atoms, each of which has the property of the predicate. By definition, this amounts to a distributive reading.[4] On the other hand, the ambiguity of the DNQ sentence can be accounted for in a fashion exactly parallel to the ambiguity of the sentence with the plural term in English, as has been discussed by Link (1984) and Landman (2000). The extension of an ordinary plural term such as English *three students* is a sum of three individuals who are students. This can be reanalyzed as a group atom by means of a group operator, as shown in (19a).

(19) a. three students: $a \sqcup b \sqcup c$ or $\uparrow(a \sqcup b \sqcup c)$

    b. san-nin no gakusei: $a \sqcup b \sqcup c$ or $\uparrow(a \sqcup b \sqcup c)$
      3-cl GEN student
      'three students'

    c. $\exists y \exists K[K \subseteq (\lambda u \exists v[nin'(v) \wedge u^{\bullet}\Pi v] \cap gakusei') \wedge |K| \geq 3$
                     'nin'   'student'
                               $\wedge \underline{\uparrow(\sqcup K)=y}] \wedge peepaa \ o \ kaita'(y)]$
                                        'wrote a paper'

---

[4] Thus, we need no special semantic mechanism such as a distributivity operator (Link 1987) to derive the distributive reading.

Under the proposed analysis, the DNQ quantification generates a sum of individuals which is exactly the same type of entity as the sum generated for a plural term. Thus, this sum can be reanalyzed as a group atom as in (19b), as occurs with an English plural term as in (19a). In the default case, a DNQ sentence is assigned a distributive reading by the same lexical semantic property that forces a distributive reading in the case of an FNQ sentence. However, unlike the FNQ, the DNQ can optionally be reanalyzed with the group operator to yield a collective reading. In that case, $\sqcup K = y$ becomes $\uparrow(\sqcup K) = y$.

It is important to see that the group operator cannot also apply to FNQ quantification, undoing the distributive reading. Consider again the interpretation of the FNQ sentence in (13a), repeated for convenience in (20).

(20) $\exists y[gakusei'(y) \wedge \exists K[K \subseteq (\lambda u \exists v[nin'(v) \wedge u^{\bullet}\Pi v] \cap peepaa\ o\ kaita'$
     'student'   'nin'   'wrote a paper'
$$\wedge |K| \geq 3 \wedge \underline{\sqcup K} = y]]$$

Applying a group operator to the sum K in (20) is not going to affect the circumstance that the intersection of the classifier and the predicate can only be a set of atoms. Thus, it is impossible in principle for the distributive reading of the FNQ sentence to be undone by an application of the group operator.

The fifth and final advantage of the proposed analysis is that it lends support to a very simple semantic explanation of the classifier-host NP agreement phenomenon. First let us note that the agreement between the classifier and the host NP does not conform to the standard pattern of true syntactic agreement. Consider (21).

(21) a. san-**bon** no **biiru**   b. san-**bai** no **biiru**
    3-CL GEN beer   3-CL GEN beer
    'three **bottles** of beer'   'three **glasses** of beer'

   c. #san-**mai** no **biiru**
     3-CL GEN beer
     'three **sheets** of beer'

Data such as (21a,b), like the minimal pair in (8) above, show that each classifier is meaningful and that the grammar allows the speaker some free choice in the selection of a classifier. The "correct" choice for the classifier depends on contextual factors, including speaker intention. For example, (21c) is ill-formed in the current actual world, because beer is not normally sold or stored in sheet-shaped packages. However, this DP could in principle become completely well-formed if beer started to be sold or packaged this way, for instance in the context of space travel. Likewise, in a context in which the speaker's intention was to make a joke of some kind, the DP in (21c) might well become perfectly well-formed. This context-sensitivity is not at all what one finds in the case of syntactic agreement. Thus, I suggest that the classifier-NP agreement observed in Japanese NQ sentences should not be analyzed as syntactic agreement but, rather, simply as a selectional restriction. A sentence interpretation is computed by function composition, or "merge", in a bottom-up fashion. Consequently, a semantically well-formed sentence must preserve coherent meaning at all points of composition. Consider now the following schema, which shows a step-by-step function composition. (22a) is an English sentence which includes a DP-internal modifier, and (22b) a Japanese DNQ sentence.

(22) a. English   #[a herd] + [students]
                  #[a herd of students] + [disobeyed the teacher]

     b. Japanese #[san-biki] + [gakusei]
                  3-CL   student
                  #[san-biki no gakusei] + [kita]
                  3-CL GEN student   came

In (22a), *a herd* and *students* must first be composed. However, since there is no entity which has the property of being a herd and the property of being students at the same time, the intersection of the two denotations is the null set. Already at this point, the composition cannot preserve coherent meaning, and thus the whole sentence is ill-formed (though possibly acceptable, thanks to accommodation). The ill-formedness of the DNQ sentence (22b) can be explained in exactly the same fashion. Next, consider (23). (23a) is an English sentence with an adverb, and (23b) a Japanese FNQ sentence.

(23) a. English   [deliberately] + [hit the car]
                  #[a branch] + [deliberately hit the car]

     b. Japanese [san-biki] + [kita]
                  3-CL   came
                  #[gakusei] + [san-biki kita]
                  student   3-CL came

In (23a), the composition of *deliberately* and *hit the car* preserves coherent meaning, since a car could be deliberately hit by some agent. However, semantic ill-formedness occurs at the next point of composition. *A branch* denotes a set of objects that cannot be agents, but *deliberately hit the car* denotes a set of agents. Consequently, the intersection of these two sets is, once again, the null set. The ill-formedness of the FNQ sentence in (23b) can be explained in exactly the same fashion. *Gakusei* 'student' denotes a set of human objects; *san-biki kita* denotes a set of animals (i.e. not human objects) that arrived. The intersection of these two sets is again null, and accommodation must take over for any sense to be made of the sentence. In sum, the agreement of the classifier and the host NP can be explained semantically in terms of a selectional restriction. There is no need to posit any covert movement to establish a syntactic agreement relation (such as the spec-head relation) to account for the Japanese classifier-host NP agreement phenomenon.

5. Conclusion

In this paper we have proposed a new approach in which the classifier functions as the domain of quantification. This approach not only captures the basic facts of the Japanese NQ sentence, but is also advantageous in that it provides (i) a unified syntactic and semantic analysis of DNQ and FNQ sentences, (ii) a straightforward syntax-semantics mapping, (iii) a unified treatment of FNQ sentences with object and event classifiers, (iv) a simple account for the obligatory distributive reading of the FNQ sentence and the ambiguity of the DNQ sentence, and finally (v) support for a simple semantic account of CL-NP agreement.

References

Bobaljik, J. 1998. Floating Quantifiers: Handle with Care. *Glot International* 3(6): 3–10.

Chierchia, G. 1998. Reference to Kinds across Languages. *Natural Language Semantics* 6:339–405.

Dowty, D., and B. Brodie. 1984. The Semantics of "Floated" Quantifiers in a Transformationless Grammar. *WCCFL 3*, eds. M. Cobler, S. Mackaye, and M. T. Wescoat, 75–90. Stanford: CSLI.

Fukushima, K. 1991. Generalized Floating Quantifiers. Doctoral dissertation, University of Arizona.

Gunji, T., and K. Hasida. 1998. Measurement and Quantification. *Topics in Constraint-Based Grammar of Japanese*, eds. T. Gunji and K. Hasida, 39–79. Dordrecht: Kluwer.

Junker, M-O. 1990. Floating Quantifiers and Georgian Distributivity. *CLS 26*, eds. M. Ziolkowski, M. Noske, and K. Deaton, 211–9. Chicago: CLS.

Kamio, A. 1983. Meishiku no kōzō. *Nihongo no kihonkōzō*, ed. K. Inoue, 77–126. Tokyo: Sanseidō.

Katō, S. 1997. Nihongo no rentaisūryōshi-to yūrisūryōshi no bunseki. *Toyama Daigaku Jinmongakubu Kiyō* 26:31–64.

Kitahara, H. 1992. Numeral Classifier Phrase inside DP and the Specificity Effect. *Japanese/Korean Linguistics 3*, ed. S. Choi, 171–86. Stanford: CSLI.

Kobuchi-Philip, M. 2003. Distributivity and the Japanese Floating Numeral Quantifier. Doctoral dissertation, CUNY Graduate Center.

Koizumi, M. 1995. Phrase Structure in Minimalist Syntax. Doctoral dissertation, MIT.

Kratzer, A. 1989. An Investigation of the Lumps of Thought. *Linguistics and Philosophy* 12:607–53.

Krifka, M. 1990. Four Thousand Ships Passed Through the Lock: Object-Induced Measure Functions on Events. *Linguistics and Philosophy* 13:487–520.

Landman, F. 2000. *Events and Plurality.* Dordrecht: Kluwer.

Link, G. 1983. The Logical Analysis of Plural and Mass Terms: A Lattice-theoretical Approach. *Meaning, Use, and Interpretation of Language*, eds. R. Bäuerle, C. Schwarze, and A. von Stechow, 302–23. Berlin: de Gruyter.

Link, G. 1984. Hydras: On the Logic of Relative Clause Constructions with Multiple Heads. *Varieties of Formal Semantics*, eds. F. Landman and F. Veltman, 245–257. Dordrecht: Foris.

Link, G. 1987. Generalized Quantifiers and Plurals. *Generalized Quantifiers: Linguistic and Logical Approaches*, ed. P. Gärdenfors, 151–80. Dordrecht: Reidel.

Nakanishi, K. 2003. Semantic Properties of (Non-)Floating Quantifiers and Their Syntactic Implications. *Japanese/Korean Linguistics 12*, ed. W. McClure, 365–76. Stanford: CSLI.

Sasaki Alam, Y. 1997. Numeral Classifiers as Adverbs of Quantification. *Japanese/Korean Linguistics 6*, eds. H. Sohn and J. Haig, 381–97. Stanford: CSLI.

Terada, M. 1990. Incorporation and Argument Structure in Japanese. Doctoral dissertation, University of Massachusetts, Amherst.

On the Singular [+Specific] Reading of WH-Doublets in Korean

YONGEUN LEE*
Northwestern University

1. Introduction

Korean simple indefinite pronouns are built on (or morphologically related to) WH-words in the language. Thus, for example, *eti* in (1) can be interpreted either as a WH-word 'where' or as an indefinite pronoun 'somewhere' depending on the particular pitch contours associated with the WH-word and the sentence (Jun and Oh 1995). The two readings are (1a) and (1b).

(1) Tom-i cinan cumal-ey   eti   ka-ss-ni?
    -NOM last weekend-LOC where go-PAST-Q
    a. 'Where did Tom go last weekend?'
    b. 'Did Tom go somewhere last weekend?'

Of particular interest in this paper is the fact that such WH-words as *eti* can be reduplicated in the language, and that the meanings associated with them slightly change in that case. Specifically, use of the reduplicated form *eti.eti* in (1) instead of its simple correspondent *eti* with the question opera-

* Thanks to Stefan Kaufmann, Chris Kennedy, and Jeff Lidz for helpful comments. All remaining mistakes are my own.

tor in presence at the end of the sentence yields a question that solicits from the listener two or more places to which Tom went last weekend. This is not an unexpected interpretation of the reduplicated form, since many languages are known to map the reduplication of simple lexical items to the concept of distributive plurality (see Haspelmath 1997 for a cross-linguistic survey of reduplication of indefinites). However, what is particularly interesting to us is the fact that sentence (2) is not ambiguous in the way that sentence (1) is. That is, sentence (2), containing the reduplicated pronoun, only allows the (2a) interpretation. If, however, sentence (2) contained the non-reduplicated form, then in that case both (2a) and (2b) would be available readings. The example is from Chung 1999.[1]

(2) yeysnal-ey sokumcangswu-ka **eti.eti**-lul ka-ess-nuntey,
    long.time.ago salt.seller-NOM **where.where**-ACC go-PAST-when
    a. 'A long time ago, a salt seller went to a certain place [+specific].'
    b. #'A long time ago, a salt seller went someplace or other [−specific].'

A major goal of this paper is to state precisely how the reduplication of the simple indefinite pronouns changes their meaning such that the logically possible interpretation of (2b) becomes unavailable. What has been noted of these reduplicated WH-forms in previous literature (e.g. Chung 1999) is that when used in an indefinite sense they only go with a singular reading, while when used in their interrogative sense they have the plural reading only.

One of the key claims in this paper is that singularity of reference is not in fact the defining characteristic of reduplicated indefinite pronouns. Instead, I will argue that reduplicated WH-forms obligatorily have what is usually called a "specific" reading.

As far as I am aware, this particular semantic property of the reduplicated indefinites has not received much discussion in the literature. The standard view, as I mentioned above, has been that the two types of Korean indefinites (i.e. reduplicated and simplex) that come from WH-words (see Lee 1989 for this assumption) differ only in the number readings available for them, but are otherwise semantically the same.

The claim that reduplicated indefinite pronouns in Korean are obligatorily specific requires an account of what exactly specificity is, in particular

---

[1] Chung (1999) discusses his observation that regarding the number interpretation of the reduplicated indefinites, some native speakers of Korean seem to allow plural readings, contrary to the claim in this paper that they have singular interpretation only. Using a range of data, however, Chung demonstrates that for those speakers, the plural (indefinite) readings arise since they take the reduplicated indefinites to be some sort of "reduced conjoined phrases". The current paper (as well as Chung 1999) deals with the intuitions of speakers who view the reduplicated indefinites not to be reduced conjoined phrases, but to be a single word (though of course two identical WH-words appear inside it). See §3 in Chung 1999 for details.

with regard to indefinites. The notion of specificity and of specific indefinites in the literature is a poorly defined and controversial one (see Fodor and Sag 1982, Farkas 1995, and Yeom 1998). In the sections that follow, I will discuss these issues more in detail.

The rest of the paper is organized as follows. §2 will introduce Korean data involving the reduplicated indefinites as they appear in sentences containing operators, such as negation and conditionals. These data will support my claim that reduplicated indefinites obligatorily receive a specific reading. In §3 I will provide an explicit analysis of specificity associated with reduplicated indefinites utilizing a framework proposed by Hamblin (1973), which was recently adopted by Kratzer and Shimoyama (2002). The key concept explored there will be that indefinites introduce a set of contextually relevant individuals (or "alternatives"), and importantly that Korean specific indefinites can be accounted for as a case that involves (maximal) domain shrinking. This operation is the converse of domain widening, which Kratzer and Shimoyama (2002) employed to explain free choice indefinites in German.

2. Korean WH-Doublets and Specificity

The specificity effect is most apparent when an indefinite NP scopally interacts with other operators in a given sentence. Thus, I consider the reduplicated indefinites contained within *if*-clauses.

The sentence in (3), which contains a reduplicated indefinite, could in principle have two readings, roughly schematized in (4).

(3) Mary-nun [nwuku.nwuku-ka ipen senke-eyse tangsentoe-lsuissu]-myen
        -TOP [who.who-NOM this election-LOC get.elected-be.able]-if
      kippu-ulkeya
      happy-will.be
      'Mary will be happy if someone can get elected in the coming election.'

(4) a. $\exists x$ [person (x) & [win (x) $\rightarrow$ happy (Mary)]] (specific reading)
     b. [$\exists x$ [person (x) & win (x)]] $\rightarrow$ happy (Mary) (non-specific)

Note that the reading represented in (4a), not the reading in (4b), is the one that is most consistent with the context described in (5). The fact that the sentence in (3) is accepted in this context therefore first shows that the specific interpretation (4a) is indeed available.

(5) Context: There are a bunch of politicians who want to be elected in the coming election. Mary dislikes most of them and doesn't want them to be elected. There is just one certain person who she wants to be elected. [sentence (3) in context (5): accepted]

Furthermore, the specific interpretation is the only one available for the reduplicated pronoun in (3). This is shown by the fact that sentence (3) is rejected in the context described in (6). This context is most consistent with a configuration where the operator takes scope over the WH-word and not the other way around, i.e. (4b) and not (4a). If (3) has reading (4a) only, as I claim, it follows that (3) should be rejected in context (6), which allows reading (4b) only.

(6) Context: Mary will be happy if any politicians get elected, but that's impossible, because no politicians in the district she lives in are eligible for reelection any more. [sentence (3) in context (6): rejected]

If the reduplicated pronoun is replaced with a simplex one as in (7), the sentence allows both a specific reading (7a) and a non-specific reading (7b), and it is accepted both in context (5) and in context (6).

(7) Mary-nun [nwuka ipen senkeo-eyse tangsentoe-lsuissu]-myen
    -TOP [who   this election-LOC get.elected-be.able]-if
    kippu-ulkeya
    happy-will.be
    a. Mary will be happy if someone [+specific] can get elected in the coming election.
    b. Mary will be happy if someone [−specific] can get elected in the coming election.

Turning to other operators, we find that reduplicated indefinite pronouns appear to take obligatory wide scope with respect to negation, as shown in (8), which only allows a specific reading for the indefinite.[2]

(8) nollapketo   ku totuk-un mwues.mwues-ul an   kacieka-ss-e.
    surprisingly the thief-TOP   what.what-ACC NOT take-PAST-DEC
    'Surprisingly, the thief didn't steal something.' (= 'There is something which the thief didn't steal.')
    $= \exists x$ [thing (x) & $\neg$[steal (x) (thief)]] (available reading)
    $\neq \neg[\exists x$ [thing (x) & steal (x) (thief)]] (unavailable reading)

Furthermore, the following examples show that the reduplicated pronoun obligatorily has a wide-scope reading relative to quantified NPs located in surface subject position. Thus, a quantified subject does not distrib-

---

[2] Note that I say that reduplicated pronouns "appear to" take wide scope, in anticipation of my adoption of Schwarzschild's (2002) account of apparent wide scope with respect to specific indefinites. For details, see the discussion below.

ute over a reduplicated indefinite, as shown in (9). A distributive reading is, however, possible with the simplex counterpart, as shown in (10).

(9) ku   pan haksayng twul ta **nwuku.nwuku**-lul coahay
     the class student   two all who.who-ACC   like
     'Two students in the class both like a person.'
     (rejected in context where each student likes a different person)

(10) ku   pan haksayng twul ta **nwuku**-lul coahay
     the class student   two all who-ACC   like
     'Two students in the class like a different person.'
     (non-distributive reading also possible)

As mentioned above, previous research has focused on the available number readings as the only semantic difference between the reduplicated and the simplex indefinite pronouns. In this section, I have provided several pieces of evidence that the two sets of indefinite pronouns most crucially differ in terms of specificity: the reduplicated series obligatorily take a specific reading, and this reading is absent in the case of simplex indefinite pronouns. It will be clear in the following section that, although specificity and singularity are not the same thing, my analysis will in fact imply that the reading of reduplicated indefinite pronouns in Korean is both specific and singular.

3. Proposed Analysis: WH-Specific Indefinites as Singleton Sets

In previous work on specificity, specific readings associated with indefinite NPs were often attributed to some special semantics associated with the determiners as in most Indo-European languages, including English (e.g. Matthewson 1999). However, Korean reduplicated pronouns, based on WH-words, lack overt determiners. Unless one posits a null D° in Korean indefinites, for which I have not been able to find any compelling independent evidence, an alternative explanation for the specificity effects is required.

Crucially, most previous analysis cannot capture the fact that Korean specific indefinites are directly based on (interrogative) WH-words. Thus, I propose that a better way of understanding specific indefinites may be found if we assume, following Kratzer and Shimoyama (2002), that all indefinite pronouns and phrases alike (with or without overt determiners) create sets of alternatives in the sense of Hamblin (1973). There are two interrelated facts that make this hypothesis attractive: (i) the Korean indefinite pronouns are morphologically directly related to question words in the language, and (ii) questions have been successfully analyzed in terms of alternatives.

Kratzer and Shimoyama (2002) adopt Hamblin's (1973) semantics for their analysis of German indefinite *irgendein*. The core of their proposal is that simple indefinite DPs denote a set of contextually relevant "alterna-tives" that satisfy the extension of the NP. Thus, for example, the denotation of a simple indefinite NP, *a boy*, under their system will be the set of boys in a contextually given domain. This point is illustrated in (11). Let us say that $g_2(C)$ is such that it is a set of people with whom I went to a Chicago Cubs game last weekend, namely {Tom, John, and Mary}. Then the denota-tion of *a boy* would be essentially a set consisting of Tom and John, since Mary, being a woman, is outside of the extension of the NP.

(11) a. Let **C** be a (domain) variable ranging over sets of individuals.
   $g(C) \subseteq D$ (D is the set of possible individuals.)
   $[[a_D \text{ boy}]]^{w,g} = \{x: x \text{ is a boy in } w \ \& \ x \in g(C)\}$

   b. graphically: the intersections of $g_1(C)$ and boy′, and $g_2(C)$ and boy′, etc.

D (set of possible individuals)

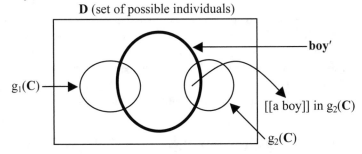

According to Kratzer and Shimoyama (2002), the sets containing alter-natives can expand via domain widening, which according to them derives the free choice meaning of German indefinite *irgendein* NP. (For example, '*irgendein* boy' would be the entire bold oval in (11b).

If some indefinites induce widening, then we might also expect indefi-nites that do the exact opposite, namely, induce maximal domain shrinking. In other words, I propose that reduplication of simple indefinites in Korean is an overt morphological signal that the set denoted by a given indefinite pronoun is a singleton. In this sense, Korean reduplicated indefinite pro-nouns may be what Schwarzschild (2000) calls singleton indefinites. The idea pursued here has some cross-linguistic support. Haspelmath (1997) provides a cross-linguistic survey of indefinite pronouns and phrases. There he observes that the free choice indefinites and specific indefinites are posi-tioned at the opposite side of what one might call a scale of specificity. See Figure 1 for this point.

```
                                    indirect __ direct
                       question __ negation  negation
specific__ specific __ irrealis   /
known    unknown   non-specific  \
                                    conditional — comparative — free-choice
```

Figure 1. Implicational Map for Indefinite Pronoun Series (Haspelmath 1997:119)

Given these assumptions, I now provide an analysis of simple sentences containing simple and doublet indefinite WH-words. First, let us consider the sentence in (13), which contains a simple indefinite WH-word.

(13) nwuka o-esse
     who come-PAST
     'Someone [−specific] came.'

Note that indefinites including Korean WH-words under the current system denote sets of individuals. Thus, *nwuka* 'who' denotes the characteristic function of a set of possible humans (a possibly proper subset of the set of all possible humans). See (14a) for a definition of this. Predicates like 'came' are functions from individuals to truth values and thus have the semantic type $<e,t>$.

(14) a. $[[who]]^{w,g} = \lambda x.$ human $(x) \in D_{<e,t>}$
     b. $[[came]]^{w,g} = \lambda x \lambda w'.$ came (x) (w')

We see that there is one problem with (14). It is that during composition we run into a type mismatch: [[came]] needs an $<e>$ type argument, but it actually gets a set of person-type things. I follow Hamblin (1973), along with Kratzer and Shimoyama (2002) and Hagstrom (1998), and assume that the predicate function applies to each individual in the set separately (i.e. "pointwise") and returns not just one proposition but the set (or collection) of results, thus obviating the potential type-mismatch problem.[3]

The meaning of a simple sentence like (13) containing a simple indefinite pronoun like *nwuka* 'who' then can be derived by composing (14a) and (14b), as shown in (15).

---

[3] A rule that shows how the pointwise application works can be formulated something along the following lines (I thank Stefan Kaufmann for suggesting this rule to me).

Pointwise application: A structure [A[B C]], where B is of type $<\alpha,t>$; C is of type $<\alpha, \beta>$; and A is of type $<\beta,t>$, is interpreted as follows:

$[[A]] = \lambda y \in D_\beta.$
$\exists x \in D_\alpha . [[B]] (x)$ & $y = [[C]] (x)$

(15)

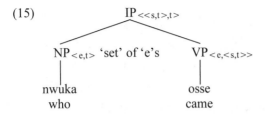

Intuitively, the denotation of (14) is (the characteristic function of) a set of the form {'A came', 'B came', 'C came', (etc)}, i.e. the set of propositions of the form '*x* came for *x* a person', which can be written as (16). Thus, the meaning of *someone came* is the set whose members are the propositions denoted by 'Mary came', 'John came', and so on for all individuals.[4]

(16) $\{\lambda p: \exists x\ [human(x)(w)\ \&\ p = \lambda w'.\ came(x)(w')]\}$

Having discussed how to derive the meaning of sentences containing simple indefinites, I now turn to deriving the meaning of a sentence that contains a WH-doublet, as in (17). Recall that our core proposal is that the reduplicated indefinites involve domain shrinking. That is, the indefinites that have undergone reduplication denote sets that are (maximally) reduced to a singleton set.

(17) nwuku.nwuku-ka o-esse
     who-NOM   come-PAST
     'A certain person came.'

First, the proposed definition of domain shrinking for reduplicated in-definite pronouns in Korean is given in (18) (along the lines of Kratzer 2003). Here, RED, taking a set of humans <e,t>, yields a non-empty set containing just single member of the set. That is, I propose that RED intro-duces a choice function variable selecting a non-empty (singleton) subset from any set in the domain.

(18) $[[WHO + RED]]^{c,w,g} = f_c\ (\lambda x\ [human\ (x)\ (w)])$
     where RED = reduplication

Given this, the proposed constituency and derivation of (17) is as in (19).

---

[4] One may notice that (13) can also be interpreted as a question. I assume, however, that there is an assertion operator in (15) as a sister node to the IP. That makes it a statement, not a ques-tion. See the diagram in (18).

(19)

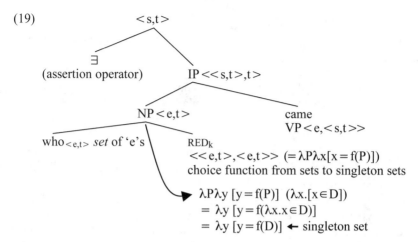

There are two things to note from (19). First, since RED returns (the characteristic function of) a singleton set during the composition, the denotation of the NP in (19), in contrast to the NP in (15), is a singleton set. Thus, the denotation of the whole sentence (19) is a set containing a single proposition of the form {'X came'}, which we set out to derive from sentences containing reduplicated indefinite pronouns. Second, note that I assume that there is an assertion operator ($\exists$) in the sister node of the IP. This operator is a speech act operator, which makes (19) a statement, not a question.

I would like to add that analyzing specific indefinites as singleton sets as a result of domain shrinking has the following advantages. First, there is the observation in previous literature that reduplicated indefinites only go with a singular reading. This is a consequence of the assumption that their domain is a singleton set (although the two claims are not equivalent). Second, the fact that reduplicated pronouns apparently take wide-scope only in sentences that contain operators can now be analyzed differently from an approach exclusively relying on the scope interaction. More specifically, the unusual scope property of specific indefinites is just apparent, as Schwarzschild (2002) puts it. Concretely, under the current assumption that (20) is understood such that the domain of the indefinite contains only one person, (20a) is always truth-conditionally the same as (20b). Thus, there is no need to posit a special scope property for specific indefinites.

(20) ku   pan haksayng twul ta **nwuku.nwuku**-lul coahay
      the class student two all who.who-ACC   like
      'Two students in the class both like someone.'
      a. The two students like someone.
      b. Someone was such that the two students like him/her.

4. Conclusion

In this paper, I have shown that Korean reduplicated indefinite pronouns obligatorily take specific readings. Evidence that the specific reading of reduplicated indefinites is obligatory includes, among other things, the fact that the reduplicated indefinites do not allow distributive readings and that they take obligatory wide scope over other operators. Characteristics such as these are traditionally considered to be hallmarks of specific indefinites (von Heusinger 2002).

To explain the facts, following Hamblin (1973) and Kratzer and Shimoyama (2002), I proposed that all indefinite pronouns and phrases alike (with or without determiners) create sets of "alternatives". This was shown to be a compelling hypothesis because Korean indefinite pronouns come directly from WH-words, and questions have been successfully analyzed in terms of alternatives (Hamblin 1973). I proposed that the core effect of reduplication of Korean simple indefinites is the reduction of the alternative set to a singleton.

The primary significance of this paper is that it introduces into the body of literature on specific indefinites a previously unnoticed way of marking specificity. More generally, this paper provides additional evidence that the semantics of questions and indefinites should both be characterized in terms of alternatives, showing that alternatives can not only expand, as argued by Kratzer and Shimoyama (2002), but can also shrink. This latter property is what derives specificity.

References

Chung, D. 1999. On WH-Doublets in Korean. *Journal of the Linguistic Society of Korea* 25:281–301.

Farkas, D. 1995. Evaluation Indices and Scope. *Ways of Scope Taking*, ed. A. Szabolcsi, 183–215. Dordrecht: Kluwer.

Fodor, J. D., and I. A. Sag. 1982. Referential and Quantificational Indefinites. *Linguistics and Philosophy* 5(3):355–98.

Hagstrom, P. 1998. Decomposing Questions. Doctoral dissertation, MIT.

Hamblin, C. L. 1973. Questions in Montague English. *Foundations of Language* 10: 41–53.

Haspelmath, M. 1997. *Indefinite Pronouns*. Oxford Studies in Typology and Linguistic Theory. Oxford: Oxford University Press.

Jun, S., and M. Oh. 1995. A Prosodic Analysis of Three Types of Wh-phrases in Korean. *Language and Speech* 39(1):37–61.

Kratzer, A. 2003. Indefinites and Functional Heads: From Japanese to Salish. Paper presented at SALT 13, Seattle.

Kratzer, A., and J. Shimoyama. 2002. Indeterminate Pronouns: The View from Japanese. Paper presented at the 3rd Tokyo Conference on Psycholinguistics.

Lee, C. 1989. (In)definites, Case Markers, Classfiers, and Quantifiers in Korean. *Harvard Studies in Korean Linguistics* 3:297–308.

Matthewson, L. 1999. On the Interpretation of Wide-scope Indefinites. *Natural Language Semantics* 7:79–134.

Schwarzschild, R. 2002. Singleton Indefinites, *Journal of Semantics* 19(3):289–314.

von Heusinger, K. 2002. Specificity and Definiteness in Sentence and Discourse Structure. *Journal of Semantics* 19:245–74.

Yeom, J. 1998. A Presuppositional Analysis of Specific Indefinites. Doctoral dissertation, University of Texas at Austin.

Locality in Syntax and Floated Numeral Quantifiers in Japanese and Korean

SHIGERU MIYAGAWA*
Massachusetts Institute of Technology

1. Introduction

Much of syntax is study of locality. Throughout history of generative grammar, linguists have attempted to reduce various linguistic phenomena to some kind of locality—adjacency, specifier-head, "governing domain", "phase", etc. The reason is simple: characterizing a problem in terms of locality substantially decreases the complexity of the problem by reducing the possible grammars that can be deduced. Floated quantifiers comprise a classic case study in syntactic locality. What is particularly interesting about floated quantifiers is that the study of their local nature has made it possible to extract empirical evidence for some of the most basic notions in linguistics. Sportiche's (1988) study of floated quantifiers in English and French gives evidence for predicate-internal subject position. McCloskey (2000) shows that the distribution of floated quantifiers in West Ulster English gives evidence for intermediate traces left by wh-movement. In Miyagawa

---

* I am grateful to the audiences at the 14th J/K Conference in Tucson, Arizona, Aoyama Gakuin University, Leiden Workshop on Ellipsis and Empty Categories, and Yokohama National University for useful discussion and suggestions.

270

(1989) I argue that floated numeral quantifiers in Japanese point to the existence of NP trace in A-movement.

In this paper I will further explore issues of locality in floated numeral quantifiers by looking at Japanese and Korean. Some of the points are based on Miyagawa and Arikawa 2004.

2. Original Observed Locality of Floated Numeral Quantifiers

The starting point for the study of locality of floated numeral quantifiers (FNQ) is the observation made by Haig (1980) and Kuroda (1980).

(1) a. Gakusei ga   san-nin   sake o nonda.
       student NOM 3-CL$_{SUB}$ sake ACC drank
       'Three students drank sake.'

   b. *Gakusei ga   sake o   san-nin nonda.
       student NOM sake ACC 3-CL$_{SUB}$ drank
       'Three students drank sake.'

   c. Hon   o gakusei ga go-satu   katta.
       book ACC student NOM 5-CL$_{OBJ}$ bought
       'Students bought five books.'

The subject FNQ *san-nin* is fine when occurring adjacent to the subject DP as in (1a), but if it occurs away from the subject, as when it is separated from the subject by the object as in (1b), the sentence is ungrammatical. The idea is that the FNQ and its associate DP require locality, and this locality is violated in (1b). The same point is observed in Korean.

(2) a. Haksayng-i sey-myeng photocwu-lul masiessta.
       student-NOM 3-CL$_{SUB}$ wine-ACC   drank
       'Three students drank wine.'

   b. *Haksayng-i photocwu-lul sey-myeng masiessta.
       student-NOM wine-ACC   3-CL$_{SUB}$ drank
       'Three students drank wine.'

In (1c), we see an instance of object FNQ; here the FNQ is separated from the object by the subject, yet, unlike (1b/2b), this separation does not lead to ungrammaticality. The assumption is that the locality requirement of the object FNQ is fulfilled by the trace left by the scrambling of the object.

Why can't the subject and the subject FNQ fulfill locality in (1b/2b)? There are two ways to ask this question. First, given that Japanese and Korean are scrambling languages, why can't there be the following derivation?

(3) Gakusei ga sake o ___ san-nin ___ nonda.
students NOM sake ACC 3-CL_{SUB} drank

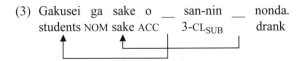

Saito (1985) answered this question by giving the following (the first is implicit but important).

(4) (i) FNQ and the associated noun phrase observe strict locality.
     (ii) The subject in Japanese cannot scramble.

The second condition in (4) prohibits the derivation in (3) by blocking the scrambling of the subject *gakusei ga* 'student NOM'. A second way to ask the question above is, why can't Japanese and Korean have the "Sportiche-style" A-movement that fulfills locality?

(5) Les enfants ont tous ___ vu ce film.
    the children have all seen this movie (Sportiche 1988:426)

The underline indicates the VP-internal subject position where the trace of the A-moved subject *les enfants* is located. This trace fulfills the locality requirement of *tous*. Note that in order for this "Sportiche-style" derivation to apply to (1b/2b), the object must scramble internal to the sentence to vP.

(6) *[$_{TP}$ Haksayng-i [$_{vP}$ photocwu-lul [$_{vP}$ t$_s$ sey-myeng [$_{VP}$ t$_o$ ...]]]]
     student-NOM wine-ACC 3-CL

Later I will argue that the culprit in this example is the A-chain; the copy of this A-chain (t$_S$) is not visible, hence locality with FNQ is violated.

3. "Exceptions" to Locality

It is not the case that whenever a subject FNQ is separated from the subject, the sentence is ungrammatical. The following is a Korean example (see Jung 2004, Kang 2002, and references therein).

(7) Cased FNQ in Korean
    Haksayng-i photocwu-lul sey-myeng-i masiessta.
    student-NOM wine-ACC 3-CL-NOM drank
    'Three students drank wine.'

In this example the stranded subject FNQ has case marking—the same nominative case marking as its associated subject DP *haksayng* 'students'. Why does case marking the FNQ "save" the example?

  To answer this question we need to understand the nature of ungrammaticality of the original observation by Haig and Kuroda about (1b) and (2b). I repeat (1b) below.

(8) *Gakusei ga sake o san-nin nonda.
student NOM sake ACC 3-CL$_{SUB}$ drank
'Three students drank sake.'

When one listens to how a native speaker pronounces this sentence, it is clear that the nuclear stress is placed on the object *sake* (Miyagawa and Arikawa 2004). Because the nuclear stress rule places the stress on the lowest entity in the structure (Cinque 1993), this means that nothing can follow this object that is not a part of the object (I leave aside the verb, which has a special status in Cinque's theory). This means that the FNQ *san-nin* cannot be a syntactically independent entity, but instead must be interpreted as being part of the object phrase.[1] This, then, explains the ungrammaticality. The subject FNQ has the classifier *-nin*, which is used to count people. This is incompatible with *sake*. It is a clash of agreement.

Returning to the Korean example in (7), we can see that the nominative case marking on the FNQ would block the FNQ from being interpreted with the object, which has accusative case marking. As a result the nuclear stress falls not on the object as in the case of the Japanese example in (8), but on the stranded subject FNQ. Later we will see that this case marking has a second important function. Korean helps us to see that the Haig/Kuroda-type locality violation can be saved if the stranded subject FNQ can somehow be kept separate from the object DP. Korean can resort to case marking—something not allowed in Japanese. But now the question arises, in the Korean example with the case-marked FNQ, how is locality fulfilled?

Before answering this question, I note that, although Japanese does not allow case-marked FNQs, a number of linguists have given examples that "save" the Haig/Kuroda-type locality violation.

(9) ?Gakusei ga sake o **imamadeni** san-nin nonda
student NOM sake ACC so far 3-CL$_{SUB}$ drank
'Three students drank sake so far.' (Gunji and Hasida 1998:57)

(10) Gakusei ga watasi no hon o **huta-ri sika** kaw-anakat-ta
student NOM I GEN book ACC 2- CL$_{SUB}$ only buy-not-PAST
'Only two students bought my book.' (cf. Takami 1998(1):92)

As noted in Miyagawa and Arikawa 2004, virtually all counterexamples given to the Haig/Kuroda locality typically have one of the forms shown. In (9) an adjunct phrase ('so far') is inserted between the object and the subject FNQ. In (10) a focus item ('only') is attached to the subject FNQ. In both cases the result is that the subject FNQ is kept separate from the object DP,

---

[1] See Kawashima 1998 and Watanabe 2004 for an analysis that the FNQ immediately following the associated DP may be in the same phrase as the DP.

thereby avoiding the problem originally observed by Haig and Kuroda. The adjunct phrase in (9) keeps the FNQ away from the object. The focus item on the FNQ in (10) attracts stress onto the FNQ, which prevents the nuclear stress from falling on the object, in turn keeping the FNQ phrasally separate from the object. Now we can ask the same question of these examples that we posed for the case-marked FNQ example in Korean. How is the locality requirement of the FNQ fulfilled?

4. Locality Is Respected After All

To understand the nature of the case-marked FNQ example in Korean and (9) and (10) in Japanese, which are basically fine despite the apparent violation of locality, let us again reflect on Saito's (1985) explanation of the ungrammatical Haig/Kuroda example.

(11) (i) FNQ and the associated noun phrase observe strict locality.
      (ii) The subject in Japanese cannot scramble.

Every Japanese linguist who has offered a counterexample to the Haig/Kuroda locality violation has concluded that in (11) it is (i) that is wrong (e.g. Fukushima 2003, Gunji and Hasida 1998, Ishii 1998, Kuno 1978, Kuno and Takami 2003, Nishigauchi and Ishii 2003, Takami 1998). No one has considered the possibility that the other condition, which prohibits subjects from scrambling, might be questioned. If subjects can scramble, there is no problem in maintaining the "locality" analysis of FNQs. This has not been considered before because of Saito's (1985) influential work. To challenge it, Ko (forthcoming) gives a series of arguments that the subject in Japanese and Korean may scramble. If it can be shown that the subject is scrambled in the "nonlocal" subject FNQ examples, it is a sure sign that the FNQ is asserting its locality requirement.

5. Miyagawa and Arikawa 2004

If the linguists who have offered counterexamples to the Haig/Kuroda locality are right that the FNQ does not require locality, the nonlocal subject FNQ examples in (9) and (10) would have the following structure.

(12) $[_{TP}$ SUB ... $[_{VP}$ OBJ FNQ_{SUB} V] ...]

There is nothing adjacent to the FNQ to connect it to the subject. A question immediately arises as to how the "agreement" phenomenon is accounted for; an FNQ has a classifier that agrees with the entity being counted by the associated DP (e.g. -nin for people). Similarly, we wonder how the case marking on the FNQ in Korean would be licensed if the FNQ is not at all connected syntactically to its associated DP, which has the same case marking. In fact Jung (2004) argues convincingly that the nominative DP and the cased FNQ form a "split" NP. By demonstrating sensitivity to islands, she shows that the subject DP has moved out of a structure that also contains the FNQ, thereby giving evidence that the trace of the moved DP fulfills the locality requirement of the case-marked FNQ.

What about the Japanese examples? If it can be shown that the subject has scrambled in (9) and (10), it is a clear sign that the FNQ is meeting locality. Miyagawa and Arikawa (2004) show that this is the correct way to view the nonlocal subject FNQ examples. I will give two pieces of evidence, the first showing that the object DP in these examples does not stay in the *v*P/VP, but moves to the Spec of TP, which, in turn, shows that the subject to the left of this object must have moved there. Second, I will show that the subject in this construction cannot bind an anaphor, showing that the subject is in an A'-position, i.e. a scrambled position. Both arguments are drawn from Miyagawa and Arikawa 2004.

5.1. Negation and 'all'

In this argument we will see that the object in the nonlocal subject FNQ examples is in the Spec of TP, not in the *v*P/VP. The argument involves the interpretation of *zen'in* 'all' relative to sentential negation. If *zen'in* occurs in the object position, it is easily interpreted inside negation.

(13) Taroo ga **zen'in** o   sikar-anakat-ta.
      NOM all ACC scold-NEG-PAST
      'Taro didn't scold all.' (not > all, all > not)

If, however, *zen'in* occurs in the subject position, it is difficult to interpret it inside negation (Kato 1988).

(14) **Zen'in** ga tesuto o   uke-nakat-ta.[2]
      all NOM test ACC take-NEG-PAST
      'All did not take the test.' (*not > all, all > not)

Turning to examples relevant to our discussion, note the following (Miyagawa and Arikawa 2004). (15a) illustrates the first point: *zen'in* 'all' in the object position may get the partial negation reading.

(15) a. Gakusei ga huta-ri **zen'in** o   mi-nakat-ta.
          student NOM 2-CL   all ACC see-NEG-PAST
          'Two students did not see all.' (not > all, all > not)

      b. Gakusei ga **zen'in** o huta-ri tomo mi-nakat-ta.
          student NOM   all ACC 2-CL both see-NEG-PAST
          'Neither of the two students saw all.' (*not > all, all > not)

---

[2] It is important to maintain neutral intonation for this test; the nuclear stress should fall on the object.

   c. Gakusei ga **zen'in** o huta-ri dake mi-nakat-ta.
      student NOM all ACC 2-CL only see-NEG-PAST
      'Only two students did not see all.' (*not > all, all > not)

However, as shown in (15b,c), which are "nonlocal" instances of subject FNQ, the object *zen'in* can only be interpreted outside the scope of negation. This means that the object has moved outside not only the VP but also the *v*P. Based on the "EPP" analysis of scrambling, this is an instance in which the object has moved to the Spec of TP to meet the EPP requirement of T (Miyagawa 2001). This is shown below.

(16) $[_{XP}$ SUB $[_{TP}$ **zen'in o** $[_{vP}$ t_{SUB} NQ$_{SUB}$ $[_{VP}$ t_{OBJ} V] NEG] T]

The fact that the object *zen'in* moves into the Spec of TP is an indication that the subject has scrambled to some position above the "basic" Spec of TP. As we will see, this is an A'-position, which means that this subject scrambling is an instance of A'-movement.

5.2. Anaphor Binding

Note the distinction below.

(17) a. Gakusei$_i$ ga san-nin dake zibunzisin$_i$ o hihansita.
        student NOM 3-CL only self ACC criticized
        'Only three students criticized himself.'

      b. ???Gakusei$_i$ ga zibunzisin$_i$ o san-nin dake hihansita
        student NOM self ACC 3-CL only criticized
        'Only three students criticized himself.'

(17b) is an instance of a "nonlocal" use of FNQ. The subject cannot be an antecedent for the anaphor, unlike in the "normal" case in (17a). It is in an A'-position, in other words.[3] By definition, the subject could not have been externally merged in this position, but must have moved there. This, again, is an indication that the subject in these "nonlocal" subject FNQ cases has scrambled, in turn giving evidence that the FNQ is meeting locality even in these "nonlocal" cases. Below, we turn to what all this is telling us.

6. A-chains and A'-chains

Is it the case that all instances of nonlocal subject FNQ have a derivation in which the subject undergoes A'-scrambling? As it turns out, in Korean, it is possible for the subject to undergo A-movement and strand an FNQ. The FNQ must be case marked. Note the following.

[3] See Hoji and Ishii 2004 for counterexamples to this claim. See Miyagawa and Arikawa 2004 for a response.

(18) **Sensayngnim-(tul)-i** caki-uy haksaying-ul **3-myeng-i** honnay-ss-ta.
      teacher-(pl)-NOM self-GEN student-ACC 3-CL-NOM   criticized
      'Three teachers criticized self's students.'

As noted earlier, case marking on the subject FNQ makes it possible for it to be stranded. We can also see that the chain created by the movement of the subject is due to A-movement, because the head of the chain is able to bind an anaphor. This contrasts minimally with Japanese, in which the subject DP that strands an FNQ cannot bind an anaphor, showing that the subject undergoes A'-movement.

What is the source of the difference between Japanese and Korean? Let us begin with Japanese. The fact that the subject cannot undergo A-movement to the Spec of TP if it strands an FNQ is tantamount to saying that Japanese does not have "Sportiche-style" A-movement for floated quantifiers. In English and French, the floated quantifier may be stranded in the Spec of *v*P, and locality is met by the NP-trace of the subject that has undergone EPP-triggered movement to the Spec of TP. Why isn't this movement available in Japanese? Miyagawa and Arikawa (2004) appeal to an observation by Nevins and Anand (2003), who make the following point about A-movement. Unlike Lasnik (1999), who argues that A-movement simply does not reconstruct (i.e., the lower copy is not visible), Nevins and Anand show on the basis of cross-linguistic data that the visibility of the lower copy of A-chains varies depending on the occurrence of agreement on the A-chain. If agreement occurs, the lower copy is visible. This is English and French, in which the lower copy of the A-chain is visible and can fulfill the locality requirement of floated quantifiers. If there is no agreement, the lower copy is invisible, hence the lower copy cannot be used to meet the locality of floated quantifiers. This is Japanese. If there is to be a copy that could fulfill locality, it must be the lower copy of the A'-chain. This is precisely what we see in Japanese.

What about the Korean case-marked FNQ construction? Like Japanese, Korean lacks agreement of the type found in English/French. Apparently the case marking on the FNQ and the same case marking on the moved subject together function as a form of agreement, which makes the lower copy of the A-chain visible. Thus, the case marking on the subject FNQ in Korean has two functions. As noted earlier, it avoids the subject FNQ from mistakenly being construed as part of the object phrase. Second, the case marking allows an A-chain in which the lower copy is visible.

6.1. Object FNQ

We saw above that the stranded subject FNQ in Japanese is connected to its associated subject DP by an A'-chain. Does this requirement of A'-scrambling for FNQs carry over to object FNQs? Let us look at stranding of object FNQ (Haig 1980, Kuroda 1980).

(19) Hon o gakusei ga go-satu katta.
     book ACC student NOM 5-CL$_{OBJ}$ bought
     'Students bought five books.'

Does the object DP that strands its FNQ in this example move by A- or A'-scrambling? Two kinds of evidence point to the fact that it is A'-scrambling. First, as observed by Hasegawa (1993), a sentence such as the following is scopally unambiguous.

(20) Hon o dareka ga t$_o$ san-satu yonda.
     book ACC someone NOM   3-CL   read
     'Someone read three books.' (some > 3, *3 > some)

The scrambled object must necessarily reconstruct, a sign that the operation that moved the object is A'-scrambling. Second, recall the *zen'in* 'all'/negation test. If *zen'in* 'all' occurs in the subject position, it is not possible (or is difficult) to interpret it inside the scope of negation.

(21) **Zen'in** ga tesuto o   uke-nakat-ta.
     all NOM test ACC take-NEG-PAST
     'All did not take the test.' (*not > all, all > not)

However, as I noted in Miyagawa (2001), if the object scrambles to the head of the sentence, it is much easier to interpret *zen'in* inside negation.

(22) Tesuto o **zen'in** ga t$_o$ uke-nakat-ta.
     test ACC all NOM   take-NEG-PAST
     'Test, all didn't take.' (not > all, all > not)

This is evidence that the object moves into the Spec of TP to satisfy the EPP on T. This is A-movement. Because the EPP is satisfied, the subject, *zen'in*, can stay in its original Spec of *v*P, making it possible to interpret it inside negation. In (21), it is the subject *zen'in* that must move into the Spec of TP to meet the EPP requirement of T, hence it cannot be interpreted inside negation. These are illustrated below (see Miyagawa 2001).

(23) a. [$_{TP}$ **Zen'in** ga [$_{vP}$ t$_s$ [$_{VP}$ tesuto o uke]]-nakat-ta]
        all NOM   test ACC take-NEG-PAST

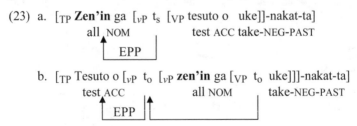

     b. [$_{TP}$ Tesuto o [$_{vP}$ t$_o$ [$_{vP}$ **zen'in** ga [$_{VP}$ t$_o$ uke]]]-nakat-ta]
        test ACC   all NOM   take-NEG-PAST

I have made the movement of the object a "two-step" one; this is based on the assumption that vP is a "phase" (a sort of a barrier), and to get out of it the object must adjoin to it (Chomsky 2000, 2001).

What is of interest is that Yamashita (2001) has noticed that if we add a stranded FNQ to the original example I gave, we get a very different result.

(24) Tesuto o **zen'in** ga t_o mit-tu uke-nakat-ta.
     test ACC all NOM   3-CL take-NEG-PAST
     'Three tests, all did not take.' (*not > all, all > not)

This shows that when the object strands an FNQ, the object can only undergo A'-scrambling. Here, the subject is meeting the EPP requirement of T by undergoing A-movement to the Spec of TP. This is why it cannot be interpreted inside negation.

(25) [$_{XP}$ Tesuto o [$_{TP}$ **zen'in** ga [$_{vP}$ t_o [$_{vP}$ t_s [$_{VP}$ t_o FNQ$_{OBJ}$ uke]]]-nakat-ta]]
     test ACC   all NOM   take-NEG-PAST

One question that arises is, which portion of the chain is A'? Is it the entire "two-step" chain, or is it just the top portion? If it is the latter, we have a nice generalization.

(26) Generalization about "invisible" copy in Japanese
     The trace in the vP domain is invisible in A-chain—whether the moved element is the external argument (subject) or the object.

Below we will see that this is, indeed, the case.

6.2. A-movement Also Possible for FNQ

Are there cases even in Japanese in which A-movement can license an FNQ? In Miyagawa 1989 evidence is given that A-movement in passive and unaccusative constructions licenses FNQs (see also Ueda 1986).

(27) a. Kuruma$_i$ ga doroboo ni t_i san-dai nusum-are-ta.
        cars NOM thief by   3-CL steal-PASS-PAST
        'Three cars were stolen by a thief.'

    b. Doa$_i$ ga kono kagi de t_i futa-tu aita.
        door NOM this key with   2-CL opened
        'Two doors opened with this key.'

    c. *Kodomo ga geragerato san-nin waratta.
        kids NOM loudly   3-CL laughed
        'Three kids laughed.'

The example in (27a) has a passive verb, and the example in (27b) has an unaccusative verb. We expect to find A-chains in these constructions; we see it with the stranding of the FNQ. In (27c) the verb is unergative, hence the only possible A-chain is the kind in which the lower copy in the Spec of vP is invisible. The following shows that, for example, the passive involves A-movement.

(28) ?Gakusei$_i$ ga zibunzisin$_i$ no sensei ni t$_i$ san-nin sikar-are-ta.
     student NOM   self   GEN teacher by   3-CL scold-PASS-PAST
     'Three students were scolded by his own teacher.'

This shows that the A'-movement requirement we saw earlier is imposed on a chain whose tail is at vP. The subject is one, as we have seen. For object scrambling that strands an FNQ, the object must move through vP, and it is this second step that must be A'-scrambling. What this means is that in the passive and unaccusative constructions, the internal argument moves directly to Spec of TP, bypassing the v. This suggests that the v is a "weak" phase with passives and unaccusatives (see Chomsky 2000), contra Legate (2003). The trace in the internal argument position is visible presumably because of lexical θ-marking.

7. Concluding Remarks

Syntactic locality is basic to UG, and floated numeral quantifiers provide a clear case of how locality can be exploited to reveal insights about human language. What the challenges by linguists who tried to argue against the local nature of FNQs led us to understand is that syntax taps whatever resources it has to maintain the locality of FNQs, as we saw with the A'-scrambling of subjects in Japanese. Korean need not resort to A'-movement because of the availability of case marked FNQs, which makes it possible to construct an A-chain in which the lower copy is visible.

References

Chomsky, N. 2000. Minimalist Inquiries: The Framework. *Essays on Minimalist Syntax in Honor of Howard Lasnik*, eds. R. Martin, D. Michaels, and J. Uriagereka, 89–156. Cambridge: MIT Press.

Chomsky, N. 2001. Derivation by Phase. *Ken Hale: A Life in Language*, ed. M. Kenstowicz, 1–52. Cambridge: MIT Press.

Cinque, G. 1993. A Null Theory of Phrase and Compound Stress. *Linguistic Inquiry* 24:239–98.

Fukushima, K. 2003. Verb-Raising and Numeral Quantifiers in Japanese: Incompatible Bedfellows. *Journal of East Asian Linguistics* 12:313–47.

Gunji, T., and K. Hasida. 1998. Measurement and Quantification. *Topics in Constraint-Based Grammar of Japanese*, eds. T. Gunji and K. Hasida, 39–79. Dordrecht: Kluwer.

Haig, J. H. 1980. Some Observations on Quantifier Floating in Japanese. *Linguistics* 18:1065–83.

Hasegawa, N. 1993. Floating Quantifiers and Bare NP Expressions. *Japanese Syntax in Comparative Grammar*, ed. N. Hasegawa, 115–45. Tokyo: Kurosio.

Hoji, H., and Y. Ishii. 2004. What Gets Mapped to the Tripartite Structure of Quantification in Japanese. *Proceedings of the 23rd West Coast Conference on Formal Linguistics*, 101–14. Stanford: CSLI.

Ishii, Y. 1998. Floating Quantifiers in Japanese: NP Quantifiers vs. VP Quantifiers, or Both? Grant-in-Aid for COE Research Report (2), 149–71. Kanda University of International Studies.

Jung, Y.-J. 2004. NP-Splits, Word Order and Multiple Case Mystery. *Korean Journal of Linguistics* 29(4):547–87.

Kang, B.-M. 2002. Categories and Meanings of Korean Floating Quantifiers—With Some References to Japanese. *Journal of East Asian Linguistics* 11:375–98.

Kato, Y. 1988. Negation and the Discourse-Dependent Property of Relative Scope in Japanese. *Sophia Linguistica* 24–5:31–7.

Kawashima, R. 1998. The Structure of Extended Nominal Phrases: The Scrambling of Numerals, Approximate Numerals, and Quantifiers in Japanese. *Journal of East Asian Linguistics* 7:1–26.

Ko, H. Forthcoming. Cyclic Linearization and Asymmetry in Scrambling. *Natural Language and Linguistic Theory*.

Kuno, S., and K. Takami. 2003. Remarks on Unaccusativity and Unergativity in Japanese and Korean. *Japanese/Korean Linguistics 12*, ed. W. McClure, 280–94. Stanford: CSLI.

Kuroda, S.-Y. 1980. Bun kōzō no hikaku [The comparison of sentence structures]. *Niti-Eigo hikaku kōza 2: bunpō* [Lectures on Japanese-English comparative studies 2: grammar], ed. T. Kunihiro, 23–61. Tokyo: Taishūkan.

Lasnik, H. 1999. Chains of Arguments. *Working Minimalism*, eds. S. Epstein and N. Hornstein, 189–216. Cambridge: MIT Press.

Legate, J. 2003. Some Interface Properties of the Phase. *Linguistic Inquiry* 34:506–16.

McCloskey, J. 2000. Quantifier Float and wh-Movement in an Irish English. *Linguistic Inquiry* 31:57–84.

Miyagawa, S. 1989. *Structure and Case-Marking in Japanese*. New York: Academic Press.

Miyagawa, S. 2001. The EPP, Scrambling, and wh-in-situ. In M. Kenstowicz (ed.) *Ken Hale: A Life in Language*. Cambridge: MIT Press.

Miyagawa, S., and K. Arikawa. 2004. Syntactic Locality and Floated Numeral Quantifiers in Japanese. Manuscript, MIT and St. Andrews College.

Nevins, A., and P. Anand. 2003. Some AGREEment Matters. *WCCFL 22 Proceedings*, eds. G. Garding and M. Tsujimura, 370–83.

Nishigauchi, T., and Y. Ishii. 2003. *Eigo kara Nihongo o miru* [Looking at Japanese from English]. Tokyo: Kenkyūsha.

Saito, M. 1985. Some Asymmetries in Japanese and Their Theoretical Implications. Doctoral dissertation, MIT.

Sportiche, D. 1988. A Theory of Floating Quantifiers and Its Corollaries for Constituent Structure. *Linguistic Inquiry* 19:425–49.

Takami, K. 1998. Nihongo no sūryōshi yūri ni tsuite [Quantifier float in Japanese]. *Gekkan Gengo* 27(1):86–95; (2):86–95; (3):98–107.

Ueda, M. 1986. On Quantifier Float in Japanese. *University of Massachusetts Occasional Papers in Linguistics* 11:263–309.

Watanabe, A. 2004. Indeterminates and Determiners. *Proceedings of the Workshop on Altaic Formal Linguistics* (*MIT Working Papers in Linguistics* 6), eds. A. Csimarz, Y. Lee, and M. A. Walter, 390–405. Cambridge: Department of Linguistics and Philosophy, MIT.

Yamashita, H. 2001. EPP and the Ordering Effects on Interpretation: A Preliminary Study. *Nanzan Studies in Japanese Language Education* 8:300–38.

On Exceptional *zibun* Binding: An Experimental Approach

DAVID Y. OSHIMA*
Stanford University

1. Introduction

In past studies, it has been widely acknowledged that the Japanese anaphor *zibun* is subject-oriented, i.e. must be (locally or long-distance) bound to a subject, unless it is logophorically bound (Oshima 2004, Kameyama 1984, among others). For example, in the following example, *zibun* must be bound to the matrix subject and cannot be bound to the dative argument of the matrix clause.

(1) Taroo$_i$ wa Hanako$_j$ ni [zibun$_{i/*j}$ ga sekkei-si-ta] ie   de   at-ta
       TOP   DAT self   NOM design-PAST house LOC meet-PAST
     'Taro$_i$ met Hanako$_j$ in the house that he$_i$/*she$_j$ designed.'

The subjecthood condition of (non-logophoric) *zibun* binding has been challenged by several authors (Iida 1996, Momoi 1986, among others) with certain types of alleged counterevidence. There is, however, a considerable

---

* I would like to thank Peter Sells, Ivan A. Sag, and Paul Kiparsky for valuable comments and discussions. Thanks also to Sandra Y. Okita and Yuko Tsukada for their help with statistical analysis, and to the subjects of this study for their cooperation. Any remaining errors are my own.

variance among speakers as to the grammaticality judgments on sentences that involve non-subject *zibun* binding. To evaluate the validity and significance of such data, it is thus essential to examine their acceptability in an experimentally controlled manner (see Bard et al. 1996, Asudeh and Keller 2001 for the effectiveness of experimental methodology for measurements of linguistic intuitions).

The goal of this paper is two-fold. First, the results of an experimental survey are reported, which demonstrate that two types of non-subject *zibun* binding, namely (i) binding by the causee of a lexical causative and (ii) so-called "backward" binding, are judged as (to varying degrees) grammatical by most speakers, with the acceptability comparable to that of other types of *zibun* binding which have been commonly assumed to be grammatical. Second, I discuss how the two types of non-subject binding can be incorporated to the existing theory of *zibun* binding, with minimum modification of the subjecthood condition.

2. Challenge for the Subjecthood Condition

This section clarifies certain theoretical assumptions for the present work (§2.1), and then illustrates two types of data that pose challenge for the subjecthood condition (§2.2 and §2.3).

2.1. Preliminaries

As background theory of *zibun*, I will assume the following.

(2) (i) Logophoric *zibun* must be distinguished from non-logophoric *zibun* (Kuno 1978, Kameyama 1984). Logophoric *zibun* is an instance of "shifted indexicals" (*de se* pronouns) (Schlenker 1999), and it does not have to be bound to a subject.[1]

(ii) Non-logophoric *zibun* must be, as a rule, bound to a subject syntactically commanding it. Non-logophoric *zibun* subsumes the reflexive and empathic uses of *zibun* (Oshima 2004).

An example of logophoric, non-subject *zibun* binding (adapted from Kameyama 1984:230) is given in (3).[2]

---

[1] In the present work, "logophoricity" is to be understood in its original (narrow) sense, and thus, for instance, empathic *zibun* which is long-distance bound in a relative or adverbial clause is not considered logophoric (see Oshima 2004, forthcoming; Culy 1997).

[2] Kameyama's judgments on the type of data shown in (3) have been questioned by several authors (Iida 1996, Mihara 1998, among others). The experimental results reveal that the acceptability of *zibun* binding by an oblique logophoric source is considerably lower than that of canonical subject binding (§3.2).

(3) Hanako wa Taroo$_i$ kara [zibun$_i$ ga   kat-ta] koto o   kii-ta.
      TOP   from   self NOM win-PAST fact ACC hear-PAST
      'Hanako heard from Taro$_i$ that he$_i$ had won.'

Logophoric binding includes binding into environments called represented speech and thought (RST; a.k.a. free indirect speech), which is also referred to as intersentential binding (Hirose 1997):

(4) (Tokiko$_i$ wa aozame-ta. 'Tokiko turned pale.')
      Masaki wa zibun$_i$ o   okizari ni site itte   simat-ta   no da.
      TOP   self ACC leave.behind   go end.up-PAST EMPH
      'Masaki had gone leaving her behind.'

In the remainder of the paper, I will mainly discuss non-logophoric *zibun*, and by the term *zibun* I will refer to non-logophoric *zibun* unless otherwise noted.

2.2. Lexical Causatives

In the literature, it has been widely assumed that the causee argument of a morphological causative can be a binder of *zibun*, while that of a lexical causative cannot (Shibatani 1976, Kameyama 1984, Manning et al. 1999, among others).[3]

(5) a. morphological causative
      Taroo$_i$ wa Hanako$_j$ o zibun$_{i/j}$ no zitensya ni   nor-ase-ta.
      TOP   ACC self   GEN bicycle DAT get.on-CAUS-PAST
      'Taro$_i$ made Hanako$_j$ ride on his$_i$/her$_j$ bicycle.'

      b. lexical causative
      Taroo$_i$ wa Hanako$_j$ o zibun$_{i/*j}$ no zitensya ni   nose-ta.
      TOP   ACC self   GEN bicycle DAT put-PAST
      'Taro$_i$ put Hanako$_j$ on his$_i$/*her$_j$ bicycle.'

(6) a. morphological causative
      Taroo$_i$ wa kodomo$_j$ ni zibun$_{i/j}$ no   huku   o   ki-sase-ta.
      TOP   child DAT self   GEN clothes ACC put.on(tr.)-CAUS-PAST
      'Taro$_i$ made the child$_j$ put on his$_{i/j}$ clothes.'

      b. lexical causative
      Taroo$_i$ wa kodomo$_j$ ni zibun$_{i/*j}$ no huku   o   kise-ta.
      TOP   child DAT self   GEN clothes ACC put.on(dtr.)-PAST
      'Taro$_i$ put his$_{i/*j}$ clothes on the child$_j$.'

This contrast has been attributed to the biclausality of morphological causatives and the monoclausality of lexical causatives. The causee argument of a

---

[3] The asterisks in (5) and (6) are merely to illustrate the standard assumption in the literature.

morphological causative is the subject of the embedded clause, and thus is a possible *zibun* binder. By contrast, a lexical causative is monoclausal, and thus its only subject (= the only possible *zibun* binder) is the nominative argument. According to some authors, however, the contrast between mophological and lexical causatives with regard to *zibun* binding is not clear-cut. Iida (1996:211–3), for example, claims that the causee of a lexical causative can be the binder of *zibun*, especially with appropriate contextual information (see also Momoi 1986, Kitagawa 1981).

In §3, the results of an experimental survey will be presented, which prove that *zibun* binding by the causee of a lexical causative is judged as acceptable by many speakers. In §4, I will discuss what makes this type of binding possible.

2.3. Backward Binding

Another type of non-subject *zibun* binding is so-called backward binding (or backward reflexivization), which is exemplified below (Inoue 1976; Ue 1982; Momoi 1986; Iida 1996).

(7) a. Zibun$_i$ ga sodate-ta desi ga Yamada-kyoozyu$_i$ ni
    self NOM train-PAST pupil NOM   -professor DAT

    meisei   o motarasi-ta.
    reputation ACC bring-PAST

    'The pupil who he$_i$ trained brought reputation to Prof. Yamada$_i$.'

   b. Zibun$_i$ no desi ga Yamada-kyoozyu$_i$ ni   meisei   o
    self GEN pupil NOM   -professor DAT reputation ACC

    motarasi-ta.
    bring-PAST

    'His$_i$ pupil brought reputation to Prof. Yamada$_i$.'

What is peculiar about *zibun* binding in (7) is that the binder is a non-subject and the bindee (*zibun*) occurs within the co-argument subject of the binder. I will take this as the defining property of backward binding. Note that the term backward binding is somewhat misleading, since it sounds as if it is defined in terms of linear order. I will keep using this term, however, for the lack of a better alternative.[4]

To account for such data, Momoi proposes that the binding condition of *zibun* must refer to the semantic role hierarchy. NPs that carry one of the highest roles in the hierarchy (Experiencer, Agent, etc.) are always good candidates for the antecedent of *zibun*, but in the absence of a higher role, an NP that bears a relatively lower role (Goal, etc.) may bind *zibun* (see also

---

[4] The effect of linear order on backward binding will be discussed in §4.2.

Uda 1994). One difficulty of semantic role-based analyses along the lines of Momoi 1986 is that they make different predictions depending on which version of the theory of semantic roles one adopts (e.g. whether Recipient and Goal are distinct or not, which of Goal or Theme is ranked higher, whether the oblique argument of 'receive' is assigned Agent or Source). In other words, they involve a risk of tailoring otherwise unmotivated theoretical assumptions to meet the empirical data (see Iida 1996:68–72 for a similar criticism). In §4, I will pursue an alternative, more syntax-oriented way to account for backward binding, still leaving open the possibility of the semantic role-based approach.

Whether we adopt the syntax-based or the semantics-based approach, the following two factors that affect the acceptability of backward binding must be taken into consideration: (i) the presence of a potential subject binder, and (ii) the "agentivity" of the antecedent. These points will be illustrated in §3 with experimental data and further discussed in §4.

3. Experiment

This section reports the results and key findings of an experimental survey of the acceptability of non-subject *zibun* binding.

3.1. Design

To investigate the acceptability of the types of non-subject *zibun* binding discussed above, I conducted a questionnaire-based experiment with 44 native speakers of Japanese (Experiment A). 10 subjects had experience in linguistics, and the other 34 were naive to linguistic theory.

The subjects were asked to evaluate the acceptability of stimuli sentences (with specification of coreference) by assigning them numerical scores from 1 to 5 (1 = "(the intended interpretation is) impossible", 2 = "possible, but nearly impossible", 3 = "possible, but considerably difficult", 4 = "possible, but slightly difficult", and 5 = "fully acceptable and natural"), which are assumed to form an interval scale. The questionnaire included the following sets of experimental sentences, as well as 17 fillers. In the experiment, each sentence was transcribed in standard Japanese orthography and included a single pair of coreference markers.

(9) [CSB]: canonical subject binding ((1) on the *i* interpretation)

[MPC](a,b): binding by the causee of a morphological causative ((5a) and (6a) on the *j* interpretation)

[LXC](a,b): binding by the causee of a lexical causative ((5b) and (6b) on the *j* interpretation)

[BWB]: backward binding

    [BWB-NPSB-AG](a,b): backward binding without a potential subject binder/with an agentive (i.e. recipient) antecedent ((7a), (7b))

    [BWB-PSB-AG]: backward binding with a potential subject binder/with an agentive antecedent ((10) below)

    [BWB-NPSB-NA]: backward binding without a potential subject binder/with a non-agentive (i.e. patient) antecedent ((11) below)

[LOGOBL]: logophoric binding by an oblique source ((3))

[NSB]: non-subject binding that satisfies neither of the MSC, BWB, or LOGOBL conditions ((1) on the *j* interpretation)

(10) Zibun$_i$ o takaku hyooka-site-i-ru desi ga Yamada-kyoozyu$_i$ ni
self ACC highly evaluate-ASP-PRES pupil NOM -professor DAT
meisei o motarasi-ta.
reputation ACC bring-PAST
'The pupil who thinks highly of him$_i$ brought reputation to Prof. Yamada$_i$.'

(11) Zibun$_i$ ga sodate-ta desi ga Yamada-kyoozyu$_i$ o hihan-si-ta.
self NOM train-PAST pupil NOM -professor ACC criticize-PAST
'The pupil who he$_i$ trained criticized Prof. Yamada$_i$.'

3.2. Results and Findings

The mean scores and standard deviations of the stimuli sentences are summarized in Table 1.

	MS	SD	1	≥2	≥3
CSB	4.48	0.73	0 (0%)	44 (100%)	44 (100%)
MPC (a)	3.18	1.39	6 (14%)	38 (86%)	28 (64%)
MPC (b)	3.52	1.41	6 (14%)	38 (86%)	33 (75%)
LXC (a)	2.70	1.58	15 (34%)	29 (66%)	22 (50%)
LXC (b)	2.75	1.50	13 (30%)	31 (70%)	23 (52%)
BWB-NPSB-AG (a)	3.41	1.28	5 (11%)	39 (89%)	33 (75%)
BWB-NPSB-AG (b)	2.80	1.25	9 (20%)	35 (80%)	27 (61%)
BWB-PSB-AG	2.39	1.10	12 (27%)	32 (73%)	18 (41%)
BWB-NPSB-NA	2.52	1.25	13 (30%)	31 (70%)	23 (52%)
LOGOBL	2.48	1.47	18 (41%)	26 (59%)	22 (20%)
NSB	1.65	0.99	26 (59%)	18 (41%)	7 (16%)

Table 1. Results of Experiment A (44 subjects; MS = mean score, SD = standard deviation, 1 = number of subjects who assigned 1 (unacceptable), ≥ x = number of subjects who assigned a score higher than or equal to x)

The results show that both binding by the causee of a lexical causative and backward binding were judged as at least marginally acceptable (i.e. ≥ 2) by most speakers. The mean score (MS) of LXC was slightly lower than that of MPC, but significantly higher than that of NSC (p < 0.01 determined by the Wilcoxon signed rank test with Holm's correction) and slightly higher than LOGOBL (which was reported to be grammatical by Kameyama 1984).

Backward binding without a potential binder and with an agentive antecedent (BWB-NPSB-AG) was judged highly acceptable (comparable to MPC), especially when *zibun* appears in a relative clause modifying the subject rather than directly modifying the subject as a possessive. The acceptability decreased when there is a potential subject binder (BWB-PSB-AG) or the antecedent is non-agentive (BWB-NPSB-NA).

4. Discussion and Proposals

4.1. Lexical Causatives and Coercion

The results of Experiment A revealed that the causee of a lexical causative is a possible *zibun* binder for many speakers, despite the fact that it has not been considered a subject in the standard syntactic analysis.

To account for the (degraded or marginal) acceptability of LXC, I propose that a lexical causative can be coercedly interpreted as having two "subjects" while still having a monoclausal syntactic structure. Such a solution is possible within syntactic frameworks like HPSG and LFG, where subjecthood is defined in a syntax-semantics interface component (i.e. ARG-ST list in HPSG, f-structure in LFG; see Asudeh and Keller 2001). In the

HPSG framework, for example, a subject is defined as the first member of an ARG-ST list, and the marginal acceptability of LXC can be formally captured by a coercion rule that assigns a nested ARG-ST list like (12a) (which is similar or identical to that of the corresponding morphological causative) to a lexical causative, which canonically has a simplex ARG-ST like (12b) (see Manning et al. 1999).

(12) a. argument structure of *noraseru* 'cause X to get on Y' and *noseru* in (5b) (for those speakers who accept the *j* interpretation)
$$[\text{ARG-ST} \ < \text{NP[NOM]}, \text{NP[ACC]}_i, < \text{PRO}_i, \text{NP[DAT]} > >]$$

   b. canonical argument structure of *noseru* 'put X on Y'
$$[\text{ARG-ST} \ < \text{NP[NOM]}, \text{NP[ACC]}, \text{NP[DAT]} >]$$

4.2. A Revised Subjecthood Condition

To accommodate backward binding exemplified by BWB-NPSB-AG, I propose to revise the subjecthood condition as follows.

(13) **Revised Subjecthood Condition**: (Non-logophoric) *zibun* must be bound to a subject syntactically commanding it **if there is any**; when there is no potential subject binder, it can be bound to a non-subject antecedent in an argument position of the same clause or a clause dominating it.

This "weakened" version of the subjecthood condition is somewhat reminiscent of Principle A proposed by Pollard and Sag (1992) ("A locally o-commanded anaphor must be o-bound."), which allows an (English) anaphor to be bound by a non-local antecedent when there is no local possible antecedent. The common idea of the revised subjecthood condition and Pollard and Sag's Principle A can be put this way: when an anaphor cannot be bound by a canonical binder (i.e. a local antecedent for English anaphors/a subject antecedent for *zibun*), it can be bound by a non-canonical binder. Note that the revised subjecthood condition still makes correct predictions as to the (nearly categorical) acceptability of CSB and (nearly categorical) unacceptability of NSB.

There remain, however, two questions yet to be addressed. First, why is a sentence like (10) (BWB-PSB-AG), which involves backward binding with a potential binder, at least marginally acceptable to many speakers, despite the fact that it does not satisfy (even) the revised subjecthood condition? Second, why does the acceptability of backward binding decrease with an antecedent with low agentivity (e.g. patient) while it increases with an antecedent with high agentivity (e.g. recipient)?

To account for the contrast between NSB (nearly categorically unacceptable), and BWB-PSB-AG (marginally acceptable), I submit the following hypothesis.

(14) **Linear Order Effect**: The effect of a potential subject binder is highly significant when it linearly precedes *zibun*, but relatively mild when it follows *zibun*.

To examine this hypothesis, I conducted a follow-up experiment with 36 speakers (Experiment B; 8 subjects had experience in linguistics) that included the following experimental sentences.[5]

(15) a. Suzuki-kyoozyu wa [[zibun$_i$ ga sodate-ta] desi ga
         professor TOP   self NOM train-PAST pupil NOM
         Yamada-kyoozyu$_i$ o   hihan-su-ru] bamen ni   dekuwasi-ta.
         -professor ACC criticize-PRES scene DAT come.across-PAST
         'Prof. Suzuki witnessed the scene where the pupil he$_i$ trained criticized Prof. Yamada$_i$.'

     b. [[Zibun$_i$ ga sodate-ta] desi ga Yamada-kyoozyu$_i$ o
         self NOM train-PAST pupil NOM   -professor ACC
         hihan-su-ru] bamen ni Suzuki-kyoozyu wa   dekuwasi-ta.
         criticize-PRES scene DAT   -professor TOP come.across-PAST

Both (15a) and (15b) involve a potential subject binder (i.e. *Suzuki-kyoozyu*), but they differ with respect to word order. Hypothesis (14) predicts that (15b) would be judged more acceptable than (15a), and that both (15a) and (15b) would be judged less acceptable than (11), repeated below as (16).

(16) Zibun$_i$ ga sodate-ta desi ga Yamada-kyoozyu$_i$ o   hihan-si-ta.
     self NOM train-PAST pupil NOM   -professor ACC criticize-PAST
     'The pupil who he$_i$ trained criticized Prof. Yamada$_i$.'

Table 2 shows the relevant part of the results of Experiment B (note the change in the number of subjects).

---

[5] The questionnaire for Experiment B contained 8 experimental sentences ((1-*i*), (1-*j*), (15a), (15b), (16), (17a), (17b-*i*), (17b-*j*)) and 11 fillers.

	MS	SD	1	≥ 2	≥ 3
CSB	4.61	0.60	0 (0%)	36 (100%)	36 (100%)
(16)	2.69	1.26	7 (19%)	29 (81%)	19 (53%)
(15a)	1.97	1.11	17 (47%)	19 (53%)	13 (36%)
(15b)	2.31	1.19	12 (33%)	24 (67%)	16 (44%)
NSB	1.56	1.05	25 (69%)	11 (31%)	5 (14%)

Table 2. Partial Results of Experiment B (36 subjects)

These results bear out the effect of linear order between *zibun* and the potential subject binder. While the acceptability difference between (16) and (15a) is significant (p < 0.01), the difference between (16) and (15b) is rather small.[6]

Next, let us address the effect of agentivity of the antecedent. A possible source of this effect is the "coerced subject" status of the antecedent (note that the verb *motarasu* 'bring' can be semantically paraphrased as 'cause to have'). That is, although in backward binding the subjecthood of the antecedent is not a necessary requirement, it still serves as a factor that improves acceptability. I do not assume, however, that "backward subject binding" can be assimilated to ordinary (forward) subject binding, since only the former is highly sensitive to the effect of a potential subject binder. In (17), for example, the acceptability of backward *zibun* binding is considerably degraded with a potential subject binder, despite the fact that the antecedent (*Yamada-kyoozyu*) is the causee of a morphological causative (and hence is a subject without coercion).

(17) a. [Zibun$_i$ ga   sodate-ta] desi   ga Yamada-kyoozyu$_i$ o
       self NOM train-PAST pupil NOM   -professor ACC
       komar-ase-te-i-ru.
       be.annoyed-CAUS-ASP-PRES
       'The pupil he$_i$ trained is embarrassing Prof. Yamada$_i$.'

---

[6] The effect of a potential binder in (15a) is not as strong as in (1). The interference of a potential binder appears to be most prominently felt when it is a clause-mate of the intended binder. Hypothesis (14) also predicts that the following sentence is more acceptable than (1-*j*):

Hanako$_i$ ni wa [zibun$_i$ ga   sekkei-si-ta]   ie   de Taroo ga   at-ta.
DAT TOP   self NOM design-PAST house LOC   NOM meet-PAST
'Taro met Hanako$_i$ in the house that she$_i$ designed.'

Unfortunately, I have no experimental data at hand about the relative acceptability of (i) and (1-*j*). My own judgments, however, conform to the prediction.

b. Suzuki-kyoozyu$_i$ wa [[zibun$_{i/?*j}$ ga sodate-ta] desi ga
    -professor TOP   self   NOM train-PAST pupil NOM
    Yamada-kyoozyu$_j$ o   komar-ase-te-i-ru]   bamen ni
    -professor ACC be.annoyed-CAUS-ASP-PRES scene DAT
dekuwasi-ta.
come.across-PAST
'Prof. Suzuki$_i$ witnessed the scene where the pupil he$_{j/?*j}$ trained
was embarrassing Prof. Yamada$_j$.'

	MS	SD	1	≥ 2	≥ 3
(17a)	2.75	1.36	10 (28%)	26 (72%)	22 (61%)
(17b) (*i*)	4.78	0.59	0 (0%)	36 (100%)	35 (97%)
(17b) (*j*)	1.89	0.92	16 (44%)	20 (56%)	11 (31%)

Table 3. Partial Results of Experiment B (36 subjects)

5. Summary

In this paper, I examined two types of non-subject *zibun* binding. With experimental data, I demonstrated that (i) *zibun* binding by the causee of a lexical causative, which has been assumed to be ungrammatical in the syntactic literature, is acceptable to many speakers, and (ii) so-called backward binding is highly acceptable, while the acceptability decreases either (a) if the agentivity of the antecedent is low, or (b) if there is a potential subject binder. To accommodate these two types of non-subject binding into the existing theory of *zibun*, I proposed that the causee of a lexical causative can be interpreted as a (predicationally defined) subject by coercion, and that the subjecthood condition must be slightly revised so that non-subject binding is licensed when there is no potential subject binder. I also pointed out that the effect of a potential binder is relatively mild when it linearly follows *zibun*.

References

Asudeh, A., and F. Keller. 2001. Experimental Evidence for a Predication-Based Binding Theory. *CLS* 37(1):1–14.

Bard, E. G., D. Robertson, and A. Sorace. 1996. Magnitude Estimation of Linguistic Acceptability. *Language* 72(1):32–68.

Culy, C. 1997. Logophoric Pronouns and Point of View. Linguistics 35:845–59.

Hirose, Y. 1997. Hito o arawasu kotoba to shōō. *Nichieigo hikaku sensho*. Vol.4, *Shiji to shōō to hitei*, ed. M. Nakau, 2–89. Tokyo: Kenkyūsha.

Iida, M. 1996. *Context and Binding in Japanese*. Stanford: CSLI.

Inoue, K. 1976. Reflexivization: An Interpretive Approach. *Syntax and Semantics 5: Japanese Generative Grammar*, ed. M. Shibanani, 117–200. New York: Academic Press.

Kameyama, M. 1984. Subjective/Logophoric Bound Anaphor *zibun*. *CLS* 20:228–38.

Kitagawa, C. 1981. Anaphora in Japanese: *kare* and *zibun*. *Coyote Papers 2*, eds. A. K. Farmer and C. Kitagawa, 61–75.

Kuno, S. 1978. *Danwa no bunpō*. Tokyo: Taishūkan.

Manning, C, I. A. Sag, and M. Iida. 1999. The Lexical Integrity of Japanese Causatives. *Studies in Modern Phrase Structure Grammar*, eds. R. Levine and G. Green, 39–79. Cambridge: Cambridge University Press.

Mihara, K. 1998. *Nihongo no tōgokōzō: Seiseibunpōriron to sono ōyō*. Tokyo: Shōhakusha.

Momoi, K. 1986. Syntactic Roles, Variation, and the Japanese Reflexive. *University of Chicago Working Papers in Linguisitics* 1:73–92.

Oshima, D. Y. 2004. *Zibun* Revisited: Empathy, Logophoricity and Binding. *University of Washington Working Papers* 23 (*Proceedings of the 20th NWLC*):175–90.

Oshima, D. Y. Forthcoming. On Empathic and Logophoric Binding. *Research on Language and Computation*.

Pollard, C., and I. A. Sag. 1992. Anaphors in English and the Scope of the Binding Theory. *Linguistic Inquiry* 23:261–303.

Shibatani, M. 1976. The Grammar of Causative Constructions: A Conspectus. *Syntax and Semantics 5: Japanese Generative Grammar*, ed. M. Shibatani, 239–94. New York: Academic Press.

Uda, C. 1994. *Complex Predicates in Japanese*. New York: Garland.

Ue, N. 1982. A Crossing Constraint in Japanese Syntax. Doctoral dissertation, University of Michigan.

Jussive Clauses and Agreement of Sentence Final Particles in Korean

MIOK DEBBY PAK*
Georgetown University

1. Introduction

Korean is often said to have sentence final particles that mark clause types. Hence, in (1), the sentence final particles *-la*, *-ca*, and *-ma*, for example, are traditionally viewed as markers of imperatives, exhortatives, and promissives, respectively. In this paper, I investigate the role(s) of the sentence final particles in Korean, focusing on the three types of clauses in (1).[1]

---

* The work in this paper is part of the project funded by NSF grant BCS-0234278 "Clause Types: Form and Force in Grammatical Theory" to Paul Portner and Raffaella Zanuttini. I thank Paul Portner, Raffaella Zanuttini, and Simon Mauck for their valuable comments, and also the audience at J/K14 for useful comments. The usual disclaimer applies.

[1] In glossing the data, the following abbreviations are used: ACC – accusative case marker, APE – apperceptive mood marker, APR – apprehensive mood marker, COMP – complementizer, DAT – dative marker, DEC – declarative marker, EXH – exhortative particle, FOC – focus marker, FUT – future tense marker, HON – honorific morpheme, IMP – imperative particle, INT – interrogative marker, NEG – negative marker, NMN – nominalizer, NOM – nominative case marker, PAST – past tense marker, POL – politeness particle, PRES – present tense marker, PRM – promissive particle, RTR – retrospective mood marker, SP – speech style particle, SUP – suppositive mood marker.

(1) a. IMPERATIVES   b. EXHORTATIVES
    Cemsim-ul mek-e-**la**   Icey kongpwuha-**ca**
    lunch-ACC eat-IMP   now   study-EXH
    'Eat lunch!'   'Now, let's study.'

    c. PROMISSIVES
    Nayil   nay-ka cemsim-ul sa-**ma**[2]
    tomorrow I-NOM lunch-ACC buy-PRM
    'I will buy lunch tomorrow.'

Within the GB/Minimalism framework it is proposed that force is directly represented in the syntax via a feature for imperatives or operator for interrogatives residing in a high position in grammatical structure (Chomsky and Lasnik 1977, Cheng 1991, Han 1998, Rizzi 1996, 1997, and Rivero and Terzi 1995, among others). These elements in the syntax play the role of marking the clause in which they occur as a member of a certain clause type. In line with such claims, Ahn and Yoon (1989), Whitman (1989), and Bradner (2004), among others, have proposed that the sentence final particles in Korean mark "sentential mood" (i.e. declarative, interrogative, imperative, etc.) and have argued that they head a MoodP positioned higher than IP. However, despite allowing different subjects and sentence final particles, imperatives, exhortatives, and promissives share a significant number of similarities that cannot be put aside as a mere coincidence. Given such facts, in this paper I propose a novel theory of clause types. Within this new theory, I claim that the sentence final particles in (1) are not force markers. Rather they mark persons such as addressee and/or speaker specified by the subject of the clause through an agreement mechanism between the subject and a sentence final particle.

2. Similarities Shared by Imperatives, Exhortatives, and Promissives

The similarities among the three types are as follows. First, when imperatives, exhortatives, and promissives are embedded, the embedded subjects show the same restrictions. Consider the following data.

---

[2] The sentence final particle -*ma* in promissives actually consists of -*m* and -*a*, the latter of which is classified as a speech style particle. For details on sentence final particles in Korean, see Pak 2004.

(2) a. Imperative

      John-i Tom-ekey [(*ney-ka/*Tom-i) cip-ey ka-**la**]-ko

      -NOM   -DAT [(you-NOM/ -NOM) home-to go-IMP]-COMP

      mal-ha-ess-ta

      say-do-PAST-DEC

      (intended meaning) 'John ordered Tom to go home.'

   b. Exhortative

      John-i Tom-ekey [(*wuli-ka) cip-ey ka-**ca**]-ko

      -NOM   -DAT [(we-NOM) home-to go-EXH]-COMP

      mal-ha-ess-ta

      say-do-PAST-DEC

      (intended meaning) 'John said to Tom let's go home.' (indirect speech)

   c. Promissive

      John-i Tom-ekey [(*nay-ka/*John-i)   nayil   tasi

      -NOM   -DAT [(I-NOM/   -NOM) tomorrow again

      o-**ma**]-ko   mal-ha-ess-ta

      come-PRM]-COMP say-do-PAST-DEC

      (intended meaning) 'John promised Tom that he would come back tomorrow.'

The examples in (2) show that nominative case marked subjects cannot appear in the embedded subject position of imperatives, exhortatives, and promissives.

    Second, all three types use the negative marker -*mal* in negative formation.[3]

---

[3] Some native speakers of Korean do not find promissives with -*mal* grammatical at first, but when given a context such as the following, they find them fully grammatical. Imagine a mother bringing six pieces of cake for dessert for family members. Because there are actually seven people, the mother tells one of her children not to eat, so that others (older people) can have one each. The father, feeling bad for the child, says he won't eat one. Now, the grandmother, feeling bad for her own son, says she won't eat. The following is the dialogue.

    Mother: Minsoo-ka mek-ci mal-a-la

               -NOM eat-NMN NEG-SP-IMP

               'Minsoo, do not eat (the cake).'

    Father: Aniya, nay-ka an mek-ci.

              no   I-NOM NEG eat-DEC

              'No, I won't eat.'

 Grandmother: Anita, nay-ka mek-ci mal-u-ma

               no   I-NOM eat- NMN NEG-u-PRM

              'No, I won't eat.'

(3) a. Imperative
    Mek-ci *an(i)/mal-a-la
    eat-NOM NEG-a-IMP
    'Do not eat.'

    b. Exhortative
    Mek-ci *an(i)/mal-ca
    Eat-NOM NEG-EXH
    'Let's not eat.'

    c. Promissive
    Mek-ci   an(i)h/mal-u-ma
    Eat-NOM NEG(+do)-u-PRM
    'I promise not to eat.'

While the negative marker -*ani* is used in declaratives and interrogatives, imperatives and exhortatives allow -*mal* only, and promissives allow both.

Third, imperatives, exhortatives, and promissives do not allow certain mood particles, such as the retrospective mood particle -*te*, the apperceptive mood particle -*kwun*, the suppositive mood particle -*ci*, and the apprehensive mood particle -*ney*.[4]

(4) a. Imperative
    *Ne cemsim-ul mek-te/kwun/-ci/-ney-la.
    you lunch-ACC eat-RTR/APE/SUP/APR-IMP

    b. Exhortative
    *Wuli cemsim-ul mek-te/kwun/-ci/-ney-ca.
    we lunch-ACC eat-RTR/APE/SUP/APR-EXH

    c. Promissive
    *Nay-ka nayil cemsim-ul sa-te/kwun/-ci/-ney-ma.
    I-NOM tomorrow lunch-ACC buy-RTR/APE/SUP/APR-PRM

All of these special mood particles are compatible with declaratives, and the retrospective -*te* and the suppositive -*ci* are allowed in interrogatives. However, in imperatives, exhortatives, and promissives none of them can be used:

---

[4] The retrospective mood denotes the speaker's past perception, observation, or experience. Hence, it is sometimes referred to as the reportive mood, and in Cinque 1999 it is called evidential mood. The apperceptive mood is used when the speaker realizes some fact that s/he did not know before the time of the utterance, and the speaker does not assume anything of the hearer's awareness of this fact. This mood is referred to as evaluative mood in Cinque 1999. The suppositive mood is used when the speaker presupposes that the hearer already knows or agrees on the proposition expressed by the utterance. Finally, the apprehensive mood is very similar to the apperceptive mood in that it is used when the speaker comes to the realization of certain fact at the time of the utterance, but it differs in that the speaker assumes that the hearer does not know about this fact.

(5) a. John-i   cemsim-ul   mek-ess-**tey-yo**./?
     -NOM lunch-ACC eat-PAST-RTR-POL
     'John ate lunch./Did John eat lunch?'

    b. John-i   cemsim-ul   mek-ess-**ci-yo**./?
     -NOM lunch-ACC eat-PAST-SUPP-POL
     '(Of course,) John ate lunch./John ate lunch, right?'

    c. John-i   cemsim-ul mek-ess-**kwun-yo**./*?
     -NOM lunch-ACC eat-PAST-APPE-POL
     '(Ah,) you ate lunch.'

    d. John-i   cemsim-ul   mek-ess-**ney-yo**./*?
     -NOM lunch-ACC eat-PAST-APPR-POL
     'John ate lunch.'

Fourth, they do not allow tense markers:

(6) a. Imperative
    *Mek-ess/-ul/-nun-e-**la**
    eat-PAST/-FUT/-PRES-SP-IMP

    b. Exhortative
    *Mek-ess/-ul/-nun-**ca**
    eat-PAST/-FUT/-PRES-EXH

    c. Promissive
    *Mek-ess/-ul/-nun-u-**ma**
    eat-PAST/-FUT/-PRES-PRM

The data in (6) illustrate that none of the past, future, and present tense markers can occur in these clauses.

Finally, they can all be conjoined using -*ko* 'and':

(7) a. Declarative and Interrogative
    *John-un sakwa-lul mek-ess-**ko** ne-nun   pay-ul   mek-ess-ni?
      -FOC apple-ACC eat-PAST-and you-FOC pear-ACC eat-PAST-INT
    (intended meaning) 'John ate an apple, and did you eat a pear?'

    b. Imperative and Promissive
    Ne-nun   sakwa-lul mek-**ko** na-nun pay-lul   mek-u-ma
    you-FOC apple-ACC eat-and   I-FOC pear-ACC eat-u-PRM
    (intended meaning) 'You eat an apple, and I promise to eat a pear.'

    c. Imperative and Exhortative
    Minwoo-nun cip-ey   ka-**ko** Yenghee-wa na-nun hakkyo-ey ka-ca
        -FOC home-to go-and   -and I-FOC school-to go-EXH
    (intended meaning) 'Minwoo go home, and Yenghee, let's go to school.'

The coordinator -*ko* can conjoin only clauses of the same type, as shown in (7a). Note that an imperative and a promissive can, however, be conjoined by -*ko*, as in (7b), and the coordination of an imperative and an exhortative is also good, as shown in (7c).

If we follow the traditional classification that treats imperatives, exhortatives, and promissives as belonging to distinct clause types and views the sentence final particles -*la*, -*ca*, and -*ma* as marking the clause types imperative, exhortative, and promissive, respectively, then these similarities are a mere coincidence. That is, there is no natural explanation for the similarities. However, given the number of similarities, we suspect that something beyond coincidence is at work. In what follows, I explore a different view of clause types, which can provide an explanation for the phenomena under investigation.

3. Jussives

Given the discussion in the previous section, I argue that Korean imperatives, exhortatives, and promissives belong to a single clause type: **jussive**. The jussive clause type expresses a property which is required of some individual, metaphorically added to this individual's "to-do list" (Han 1998, Hausser 1980, Portner 2004, Portner and Zanuttini 2002, Potts 2003). A fundamental hypothesis in this paper is that imperatives, exhortatives, and promissives, while all being jussive in this sense, differ in the person of their subjects. When the subject is second person, referring to the addressee, the result is an imperative; when it is first person, the result is a promissive; and when it is first person inclusive of the addressee, it is an exhortative.

I hypothesize that the semantics of the jussive is built up from three components represented in the syntax. The first is a property P—in the case of (1a), the property of eating lunch. The second is a representation of the individual i to whose to-do list the property is to be added. In the case of (1a), an imperative, i is the addressee, while in the corresponding exhortative i would be the speaker and the addressee. In the corresponding promissive i would be the speaker. The third component is an intensional variable-binding operator *Modal*, which binds i as well as the predicate's world variable and makes it the case that the whole jussive denotes a property. Intuitively, the resulting jussive clause denotes the property P restricted to the individual i. Example (1a) denotes the property of eating lunch restricted to the addressee, formally (8).

(8) $[\lambda \, w \, \lambda \, x : x = \text{addressee(context)} . \, x \text{ eats lunch in } w]$

In any world in which the addressee eats lunch, this property is true of the addressee and nobody else; in any other world, it is not true of anyone. Similarly, the example (1c) denotes the property of buying lunch restricted to the speaker. Hence, a promissive would only differ in having "$x =$ speaker(context)" as the restriction on argument x, while an exhortative like

(1b) would denote the property of studying restricted to the speaker and the addressee. So a formal representation of an exhortative would have "x = speaker and addressee".

Given this proposal that imperatives, exhortatives, and promissives are all members of the same clause type called jussives, the similarities discussed in §2 are not a mere coincidence any more. Rather, they are a natural result. See Pak et al. 2004 for a theoretical account of the similarities.

4. The Role of the Particles: Agreement Markers for Addressee/ Speaker

Given the claim above, the sentence final particles *-la, -ca*, and *-ma* are not force markers. What, then, is/are the role(s) of these particles in Korean? I claim that they are agreement markers marking person(s) of the subject of the sentence in terms of [addressee and/or speaker].

4.1. Agreement of Sentence Final Particles with the Subject in Jussive Clauses

In jussives, the subject is always the addressee in imperatives, the speaker in promissives, and the addressee and speaker in exhortatives. The idea, then, is first, the sentence final particles convey information concerning the subject. More specifically, their job is to express the person(s) whose to-do list is to be updated. Thus, *-la* indicates that the subject is the addressee, grammatically realized as second person. The sentence final particle *-ca* in exhortatives indicates that the subject is the speaker and the addressee, grammatically realized as first person inclusive of the addressee. The *-ma* in promissives indicates that the subject is the speaker—grammatically first person. Second, this role of the particles is achieved through an agreement mechanism between the persons and the particles.

To implement this idea, I make the following claims.

- Cross-linguistically, in jussives the subject must coincide with the addressee/speaker (Mauck et al. 2005). Hence, the individual whose to-do list needs to be updated must coincide with the addressee/ speaker. This restriction on the subject of jussives can be captured by the presence of an Addressee/Speaker Projection in the syntax of jussives.

- The sentence final particles are spell outs of the addressee/speaker head and the modal head which are the composite of [+modality, addressee and/or speaker] features in the Distributed Morphology framework.

> -*la*: [+modality, +addressee, −speaker]
> -*ma*: [+modality, −addressee, +speaker]
> -*ca*: [+modality, +addressee, +speaker][5]

- The Modal in jussives is a raising predicate, like other modals, hence the subject raises to the specifier position of ModalP.

- The Addressee/SpeakerP semantically binds a variable of the subject in jussives, and this achieves the interpretive restriction on the subject that it always coincides with the addressee/speaker (see Mauck and Zanuttini 2005 for details).

- Since the sentence final particles are spell outs of the Modal and addressee/speaker head, and the subject in jussives is semantically bound by the Addressee/SpeakerP, there is a vacuous agreement between the subject and the sentence final particles.

The proposed clausal structure is shown in Figure 1.

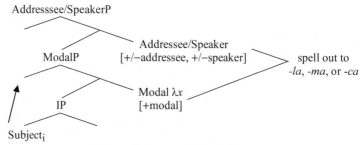

Figure 1. Proposed Clausal Structure

4.2. Honorific Agreement

Normally Korean is considered to be one of those languages that lack agreement (like Japanese, Chinese, etc). It is true that Korean does not have

---

[5] Alternatively, it is possible to posit [+deictic] feature along with the [+/−addressee] feature to distinguish the system of +deictic (first and second person) from the system of non-deictic (third person) (Benincà and Poletto 2004). Specifically, [+deictic, +addressee] would be the subject features for imperatives, [+deictic, −addressee] for promissives, and [+deictic, +/−addressee] for exhortatives. However, in this paper, I prefer to use the [+addressee, +speaker] features for two reasons: simplicity and presence of third person subject imperatives. Consider the following.

Taum hwanca tul-e oseyyo.
next patient in come
Next patient come in.'

This imperative has a third person subject. This kind of data cannot be explained with the [+deictic, +/−addressee] features, which exclude a third person subject, but can be explained with the features [+addressee, +speaker].

subject-verb agreement and does not have agreement affixes (for person, number, and gender). But there is another kind of agreement that some researchers have argued involves an agreement mechanism. This is **honorific agreement**.

Honorific agreement in Japanese and Korean has been claimed by many researchers (Harada 1976, Shibatani 1977, Toribio 1990, Boeckx and Niinuma 2004 for Japanese; Ahn 2002 and references therein for Korean). These researchers have claimed that honorific agreement involves at least some kind of syntactic agreement. One argument for this is that when both an indirect object and a direct object are present, only the indirect object can trigger honorific agreement on the predicate (Toribio 1990, Boeckx and Niinuma 2004, among others).

(9) Japanese (Boeckx and Niinuma 2004)

    a. Boku ga Tanaka-sensei ni Mary o   go-syookai-si-ta
          I NOM   -teacher to   ACC HON-introduce-do-DEC
          'I introduced Mary to Prof. Tanaka.'

    b. *Boku ga Mary ni Tanaka-sensei o   go-syookai-si-ta
          I NOM   to   -teacher ACC HON-introduce-do-DEC
          'I introduced Prof. Tanaka to Mary.'

(10) Korean

    a. Mina-ka kyoswunim-ekey tongsayng-ul   sokaysiykye
          -NOM   professor-to younger.sibling-ACC introduce
      tuli-ess-ta
      give(HON)-PAST-DEC
      'Mina introduced the younger sibling to the professor.'

    b. Mina-ka   tongsayng-ekey kyoswunim-ul sokaysiykye
          -NOM younger.sibling-to professor-ACC   introduce
      cwu-ess-ta
      give-PAST-DEC
      'Mina introduced the professor to the younger sibling.'

    c. */??Mina-ka   tongsayng-ekey kyoswunim-ul sokaysiykye
            -NOM younger.sibling-to professor-ACC   introduce
      tuli-ess-ta
      give(HON)-PAST-DEC

    d. *??Mina-ka kyoswunim-ekey tongsayng-ul   sokaysiykye
           -NOM   professor-to younger.sibling-ACC introduce
      cwu-ess-ta
      give-PAST-DEC

A second argument is that honorific agreement always requires a syntactically present trigger.

(11) *Boku ga o-iki-simasu (Toribio 1990)
     I NOM HON-go
     'I will go for you.'

4.2. Agreement and AgrP

How should we reconcile the facts that Korean (and Japanese) lacks regular subject-verb agreement and that it allows honorific agreement as well as the jussive particle agreement with the subject? Speas (1995) claims that agreement affixes in languages (such as Italian) that have rich agreement (i.e. a full agreement paradigm) are strong in that they are listed as individual lexical items in the lexicon and hence project as head of AgrP in the syntax. On the other hand, those in the languages that have partial agreement (such as English) are weak in that they are only part of a morphological paradigm in the lexicon and are not listed as individual lexical items. As such, they do not project as head of AgrP. Rather, they are inserted in the syntax as a part of verbs. But they need to check the affixal features, and hence AgrP is needed. In languages that do not have agreement at all (such as Japanese and Korean), there is no agreement affix and hence no features to check. So there is no AgrP in the syntax.

Speas further claims that the lack of phi-feature agreement in languages such as Korean (and Japanese) should not be taken as the absence of other kinds of agreement relation. What is lacking is the AGR head, not the agreement relation. In line with Speas' claim, I also take it that the lack of phi-feature agreement (and agreement affixes) in Korean only means that there is no AgrP in the syntax and does not preclude the presence of an agreement relation of one kind or another. Other kinds of agreement such as the sentence final agreement with the subject in jussive clauses, as well as the honorific agreement, need not require the presence of AgrP, and the agreement relation can be established through other projections.

5. Conclusion

I have argued for the existence of a clause type "jussive" which arises when its three meaning components are encoded in the syntactic structure. In Korean, this clause type encompasses imperatives, exhortatives, and promissives. In this new theory of clause types, the sentence final particles are viewed as marking agreement with the subject of jussives in terms of Addressee/Speaker.

References

Ahn, S.-H. 2002. Honorification and AgrP. Paper presented at the 2002 Winter Conference of the Linguistic of Society of Korea, Seoul.

Ahn, H.-D., and H.-J. Yoon. 1989. Functional Categories in Korean. *Harvard International Studies on Korean Linguistics III*, eds. S. Kuno et al., 79–88. Seoul: Hanshin.

Boeckx, C., and F. Niinuma. 2004. Conditions on Agreement in Japanese. *Natural Language and Linguistic Theory* 22(3):453–80.

Brandner, E. 2004. Head-Movement in Minimalism, and V2 as Force-Marking. *Interface Explorations 9: Syntax and Semantics of the Left Periphery*, eds. H. Lohnstein and S. Trissler. Berlin: Mouton de Gruyter.

Cheng, L.-S. 1991. On the Typology of Wh-Questions. Doctoral dissertation, MIT.

Chomsky, N., and H. Lasnik. 1977. Filters and Control. *Linguistic Inquiry* 8(3): 425–504.

Cinque, G. 1999. *Adverbs and Functional Heads: A Cross-Linguistic Perspective*. Oxford: Oxford University Press.

Han, C. H. 1998. The Structure and Interpretation of Imperatives: Mood and Force in Universal Grammar. Doctoral dissertation, University of Pennsylvania.

Han, C. H., and C. Lee. 2002. On Negative Imperatives in Korean. *Proceedings of the 16th Pacific Asia Conference on Language, Information and Computation*, 59–68. Seoul: The Korean Society for Language and Information.

Harada, S. I. 1976. Honorifics. *Syntax and Semantics 5: Japanese Generative Grammar*, ed. M. Shibatani, 299–361. New York: Academic Press.

Hausser, R. 1980. Surface Compositionality and the Semantics of Mood. *Speech Act Theory and Pragmatics*, eds. J. Searle, F. Kiefer, and M. Bierwisch, 71–95. Dordrecht: D. Reidel.

Mauck, S., M. Pak, P. Portner, and R. Zanuttini. 2005. Clause Typing in Imperatives: A Cross-Linguistic Perspective. *Georgetown University Working Papers in Theoretical Linguistics*, eds. C. Brandstetter and D. Rus, 135–52. Washington: Georgetown University.

Mauck, S., and R. Zanuttini. 2005. Subjects of English Imperatives. *Georgetown University Working Papers in Theoretical Linguistics*, eds. C. Brandstetter and D. Rus, 53–86. Washington: Georgetown University.

Pak, M. 2004. Investigating the Role of Sentence End Particles in Korean. Manuscript, Georgetown University.

Pak, M., P. Portner, and R. Zanuttini. 2004. Deriving Clause Types: Focusing on Korean. *Proceedings of Linguistic Society of Korea 2004*, 359–68. Seoul: Yonsei Institute of Language and Information Studies.

Platzack, C., and I. Rosengren. 1998. On the Subject of Imperatives: A Minimalist Account of the Imperative Clause. *Journal of Comparative Germanic Linguistics* 1:177–224.

Portner, P. 2004. The Semantics of Imperatives within a Theory of Clause Types. Paper presented at SALT 14, Evanston, Illinois.

Portner, P., and R. Zanuttini. 2002. Form and Force in Grammatical Theory, Ppaer presented at the workshop on the Syntax-Semantics Interface in the CP Domain, Berlin.

Potsdam, E. 1996. Syntactic Issues in the English Imperative. Doctoral dissertation, University of California, Santa Cruz.

Potts, C. 2003. Keeping World and Will Apart: A Discourse-Based Semantics for Imperatives. Paper presented at the NYU Syntax/Semantics Lecture Series, New York. (Handout available at http://www-unix.oit.umass.edu/% 7Epotts/)

Rivero, M. L., A. Terzi. 1995. Imperatives, V-Movement and Logical Mood. *Journal of Linguistics* 31:301–22.

Sadock, J. M., and A. Zwicky. 1985. Speech Act Distinctions in Syntax. *Language Typology and Syntactic Description*, ed. T. Shopen, 155–96. Cambridge: Cambridge University Press.

Shibatani, M. 1977. Grammatical Relations and Surface Cases. *Language* 53:780–809.

Speas, M. 1995. Economy, Agreement and the Representation of Null Arguments. Manuscript, University of Massachusetts.

Toribio. A. J. 1990. Specifier-Head Agreement in Japanese. *Proceedings of WCCFL* 9:535–48.

Whitman, J. 1989. Topic, Modality, and IP Structure. *Harvard International Studies on Korean Linguistics III*, eds. Susumo Kuno et al., 341–56. Seoul: Hanshin.

Zanuttini, R. 2003. Imperative and Clause Types. Paper presented at the North American Syntax Conference, Montreal.

Zanuttini, R., and P. Portner. 2003. Exclamative Clauses: At the Syntax-Semantics Interface. *Language* 79:39–81.

Part V

Discourse

Zero-Marked Topics, Subjects, and Objects in Japanese

Mutsuko Endo Hudson
Michigan State University

Yoshimi Sakakibara
Michigan State University

Junko Kondo
University of Michigan

1. Introduction

It is well known that Japanese has particles for topics (most notably *wa*), subjects (*ga*), and direct objects (*o*). Although these markers usually appear in formal writing, they are often absent in natural speech. In (1), for example, the topic *B-chan* (line 1), the subject *watashi* 'I' (line 2), and the object *kii* 'attention' (lines 1 and 2) are all without particles, or zero-marked.

(1) [#3 '2 bottles'][1]

   1 A: Kii Ø   tsukatte-n no yone. B-chan Ø tsukareru yo.
          attention are-using EP FP   get-tired FP
          'You're worrying about us. B, you'll be tired.'

   2 B: Watashi Ø   kii Ø tsukatte-nai yoo.
          I   attention am-not-using FP
          'I'm not worried.'

---

[1] Numbers and topics in square brackets refer to those in our data. All names are pseudonyms. Due to space limitations, longer stretches of discourse cannot be included. Abbreviations in the examples are: ACC: accusative; COP: copula; EMP: emphatic; EP: extended predicate; FP: final particle; GEN: genitive; NOM: nominative; Q: question particle; TQ: tag question; TOP: topic.

310 / E<small>NDO</small>, S<small>AKAKIBARA</small>, <small>AND</small> K<small>ONDO</small>

A number of analyses have been proposed on zero-marked topics and subjects (e.g. Hudson and Kondo 2001, Ito 1998, Kusumoto 2002, D.-Y. Lee 2002, K. Lee 2002, Maruyama 1996, Niwa 1989, Noda 1996, Ono, et al. 2000, Suzuki 1995, Terakura 1997), and objects (Fujii and Ono 2000, Himeno 1999, Ōtani 1995). The present study examines zero-marked topics, subjects, topic-sentence subjects, and objects in Prince's (1992) framework. Our data consist of 400 tokens in total, taken from a naturally-occurring informal conversation. While zero-marking has traditionally been attributed to particle deletion/ellipsis (e.g. Iwasaki 2002, Kuno 1973, Makino and Tsutsui 1986, Tsujimura 1996, Tsutsui 1983, 1984), we contend that it is actually "unmarked", as do Fujii and Ono (2000) concerning objects, and that particles are added for pragmatic effects. Our objectives are to illustrate the abundance of zero markings in informal speech and to show the usefulness of Prince's (1992) three-way classification of information status.

In the present study, "topic" refers to X in a base-generated topic sentence $[X\ wa\ Y\ ga\ Z]$ and in an *unagi* 'eel' sentence $[X\ wa\ Z]$. "Topic-sentence subject" refers to Y in base-generated $[X\ wa\ Y\ ga\ Z]$, whether it is like the subject or the object of Z. "Subject" refers to X in a nominal sentence $[X\ wa/ga\ NP\ da]$, an adjectival sentence $[X\ wa/ga\ AP]$, and a verbal sentence $[X\ wa/ga\ (Y\ o)\ VERB]$. "Object" refers to Y in both types of verbal sentences $[X\ wa/ga\ Y\ o\ VERB]$ and $[Y\ wa\ X\ ga\ VERB]$. The same definitions apply to zero-marked NPs. "Subject" and "object" may or may not be topicalized; the former may be marked with *wa*, *ga*, or Ø, and the latter, by *wa*, *o*, or Ø. This classification assures consistency in analyzing all NPs, eliminating the futile efforts of deciding what an NP is "supposed to be" marked with if particles are absent. Consider *kore* 'this' in line 3 in (2), for example.

(2) [#43 'Evidence']

    1 A: Un, soo yo. Shooko ga   aru   kara, kore Ø uso Ø tsukenai.
           yeah so FP evidence NOM exist so   this   lie   can't-tell
           'Yeah, really. There is evidence, so you can't lie about this.'

    2 B: Soo.
           right   'Right.'

    3 A: Soshitara **kore Ø**.
           in-that-case this   'In that case, **this**.'

    4 B: Mottette moraoo.
             take   let's-ask   'Let's ask them to take it.'

Kore 'this' can potentially be marked with *wa* or *o*, which is of no consequence in our analysis. It will simply be classified as "object", based on its grammatical relation to the verb *mottette* 'take' in line 4. Similarly, an NP functioning as subject, whether marked with *wa*, *ga*, or Ø, is classified as subject. To put it differently, a *wa*-marked NP may be classified as a "topic", a "subject", or an "object", depending on its grammatical function in the sentence, and a *ga*-marked NP may be classified as a "subject" or a "topic sentence subject". Base-generated topic sentences turned out to be relatively rare in our data; hence, "topics" and "topic-sentence subjects" are much fewer than are other categories.

2. Prince's (1992) Framework

Prince (1992) distinguishes information status into four types: old and new in the "Hearer's Head" and old and new in the "Discourse-Model". According to her (1992:301), "Information, by which is . . . generally meant 'entities'/referents, may be old/new with respect to (the speaker's beliefs about) the hearer's beliefs." Hearer-old information is what was termed "Unused" in Prince 1981 and "in the permanent registry" in Kuno 1972. Hearer-new information is "an entity assumed not to be already known to the hearer," or "Brand-new" (Prince 1981). Discourse-old information is represented by an NP that refers to "an entity that has already been evoked in the prior discourse-stretch" and Discourse-new information, by "an NP that evokes an entity which has not previously occurred in the prior discourse-stretch" (Prince 1992:303). Although "[d]iscourse-newness tells us nothing about an entity's Hearer-status, if a piece of information is Hearer-new, it would necessarily be Discourse-new" (Prince 1991:303). In other words, there is no such category as "Hearer-new, Discourse-old" (Prince 1992:303). Data sets (3)–(5) offer examples from our data.

(3) ⟨Hearer-new, Discourse-new⟩

    a. TOPIC — PARTICLE MARKED: NONE
    TOPIC — ZERO MARKED: NONE

    b. SUBJECT — PARTICLE MARKED: [#16 "Paper"]
    A: Dareka no, ano, **denwa   ga**   natteru.
    someone's um telephone NOM is-ringing
    'Someone's phone is ringing.'

    SUBJECT — ZERO MARKED: [#17 "Superwoman"]
    B: Demo nee,   sugoi   no yo, minna. **Hon   dashiteru   hito Ø**
    but   FP impressive EP FP   all   book has-published people
    nanninka iru   no nee.
    several exist EP   FP
    'But they're all impressive. There are several **people who have published books.**

    c. TOPIC-SENTENCE SUBJECT — PARTICLE MARKED: [#17 "Super-woman"]

    A: **Minna**   **ga** soo yatteru wake?
      everyone NOM so are-doing EP
      '(As for your department,) is **everyone** doing that?'

    TOPIC-SENTENCE SUBJECT — ZERO MARKED: [#19 "Video"]

    C: Nanka **ii aidia** Ø nai?
      some good idea   not-exist
      '(As for you,) is there any **good idea**?'

   d. OBJECT — PARTICLE MARKED: [#62 "Medicine (2)"]

    A: Dakara, takusan non-de takusan ase   kaite ne?
      so   much drink-and much sweat produce FP
      (C: Soo soo soo.) Ano, **doku** o   dasu   toka.
      right right right um poison ACC get-rid or-something
      'So, (you should) drink a lot and sweat a lot. (C: Right, right,
      right.) Um, (you should) get rid of **bad things**.'

    OBJECT — ZERO MARKED: [#61 "Illness"]

    A: Koo, moo, kyonen wa ne, **suggoi kaze** Ø hiite.
      um really last-year TOP FP terrible cold   caught
      'Um, really, last year, I caught **a terrible cold**.'

(4) ⟨**Hearer-old, Discourse-new**⟩

    a. TOPIC — PARTICLE MARKED: [#3 "2 bottles"]

    C: Futatsu nante, **watashi wa**   kekkoo.
      two   TOP   I   TOP no-thanks
      'Two! As for **me**, no thanks.'

    TOPIC — ZERO MARKED: [#6 "Can you drink?"]

    A: Shooga   ii, **watashi** Ø.
      ginger no-thanks I
      '**I** don't want ginger.'

   b. SUBJECT — PARTICLE MARKED: [#16 "Paper"]

    A: Dakedo, **uchi no kareshi ga**   itte-kureta no.
      but   I GEN husband NOM went-for-me FP
      'But, **my husband** went for me.'

    SUBJECT — ZERO MARKED: [#44 "John and tennis"]

    B: Demo, kyoo **Jon-san** Ø kawaisoo janai?
      but today John   lonely TQ
      'But, today, **John** is lonely (without you), isn't he?'

c. TOPIC-SENTENCE SUBJECT — PARTICLE MARKED: [#4 "Restaurant Fuji"]

C: Fuji, **ocha ga** ne.
    tea NOM FP
'As for Fuji, **their tea** (leaves something to be desired).'

TOPIC-SENTENCE SUBJECT — ZERO MARKED: [#17 "Superwoman"]

A: Un, demo   wakaru   **sono kimochi Ø**.
   yeah but understandable that feeling
'Yeah, but, as for me, **that feeling** is understandable.'

d. OBJECT — PARTICLE MARKED: [#63 "Resistance"]

C: De, kaze o   hiitemo,   **kusuri**   o nondewa ikenai toka ne.
   and cold ACC even-catch medicine ACC take   can't like FP
'And, like, even if you catch a cold, you can't take **medicine**.'

OBJECT — ZERO MARKED: [#60 "Salt"]

A: **Oshio Ø** itadaitemo-ii-deshoo ka?
   salt   could-have   Q
'Could I have **salt**?'

(5) ⟨Hearer-old, Discourse-old⟩

a. TOPIC — PARTICLE MARKED: [#42 "Telephone"]

B: Watashi no   uchi wa, **watashi wa** Supurinto.
   I   GEN home TOP   I   TOP   Sprint
'As for my home, as for **me**, it's Sprint.'

TOPIC — ZERO MARKED: [#4 "Restaurant Fuji"]

C: **Fuji Ø**, ocha ga   ne.
   Fuji   tea NOM FP
'As for **Fuji**, their tea (leaves something to be desired).'

b. SUBJECT — PARTICLE MARKED: [#36 "John and Sushi"]

C: **Sore wa** kitsui wane.
   that TOP tough   FP
'**That** is tough.'

SUBJECT — ZERO MARKED: [#4 "Restaurant Fuji"]

C: **Sore Ø** chotto kitsui wane.
   that   a-little tough FP
'**That** is a little tough.'

c. TOPIC-SENTENCE SUBJECT — PARTICLE-MARKED: [#25 "Sea urchin"]

A: Kore,   uni   tanonda no watashi dake na no?
   this sea-urchin ordered one   I   only COP FP
'Am I the only one who ordered this, sea urchin?'

B: Hai, soo, soo.
   yes right right
   'Yes, that's right.'

A: Watashi suki na no, **uni**   **ga.**
   I   fond am FP sea-urchin NOM
   'I am fond of **sea urchin**.'

TOPIC-S SUBJECT — ZERO-MARKED: [#39 "Strange mail"]

B: Nihongo de kaite-atta desho? are.
   Japanese in was-written TQ   that
   'That was written in Japanese, right?'

A: Watashi **Nihongo** Ø yomenakatta.
   I   Japanese   couldn't-read
   'I couldn't read **the Japanese**.'

    d. OBJECT — PARTICLE MARKED: [#8 "Dormitory"]

B: Reizooko   karite, saisho nakatta kara, moo, ocha mo
   fridge borrow-and first didn't-have so EMP   tea even
   dekinai   shi, nannimo   dekinai kara, tsuini **reizooko o**
   couldn't-make and anything couldn't-do so finally   fridge ACC
   katte . . .
   bought-and
   'He borrowed a fridge, and since he didn't have it first, he
   couldn't even make tea, and couldn't do anything, so he finally
   bought **a fridge** and . . .'

OBJECT — ZERO MARKED: [#19 "Video"]

A: Bideo. (1 sec.) **Bideo** Ø tsukawanai no wa kangaerarenai.
   video   video   not-use   to TOP unthinkable
   'Video. ... It's unthinkable not to use **video**.'

3. Data, Results, and Discussion

Our data consist of a naturally-occurring informal conversation at a dinner
table, which took place in 2003. Three female native speakers participated,
all about 50 years of age. The whole conversation was audio-taped, of
which the first 60 minutes (after the initial three minutes) were analyzed.
There were 29 topics, 164 subjects, 27 topic-sentence subjects, and 180
objects, a total of 400 tokens.[2] Table 1, on the next page, presents a summary of zero- and particle-markings in our data (TSb: topic-sentence subject).

---

[2] Topics marked with *nanka*, *tte mo*, etc., are excluded from the present analysis.

	Ø-Marked Ø	Particle-Marked wa	ga	o	P-Marked Total	Total
Top	19(66%)	10(34%)	0 (0%)	0 (0%)	10(34%)	29(100%)
Sub	72(44%)	38(22%)	54(33%)	0 (0%)	92(56%)	164(100%)
TSb	10(37%)	5(19%)	12(44%)	0 (0%)	17(63%)	27(100%)
Obj	113(63%)	0 (0%)	0 (0%)	67(37%)	67(37%)	180(100%)
Total	214(53.5%)	53(13%)	66(16.5%)	67(17%)	186(46.5%)	400(100%)

Table 1. Zero- and Particle-Marked NPs

Overall, zero marking was more frequent (53.5%) than overt marking (46.5%). This is consistent with the findings in previous studies. In Terakura's (1997) data, zero-marked topics accounted for 53%, and *wa*-marked topics for 47%. These numbers are strikingly close to our overall figures. The rate of zero-marked topics in our data was actually even higher: 66%, as opposed to 34% for *wa*-marked topics. Similar results obtained with objects: 63% were zero-marked, and 37% *o*-marked. Our figures are comparable to those in Fujii and Ono's (2000) study of object marking, in which 70% were zero-marked, and 30% *o*-marked. In the case of topic-sentence subjects and regular subjects, a different pattern emerged. Overt marking was more frequent than zero marking. 56% of subjects were overtly marked, while 44% were zero-marked, and 63% of topic-sentence subjects were overtly marked, whereas 37% were zero-marked. This is in stark contrast to Ono et al.'s (2000) findings, in which only 28% of subjects were *ga*-marked, and the rest were zero-marked. We must be cautious in comparing numbers, however, since our definitions of "topic" and "subject" are not identical to those of others.

Table 2, on the following page, is a summary of the information status of all the tokens in our data.[3] The totals for zero- and particle-marked phrases are almost evenly divided among the three information types (28%, 37%, 35%). Obviously, the traditional classification of just "new" and "old" information would miss such a fact. Himeno (1999) states, "Ø is the most natural marking for *o*-case when talking about something that is present at the place of speech but has not been taken up in the previous discourse, and also something that is not present but is well known to the speaker and the hearer." [4] This would be classified as ⟨Hearer-old, Discourse-new⟩ in Prince's (1992) classification. According to our data, however, this type of information is expressed least frequently (28%) by zero-marked objects, and, instead, ⟨Hearer-new, Discourse-new⟩ (36%) and ⟨Hearer-old, Dis-

---

[3] H: hearer; D: discourse; n: new; o: old.

[4] This book is written in Japanese. The translation is ours.

course-old⟩ (35%) occurred at about the same rate. On the other hand, *o*-marked objects occur with ⟨Hearer-new, Discourse-new⟩ information almost than half of the time (49%). Another finding was that an NP representing new information often appears zero-marked, despite the common belief to the contrary.

		H-n, D-n	H-o, D-n	H-o, D-o	Total
	Topic	1 (5%)	14 (74%)	4 (21%)	19 (100%)
	Subject	6 (8%)	36 (50%)	30 (42%)	72 (100%)
Ø	T-S Subj	3 (30%)	4 (40%)	3 (30%)	10 (100%)
	Object	41 (36%)	32 (28%)	40 (35%)	113 (99%)
	Subtotal	51 (24%)	86 (40%)	77 (36%)	214 (100%)
	Topic	0 (0%)	7 (70%)	3 (30%)	10 (100%)
	Subject	0 (0%)	20 (53%)	18 (47%)	38 (100%)
wa	T-S Subj	0 (0%)	4 (80%)	1 (20%)	5 (100%)
	Object	0 (0%)	0 (0%)	0 (0%)	0 (0%)
	Subtotal	0 (0%)	31 (58%)	22 (42%)	53 (100%)
	Subject	24 (44%)	19 (35%)	11 (20%)	54 (99%)
ga	T-S Subj	4 (33%)	2 (17%)	6 (50%)	12 (100%)
	Subtotal	28 (42%)	21 (32%)	17 (26%)	66 (100%)
o	Object	33 (49%)	11 (16%)	23 (34%)	67 (99%)
P-Marked Total		61 (33%)	63 (34%)	62 (33%)	186 (100%)
Grand Total		112 (28%)	149 (37%)	139 (35%)	400 (100%)

Table 2. Information Status of All Tokens

The information type that zero-marked phrases of all types represent most frequently is ⟨Hearer-old, Discourse-new⟩ (40%), then ⟨Hearer-old, Discourse-old⟩ (36%), and lastly ⟨Hearer-new, Discourse-new⟩ (24%). Zero marking can therefore be associated more with "old" information in the binary classification than with "new" information. When all particle-marked phrases are combined, the three information types are, again, evenly divided (33%, 34%, 33%), though each particle displays a different pattern. *Wa* occurs with ⟨Hearer-old, Discourse-new⟩ and ⟨Hearer-old, Discourse-old⟩ information at about a 3-to-2 ratio (58% vs. 42%), and, as expected, never with ⟨Hearer-new, Discourse-new⟩ information. Surprisingly, the particle *ga*, the "quintessential" marker of new information, occurs with ⟨Hearer-new, Discourse-new⟩ information less than half of the time (42%). *Ga* actually expresses the other two types, or "old" information, more frequently (58%). It is also surprising that *o* is used to express "new" (49%) and "old" information (51%) at about the same ratio. This will be an interesting topic for future research.

4. Zero Marking vs. Particle Marking

Traditionally, zero marking has been regarded as a result of particle "dele-tion" or "ellipsis". Martin's (1975:50) statement is typical: "The surface versions of sentences . . . often contain an optional omission of a marker, the result of ellipsis." Interestingly, Martin (1975:51) also adds that "in some cases the unmarked theme may simply be unmarked from the start." We propose that all zero-marked phrases—topics, subjects, and objects—be regarded as "unmarked", and particle-marked ones as "marked". Zero-marked subjects and topics have often been analyzed as directly expressing the speaker's emotions, pleas, evaluations, urgings, etc. (e.g. Hasegawa 1993, Onoe 1996, Shibatani 1990). We assume, as in Hasegawa 1993, that a zero-marked NP has its own "neutral" meaning, and that this meaning is different from the "thematic" and "contrastive" meanings associated with the particle *wa*, and from the "exhaustive listing" and the "neutral descrip-tion" meanings associated with *ga*. In our analysis, attachment of *wa*, *ga*, and *o* occurs to specify grammatical functions clearly and/or to add such pragmatic information. In other words, sentences with particle-marked NPs, whether spoken or written, represent more "planned discourse" (Ochs 1979) than do those with zero-marked NPs. This view is consistent with the fact that sentences in which NPs are marked with particles sound more objective and analytical than those without them. Note, however, that zero-marking is not strictly a "casual speech" (e.g. Tsujimura 1996:136) phenomenon. For-mal-style sentences with zero marked NPs are quite common (e.g. *Wataku-shi Ø X to mooshimasu* 'My name is X'). The effect of the presence or ab-sence of particles on the meanings and functions is beyond the scope of the present study (see the references cited at the end of this paper).

Below, we provide six arguments for our position that "unmarked" (i.e. zero-marked) NPs are "unmarked".

First, in traditional generative grammar, *ga* (nominative) and *o* (accusa-tive) are assumed to "occur to fulfill this requirement that the overt NPs be case marked" (Miyagawa 1989:35).[5] If so, it would seem unreasonable and uneconomical to "drop" the markers that have just "occurred".

Second, Case particles can be absent even when the associated NPs are present, unlike postpositions such as *kara* 'from' and *de* 'by', which must be there. This is because *wa*, *ga*, and *o* do not express semantic meanings but, rather, grammatical functions. This is parallel to Indo-European lan-guages like English, in which abstract Case is not overtly marked, and prepositions express semantic meanings.

Third, the uses of *ga* and *o* as case particles are attested in the earliest

---

[5] *Wa*, *ga*, and *o* could be present from the start as the head of a DP.

318 / ENDO, SAKAKIBARA, AND KONDO

records, but they were not common (e.g. Kinsui 1996, Shibatani 1990). In other words, particle marking is likely a newer phenomenon than zero marking.

Fourth, there are many NPs which resist attachment of *wa*, *ga*, or *o*. Two examples are the subject *ika* 'squid' in (6), and the object *kore* 'this' in (7). This fact calls into question whether zero marking is "optional" (e.g. Martin 1975:50, Miyagawa 1989:240). See also other examples in (1)–(5), given earlier.

(6) [#32 "Squid"]
    B: **Ika Ø** oishii.   cf. **Ika** {#**wa**/#**ga**} oishii.
       squid good   'The squid tastes good.'

(7) [#21 "Mr. K"]
    C: Chotto, **kore Ø** kesu?   cf. Chotto **kore** {#**o**/#**wa**} kesu?
       say   this turn off 'Say, shall we turn this (tape recorder) off?'

Fifth, overt marking and zero marking can occur in the same grammatical environment, representing the same information status, and when spoken by the same speaker. If two ways to say the "same" thing are available, there is expected to be some difference between them because, otherwise, there is no *raison d'être* for both. Compare (8a) and (8b).

(8) a. [#19 "Video"]
       C: Sorekara ne, X no kurasu. **Kore ga** komatteru wakena no.
          and   GEN course this NOM having-trouble EP   FP
          'And, the X course. I'm having trouble with **this**.'

    b. [#20 "Teaching methods (1)"]
       C: Watashi **sono kurasu Ø** moo   iyana   no yone.
          I   that course   really displeased EP FP
          'I'm really displeased with **that course**.'

Kore in (8a) and *sono kurasu* in (8b) are topic-sentence subjects, both representing ⟨Discourse-old, Hearer-old⟩ information, and are uttered by the same speaker C. There is a difference, however. *Kore* 'this' in (8a), with the particle *ga* attached to it, singles out the entity and expresses the "exhaustive listing" interpretation clearly, which the zero-marked *sono kurasu* 'that course' in (8b) does not. Data set (9) presents additional examples.

(9) a. [#4 "Restaurant Fuji"; Subject; ⟨Hearer-old, Discourse-old⟩]
       C: **Sore Ø** chotto kitsui wane.
          that   a little tough FP   '**That** is a little tough.'

b. [#36 "John and Sushi"; Subject; ⟨Hearer-old, Discourse-old⟩]
   C: **Sore wa** kitsui wane.
      that TOP tough   FP   '**That** is tough.'

Sixth, zero-marked NPs are ubiquitous. In our overall data, zero marking was more frequent (53.5%) than overt marking (46.5%), as in the data of Terakura (1997), Fujii and Ono (2000), and Ono et al. (2000).

5. Conclusions

Zero-marked topics, subjects, and objects are very common, especially in informal speech. The conventional wisdom that a Case particle is "sometimes dropped" cannot be maintained in the face of actual data. As may be expected, zero marking generally occurs more frequently with old information than with new. That is not the whole story, however. The information type most frequently expressed by zero-marked phrases is ⟨Hearer-old, Discourse-new⟩ (40%). With particle-marked phrases, the three information types are evenly divided: ⟨Hearer-new, Discourse-new⟩ (33%), ⟨Hearer-old, Discourse-new⟩ (34%), ⟨Hearer-old, Discourse-old⟩ (33%). An analysis adopting Prince's (1992) three-way information classification thus offers important insights. There are many interesting topics to be explored, in addition to those mentioned earlier. With objects, for example, why should both zero-marking and *o*-marking be more closely associated with ⟨Hearer-new, Discourse-new⟩ information (36% and 49%, respectively) than with the other two information types? Other topics concern the relationships between zero-marking and the types of associated NPs—demonstratives and postposed NPs, for example. Zero-marking is interesting because an "absence" speaks volumes.

References

Fujii, N., and T. Ono. 2000. The Occurrence and Non-occurrence of the Japanese Direct Object Marker *o* in Conversation. *Studies in Language* 24:1–39.

Hasegawa, Y. 1993. Hanashi kotoba ni okeru "mujoshi" no kinō. *Nihongo Kyōiku* 80:158–68.

Himeno, T. 1999. *Nihongo kyōiku no otoshiana*. Tokyo: ALC.

Hudson, M. E., and J. Kondo. 2001. Mujoshi no shugo, shudai. Paper presented at the Annual Meeting of the Association of Teachers of Japanese, Chicago.

Ito, R. 1998. Topic Coding without Marking: Topic and Information Status in Japanese. *Papers in Sociolinguistics: NWAVE* 26:199–208.

Iwasaki, S. 2002. *Japanese*. Amsterdam: John Benjamins.

Kinsui, S. 1996. Rekishiteki ni mita "kaku joshi" no kinō. http://www.sccs.chukyo-u.ac.jp/jcss/CONFs/kinsui.html.

Kuno, S. 1973. *The Structure of the Japanese language.* Cambridge: MIT Press.

Kusumoto, T. 2002. Mujoshibun ni okeru hanashite no jōi nettowāku. *Nihongo Kyōiku* 115:21–30.

Lee, D.-Y. 2002. The Function of the Zero Particle with Special Reference to Spoken Japanese. *Journal of Pragmatics* 34:645–82.

Lee, K. 2002. Nominative Case-marker Deletion in Spoken Japanese. *Journal of Pragmatics* 34:683–709.

Makino, S., and M. Tsutsui. 1986. *A Dictionary of Basic Japanese Grammar.* Tokyo: Japan Times.

Martin, S. 1975. *A Reference Grammar of Japanese.* New Haven: Yale University Press.

Maruyama, N. 1996. Hanashi kotoba ni okeru mujoshikaku seibun. http://www.sccs.chukyo-u.ac.jp/jcss/CONFs/maruyama.html.

Miyagawa, S. 1989. *Structure and Case Marking in Japanese: Syntax and Semantics 22.* San Diego: Academic Press.

Niwa, T. 1989. Mujoshikaku no kinō: Shudai to kaku to gojun. *Kokugo Kokubun* 58(10):38–57.

Noda, H. 1996. *Shin Nihongo bunpō sensho 1: "wa" to "ga".* Tokyo: Kuroshio.

Ochs, E. 1979. Planned and Unplanned Discourse. *Syntax and Semantics 12*, ed. T. Givon, 51–80. New York: Academic Press.

Ono, T., S. Thompson, and R. Suzuki. 2000. The Pragmatic Nature of the So-called Subject Marker *ga* in Japanese. *Discourse Studies* 2:55–84.

Onoe, K. 1996. Shugo ni *wa* mo *ga* mo tsukaenai bun ni tsuite. Nihon Ninchi Kagakukai Dai 13-kai Taikai Wākushoppu, *Nihongo no Joshi no Umu o Megutte.* http://www.sccs.chukyo-u.ac.jp/jcss/CONFs.

Ōtani, H. 1995. *Wa* to *o* to Ø: O-kaku no joshi no shōryaku. *Nihongo ruigo hyōgen no bunpō: Jō*, eds. T. Miyajima and Y. Nitta, 287–95. Tokyo: Kuroshio.

Prince, E. 1992. The ZPG Letter: Subjects, Definiteness, and Information-status. *Discourse Description: Diverse Linguistic Analysis of a Fund-raising Text*, eds. W. C. Mann and S. Thomposon, 295–325. Amsterdam: John Benjamins.

Prince, E. 1981. Toward a Taxonomy of Given/New Information. *Radical Pragmatics*, ed. P. Cole, 223–55. New York: Academic Press.

Shibatani, M. 1990. *The Languages of Japan.* Cambridge: Cambridge University Press.

Suzuki, S. 1995. The Functions of Topic-Encoding Zero-Marked Phrases. *Journal of Pragmatics* 23:607–26.

Terakura, H. 1997. Functions of Zero-Marked and *Wa*-Marked Topic-NPs in Conversational Japanese Discourse, *Japanese Discourse* 2:65–89.

Tsujimura, N. 1996. *An Introduction to Japanese Linguistics.* Oxford: Blackwell.

Tsutsui, M. 1983. Ellipsis of *Ga. Papers in Japanese Linguistics* 9:199–244.

Tsutsui, M. 1984. *Wa* no shōryaku. *Gekkan Gengo* 13(5):112–21.

What Does the Korean "Double Causative" Reveal about Causation and Korean? A Corpus-Based Contrastive Study with Japanese

TSUNEYOSHI ISHIHARA*
Tohoku University

KAORU HORIE
Tohoku University

PRASHANT PARDESHI
Kobe University

1. Introduction

Causative constructions, which prototypically encode a situation in which a causer acts upon a causee for the realization of an intended caused event, have occupied a privileged position in linguistic typology and cognitive-functional linguistics (e.g. Comrie 1976, Shibatani 1976, Lee 1985, Croft 1991, Kemmer and Verhagen 1994, Song 1996, Shibatani and Pardeshi 2002, just to name a few). Particular attention has been paid to the mechanism of valence-changing operations in causative constructions and to the semantics of interpersonal manipulation (e.g. direct/indirect causation).

Double causative constructions (henceforth DCCs), a subtype of causative constructions, refer to the situation in which a causer X acts upon a causee/causer Y physically or verbally, to act upon yet another causee Z. There have been rather few cross-linguistic or language-specific studies on

---

* This study was supported in part by grants from the Tohoku University 21st Center of Excellence Program in Humanities (http://www.lbc21.jp/) and the Japan Society for the Promotion of Science (#70181526). Our thanks go to Andrew Barke, Bernard Comrie, Shoichi Iwasaki, Shigeru Miyagawa, and Kanako Mori for their valuable comments and constructive criticism. The usual disclaimer applies.

the syntax and semantics of DCCs compared to their single causative counterparts, reflecting perhaps the lesser degree of prototypicality of double
causative situations. The purpose of this study is three-fold: (i) to examine
the distributional characteristics of Korean DCCs as they occur in texts, (ii)
to present a cognitive-functional account of the distributional patterns attested, and (iii) to present a contrastive study of Korean DCCs with their
Japanese counterparts from a comparative typological perspective.

2. Theoretical Preliminaries

Shibatani (1976:1), in a seminal work on causative constructions, defines a
causative construction as "a linguistic expression referring to the situation
in which a caused event is wholly dependent on a causing event". The current study extends this characterization and defines a double causative construction (DCC) as a linguistic expression referring to the situation in which
two caused events are wholly dependent respectively on two causing events.
Figure 1 illustrates a double causative situation. The symbols A, B, and C
stand for three participants, while L and T respectively indicate location and
time at which each causative event takes place. E1 stands for the causing
event which leads to E2. E2 in turn serves as a causing event for the realization of the ultimate caused event E3.

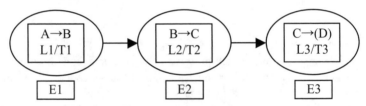

Figure 1. Double Causative Situation

As noted in §1, there have not been many typological studies on DCCs.
Kulikov 1993 is one of few extensive typological studies on this topic. It
presents a typology of morphological encoding of DCCs and the range of
semantic/pragmatic functions they convey. The information gleaned from
Kulikov is summarized in Tables 1 and 2.

Language	Morphological Encoding
Huallaga Quechua, Mansi (Vogul), Hunzib (Daghestan)	Doubling: $Y = X + X$
Turkish, Mongolian	Doubling with Alternation: $Y = X1 + X2$
Hindi, Japanese, Yukaghir	(Nontrivial) Including: $Y \supset X$
Amis	Intersecting: Y shares a common part with X but does not include it.
Dogon	Y does not share any common part with X.

Table 1. Morphological Typology of DCCs (based on Kulikov 1993)

Language	Semantic/Pragmatic Functions
Turkish	double causative
Oromo	intensive
Tuvan	iterative
Carib	plurality
Hindi	distant causation
Evenki	permissive
Cashibo	assistive
Finnish	curative
Kashimiri	deliberate vs. accidental causation
Swahili	non-agentive vs. agentive
Buryat	subject version
Divehi	style variation

Table 2. Cross-Linguistic Variation in Semantic/Pragmatic Functions of DCCs (based on Kulikov 1993)

Let us illustrate how Korean encodes double causative situations morpho-syntactically. As noted by Yeon (2003), the DCC in Korean is realized by the combination of the two distinct causative forms: the -*i*-, -*hi*-, -*li*-, -*ki*- suffixes and the -*key ha*- auxiliary, as shown in (1).

(1) John-i Tom-eykey Bill-lul cwuk-**i-key ha**-ess-ta
    -NOM   -DAT   -ACC die-CAUS-CAUS-PAST-DEC
    'John made Tom kill Bill.'

The double causative situation described in (1) can be construed as consisting of three events, as shown in (2a–c) for instance.

(2) a. John directed Tom to kill Bill.
    b. Tom stabbed Bill.
    c. Bill died.

A few words on Korean causative constructions are in order. Korean causative constructions are realized by morphological (-*i*-, -*hi*-, -*li*-, -*ki*-suffixes) and periphrastic (auxiliary -*key ha*-) means. Song (1996) notes that the -*i*-, -*hi*-, -*li*-, -*ki*- suffixes have lost their productivity, whereas the periphrastic -*key ha*- evolved from a purposive marker into the unmarked causative marker. Thus, while only a limited number of verbs can cooccur with the -*i*-, -*hi*-, -*li*-, -*ki*- suffixes, basically all verbs can cooccur with -*key ha*-. For example, while verbs such as *mek-ta* 'to eat' and *cwuk-ta* 'to die' can cooccur with the former suffixes to form *mek-i-ta* 'to make someone eat' and *cwuk-i-ta* 'to make someone die', verbs like *manna-ta* 'to meet' and *mantul-ta* 'to make' cannot cooccur with them; they need the periphrastic -*key ha*- to be turned into causative forms.

It is important to note that the order of the two causative forms (i.e. the morphological causative suffixes -*i*-, -*hi*-, -*li*-, -*ki*- and the periphrastic -*key ha*- construction) is fixed, as schematized in (3).

(3) {-*i*-, -*hi*-, -*li*-, -*ki*-} + -*key ha*-

This order is significant in that it lends support to the claim in previous studies (e.g. Kwon 1994) that the -*i*-, -*hi*-, -*li*-, -*ki*- suffixes have become lexicalized with the cooccurring verbs, thereby necessitating the productive -*key ha*- construction to encode causative meaning explicitly.

As for their morphological encoding, Korean DCCs can be classified as the second type in Table 1: "Doubling with Alternation (Y = X1 + X2)".

As seen in Table 2, it should be noted that DCCs do not invariably encode double causative situations, but can encode other semantic and pragmatic meanings. This observation will be relevant to our contrastive study of Korean and Japanese DCCs in §4.

3. Double Causative Constructions in Korean: A Corpus-Based Study

The corpus linguistic approach is known to be particularly helpful in analyzing grammatical phenomena that are relatively low in frequency such as DCCs. In this study we collected tokens of Korean DCCs from the KAIST (Korea Advanced Institute of Science and Technology) corpus (300MB), which is available on the web (http://csfive.kaist.ac.kr/kcp/) for analysis.

The following are prototypical examples of Korean DCCs attested in the KAIST corpus.

(4) yutan-i motun nongpwu-lohayekum so-eykey mwul-ul
    -NOM all   farmer-DAT   cows-DAT water-ACC

mek-**i-key ha**-n-kes
drink-CAUS-CAUS-PAST/REL-NOML

'. . . that Yutan made all farmers have cows drink water.'

(5) isulaeyl-i   ywuta-lul   caki-pota aphseywese yoseyp-eykeylo
    Israel-NOM Judah-ACC himself-than   earlier   Joseph-DAT
    ponayse yakep   ilhayng-i koseyn-ulo ka-nta-nun kes-ul
    send-and   Jacob group-NOM Goshen-to go-QUOT-REL-ACC
    al-**li-key ha**-yess-ta
    learn-CAUS-CAUS-PAST-DEC
    'Israel sent Judah to Joseph earlier than himself and made Judah make
    Joseph learn that Jacob's group would go to Goshen.'

The foregoing examples of Korean DCCs depict a double causative situation in which a causer X acts upon a causee/causer Y, physically or verbally,
to act upon yet another causee Z (see Figure 1).

To explore the semantic characteristics of Korean DCCs, we paid special attention to the verbs occurring in DCCs. To begin with, we first
identified all the tokens of the verbs capable of occurring in DCCs on morpho-syntactic grounds (i.e. compatibility with *-i-*, *-hi-*, *-li-*, *-ki-* suffixes).
We then confirmed whether they were attested in DCCs. Table 3 on the
following page shows the token frequency of the verbs capable of occurring
in DCCs. The left column indicates the total token frequency of a verb attested in the corpus in non-causative use, while the right column indicates
the frequency of its actual occurrence in DCCs in the corpus.

We can see from Table 3 that DCCs are by and large not very frequently attested in the corpus. The relative infrequency of DCCs arguably
reflects the lesser degree of prototypicality of double causative situations.
We can also see that, among verbs capable of occurring in DCCs, not all are
attested, and that some are more frequently attested than others. What determines the occurrence/non-occurrence of a verb in DCCs and the frequency patterns of the verbs that do occur?

We argue that the distribution of verbs occurring frequently in DCCs is
not random but rather is well-motivated and dictated by semantic and pragmatic factors. First, the distribution depends on the notion of "manipulability", that is, the degree of control that the causer exercises on the causee
(see Givón 2001). Verbs likely to occur in DCCs (e.g. *tol-ta* 'to turn' (intransitive), *olm-ta* 'to move' (intransitive), *cwuk-ta* 'to die') are those involving either an inanimate entity or a non-volitional human being as the
ultimate causee Z, which prototypically has no control over the motion/
change-of-state or action he/she/it is involved in. In other words, the ultimate causee Z is the passive recipient of the action performed on it by the
intermediate causer Y. These verbs arguably index high manipulability in
terms of transmission of force in the causal chain—from the ultimate causer X through the intermediate causer Y to the ultimate causee Z. DCCs can
thus be interpreted as a special construction type representing a highly ma-

tol-ta	'to turn'	7,677	tol-li-key ha-ta	109
cwuk-ta	'to die'	9,261	cwuk-i-key ha-ta	53
olm-ta	'to move'	28	olm-ki-key ha-ta	34
pwuth-ta	'to cling'	1,583	pwuth-i-key ha-ta	26
cwul-ta	'to decrease'	197	cwul-i-key ha-ta	13
noph-ta	'be tall'	1,715	noph-i-key ha-ta	11
mek-ta	'to eat'	6,592	mek-i-key ha-ta	8
ip-ta	'to wear'	3,499	ip-hi-key ha-ta	7
kwut-ta	'be hard'	1,272	kwut-hi-key ha-ta	7
nam-ta	'to remain'	3,576	nam-ki-key ha-ta	7
sal-ta	'to live'	10,423	sal-li-key ha-ta	4
nol-ta	'to play'	990	nol-li-key ha-ta	4
nok-ta	'to melt'	305	nok-i-key ha-ta	3
pes-ta	'to take off'	2,370	pes-ki-key ha-ta	3
nelp-ta	'be large'	1,009	nelp-hi-key ha-ta	3
anc-ta	'to sit'	9,490	anc-hi-key ha-ta	2
nul-ta	'to stretch'	1,315	nul-li-key ha-ta	2
kkulh-ta	'to boil'	356	kkulh-i-key ha-ta	1
kalaanc-	'to sink'	605	kalaanc-hi-key ha-ta	0
kwulm-ta	'to be hungry'	254	kwulm-ki-key ha-ta	0
wus-ta	'to laugh'	6,800	wus-ki-key ha-ta	0
nwup-ta	'to lie down'	2,285	nwup-hi-key ha-ta	0
koylop-ta	'to be painful'	770	koylop-hi-key ha-ta	0
mwuk-ta	'to stay'	478	mwuk-ki-key ha-ta	0
pak-ta	'to drive a nail'	465	pak-i-key ha-ta	0
sin-ta	'to wear (shoes)'	297	sin-ki-key ha-ta	0

Table 3. Token Frequency of Verbs Capable of Occurring in DCCs

nipulable subset of causative events that can be expressed by "regular" causative constructions. By contrast, verbs not likely to occur in DCCs are those encoding actions/states over which an ultimate causee Z retains control (e.g. *wus-ta* 'to laugh', *nwup-ta* 'to lie down', *kwulm-ta* 'to be hungry') or, to put it differently, can offer resistance to the intermediate causer Y. These verbs are low on the manipulability scale.

Secondly, the probability of the chain of events encoded by DCCs is significant. Shibatani (1996) noted that certain linguistic expressions are based on a specific schema, which functions as a construal of scenes or situations. Double causation should be the combination of direct and manipulative causations because there is no need for the three participants to be at the same place. What is less acceptable about DCCs such as *wus-ki-key ha-ta* is that the situation in which X makes Y make Z laugh is not construable in terms of the schema underlying DCCs.

As we have seen, semantic/pragmatic notions, which play crucial roles in determining the occurrence/nonoccurrence of the verbs in DCCs, are expected to be operative in other languages that have DCCs. In the next section, we will contrast Korean DCCs with their Japanese counterparts.

4. A Contrastive Study with Japanese

As noted in §2, DCCs are reported to exist not only in Korean but also in many other languages such as Japanese, Marathi, Mongolian, Quechua, and Turkish (see Table 1). This section presents a contrast between Korean DCCs and their Japanese counterparts in terms of the form-meaning mapping exhibited therein.

Japanese has both morphological and lexical means of encoding causation. The former is the causative suffix -(s)ase-. Basically it can cooccur with any verb and turn it into a causative form. The latter, by definition, is not productive and is limited to only a handful of verbs. Occasionally, one and the same verb can have both lexical and morphological causative counterparts, with subtle semantic differences in terms of directness of causation, as shown in (6) (see Shibatani 1976).

(6) *kiru* 'to put clothes on oneself'
     ki-seru (lexical causative) 'for someone to put clothes on another'
        (contact causation)
     ki-saseru (morphological causative) 'to make/let/help someone put
        (clothes) on him/herself' (indirect causation)

Kuroda (1993) and Miyagawa (1998) noted that DCCs in Japanese are possible when the first causative marker is lexical. It is interesting to note there is a parallel between Korean and Japanese in that first causatives have become lexicalized in both languages. This observation correlates with the semantic observation that a double causative situation consists of direct and manipulative causatives. Unlike Korean, Japanese can employ "doubling" of the same causative suffix: -(s)ase-sase-. As noted by Miyagawa (1999), there is in principle nothing to block a multiple occurrence of (s)ase. In reality, however, this double encoding is not favored by some speakers. For these speakers, the regular causative can convey the meaning of double causation, as in (7) and (8).

(7) Hanako wa Taroo ni Jiroo o   aruk-**ase**-ta
        TOP   DAT   ACC   walk-CAUS-PAST

(8) ?Hanako wa Taroo ni Jiroo o   aruk-**ase-sase**-ta (Okada 2003: 30)
        TOP   DAT   ACC   walk-CAUS-CAUS-PAST
     'Hanako made Taroo make Jiroo walk.'

Okada (2003) observes that Japanese DCCs occur most frequently in highly conventionalized benefactive expressions indexing humbleness and politeness, such as -(s)ase-sase-te itadaku 'to have someone allow one to do something', as in (9).

(9) Otayori   yom-**as-ase**-te-itadakimasu. (Okada 2003:29)
    letter read-CAUS-CAUS-TE-AUX.POL.NONP
    'Allow me to read this letter.'

Table 4 summarizes Okada's (2003) findings on the frequency and patterns of Japanese verbs occurring in DCCs.

Verb	Meaning	S+L	L+L	S+S	L+S
owar-u	'to end'	123	13	9	1
ik-u	'to go'	119	2	20	0
mi-ru	'to see'	18	1	6	0
tabe-ru	'to eat'	10	8	1	0
su-ru	'to do'	3	15	0	0
yom-u	'to read'	1	12	0	0
kangae-ru	'to think'	7	5	0	0
tor-u	'to take'	0	1	0	0
tsuka-u	'to use'	0	0	0	0
kak-u	'to write'	1	0	0	0
Total: 381		282	57	36	1

Table 4. Frequency and Morphological Patterns of Japanese Verbs Occurring in DCCs (adapted from Okada 2003:34) S = short form -(s)as-, L = long form -(s)ase-

It can be inferred from Table 4 that the verbs likely to occur in DCCs typically encode actions/changes-of-state that a causer can act upon a causee to perform/bring about, suggesting that the notion of manipulability is operative in Japanese DCCs as well. It should also be added that, in the case of Japanese DCCs employed in humble expressions like (9), the first causee (= the second causer) and the third/final causee are almost invariably the same person, i.e. the speaker. This accounts for the high frequency of verbs encoding actions that one can induce oneself to perform voluntarily and ordinarily, such as *taberu* 'to eat', *yomu* 'to read', and *kaku* 'to write'.

As pointed out by Okada (2003), in many cases Japanese DCCs do not encode prototypical double causation but merely serve to reinforce politeness. This "added politeness" usage is absent in Korean DCCs, which prototypically encode double causation, i.e. chains of causative events (see Table 2 for the cross-linguistic variation in semantic/pragmatic functions encoded by DCCs).

That Korean and Japanese DCCs show a striking contrast in form-meaning mapping is intriguing from a contrastive linguistic perspective, since the two languages are known to show remarkable similarity in grammatical structure. We argue that this contrast in the function and usage of DCCs between Korean and Japanese is not accidental. As extensively discussed by Horie (1998, 2002a, 2002b), in many domains of grammar (e.g. tense-aspect auxiliaries), Korean tends to preserve a tighter correspondence between form and meaning than Japanese, which exhibits more ambiguity/opacity. Table 5 summarizes the contrasts in form-meaning mapping between the two languages.

Phenomenon	Japanese	Korean
surface syntactic structures that allow for two (or more) semantic interpretations	common	uncommon
case-marking particles that develop adverbial clause marking functions	common	uncommon
case-particle conversion phenomena	common	uncommon

Table 5. Differing Form-Meaning Correspondence Patterns in Korean and Japanese (adapted from Horie 2003:381)

It is thus natural that Korean DCCs employ two causatives to index "double causation" straightforwardly, thereby exhibiting transparency in form-function mapping. In contrast, Japanese DCCs take on an extended politeness meaning, thereby showing less transparency in that reduplicated causatives do not directly map onto double causation.

5. Conclusion

This study has examined the syntactic and semantic characteristics of double causative constructions (DCCs) in Korean based on their patterns of occurrence in the KAIST corpus. The notions of manipulability and probability are found to be operative in determining the frequency patterns of verbs attested in Korean DCCs. A contrastive linguistic analysis of Korean and Japanese DCCs was also presented, arguing that the cross-linguistic difference in prototypical meaning coded by DCCs ("double causation" in Korean vs. "added politeness" in Japanese) correlates with the overall patterns of form-meaning mapping in the two languages. Investigation into the morphological encoding and semantic/pragmatic functions of DCCs in other Asian languages (e.g. Mongolian, Marathi) is next on our agenda.

Appendix: Abbreviations

ACC: Accusative	CAUS: Causative	DAT: Dative	DEC: Declative
NOM: Nominative	NOML: Nominalizer	NONP: Nonpast	PAST: Past
POL: Polite	QUOT: Quotative	REL: Relativizer	TOP: Topic

References

Comrie, B. 1976. The Syntax of Causative Constructions: Cross-Language Similari-

330 / ISHIHARA, HORIE, AND PARDESHI

ties and Divergences. *Syntax and Semantics 6*, ed. M. Shibatani, 261–312. New York: Academic Press.

Croft, W. 1991. *Syntactic Categories and Grammatical Relations*. Chicago: University of Chicago Press.

Givón, T. 2001. *Syntax*. Vol. 2. Amsterdam: John Benjamins.

Horie, K. 1998. Functional Duality of Case-Marking Particles in Japanese and Its Implications for Grammaticalization: A Contrastive Study with Korean. *Japanese/Korean Linguistics 8*, ed. D. Silva, 147–59. Stanford: CSLI.

Horie, K. 2002a. A Comparative Typological Account of Japanese and Korean Morpho-Syntactic Contrasts. *Eonehag* 32: 9–32.

Horie, K. 2002b. Verbal Nouns in Japanese and Korean: Cognitive Typological Implications. *Culture, Interaction, Language*, eds. K. Kataoka and S. Ide, 77–101. Tokyo: Hitsuji.

Horie, K. 2003. What Cognitive Linguistics Can Reveal about Complementation in Non-IE Languages: Case Studies from Japanese and Korean. *Cognitive Linguistics and Non-Indo-European Languages*, eds. E. Casad and G. Palmer, 363–88. Berlin: Mouton de Gruyter.

Kemmer, S., and A. Verhagen. 1994. The Grammar of Causatives and the Conceptual Structure of Events. *Cognitive Linguistics* 5:115–56.

Kulikov, L. 1993. The "Second Causative": A Typological Sketch. *Causatives and Transitivity*, eds. B. Comrie and M. Polinsky, 121–54. Amsterdam: John Benjamins.

Kuroda, S. 1993. Lexical and Productive Causatives in Japanese: An Examination of the Theory of Paradigmatic Structure. *Journal of Japanese Linguistics* 15:1–81.

Kwon, J.-I. 1994. *Hankwuke mwunpep uy yenku*. [A study of Korean grammar] Seoul: Sekwang Hakswulcalyosa.

Lee, H.-S. 1985. Causatives in Korean and the Binding Hierarchy. *CLS* 21:138–53.

Miyagawa, S. 1998. (*S*)*ase* as an Elsewhere Causative and the Syntactic Nature of Words. *Journal of Japanese Linguistics* 16:67–110.

Miyagawa, S. 1999. Causatives. *The Handbook of Japanese Linguistics*, ed. N. Tsujimura, 236–68. Oxford: Blackwell.

Okada, J. 2003. Recent Trends in Japanese Causatives: The *sa*-Insertion Phenomenon. *Japanese/Korean Linguistics 12*, ed. W. McClure, 28–39. Stanford: CSLI.

Shibatani, M. 1976. The Grammar of Causative Constructions: A Conspectus. *Syntax and Semantics 6*, ed. M. Shibatani, 1–40. New York: Academic Press.

Shibatani, M. 1996. Applicatives and Benefactives: A Cognitive Account. *Grammatical Constructions—Their Form and Meaning*, eds. M. Shibatani and S. Thompson, 157–94. Oxford: Clarendon Press.

Shibatani, M., and P. Pardeshi. 2002. The Causative Continuum. *The Grammar of Causation and Interpersonal Manipulation*, ed. M. Shibatani, 85–126. Amsterdam: John Benjamins.

Song, J.-J. 1996. *Causatives and Causation*. London: Longman.

Yeon, J-H. 2003. *Korean Grammatical Constructions*. London: Saffron Books.

The Structure of Internal-State Expressions in Japanese and Korean

SHOICHI IWASAKI*
University of California, Los Angeles

1. Introduction

It is widely discussed among Japanese and Korean linguists that the predicates referring to internal states such as sensations and emotions have morphological peculiarities (e.g. Kuroda 1973, Lee 1976, Iwasaki 1993:24–8, Kamio 1997:60–6, Sohn 1999:382–4). An unmodified predicate form can appear with a first person experiencer, as in (1), but a modified form with an evidential morpheme must be used with a third-person experiencer, as in (2).

(1) (J) samui!   (K) chwuwe!
      cold   cold
      '(I am) cold!'

(2) (J) ano ko samu-soo   (K) cay   ka chwuwe-he
      that child cold-EVI   child NOM cold-EVI
      'That child looks cold.'

---

* I received much help from the following people for this study: Chung-min Lee, Yukinori Takubo, Mary Kim, Jini Noh, Jane Choi, and especially Jieun Kim. I also had interesting discussions on the issue of internal-state expressions with Sun-Ah Jun and Barry Griner. Any remaining problems in the discussion are, of course, all mine.

Not discussed widely, however, is the fact that these morphological distinctions are in fact based on a more fundamental division between two distinct modes in language, namely, the mode of "expression" and the mode of "description" (see Maynard 2002). Though recognized in the *kokugogaku* tradition of Japanese language research (e.g. Yamada 1956) as *kantai* and *juttai*, respectively, it is mostly *juttai* ("descriptive" mode) sentences that have attracted researchers' attention (Suzuki 1987:129). This tendency is even more striking in the linguistics tradition of the West.

Without understanding the grammar of "expression" and its relationship to the grammar of "description", however, our understanding of grammar will remain incomplete. We will attempt in this paper to come closer to a fuller understanding of grammar by laying out a general matrix for the expressive and descriptive modes in language. We will pay special attention to the details of how internal states are **expressed** and **described**. This is the first goal of the paper. The second goal is to show that the expressive and descriptive modes are closely associated with the neurological processes of reflex, perception, and cognition. More precisely, the expressive mode is used to code reflex and perception, while the descriptive mode is used to code higher cognitive behaviors. The third goal is to consider to what extent Japanese and Korean are similar and dissimilar with respect to the expression and description of internal states.

The diagram in Figure 1 below shows the basic matrix of expressions and descriptions for Japanese and Korean. A reflex expression takes a one-word form, as shown in (a); a perception expression uses the nominative particle (J *ga*, K *ka/i*), as shown in (b); and a cognition sentence uses the topic marking particle (J *wa*, K *(n)un*), as shown in (c).

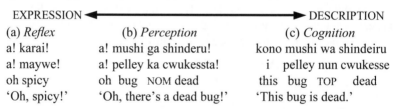

EXPRESSION ◄──────────────────────► DESCRIPTION

(a) *Reflex*	(b) *Perception*	(c) *Cognition*
a! karai!	a! mushi ga shinderu!	kono mushi wa shindeiru
a! maywe!	a! pelley ka cwukessta!	i pelley nun cwukesse
oh spicy	oh bug NOM dead	this bug TOP dead
'Oh, spicy!'	'Oh, there's a dead bug!'	'This bug is dead.'

Figure 1. Matrix of Expressions and Descriptions for Japanese and Korean

In addition to the discussion of how internal states are typically coded as reflexes, perceptions, and cognitions, we will also show how subtly modified forms are used to code finer distinctions along the continuum between reflex and perception as well as between perception and cognition.

2. Expression of Internal States

An internal-state expression is defined as follows.

(i) It expresses (rather than describes) the internal state of feeling, sensa-tion, or perception of the speaker.

(ii) It is deictic in nature and is tied to the current speech situation.

(iii) It is self-speech, not intended for communication in principle.

(iv) It consists of one or more of the three specific semantic primitives 'ex-perience', 'stimulus', and 'receptor'.

(v) It indexes the "experiencer" (= speaker) but cannot code the experi-encer linguistically.

An internal-state expression is a linguistic coding of a sensation, feeling, or perception at the time when an experiencer (= speaker) experiences it. It is a self-revelation, not intended for communication. This feature of non-communication ascribed to internal-state expressions makes this kind of deictic expression distinct from the deictic linguistic action of directives. It should be noted, however, that people around a speaker who utters internal-state expressions may react to the expressions upon hearing them (e.g. "Are you OK?"), but genuine internal-state expressions are non-communicational. One of the consequences of the non-communicational nature of internal-state expressions is their inability to take the polite and formal predicate forms and other interactional features such as pragmatic or interactional particles (e.g. *ne* and *yo* in Japanese).[1]

An internal-state expression has drastically different internal semantic composition from a sentence of external description. While a state of affairs that an external descriptive sentence depicts is composed of such primitives as 'agent', 'patient', 'theme', 'instrument', 'action', and 'state', among oth-ers, a state of affairs that an internal-state expression refers to is composed of 'experience', 'stimulus', and 'receptor'. 'Experience' is the quality of an internal state the experiencer is currently undergoing such as pain, elation, smell, and so forth, and a 'stimulus' is something that causes a particular experience. A 'receptor' is the location of an experience, where a sensation, feeling, or perception is believed to be registered. For example, a flickering of light (a stimulus) reaches one's eyes (a receptor) and causes a glaring or blinding sensation (an experience).

One of the most peculiar aspects of internal-state expressions is that an experiencer (= speaker) is always present, but it can never be coded linguis-tically; it can be only indexed by the act of exclamation.

---

[1] The speaker may also exploit an internal-state expression, intending it to be heard as a direc-tive such as a complaint. When an internal expression is used purposely as a directive, it per-forms the function of indirect speech act. Note also that while *itai!* 'Ouch!' (< 'painful') may be a genuine internal-state expression, *itai yo* 'It hurts, you know!', with the pragmatic particle *yo*, is a directive communicating a complaint to the assailant.

2.1. Reflex

A pre-linguistic outcry directly indexes the existence of the experiencer-speaker. Japanese speakers may utter an exclamatory expression such as *a!*, *aa!*, or *waa!*, and Korean speakers may similarly utter *a!*, *aa!*, *wa!*, or *aya!*[2] When a reflex is coded linguistically, it takes a one-word expression with or without an exclamatory marker to reveal one of the three primitives. A one-word expression consists only of the predicate and lacks the subject. For example, upon biting into a chili pepper, one might utter *a! karai!* (J) or *aya! meypta!/mewe!* (K) (see more examples in Table 1 on the next page). One-word expressions are a revelation of an immediate and automatic reaction that occurs before we know, for example, what hit us, or why we removed our finger from an object. The neurological process that is behind this automatic reaction is the process of reflex. Although a stimulus that causes a neurological experience such as pain may travel through the spinal cord to the brain, where appropriate instructions are formed and sent to the motor nerves to react accordingly, a sudden and strong stimulus may be directly transmitted to the motor nerve via the spinal cord, bypassing the brain. It is interesting to observe that this short-circuited neurological activity is reflected in the abbreviated linguistic form of one-word expressions. Further, in Japanese, some adjectives are expressed in their clipped form, e.g. *ita!* < *itai!* 'Ouch!' for sudden physical pain and *achi!* < *atsui!* 'Hot!' for sudden heat-induced pain.[3] In Korean, some adjectives may end in the dictionary form, i.e. the *-ta* form without tense-aspect morphology. These forms in both languages are morphologically less developed forms and thus are iconically motivated forms for the expression of reflexes that circumvent full processing involving the brain.

Although Japanese and Korean reflex expressions are similar in their one-word and reduced-predicate forms, there is also a striking difference. While most types of experience can be expressed by adjectives as a one-word reflex expression in Japanese, as shown in Table 1, only certain types of experience can be coded as such by Korean adjectives, leaving certain types of pain, olfactory, tactile, and emotional experiences to be expressed pre-linguistically.

---

[2] English has a variety of outcry expressions: *ah, aw, ay, gee, hey, huh, jeez, man, my, oh, ooh, oops, ouch, ow, phew, poof, pooh, shoot, ugh, whee, wow, yikes, yippee, yuk, yuck*, and explicatives such as *damn, fuck*, and *shit* (courtesy of Barry Griner). Some of these (*ouch* and *ugh*, for example) are closer to Japanese and Korean outcry expressions, while others (*shoot* and *yippee*, for example) are more intentional and may not be true outcry expressions.

[3] Also note partially reduplicated forms such as *a itatata!* 'Ouch!' and *atchitchi!/achichichi-chi!* 'Hot!'.

Experience Type	Japanese	Korean	
1 gustatory	a! karai!	a! maywe!/maypta!	'Oh, spicy!'
2 temperature	a! atui!	a! ttukewe!/ttukepta!	'Oh, hot!'
3 auditory	a! urusai!	a! sikkulewe!	'Oh, noisy!'
4 visual	a! mabushii!	?a! nwunpwusye!	'Oh, too bright!'
5 tactile	a! katai!	??a! ttakttakhay!	'Oh, too hard!'
6 pain	a! itai!	??a! apha/aphe![4]	'Ouch!'
7 emotion	waa! ureshii!	*a! hayngbokhay!/kippe!	'Oh, so happy!'
8 olfactory	a! kusai!	*a! kwulye!	'Yuck, it stinks!'

Table 1. Reflex Expressions Encoding "Experience"

The data presented in Table 1 are based on the results obtained from a questionnaire survey of 20 native speakers of Korean. Expressions 1 and 2 were accepted by more than 18 respondents, expressions 3 and 4 by 15 and 14 respondents, respectively, and expressions 5–8 by 7, 5, 3, and 2 respondents, respectively.

Some one-word expressions are onomatopoeic words. They essentially denote experience as it refers to the sensation that the experiencer is experiencing: *a! makkura!* (J), *khamkham hata!* (K) 'Oh, so dark!'; *a! zarazara!* (J), *aya! kechilkechil hata!* (K) 'Oh, it's so rough!' (as in the case of the surface of a wall). Some other one-word expressions code a receptor. This type of expression is found more in Korean, as in *meri ya!* 'Oh, my head (hurts).'

2.2. Perception

When sensory information reaches the brain, the brain checks it against prior experiences and tries to understand the senses that the body is currently experiencing. This is the neurological process of perception. One-word expressions are still used to code the perception of a simple stimulus of an entity that reaches a speaker's receptor. For example, upon seeing a bug, one may utter *a! mushi!* (J) / *a! pelley ta!* (K), to code the stimulus entity ('bug'). Or, upon hearing the sound of ambulance siren, one may utter *a! kyuukyuusha da!* (J) / *a! aymbullansu ta!* (K). However, when a stimulus to be described is more complex and refers to an entity in its particular temporal situation, grammar codes it as a bipartite expression. Thus, upon seeing a dead bug, a speaker may utter *a! mushi ga shindeiru!* (J) / *a! pelley ka cwukessta!* (K) 'A dead bug!' (lit. 'A bug is dead'). Or, upon hearing the sound of an approaching ambulance siren, s/he may utter *a! kyuukyuusha ga kita!* (J) / *a! aymbullansu ka wassta!* (K) 'An ambulance is coming!'. In

---

[4] Korean has many different pain expressions. *Appa/appe* refers to a sharp pain as one feels, e.g., when one accidentally hits one's thumb with a hammer. Other pain adjectives such as *cokssurye* (for a stomach ache) and *ttakewe* (e.g. for a pin prick) are more easily used as reflex expressions.

these expressions referring to complex stimulus perceptions, the entity and its temporary situation are connected with the nominative particle: *ga* (J), *ka/i* (K).[5] (3) and (4) give more examples. As long as one comprehends the situation, either visually or auditorily, one can utter these sentences.

(3) Visual Perception

    (J) a! inu   ga   hashitteru!   (K) a! kay ka   cinakanta!
       oh dog NOM run:ASP:NPST   oh dog NOM pass:ASP:DCL
              'Oh, (I see) a dog running/passing by!'

    (J) a! hebi ga   detekita!   (K) a! paym i   nathanassta!
       oh snake NOM come.out:PST   oh head NOM come.out:PST:DCL
              'Oh, (I see) a snake coming out!'

    (J) a! kao ga akai!   (K) a! elkwul i ppalkahta!
       oh face NOM red   oh face NOM red:DCL
              'Oh, (his) face is red!'

(4) Auditory Perception

    (J) a! mushi ga   naiteru!   (K) a! pelley ka   wunta!
       oh bug NOM cry:ASP:NPST   oh bug NOM cry:ASP:DCL
              'Oh, (I hear) a bug chirping!'

    (J) a! mizu ga   nagareteru!   (K) a! mwul i   hulunta!
       oh water NOM flow:ASP:NPST   oh water NOM flow:ASP:DCL
              'Oh, (I hear) water flowing!'

According to Kuroda (1984, 1992), these perception sentences are sentences of "thetic judgment", which represent "a simple recognition of the existence of an actual situation" (Kuroda 1992: 22–3). In other words, when the speaker utters these sentences, s/he perceives the situation as a (complex) stimulus without any particular focus on either the entity or its temporary situation; s/he is simply conveying the whole scene as a stimulus.

To summarize so far, reflex and perception are two neurological experiences that are coded in the expressive mode of language in both Japanese and Korean. Reflex is represented by one-word expressions which refer to a stimulus, experience, or receptor. Perception of a simple stimulus is also coded in the form of one-word expressions, but that of a more complex stimulus is coded in a morphosyntactically more developed form in which a nominative case marker connects an entity and its temporary situation.

---

[5] The nominative case particles *ga* (J) and *i/ka* (K) are the particles of so-called "neutral description" and can cooccur with an exclamatory marker such as *a!*. The same particles are also used for "exhaustive listing", but this function is not discussed in this paper. See Kuno's (1973) discussion of the two functions of *ga* in Japanese.

2.3. Linguistic Forms of Intermediary Type of Internal States

Reflex and perception are two broad neurological events that are coded in the expressive mode in language. There are forms, however, that code some subtly different neurological events. We will examine in this section, first, sentences of non-visual and non-auditory perceptions that are intermediate events between reflex and perception. We will then examine underdeveloped descriptive sentences, which code intermediate experiences between perception and cognition.

While the examples of perception expression so far all refer to a visual or auditory perception, other types of stimuli can also be expressed similarly:

(5) Non-visual, Non-auditory Perception

Gustatory (upon tasting sweet rice)
(J) a! gohan ga amai!   (K) a! pap   i   talta!
    oh rice NOM sweet   oh rice NOM sweet
              'Oh, the rice is sweet!'

Olfactory (upon smelling burning rice)
(J) a! gohan ga   kogeteru!   (K) a! pap   i   thanta!
    oh rice NOM burn:ASP:NPST   oh rice NOM burn:ASP:NPST
              'Oh, the rice is burnt!'

Temperature (upon feeling lukewarm water)
(J) a! oyu   ga   nurui!   (K) a! mwul   i   sikessta!
    oh water NOM lukewarm   oh water NOM lukewarm
              'Oh, the water is lukewarm!'

The examples in (5) suggest that a wider range of perceptions can be articulated within the expressive mode. However, in Japanese, non-visual and non-auditory stimuli do not always produce acceptable expressions.

(6) Gustatory (upon biting into spicy *kimchi*)
     ?a! kimuchi ga   karai!
      oh kimchi NOM spicy
     'Oh, the *kimchi* is spicy!'

Gustatory (upon tasting spoiled rice)
     *a! gohan ga   kusatteru!   (This is acceptable as a visual
      oh   rice NOM spoil:ASP:NPST   response upon **seeing** rather than
     'Yuck, the rice is spoiled!'   **tasting** spoiled rice.)

Olfactory (upon smelling a stinky bug)
     *a! mushi ga   kusai!
      oh bug NOM stinky
     'Yuck, the bug is stinky!'

Temperature (upon touching ice)
*a! koori ga tsumetai!
oh ice NOM cold
'Oh, the ice is cold!'

The awkwardness of these expressions, however, is reduced dramatically when the particle *ga* is removed:

(7)   Gustatory: a! kimuchi __ karai!   'Oh, the *kimchi* is hot!'
       Gustatory: a! gohan __ kusatteru!   'Yuck, the rice is spoiled!'
       Olfactory: a! mushi __ kusai!   'Yuck, the bug is stinky!'
       Temperature: a! koori __ tsumetai!   'Oh, the ice is cold!'

In the expressions in (7), the stimulus and experience are put together without a formal linkage through the nominative particle. These sentences, in other words, take less elaborate morphosyntactic forms. The reason that some non-visual, non-auditory sensations are not expressed as full-fledged perception is obvious from a neurological point of view. Smell and taste are "phylogenetically primitive sensibilities" (Dodd and Castellucci 1991:512) and are qualitatively different from vision and hearing. The stimuli for smell and taste are chemical substances which must come in close contact with a receptor. In contrast, stimuli for visual and auditory senses are non-chemical and can be away from a receptor. For the visual and auditory senses, in other words, the speaker can take a less immediate and a more objective stance. This less immediate and more objective stance allows the process of more fully developed perception. In contrast, a more immediate and less objective stance does not allow such a process for smell and taste. Japanese grammar is responding to these different neurological processes. Korean data are similar in this aspect; 13 of 20 respondents on the survey did not accept *kimchi ka meyphuta!* 'The kimchi is spicy!' with the nominative particle, and 19 respondents did not accept *elim i ca ta!* 'The ice is cold!' with the particle.

Pain perceptions are interesting in several respects. First, both in Japanese and in Korean they do not appear with the exclamatory expression *a!*, a marker of sudden realization of a situation, but with *aa!*, an exclamatory marker for a slower realization. (When a pain is expressed with *a!*, it has to be expressed as a reflex: *a! itai!* (J) / *a! pay ya!* (K); see §2.1.) Second, in both languages, the nominative marker is often omitted, but resistance to the particle seems stronger in Korean than in Japanese. In Korean, the particle is almost always omitted:

(8) Pain Perception

    (J) aa! onaka   ga   itai!   (K) aa! pay __ aphpa!
    oh stomach NOM painful   oh stomach painful
       'Oh, (I have) a stomach ache.'

    (J) aa! me ga kayui!   (K) aa! nwun __ kancilewe
    oh eye NOM itchy   oh eye   itchy
       'Oh, (my) eyes are itchy.'

We now move to the second type of sentence that does not allow the nominative case particle. We noted earlier that in a sentence of thetic judgment, i.e. [NP – Nominative particle – Predicate] as in (9) below, neither the NP nor the predicate can receive saliency. This means that if the NP is singled out through modification by a demonstrative, the sentence will become ungrammatical, as shown in (10). Perception expressions do not allow this process in either Japanese or Korean.

(9) Perception Expressions

    (J) a! mushi ga shinderu!   (K) a! peley ka cwukessta!
    oh bug NOM dead   oh bug NOM dead
       'Oh, a bug is dead!'

    (J) waa! hoshi ga   kiree!   (K) wa! pyel i   yepputa!
    wow   star NOM beautiful   wow star NOM beautiful
       'Wow, the stars are beautiful!'

(10) Perception Expressions with a Demonstrative

    (J) *a! kono mushi ga shinderu!   (K) *a! i pelley ka cwukessta!
    oh this   bug NOM dead   oh this bug NOM   dead
       'Oh, this bug is dead!'

    (J) *waa! ano hoshi ga   kiree! (K) *wa! ce pyel i   yepputa!
    wow that star NOM beautiful   wow that star NOM beautiful
       'Wow, that star is beautiful!'

To make the sentences in (10) grammatical, the nominative particle must be removed, as in (11).

(11) (J) a! kono mushi __ shinderu! (K) a! i pelley __ cwukessta!
    (J) waa! ano hoshi __ kiree! (K) wa! ce pyel __ yepputa!

We have seen in this section two different cases where the nominative case particle cannot appear in a sentence. In one case, the nominative case particle cannot appear due to the limited processing of non-visual and non-auditory perceptions; the less developed linguistic form mirrors the less developed neurological process. In the other case, the nominative case particle cannot appear due to saliency placed on the NP referent; a sentence with a nominative case particle must represent a situation where no saliency is detected either on the NP or on the predicate.

3. Description of Internal States

The sentences shown in (11) in the previous section are not typical sentences of internal states in the expressive mode, but they are not typical sentences of internal states in the descriptive mode either. A sentence becomes fully descriptive when the noun phrase is marked with *wa* (J) or (*n*)*un* (K), as shown in (12) below.

(12) Descriptive Mode

    (J) kono mushi wa   shindeiru   (K) i pelley nun cwukesse
       this bug TOP die:ASP:NPST   this bug TOP die:ASP:DCL
            'This bug is dead.'

    (J) ano hoshi wa   kiree da   (K) ce pyel un   yeppe
       that star TOP beautiful COP   that star TOP beautiful:DCL
            'That star is beautiful.'

These sentences in the descriptive mode represent a process of higher cognition. They are sentences characterized by "double (or categorical) judgment" (Kuroda 1984, 1992), in which the speaker deliberately attributes a certain property to an entity. From the neurological point of view, a sentence in this mode represents the process of cognition, which is called for when the automatic process of perception is unable to sort out the complex stimulus. In other words, a sentence in the descriptive mode codes a speaker's conclusion regarding the state of affair s/he has processed. This deliberate process precludes marking the sentence with an exclamation such as *a!*, *aa!*, etc.

Descriptive mode sentences can be used as sentences of communication. This means that, unlike expressive mode sentences, they can cooccur with features of interaction such as polite and formal predicate forms and, in the case of Japanese, interactional particles:

(13) Descriptive Mode with Interactional Features

    (J) kono mushi wa   shindeimasu   yo
       this   bug TOP die:ASP:NPST:POL PP

    (K) i pelley nun cwuk-ess-eyo
       this bug TOP die-ASP-POL

    'This bug is dead.'

(J) ano hoshi wa   kiree   desu nee
    that star TOP beautiful COP:POL PP

(K) ce pyel un   yeypp-eyo
    that star TOP beautiful-POL

'That star is beautiful.'

Descriptive mode sentences can be also mobilized to portray third-person experiencers' internal states, as shown in (2) at the outset of the paper.

4. Conclusion

In this paper, we showed the importance of distinguishing the expressive and descriptive modes of language, and how neurological factors explain the structure of various internal-state expressions. Linguists have been trying to understand the structure of descriptive mode sentences extensively, but they have been neglecting to investigate the structure of expressive mode sentences (see Zwicky et al. 1971 as a rare exception). The reason is partly because English, the leading language in linguistic research, does not show many interesting structural patterns associated with expressive mode sentences (but see e.g. Dong 1971). Japanese, Korean, and most likely some other languages, however, have developed an intricate system in the expressive mode. I did not discuss the implications of some subtle differences between Japanese and Korean internal-state expressions in this paper, but they should be addressed within the developing field of the contrastive study of the two languages in the future.

References

Dong, Q. P. 1971. English Sentences without Overt Grammatical Subject. *Studies out in Left Field: Defamatory Essays Presented to James D. McCawley*, eds. A. Zwicky et al., 3–10. Edmonton: Linguistic Research.

Dodd, J., and V. F. Castellucci. 1991. Smell and Taste: The Chemical Senses. *Principles of Neural Science*, 3rd ed., eds. E. Kandel, J. Schwartz, and T. Jessell, 512–29. Amsterdam: Elsevier.

Iwasaki, S. 1993. *Subjectivity in Grammar and Discourse: Theoretical Considerations and a Case Study of Japanese Spoken Discourse*. Amsterdam: John Benjamins.

Kamio, A. 1997. *Territory of Information*. Amsterdam: John Benjamins.

Kuno, S. 1973. *The Structure of the Japanese Language*. Cambridge: MIT Press.

Kuroda, S.-Y. 1973. Where Epistemology, Style, and Grammar Meet. *A Festschrift for Morris Halle*, eds. S. Anderson and P. Kiparsky, 377–99. New York: Holt.

Kuroda, S.-Y. 1984. *The Categorical and the Thetic Judgment Reconsidered. Mind,*

Meaning and Metaphysics – The Philosophy and Theory of Language of Anton Marty. Fribourg, Switzerland: Nijhoff.

Kuroda, S.-Y. 1992. *Japanese Syntax and Semantics: Collected Papers*. Dordrecht: Kluwer.

Lee, C.-M. 1976. Cases for Psychological Verbs in Korean. *Ene (Journal of Linguistic Society of Korea)* 1:256–96.

Maynard, S. K. 2002. *Linguistic Emotivity*. Amsterdam: John Benjamins.

Sohn, H-M. 1999. *The Korean Language*. Cambridge: Cambridge University Press.

Suzuki, H. 1987. Yamada bunpō. *Kokubunpō kōza 1 – Bunpō no taikei*, ed. A. Yamaguchi, 103–33. Tokyo: Meiji Shoin.

Yamada, Y. 1956. *Nihon bunpōgaku gairon*. Tokyo: Hōbunkan.

Zwicky, A., et al., eds. 1971. *Studies out in Left Field: Defamatory Essays Presented to James D. McCawley*. Edmonton: Linguistic Research.

Aspectual Markers in Japanese and Korean: A Corpus Linguistics Study

KAORI KABATA*
Univesity of Alberta

JEONG-HWA LEE
Korea Digital University

1. Introduction

Aspect, which refers to "the way the grammar marks the duration or type of temporal activity denoted by the verb" (Crystal 1991), is considered as fundamental a morphological system in languages as **tense**, which refers to "the way the grammar marks the time at which the action denoted by the verb took place" (Crystal 1991). Within the former, the most basic distinction is made between perfective and imperfective aspects, which are expressed by different morphemes in many languages (Comrie 1976), and which often exhibit two separate grammaticalization patterns (Bybee et al. 1994).

This paper deals with aspectual markers in Japanese and Korean, with the focus on the progressive and resultative senses. While the two languages exhibit a remarkable similarity in various other linguistic features, they have different form-function mapping relations in marking these two aspectual

* We are grateful to Tim Vance and Kim Jones for their comments and input, and to John Newman for letting us use the LDC corpora for Japanese and Korean for this study, and for sharing with us helpful information about corpus studies. We received many insightful comments at the J/K conference, for which we are also very grateful.

343

senses. The Japanese aspect marker *-te iru*, which is formed by combining a connective particle *-te* and a verb *iru* 'exist', presents a unique case by denoting either the progressive, a type of imperfective aspect, or the resultative, which is generally treated as perfective. In Korean, on the other hand, the verb *issta* 'exist' is combined with two different connective particles to form two aspectual constructions: *-ko issta* indicates the progressive aspect, and *-e issta* indicates the resultative. Taking a corpus-linguistics approach, this study aims to examine the similarities and differences of aspectual markers in Japanese and Korean. We are particularly interested in how aspectual meanings interact with the semantics of main verbs. By comparing the distribution patterns of these markers in Japanese and Korean, we will show that while the two languages share a basic conceptualization of aspectual events, different semantic factors seem to underlie the distinctions between progressive and resultative marking. Moreover, despite the morphosyntactic distinction between aspectual events in Korean, the two semantic fields are not as clear-cut as they appear to be and exhibit some semantic overlap. Our study reveals some of the complex interactions between the semantics of linguistic items and their surface structures that reflect the flexibility and elasticity of speakers' conceptualizations of the world.

2. Description of Aspectual Markers

Japanese and Korean exhibit contrastive form-function mapping in the aspectual field. Japanese *-te iru* serves as a versatile aspectual marker and is used to describe not only the progressive and the resultative senses, as shown in (1) and (2), but also the habitual and perfect senses, shown in (3) and (4), which are related to, but distinctive from, the other two (Kudō 1995, Shirai 1998). The Korean aspectual markers *-ko issta* and *-e issta*, on the other hand, have more restricted distributions. The habitual and perfect aspects, denoted by *-te iru* in Japanese, are usually described by the paraphrastic expressions *-n ta* and *-ess-ta*, respectively.[1]

(1) **Progressive**: 'Taro/Inho is eating rice.'
    [JPN] Taroo wa gohan o tabe-**te iru**.
            TOP rice ACC eat-TE IRU
    [KOR] Inho-nun pap-ul mek-**ko issta**.
           -TOP rice-ACC eat-KO ISSTA

---

[1] Abbreviations used in this paper are: ACC accusative, ALL allative, CONN connective, CONJ conjunctive, COP copula, GEN genitive, LOC locative, NML nominaliizer, NOM nominative, DC declarative, FP final particle, PAST past, PRES present, TOP topic marker.

(2) **Resultative**: 'Taro/Inho has sat (and is sitting) in the chair.'
[JPN] Taroo wa isu ni suwat-**te iru**.
　　　 TOP chair ALL sit-TE IRU
[KOR] Inho-nun uyca-ey anca-**a issta**.
　　　 -TOP chair-ALL sit-E ISSTA

(3) **Habitual**: 'Taro/Inho runs every day.'
[JPN] Taroo wa mainichi hashi-**te iru**.
　　　 TOP everyday run-TE IRU
[KOR] Inho-nun mayil talliki(-lul) ha-n-ta.
　　　 -TOP everyday running(-ACC) do-PRES-DC

(4) **Perfect**: 'Taro/Inho has studied abroad before.'
[JPN] Taroo wa mae ni ryuugakushi-**te iru**.
　　　 TOP before study.abroad-TE IRU
[KOR] Inho-nun cen-ey yuhak-ul hay-ss-ta.
　　　 -TOP before study.abroad-ACC do-PAST-DC

It should be noted, however, that -*ko issta* does overlap semantically with -*e issta*, and marks the resultative when used with verbs of contact, such as *ipta* 'put on' and *kkita* 'put on (gloves)', as discussed in more detail in the next section. There is also some evidence in today's Korean that -*ko issta* can mark the habitual and the perfect, though in limited contexts (Cho 2000, Wako et al. 2003).

The polyfunctionality of Japanese -*te iru* is discussed by a number of Japanese grammarians and linguists, with their primary interest being in the interaction between the type of verb and the aspectual sense when used in the -*te iru* construction. Shirai (2000) proposes what he calls a two-component theory approach, which he claims resolves the disagreements in claims of previous studies, such as Kindaichi's (1950) duration account and Okuda's (1978a, 1978b) syntactic approach. Shirai's approach is one that integrates the inherent aspectual meaning of verbs (state, activity, accomplishment, or achievement) and the viewpoint aspect denoted by the aspectual marker, which he argues has the function of focusing on "the durative phrase of a situation" (Shirai 1998:333), thus yielding the four distinct meanings, as illustrated in (1)–(4) above.

There seems to be ample historical evidence that -*te iru* developed as a progressive marker and later acquired the resultative meaning.[2] Around the

---

[2] While Shirai (1998:678–9) claims that the basic sense of -*te iru* is progressive, he makes no reference to the usage of -(*te*) *iru* in Classical Japanese. He points out, on the other hand, that -*tari* and -*ri* were used to indicate the progressive with some non-telic verbs. While it is beyond the scope of this paper, we follow Yamaguchi and Akimoto (2001), who maintain that -*te iru* co-existed with -*tari* and -*ri* and was the primary progressive marker in Classical Japanese.

14th century *-te iru* began to take on the resultative sense, which was mainly marked by *-tari* or *-ri* in Classical Japanese (Yamaguchi and Akimoto 2001:60–2). It is worth noting that the two aspectual senses are kept distinct in some dialects in Japan, including the Uwajima dialect, in which *-yoru* marks the progressive and *-toru* the resultative (Kudō 1995).

While studies of Japanese *-te iru* have focused on the interaction between main verbs and aspectual meaning, Korean linguists have been more interested in the semantic similarity or difference between the two aspectual constructions (Koo 1987, Lee 2000, Rhee 1996). Kim (1981) and Sohn (1994) maintain that both *-ko issta* and *-e issta* denote the durative aspect, but that they differ from each other in that the former describes the duration of an on-going activity and the latter the duration of a resultative state. Kim (1981) also points out that *-ko issta* is aspectually ambiguous in that it can describe not only the result of a completed action but also the duration of an action. Lee (1993), on the other hand, claims that *-e issta* denotes the end point of a process, be it the goal of locomotion when used with an intransitive verb, or the recipient of an action when used with a passivised verb. More recently, Cho (2000) studied the interaction between main verbs and aspectual meaning, classifying aspects of Korean verb phrases from a lexical semantics viewpoint. She argues that each compound aspect, including *-ko issta* or *-e issta*, can convey different meanings depending on the semantics of the verb phrase with which it is combined, and the distributional restrictions such aspect markers have acquired.

The development of the two aspectual markers in Korean exhibits similarities to that of their Japanese counterparts, *-te iru* and *-tari/-ri*. According to Rhee (1996), *-ko issta* developed much later than *-e issta* as a syntactic variant in Middle Korean, and both were used to express the same "state-persistence", that is, the resultative meaning. However, the progressive use of *-ko issta* has become predominant in Modern Korean, partially because it has gained more conceptual saliency, thus stressing its paratactic function and forcing *-e issta* further toward a hypotactic status. Rhee examined two different versions of a Korean text called *Nokeltay* and found that the occurrence of *-ko issta* as a progressive marker has increased markedly in the 1995 version compared to the 1577 version. Rhee further claims that the preference for the progressive marker *-ko issta* over the resultative *-e issta* is semantically motivated due to the nature of the former, which is associated with two components since it describes "the subject located in the midst of doing something at a given moment of time", as argued by Bybee et al. (1994:136).

Some of the claims made in previous studies on these aspectual markers in the two languages are tested on the corpus data in our study. For example, is the progressive sense of Japanese *-te iru* more frequent than the resultative sense, as implied by the claims about their historical development? To what degree are the Korean aspectual markers ambiguous? Based on parallel data, taken from both spoken and written corpora, we are particularly interested in the similarities and differences in the lexical distributions of the aspectual markers in Japanese and Korean.

3. A Corpus-Based Study of Aspectual Markers

A corpus study was conducted in order to examine the usage distribution of the aspectual markers, -*te iru* in Japanese and -*ko issta* and -*e issta* in Korean. Data was collected to study the distributional frequency of the progressive and resultative aspects, and the patterns of distribution of the verbs used in each aspectual construction.

3.1. Methodology

Our study was based on comparative corpora of both spoken and written texts. For the spoken corpora (henceforth SPK), we used a collection of telephone conversations from the Linguistic Data Consortium, which are available both for Japanese and Korean.[3] The corpus consisted of 120 files for the Japanese corpus (CALLHOME Japanese Speech) and 100 for Korean (Korean Telephone Conversation Speech). Each file covered a continuous 5- or 10-minute segment taken from a recorded conversation between native speakers, most of whom were family members or close friends. The written corpora (WRT) consisted of 10 texts in each language, which were novels or essays available online.[4] Each instance of the -*te iru* construction was categorized into one of the four senses described in (1)–(4), following the criteria proposed by Shirai (2000).

---

[3] Information about LDC corpora is available at <http://www.ldc.upenn.edu/Catalog>.

[4] The texts used in the study are as follows. Japanese (all taken from http://www.aozora.gr.jp/): Akino, T. 1993. *Rokku nanajūnendai* [Rock in the '70s]; Hamano, S. 1998. *Shintoshi ongaku nōto* [A music note in new towns]; Ichikawa, Y. 2000. *Hōkago no Rock'n Roll* [Rock'n Roll after school]; Kareha. 2001. *Great Gatsby* (Translation of *The Great Gatsby* by F. S. Fitzgerald); Koba, T. 1999. *Sophia*; Koizumi, H. 1999. *Mimizu monogatari 2* [An earthworm story]; Kuwahara, I. 1998. *Ningen no kihon* [The foundation of human beings]; Sano, R. 1993. *Warera rifutā* [We weightlifters]; Takahashi, Y. 1997. *Ongaku no han-hōron josetsu* [Introduction to anti-music methodology]; Yamagata, H. 1999. *Garan to bazāru* (Translation of *The Cathedral and Bazaar* by E. Raymond). Korean (all taken from http://www.sejong.or.kr/ sejong_kr/): Ha, I.-C. 1993. *Kyengmacangeyse sayngkin il* [The story that happened at a horse-race track]; Kwu, H.-S. 1995. *Nachsen yelum* [A strange summer]; Hong, S.-W. 1993. *Mendong 1* [The dawning sky]; Pak, I.-M. 1992. *Sala namun cauy sulphum* [The sadnesss that a surviver feels]; Kwak, C-K. 1992. *Aki chamsay Ccikkwu* [The little sparrow Ccikkwu]; Kim, S.-D. 1993. *Yenkkochkwa cinhulk* [A lotus flower and mud]; Kim, S.-C. 1993. *Yellin sahoywa ku cektul* [The open society and its enemy]; Kim, H.-K. 1990. *Wancenhan mannam* [A perfect meeting]; Han, S.-W. 1994. *Phokwu* [A port]; An, C.-H. 1993. *Heliwutu khituuy sayngay* [A Hollywood kid's life].

3.2. Results

Examination of the spoken and written corpus data, summarized in Tables 1 and 2 (see Appendix for details), reveals both similarities and differences in the usage distribution of the progressive and resultative constructions in Japanese and Korean. Regardless of its foundational semantic importance (Shirai 1998), the overall token frequency of the progressive in Japanese, when both the SPK and WRT are examined, was not any higher than that of the resultative. This was in line with the findings of Shirai and Nishi (2004), whose study was based on conversational data. On the other hand, the Korean progressive marker *-ko issta* had a higher frequency of usage than the resultative marker *-e issta*. The former was used 427 times and the latter only 93 times in SPK. While the difference was not as large in WRT as in SPK, *-ko issta* was used almost one and a half times as often as *-e issta*, illustrating the dominance of *-ko issta* in Korean.

	Progressive		Resultative	
	Japanese	Korean	Japanese	Korean
Total Tokens	1,472	427	1,131	93
Total Types	210	116	230	31
Transitive	1,135 (77%)	326 (76%)	336 (30%)	0 (0%)
Intransitive	301 (20%)	101 (24%)	763 (67%)	65 (70%)
Passive	36 (2%)	0 (0%)	32 (3%)	28 (30%)

Table 1. Token and Type Frequencies and Cooccurring Verb Types in Spoken Corpora

	Progressive		Resultative	
	Japanese	Korean	Japanese	Korean
Total Tokens	2,127	3,918	2,558	2,639
Total Types	727	979	960	401
Transitive	1,286 (60%)	2,669 (68%)	691 (27%)	0 (0%)
Intransitive	754 (35%)	1,250 (32%)	1,398 (55%)	1,883 (71%)
Passive	87 (4%)	0 (0%)	469 (18%)	756 (29%)

Table 2. Token and Type Frequencies and Cooccurring Verb Types in Written Corpora

The limited distribution of the resultative marker *-e issta* in Korean is associated with its syntactic restrictions. While the progressive marker *-ko issta* was used both with transitive verbs and intransitive verbs, the resultative marker *-e issta* was never used with transitive verbs. At the same time, the passive forms of transitive or intransitive verbs, and verbs that convey passive meanings, were used exclusively with *-e issta* and never with *-ko issta*. While Japanese shows similar patterns of interaction between transitivity of verbs and aspectual sense, the distribution is not mutually exclusive as in the case of Korean.

A closer look at the distribution of the two aspectual markers in Japanese and Korean reveals complex interactions between the semantics of verbs and their syntactic functions. In both languages, the progressive frequently cooccurred with verbs like 'do', 'see', 'listen to', 'eat', 'live', and 'sleep' (some transitive and some intransitive), which describe certain types of actions or activities. The resultative, on the other hand, was frequently used with verbs like 'become', 'enter', 'sit', and 'stand', all of which are achievement verbs describing change of state according to Shirai and Nishi (2004), who also found them most compatible with the resultative.

However, the lexical distributions were not always parallel in Japanese and Korean. The verbs 'go' and 'come', shown in (5)–(7), exhibit an interesting pattern.

(5) a. tamatama hayaku gakkoo   **it-teta**   n   da kedo sa.
         by.chance early   school **go-TE.IRU.PAST** NML COP but FP
         'I happened to have gone to school early, but . . .' [J.SPK]

     b. sensee kara   nanka   hagaki ga   **ki-tete** . . .
         teacher from   somehow postcard NOM **come-TE.IRU.PAST**
         'A postcard had somehow come from my teacher.' [J.SPK]

(6) a. nolan   pesu-ka cilcwuha-e **o-ko**   **iss**-ess-ta.
         yellow   bus-NOM rush-CONN **come-KO ISSTA**-PAST-DC
         'A yellow bus is coming, rushing at full speed.' [K.WRT]

     b. tomi nwuna-ka   yeki **o-a**   **iss**-eyo.
         elder.sister-NOM here **come-E ISSTA**-DC
         'Elder sister Tomi came and is here, as a result.' [K.WRT]

(7) a. ku-nun   pokto-lul   ttal-a   **ka-ko**   **iss**-ess-ta.
         he-TOP corridor-ACC follow-CONN **go-KO ISSTA**-PAST-DC
         'He was going along the corridor.' [K.WRT]

     b. ku-nun sewul-ey ka-(a)   iss-ta.
         he-TOP Seoul-ALL go-(E) ISSTA-DC
         'He went to Seoul and is there now.'

In Japanese, *iku* 'go' and *kuru* 'come' as main verbs describing locomotion were used primarily with the resultative, as shown in (5). In Korean, on the other hand, *ota* 'come' was used both with the progressive and the resultative, but with different meanings. With the progressive, shown in (6a), the focus is on the process of going or coming, and with the resultative, shown in (6b), the focus is on the end point. While *kata* 'go' is generally acceptable in both the progressive and resultative constructions, as shown in (7), no instance of *ka-(a) issta* was found in either corpus. In contrast, 24 instances of *o-a issta* 'come-E ISSTA' were found in WRT, while none were found in SPK. The verb *toyta* 'become' also appeared with both *-ko issta* and *-e issta*, as shown in (8).

(8) a. ta   cikum noum   **toy-ko**   **iss**-e.
    everything now recording become-KO ISSTA-DC
    'Now everything is getting recorded.' [K.SPK]

   b. ilehkey   sahoy-ka   anceng-i   **toy-e issta**.
    like.this society-NOM stability-NOM become-E ISSTA
    'The society has become stable like this.' [K.SPK]

While (8a), used with the progressive *-ko issta*, focuses on the process of the recording, (8b), with the verb *toyta* 'become' used with *-e issta*, clearly represents the resultative meaning. Japanese *naru* 'become' is only compatible with the resultative sense.

Similar cases of this "split" in the Korean data were found with the verb *salta*, which means either 'be alive' or 'live'. The former meaning is compatible with the resultative sense, and the latter with the progressive, which conveys a more active sense of living.

(9) a. nu   noin-i   acikto **sal-a**   **iss**-ey.
    the old.man-NOM still **live-E ISSTA**-DC
    'The old man still is alive.' [K.WRT]

   b. ku-nun   cel-eyse   **sal-ko issta**.
    he-TOP temple-LOC **live-KO ISSTA**
    'He is living in a Buddhist temple.' [K.WRT]

The semantic difference between (9a) and (9b) can be explained in Sohn's (1973:242) terms: *-e issta* is used for "stative existence", referring to "being in a state resulting from or is done", while *-ko issta* for "activity existence". Thus, (9a) describes the old man in the continuous state of staying alive, while (9b) has more focus on the activity of living. In Japanese, these two events are denoted by two different verbs, *ikiru* 'be alive' and *sumu* 'live', both compatible with the progressive.

Verbs like 'put on', '(get to) know', and 'have', which are generally categorized as achievement verbs in Japanese and Korean, are therefore associated with the resultative sense in Japanese, as shown in (10a), (11a), and (12a). In Korean, however, these verbs were used with *-ko issta*.

(10) a. midori no doresu o   **ki-te**   **iru**.
     green GEN dress ACC **put.on-TE IRU**
     '(She) is in a green dress.' [J.WRT]

    b. kulen thi-syechu-lul **ip-ko**   **iss**-nun keya.
       such T-shirt-ACC **put on-KO ISSTA**-PRES DC
       '(He) has put on such a T-shirt and is (still) in it.' [K.SPK]

(11) a. kore wa kimi-jishin ga ichiban yoku **shit-te iru** hazu da.
       this TOP you-self NOM best   well **know-TE IRU** should COP
       'As for this, you yourself should know it the best.' [J.WRT]

    b. ne-to   **al-ko iss**-keyss-ciman.
       you-also **know-KO ISSTA**-CONJ-but
       'You too already know (something), but . . .' [K.WRT]

(12) a. kogitte ne, watashi mada **mot-te iru** n da wa.
       check FP   I   still **have-TE IRU** NML COP FP
       'I still have the check.' [J.WRT]

    b. na-nun chayk-ul **kaci-ko iss-ta.**
       I-TOP book-ACC **have-KO ISSTA**
       'I still have a book.' [K.WRT]

    The case of the verb *ipta* 'put on/slip on', shown in (10), has been discussed by Korean linguists, including Sohn (1994) and Rhee (1996). While *ipta* can be used both with the progressive sense, describing the process of putting on clothing, and with the resultative sense, describing the change of state, all the instances in our data were associated with resultative sense. Our data also revealed similar patterns of cross-categorical marking with the verbs 'know' and 'have', as shown in (11) and (12). As in Japanese, these Korean verbs are usually associated with the resultative sense, describing the change of state, and yet, they were used only with *-ko issta*, and not with *-e issta*.

4. Discussion

Our corpus-based study of the aspectual constructions in Japanese and Korean indicated complex interactions between the semantics and syntactic functions of verbs in the two languages.

    The overall token frequencies indicate that the resultative sense of *-te iru* in Japanese has become as salient as the progressive sense, if not more. On the other hand, the progressive *-ko issta* is predominant in Korean, especially in the spoken data. What was striking, moreover, was the complementary distribution of the two aspectual constructions: *-e issta* was used only with intransitive verbs or passivized verbs, and never with transitive verbs, while *-ko issta* never occurred with passivized verbs. While Japanese *-te iru* exhibited similar distributional patterns, they were not as clear-cut as in Korean.

    A closer examination of the lexical distribution revealed both the persistence and fluidity of the semantics of the two aspectual markers in Korean. On the one hand, intransitive verbs like *salta*, which means either 'be alive' or 'live', or *ota* 'come' and *toyta* 'become', interacted with the two aspectual senses, indicating the persistent semantic distinction between them. On the other hand, *-ko issta* was used to describe the resultative meaning when used with verbs like *ipta* 'put on', *kacita* 'have', and *alta* 'know', indicating the semantic ambiguity of *-ko issta* that allows it to denote both the progressive and resultative aspects when used with certain achievement verbs, all of which are transitive in our data. Cho (2000:160–3) attributes the polyfunctionality of *-ko issta* to the "compound aspect" of the achievement verb phrase rather than to the intrinsic semantics of *-ko issta* alone. Since achievement verbs describe instantaneous events and therefore do not have a time span, the events designated by those verbs cannot continue. However, a completed state, after the momentary event reaches the completion point, can be continuous. Thus, for example, as soon as the possessing event designated by the verb *kacita* 'have' has been completed, the possessed state persists, and the combination of the achievement verb and *-ko issta* refers to only to the state persistence of a completed event instead of to the process of an action or activity. While Cho's argument provides an explanation for the cases with transitive verbs, it fails to explain why intransitive verbs are used with *-e issta*. We argue that there is a strong syntactic constraint in Korean, at least at this point, as we have seen from the complementary distribution of *-e issta* and *-ko issta*. For these transitive achievement verbs to have the resultative aspect, the only option is for them to be used with *-ko issta*.

Interestingly enough, the semantic extension of the progressive marker *-ko issta* to take on some resultative senses, as found in the Korean data, is what Japanese *-te iru* had undergone before becoming established as the versatile aspectual marker which can indicate not only the progressive and resultative, but also the habitual and even the perfect aspects. At present, the Korean progressive *-ko issta* combines with only a limited number of achievement verbs, but it could plausibly extend semantically, as Japanese *-te iru* has done.

5. Conclusion

Based on comparative corpus data of both spoken and written texts, we have shown that the aspectual systems in Japanese and Korean, which appear to differ, share many semantic characteristics and are possibly undergoing very similar developmental processes. What is unknown to us at this point, however, is whether the various meanings of *-te iru* are perceived as distinct by native speakers of Japanese. Our findings should also be tested on a larger corpus which includes samples of different types of discourse.

Very few studies have examined the similarities and differences of grammatical morphemes in two languages, despite the rather apparent contribution this line of investigation can make to typological and cognitive linguistic research (see Strauss 2002). This kind of study has pedagogical implications as well, since the differences between grammatical and aspectual encoding often proves challenging to language learners (Shirai and Kurono 1998).

Appendix: Frequently Cooccurring Verbs in the Corpus Data

(T = transitive, I = intransitive, P = passive, P_L = lexicalized passive)

SPK (= 10)

Japanese   Progressive

VERB	TOKENS	CLASS
iu 'say'	319	T
suru 'do'	152	T
yaru 'do'	144	T
omou 'think'	88	T
miru 'see'	48	T
neru 'sleep'	32	I
tsukau 'use'	30	T
uru 'sell'	29	T
hataraku 'work'	24	I
sumu 'live'	22	I
matsu 'wait'	21	T
taberu 'eat'	17	T
kiku 'listen to'	17	T
hashiru 'run'	17	I
ganbaru 'try best'	17	I
aruku 'walk'	17	I
naku 'cry'	15	I
kaku 'write'	15	T
kangaeru 'ponder'	14	T
hanasu 'talk'	14	T
sagasu 'search for'	13	T
shaberu 'chat'	12	I
nomu 'drink'	12	T
hayaru 'prosper'	12	I
toru 'take (photos)'	11	T
rokuonsareru 'be taped'	11	P
asobu 'play'	11	I
tsukuru 'make'	10	T

Resultative

VERB	TOKENS	CLASS
naru 'become'	83	I
hairu 'enter'	81	I
shiru 'know'	80	T
iku 'go'	77	I
kuru 'come'	76	I
motsu 'have'	63	T
deru 'exit'	43	I
wakaru 'understand'	40	I
suru 'do'	33	I
oboeru 'remember'	22	T
kimaru 'be decided'	18	P_L
tsuku 'arrive'	16	I
kaku 'write'	15	T
ireru 'put in'	15	T
wasureru 'forget'	14	T
tamaru 'be saved'	13	I
todoku 'reach'	12	I
tsuku 'attach'	12	I
kawaru 'change'	11	I
nokoru 'remain'	10	I

Korean   Progressive

VERB	TOKENS	CLASS
hata 'do'	110	T
kacta/kacita 'have'	37	T
pota 'see'	18	T
salta 'live'	12	I
toyta 'become'	11	I
mekta 'eat'	10	T
cata 'sleep'	10	I

Resultative

VERB	TOKENS	CLASS
ancta 'sit'	20	I
ttelecita 'fall'	14	I

WRT (= 20)

Japanese	Progressive			Resultative		
	VERB	TOKENS	CLASS	VERB	TOKENS	CLASS
	suru 'do'	213	T	*naru* 'become'	181	I
	miru 'see'	169	T	*shiru* 'know'	90	T
	omou 'think'	72	T	*motsu* 'have'	82	T
	iu 'say'	43	T	*tatsu* 'stand'	47	I
	kiku 'hear'	42	T	*nokoru* 'remain'	35	I
	matsu 'wait for'	37	T	*wakaru* 'understand'	28	I
	ikiru 'be alive'	33	I	*narabu* 'line up'	28	I
	yaru 'do'	26	T	*suwaru* 'sit down'	27	I
	kangaeru 'ponder'	20	T	*oboeru* 'rememeber'	26	T
				suru 'do'	25	I
				dekiru 'be able'	24	I
				kakareru 'be written'	24	P
				hairu 'enter'	24	I
				niru 'resemble'	23	I
				deru 'exit'	22	I
				kuru 'come'	21	I
				tsuku 'adhere'	20	I

Korean	Progressive			Resultative		
	VERB	TOKENS	CLASS	VERB	TOKENS	CLASS
	hata 'do'	282	T	*seta* 'stand'	280	I
	alta 'know'	169	T	*ancta* 'sit'	245	I
	pota 'see'	66	T	*toyta* 'become'	122	I
	salta 'live'	65	I	*tulta* 'enter'	98	I
	kitalita 'wait for'	61	T	*namta* 'remain'	91	I
	ipta 'put on'	58	T	*pwuthta* 'stick to'	76	I
	kacita 'have'	57	T	*noh-I-ta* 'be put'	73	P
	tulta 'lift/raise'	53	T	*nwupta* 'lie down'	73	I
	kata 'go'	49	I	*salta* 'live'	57	I
	pala-pota 'look at'	47	T	*kel-li-ta* 'be hanged'	50	P
	moshata 'cannot do'	41	T	*camkita* 'soak in'	31	I
	tutta 'listen'	40	T	*ssah-I-ta* 'be piled up'	29	P
	tuli-e ota 'come to be heard'	31	I	*piwuta* 'be emptied'	28	P
	ilkta 'read'	25	T	*ttelecita* 'fall down'	27	I
	twuta 'put'	24	T	*swumta* 'hide'	26	I
	moluta 'don't know'	24	T	*tal-li-ta* 'depend on'	25	P
	ttelta 'tremble'	24	I	*pak-hi-ta* 'be nailed'	25	P
	ssuta 'write'	23	T	*na-ota* 'come out'	24	I
	cata 'sleep'	21	I	*ota* 'come'	24	I
	ota 'come'	20	I	*kkal-li-ta* 'be spread'	24	P
				ppacita 'fall into'	23	I
				eptulita 'lie face down'	22	I

References

Bybee, J., R. Perkins, and W. Pagliuca. 1994. *The Evolution of Grammar: Tense, Aspect and Modality in the Language of the World.* Chicago: University of Chicago Press.

Cho, M-J. 2000. *Kwuke-uy sang-ey tayhan yenkwu* [A study on the Korean aspect]. Doctoral dissertation, Yonsei University.

Comrie, B. 1976. *Aspect.* Cambridge: Cambridge University Press.

Crystal, D. 1991. *A Dictionary of Linguistics and Phonetics.* 3rd ed. Oxford: Blackwell.

Kim, S. 1981. Wulima-uy sisang [Korean tense/aspect]. *Aysanhakpo* 1: 25–70.

Kindaichi, H. 1950. Kokugo dōshi no ichibunrui [A classification of Japanese verbs]. *Gengo Kenkyū* 15:48–63.

Koo, H.-G. 1987. Ssikkuth {-a, -key, -ci, -ko} uy ssuim-kwa uymi [The usage and semantics of the suffixes -a, -key, -ci, and -ko]. *Konkuk Emwunhak* 11/12:167–88.

Kudō, M. 1995. *Asupekuto-tensu taikei to tekusuto* [Aspect-tense system and text]. Tokyo: Hitsuji Shobō.

Lee, K.-D. 1993. *A Korean Grammar on Semantic-Pragmatic Principles.* Seoul: Hankuk Munhwasa.

Lee, J.-H. 2000. A Cognitive Approach to Connective Particles -e and -ko: Conceptual Unity and Conceptual Separation in Korean Motion Verbs. *Japanese/Korean Linguistics 9*, eds. Mineharu Nakayama and Charles J. Quinn, Jr, 225–38. Stanford: CSLI.

Okuda, Y. 1978a. Asupekuto no kenkyū o megutte (jō) [On the study of aspect I]. *Kyōiku Kokugo* 53:33–44.

Okuda, Y. 1978b. Asupekuto no kenkyū o megutte (ge) [On the study of aspect II]. *Kyōiku Kokugo* 54:14–27.

Rhee, S.-H. 1996. Semantics of Verbs and Grammaticalization. Doctoral dissertation, University of Texas at Austin.

Shirai, Y. 2000. The Semantics of the Japanese Imperfective -teiru: An Integrative Approach. *Journal of Pragmatics* 32:327–61.

Shirai, Y. 1998. Where the Progressive and the Resultative Meet: Imperfective Aspect in Japanese, Korean, Chinese and English. *Studies in Language* 22:661–92.

Shirai, Y., and A. Kurono. 1998. The Acquisition of Tense-Aspect Marking in Japanese as a Second Language. *Language Learning* 48:245–79.

Shirai, Y., and Y. Nishi. 2004. Kaiwa ni okeru te iru no imi [The meaning of te iru in conversation]. *Linguistics and Japanese Language Education III*, eds. M. Minami and M. Asano, 31–49. Tokyo: Kuroshio.

Sohn, H.-M. 1994. *Korean.* London: Routledge.

Strauss, S. 2002. Distinctions in Completiveness: The Relevance of Resistance in Korean V-a/e pelita and V-ko malta and Japanese V-te shimau. *Journal of Pragmatics* 34:143–66.

Wako, M., S. Sato, and K. Horie. 2003. From Progressive to Perfect: A Corpus-Based Study of the "Perfect" Meaning of the Korean Progressive Form -ko iss-. *Japanese/Korean Linguistics 12*, ed. W. McClure, 64–74. Stanford: CSLI.

Yamaguchi, A., and M., Akimoto. eds. 2001. *Nihongo bunpō daijiten* [Dictionary of Japanese grammar]. Tokyo: Meiji Shoin.

Retroactive Elaboration in Korean Conversation

HAEYEON KIM
Chung-Ang University

1. Introduction

In naturally occurring conversation, it is not uncommon that speakers regularly repeat, revise, elaborate, or specify retroactively what they have said in the turn-in-progress or in the immediately following turn. Such a practice of retroactive elaboration has been explained in terms of repetition, repair, turn extensions and increments, or word order variability (Banno 1998, Ford, Fox and Thompson 2002, H. Kim 2003, K. Kim 2001, Ono and Suzuki 1992, Schegloff 1979, 1997, 2000, Schegloff et al. 1977). In conversation analysis, the term **repair** has often been used as a broad cover term which refers to practices for dealing with problems or troubles in speaking, hearing, and understanding the talk in conversation, including phenomena such as change of topic, word search, false starts, and so on. Among these diverse phenomena of repair, this research will deal with a particular type of non-error self-repair, here termed **retroactive elaboration**, in which the current speaker backtracks to an earlier part of the on-going turn, and elaborates, expands, revises, or reformulates it to fulfill the contingent needs of participants such as the need for additional, specific information.

The purpose of this research is to examine the types and functions of retroactive elaboration in Korean conversation from an interactive perspective. In the present research, some instances of the retroactive elaboration phenomena that will be dealt with are illustrated in (1).[1]

(1) P: ... kuliko eymeysuci-to an   tule-kass-tapni-ta,
          and   MSG-too   not add-PST-QUOT-DECL
        .. hwahak-comilyo   chenyen-comilyo,
        chemical-seasoning natural-seasoning,
        ... kulayse lamyen-i pissacyanh-ayo chenpayk wen.
        so   ramen-NM expensive-DECL 1,100   won
        'And MSG, chemical seasonings, are not added, (only) natural sea-
        sonings (are added), so the ramen is expensive (you know), 1,100
        won.'

As shown in (1), the lexical NP *eymeysuci* 'MSG (monosodium glutamate)' is followed by the replacement NP *hwahakcomilyo* 'chemical seasonings (compound)', repairing the preceding NP retroactively. Then, P adds *chenyencomilyo* 'natural seasonings' as a way of providing (contrastive) additional information. In addition, P adds another unattached NP '1,100 won' (i.e., the price) as a way of justifying his statement after stating that the noodles are expensive. Based on this observation, I will discuss the types and functions of retroactive elaboration. After that, I will discuss motivations for the occurrence of retroactive elaboration in terms of a lack of recipient uptake and recipient design. In sum, this research will show the interactive nature of conversation manifested in the act of retroactive elaboration, performed in the manner of revising, specifying, and extending what has been said in the preceding turn-constructional unit (TCU), reflected in the negotiation among participants in shaping forms of TCUs and determining transition-relevance places (TRPs).

2. Context of the Research

Since the research on repair in conversation done by Jefferson (1975) and Schegloff et al. (1977), a great amount of research has been carried out to characterize repair phenomena in conversation from a conversation-analytic,

---

[1] The Korean conversational data are transcribed basically following the transcription conventions proposed by Du Bois et al. (1993), each line representing an intonation unit. The transcription of Korean examples in this research follows the conventions of the Yale Romanization system. The abbreviations used in glossing Korean examples are as follows:

ATTR: attributive	COMM: committal connective	COMP: complementizer
DECL: declarative ending	HEAR: hearsay marker	IE: informal sentence-ender
LOC: locative marker	NM: nominative case marker	POL: polite ending
PST: past tense marker	QUOT: quotative	RESN: reason connective
RETRO: retrospective	TM: topic marker	

interactional perspective. In conversation analysis, as Jefferson and Schegloff et al. state, repair is not viewed as mere correction of "errors" or "mistakes" caused by a speaker's sloppiness or carelessness. Rather, Schegloff et al. (1977) and Schegloff (1997:503) define repair as "practices for dealing with problems or troubles in speaking, hearing, and understanding the talk in conversation". Such a definition provides a new way of examining repair phenomena in conversation in terms of interactional needs and motivations (Jefferson 1975, Schegloff 1979, 1997, Schegloff et al. 1977).

Jefferson (1975) claims that error correction should be viewed as an interactional resource which performs a social action in conversation. Schegloff (1979) shows that same-turn self-repair and syntax are interdependent and co-organizing, illustrating how forms of syntax are determined by the operation of same-turn repair. The research by Fox et al. (1996) is a cross-linguistic study of syntax and repair in English and Japanese, showing how repair is shaped by the syntactic practices of the speakers of a language, and the ways in which repair shapes these practices. Geluykens (1994) observes many instances of "informativeness-repair" in English conversation, in which problematic spots with potential ambiguity are repaired by more specific or informative expressions. Banno (1998) is a study of elaboration repair with a marked rising pitch movement, in which a speaker elaborates the utterance using an abrupt rise in pitch on the final syllable of the prosodic unit. Some other studies which are closely related to the present study are those on turn extensions or increments (Ford, Fox, and Thompson 2002, Kim 2001, Ono and Suzuki 1992, Schegloff 2000). These researchers show that turn increments are closely related to interactional contingencies, including a lack of recipient uptake.

As discussed above, interaction-based research on the organization of repair has provided a way of exploring how forms of syntax are interactionally determined by the negotiation between participants in the process of performing a social action of repair. In this regard, it is necessary to examine instances and types of retroactive elaboration in their sequential and interactional contexts as a way of understanding the organization of repair.

In carrying out the research on retroactive elaboration as a type of non-error repair phenomenon, I chose four audio-taped face-to-face conversations in Korean, totaling approximately 85 minutes. Based on the four conversations, I will explore the questions of in what contexts retroactive elaboration occurs, what interactional motivations are at work, and what social actions are involved in the production of retroactive elaboration. In the present data, a total of 36 instances of retroactive elaboration were found. Based on these statistics, I will try to characterize retroactive elaboration from an interactional perspective.

3. Types and Functions of Retroactive Elaboration

In naturally occurring conversation, speakers repeat, reformulate, elaborate, or specify what they have said by backtracking to preceding TCUs of the turn-in-progress. Such an action has been termed a repair activity in conversation analysis and has been analyzed in terms of the cover term **repair**. As a type of non-error repair, retroactive elaboration can be schematized as [repairable segments (trouble sources) . . . (intervening elements) . . . + repairing segments]. In a study of repair in Japanese, Banno (1998) claims that there are three types of elaboration-repair marked with a rising pitch movement: (i) repetition, (ii) reformulation, and (iii) definitions. In this research, I will classify types of retroactive elaboration into the following three categories: (i) lexical elements followed by repairing lexical elements which are elaborated, expanded, incremented, or reformulated, (ii) pronominal elements followed by repairing lexical elements, and (iii) added non-constituent segments, usually occurring as unattached NPs. Based on this categorization, this research will examine interactional functions of the three types of retroactive elaboration in their sequential contexts.

3.1. Reformulation Repair

The first type of retroactive elaboration can be termed reformulation repair in the sense that repairable lexical elements are reformulated, replaced, revised, or expanded by repairing elements. In this case, the repairable segments are either partially repeated with added elements or replaced by other lexical elements. In other cases, the repairables are reformulated into repairing segments, being specified by additional information. In some other cases, the repairable segments are replaced with other terms which are more transparent to the listener.

First, in the course of producing an utterance, when the current speaker realizes that s/he needs to make a repair, s/he revises or reformulates what s/he has said before by partially repeating or replacing the repairables.

(2) S: (3 IUs omitted)
      .. waynyahamyen,
         the:reason:why
      ... cikum malathon,   ←A
         now marathon
      '(I got here late) because now the marathon (is going on),'
      P: .. malathon,   ←B
         'marathon,'
      S: ... yey tonga malathon.   ←C
         yeah Dong-a Marathon
      'Yeah, Dong-a Marathon.'

P: tonga   mala- a macta,   ←D
Dong-a Mara- ah right
onul   malathon   ha-ci.
today marathon do-COMM
(one IU omitted)
'Dong-a Mara-, ah, (that's) right. Today they have a marathon race.'

In (2), Speaker S says that he is late because of the traffic jam caused by a marathon race on the street. In this context, when S produces the NP *malathon* 'marathon', P, the next speaker, partially repeats what S has said, which functions as a next-turn repair initiator (NTRI). Then, S, with an affirmative response, revises his previous utterance by providing specific information, saying that the race is the Dong-a Marathon Race, which is sponsored by the Dong-a Daily Newspaper Agency. As this excerpt shows, the current speaker revises or reformulates retroactively what s/he has said before by partially repeating or replacing the repairable segment.

Second, the repairable segments are reformulated or revised into more specific elements (sometimes from broad categories to narrow ones), being specified by additional information.

(3) M: .. kulay kaciko,
            such   that
        .. wenlay kekise sensayngnim-i-ess-tay-yo,
           originally there teacher-be-PST-HEAR-POL
        .. sayngmwul sensayngnim-i-nci.   ←
            biology   teacher-be-maybe
'And (she) was a teacher there, maybe a biology teacher.'

In (3), Speaker M talks about a newly employed foreigner at the university career information center. In this excerpt, M first says that the referent was a *sensayngnim* 'teacher', which is a rather broad and vague term. Then, she reformulates the problem spot by adding *sayngmwul* 'biology', which results in a more specific term. As this excerpt shows, speakers often reformulate what they have said before into more specific elements by providing additional, specific information retroactively.

Third, speakers often replace what they have said before with other related, transparent terms for the benefit of the listener's better understanding.

(4) M: ... kuntey kekiey=,
            by:the:way there
        ... ku oykwukin sangcwu--,   ←A
            that foreigner regular-job
'by the way, there, there is a regular-job foreigner-.'

S: .. e,
    'Yeah,'

M: .. ku-   cikwen-i   hana iss-ketun-yo,   ←B
    such employee-NM one be-RETRO-POL
    .. caneys-ila-ko.   ←C
    Janet-named-COMP
    'such that, there is an employee named Janet.'

In (4), Speaker M talks about a foreign (American) employee in an office at the university. In her utterance, M falters in the TCU marked A, and the TCU functions as a repairable. Then she makes a repair in the TCU marked B, which results in self-initiated self-repair. However, M adds another TCU, here marked C, which replaces the lexical NP *cikwen* 'employee' in the immediately preceding TCU. As this excerpt shows, speakers often make an elaboration repair by replacing problem segments with other specific and transparent terms retroactively.

3.2. Replacement Repair of Pronominal Elements

In conversation, speakers often produce utterances with pronominal elements, assuming that the hearer shares the information with the speaker or infers the information from the context or world knowledge. But such a use of pronominal elements often calls for repair because of a lack of shared information between speaker and hearer. Excerpt (5) is a case in which the current speaker's use of a pronominal element causes a problem in the next speaker's turn.

(5) M: .. nay-ka maynnal tayhakkyo-ttay,
           I-NM every:day college-time
        .. kulen kes-man   ccochatany-ess-ketun.   ←A
           such thing-only chase:after-PST-RETRO
        'When I was at college, I always chased after such things.'

    S: ... (0.7) kulen ke,   ←B
               such thing
        .. kangcwa tutnun ke?   ←C
           lecture attend thing
        'such things, attending (English) classes?'

    M: .. ung,
        'Yeah,'

In (5), the two speakers are talking about attending English classes during the summer vacation. Speaker M talks about her experience of attending many English classes in her college life. In her talk, she uses the pronominal *kulen ke* 'such things' (marked A) in referring to attending English classes. However, the information expressed in the pronominal form is not shared with Speaker S. In such a context, Speaker S, after a 0.7-second pause, repeats the pronominal expression which functions as an NTRI (marked B). Immediately after that, she produces a candidate NP (marked C), which gets an affirmative response in the next turn. As this excerpt shows, the current speaker's use of prononimal elements sometimes causes problems in the next speaker's understanding when there is a lack of shared information concerning the referent being talked about.

In discourse, it is normal for speakers to use lexical NPs first. In the following discourse, the lexical NPs are usually replaced by pronominal expressions. However, sometimes, this way of using pronominal elements is reversed in conversation. In such a context, the pronominal elements function as repairables, and the problem sources are repaired either by the current speaker, initiated by an NTRI, as shown in (5), or by the current speaker's self-initiation.

(6) a. A: .. e kulay,
        oh right
        .. ani,
        well
        .. naykke-y,   ←A
        my:thing-NM
        ... nay-ka ku ttay sa   o-ass-ten   thong-i ←B
        I-NM that time buy bring-PST-ATTR container-NM
        ... com   te khun thong-i-ess-cyanha.
        a:bit more big container-be-PST-IE
        'oh right, well, mine, the (cosmetic) container that I bought was a bit bigger one (you know).'

    b. J: .. cepen cwu-ey,
        last week-LOC
        yeki   o-ass-ess-ketun-yo,   ←C
        here come-PST-PST-RETRO-POL
        '(He) came here last week,'

      Y: .. ung.
        'Yeah.'

      J: .. kkwasa-ey.   ←D
        dept.:office-LOC
        'the department office.'

As shown in (6), in conversation, speakers sometimes use pronominal elements first, then they backtrack to the repairable pronominals and replace them with full lexical NPs. In (6a), Speaker A, talking about a cosmetic container, first produces the pronominal expression *naykkey* 'mine (my thing)' (marked A), and then she replaces it with a full lexical NP with a pre-modifying clause (marked B). Likewise, in (6b), Speaker J, talking about a fellow graduate student, produces the deictic expression *yeki* 'here' first, and then she replaces it with the full lexical NP *kkwasa* 'department office'. As these excerpts show, speakers sometimes use pronominal elements based on the assumption that the information being delivered is shared between speaker and hearer. However, when such an assumption fails or when the current speaker feels the need to provide more explicit information, s/he replaces the pronominal elements with more informative expressions such as full lexical NPs, performing an act of retroactive elaboration.

3.3. Retroactive Elaboration with Unattached NPs

In conversation, speakers often add certain elements which are not constituents of the preceding TCUs. In discussing turn increments, Ford, Fox, and Thompson (2002) classified turn increments into extensions and unattached NPs. They define unattached NPs as noun phrases that occur as increments after a possible completion point but that are not interpretable as syntactic constituents, or syntactically integrated continuations, of that immediately prior turn (cf. Ono and Thompson 1994). Examination shows that unattached NPs are often used after a possible completion point, as shown in Excerpt (7).

(7) S: ... hanpen-un tul-ulmanhan kes   kath-a,
           one:time-TM take-worth thing seem-IE
           .. hanpen-un.
           once-TM
           'It is worth taking once, (at least) once.'

     M: ... kuntey=,
           but
           ... (0.7) sikan-i an   mac-ase-yo,
           time-NM not match-RESN-POL
           ... (0.7) tasessi   pan.   ←
           five:o'clock half.
           'but, I cannot meet the class schedule, five thirty.'

In (7), in response to Speaker S's suggestion that it would be worth taking English classes at least once, Speaker M says that she could not attend the class. After that, she produces an unattached NP, which serves as a reason for her dispreferred response. As this excerpt shows, speakers often produce unattached NPs after a possible completion point. Such NPs are used to elaborate or justify retroactively what they have said immediately before.

4. Motivations for Retroactive Elaboration

In this section, let us explore interactional motivations for the occurrence of retroactive elaboration. This research will show that two major motivations for the occurrence of retroactive elaboration are: (i) lack of recipient uptake (Ford, Fox, and Thompson 2002, Schegloff 2000, Kim 2001), and (ii) recipient design (Sacks and Schegloff 1979).

First, instances of retroactive elaboration in the next intonation unit which function as a turn increment can be explained in terms of a lack of recipient uptake. As has been suggested by Ford, Fox, and Thompson (2002), speakers add segments which occur after a possible completion point in the absence of recipient uptake as a way of providing another possible transition-relevance place (TRP), inviting uptake from the recipient, as shown in (8).

(8) B: ... ku ttay 235 kulaym-i-ess-na?
       that time   gram-be-PST-IE
    ... onsu-i-ess-na?
       ounce-be-PST-IE
    .. 235 onsu-i-ess-na?
       ounce-be-PST-IE
    'at that time, did it weigh 235 grams? Or was it ounces? Was it 235 ounces?'

    A: ... al   swu-ka   eps-ci.
       know way-NM not-COMM
       '(We) cannot know.' (or: 'I have no idea.')

In (8), the two speakers are talking about a cosmetic, and B is wondering about its weight. She first asks whether it was 235 grams or not, but she does not receive a response from the hearer. Then, she revises the measurement units from grams to ounces, but she still does not get a response. Next, she partially revises and repeats what she said, and then she gets a response from the next speaker. As this excerpt shows, added segments which are used to modify, revise, modulate, or extend the immediately preceding host TCU function as devices for creating a renewed TRP (Ford, Fox, and Thompson 2002, Kim 2001, Schegloff 2000).

Another motivation for retroactive elaboration can be explained in terms of recipient design (see Sacks and Schegloff 1979). Recipient design is a motivation which is at work when speakers produce turns to be understood in terms of what the speaker knows or assumes about the existing mutual knowledge among participants.

(9) S: .. ung,
        ... heylaltu,   ←A
        'Yeah, herald,'

     M: .. ung,
        'Yeah,'

     S: .. ni-ka   malhay-ss-ten,
        you-NM mention-PST-ATTR
        .. heylaltu sinmwun,   ←B
        herald newspaper,
        ... (0.7) hakkyo ku   ke--,
                school that thing
        'the one you mentioned, the Herald News, school thing . . .'

     M: .. enni,
        'Sister,'

     S: ... cwungang heylaltu,   ←C
        'the Chung-Ang Herald,'

In (9), the speakers are talking about *The Chung-Ang Herald*, the University English magazine. Here, Speaker S first produces the NP 'Herald' (marked A). She receives a backchanneling response only. She then revises her utterance into a more specific NP with a pre-modifying clause (marked B) and a partial repeat of the preceding utterance, but the next speaker still does not take a turn. So, with a slight pause, S provides additional information in the form of an NP. After that, she gets another response in the form of an address term. She then provides the proper name of the magazine, specifying what she has said before. As this excerpt shows, the current speaker revises or reformulates what s/he has said before to help the recipient understand it.

As has been discussed above, when these motivations are at work, the current speaker elaborates, modifies, or revises the turn-so-far or provides additional information to fulfill the demand for more clear and specific information signaled by the recipient.

5. Summary and Conclusions

So far, we have discussed types and functions of retroactive elaboration in Korean conversation. In this research, retroactive elaboration is defined as a particular type of non-error self-repair, in which the current speaker backtracks to an earlier part of the on-going turn, and elaborates, revises, or reformulates it to fulfill the contingent needs of participants. Based upon this definition, this research has shown retroactive elaboration of the following three types: (i) reformulation repair, (ii) replacement repair of pronominal elements, and (iii) retroactive elaboration with unattached NPs.

As a first type of retroactive elaboration, this research has discussed reformulation repair in terms of three subtypes. In the first subtype, the repairable segments are either partially repeated with added elements or replaced by other lexical elements. In the second subtype, the repairables are reformulated into repairing segments, being specified by additional information. In the third subtype, the repairable segments are replaced by other terms. As a second type of retroactive elaboration, this research has shown that pronominal elements are replaced by full lexical NPs retroactively. In conversation, speakers sometimes produce utterances with pronominal elements on the assumption that the hearer shares the information with the speaker. However, such a use of pronominal elements often calls for repair because of a lack of shared information between speaker and hearer. In such a context, the pronominal elements are replaced by full lexical NPs in repairing segments, providing more explicit information. As a third type of retroactive elaboration, this research has shown the role of unattached NPs as a device for retroactive elaboration. In conversation, speakers sometimes produce unattached NPs after a possible completion point. Some such unattached NPs are used to elaborate or justify preceding TCUs retroactively.

Based on the types and functions of retroactive elaboration, this research has discussed interactional motivations in terms of a lack of recipient uptake and recipient design. First, as Ford, Fox, and Thompson (2002) and Schegloff (2000) show, speakers add segments which function as retroactive elaboration after a possible completion point in the absence of recipient uptake. Such instances of retroactive elaboration can be explained as an action of providing another possible TRP, inviting uptake from the recipient. Second, this research has shown that the occurrence of retroactive elaboration can be explained in terms of recipient design (see Sacks and Schegloff 1979). Speakers produce turns to be understood in terms of what the speaker knows or assumes about existing mutual knowledge among participants as an action of performing recipient design.

In sum, through an examination of types and functions of retroactive elaboration, this research has shown the interactive nature of conversation manifested in the act of retroactive elaboration. In particular, explanation of the occurrence of retroactive elaboration in terms of a lack of recipient uptake and recipient design shows the interactive nature of retroactive elaboration, reflecting how negotiation among participants is done in shaping forms of TCUs and determining TRPs.

References

Banno, M. 1998. Repetition, Reformulation, and Definitions: Prosodic Indexes of Elaboration in Japanese Discourse. *Japanese/Korean Linguistics 8*, ed. D. Silva, 3–16.

Du Bois, J., S. Schuetze-Coburn, D. Paolino, and S. Cumming. 1993. Outline of Discourse Transcription. *Talking Data: Transcription and Coding Methods for Language Research*, eds. J. Edwards and M. Lampert, 221–60. Hillsdale, N.J.: Erlbaum.

Fox, B., M. Hayashi, and R. Jasperson. 1996. A Cross-linguistic Study of Syntax and Repair. *Interaction and Grammar*, eds. E. Ochs, E. Schegloff, and S. A. Thompson, 185–237. Cambridge: Cambridge University Press.

Ford, C., B. Fox, and S. A. Thompson. 2002. Constituency and the Grammar of Turn Increments. *The Language of Turn and Sequence*, eds. C. Ford, B. Fox, and S. A. Thompson, 14–38. Oxford: Oxford University Press.

Geluykens, R. 1994. *The Pragmatics of Discourse Anaphora in English: Evidence from Conversational Repair*. Berlin: Mouton.

Jefferson, G. 1975. Error Correction as an Interactional Resource. *Language in Society* 3:181–99.

Kim, H. 2003. Turn Extensions as Turn-Constructional Practice: Word Order Variability in Korean Conversation. Paper presented at the 13th Japanese/Korean Linguistics Conference. East Lansing, Michigan.

Kim, K. 2001. Turn-constructional Practice in Korean Conversation: Organization of Turn Increments. *Language Research* 37(4):885–922.

Ochs, E., E. Schegloff, and S. A. Thompson. 1996. *Interaction and Grammar*. Cambridge: Cambridge University Press.

Ono, T., and R. Suzuki. 1992. Word Order Variability in Japanese Conversation: Motivations and Grammaticization. *Text* 12(3):429–55.

Ono, T., and S. A. Thompson. 1994. Unattached NPs in English Conversation. *Berkeley Linguistics Society* 20:402–19.

Sacks, H., E. Schegloff, and G. Jefferson. 1974. A Simplest Systematics for the Organization of Turn-taking Conversation. *Language* 50:696–735.

Sacks, H., and E. Schegloff. 1979. Two Preferences in the Organisation of Reference to Persons in Conversation and their Interaction. *Everyday Language: Studies in Ethnomethodology*, ed. G. Psathas, 15–21. Hillsdale, N.J.: Erlbaum.

Schegloff, E. 1979. The Relevance of Repair to Syntax-for-Conversation. *Syntax Semantics*, vol. 12, ed. T. Givón, 261–86. New York: Academic Press.

Schegloff, E. 1996. Turn Organization: One Intersection of Grammar and Interaction. *Interaction and Grammar*, eds. E. Ochs, E. Schegloff, and S. A. Thompson, 52–133. Cambridge: Cambridge University Press.

Schegloff, E. 1997. Practices and Actions: Boundary Cases of Other-Initiated Repair. *Discourse Processes* 23:499–545.

Schegloff, E. 2000. On Turn's Possible Completion, More or Less: Increments and Trail-offs. Manuscript, UCLA.

Schegloff, E., H. Sacks, and G. Jefferson. 1977. The Preference for Self-Correction in the Organization of Repair in Conversation. *Language* 53:361–82.

Rethinking the Temporal Approach to Stativity Denoted by -*te iru*: The Application of the Two-Component Theory of Aspect

YUMIKO NISHI*
Cornell University

YASUHIRO SHIRAI
Cornell University and Chinese University of Hong Kong

1. Introduction

This paper examines the nature of stativity realized by the Japanese imperfective aspect -*te iru*, which has long been a controversial issue in aspectual theory in Japanese linguistics. By applying Smith's (1997) two-component theory of aspect, which is claimed to have universal validity, we attempt to show that a temporal approach systematically accounts for the semantics of -*te iru*. We discuss varieties of stative construction expressed by -*te iru* that have been considered problematic in pursuing a temporal account, including the ones that are associated with Kindaichi's (1950) class IV verbs. We also provide some evidence from historical data.

* We thank Peter Sells, Tai Suzuki, Natsuko Tsujimura, and John Whitman for their valuable comments on the earlier version of the paper. We are also grateful to the participants in the 14th Japanese/Korean Linguistics Conference, especially to Shigeto Kawahara and Kiyota Hashimoto. Needless to say, we are responsible for all remaining errors. This paper is partly based on a paper presented at the 3rd International Conference on Practical Linguistics of Japanese (San Francisco State University, March 2002), which appeared in the selected proceedings in Japanese (Nishi and Shirai 2004). The second author gratefully acknowledges a conference grant from Shaw College, the Chinese University of Hong Kong.

1.1. Semantics of *-te iru* in Japanese

The Japanese imperfective aspect *-te iru* denotes not only an action-in-progress meaning, as in (1), but also a resultative state meaning, as in (2).

(1) Ken ga   utat-te i-ru.   (action-in-progress)
    NOM sing-ASP-NONPAST
    'Ken is singing.'

(2) Hebi   ga   sin-de i-ru.   (resultative)
    snake NOM die-ASP-NONPAST
    'A snake is dead (as a result of having died).'

As in many other languages, Japanese expresses stativity by using stative verbs, but it is also common to refer to a stative situation by using imperfective aspect *-te iru* for a state that has resulted from some change (Nishi and Shirai forthcoming, Shirai and Nishi 2002, 2005). Although *-te iru* denotes meanings such as perfect and habitual in addition to progressive and resultative, the present paper focuses on examining the conditions under which resultative meaning arises.

1.2. Previous Studies

In order to account for the meanings that *-te iru* denotes, Kindaichi (1950) proposed that it is verb punctuality that triggers resultative meaning. That is, when *-te iru* is combined with verbs that have duration (**keizoku doosi**), it denotes action-in-progress meaning, and when it is combined with verbs with no duration (i.e. punctual: **syunkan doosi**), resultative meaning is obtained.

Shirai (2000) proposed a system that explains the semantics of *-te iru* by applying Smith's (1997) two-component theory of aspect. This theory of aspect claims that the aspectual meaning of a sentence is primarily determined by the interaction between grammatical (or, viewpoint) aspect and lexical (or, situation) aspect. According to Shirai (2000), the imperfective aspect *-te iru* denotes progressive meaning when combined with durative verbs, and a resultative state interpretation is obtained when it is combined with achievement verbs. This is because imperfective aspect, which imposes an internal view, requires duration. In the case of achievement verbs, which have no duration, the focus has to be on the duration of the resultant state that obtains as a result of a punctual change of state. In (2), *hebi ga sinde iru* 'a snake is dead', the focus has to be on the state after 'dying' occurs, as shown in Figure 1, since the verb *sinu* 'die' is punctual and does not have duration.

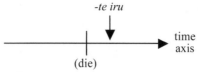

-te iru

(die)

Hebi ga sin-de i-ru.
'A snake is dead (as a result of dying).'

Figure 1. Resultant State Realized by "Achievement + Imperfective *-te iru*"

Shirai's (2000) system for the semantics of *-te iru* has recently been empirically tested by Shirai and Nishi (2005), who analyzed 518 tokens of *-te iru* in a conversational corpus compiled by Ide et al. (1984). All 518 tokens of *-te iru* analyzed in this study were classified according to the aspectual meanings they denote: progressive, resultative, perfect, and habitual. Independent of this classification, all verb phrases to which *-te iru* was attached were classified into four inherent aspectual values: state, activity, accomplishment, and achievement, using linguistic tests from Shirai 1998a.[1] The results showed that the meaning of *-te iru* was determined by the interaction between lexical aspect and grammatical aspect, which supports Shirai's system, and by extension, the two-component theory of aspect (Smith 1997). This indicates that punctuality of verbs does play an important role in determining the conditions under which different meanings of *-te iru* occur.

However, the temporal approach has long been questioned by some researchers (Kudō 1995, Okuda 1978a, 1978b, Tsujimura 2001), partly because of a unique set of stative constructions realized by *-te iru* in which verbs do not seem to involve a "change-of-state". For example, although (3) describes a situation as if a street is in the state of being 'not straight' as a result of a change, there is obviously no change involved in reality.

(3) Kono miti wa   magat-te i-ru.
    this street TOP turn-ASP-NONPAST
    'This street curves.'

Therefore, it may seem peculiar to characterize such sentences as expressing a resultant state.

1.3. Goals

In this paper, we discuss how the notion of stativity is expressed by means of the *-te iru* imperfective and show that a temporal approach systematically accounts for the stative meanings expressed by *-te iru*, including the set of stative constructions that has been argued to be problematic. Corresponding

---

[1] For example, the stative and dynamic distinction was determined by the test "Can it refer to a present state in simple present tense without having a habitual or vivid-present interpretation?" For reasons of space, we refer the reader to Shirai 1998b for the complete list of tests.

stative expressions used in the Early Modern Period, when imperfective aspect -*te iru* had not yet developed, will also be analyzed.

2. Stativity Expressed by the Imperfective -*te iru*

In our study, we use Vendler's (1957) four-way classification of inherent lexical aspect. Vendler categorized verbs into four aspectual types: state, activity, accomplishment, and achievement, which are defined by semantic features of punctuality, telicity, and dynamicity, as shown in Table 1.

	Punctual	Telic	Dynamic
State	−	−	−
Activity	−	−	+
Accomplishment	−	+	+
Achievement	+	+	+

Table 1. Semantic Features of the Four Categories of
Inherent Lexical Aspect (Andersen 1991)

All the verbs referred to in this paper were tested for their aspectual values, using the linguistic tests from Shirai 1998a.

2.1. Resultative Aspect and Change-of-State

Resultative state meaning is obtained when -*te iru* is attached to an achievement verb (Shirai 2000). Resultative aspect can be defined as a grammatical category that "denotes a state that was brought about by some action in the past" (Bybee, Perkins, and Pagliuca 1994:63). The resultative state in Japanese usually involves a real change, as we have seen in (2): *hebi ga sinde iru* 'a snake is dead'. However, there are cases that do not involve change-of-state. Examples (4)–(6) are such cases, which we found in the corpus used in Shirai and Nishi's (2005) study.

(4) (seki ga)   ai-te i-reba . . .
    seat NOM open-ASP-COND
    'If seats are available . . .'

(5) hudan   wa konnani   hissorisi-te-te [2]
    normally TOP like:this become:quiet-ASP-and
    'It is usually quiet like this around here.'

---

[2] There were some problematic cases as we analyzed the lexical aspect of verb phrases, which we mention here. One of them is the lexical aspect of the light verb *suru* 'do', which varies depending on the argument it takes. For each case of a verb phrase with *suru* inflected for -*te iru* identified in the corpus, we tested for its lexical aspect using the linguistic tests, as we did for all the other verbs inflected for -*te iru*. As long as we were able to identify the lexical aspect, we included them in the analysis. In the case of *hissori suru* in (5), it was identified as an achievement verb. In contrast, *gorogoro suru* was excluded from the analysis because we could

(6) karotin   ga   hukum-are-te i-ru   kara
    carotene NOM contain-PASS-ASP-NONPAST because
    '. . . because carotene is contained.'

2.2. Three Types of Resultative State Expressed by -te iru

To account for the above stative meanings denoted by -*teiru*, we introduce the notions of **conceptual change, spurious change**, and Matsumoto's (1996) **subjective change**.

Example (4) is a case of subjective change, the notion proposed by Matsumoto (1996). Subjective change involves hypothetical change from the normal (expected) state to an unusual (unexpected) state, as in (7) (Matsumoto 1996:124; gloss modified).

(7) Sono heya wa maruku   nat-te i-ru.
    The room TOP round become-ASP-NONPAST
    (lit. 'The room is in the state of having become round.')
    'The room is round.'

Rooms are usually rectangular, and that is our normal expectation. In this case, we conceive of it as if there was a change from a normal state (of a room being square) to an unusual state of a room being round, even if there is no such change in reality. Therefore, in the case of (4), if we assume the normal state of the theater under discussion as being full (perhaps at a busy time of the year), it can be interpreted as a subjective change expression.

However, (5) and (6), repeated here as (8) and (9), still seem to be problematic.

(8) hudan   wa   konnani   hissorisi-te-te   =(5)
    normally TOP this much become:quiet-ASP-and
    'It is usually quiet like this around here.'

(9) karotin   ga   hukum-are-te i-ru   kara   =(6)
    catrotene NOM contain-PASS-ASP-NONPAST because
    '. . . because carotene is contained.'

These sentences cannot be explained by the notion of subjective change, because Matsumoto's defining feature "deviation from a norm" is not pre-

---

not identify the lexical aspectual value. This is because, in the case of *gorogoro si-te iru* 'be abundant', if we change the form into simple nonpast tense, which is necessary in order to test the aspectual value (Shirai 1998b), the lexical meaning changes from 'be abundant' to 'rumble' or 'roll'. Aspectual meanings of mimetic verbal expressions seem to be very complex (Nishi 2000) and will require an in-depth analysis of their own. The aspectual difference between "adverbial + *suru* + -*te iru*" as in *hissori si-te iru* and "adverbial + *to* + *suru* + -*te iru*" as in *hissori to si-te iru* is also an issue to be further investigated.

sent. Therefore, we propose a new category, spurious change, which does not involve real change and does not entail any type of unexpectedness.

We thus propose the system in Figure 2 for the resultative state meaning denoted by *-te iru*. There are two types of resultative state sentence; one involves a real change-of-state, and the other involves no real change, which we refer to as conceptual change. We further propose two notions as subtypes of conceptual change: subjective change and spurious change.

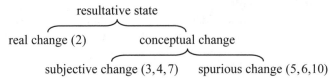

Figure 2. Resultative State Meanings Expressed by *-te iru*
(corresponding examples in parentheses)

What is important here is that resultative state meaning is always expressed by the combination of an achievement verb and *-te iru*.[3] That is, these cases always involve achievement verbs, whether the change is real or conceptual. All the verbs in (2)–(9) that we have examined are achievement verbs. Therefore, even if no real change is involved, the fact remains that only achievement verbs can express resultative state meaning when combined with *-te iru*, as proposed by Shirai (2000).

2.3. Why Conceptual Change?

An interesting issue here is how native speakers of Japanese treat real vs. conceptual change in their description of resultative states. In the real world, only one of two possibilities holds; either there was a change or there was not a change. However, when we talk about a resultant state, it is not always the case that we are clearly aware of the nature of the change. (10) is a good example (Tai Suzuki, p.c.).

(10) Ike ni happa ga   ukan-de iru.
pond LOC leaf NOM float-ASP-NONPAST
'A leaf is floating in the pond.'

This sentence describes a scene where a leaf is floating on the surface of a

---

[3] Tsujimura's (2001) "stative construction" does not belong to the resultative state class in our system, even though it denotes stativity. We treat the stative expressions that involve *-te iru* attached to dynamic durative verbs, such as the following (Tsujimura 2001:602), as metaphorical expressions that originated due to a product-oriented generalization—the notion to be discussed in §2.4.

Koosokudooro ga mati no mannaka o   hasitte iru
highway   NOM town GEN middle ACC run-ASP-NONPAST
'A highway runs in the middle of the town.'

pond, and it is generally considered a resultant state expression. However, in most cases, the speaker is not aware of, or interested in, the nature of the change.[4] The meaning of the achievement verb *ukabu* 'float' is that something floats up from below the surface of the water. However, most speakers do not care whether it comes from under the water or just fell from a tree, and as long as it is floating on the water, one can use this expression. In reality, it is almost always the case that leaves fall from a tree, and they almost never float up from the bottom of a pond. This suggests that the way we conceptualize events or states does not always reflect reality. Thus, we consider examples like (10), (5), and (6), which do not involve an actual change **denoted by the verb**, as spurious change in our system, since these examples neither involve a real change (denoted by the verb) nor "unexpectedness", a defining feature of subjective change.[5] Note that in using spurious change, speakers do not appear to mind whether or not the real-world situation actually corresponds to the change denoted by the verb.

2.4. Product-Oriented Generalization

Why, then, are speakers not concerned about the nature of change? Why do we refer to a stative situation as if there were a change involved using *-te iru*? We suggest the following scenario with respect to stative situations in Japanese.

As the aspectual system of Japanese developed over time, it became conventional to express resultative state by attaching *-te iru* to achievement verbs that involve a real change. This, in turn, brought about a situation in which the formal unit "achievement + *-te iru*" itself is directly mapped onto stativity, which makes speakers less concerned about the nature of change itself and renders it possible to refer to a stative situation regardless of whether there was a real change or whether there is a logical contradiction between the reality and the linguistic expression as in (10).[6]

This type of generalization is reminiscent of what is called a "product-oriented generalization" (e.g. Bybee 1995). Normally, morphological derivation is from the zero form to a derived form (as in *jump* > *jumped*, *eat* >

---

[4] See also Suzuki 1998.

[5] This of course specifically refers to the case of stativity denoted by *ukabu* + *-te iru* when it has 'a leaf' as its argument. The analysis of spurious change does not apply if *ukabu* 'float' has an argument such as 'a dead goldfish', since it is most probably the case that a goldfish did float up, which involves a change-of-state (i.e. real change).

[6] When the speaker's focus is more on the event than on the consequence of the change, it expresses perfect and not resultant state. This explains why achievement verbs such as *itibe-tusuru* 'glance' or *mokugekisuru* 'witness' usually denote perfect rather than resultative meaning when combined with *-te iru*. See Shirai 2000:354 for further details. See also Kunihiro's (1985) discussion of non-prototypical resultant states.

eats), but sometimes there are cases that do not involve this process and where generalization through derived forms is observed. Although Bybee (1995) discusses the case of Hausa, it appears that Japanese also has such an example. In colloquial Japanese, we have an adjectival form that lacks the most basic form, as shown in (11).

(11)   'delicious'   'different'
            Nonpast   *oisi-i*   **tiga-i*
            Past   *oisi-katta*   *tiga-katta*
            Adverbial   *oisi-ku*   *tiga-ku*
            Conditional   *oisi-kereba*   *tiga-kereba*

On the left is the regular conjugation of adjectives, but the adjective in question, which presumably was derived from the stative verb *tigau* 'differ', does not have the most basic, nonpast form (**tigai*). The absence of the basic form suggests that this adjective arose as a result of product-oriented generalization—generalization based on derived forms. This is a product-oriented generalization at the morphological level.

What does product-oriented generalization tell us about the stativity denoted by *-te iru*? We argue that the conceptual change expressions discussed earlier are analogous in that the derived forms directly map onto stative meaning. That is, instead of deriving resultative aspect by attaching *-te iru* to achievement verbs, stative meaning is directly attached to the frame "achievement verb + *-te iru*". This scenario of course needs to be tested against historical data. For example, if the scenario here is correct, we expect to observe real change expressions before conceptual change expressions as we trace the development of the resultative use of *-te iru*. The results of our analysis of historical data will be discussed momentarily.

2.5. Kindaichi's Class IV Verbs

How do we account for the stativity denoted by *-te iru* attached to Kindaichi's class IV verbs, such as *sobieru* 'tower', *sugureru* 'excel', *arihureru* 'be ordinary'? These verbs express stativity when combined with *-te iru*, but they differ from other achievement verbs in that they usually accompany *-te iru* and are rarely used without it except in adnominal clauses.[7] An example of a class IV verb is given in (12) (Shirai 2000:337).

---

[7] Class IV verbs are often used without *-te iru* in adnominal clauses, as in *sobieru yama* 'mountain that towers', and are occasionally used in matrix clauses, as in *tainetusei ni sugureru* 'excels in heat-resistance'. However, in both cases, class IV verbs express stativity and do not refer to a dynamic event in simple present form, which is different from other achievement verbs. In other words, if class IV verbs are used without *-te iru*, they represent an attribute of the nominal that follows or an attribute of the subject or topic in matrix clauses. See also note 11 below.

(12) Yama   ga takaku   sobie-te i-ru   /   *sobie-ru.
mountain NOM high tower-ASP-NONPAST / tower-NONPAST
'The mountain towers high above.'

Why this set of verbs lacks simple nonpast forms needs to be explained.

3. Evidence from Historical Data

To address this issue, we examined the use of these verbs in the Early Modern Period, using a web-based database of classical literary texts.[8] Although we did not find any class IV verbs used with -te iru, we found some cases where these verbs were used with and without -tari, which is an aspect marker of Classical Japanese that denotes resultative, perfect, and perfective. For example, we found a case of *sobiyu* without -tari (13) and a case of *sobiyu* with -tari (14), both in *Chinsetsu Yumiharizuki* (1806).

(13) kozyoo takaku sobiyu   sirakumo   no . . .
old:castle tall   tower white:clouds GEN
'the white clouds where the old castle towers . . .'

(14) maezura ni takaku sobie-taru wa kiharayama . . .
in:front LOC tall   tower-ASP TOP Mt. Kihara
'Mt. Kihara, which towers tall in front of us . . .'

We need to explain the two patterns of use of *sobiyu* that existed concurrently, one with -tari and one without -tari.

One possibility is that the simple nonpast forms of verbs like *sobiyu* or *suguru* used to be achievement verbs, and that -tari was attached in order to express a result state.[9] However, since these verbs are usually used to denote stative situation rather than change-of-state, eventually the simple nonpast form lost its place, and as a consequence, we do not see these verbs used without -te iru in the Modern Japanese.[10]

Another possibility is that these verbs were intrinsically stative, and

---

[8] We used *Nihon koten bungaku honbun dētabēsu*, compiled by Kokubungaku Kenkyū Shiryōkan [Department of Historical Documents, National Institute of Japanese Literature] (URL: http://base3.nijl.ac.jp/Rcgi-bin/hon_home.cgi). This is a collection of Classical Japanese literature *Nihon koten bungaku taikei* published by Iwanami Shoten. All the literary texts from the Early Modern Period (1603–1868) included in the database were examined.

[9] According to McClure (1993), most of the Class IV verbs are identified as achievement type if one applies the linguistic tests from Dowty 1979, etc., for verb classification. Ogihara (1998) and Shirai (2000) take the same view. Under this view, stativity expressed by -te iru can be characterized as a state brought about by a spurious change in our system.

[10] We note here that there seems to be no means of identifying whether the simple nonpast form of these verbs expressed dynamicity, even if we examine historical data back to the 8th century (Tai Suzuki, p.c.).

they always denoted stative situations, with or without *-tari*. In other words, these verbs were originally stative verbs.[11] If so, why do we see these verbs used with *-tari* when there was actually no need? Here, we can apply the notion of product-oriented generalization again. Under this scenario, we assume that when *-tari* and *-ri* established their functions as stative markers, they came to be attached not only to achievement verbs but also to stative verbs that actually did not require aspect markers, and that they expressed stative situations as if there were a conceptual change.

To summarize, if the first scenario is the case, these class IV verbs were originally achievement verbs, and with *-te iru* they expressed a resultative state meaning. If the second scenario is the case, they were originally stative verbs. The seemingly redundant use of *-te iru* with stative verbs can subsequently be explained by using the concepts of product-oriented generalization and conceptual change.

4. Conclusion

In this paper, we discussed varieties of stative meaning denoted by *-te iru* by introducing the notions of conceptual change and product-oriented generalization. We have shown that the temporal approach accounts for the semantics of *-te iru* without excluding the kinds of sentences that have been considered problematic in pursuing a temporal account. We have also shown that our proposal is consistent with historical facts, based on the findings from our corpus analysis of the Early Modern Japanese.

References

Andersen, R. W. 1991. Developmental Sequences: The Emergence of Aspect Marking in Second Language Acquisition. *Crosscurrents in Second Language Acquisition and Linguistic Theories*, eds. T. Huebner and C. A. Ferguson, 305–24. Amsterdam: John Benjamins.

Bybee, J. 1995. Regular Morphology and Lexicon. *Language and Cognitive Processes* 10:425–55.

Bybee, J., R. Perkins, and W. Pagliuca. 1994. *The Evolution of Grammar: Tense, Aspect, and Modality in the Languages of the World.* Chicago: University of Chicago Press.

Dowty, D. R. 1979. *Word Meaning and Montague Grammar.* Dordrecht: Reidel.

Ide, S., S. Ikuta, A. Kawasaki, M. Hori, and H. Haga. 1984. *Shufu no isshūkan no danwa shiryō.* Tokyo: Japan Women's University.

---

[11] Under this hypothesis, the stativity denoted by the class IV verbs is not realized as a resultant state. In regard to the class IV verbs that appear in adnominal clauses (e.g. *sobieru* 'tower' in *sobieru yama* 'mountain that towers'), the verb expresses stativity with or without an aspectual marker *-tari* or *-ri*, since the structure of adnominal clause requires that the adnominal denote an attribute of the argument (Tai Suzuki, p.c.).

Kindaichi, H. 1950. Kokugo dōshi no ichibunrui. *Gengo Kenkyū* 15:48–63.

Kudō, M. 1995. *Asupekuto/tensu taikei to tekusuto: Gendai Nihongo no jikan no hyōgen.* Tokyo: Hitsuji Shobō.

Kunihiro, T. 1985. Ninchi to gengo hyōgen. *Gengo Kenkyū* 88:1–19.

Matsumoto, Y. 1996. Subjective-Change Expressions in Japanese and Their Cognitive Linguisitc Bases. Spaces, Worlds, and Grammar, eds. G. Fauconnier & E. Sweetser, 124-156. Chicago: University of Chicago Press.

McClure, W. T. 1993. A Semantic Parameter: The Progressive in Japanese and English. Japanese/Korean Linguistics 3, eds. , 254–79. Stanford: CSLI.

Nishi, Y. 2000. A Corpus Analysis of the Semantics of *-teiru*. Manuscript, Cornell University.

Nishi, Y., and Y. Shirai. 2004. Kaiwa ni okeru *-te iru* no imi [Semantics of *-te iru* in conversation]. *Gengogaku to Nihongo kyōiku III* [Linguistics and Japanese language education III], eds. M. Minami and M. Asano, 231–49. Tokyo: Kurosio.

Nishi, Y., & Y. Shirai. Forthcoming. How Aspectual Notions are Lexicalized: A Comparative Analysis of Predicates in *The Little Prince* in English and Japanese. *Japanese Linguistics European Chapter*, eds. V. Eschbach-Szabo and A. Wlodarczyk. Tokyo: Kurosio.

Ogihara, T. 1998. The Ambiguity of the *-te iru* Form in Japanese. *Journal of East Asian Linguistics* 7:87–120.

Okuda, Y. 1978a. Asupekuto no kenkyū o megutte (ge). *Kyōiku Kokugo* 54:14–27.

Okuda, Y. 1978b. Asupekuto no kenkyū o megutte (jō). *Kyōiku Kokugo* 53:33–44.

Shirai, Y. 1998a. The Emergence of Tense-Aspect Morphology in Japanese: Universal Predisposition? *First Language* 18:281–309.

Shirai, Y. 1998b. Where the Progressive and the Resultative Meet: Imperfective Aspect in Japanese, Chinese, Korean and English. *Studies in Language* 22:661–92.

Shirai, Y. 2000. The Semantics of the Japanese Imperfective *-teiru*: An Integrative Approach. *Journal of Pragmatics* 32:327–61.

Shirai, Y., and Y. Nishi. 2002. Lexicalisation of Aspectual Structures in English and Japanese. *Typology and Second Language Acquisition*, ed. A. Giacalone Ramat, 267–90. Berlin: Mouton de Gruyter.

Shirai, Y., and Y. Nishi. 2005. How What We Mean Impacts How We Talk: The Japanese Imperfective Aspect Marker *-teiru* in Conversation. *The Power of Context in Language Teaching and Learning*, eds. J. Frodesen and C. Holten, 39–48. Boston: Heinle & Heinle.

Smith, C. S. 1997. *The Parameter of Aspect*, 2nd ed. Dordrecht: Kluwer.

Suzuki, T. 1998. 'Tari' to 'ri' = keizoku to kansei no hyōgen. *Kokubungaku* 43(11): 70–7.

Tsujimura, N. 2001. A Constructional Approach to Stativity in Japanese. *Studies in Language* 25:601–29.

Vendler, Z. 1957. Verbs and Times. *Philosophical Review* 66:143–60.

Postpredicate Elements in Japanese Conversation: Nonmodularity and Panchrony

TSUYOSHI ONO*
University of Alberta

1. Introduction

Japanese, a predicate-final language, actually exhibits various types of elements occurring after predicates and their associated elements (e.g. final particles), as illustrated in (1) (Inoue 1976:176; romanization, glosses, and translation are mine).

(1) <u>subarashii hon ga puresento   sareta   soo desu</u> **kodomotachi kara**
    wonderful book GA present do:PASS:PAST I.hear COP   child:PL   from
    'I hear (she) was given a wonderful book, from (her) children.'

In this paper, the first part (underlined) is called the **host**, and the sec-

* I should thank friends at and from the University of Arizona, particularly Hiromi Aoki, Maggie Camp, Kim Jones, Yuka Matsugu, Takako Ogawa, Tomoko Takeda, and Tim Vance, as well as Diana Benschop, Betty Couper-Kuhlen, Makoto Hayashi, Yuri Hosoda, and Sandy Thompson, for all their help which made it possible for me to give a presentation at J/K14 and to complete this version. This study was financed in part by the German Science Foundation (*Deutsche Forschungsgemeinschaft*) through a grant entitled "Speech as communicative practice: The interplay of linguistic structures and interaction" (*Praktiken der mündlichen Kommunikation: Zur Wechselwirkung zwischen Sprach- und Interaktionsstrukturen, Sonderforschungbereich 511 Literatur und Anthropologie*) at the University of Konstanz, 2001.

ond part (bolded), the **tail**. This phenomenon has been studied under various labels, including **postposing**, **right dislocation**, and more recently **increment**. It has been given various functional characterizations, such as after-thought, repair, and defocusing. Recent conversation-based investigations (Koike 2003, Mori 1999, Ono and Suzuki 1992, Tanaka 2001) have high-lighted some specific types of **postpredicate element** (PPE hereafter). Though these studies have allowed us to see an interesting array of what a "strict predicate-final language" can do in a live setting, we have yet to see how these types fit together in the grammar of Japanese. Based on the findings of earlier studies and my own data, I will review and identify vari-ous PPEs. In particular, I would like to establish three distinct types, each of which is associated with a particular combination of disparate prosodic, syntactic, semantic, and interactional features. That is, by focusing on what happens after the "final" predicate in Japanese conversation, we will find that some linguistic units are defined by features from various "modules" of grammar which have traditionally been understood to be distinct. We will also find that many instances of PPEs are associated with various degrees of fixedness, a situation best understood as reflecting on-going change. These results thus lend support to recent nonmodular and panchronic views of grammar (e.g. Bybee and Hopper 2001, Hopper 1998, Langacker 1987, 1991, Sohn 2004) while demonstrating that such a conception is a first step in our attempt to identify and represent Japanese syntax.[1]

2. Increment

The first type of PPE, called **increment** here and illustrated in (2), involves a grammatically and prosodically completed host, followed by some ele-ment which seems to be syntactically fitted to it. That is, the tail *fudoosan tte* 'as for real estate (companies)' in line 2 can be inserted in the host in line 1. The @ sign in the host marks a place where the tail may be inserted.

---

[1] What is observed by linguists is simply what is captured at one point in the everlasting change of a particular language, and thus it exhibits variation. This is an obvious fact consider-ing that human language constantly changes and thus in principle can never be fixed, but it has not been recognized in most models of grammar (see Hopper 1998 for an exception), which is part of the motivation for framing the present paper in this way. For a discussion of the non-modularity of human language, see Langacker 1987, 1991. This idea has also been elaborated in relation to so-called first person pronouns in Japanese (Ono and Thompson 2003).

As a methodology, it might be possible to look at different modules of language at the same time. But that should belong only to methodology; as part of a theory of language it needs to be tested against data.

(2) A couple is talking about someone in real estate.

1 H: <u>@ goorudenuiiku tte yasumi ja   nai no?</u>[2]
   Golden.Week TOP break COP not FP
   'Isn't Golden Week a break?'

2 **fudoosan tte**
   real.estate TOP
   'as for real estate (companies)'

As demonstrated by the sound waves and F_0 curves presented in Koike 2003, the tail is prosodically subordinated by being lower in pitch and amplitude than the host.[3] Further, the prosodic break between the host and the tail for this type is typically associated with a pause, often along with intervening contributions by other interactants, as seen in (3).

(3) K asks A if Nanno was checking if the address list from their high school was current.

1 K: <u>a Nanno ga @ sooyatte   shirabeteta wake?</u>
   oh Nanno GA   in.that.way examining:PAST FP
   'Oh, Nanno was checking (them) out in that way?'

2 A: un
   'mhm'

3 K: **hitori hitori o**?
   one   one   O
   'one by one?'

4 A: un
   'mhm'

Again, *hitori hitori o* 'one by one' in line 3 can be inserted in the utterance in line 1, which is grammatically and prosodically complete. Examples like (3), however, show that a PPE is not merely a syntactic fact but instead involves interaction where each step of the speaker's utterance is produced in coordination with other interactants.

In (4), the utterance in line 3 can be understood to be a subordinate clause to the clause in line 1. (Square brackets mark overlapped speech.)

---

[2] Golden Week is a week-long holiday in Japan, running from the end of April to the beginning of May.

[3] Koike (2003), however, does not discuss amplitude in her paper.

(4) Discussing the difficulty of M's being accepted into a graduate program.

   1 H: <u>demo @ wakannai jan</u>.
         but   understand:not FP
         'But (you) don't know'

   2 M: un   wakan[nai   ne]
         mhm understand:not FP
         'mhm, don't know'

   3 H: **[sonna koto]**   **itteta**   **tte**   **sa**.
                       such thing say:STAT:PAST even.though FP
                       'even though (you) are saying such a thing'

We have thus seen examples where the tail seems to be filling in a syntactic slot in the host. Interestingly, however, other examples, such as (5), suggest that the process may not be syntactic.

(5) A couple is talking about a friend, Aki, who had to cancel a trip to Australia.

   1 R: <u>@ soshitara oo- asoko ikanakattan da   tte</u>.
             then   Au- there go:not:PAST COP I.hear
             'I hear (she) didn't go (to) Au- there then'

   2 H: [doko e]?
         where to
         'to where?'

   3 R: **[oosutora]ria**
         'Australia'

   4   **akichan**
         'Aki'

R's *oosutoraria* 'Australia' in line 3 and *akichan* 'Aki' in line 4 both appear to be syntactically fitted to the host in line 1.[4] Notice, however, that the utterance in line 1 can accommodate *akichan*, but not *oosutoraria*, because the location is already specified in the clause with *asoko* 'there'. One might then suggest that *oosutoraria* 'Australia' replaces the less specific *asoko* 'there' (called "replacement repair" in Kim 2006). This suggestion, however, results in two different analyses for the two utterances: insertion for *oosutoraria* and replacement for *asoko*. Yet, occurring next to each other, these two PPEs seem to be doing the same type of semantic work: specifying some referents which are part of the event described in the host.

---

[4] H's *doke e* 'to where?' in line 2 and R's *oosutoraria* 'Australia' in line 3 are overlapped speech and thus do not constitute a question-answer sequence.

Example (6), taken from the same conversation as (5), further suggests the semantic nature of the process involved in the occurrence of increment.

(6) 1 H: <u>koara ni   aenakattan   da ne ja</u>.
         koala with meet:can:not:PAST COP FP then
         '(She) wasn't able to meet with koalas then'

     2 R: soo soo
         'right right'

     3 H: **kangaruu toka ni**
         kangaroo etc. with
         'with kangaroos and others'

H is jokingly talking about one outcome of canceling a trip to Australia: not being able to see certain animals. In line 3, he adds *kangaruu toka ni* 'with kangaroos and others' as another example of such animals. What is interesting about this example is that a simple insertion of the tail in the host does not produce a well-formed utterance, as illustrated in (6'), though its interpretation is still dependent on the host.

(6') ? koara ni **kangaruu toka ni** aenakattan da ne ja

Though the tails in (5) and (6) do not fit in the host syntactically, functionally they do not seem to be any different from the tails in examples (2)–(4), which can be inserted into the host. This suggests a hypothesis that the use of the first type of PPE is essentially a semantic process where the tail is produced in order to repair and further specify what is expressed by the host.

3. Cognitive Shift

The second type of PPE involves what Tanaka (2001) calls "cognitive shift", in which the tail reframes the grammatical and semantic understanding of the host. That is, unlike the first type of PPE, the tail in this type is not part of or subordinate to the host but can instead be analyzed as including the host grammatically and semantically.[5] In (7) (from Tanaka 1999:144; slightly modified) we observe that the husband first agrees with the wife's critical remark about himself, and then, after a long pause, turns his position into a self-deprecation by restructuring the host into a quote marked by the verb 'say', introduced in the tail.

---

[5] It is treated together with the other two types of PPE in this paper because it is similar to them in the sense that the final predicate is followed by some elements, which can be analyzed as being syntactically connected to it.

(7) 1 W: ((complains about H))

    2 H: <u>sore wa soo ne</u>
          that TOP so FP
          'That's right, isn't it'

          (1.2 second pause)

    3 **tto   iu   kara   ikenai no**
       QUOT say because wrong FP
       '(It's) wrong because (I) say that ("that's right, isn't it")'

Tanaka (2001:89) states that in examples such as this "the original turn can thereafter be retroactively re-directed, re-processed, re-formulated, re-constructed, negated, and so forth." That is, the utterance in line 3 can be understood to constitute an action separate from the action performed by the utterance in line 2: self-deprecation versus agreement. In this type, the tail is prosodically independent of the host, often exhibiting either a pause, as in (7), or contributions by other interactants.[6] This iconically mirrors the independent actions performed by the two parts.

Now consider (8). In line 1, talking about a graduate program, M says that there are not many (undergraduates) who stay on, which is grammatically and prosodically complete. Notice that her utterance does not contain a lexical item meaning 'undergraduate' (so-called zero anaphora).

(8) Talking about the fact that more graduate students come from elsewhere.

    1 M: <u>anmari datte yappari nokkotteru hito tte inai mon ne</u>.
          'There aren't many (undergraduates) who stay on.'

    2 **te   yuu ka**
       QUOT say or
       'saying that or' → 'rather'

    3 **gurajueeto no hito datte sa dokka kara kita hito ga ooi desho**
       'More graduate students come from (other) places, don't they?'

In lines 2 and 3, M reformulates her utterance, perhaps because she did not receive an appropriate uptake from the other speaker (Ford, Fox, and Thompson 2002). It is interesting that *te yuu ka* 'saying that or', seen in line 2, seems to have been lexicalized as a type of conjunction (or discourse marker) meaning 'rather', which presents a revised view. And as is common with this type of change, reduced forms are observed: *te ka*, *tsuuka*, and *tsuka*. Apparently, this use has further developed to simply introduce a new theme/story (Martin 1975:1015, Wakamatsu and Hosoda 2003).

In fact, fixed expressions are rather common with the cognitive shift

---

[6] Pause can be interpreted as deliberate non-contribution by other interactants.

type of PPE, which includes *tte iu no wa* 'because . . .' and *tte ieba, to ittara, to ii masu to* 'speaking of which'. New ones seem to keep being created, sometimes with rather clear social meanings. For instance, about ten years ago the above-mentioned *te iu ka* with lengthening and a marked pitch contour, as in (9), became extremely popular among younger speakers, perhaps particularly among female speakers.

(9)

teyuu=ka=
QUOT:say:QUES
'rather than that' (starting a turn)

Searching for this expression on the Internet confirms my observation with the indication that speakers have a rather clear sense about its lexicalized status. One webpage, for example, translates it as 'in other words . . .' and reports a situation in a TV program participated in by youth where ". . . almost every sentence will start with this phrase, no matter whether other person has said anything or not. It's about equivalent to the way North American teen-agers use 'like' and 'you know'."

Further, starting about twenty-five years ago the expressions *na(=)n-chatte, na=nte, toka (i)tte* 'saying that . . .' and their variants became particularly popular and are used to turn the previous serious/offensive-sounding utterance into a joke. These expressions mean something like '(I'm only) saying that; (I'm not serious)'.

It is interesting to note also that this type of PPE was already available at least 100 years ago in the form *to moosu no wa* 'saying that . . .' (Miller et al. 1997:47). It shows that the grammatical practice of cognitive shift and its lexicalized nature has been with Japanese for some time.

In sum, the cognitive shift type of PPE is used to reframe what has been expressed in the host, and many instances of this type are lexicalized.

4. Emotive[7]

The third type, briefly discussed by Ono and Suzuki (1992) and called "emotive" here, seems to be used when the speaker expresses a certain type of emotive reaction, as in (10) and (11).

(10) <u>hen   da yo ne</u> **are mo ne**
     strange COP FP FP that also FP
     'Strange, that also is'

---

[7]This type is much more thoroughly treated in Ono forthcoming.

(11) <u>zettai   wakai no</u> **minna**
     absolutely young FP   all
     'Absolutely younger (than me), everyone (is)'

This type is typically short, and the acoustic signal for (10), given in Figure 1, shows neither a pause nor a prosodic break between the host and the tail. The host is associated with high amplitude and pitch which suddenly drop. These characteristics seem to result in an auditory impression that the host and the tail of this type are planned and produced together and that it has an "emotionally charged" intonation.

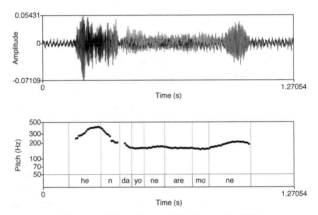

Figure 1. Waveform and F_0 Curve for (10)

It should also be noted that, unlike the other two types of PPE, in the emotive type the next speaker does not come in until after the tail is expressed, suggesting that the tail in this type probably is neither an "afterthought" nor a repair.

Further, there is distributional skewing in elements occurring in the host and the tail of this type, which suggests a pragmatically-based principle of ordering elements. As seen in the above and following examples, the element in the host expresses some emotion or feeling of the speaker, or at least is expressed with some emotion.

(12) <u>damena no</u> **atashi**
     bad   FP   I
     'I'm hopeless'

(13) <u>ii   jan</u> **betsuni**
     good TAG particularly
     'Isn't (it) OK, really?'

(14) <u>uso nanda</u> **aitsura   tte**
      lie   COP   that.guys TOP
      '(It's) a lie, those guys'

(15) <u>okashina ie   da na</u> **honto**
      funny family COP FP really
      'Funny family, really'

(16) <u>dokidoki   shichau mon</u> **nanka**
      heart.pounding do:end.up FP somehow
      '(I) get nervous, for some reason'

(17) <u>zettai   kuru   beki   datta   yo</u> **are wa**
      absolutely come should COP:PAST FP that WA
      '(You) absolutely should have come, to that'

(18) <u>shiten   da yo</u> **kore demo**
      doing:NOML COP FP this even
      '(I) am (dieting), even this'

(19) <u>kawatteru desho</u> **uchi no   papa**
      strange   COP house GEN father
      '(He) is strange, my dad'

In these cases, the tail relates the attribute expressed in the host to a referent already available in the discourse ("given" information in the sense of Chafe 1994), in the form of demonstratives, pronouns, or proper nouns, as seen in (11), (12), (14), (17), and (19). This analysis is partly supported by the fact that some tails include so-called topic markers such as *wa* in (17) and *tte* in (14), which have been said to mark "given" information.

Alternatively, the tail reframes the attribute expressed in the host with adverbs, as seen with 'particularly' in (13), 'really' in (15), and 'somehow' in (16). It is interesting that some tails, such as 'that also' in (10) and 'even this' in (18), seem to be a combination of these two types; the tail not only relates the attribute to certain "given" referents but also reframes it.

The prosodic characteristics, along with the distributional skewing of elements appearing in the host and in the tail, suggest that the emotive type may have developed into a grammaticized template (or schema) which encodes a certain type of emotive reaction.

5. Concluding Remarks

We have seen that PPEs in Japanese actually can be examined as three separate types, each associated with a specific set of phonological, syntactic, semantic, and interactional features, suggesting that they do not form a unified category. To the extent that the three types are defined with features from what have been assumed to be distinct modules of grammar, the present study does not support the standard idea that grammar is modular, nor that it can or even should be studied one module at a time. It has instead shown us that (pieces of) grammar may be better understood as an aggregate of various, disparate features.

We have also seen that many instances of PPEs are associated with various degrees of fixedness. Specifically, we have seen that the emotive type has grammaticized as a template to express a certain type of emotive reaction. We have also seen that the cognitive shift type involves various lexicalized expressions which reframe the previous talk, start a new theme/story, etc. The fixedness associated with PPEs seems to be best understood as traces of the constant change momentarily captured at various points in its course. That is, grammar is not a stable synchronic entity as has often been assumed, but instead very much a living entity, so that what linguists observe is simply a temporarily captured sample of the ongoing change, a process which naturally results in variation.

We have thus seen that what may be considered as a core area of syntax—word order—cannot be understood simply as a syntactic phenomenon; it is better captured as nonmodular and as reflecting on-going change. I hope this paper has added to our interactional and diachronic understanding of Japanese grammar and human language (Bybee and Hopper 2001, Hopper 1998, Ochs, Schegloff, and Thompson 1996).

References

Bybee, J., and P. Hopper. 2001. *Frequency and the Emergence of Linguistic Structure*. Amsterdam: Benjamins.

Chafe, W. 1994. *Discourse, Consciousness, and Time: The Flow and Displacement of Conscious Experience in Speaking and Writing*. Chicago: University of Chicago Press.

Ford, C. E., B. A. Fox, and S. A. Thompson. 2002. Constituency and the Grammar of Turn Increments. *The Language of Turn and Sequence*, eds. C. E. Ford, B. A. Fox, and S. A. Thompson, 14–38. Oxford: Oxford University Press.

Hopper, P. J. 1998. Emergent Grammar. *The New Psychology of Language: Cognitive and Functional Approaches to Language Structure*, vol. 1, ed. M. Tomasello, 155–75. Mahwah, N.J.: Erlbaum.

Inoue, K. 1976. *Henkei bunpō to Nihongo, jō: Tōgo kōzō o chūshin ni* [Transformational grammar and Japanese, vol. 1: Centering on syntactic structure]. Tokyo: Taishūkan.

Kim, H. 2006. Retroactive Elaboration in Korean Conversation. *Japanese/Korean Linguistics 14*, eds. T. J. Vance and K. Jones, 356–68. Stanford: CSLI. [this volume]

Koike, C. 2003. An Analysis of Increments in Japanese Conversation in Terms of

Syntax and Prosody. *Japanese/Korean Linguistics 11*, ed. P. M. Clancy, 67–80. Stanford: CSLI.

Langacker, R. W. 1987. *Foundations of Cognitive Grammar Vol. I: Theoretical Prerequisites*. Stanford: Stanford University Press.

Langacker, R. W. 1991. *Foundations of Cognitive Grammar Vol. II: Descriptive Applications*. Stanford: Stanford University Press.

Martin, S. E. 1975. *A Reference Grammar of Japanese*. New Haven: Yale University Press.

Miller, J. S., U. Miyakoya, et al. 1997. *Yomigaeru Oppekepē: 1900-nen Pari banpaku no Kawakami Ichiza*. Toshiba EMI TOCG-5432.

Mori, J. 1999. *Negotiating Agreement and Disagreement in Japanese: Connective Expressions and Turn Construction*. Amsterdam: John Benjamins.

Ochs, E., E. A. Schegloff, and S. A. Thompson, eds. 1996. *Interaction and Grammar*. Cambridge: Cambridge University Press.

Ono, T. Forthcoming. An Emotively Motivated Post-Predicate Constituent Order in a 'Strict Predicate Final' Language: Emotion and Grammar Meet in Japanese Everyday Talk. *Emotive Communication*, ed. S. Suzuki.

Ono, T., and R. Suzuki. 1992. Word Order Variability in Japanese Conversation: Motivations and Grammaticization. *Text* 12:429–45.

Ono, T., and S. A. Thompson. 2003. Japanese (*w*)*atashi/ore/boku* 'I': They're Not Just Pronouns. *Cognitive Linguistics* 14:321–47.

Sohn, H. 2004. A Grammar of *pota* 'to see': A Panchronic Perspective. Paper presented at the 14th Japanese/Korean Linguistics Conference, Tucson, Arizona.

Tanaka, H. 1999. *Turn-Taking in Japanese Conversation: A Study in Grammar in Interaction*. Amsterdam: John Benjamins.

Tanaka, H. 2001. The Implementation of Possible Cognitive Shifts in Japanese Conversation: Complementizers as Pivotal Devices. *Studies in Interactional Linguistics*, eds. M. Selting and E. Couper-Kuhlen, 81–109. Amsterdam: John Benjamins.

Wakamatsu, M., and Y. Hosoda. 2003. Sōgokōi, bunpō, yosokukanōsei: 'Teiuka' no bunseki o rei ni shite [Interaction, grammar, and projectability: Using an analysis of *teiuka* as an example]. *Goyōron Kenkyū* 5:31–43.

The Relationship Between Prosodic Features and Modal Expressions in Discourse: A Case Study of the Japanese Sentence-Final Particle *yo*

MAKI SHIMOTANI*

University of Wisconsin–Madison

1. Introduction

Prosody and grammar are often said to be pragmatically interdependent and to cooperate in expressing the speaker's feelings most directly (Bolinger 1989). In Japanese, it has been pointed out that the choice of pitch type in the terminal intonation is important specifically in using sentence-final particles such as *yo, ne*, etc. This is because they typically occur in face-to-face interaction and function as a conversational device signaling the speaker's affective attitudes (McGloin 1990, Cook 1992, Maynard 1993). For instance, *yo* in a command sentence, as in example (1) below (from Moriyama 1990: 182), is pronounced with falling pitch.[1] The combination of *yo* and falling pitch is generally said to express the speaker's affective attitudes such as reproach or irritation toward the addressee (Alfonso 1966, Moriyama 1990).

---

* I am indebted to Naomi H. McGloin and Junko Mori for providing me with invaluable comments and suggestions to improve this paper. I am also grateful to the audience at J/K14 and the following people for their insightful comments and kind help: Tim Vance, Sun-Ah Jun, Makoto Hayashi, Masatsugu Yamazaki, Mieko Kawai, Naomi F. Geyer, Yan Wang, Kasumi Kato, Beth Schewe, and Tomoyuki Kitamura. Of course, all remaining errors are my own.

[1] Here, I use ↗ for rising pitch and ↘ for falling pitch for convenience (see §3).

(1) (with gruff tone) Katteni   shiro **yo ↘/*↗**
    at-one's-discretion do
    'Suit yourself *yo* ↘/*↗'

On the other hand, it has been thought that *yo* is pronounced with rising pitch when the speaker provides a piece of information which the addressee does not have and expresses a notification or warning. Observe (2) and (3) (from Koyama 1997:105).[2]

(2) 10-pun   go ni genkan   no tokoro ni dete choodai.
    minutes later at front-door GEN place at out please
    onegai **yo ??↘/↗**
    please
    'Please be outside of the front door 10 minutes later. Please *yo* ??↘/↗'

(3) kami ni   nanika tsuitemasu **yo ??↘/↗**
    hair on something stick
    'Something is on your hair *yo* ??↘/↗'

In natural conversations, however, *yo* often occurs with falling pitch when the speaker gives the addressee new information, and it does not always express the speaker's affect (cf. example (1)). Observe (4).[3]

(4) 1.   K: ato umai tokoro tte ittara:: (1.06) ore wa ne:: ano
             other good place QT say.if   I TOP FP well
             'Speaking of other good places (to eat), I um,'

    2. → asameshi taberu no ga sukina n desu **yo↘** resu[toran de (.) wa
             breakfast eat NML NOM like NML COP   restaurant at   TOP
             'I like to eat breakfast *yo*↘, at a restaurant.'

    3.   H: [u::n
                                                        'uh-huh'

    4.   K: ie de (.) koko de shiriaru taberu koto mo ooi desu ke[do
             home at here at cereals eat NML also many COP but
             'I often eat cereals at home here, too, though.'

    5.   H: [un
                                                                 'yeah'

    6.   K: ano:: tamani   wa tabeni iku to:: (continues until line 62)
             well sometimes TOP eat go when
             'Well, sometimes when I eat out (for breakfast) . . .'

---

[2] The abbreviations used in this paper are: ACC accusative, COP copula, FP final particle, GEN genitive, NEG negative, NML nominalizer, NOM nominative, PST past tense, PSV passive, QP question particle, QT quotation, TOP topic marker.

[3] K and H live in the same dormitory, where K has lived for more than two years while H has just moved in. Here, K is telling H about his favorite restaurants around their dormitory.

In (4) K starts telling H that he likes to eat breakfast at a restaurant. In line 2, K uses *yo* with falling pitch simply to give H new information. Why did he use *yo* with falling pitch instead of rising pitch? Moreover, the speaker in line 2 does not seem to express any particular affective stance by the use of *yo* (cf. example (1)). This paper focuses on such uses of *yo* in natural conversation and investigates the relationship between the uses of *yo* and its prosodic features in Japanese discourse. The primary goals of this paper are (1) to elucidate what underlies the choice of the pitch type for *yo* in the discourse context, and (2) to examine how the uses of *yo* with these pitches are related to the speaker's affective attitude in discourse.

2. Past Studies

Yo has been analyzed as a modality marker for expressing the speaker's "insistive emphasis" on what he is saying (Alfonso 1966) and to draw the hearer's attention to the information (Uyeno 1971). Maynard (1993:208) also characterized *yo* as an interactional particle and argued that it functions to foreground information specifically when "the speaker has exclusive or more relative information accessibility and/or possessorship." These past studies are insightful; however, their analyses focus mainly on the semantic and pragmatic functions of the usages of *yo*. They lack analyses of the prosodic aspects of *yo* in the discourse context.

Moriyama (1990) claimed that the basic function of sentence-final rising pitch is to draw the addressee's attention and check his reaction; i.e., it is used when the speaker requests or waits for the addressee's reaction. Thus, rising pitch may add mild tone and be used in polite commands, as in (5) (from Moriyama 1990:182), although only falling pitch is used in strong commands (cf. example (1)).

(5) Ki   o tsukete kudasai **yo** ↘/↗
    mind ACC keep   please
    'Please be careful *yo* ↘/↗'

According to Moriyama, falling pitch indicates that the utterance does not require the addressee's reaction. Thus, it is used when the speaker ignores the addressee's reaction and conveys information with strong feeling.

Koyama (1997) argued that the choice between the pitch types depends on the degree of disagreement in informational realization between the discourse participants. He claimed that *yo* with falling pitch is used when there is a conflicting standpoint between the discourse participants. Observe (6) (from Koyama 1997:106).

(6) Hayaku koi yo↘
 quickly come
 'Come right away *yo* ↘/↗'

According to Koyama, (6) implies that, contrary to the speaker's expectation that the addressee would come soon, he did not. Thus, *yo* with falling pitch in (6) functions to emphasize the conflicting standpoint between them and express the speaker's feelings such as reproach.

In natural conversation, however, *yo* with falling pitch often occurs when there is no conflicting standpoint between the discourse participants. For example, in (4) it is difficult to suppose that K and H have a conflicting standpoint because K gives H new information in lines 2 and 3. In other words, it is unlikely that K assumes that H does not like eating breakfast at a restaurant at this point in the conversation. In my data, I found more cases of *yo* with falling pitch, like line 2 in (4), than cases of the type shown in past studies, like (1) and (6). The past studies are problematic in that their analyses are based only on constructed sentences. In the following sections, I will consider cases of *yo* found in naturally occurring conversations and examine in what discourse context and structure *yo* occurs with rising pitch or with falling pitch. Then, I will analyze what controls the choice of the pitch types for *yo* in the context of discourse and what type of pitch occurring with *yo* functions to express the speaker's affective attitudes.

3. Data and Definition of the Pitch Types of *yo*

The data used for my analysis include twelve sets of conversations (Data [a]–[l]). They include informal talk between close friends (Data [a]–[g]) and between participants who are in senior-junior relationships (Data [h]–[k]). Data [l] is a semi-informal conversation between a Japanese language instructor and two teaching assistants. The length of these conversations ranges from 4.5 to 30 minutes. All of them were digitally recorded and transcribed by myself.[4] A total of 128 cases of *yo* were found in these conversations.

In order to determine the pitch types of *yo*, I first analyzed the pitch contour of each case of *yo* using the acoustic analysis software package PRAAT. Figures 1 and 2 show acoustic records of utterances with *yo*.[5]

---

[4] The transcription conventions are based on Goodwin 1990:25, with a few exceptions, which fol-low the transcription system described in Sacks, Schegloff, and Jefferson 1974.

[5] The upper part of the figure shows waveform. The pitch contour, with a broad transcription, is below it. The shadowed part shows the pitch contour of *yo*.

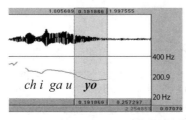
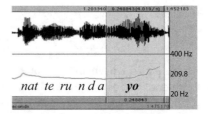

Figure 1. *Yo* with Falling Pitch   **Figure 2.** *Yo* with Rising Pitch

The pitch contour of *yo*, however, varies depending on whether the pitch level of a word immediately before *yo* is high or low, as well as on whether or not the word has an "accentual fall" immediately before *yo*.[6] In natural conversations, of course, many utterances overlap with another participant's utterances, which often makes it difficult to determine pitch contours. Noises, laughter, whispered utterances, etc., can also make it difficult to determine the pitch contour of *yo*. In my data, 31 of 128 cases did not show a clear pitch trace, although they were audible. For those cases, I asked ten native speakers of Japanese to listen to each segment of conversation where an unclear case of *yo* occurred and auditorily judge whether the pitch was rising, falling, or level.[7] I then excluded 22 cases whose auditory pitch was judged differently by more than three listeners. Thus, I used a total of 106 cases in my analysis. In many of these cases it was unclear from the acoustic analysis whether there was a small rise or a level pitch, and these cases were auditorily perceived by the listeners as ambiguous between rising and level pitch. Therefore, combining rising and level pitch into one type, I categorized *yo* prosodically into two types: *yo*[+fall] and *yo*[−fall].[8] The definitions of these pitch types are as follows.

yo[+fall] shows a pitch lower than that of the word immediately before *yo*, although the pitch difference may be small.

yo[−fall] shows a pitch not lower than that of the word immediately before *yo*, i.e., the pitch on *yo* may be the same as or higher than that of the word immediately before *yo*.

4. The [+fall] and [−fall] Pitches in the Context of Discourse

Table 1 shows the frequencies of *yo*[+fall] and *yo*[−fall] in my conversational data ([a]–[l]). In the 106 total cases, *yo*[+fall] (78 cases) was more than twice as frequent as *yo*[−fall] (28 cases).

---

[6] See Kindaichi (1967) for the pitch accent pattern of the Tokyo dialect of Japanese.

[7] All participants in this experiment are speakers of the Tokyo dialect of Japanese.

[8] Although I cannot provide more specific pitch contours of *yo* in this paper due to space limitations, more detailed acoustic analysis will be necessary in my future studies.

Data	a	b	c	d	e	f	g	h	i	j	k	l	Total
yo[+fall]	10	3	2	2	9	8	19	3	7	6	6	3	78 (73.6%)
yo[−fall]	2	3	0	1	4	1	2	0	4	3	3	5	28 (26.4%)
Total	12	6	2	3	13	9	21	3	11	9	9	8	106 (100%)

Table 1. Frequencies of yo[+fall] and yo[−fall] in Natural Conversation

In what follows, I will discuss my analysis of the discourse structures in which yo[+fall] and yo[−fall] occur. The pitches that occur in more typical discourse structures are hereafter referred to as unmarked cases of yo[±fall] and, and those that occur in less typical discourse structures as marked cases of yo[±fall]. Table 2 shows the frequencies of unmarked and marked cases.

	Data	a	b	c	d	e	f	g	h	i	j	k	l	Total
Unmarked yo (84 cases)	[+fall]	6	2	2	2	5	5	15	3	6	5	6	3	60 (56.6%)
	[−fall]	2	2	0	1	4	0	2	0	3	3	2	5	24 (22.6%)
Marked yo (22 cases)	[+fall]	4	1	0	0	4	3	4	0	1	1	0	0	18 (17.0%)
	[−fall]	0	1	0	0	0	1	0	0	1	0	1	0	4 (3.8%)
	Total	12	6	2	3	13	9	21	3	11	9	9	8	106 (100%)

Table 2. Unmarked vs. Marked Cases of yo[+fall] and yo[−fall]

4.1. Unmarked Cases of yo[+fall] and yo[−fall]

Unmarked cases of yo[+fall] occur in a discourse context in which the speaker knows or assumes that he/she shares a given piece of information with the addressee. Observe (7).[9]

(7) 1. S: mata semerareru no wakatten noni (.) iku n   da ne:: (0.3)
           again taunt.PSV NML know although go NML COP FP

    2.   isshoni:: =e- [dare] to   itte-ta no?
            together um   who with go-PST QP

            'Although (K) knew that he would be taunted again, he went (with
            another girl). Well, who did he go with?'

    3. Y: °kondo° (hh) kiku? so- (sh) atete mite kudasai [eh eh eh
            this.time   listen   guess try   please
            'This time you wanna know? Guess who, please.'

    4. S: [shitteru hito? atashi.
                                                 know person   I
            'Is she the one I know?'

---

[9] Here, S and Y are talking about their male friend K, who likes to flirt with girls (Data [j]).

5.   (0.66)

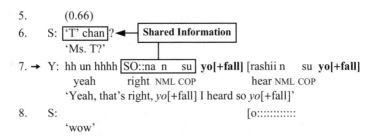

6.   S: 'T' chan ? ◄— Shared Information
       'Ms. T?'

7. → Y: hh un hhhh SO::na n su **yo[+fall]** [rashii n su **yo[+fall]**
           yeah   right NML COP   hear NML COP
           'Yeah, that's right, *yo*[+fall] I heard so *yo*[+fall]'

8.   S: [o::::::::::::
       'wow'

In line 3, knowing who went out with K, Y asks S to guess who she was. After S correctly guesses, Y confirms that the information has been shared with S in line 7. In this example the speaker uses *yo*[+fall] is used to show his confirmation of or agreement on shared information with the addressee.

Example (8) (from Data [b]) represents another case of *yo*[+fall]. Here, it is used when the speaker expects the addressee to share some information as background in order to project her turn and initiate her talk.

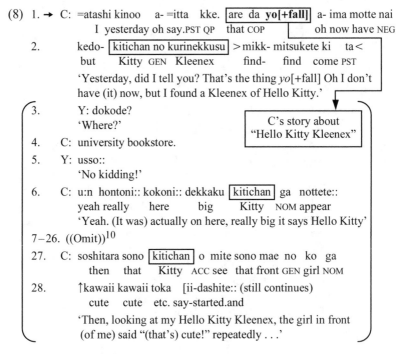

(8) 1. → C: =atashi kinoo   a- =itta   kke. are da **yo[+fall]** a- ima motte nai
          I yesterday oh say.PST QP that COP   oh now have NEG

  2.   kedo- kitichan no kurinekkusu >mikk- mitsukete ki ta<
          but   Kitty GEN Kleenex   find-   find   come PST
          'Yesterday, did I tell you? That's the thing *yo*[+fall] Oh I don't have (it) now, but I found a Kleenex of Hello Kitty.'

  3.   Y: dokode?
         'Where?'

                                 C's story about
                            "Hello Kitty Kleenex"
  4.   C: university bookstore.

  5.   Y: usso::
         'No kidding!'

  6.   C: u:n hontoni:: kokoni:: dekkaku kitichan ga nottete::
         yeah really   here   big   Kitty NOM appear
         'Yeah. (It was) actually on here, really big it says Hello Kitty'

 7–26. ((Omit))[10]

 27.   C: soshitara sono kitichan o mite sono mae no ko ga
         then   that   Kitty ACC see that front GEN girl NOM

 28.   ↑kawaii kawaii toka [ii-dashite:: (still continues)
         cute   cute   etc. say-started.and
         'Then, looking at my Hello Kitty Kleenex, the girl in front (of me) said "(that's) cute!" repeatedly . . .'

After a minor topic shift in the preceding context, C uses *yo*[+fall] in line 1,

---

[10] Lines 7–26 are omitted due to limited space. Here, C mainly talks about what happened in her Italian class, where she first had to use her favorite Hello Kitty Kleenex.

although no information is yet shared between C and Y at this point. This is because, by expecting that Y would share some background about C's forthcoming story, C attempts to project her turn and initiate telling a story. *Yo*[+fall] is often used in such a "pre-story-telling" discourse structure, in which assumedly shared background knowledge is necessary.[11]

Now, let us go back and consider the use of *yo*[+fall] in line 2 in (4), which appears above in the introduction. Here, *yo*[+fall] performs a "pre-story-telling" function; K attempts to initiate his story, which continues until line 62, by providing the background information that H must share to understand K's forthcoming story. This account of the use of *yo*[+fall] is further supported by the fact that it typically cooccurs with other grammatical expressions that indicate information shared (or mutually understood) between the speaker and the addressee, including the marker of known information *ndesu* (line 2 in (4), line 7 in (7)), the anaphoric expression *so::* (line 7 in (7)), and the demonstrative pronoun *are* (line 1 in (8)).[12] It is thus the existence of shared (or assumedly shared) information and/or "mutual understanding" between the discourse participants that *yo*[+fall] functions to mark.

Unmarked cases of *yo*[−fall], on the other hand, occur in a discourse structure in which the speaker knows or assumes that there is no shared information with the addressee. That is, as suggested in the previous studies, they occur when the speaker gives new information to the addressee. Thus, unmarked *yo*[−fall] typically occurs in the second member of an adjacency pair consisting of a question (or confirmation) and its answer, as in (9).[13]

(9) 1.   Y: demo masaka tsukiau to wa omowa-nakat-ta n   da yone.
              but   indeed date QT TOP think-NEG-PST NML COP FP
              'But I really didn't expect they would start to date.'

     2.   (2.3)

     3.   H: demo masaka hontoni- sh- e::to 'S₁' toka shitteru no?
              but   indeed really-   um   etc. know QP
              'But I really- sh- um does S₁ know about that?'

     4.   (0.69)

     5. → Y: 'M'san wa shitteru tsu tte-ta **yo[−fall]**
              Mr. TOP know   QT say-PST
              'Mr. M knows, he said *yo*[−fall]'

---

[11] See Goodwin 1984 for detailed analysis of sequential organization of pre-story-telling.

[12] *N(o)desu* functions to "mark a certain piece of information as known in the context of discourse" (McGloin 1981:152). Cataphoric uses of the demonstrative *are* function to "solicit the addressee's alignment" to "project a prospective specification of its referent in the subsequent talk" (Hayashi 2004:1335).

[13] Y and H are talking about their friends, who have started dating recently (Data [e]).

6.   H: a::. tte koto wa 'S₂' san   mo shitteru.
            oh QT NML TOP   Ms. also   know
            'Oh, I see. That means Ms. S₂ also knows (about that, correct).'

7.   (1.5)

8. → Y: 'S₂' san wa shira-nakat-ta mitai da **yo[−fall]**
            Ms. TOP know-NEG-PST seem COP
            'It seems that Ms. 'S₂' didn't know *yo*[−fall]'

The utterances of H and Y in lines 3/5 and 6/8 form adjacency pairs consisting of question/answer and confirmation/answer, respectively. In this context, Y can know or assume from H's utterances that there is an informational gap between them. Thus, in line 5 and line 9, by responding to H with the use of *yo*[−fall], Y tries to fill in the informational gap.

Another typical case in which this type of *yo*[−fall] is used is when the speaker suddenly inserts a piece of information which is not known to the addressee to supplement his/her statement. Observe (10).[14]

(10) 1.   H: daka- kekkyoku kinoo (..) itte   nan-ji   goro   made yatte-ta no?
               so   finally yesterday   go what-time around until   do-PST QP
               'So, yesterday you went to (..), till what time did you have (a party there)?'

     2.   (1.6)

     3.   Y: su- e- juuichi-ji. (sniff)
               '(until) eleven o'clock.'

     4.   H: naga-
               '(That's) long'

     5. → Y: (sniff) (0.6) =demo   hachi-ji-han   kara da **yo[−fall]**
               but eight-o'clock-half from COP
               'But (that was) from eight thirty *yo*[−fall]'

     6.   (0.43)

     7.   H: ni-jikan-han   mo   i-ta   no?
               two-hours-half even stay-PST QP
               'You were (there) for two and half hours (that long)?'

In line 1, H asks until what time Y was at the party, and Y answers *juuichi-ji* in line 3. Hearing H's complaint *naga-* in line 4, Y hastily inserts more information (=*demo* . . .) with *yo*[−fall] in line 5 to supplement her statement in line 3 because H does not know what time the party started.

As these examples show, in order to have an effectual conversation, it is necessary for the speaker to know or assume how much information is

---

[14] In this conversation, H complains to his girlfriend Y about the fact that she went to a party without him on the previous night (Data [e]).

shared or mutually understood with the addressee. Based on such knowledge or assumptions, information is exchanged (Levinson 1983, Katagiri 1997). *Yo*[−fall] is used based on the speaker's knowledge or assumption that a piece of information is not shared with the addressee. It is hence a lack of shared information that *yo*[−fall] marks. Therefore, it typically functions to offer new information to the addressee in order to develop mutual understanding for an effectual conversation.

Considering the unmarked cases of *yo*[+fall] and *yo*[−fall] discussed above, I find that they both occur in an information-oriented discourse context where an existence or lack of shared information is marked.

4.2. Marked Cases of *yo*[+fall] and *yo*[−fall]

Marked cases of *yo*[±fall], as opposed to unmarked cases, occur in more affect-oriented discourse, in which the speaker reacts by showing affect toward the addressee's conflicting viewpoint observed in the previous context. First, observe the marked case of *yo*[+fall] in (11).[15]

(11) 1. Y: eigo   de mo onnaji koto an   no kane.
         English in also same thing exist NML FP
         'I wonder if there are the same things (= particles) in English'

     2.   (1.2)

     3. Y: demo eigo   tte 'ne' toka nai jan.
            but English QT   etc NEG TAG
            'But English doesn't have an expression like *ne*, does it'

     4. H: e-?   an ja   nai no? °nanka°
            what exist COP NEG QP   um
            'what? I guess it does.'

     5. → Y: =nai **yo [+fall]** zettai.
            NEG   definitely
            'No, it doesn't *yo*[+fall] Definitely.'

In (11), it is obvious that Y knows that H realizes their opposing opinions. This is because, hearing Y's opinion that English does not have such an expression as *ne* in line 3, H contradicted it in line 4. Thus, *yo*[+fall] here is used to further emphasize Y's opposing opinion and functions to express Y's dogmatic attitude.

Marked cases of *yo*[−fall] also occur when the discourse participants have conflicting viewpoints, and it expresses the speaker's affect. *Yo*[+fall] is used when the speaker knows or assumes that the addressee realizes that their opinions are conflicting. *Yo*[−fall], on the other hand, is used when the speaker knows or assumes that the addressee does not realize the conflict. Compare (12) (from Data [i]) with (11) above.

---

[15] Y and H are talking about the differences between English and Japanese (Data [e]).

(12) 1.   (2.32)

   2. K: ⌈sore ga   tabehoodai⌉ deshi-ta (.) ato wa::
           that NOM all.you.can.eat COP-PST others TOP
           'That's it for the all-you-can-eat restaurants. Others are::'

   3.   (1.3)

   4. K: hiru   dake ⌈tabehoodai⌉ tte yuu:: (0.59) ano[:::
           afternoon only all-you-can-eat QT say   um
           '(There's a place which is) all-you-can-eat during lunch time only.'

   5. H: [°u:::n°
                                                  'yeah'

   6. K: indo-ryoori-ya   ga:::=
           Indian-cuisine-restaurant NOM
           '(There is an) Indian food restaurant'

   7. → H: =a- ⌈demo- tabehoodai   ja naku-temo juubun⌉ da °yo°[−fall]
           um   but all-you-can-eat COP NEG-even.if enough COP
           'But it does not have to be all-you-can restaurants yo[−fall].'

   8. K: °un. ma::°
           'yeah, well'

   9.   (1.1)

   10. K: °ato umai tokoro tte ittara::° (1.06) ore wa ne:: ano
           'Speaking of other good places (to eat), I um'
           (continues to line 2 in (4) above)

In this segment, K has been telling H about all-you-can-eat restaurants in the preceding context. After a long pause in line 1, K seems to close his talk about this topic in line 2. Unexpectedly, however, he again starts talking about the same topic in line 4, and then H interrupts K in line 7. That is, there is a mismatching view between K and H about the topic of their conversation. Hence, yo[−fall] here functions to alert K to H's conflicting viewpoint and to express H's affective attitudes such as discomfort. Interestingly, if yo[+fall] were used here, it would be odd because it would sound as if H were reproaching K for talking repetitiously despite knowing of H's discomfort. Because of this function, marked cases of yo[+fall] as well as yo[−fall] can be face threatening (Brown and Levinson 1987). Cases of yo[−fall] can be particularly face threatening because the more clearly its rising pitch is uttered, the more directly it reflects the speaker's conflicting viewpoint with the addressee. It is thus very rare and tends to be avoided in natural conversation. Therefore, when it is used, it tends to be whispery, as in line7, and its pitch is often a small rise or level in order to mitigate a possible face-threatening act.

In my data, marked cases of yo[−fall] are rare regardless of the formality of conversation and of the relationship between the speaker and the addressee. Most marked cases of *yo*[+fall], however, can be observed in casual conversations between close friends (see Data [a]–[g] and [h]–[l] in Table 2). Furthermore, it is significant that *yo*[−fall] is much less frequent than *yo*[+fall] overall. This fact implies that the use of *yo*[−fall] has more face-threatening characteristics because it indicates the addressee's lack of knowledge about a piece of information or lack of realization of the speaker's viewpoint/opinion.

5. Concluding Remarks

In this paper, I have examined what underlies the choice between *yo*[+fall] and *yo*[−fall], in what discourse structures they tend to occur, and how they are related with to the speaker's affective attitudes. In particular, I have argued that **an existence (or assumed existence) of mutual understanding (or realization) between the discourse participants** underlies the use of *yo*[+fall], whereas **a lack of "mutual understanding (or realization)" as to shared information as well as viewpoints/opinions** underlies the use of *yo*[−fall]. More specifically, unmarked cases of *yo*[±fall] occur in information-oriented discourse where the speaker indicates shared (or assumedly shared) information with the addressee and/or gives the addressee new information. Marked cases of *yo*[±fall], on the other hand, occur in affect-oriented discourse in which there are conflicting viewpoints/opinions between the discourse participants. It is thus marked cases of *yo*[±fall] that strongly relate to the speaker's affective attitudes and therefore tend to be face threatening and avoided in natural conversation.

References

Alfonso, A. 1966. *Japanese Language Patterns: A Structural Approach*, vol. 2. Tokyo: Sophia University.

Bolinger, D. 1986. *Intonation and Its Parts: Melody in Spoken English*. Stanford: Stanford University Press.

Brown, P., and S. Levinson. 1987. *Politeness: Some Universals of Language Usage*. Cambridge: Cambridge University Press.

Cook, H. M. 1992. Meanings of Non-referential Indexes: A Case Study of the Japanese Sentence-Final Particle *ne*. *Text* 12(4):507–39.

Goodwin, C. 1984. Notes on Story Structure and the Organization of Participation. *Structures of Social Action*, ed. M. Atkinson and J. Heritage, 225–46. Cambridge: Cambridge University Press.

Goodwin, M. H. 1990. *He-Said-She-Said: Talk as Social Organization among Black Children*. Bloomington: Indiana University Press.

Hayashi, M. 2004. Projection and Grammar: Notes on the "Action-Projecting" Use of the Distal Demonstrative *are* in Japanese. *Journal of Pragmatics* 36:1337–74.

Katagiri, Y. 1997. Japanese Sentence-Final Particles and Utterance-Final Intonation, *Speech and Grammar 1*, ed. Spoken Language Working Group, 235–56. Tokyo: Kuroshio.

Koyama, T. 1997. Sentence-Final Particles and Final Intonation in Japanese. *Speech and Grammar 1*, ed. Spoken Language Working Group, 97–119. Tokyo: Kuroshio.

Kindaichi, H. 1967. *Nihongo on'in no kenkyū*: Tokyo: Tōkyōdō.

Levinson, S. 1983. *Pragmatics*. Cambridge: Cambridge University Press.

Maynard, S. 1993. *Discourse Modality: Subjectivity, Emotion and Voice in the Japanese Language*. Philadelphia: John Benjamins.

McGloin, N. H. 1981. Discourse Functions of No Desu. *Papers from the Middlebury Symposium on Japanese Discourse Analysis*, ed. S. Makino, 151–76. Urbana, Ill.: Toyota Foundation.

McGloin, N. H. 1990. Sex Differences and Sentence-Final Particles. *Aspects of Japanese Women's Language*, eds. S. Ide and N. H. McGloin, 23–41. Tokyo: Kuroshio.

Moriyama, T. 1990. Bun no imi to intonēshon, *Kōza Nihongo to Nihongo kyōiku I: Nihongogaku yōsetsu*, ed. Y. Miyaji, 172–96. Tokyo: Meiji Shoin.

Sacks, H., E. Schegloff, and G. Jefferson. 1974. A Simplest Systematics for the Organization of Turn-taking Conversation. *Language* 50:696–735.

Uyeno, T. 1971. A Study of Japanese Modality: A Performative Analysis of Sentence Particles. Doctoral dissertation, University of Michigan.

Obliqueness and Postpositional Marking in Japanese

TOMOKO TAKEDA*
University of Oregon

1. Introduction

Thompson (1997) discusses the distinction between core and oblique argu-ments in terms of their roles. She points out that a number of analysts have proposed a distinction between "syntactic" and "semantic" nominal mark-ing, where "syntactic" marking is generally used for A, S, or O (core argu-ments) with no direct association with any semantic role, and "semantic" marking refers to those with direct association with a semantic role (oblique arguments), such as Instrumental, Goal, Dative, and Locative. As opposed to the discrete core-oblique distinction, Thompson takes the view that these argument roles are to be classified as a **continuum** of verbal dependents, from those that are required by the majority of verbs (most core) to those that occur most frequently independently of verb semantics (most oblique). Thompson analyzes a small set of English conversation data to examine the information flow of core and oblique arguments employing three parame-

* I would like to express my sincere gratitude to Dr. Noriko Fujii, who read an earlier draft and offered helpful comments. I particularly appreciate valuable comments from Dr. Paula Ra-detzky in the preparation of this paper. I also thank Miyoko Nakajima, Yuka Matsugu, and Brent Wright for their help and input.

ters: **Identifiability**, **Activation State**, and **Tracking State**. For Identifiability, Thompson (1997:66) states that "an identifiable NP is one whose referent the speaker assumes the listener can identify" and "a Non-Identifiable NP is one whose referent the speaker assumes that the listener is not able to identify." In English, the definite article generally marks Identifiability. As for Activation State, Thompson adopts Chafe's (1987, 1994) "Given" and "New". According to Chafe, Given information is what the speaker assumes to be already active in the hearer's mind, whereas New information is in an inactive state and the speaker assumes that it has to be newly activated in the hearer's mind. Regarding Tracking State, an NP is identified as **tracking** if "the speaker is judged to be mentioning it for the purpose of either introducing it for further tracking or continued tracking of earlier mention information" (Thompson 1997:69). Based on this analysis, Thompson proposes that the core-oblique distinction can be explained as follows: Cores (A, S and O), are predicted to show tendencies towards being Given, Identifiable, and Tracking, while obliques are much less likely to be Given, Identifiable, and Tracking. Thompson further hypothesizes this core-oblique distinction's universality in all languages.

There are languages, including Japanese, which possess core-marking and oblique-marking adpositions. The difference between these two types of postpositions is generally explained in terms of their relationship to the verb and semantics. Blake (2001) states that core-marking postpositions are those that mark dependent nouns for the type of relationship they bear to the head. The head of the clause is the verb, since it determines what dependents may be present. On the other hand, oblique-marking postpositions mark those dependents that are not licensed by the verb. They convey such semantic roles as location and time. Tsujimura (1996) uses two terms, "case particles" and "postpositions", to refer to these core- and oblique-marking postpositions in Japanese. She says that postpositions in Japanese are counterparts of English prepositions and that case particles include nominative *ga*, accusative *o*, dative *ni* and genitive *no*, as well as the topic marker *wa*. Tsujimura (1996:135) asserts that "while case particles can often be absent in a sentence particularly under a casual speech situation, postpositions must be present in order to retain their meanings." This probably explains why the vast majority of studies that examine the occurrence/non-occurrence patterns of postpositions (both case particles and postpositions in Tsujimura's term) in Japanese deal with core-marking postpositions (e.g. Tsutsui 1984, Mori and Givón 1987, Masunaga 1988, Matsuda 1996, Ono, Thompson, and Suzuki 2000, Fujii and Ono 2000).

The present study analyzes oblique arguments in Japanese conversations to examine how they interact with the core-oblique continuum. Specifically, the study investigates whether different degrees of obliqueness among various oblique arguments can be found in the data. Following Thompson (1997), the three parameters (Identifiability, Activation State, and Tracking State) are employed to measure information flow. In addition to the investigation of information flow patterns, the present study examines oblique arguments in conversational Japanese in terms of the occurrence/ non-occurrence pattern of their postpositions for its possible interaction with the continuum of obliqueness.

2. Data and Methodology

2.1. Data

The data consists of five tape-recorded spontaneous dyadic conversations between friends, totaling approximately eighty minutes. Each conversation consists of 900 intonation units, and the length varies from ten to fifteen minutes. The data consists of conversations involving only standard dialect speakers in order to avoid possible effects of particular occurrence/non-occurrence patterns of postpositions unique to specific non-standard dialects (e.g. Nitta 1992, Inoue 1992).

2.1. Coding

First, all the oblique markers are identified in terms of their semantics (in-strument, location of action, etc.). To measure the degree of obliqueness, all the oblique arguments were then examined for their information flow in terms of the three parameters of Identifiability, Activation State, and Track-ing State. All three information types—Given, Accessible, and New—were adopted from Chafe (1987, 1994) for a finer distinction. As mentioned ear-lier, Given information is what the speaker assumes to be already active in the hearer's mind, whereas New information is in an inactive state and the speaker assumes that it has to be newly activated in the hearer's mind. The third information type, *Accessible* information, refers to concepts which are in a semi-active state and are assumed by the speaker to be accessible in the hearer's mind. Chafe (1987:86) further specifies the following three dis-course factors for an activated referent that may be Accessible rather than New. It may be a referent that (a) was active at an earlier time in the dis-course, (b) is directly associated with an idea that is or was active in the discourse, or (c) is associated with the nonlinguistic environment of the conversation. Chafe (1987:29) elaborates on the Accessible concept of (b) in terms of a "schema"—a cluster of interrelated expectations. That is, con-cepts may become semi-active when they belong to the set of expectations associated with a schema. In addition to these three parameters, the occur-rence and non-occurrence of the postpositional markings of the oblique ar-guments were examined.

3. Identified Oblique Markers

The following three oblique marking postpositions and sixteen semantically-based argument roles are identified in the data.[1]

NI – *ni* marks NPs that express Goal, Location of Existence, Result, Recipient, Purpose, Agent, Base for Frequency, Point of Reference, or Time.

DE – *de* marks NPs that express Location of Action, Means, General Location, or Cause.

KARA – *kara* marks NPs that express Starting Point (including Source).

MADE – *made* marks NPs that express Ending Point.

TO – *to* marks NPs that express an Associative Argument.

Examples of all sixteen argument roles are given below.

(1) Goal (*ni*)
    Natsuyasumi Nihon **ni** kaetta no.
    'I went back to Japan during the summer vacation.'

(2) Location of Existence (*ni*)
    Atashi wa kyooshitsu **ni** itakatta no.
    'I wanted to stay in the classroom.'

(3) Result (*ni*)
    Shingoo aka **ni** natta yo.
    'The traffic signal turned to red.'

(4) Recipient (*ni*)
    Kotchi wa otagai **ni** purezento suru n da yo ne?
    'Here, they give presents to each other, right?'

(5) Purpose (*ni*)
    Kinoo kaimono **ni** itta?
    'Did you go shopping yesterday?'

(6) Agent (*ni*)
    Sensee **ni** soo iwarete sa.
    'I was told so by the teacher.'

(7) Base for Frequency (*ni*)
    Isshuukan **ni** ikkai sentaku suru.
    'I do laundry once a week.'

---

[1] The classifications are based on Iori et al. 2000 and Kabata and Rice 1997.

(8) Point of Reference (*ni*)
Watashi no uchi wa gakkoo **ni** chikai.
'My house is close to the school.'

(9) Time (*ni*)
Nan-ji **ni** okita?
'What time did you wake up?'

(10) Location of Action (*de*)
Sakki sutaa-kafe **de** benkyoo shiteta.
'I was studying at a Star café a little while ago.'

(11) Means (*de*)
Kesa wa jitensha **de** gakkoo ni kita.
'I came to school by bicycle this morning.'

(12) General Location (*de*)
Kono resutoran kororado **de** wa yuumee na n da tte.
'I heard that this restaurant is famous in Corolado.'

(13) Cause (*de*)
Byooki **de** gakkoo o yasunda.
'I didn't go to school because of being sick.'

(14) Starting Point (*kara*) and Ending Point (*made*)
Mainichi uchi **kara** gakkoo **made** aruku.
'I walk from my house to the school every day.'

(15) Associative Argument (*to*)
Yuki-chan **to** ryokoo suru tsumori na n da.
'I am planning on going on a trip with Yuki-chan.'

4. Results and Discussion

4.1. Activation State

Table 1 shows the activation states of the oblique arguments in the data.

New	Accessible	Given
131 (56%)	54 (23%)	50 (21%)

Table 1. Overall Activation States (Total: 235)

Of a total 235 oblique arguments, only 21% (50/235) are Given, and more than half of them carry New information (131/235 = 56%). This confirms one of the characteristics of oblique arguments proposed by Thompson (1997), namely, that oblique arguments rarely code Given information.

Closer examination of each oblique semantic role suggests that in all but one semantic role, more than half code Non-Active information and are thus consistent with Thompson's argument. The semantic role which does not follow this tendency is Cause (marked by *de*), all three instances of which code Given information. Due to the low frequency, it is hard to determine what accounts for this phenomenon.

4.2. Activation State and Oblique Marking

By examining the postpositional marking of the oblique arguments, it is found that all but four oblique types **always** appear marked by their postpositions. The four oblique types which appear both marked and unmarked are Goal, Location of Existence, Base for Frequency, and Time. Note that they are all marked by the postposition *ni*, if marked. I further examined the Activation State of these three semantic roles separately for those marked and those unmarked. In Table 2 below, + and − in the postposition column indicate the occurrence and non-occurrence of the postposition *ni* with each semantic role.

	Postposition	New	Accessible	Given	Total
Goal	+	14	10	9	33
	−	**13**	**6**	**3**	22
Location of Existence	+	27	9	9	45
	−	**1**	**2**	**0**	3
Base for Frequency	+	3	0	0	3
	−	**1**	**0**	**0**	1
Time	+	10	2	0	12
	−	**1**	**1**	**0**	2

Table 2. Activation State of Marked and Unmarked Obliques for *ni*

We can see from Table 2 that unmarked NPs occur in New arguments of all four semantic role types. Moreover, a particularly high frequency of unmarked Goal NPs is observed, especially among New arguments (13/27 = 48%). This correlates with the tendencies found by Maruyama (1996) and Masuda (2000).

4.3. Identifiability and Tracking State

In order to verify Thompson's proposal that oblique arguments are much less likely to be Identifiable and Tracking, all oblique arguments in the data were examined for their Identifiability and Tracking State. Table 3 shows the results.

| Identifiability | Identifiable | 120 (51%) |
| | Non-Identifiable | 115 (49%) |

| Tracking State | Tracking | 102 (43%) |
| | Non-Tracking | 133 (57%) |

Table 3. Identifiability and Tracking State of All Obliques

There is no strong tendency for oblique arguments to be either Identifiable or Non-Identifiable or to be either Tracking or Non-Tracking. The results therefore do not confirm Thompson's universal in terms of Identifiability and Tracking State.

In summary, of the three parameters adopted from Thompson (1997), only Activation State of oblique arguments in my Japanese conversation data shows an information flow pattern similar to that observed in Thompson's English conversation data. Regarding postpositional marking, of the four semantic roles that appear in both marked and unmarked forms, Goal NPs show the highest ratio of unmarked instances. That is, the pattern of postposition marking distinguishes Goal NPs from other oblique arguments, suggesting that the locus of Goal NPs on the continuum of obliqueness is at a different point from other oblique arguments. The rest of the discussion below will focus on the properties of Goal NPs which account for their distinct status among oblique arguments.

5. Goal NPs

In this final section, Goal NPs are closely examined in terms of Identifiability, Tracking State, and postpositional marking, as well as their predicate types and referential forms. The last two additional aspects are adopted from previous studies (Matsuda 1996, Fujii and Ono 2000) which investigate core arguments and their postpositional marking patterns.

5.1. Identifiability and Tracking State

Table 4 below shows the results of the examination of all Goal NPs, both marked and unmarked, in terms of their Identifiability and Tracking State.

		Marked	Unmarked	Total
Identifiability	Identifiable	22	10	32
	Non-Identifiable	11	12	23
Tracking State	Tracking	16	10	26
	Non-Tracking	17	12	29

Table 4. Identifiability and Tracking State of Goal NPs

Overall, Goal NPs have a weak tendency to be Identifiable (32/55 =

58%), which goes against Thompson's proposal. Regarding Tracking State, no strong tendency is observed. In looking at the possible interaction between the postpositional marking of Goal NPs and their Identifiability or Tracking State, I found no observable correlation except that marked Goal NPs are more likely to be Identifiable (22/33 = 67%). This tendency of marked Goal NPs is strongly in opposition to Thompson's proposal.

5.2. Predicate Types

Goal NPs were further analyzed in terms of predicate types. This examination reveals the following.

1. Goal NPs take a limited set of verbs. Specifically, 85% (47/55) of predicates of Goal NPs in the data consist of *iku* 'to go', *kaeru* 'to return', and *kuru* 'to come.' (The remaining verbs include *tobasareru* 'to be transferred', *tsurete iku* 'to take someone along', and *kayou* 'to commute'.)
2. An especially strong relationship is observed between Goal NPs and *iku* 'to go', which accounts for 55% (30/55) of all predicates of Goal NPs.
3. In relation to the occurrence or non-occurrence of postpositions, 82% of unmarked Goal NPs (18/22) occur with *iku*. This strong relationship between Goal NPs and *iku* is suggested by Maruyama (1996) and Masuda (2000) as well.

The last observation indicates that the stronger the co-occurrence relationship between the Goal NP and a verb, the more likely the Goal NP is to be unmarked.

5.3. Referential Forms of Unmarked Goal NPs

Examination of referential forms suggests that there are two forms that often represent unmarked Goal NPs. 36% (8/22) are **interrogative pronouns**, as in (16) below.[2]

(16) M: **dokka** itta.   M: 'I went **somewhere**.
     ...sore mo kurai kara,   And even worse it was dark, so
     sara ni yoku wakanne=   I don't know
     doko itta no ka.   **where** I went.'

23% (5/22) unmarked Goal NPs are represented by **locational demonstratives**, as in (17) below.

(17) C: **kotchi** ichinenkan kite=,   C: 'I was **here** for a year, and went
     Nihon ni kaetta no ne   back to Japan.'

---

[2] The transcription conventions in (16) and (17) are based on Du Bois et al. 1992: final (.), continuing (,), medium pause (...), short pause (..), lengthening (=), speech overlap ([ ]).

The same tendencies are observed in the non-occurrence of nominative *ga* in Ono, Thompson, and Suzuki 2000, accusative *o* in Fujii and Ono 2000, and the Goal marker *ni* in Masuda 2000. Fujii and Ono (2000) argue that NPs marked by *o* are salient in either a local or global discourse context, or have referents that are difficult to identify. In other words, object NPs that are already "activated" or do not need to be "activated" (non-salient) are left unmarked. Specifically, they state that demonstratives tend to be unmarked because they encode already "activated" entities. Regarding interrogative pronouns unmarked by *o*, they explain that they refer to "non-salient" entities and thus do not need to be "activated". Ono, Thompson and Suzuki (2000) investigate nominative *ga* in spontaneous conversations and claim that NPs that convey "shared" or "predictable" information tend to be unmarked. The similarity between the non-occurrence of nominative *ga* and accusative *o* and the non-occurrence of goal-marking *ni* appears to be another property that indicates the divergence of Goal NP from other oblique arguments and its proximity to core arguments.

6. Conclusion

In this paper, I have analyzed oblique arguments in Japanese conversation data in order to examine how they interact with Thompson's (1997) continuum core-oblique distinction. Of the three parameters adopted from Thompson, my Japanese conversation data shows a similar information flow pattern to her English data in terms of Activation State, but not Identifiability or Tracking. Among all the oblique arguments in the data, Goal NPs exhibit several properties that distinguish them from other obliques. First, they show a strong relationship with a certain set of verbs, namely, *iku* 'to go', *kuru* 'to come', and *kaeru* 'to return', whereas other oblique arguments do not show any such strong relationships with particular verbs. Goal NPs also display the following characteristics similar to those observed among core arguments: (1) they are likely to be Identifiable, and (2) they show an especially high ratio of unmarked instances (as shown in Table 2). In addition, many unmarked Goal NPs are expressed by interrogative pronouns and locational pronouns, which tend to be unmarked by accusative *o* and nominative *ga* as well. These findings suggest that Goal NPs have properties that distinguish them among oblique arguments and which locate them closer to core arguments on the core-oblique continuum.

References

Blake, B. J. 2001. *Case*. 2nd ed. Cambridge: Cambridge University Press.

Chafe, W. 1987. Cognitive Constraints on Information Flow. *Typological Studies in Language*, vol. 11, ed. R. Tomlin, 21–51. Amsterdam: John Benjamins.

Chafe, W. 1994. *Discourse, Consciousness and Time: The Flow and Displacement of Conscious Experience in Speaking and Writing*. Chicago: University of Chicago Press.

Du Bois, J. W., S. Schuetze-Coburn, D. Paolino, and S. Cumming. 1992. Discourse Transcription. *Santa Barbara Papers in Linguistics* 4:1–225.

Fujii, N., and T. Ono. 2000. The Occurrence and Non-occurrence of the Japanese Direct Object Marker *o* in Conversation. *Studies in Language* 24(1):1–39.

Inoue, F. 1992. Shakaigengogaku to hōgenbunpō [Sociolinguistics and dialect grammar]. *Nihongogaku* 11(6):94–105.

Iori, I., K. Nakanishi, S. Takanashi, and T. Yamada 2000. *Nihongo bunpō handobukku* [A handbook of Japanese grammar]. Tokyo: Three A Network.

Kabata, K., and S. Rice, 1997. Japanese *ni*: The Particulars of a Somewhat Contradictory Particle. *Lexical and Semantical Constructions and the Construction of Meaning*, eds. M. Verspoor, K. D. Lee, and E. Sweetser, 107–27. Amsterdam: John Benjamins.

Maruyama, N. 1996. Hanashikotoba ni okeru mujoshi kakuseibun no kaku [Functions of case particle ellipsis in spoken language]. *Mathematical Linguistics* 9(8): 365–80.

Masuda, K. 2000. The Occurrence and Non-occurrence of Japanese Locative Postpositions *ni* and *de* in Conversation. *Proceedings of the Third Annual High Desert Conference in Linguistics*, eds. K. A. Smith and D. Nordquist, 85–92. Albuquerque: High Desert Linguistics Society.

Masunaga, K. 1988. Case Deletion and Discourse Context. *Papers from the Second International Workshop on Japanese Syntax*, ed. P. J. William, 145–56. Stanford: CSLI.

Matsuda, K. 1996. Variable Zero-Marking of (o) in Tokyo Japanese. Doctoral dissertation, University of Pennsylvania.

Mori, T., and T. Givón. 1987. Zero-Object Marking in Colloquial Japanese: The Pragmatics of 'Optional Deletion'. Manuscript, University of Oregon.

Nitta, Y. 1992. Kakuhyōji no arikata o megutte – Tōhoku hōgen to no taishō o moto ni [On case expressions: Based on comparison with Northeastern dialect). *Nigongogaku* 11(6):33–45.

Ono, T., S. A. Thompson, and R. Suzuki. 2000. The Pragmatic Nature of So-called Subject Marker *ga* in Japanese: Evidence from Conversation. *Discourse Studies* 2: 35–63.

Thompson, S. A. 1997. Discourse Motivations for the Core-Oblique Distinctions as a Language Universal. *Directions in Functional Linguistics*, ed. A. Kamio, 59–82. Amsterdam: John Benjamins.

Tsujimura, N. 1996. *An Introduction to Japanese Linguistics*. Oxford: Blackwell.

Tsutsui, M. 1984. Particle Ellipsis in Japanese. Doctoral dissertation, University of Illinois.

On the Optionality of *to*-Marking on Reduplicated Mimetics in Japanese

KIYOKO TORATANI*
York University

1. Introduction

This paper examines the function of the particle *to* (a "complementizer" otherwise), which marks adverbial mimetics in Japanese. The mimetics under investigation are the fully reduplicated mimetics whose initial vowels are accented, such as *kíra-kira* 'manner of glittering' and *póro-poro* 'manner of small drops falling continuously'. These adverbial mimetics denote a manner of the host predicate and can appear within a sentence marked by *to*, as in (1a), or without any marking, as in (1b).

---

* I am deeply indebted to Len Talmy for his helpful comments on the earlier versions of this paper. I also thank the audience at the 14th J/K Linguistics Conference for providing me with encouragement and valuable feedback, in particular, Shoko Hamano, Yongeun Lee, Mana Kobuchi-Philip, and Masa Yamazaki. I am also grateful to John Dingley for his time in reading the paper and providing me with insightful comments. All remaining errors and shortcomings are, of course, mine.

(1) a. namida ga póro-poro-to oti-ta
        tear NOM (mimetic)-*to* drop-PST[1]
        'Tears ran down continuously.'

    b. namida ga póro-poro oti-ta
        tear NOM (mimetic)-Ø drop-PST
        'Tears ran down continuously.'

The two sentences in (1) stand on a par with each other in terms of syntactic well-formedness and of denotation, despite the fact that the mimetic (*póro-poro* 'manner of small drops falling continuously') is marked differently. Thus far, little attention has been paid to the formal distinction of *to*- vs. Ø-marking, and the majority of previous studies describe *to*-marking as "optional" (Hamano 1986:15, Hamano 1998:13, Tamori and Schourup 1999: 65–8, Kakehi et al. 1996:xv). The only exception seems to be Tamori (1980), who concludes that the marking distinction is affected by the sentence-internal position of the mimetic.[2]

Building on Tamori's insight, this paper first examines the distribution of *to*- and Ø-marked mimetics in literary texts and reports the results of a frequency count. Next, this paper argues that the formal distinction between *to* and Ø is sensitive to semantic and pragmatic factors. To show this point, observations on (i) semantic predictability, (ii) distance between the mimetic and the predicate, and (iii) focus (Lambrecht 1994) are presented. Then, on the basis of the notion of "conceptual partitioning" (Talmy 2000), this paper proposes that the coding difference between *to* and Ø manifests the speaker's view of whether the event denoted by the mimetic is independent of the event denoted by the predicate.

2. Frequency Count

In order to examine whether the position of the mimetic affects its marking (*to* or Ø), 320 tokens of mimetic sentences were gathered from eight literary sources. Of the 320 instances, 11 mimetics occurred in a complex sentence which contained two potential host predicates (see e.g. (5a)). Of these 11, just one (1/320 = 0.3%) was marked by Ø, while 10 (10/320 = 3%) were

---

[1] The following abbreviations are used: ACC = accusative, DAT = dative, GEN = genitive, LINK = linker, NOM = nominative, NPST = non-past, P = particle, PST = past, and TOP = topic.

[2] Shoko Hamano brought to my attention that Asano (2003) offers a phonological account for the optionality of *to*-marking. Asano's argument is that *to*-marking is "optional" as long as the mimetic is coded with the required phonological information. Contra this view, this paper argues that both the overt *to*-marking and the covert Ø-marking bear significance. As far as the fully reduplicated mimetics (which this paper deals with) are concerned, a purely phonological account would fail to explain why a mimetic is likely to be *to*-marked if it occurs away from the verb (see the discussion in §2 and §3.2.).

marked by *to*. This suggests that the mimetic in a complex sentence is more likely to be marked by *to*. On the other hand, the remaining 309 mimetics occurred in a simple sentence (see e.g. (4a)). Of these 309, 187 (187/320 = 58%) were marked by Ø, while 122 (122/320 = 38%) were marked by *to*. To further examine the relationship between the marking and the mimetic position in a simple sentence, the distance between the mimetic and the host predicate was examined. Adapting Givón's (1983) idea of "referential distance" to sentence-internal elements, a number was assigned according to how many phrasal elements occurred between the mimetic and the host predicate. For example, the immediately preverbal position was assigned the value 1, since the mimetic is the first phrasal element from the verb, and the next position to the left was assigned the value 2, since the mimetic is the second phrasal element. Table 1 shows the results.

Marking	Position 1	Position 2	Position 3	Total
Ø	151/187 (81%)	34/187 (18%)	2/187 (1%)	187/187 (100%)
to	58/122 (48%)	55/122 (45%)	9/122 (7%)	122/122 (100%)

Table 1. Distribution of Mimetics in Simple Sentences

Table 1 shows that the immediately preverbal position (Position 1) was the most frequent for both Ø- and *to*-marked forms. However, the percentage was much higher for the Ø-marked forms (81%) than for the *to*-marked forms (48%). With *to*-marked mimetics, the ratio was roughly the same for Position 1 (48%) and Position 2 (45%). The mean position for each marking type was also calculated: 1.2 for Ø-marking and 1.6 for *to*-marking. This implies that *to*-marked mimetics are more likely to occur away from the host predicate than the Ø-marked mimetics. The results of the frequency count here show that there is a tendency in the distribution of mimetic coding that is consistent with Tamori's (1980) observation that the marking distinction between Ø and *to* is not quite random.

3. Factors

Having observed a tendency for *to*-marked mimetics to occur away from the host predicate, the factors that affect the marking choice are now considered.

3.1. Semantic Predictability

The first factor is semantic predictability. Mimetic-host combinations can be first divided into (i) unacceptable combinations and (ii) acceptable combinations. An unacceptable combination is a case in which the lexical in-

formation of the mimetic and of the predicate clash, and hence their cooccurrence is impossible. For example, *téku-teku* specifically describes a
manner of walking and hence cannot cooccur with *hasir-* 'run', as illustrated by the infelicity of (2).

(2) *téku-teku (-Ø/-to) hasir-u
    (mimetic)   run-NPST
    (intended) 'to run at a constant pace'

The acceptable combinations can be further divided into two types: predicted combinations and combinations that diverge from predicted combinations. The mimetic and the verb that are in construction with each other
are semantically constrained rather rigidly, as noted by Hamano (1986:14).
By virtue of this constraint, the hearer can in general predict which predicate will be mentioned upon hearing a mimetic word. Let us call such a predicted form a "typical host". Some mimetics can cooccur only with a typical
host. An example is *téku-teku* 'manner of walking', which can occur only
with a verb that denotes walking, such as *aruk-* 'walk' in (3) (cf. (2)).

(3) téku-teku (-Ø/-to) aruk-u
    (mimetic)   walk-NPST
    'to walk at a constant pace'

Other mimetics are semantically more lax in the sense that they can occur with an atypical host, as shown in (4).

(4) a. níko-niko-to akarui
      (mimetic)-*to* cheerful
      (lit.) '(He) is cheerful, smiling.' (Hoshi 1962:10)

   b. poketto no naka ni góro-goro-to ikutumono isi   o
      pocket GEN inside DAT (mimetic)-*to*   many stones ACC
      ire-te   ir-u
      put-LINK exist-NPST
      'In her pocket, she is carrying a lot of stones (as we can tell from
      the rumbling sound).' (Sakura 2003:239)

In (4a), the mimetic *níko-niko* 'manner of smiling' is predicted to occur
with *waraw-* 'laugh'. But it turns out that it appears with *akarui* 'cheerful'.
Analogously in (4b), the mimetic *góro-goro* 'sound/manner of a heavy object rolling' is predicted to occur with a verb such as *korogar-* 'roll' or *nar-*
'ring', but it turns out to occur with *ire-* 'put'. Despite the fact that these
mimetics occur with atypical hosts, the sentences in (4) are readily interpretable and perfectly acceptable.

A *to*-marked mimetic is often found when it accompanies an atypical host, as in (4). On the other hand, a Ø-marked mimetic is often found when it occurs with a typical host, as in (3). Given this, it can be hypothesized that *to* here is functioning as a marking to "foreshadow" (Epstein 1996: 105) a semantic mismatch between the predicted host and the host that actually cooccurs, whereas Ø-marking suggests a match.

3.2. Distance

The second factor is the distance between the mimetic and the host predicate. In the case of a complex sentence which includes two host candidates, the *to*-marked mimetic permits a wide scope interpretation (interpreting the more distant matrix predicate as its host), whereas the Ø-marked mimetic favors a narrow scope interpretation (interpreting the closer predicate as its host). For example, each sentence in (5) contains two host candidates.

(5) a. watasi wa nóko-noko-to omiyage no hanataba o   mot-te
         I   TOP (mimetic)-*to*   gift GEN bouquet ACC carry-LINK
         zinguumae no mansyon e   mukat-ta
         GEN apartment to leave.for-PST
         'Carrying a gift bouquet, I left for her apartment in Zinguumae nonchalantly.' (Mure 1984:215)

    b. ?watasi wa nóko-noko omiyage no hanataba o   mot-te
         I   TOP (mimetic)-Ø   gift GEN bouquet ACC carry-LINK
         zinguumae no mansyon e   mukat-ta
         GEN apartment to leave.for-PST
         'Carrying a gift bouquet (appearing) nonchalantly, I left for her apartment in Zinguumae.'

In (5a), the *to*-marked mimetic can modify the matrix verb *mukaw-* 'leave for', yielding a wide scope interpretation, whereas in (5b), the Ø-marked counterpart can be interpreted only as modifying the closest verb *mot-* 'carry'. In the latter case, the sentence sounds awkward because the mimetic *nóko-noko* 'manner of appearing nonchalantly' is semantically incompatible with *mot-* 'carry'. From these examples, we can hypothesize that *to* here allows the interpretation of the mimetic modifying a potential host that is not in close proximity, whereas Ø necessitates an interpretation such that the mimetic modifies the closest non-nominal element.

3.3. Focus

The third factor is focus, in the sense of Lambrecht (1994). Focus can be roughly defined as discourse-new information which cannot be predicted or recovered from the context. This contrasts with pragmatic presupposition, which is information already mentioned in the discourse or taken for granted at the time of the speech. A *to*-marked mimetic can readily receive narrow focus. The situational context of (6a) is a scene where two women are walking, and as one woman keeps on going at her own speed, she realizes that her friend is not keeping up with her. Wondering what her friend is doing, she turns back and utters this sentence (the mimetic *tóbo-tobo* expressing the 'manner of walking looking weak').

(6) hurikaeru   to   sita o mui-te   tóbo-tobo-to   arui-te   iru
    turn.back when down P turn-LINK (mimetic)-*to* walk-LINK-exist
    'I turned back, and there she was walking ploddingly looking down.'
    (Mure 1984:186)

In this context, that her friend is walking is pragmatically presupposed by the speaker, whereas the manner of how her friend was walking denoted by the mimetic is introduced as new information, i.e. focus. The Ø-marked form may occur here, but in that case the sentence should be pronounced with the prosodic peak falling on the mimetic word. Thus, to indicate that the mimetic is the target of narrow focus, a *to*-marked form seems preferred to a Ø-marked form without any prosodic cue.

Having presented observations on the three factors that affect the marking of a mimetic, I now discuss what can be induced from these observations.

4. Conceptual Partitioning

The notion of "conceptual partitioning" (Talmy 2000:215) can provide the basis for an account of the three observations presented above: "Conceptual partitioning" refers to an operation in which "the human mind in perception or conception can extend a boundary around a portion of what would otherwise be a continuum." An event can be considered a continuum. Notice that in (7) (from Talmy 2000:216) a truth-conditionally equivalent scene is expressed by a complex sentence in (a) and by a simple sentence in (b).

(7) a. The aerial toppled because I did something to it (e.g. because I
        threw a rock at it).

    b. I toppled the aerial.

Sentence (7a) consists of a matrix clause and a subordinate clause, each denoting a distinct meaning component. The former denotes the main event (that the aerial toppled), and the latter denotes the subordinate event (the causing event of the speaker doing something to it). On the other hand, (7b) consists of a simple sentence but expresses the same essence of content as a unitary event, in which the subordinate event is "conflated" (Talmy 1972, 1985, 2000) into the main event. This contrast can be illustrated as in (8).

(8) a. [[The aerial toppled] [because I did something to it]].

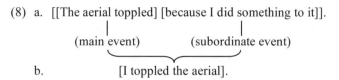

      (main event)   (subordinate event)

   b.   [I toppled the aerial].

To put it differently, in the (8a) type scheme, the main event is conceptualized as "partitioned" from the subordinate event, and each event is realized in a distinct formal unit. On the other hand, in the (8b) type scheme, the event in its entirety is realized in a single formal unit, without partitioning the main event from the subordinate event.

This (8a) type scheme can be applied to mimetic sentences, since their formal realization corresponds to the meaning units illustrated in (9).

(9)   [mimetic]   [predicate]

    (subordinate event of manner)   (main event)

This alignment seems to imply that a speaker always captures a mimetic "event" conceptually partitioned from the matrix predicate event. The behavior of mimetics that we observed, however, is not completely consistent with this simple alignment scheme. As we saw in §3, Ø-marked mimetics are associated with a tighter formal and semantic relationship to the predicate event, whereas *to*-marked mimetics are associated with formal separation from the predicate, differentiated pragmatic activation state, and semantic non-integratedness into the predicate event. In other words, the characteristics of *to* are more in line with the (a) type scheme, in which there is a one-to-one correspondence between the form and the event (i.e. the meaning component), whereas the characteristics of Ø are more in agreement with the (b) type scheme, where two formal units correspond to a unitary event.

Given this, I propose that the coding difference between *to* and Ø manifests how the speaker views the mimetic "event". The particle *to* signals that the event denoted by the mimetic is conceptualized as being independent of the event denoted by the host predicate, whereas Ø signals that the event denoted by the mimetic is conceptualized as being conflated into the event denoted by the host predicate.

4. Concluding Remarks

This paper has examined the coding alternation of *to* vs. Ø following reduplicated mimetics in Japanese. It was shown that the speaker's selection of one form over the other is not completely random. Examination of discourse data made it possible to capture characteristics that would not have emerged if we had only observed atomic sentences in isolation. It was also argued that a cognitive account based on "conceptual partitioning" (Talmy 2000) can offer an explanation for the differences between *to* and Ø forms concerning the phenomena of (i) semantic predictability, (ii) distance between the mimetic and the predicate, and (iii) focus. These differences would be difficult to account for solely on the basis of a syntax or truth-conditional semantics.

Future research will determine what other factors trigger the marking difference between *to* and Ø for reduplicated mimetics and whether the notion of "conceptual partitioning" can offer an account for such phenomena.

References

Asano, M. 2003. The Optionality of the Quotative Particle -*to* in Japanese Mimetics. *Japanese/Korean Linguistics 12*, ed. W. McClure, 91–102. Stanford: CSLI.

Epstein, R. 1996. Viewpoint and the Definite Article. *Conceptual Structure, Discourse and Language*, ed. A. Goldberg, 99–112. Stanford: CSLI.

Givón, T. 1983. Topic Continuity in Discourse: An Introduction. *Topic Continuity in Discourse: A Quantitative Cross-Language Study*, ed. T. Givón, 5–41. Amsterdam: John Benjamins.

Hamano, S. 1986. The Sound-Symbolic System of Japanese. Doctoral dissertation, University of Florida.

Hamano, S. 1998. *The Sound-Symbolic System of Japanese*. Stanford: CSLI.

Hoshi, S. 1962 [1999]. *Bonbon to akumu*. Tokyo: Shinchōsha.

Kakehi, H., I. Tamori, and L. Schourup. 1996. *Dictionary of Iconic Expressions in Japanese: A–J*. Berlin: Mouton de Gruyter.

Lambrecht, K. 1994. *Information Structure and Sentence Form: Topic, Focus and the Mental Representations of Discourse Referents*. Cambridge: Cambridge University Press.

Mure, Y. 1984 [2003]. *Gozen reiji no genmai pan*. Tokyo: Kadokawa Shoten.

Sakura, M. 2003. *Tai no okashira*. Tokyo: Shūeisha.

Talmy, L. 1972. Semantic Structures in English and Atsugewi. Doctoral dissertation, University of California, Berkeley.

Talmy, L. 1985. Lexicalization Patterns: Semantic Structure in Lexical Forms. *Language Typology and Syntactic Description, Vol. III: Grammatical Categories and the Lexicon*, ed. T. Shopen, 57–149. Cambridge: Cambridge University Press.

Talmy, L. 2000. *Toward a Cognitive Semantics, Vol. II: Typology and Process in Concept Structuring*. Cambridge: MIT Press.

Tamori, I. 1980. Cooccurence Restrictions on Onomatopoeic Adverbs and Particles. *Papers in Japanese Linguistics* 7:151–71.

Tamori, I., and L. Schourup. 1999. *Onomatope: Keitai to imi*. Tokyo: Kuroshio.

Complaint Utterances in Korean Conversation: Interrogatives with Question Words

KYUNG-EUN YOON*
University of Illinois at Urbana-Champaign

1. Introduction

Using the framework of conversation analysis, this study investigates the uses of interrogative sentences with question words in complaining actions in Korean talk-in-interaction. Through the analysis of complaints in Korean conversation, I have found that interrogatives with question words, especially with *way* 'why', are most commonly utilized in direct complaint utterances toward a co-present party.[1] Although they are grammatically formulated as questions, they do not seek new information in this context. Rather, they perform complaining by conveying the speaker's stance of

* I am deeply grateful to Professor Makoto Hayashi and Professor Irene Koshik for their inspirational advice and support. My gratitude also goes to the audience at the J/K14 conference for their invaluable questions and comments, and to Jill Knutson for her insightful suggestions. However, I remain responsible for all shortcomings of this paper.

[1] I collected a three-hour sample of data, in which 40 complaint utterances toward a co-present party occur. Out of the 40 complaint utterances, 16 are formulated as interrogatives with question words: 9 with 'why' (8 *way* and 1 *ecci*), 6 with 'what' (*mwe* or *mwusun*), and 1 with 'how' (*etteh*). Other than interrogatives with question words, reversed polarity questions (termed as such in Koshik 2003) are found in 6 complaints, and the imperative type is found in 4. The other 14 complaints are formulated as declarative statements with a variety of sentence-final suffixes.

423

negatively evaluating and thus being dissatisfied with the addressee's preceding utterance or conduct. This study explicates how and why the specific linguistic formulation of interrogatives with question words is utilized as a resource for doing complaining.

Traditionally, non-real questions have been categorized as "rhetorical questions" in studies such as Sohn 1999 in Korean, and Bolinger 1957 and Quirk et al. 1985 in English. These rhetorical questions are explained as assertions of the opposite polarity to that of the question, rather than as ordinary information-seeking questions. However, these studies have used isolated sentences, constructed on the basis of the authors' intuitions, and thus how exactly those questions operate as assertions in actual interactional context has not been investigated. More recently, research has started to focus on the actual context in which such rhetorical questions are used to display the speaker's epistemic stance in English (Koshik 2003). This research has shown that the use of WH-questions in institutional settings can display participants' orientation to institutional goals, norms, and roles. That is, institutional roles can be enacted, and goals accomplished by means of practices of talk which are not, themselves, inherently related to the institutional contexts. Following this line of research, the present study explores how interrogatives with question words come to be heard as asserting a specific epistemic stance toward the addressee's prior utterance or conduct in Korean conversation, and how this hearing enables the questions to be used as complaints about the target behavior. By doing so, this study argues that speech is an ongoing or emergent product in a social event, and that grammar provides one set of resources for accomplishing goals and tasks within that event.

2. Data

The data corpus of this study consists of ten hours of audio- and video-taped face-to-face interaction and three hours of audio-taped phone conversations. The conversations are all naturally-occurring talk, mostly among family members and/or friends who know one another very well. The participants are native speakers of Korean who range in age from their teens to their seventies, and the number of people involved is approximately sixty. The participants originally come from all the different provinces of South Korea, but most of them used standard Korean. These conversations are closely transcribed according to the conventions commonly used in conversation analysis (see Ochs, Schegloff, and Thompson 1996:461–5). Based on this data set, the following section presents an analysis of how interrogatives with question words are utilized as a resource for performing complaints.

3. Analysis: Interrogatives with Question Words as Complaints

This section describes the sequential contexts in which a complaint utterance in the format of an interrogative with a question word is produced, and demonstrates that the hearing of the utterance as a complaint is not dependent on the linguistic form of the question alone but also on the interactional environment, specifically the sequential environment of the utterance.

Fragment (1) below presents a use of an interrogative with a question word as a complaint. It is taken from a conversation among five close friends at a dinner gathering. This gathering was hosted by two female roommates, Young and Jeong. Young (the elder) has directed the table setting and cooking, and Jeong has assisted her. In the following the participants are about to start eating, and Young, as hostess, initiates a ritualistic meal-beginning sequence toward a guest, Hoon, in line 1.[2]

(1) Dinner Talk among Five Friends

```
1     Young:   ma:nhi mek-e:. hu
               a.lot   eat-IM
               ((toward Hoon)) 'Eat a lo:t ((/Help yourself)) hu'
2              (2.0)
3     Hoon:    nwuna       manhi mek-nuntey-yo,
               elder.sister a.lot eat-but    -POL
               'Sister, I will eat a lot, but'
4              (1.2)
5     Hoon:    *°swutkalak com cwu(h)-sey(h)-yo(h).°*
                spoon      please give -HON  -POL
               * *: ((stands up and goes to kitchen))
               'Please give me a spoon ((/silverware)).'
6              (.6)
7     Jeong:   °e:°
               '°O:h°'
8     Young:   ((laugh))=
9     Hoon:    =°u°=
10 →  Young:   =way(h) yay -n   ceskal [an cw-ess -e:]
               why this.one-TC chopstick not give-PST-Q
               ((toward Jeong)) 'Why didn't you give chopsticks
               ((/silverware)) to hi:m?'
11    Jeong:                            [>(isangha-ta,)<]
                                          strange-DC
12             akka *pa:p (ne/na)-ss-nuntey¿=
               before rice  put   -PST-but
               *: ((standing up))
               '>It's (strange),< I put it a little while ago ((beside the rice)), but
               then why¿'
```

---

[2] See the appendices for abbreviations and transcription conventions.

In line 3, Hoon repeats Young's ritualistic wording, adds a contrastive marker *-nuntey* 'but', and then in line 5 issues a request to give him a spoon. With this request produced in contrast to the hostess's hospitable meal-beginning ritual, Hoon brings everybody's attention to the fact that he has not been provided with silverware. Jeong, who set the table earlier, registers her notice of the fact with °*e:*° in line 7, which is similar to the change-of-state token *oh* in English (Heritage 1984). Young also registers her notice with laughter in line 8, which responds to the way that Hoon produces his request in a non-serious or jocular way with laugh tokens. Young then issues a *way* 'why' question in line 10: *way(h) yay-n ceskal an cw-ess-e:* 'Why didn't you give chopsticks (((/silverware)) to *hi:m?*'. This *way* question serves as a challenge and a complaint toward Jeong's prior conduct of setting the table. In the prior context, Hoon's action in lines 3 and 5 of bringing to everybody's attention to the fact that he has not been provided with silverware implies his normative orientation that a hostess is supposed to provide silverware to a guest before eating. Young's *way* question in line 10 then subsequently formulates the lack of silverware as Jeong's failure and also shows that she has the same normative orientation as Hoon. Her question literally asks for the reason why Jeong did not provide silverware to Hoon, but through the procedure of establishing setting out silverware as a normative standard in the preceding context, it is suggested that there is no good reason for failing to give silverware to a guest. The *way* question thus implies that Jeong will not be able to answer and therefore, rather than functioning as a real question, it challenges the ground of Jeong's action and performs a complaint which can be interpreted as asserting 'you should have given chopsticks (((/silverware)) to *him*'. Therefore, the sequential environment in which the normative standard is established and Jeong's conduct is defined as violating the standard enables the *way* question to be heard as Young's complaining. It is interesting that Young directs Hoon's request to Jeong through her complaint utterance in line 10, although Hoon targeted Young with his request in line 5. That is, her complaint utterance makes obvious that it was Jeong who was supposed to do the particular job and thereby puts the responsibility on her.

Fragment (2) below shows another example of a *way* question used as a complaint. It is a later portion of the same conversation as Fragment (1). To provide more background information for better understanding of this fragment, all the participants are single, Young is in her mid-twenties and Joo, a female guest, is in her mid-thirties. Joo and Hoon are sister and brother. In the immediately preceding talk, Young said that their rice cooker does not work very well, and Joo recommended that she buy an electronic pressure rice cooker because it makes great tasting rice. Young responded that she could not buy one because it is very expensive and it would not be necessary anyway because she would not have any chance to get married soon. That is, Joo's suggestion of buying a nice rice cooker turns into bringing up Young's socio-cultural orientation that single women do not need to buy nice appliances until they have specific wedding plans. At this point in the talk, Joo issues a complaint toward Young in line 1.

(2) Dinner Talk among Five Friends

```
1     Joo:    ya  kyelhon  an ha-myen masiss-nun  ke
              hey wedding not do-if    delicious-RL thing
2             mek-umyen an   tway?=
              eat-if        not allowed
              'Hey if not married, can we not eat delicious food?'
3     Young:  =°kule-l      il  -i    ep  -ul ke-yey-yo,°
              do.so-RL matter-NM not.exist-will  -POL
              ((irrelevant to Joo's utterance: late response to Jeong's
              encouragement to get married)):
              '°That thing ((=My wedding)) will not happen°'
4     Hoon:   ((ch[uckle))
5     Young:       [((chuckle)) ((l [a  u  g  h))]
6     Hoon:                          [((chuckle))]
7     Young: [ mianhay    s::   ((laugh)) ]
                sorry
              'I am sorry s:: ((laugh)))'
8     Joo:   [>ma masiss-nun  ke  mek ]
              de delicious-RL thing eat
9             [-eya[-ci<  (        ) ]
              -must-SUP
              '>Del-- we have to eat delicious things anyway<'
10    Young: [ ((l [ a  u  g  h)) ]
11 →  Hoon:  [way  tto  kyelhon] yayki -lul
              why again wedding  talking-AC
12 →          hay-se  tto wuli  nwuna-lul
              do-and  again our elder.sister-AC
13 →          [tto kentulye tto:]
              again irritate again
              'Why do you talk again about marriage and so irritate my
              sister again?'
14    Young: [ ((l  a  u  g  ]h)) .h
```

With her utterance in line 1, Joo claims another kind of norm that any-body, whether or not married or planning to get married, can buy a nice rice cooker for their own sake. As mentioned earlier, Joo is a single woman who is much older than Young. According to the socio-cultural norm that Young has brought up in the preceding context, Joo could be considered to have wasted money on buying an expensive rice cooker without getting married.

Joo's utterance in line 1 thus makes visible this consequential interpretation of Young's normative orientation and thereby challenges and complains about Young's act of raising the issue of marriage related to buying a rice cooker. This complaint from Joo is registered by Hoon and Young in lines 4–6 with laugh tokens, and Young (the complainee) produces an apology in line 7. At this point, Joo's younger brother, Hoon, issues another complaint toward Young in lines 11–13 in the format of a *way* question: *way tto kyel-hon yayki-lul hay-se tto wuli nwuna-lul tto kentulye tto:* 'Why do you talk again about marriage and so irritate my sister again?'. This *way* question literally asks for the reason why Young brought up the issue of marriage and irritated his sister. However, in the sequential environment where Young's target behavior has already been complained about and Young herself has apologized, there should not be reasonable grounds that Young could provide to defend her comment. Moreover, since Hoon's seeming question already defines Young's conduct as "irritating", it prevents Young from presenting a justification for her act. Therefore, Hoon's *way* question, instead of seeking a real answer, serves as a complaint with an assertion that 'you should not have talked about marriage again and irritated my sister'.

We can see another example in Fragment (3), which is a conversation among five close friends at a pizza gathering. In this segment, a guest, Min, drinks the juice provided by the host, Suh, and makes a positive assessment in line 2 that it is delicious.

(3) Pizza Gathering

```
    1       {(2.2) / ((Min drinks juice that was provided by Suh, the host.))}
    2    Min:    i   -ke      masiss-ta:.
                 this-thing delicious-DC
                 'This one is delicious!'
    3    Suh:    °yey. ku-ke° .h    pissa -n    ke-yey-yo:
                 yes  that-thing  expensive-RL thing-be-POL
                 '°Yes. that one° .h it is an expsensive one!'
    4            (1.0)
    5    Won:    [((l [ a    u    g    h))]
    6    Yeon:   [((l [    a    u    g ]  [ h)) ]=
    7 →  Min:         [.h eyi mwe-l   tto]  [pissa:]=
                      EXC what-AC again expensive
                 '.h eyi³ What are you saying is expensive? ((/How come you
                 say it's expensive?))'
```

---

³ Exclamatory tokens such as *eyi, ai* (in line 11), *aikwu* (line 4 in Fragment (4)), *aywu* (line 5 in Fragment (4)), etc., are often found in complaint utterances as a device to project the upcoming complaining action. See Yoon forthcoming for discussion of such uses of exclamatory tokens in complaints.

```
8     Yeon:   =[((l   a   u   g  ] h))=
9 →   Min:    =[ha way kulay:]
              why do.so
              'ha Why do you act like that?'
10    Yeon:   =((l [    a     u     g     h))  ]=
11    Suh:        [a(h)i(h) i   pissan(h) ke(h)-yey-yo]=
                  EXC  this expensive thing-be-POL
              'A(h)i(h)4 this is an expensive one.'
12    Yeon:   =[.h    h:  ]
13    Suh:    =[cengma:l]
              really
              'Really!'
```

In response to Min's assessment, the host, Suh, issues an agreement in line 3 with *yey* 'yes' and then upgrades the assessment by saying that it is expensive. An upgraded agreement is generally a preferred response to an assessment (Pomerantz 1984), but that is not the case in this context. Since the assessment has been produced by a guest (Min) about the juice that the host (Suh) prepared, Min's assessment also serves as a compliment to Suh. Thus, a preferred response from Suh would be simply an appreciation token. However, Suh does not issue any appreciation token and instead upgrades the assessment. Suh's upgraded assessment in response to the guest's compliment is treated as an upgraded, strong self-compliment by the other participants, and Won's and Yeon's laughter in lines 5 and 6 portrays it as an "unusual, laughable" action for the context. Min, who made the original compliment, also issues complaint utterances in lines 7 and 9: *mwe-l tto pissa: ha way kulay:* 'What are you saying is expensive? ((/How come you say it's expensive?)) Why do you act like that?' Min's complaint consists of two interrogatives with question words: one with *mwe* 'what' and the other *way* 'why'. In this context, Suh's behavior of self-complementing has been recognized by Won and Yeon as an unusual one that violates a sociocultural norm: A host should not boast about what he has provided. Therefore, the first question with *mwe* 'what' is not a real question about what Suh was saying is expensive, but an assertion that Suh should not have said so. The second question also suggests that Suh should not have acted like that; in other words, his act was not appropriate for a host.

The next fragment is a later portion of the same conversation, which shows another instance of a complaint in the format of interrogative with a question word. Of the participants of this conversation, Suh, Min, and Won are graduate students in the same department, and Won mentioned in the preceding context that he and Min were in their departmental building on

---

4 See note 3.

the fourth floor, where Won's office is located, before coming to the gathering. In line 1, Yoon asks Min as a new topic initiator in the conversation, whether he stayed on the fourth floor for a long time.

(4) Pizza Gathering

1	Yoon:	sa-chung-ey kyeysok kyeysy-ess-eyo?
		four-floor-on continuously stay(HON)-PST-POL
		'Did you stay on the fourth floor for a long time?'
2		(1.0)
3	Min:	ani mwe ccik-nun ke pwuthakha-nulakwu
		no like measure-RL thing ask.favor-because
		'Well uh because I needed to ask Won a favor, some help with measuring'
4		aikwu:[: ce inkan yw]useyha-nun=
		EXC that human.being show.arrogance-RL
		'aikwu::[5] that human being[6] was showing so much arrogance that'
5	Won:	[↑ a y w u :: ↑]
		EXC
		'↑aywu::↑'[7]
6	Min:	=ke-ttaymwuney nay-ka acwu,=
		thing-because I-NM too.much
		'I was too much,'
7	Yoon:	=AYWU::=
		EXC
		'AYWU::'
8 →	Won:	= >(mwusun)< ywusey-lul hay-yo:
		what arrogance-AC do-POL
9 →		hankkepeney celehkey ta kackwuw-akacikwu: hu
		at.one.time like.that all bring-and
		'What arrogance did I show? You brought all the materials at once like that hu'

In response to Yoon's topic-initiating question, Min begins in line 3 to answer with an account of why he was on the fourth floor, which is not the location of his own office. In the middle of telling Yoon that he went to the fourth floor because he needed to ask Won to do him a favor, Min changes the flow of the talk from account-giving into complaining toward Won, saying that Won treated him with so much arrogance. In response to Min's complaint, Won issues a counter-complaint in lines 8 and 9 in the format of a question with *mwusun* 'what': >(mwusun)< ywusey -lul hay-yo: 'What

---

[5] See note 3.

[6] The literal meaning of the word *inkan* is 'human being', but it is sometimes used as a pejorative expression for 'person', as in this example.

[7] See note 3.

arrogance did I show?' In a context where a contesting environment has been set up after an accusation or after the questioner's position is threatened, a challenge would be a relevant next action, and a WH-question is especially likely to be interpreted as a challenge in naturally occurring talk in English (Koshik 2003). Similarly, in the context given above, Min has complained toward Won, and hence a contesting environment has been established. Won's *mwusun* question is then designed to deliver an affirmative assertion ('I did not show any arrogance at all') rather than asking for information, and thereby disagree with and issue a counter-complaint toward Min's prior accusation. This is further evidenced by the fact that the speaker does not pause at the end of the question for the addressee to answer. The speaker continues to say that it was Min who had brought too many materials to handle at one time. This declaration suits the conveyed assertion ('I did not show any arrogance'), whereas it would not be a reasonable follow-up to the pure question 'what arrogance did I show?', since it is an account for the underlying claim in the *mwusun* question.

The following data segment presents a complaint utterance with the question word *ecci* 'how; why'. It is a phone conversation between two high-school girls. Nami is calling her friend Eun, and Eun opens the phone conversation with 'hello' in line 1.

(5) Phone Conversation between High-school Girls

1	Eun:	yeposeyyo:?
		'Hello:?'
2	Nami:	na Nami-ta.
		I NAME-DC
		'This is Nami.'
3	Eun:	u:ng. olayn-man-i-ney?
		yes long.time-after-be-APP
		'Yea:h. It's been a long time.'
4 →	Nami:	**ecci nay-ka cenhwa-l an ha-myen CENHWA-L**
		how I-NM call-AC not do-if call-AC
5 →		**HAN THONGHWA-TO an ha-nya?**
		one CL-even not do-Q
		'How come you NEVER MAKE A SINGLE PHONE CALL
		to me if I don't call you?'
6	Eun:	WAY::?
		why
		'WHY::?'
7		(.)
8	Nami:	encey. hay-ss -ess-e?
		when do-PST-PST-Q
		'When. Did you call me?'

Nami self-identifies in line 2, and Eun acknowledges Nami's self-identification and then greets her in line 3. Then Nami produces a question with *ecci* 'how; why' in lines 4 and 5: *ecci nay-ka cenhwa-l an ha-myen CENHWA-L HAN THONGHWA-TO an ha-nya?* 'How come you NEVER MAKE A SINGLE PHONE CALL to me if I don't call you?'. In this seeming question, Nami already characterizes the absence of Eun's effort to keep up their phone communication in definite negative terms with the expression *HAN THONGHWA-TO* ('not EVEN A SINGLE PHONE CALL'). Moreover, the subordinate clause, *nay-ka cenhwa-l an ha-myen* 'if I don't call you', strongly contrasts the absence of Eun's effort with Nami's own effort, which brings up a social normative standard that there should be mutual efforts between friends to keep up communication. Nami's utterance thus articulates the unbalanced efforts between herself and Eun, and thereby portrays Eun's lack of effort as an unacceptable action for a friend. Following Nami's definite characterization of Eun's lack of effort, there is no way for Eun to provide justifiable grounds for not having made a phone call. Therefore, the *ecci* question in this example challenges Eun's behavior and performs a complaint which strongly points to the absence of Eun's effort.

4. Conclusion

As seen in the analysis in the preceding section, interrogative sentences with question words, especially *way/ecci* 'why', are recurrently used as direct complaint utterances in Korean talk-in-interaction. The interrogatives with question words are heard as complaints in a context where a certain normative standard has been set up as a yardstick with reference to which the complainant assesses the addressee's preceding action or utterance as some kind of failure for the particular situation. The questions presented in this paper function not as real questions but as negative assessments which display the speakers' strong epistemic stances and thereby perform complaints which claim that the target behavior has violated the normative standard.

Then why is it particularly interrogatives with question words, especially *way* (or *ecci*) 'why', that are chosen most frequently in complaining rather than other grammatical formats? This type of question seems to have grammatical and interactional advantages which lead to its uses in complaint utterances. First, an interrogative with a question word challenges the ground for the addressee's prior action or utterance, implying that there is no adequate reason for it and hence that it should not have been done in the first place. In particular, a *way* question is useful as a way to "call into question" the ground of the recipient's previous action and thereby challenge and complain about it. Second, the interrogative is the first part of an adjacency pair, and the speaker makes use of the interactional requirement that the addressee respond to the question.[8] The question assumes that the addressee will not be able to give a reasonable response, and this failure becomes a resource by which the complainant can formulate the target conduct as unacceptable. This shows that the grammatical resource of interrogatives with question words is not inherently related to the complaining action. Rather, shaping this type of utterance into a direct complaint depends greatly on its sequential environment at the particular moment. Therefore, this type of grammatical sentence can operate as a complaint only when it is situated in ongoing interaction, which suggests that grammar provides one set of resources for accomplishing a task within a social event and that the organization of grammar and that of social interactional practices are deeply interrelated.

Appendix 1: Abbreviations Used in Interlinear Glosses

AC:	accusative case particle	APP:	apperceptive suffix
CL:	numeral classifier	DC:	declarative suffix
EXC:	exclamatory token	HON:	honorific marker
IM:	imperative suffix	NM:	nominative case particle
NOM:	nominalizer suffix	POL:	polite speech level
PST:	past tense suffix	Q:	interrogative suffix
RL:	relativizer suffix	SUP:	suppositive mood suffix
TOP:	topic-contrast particle		

Appendix 2: Transcription Conventions

word	stressed talk	?	rising intonation
WOrd	loud talk	,	half-rising intonation
(( ))	transcriber's remarks	° °	softer talk
:	sound stretch	:_	inflected rising intonation
(h)	laugh in the middle of an utterance	[ ]	overlapping talk
(0.0)	length of pause in tenths of a second	=	contiguous utterance
( )	words unclear	↑ ↑	high-pictched talk
.	falling intonation	> <	faster talk
.h	audible inbreath		

References

Bolinger, D. L. M. 1957. *Interrogative Structures of American English: The Direct Question*. Alabama: University Alabama Press.

Heritage, J. 1984. A Change-of-State Token and Aspects of Its Sequential Placement. *Structures of Social Action: Studies in Conversation Analysis*, eds. J. M. Atkinson and J. Heritage, 299–345. Cambridge: Cambridge University Press.

Koshik, I. 2003. WH Questions Used as Challenges. *Discourse Studies* 5:51–77.

---

[8] Sacks 1992:521–69 is a major resource on the adjacency pair.

Ochs, E., E. A. Schegloff, and S. A. Thompson, 1996. *Interaction and Grammar.* Cambridge: Cambridge University Press.

Pomerantz, A. 1984. Agreeing and Disagreeing with Assessments: Some Features of Preferred/Dispreferred Turn Shapes. *Structures of Social Action: Studies in Conversation Analysis,* eds. J. M. Atkinson and J. Heritage, 57–101. Cambridge: Cambridge University Press.

Quirk, R., S. Greenbaum, G. Leech, and J. Svartvik. 1985. *A Comprehensive Grammar of the English Language.* New York: Longman.

Sacks, H. 1992. *Lectures on Conversation.* Ed. G. Jefferson. Oxford: Blackwell.

Sohn, H. 1999. *The Korean Language.* Cambridge: Cambridge University Press.

Yoon, K. Forthcoming. Complaint Talk in Korean Conversation. Doctoral dissertation, University of Illinois at Urbana-Champaign.

An Analysis of Negative Nominalized Predicates as Prohibitives in Japanese Discourse

NINA AZUMI YOSHIDA
University of California, Los Angeles

1. Introduction

In Japanese, there exist a number of morpho-syntactic structures for delivering negative directives, or "prohibitives." Besides the negative counterparts of verbal imperative forms and negative requests, past studies have pointed out that prohibitives may also be expressed in Japanese through conditionals (e.g, Clancy, Akatsuka, and Strauss 1997, Akatsuka and Tsubomoto 1998) and by predicates nominalized by the formal nouns *no, mono*, and *koto* followed by the negated copula *da* (Noda 1995).[1]

The present study focuses on the latter, namely, on prohibitives expressed in the form of a negative nominalized predicate (NNP). The prohibitive, or "negative" counterpart of commands expressed as nominalized predicates, may potentially be realized in one of two ways: (1) by negating the verbal element in the nominalized clause/proposition (hereafter **NPP1**), or (2) by negating the copula *da* (hereafter **NNP2**).

Among the three prohibitive constructions consisting of a predicate nominalized by *no, mono*, or *koto*, however, only *koto* does not allow for

---

[1] Formal nouns, or *keishiki meishi* in Japanese, are those morphological items which possess significance as nouns in formal terms only.

the NNP2 version. Examples illustrating these NNP types as collected from authentic Japanese discourse data are provided in (1)–(5) below.[2]

(1) NNP1with *no* (a mother to her adult daughter)
Yayakoshii koto wa iwa**nai no**![3]
complicated things TOP say:NEG:NPST **NO**
'Don't fuss over the details!'

(2) NNP2 with *n(o)*[4] (a salaryman to a delinquent youth harassing him)
Sararii-man o nameru **n janee**![5]
salaryman ACC make.light.of:NPST **NO** COP:NEG:NPST
'Don't make light of salarymen!'

(3) NNP1 with *mono* (Internet advice column about wedding etiquette)
Shinseki igai no hito wa sanka shi**nai mono** yo.[6]
relatives besides GEN people TOP participation do:NEG:NPST **MONO** PP
'People (like you) who aren't relatives shouldn't participate.'

(4) NNP2 with *mon(o)* (the male protagonist to his younger sister)
Sonna kao shite joodan o iu **mon janai** zo.[7]
like.that face wearing joke ACC say:NPST **MONO** COP:NEG:NPST PP
'You shouldn't/Don't make jokes with a face like that, you know.'

(5) NNP1 with *koto* (corporate website providing job interview tips)
Yokei na koto wa iwa**nai koto** da.[8]
unnecessary COP:ATT thing TOP say:NEG:NPST **KOTO** COP:NPST
'Do not say unnecessary things/offer unsolicited information.'

(6) NNP2 with *koto* (an adaptation of example 5)
* Yokei na koto wa iu **koto janai**.
anomalous with the prohibitive reading

---

[2] In this paper, the following abbreviations are used in data glosses: ACC accusative, ASP aspect, ATT attributive form, COP copula, GEN genitive, NEG negative, NPST nonpast, PP pragmatic particle, PST past, TE conjunctive form, TOP topic.

[3] Data taken from the Japanese television drama series *Hagure keiji* (The unconventional detective), Part 15, Special episode, 2003. Tokyo: TV Asahi.

[4] In colloquial or informal spoken discourse contexts, *no* and *mono* are often contracted to *n* and *mon*, respectively, resulting in the forms *n da* and *n janai* as well as *mon da* and *mon janai*.

[5] Data taken from the Japanese television drama series *Sararii-man Kintaroo* (Kintarō the salaryman), Episode 1, 2001. Tokyo: TBS.

[6] Data taken from www.yomiuri.co.jp/komachi/reader/200405/2004051700190.htm.

[7] Data taken from the Japanese movie series *Otoko wa tsurai yo*, no. 17 (*Shiawase no aoi tori*), 1976. Tokyo: Shōchiku Co., Ltd.

[8] Data taken from www.sasajima-intl.jp/column/job/job_p13.html.

In observing the occurence of utterances such as (1)–(5) in authentic Japanese discourse, and considering that the language already allows for a number of alternative morphosyntactic means for expressing prohibitives, several questions arise which warrant addressing:

  i. What particular features of NNPs allow for their use as prohibitives in certain discourse contexts?

 ii. What are the differences in semantic and pragmatic reverberations between an NNP1 and NNP2?

iii. What particular semantic features of *koto janai* render this combination anomalous with a prohibitive reading?

2. Nominalized Predicates as Directives

Syntactically speaking, predicates nominalized by the formal nouns *no*, *mono*, and *koto* share a striking formal resemblance to the commentary predicate in that they occupy the "comment" position of topic-comment sentences.[9] Such nominalized predicates have been noted by past studies as possessing a wide variety of functions as modals (e.g. Teramura 1984, Agetsuma 1991, Tsubone 1994).

As Lyons (1977:823–4) points out, when we impose upon someone the obligation to perform (or to refrain from performing) a particular act, we are describing the desirable results that will obtain if the act in question is realized. The modality of deontic necessity, or obligation, moreover, typically derives from some source or cause. If we recognize that we are obliged to perform some act, then there is usually someone or something that we acknowledge as being responsible for our being under obligation to act in this way.

Accordingly, the deontic interpretation of nominalized predicates in Japanese typically emerges when (1) the clause modifying the predicative nominalizer contains a verb with nonpast (i.e. future) inflection, denoting an agent-controllable action, and (2) the utterance containing this nominalized predicate is directed toward an overt or implied second-person referent. The fact that the propositional content expressed by the modifying clause has been made nonchallengeable through its nominalization is what syntactically imbues this construction with the illocutionary force of a directive.

---

[9] The "comment" is the *B* (*da*) portion of an A *wa* B (*da*) type construction. The copula *da* is enclosed in parentheses here to indicate my claim that it is an optional element in this construction, namely, that its overt use marks for what Narahara (2002:178) terms the "anti-ignorative mode" or an explicit assertion of "the speaker's certainty in his/her knowledge and belief in his/her judgement about the sentential content". The term "sentence" is being used here generically to refer synonymously to the notion of "utterance" in spoken data.

As initially proposed in Yoshida forthcoming, the speaker's choice of marking this nominalized clause with *no, mono,* or *koto* functions to indicate the authoritative source or basis behind why the hearer is obligated to perform the action named by it, and in the following ways:

no Marks the source or basis as assumed known or accessible to both the speaker and hearer (i.e. established in a past context, but recoverable through the present one).

mono Marks the source or basis as having a validity which has endured throughout time; that is, it represents a generally accepted norm or truth-by-consensus, often based on common sense.

koto Marks the source or basis as known or identifiable to the speaker (but not to the hearer).

The ability to cite this source or basis, in turn, serves to mark its user (i.e. the speaker) as standing in a position of higher authority than the hearer. Next is a brief examination of the system of negation in Japanese and its conceptual ties with existence.

3. Negation in Japanese

Negative expressions in Japanese are basically formed by employing the adjectival marker *nai*, which means 'non-existent'. The "positive" or affirmative counterpart of this *nai* is the verb *aru*, whose meaning is 'to exist'. Thus, instead of using such negative terms such as 'not' or 'no' (as in English), Japanese generally employs the adjectival marker *nai* to change the meaning of a given expression from affirmative to negative. Thus, the original function of the Japanese negative marker *nai* is to negate existence, and it is substantially different from the normal verbal negation of a dynamic process or activity.

4. NNPs as Prohibitives

Based on these premises, I propose that the morphosyntax of NNP1s functions to denote, or point out to the hearer, the source or basis behind why s/he is obligated to **refrain** from performing the act named in the nominalized proposition, whereas in the case of NNP2s, it is **the existence** of this authorizing source or basis which is being negated by the speaker. I further suggest that it is such differences in the scope of negation which result in the "stronger" illocutionary impact attributed to NNP2s over NNP1s in actual Japanese discourse. Moreover, in the case of **koto janai*, I claim that a conflict in the individual semantics signaled by its two components (i.e. *koto* and *janai*) renders this combination unacceptable with a prohibitive reading. Namely, it is incongruous to negate the existence of a source or basis for necessity which is only known/identifiable to the speaker.

To provide evidence in further support of these claims, I present a context-based analysis of NNP1 and NNP2 tokens as they occur in authentic Japanese discourse data. The following data segments were taken from the scripted speeches of popular Japanese television programs and movies.

5. NNP2 with *no*

The first data segment was taken from the Japanese television drama series *Wataru seken wa oni bakari* (The road through life is full of demons) and involves a family situation.[10] The eldest daughter, Ai, has just returned home late from her first day at a new job, and she is visibly drunk. At home await her parents, grandmother, and younger brother, Shin. The parents, who have been worrying about her whereabouts, interrogate Ai about where she has been, but she coolly informs them that she had only gone drinking with her new co-workers after work. Hearing this, her parents get upset, but Ai argues back that she's a working adult now, so she can stay out and socialize as she pleases. The father, who actually wanted Ai to get married instead of getting a job, becomes irate and yells that such after-work socializing must never take place again. At this point the following exchanges takes place.

01. Ai: (to Father):
        Otoosan ni wa yokei na kuchidashi shite
        'I don't want you
02.   moraitakunai wa
        meddling in my life, Father.'
03. Father: (slaps Ai)
04. Mother: (looks at both Ai and Father with horror)
05. Ai: (to Father)
        Otoosan ni soshiki no naka de
        'Father, there's just no way you could possibly
06.   ikite ikanakya naranai ningen no
        understand the feelings of someone who has to
07.   kimochi nante wakaru mon desu ka=
        survive in a organization.'
08. Father: (to Ai)
→   =Erasoo   na   koto   yutte   n   janai   yo.
    conceited COP:ATT thing say:TE-ASP:NPST NO COP:NEG:NPST PP
    'Don't talk big!'
09.   Musume ga sake nomu nante
        'Cause I'm not going to allow

---

[10] Data segment taken from Series 7, Episode 2, 2004. Tokyo: TBS.

10.	donna riyuu ga atte mo
	(my) daughter to drink (liquor),
11.	yurusanai kara na.
	no matter what the reason!'
12.	Tsutome nanka yamero!
	'Quit that job (of yours)!'
13.	Yametchimae!
	'Just quit!'
14. Ai:	(to Father)
	Otoosan no sashizu wa ukenai.
	'I won't take orders from you, Father.'
15.	Korekara atashi no jinsei wa
	'From now on, I'll decide
16.	atashi ga kimeru.
	(what I'll do in) my life.'
17.	Otoosan no yuu koto nanka kiitetara
	'If I keep listening to what you say,
18.	atashirashiku ikiru koto nante
	I'll never be able to
19.	dekinai mon.
	live my own life.'
	(Ai storms out of the room.)
20. Shin:	(to parents, dumbstruck with shock at Ai's retort)
	Aneki mo tsuyoku natta monda.
	'Sis sure has gotten strong.'

In this segment, the father employs the NNP2 prohibitive *Erasoo na koto yuu n janai* 'Don't talk big' in line 8, because Ai continues to argue back despite her father's attempts to silence her, even with a slap. By using the NNP2 form nominalized by *no*, the father is claiming that there exists absolutely no reason or basis, known to either one of them, that authorizes or justifies the daughter to be "talking big" to him. In other words, it is similar to declaring, "You may think there exists a source or basis necessitating you to act that way, but it (actually) doesn't (exist)." Hence, its pragmatic impact is the verbal equivalent of a "slap in the face". The daughter Ai's refusal to be silenced despite being delivered this second, verbal "slap in the face" is what draws the comment *Aneki mo tsuyoku natta mon da* 'Sis sure has gotten strong' from her younger brother in line 20.

6. NNP1 with *no*

The next data segment illustrates a token of an NNP1 with *no*. It was taken from an earlier episode of the same television drama but involves a different family. This family—consisting of a middle-aged mother and father and their two grade-school children, a boy (Noboru) and his older sister (Kana) —has just moved to a new apartment, and in this scene they are in the process of having their furniture moved in with the help of two men from a moving service. This leads to the exchanges below.[11]

01. Father: (to Movers 1 and 2)
Sore.
'That (shelf).'

02.   Sono hen ni oitoi[te].
'Please leave it around there.'

03. Mover1:   [He]i.
'Okay.'

04. Mother: (to Movers 1 and 2)
Soko no tansu no ne,
'Line it up, uh

05.   yoko ni narabetoite.
next to that cabinet, please.'

06. Mover1:   Okimasu
'(We're) going put it down.'

07. Mother: (watching as movers ease the shelf in next to the cabinet)
Hai, hai.
'Okay, okay . . .

08.   hai.
okay.'

09. Noboru   (to Movers 1 and 2)
Kokoo,
'This (place)

10.   otoosan to okaasan no heya
is (going to be)

11.   nan da yo.
Mother and Father's room, you know.'

12. Movers: @[@@@]

13. Kana: (running up to Noboru and giving his head a shove)
→   [Yokei   na   koto   iwa**nai**   **no**]!
unnecessary COP:ATT thing say:NEG:NPST NO
'Don't say unnecessary things!'

14. Noboru: (to Kana)
Ii janai ka,
'What's so wrong

15.   betsu ni.
(with saying that)?'
(Noboru walks away, with Kana following after him)

16. Mother: (to Movers 1 and 2)
Doomo sumimasen.
'Please excuse (them).'
(bows to both movers)

---

[11] Data segment taken from the Japanese television drama series *Wataru seken wa oni bakari*, Part 2, Episode 2, 1993. Tokyo: TBS.

17.   Onegai shimasu.
       'Please (continue on with your work).'

As can be seen in lines 9–11, the little boy, Noboru, makes an unsolicited announcement to the two moving men, who are obviously busy at work and have no time to be listening to him. This causes the boy's older sister, Kana, to deliver the NNP1 *Yokei na koto iwanai no* 'Don't say unnecessary things', with *no*, in line 13. The NNP1 form with *no* is employed here to indicate that the basis for the necessity of refraining from 'saying unnecessary things' is something that is known or identifiable by the hearer. In other words, it is equivalent to the reprimand "You know you're not supposed to do that" or "You know better than to do that". Although Kana is older than Noboru, the fact that is she is a female sibling, only a few years older than her brother, and that Noboru's "crime" is a minor or innocent one, motivates her to employ the NNP1 form (with *no*) over the NNP2.

7. NNP2 with *mono*

The next data segment contains a token of an NNP2 with *mono* and was taken from the Japanese movie series *Otoko wa tsurai yo* (It's tough being a man). The situation involves the family of the movie's protagonist, Tora-san, who run a small *dango* 'sweet dumpling' shop in Tokyo. One day, a young boy carrying a knapsack, alone and looking worn out from travel, shows up at their storefront asking for Tora-san. When asked where he came from, the boy replies *Kooriyama*, the name of a city located quite far from Tokyo. When asked about his parents, the boy replies that his mother had abandoned him and that his father, too, has recently passed away. With no place to go, the boy came to the *dango* shop relying on the address written on a postcard his father had received from Tora-san some time ago. The scene involves the members of Tora-san's family—his teenage nephew Mitsuo and Mitsuo's mother and grandmother—along with a neighbor girl, Akemi, all of whom are standing around and questioning the boy in the store. From this ensues the following.[12]

01. Akemi: (to boy)
             Kimii
             'Hey,
02.   Satoo-kun tte yuu no?
             (so) your (last) name is Satō?'
03. Boy: (nods)
04. Akemi: Satoo nante yuu no?
             'What's your first name?'

---

[12] Data segment taken from *Torajirō monogatari*, no. 39, 1987. Tokyo: Shōchiku Co., Ltd.

05. Boy:	Hideyoshi Hideyoshi.
06. Akemi:	Heh?@ 'What?'
07.	Donna ji kaku no? 'What kind of characters do write that with?'
08. Boy:	Toyotomi Hideyoshi no Hideyoshi '(Same) as Hideyoshi of Toyotomi Hideyoshi.'
09. Akemi:	@@
10.	@Suggoi namae@! 'What a grandiose name!'
11. Boy:	(tries to wipe away the tears welling up in his eyes)
12. Mitsuo:	(to his mother) Kaasan, 'Mom,
13.	konna jinmon mitai na koto shicha to be interrogating him like this,
14.	kawaisoo da yo. it's cruel.'
15. Mother:	(to Mitsuo) Soo ne. 'You're right.'
16.	(to boy, while helping him take off his knapsack) Gomen nee. 'I'm sorry.'
17.	Nagai tabi shite kita n da mon nee. 'You made a long trip over here, didn't you?'
18.	Saa kotchi e irasshai. 'Now, come over here (with me).'
19. Grandmother:	(to boy as he follows Mother into the house) Atode oishii mon tsukutte ageru kara nee. 'I'll make you something good to eat later, okay?'
20:	(to herself, after boy is out of earshot) Kawaisoo ni nee. 'Poor thing!'
21: Mitsuo:	(to Akemi, after boy is out of earshot) → Anna toki warau mon janai yo. like.that times laugh:NPST MONO COP:NEG:NPST PP 'You shouldn't laugh at times like that, you know.'
22. Akemi:	(to Mitsuo) Wakatteru yo. 'I know (that)!'
23.	Nani erasoo na kuchi kiite! 'Who (do you think you are), talking (so) big (to me)!'

In line 21, the teenage boy, Mitsuo, delivers an NNP2 with *mono* to

Akemi, a girl older than him, who is actually just a neighbor who has come by to help out in the shop. By employing the NNP2 with *mono*, Mitsuo is claiming that there exists no general norm or common-sensical truth that might warrant the hearer (Akemi) to act in the way she had, namely, to laugh at hearing the name of a weary and defenseless child (*anna toki ni warau*), who had no control over what his parents named him. Although Mitsuo is a male, he is young and even younger than the hearer, Akemi. Thus, the fact that Mitsuo directed a prohibitive to her in the form of an NNP2 with *mono* results in the retort *Nani erasoo na kuchi kiite!* 'Who do you think you are, talking so big to me?' in line 24, because Akemi, given their social relationship, finds this prohibitive form inappropriate and impudent directed to her, even though she does not deny the accuracy of its content.

8. NNP1 with *koto*

This final data segment, which contains a token of an NNP with *koto*, was taken from a health and beauty care program called *Karada genki-ka* (The healthy body course). Each episode of this program focuses on a selected health or beauty issue and features a doctor or professional specializing in that field. The doctor or professional first provides an explanation of the issue, using much technical or professional jargon, and this is then followed up by the program's narrator (usually a female voice), who summarizes what was just said using everyday terms. The segment below was on how to care for one's cuticles.[13]

01. Narrator: Amakawa to wa
　　　　　　　'The term "cuticle"

02.　　　　　soojoohi to yobareru kono bubun
　　　　　　　refers to the part (of the fingernail) called "soojoohi".'

03.　　　　　Amakawa wa umareta bakari no
　　　　　　　'The cuticle is the area which provides protection

04.　　　　　mijuku na tsume o hogo suru basho.
　　　　　　　for the newly born, prematurely developed fingernail.'

05.　　　　　Atarashiku dekita bakari no tsume wa yawarakaku
　　　　　　　'The just-developed fingernail is soft,

06.　　　　　amakawa ga shoogeki kara mamotte kureteiru no desu.
　　　　　　　so the cuticle provides it protection from trauma.'

07.　　　　　Amakawa o muri ni kittari hagashitari suru to
　　　　　　　'If you forcefully cut or peel away the cuticle,

08.　　　　　tsume no yokojiwa no gen'in to narimasu
　　　　　　　it becomes the cause of (unsightly) vertical ridges.'

---

[13] Data segment taken from *Tsume no toraburu kaiketsuhō*, televised 10 October 2004. Tokyo: NTV.

09.   Oshare no tame ni
               'For fashionability's sake,

10.   → amakawa o   ijimenai   koto
               cuticle ACC abuse:NEG:NPST KOTO
               (you) must not abuse your cuticles!'

As seen in line 10, the narrator employs an NNP1 with *koto* in this situation because she is summarizing the words of the doctor who is the authoritative source behind why it is necessary to refrain from the act of 'abusing (one's) cuticles' (*amakawa o ijimeru*). Since the program's aim is to inform viewers, the narrator employs the NNP1 with *koto* to mark the basis behind the necessity of not abusing one's cuticles as something known/identifiable only to the speaker/narrator (but not to the hearer/ viewer) at speech time. As suggested earlier, the NNP2 with *koto* is not possible here because it would be incongruous to negate the existence of a basis for necessity that is assumed **not** known or identifiable to the hearer at speech time.

9. Conclusion

The aim of this analysis has been to account for the differences in semantic and pragmatic effects conveyed by prohibitives expressed as NNP1s and NNP2s. It has been proposed that the morphosyntax of NNP1s functions to denote or point out to the hearer the basis behind why s/he is obligated to refrain from performing the act named in the nominalized proposition, whereas for NNP2s, it is the very existence of this basis which is being negated by the speaker. It has moreover been suggested that such differences in the scope of negation is what results in the seemingly "stronger" illocutionary impact attributed to NNP2s over NNP1s when employed in actual Japanese discourse.

Finally, in the case of **koto janai*, it has been claimed that the incongruity of negating the existence of a basis for necessity that is only known or identifiable to the speaker renders this combination unacceptable with a prohibitive reading.

References

Agetsuma, Y. 1991. Jisshitsu meishi "mono" to keishikiteki yōhō to no imiteki tsunagari [The semantic link between the substantial noun "mono" and its formal uses]. *Tōhoku Daigaku Bungakubu Nihongogakka Ronshū* 1:2–11.

Akatsuka, N., and A. Tsubomoto. 1998. *Modaritī to hatsuwa kōi* [Modality and speech acts]. Tokyo: Kenkyūsha.

Clancy, P. M., N. Akatsuka, and S. Strauss. 1997. Deontic Modality and Conditionality in Discourse: A Cross-linguistic Study of Adult Speech to Young Children.

Directions in Functional Linguistics, ed. A. Kamio, 19–57. Amsterdam: John Benjamins.

Lyons, J. 1977. *Semantics*. Vol. II. Cambridge: Cambridge University Press.

Narahara, T. 2002. *The Japanese Copula: Forms and Functions*. New York: Palgrave Macmillan.

Noda, H. 1995. Mono da to koto da to no da: meishisei no jodōshi no tōiteki na yōhō. *Nihongo ruigi hyōgen no bunpō*, eds. T. Miyajima and Y. Nida, 253–62. Tokyo: Kuroshio.

Teramura, H. 1984. *Nihongo no shintakusu to imi* [Japanese syntax and semantics]. Vol. 2. Tokyo: Kuroshio.

Tsubone, Y. 1994. "Mono da" ni kansuru ichi kōsatsu [A study of "*mono da*"]. *Nihongo Kyōiku* 84:65–77.

Yoshida, N. Forthcoming. Nominalized Predicates as Directives in Japanese Discourse. *Japanese/Korean Linguistics 13*. Stanford: CSLI.

Index

447

Japanese and Korean Linguistics

For a cumulative table of contents of the entire series, please visit

http://cslipublications.stanford.edu/ja-ko-contents/jako-collective-toc.html

where articles are grouped by the following subject categories:

Phonetics and Phonology
Syntax and Morphology
Semantics
Pragmatics, Discourse and Conversation
Psycholinguistics and Cognition
L1 and L2 Acquisition
Historical Linguistics, Language Change and Grammaticalization
Sociolinguistics and Language Use

For more information on other volumes in this series, please visit

http://cslipublications.stanford.edu/site/JAKO.html